ASP.NET MVC 1.0 Website Pr
Problem – Design – Sol

ASP.NET MVC 1.0 Website Programming:

Problem – Design – Solution

ASP.NET MVC 1.0 Website Programming:

Problem – Design – Solution

Nick Berardi

Al Katawazi

Marco Bellinaso

Wiley Publishing, Inc.

ASP.NET MVC 1.0 Website Programming: Problem – Design – Solution

Published by
Wiley Publishing, Inc.
10475 Crosspoint Boulevard
Indianapolis, IN 46256
www.wiley.com

Copyright © 2009 by Wiley Publishing, Inc., Indianapolis, Indiana

ISBN: 978-0-470-41095-0

Manufactured in the United States of America

10 9 8 7 6 5 4 3 2 1

For general information on our other products and services please contact our Customer Care Department within the United States at (877) 762-2974, outside the United States at (317) 572-3993 or fax (317) 572-4002.

Wiley also publishes its books in a variety of electronic formats. Some content that appears in print may not be available in electronic books.

Library of Congress Control Number: 2009928721

To my wife, Melinda, for her love, patience, and support, in everything I do.
— Nick Berardi

To my wife Heather and loving family.
— Al Katawazi

About the Authors

Nick Berardi is the owner of Managed Fusion (`www.managedfusion.com`), a U.S.-based company that specializes in the fields of software architecture/development, usability engineering, and cloud-based computing initiatives with a strong focus on .NET, the Web, SEO, SEM, and Microsoft technologies.

In his spare time, of which there is very little, he writes on his blog, Coder Journal (`www.coderjournal.com`), about all things that interest him. Topics include, but are not limited to, ASP.NET MVC, cloud computing, social networking, scalable computing, software usability, and anything that may intrigue or pique his interest on any given day. He also does a lot of public speaking on and evangelizing of Microsoft software, specifically regarding ASP.NET and other .NET-based web technologies such as Silverlight and WCF. He has been working with the .NET Framework since the beta, creating and developing all types of applications including MVC, Silverlight, WCF, WPF, Web Forms, Windows Forms, Windows Services, and various types of back office applications.

He is also the sole developer of the Managed Fusion Rewriter and Reverse Proxy (`http://urlrewriter.codeplex.com`), which is a .NET-based URL rewriter and reverse proxy for IIS 6 and IIS 7 based off of the syntax made popular by the Apache mod_rewrite module. His rewriter is currently deployed on everything from small, home-based servers running Microsoft Home Server to very large government websites running high-access-high-availability applications.

If you want to contact Nick to talk about the book, about MVC, or any random questions you may have, please use the contact form on his site (`www.managedfusion.com`) or his blog (`www.coderjournal.com`).

Al Katawazi is owner of Blue Shift Technologies Inc. (`www.blueshifttechnologies.com`), a software consulting company based out of Upstate New York. He is very fortunate to have worked on a variety of different projects for many notable clients. Most recently his focus has been on creating SaaS-based solutions leveraging the MVC framework. Al is also the author of his own blog (`www.codingsmarter.com`), which he has tried to keep up to date even though writing a book is a great excuse not to. When Al is not programming he enjoys kayaking with his dog Scout and card sharking with his wife Heather.

If you want to contact Al to talk about the book, please use the contact form on his site (`www.blueshifttechnologies.com`) or his blog (`www.codingsmarter.com`).

Marco Bellinaso lives in Bologna, Italy, and works as a freelance consultant, developer, and trainer specialized in all "web-things" that run on the Microsoft platform, such as ASP.NET, AJAX, and SharePoint. He's been working with the .NET Framework since the Beta 1 on applications of all types, including Web Services, Windows Forms, Windows Services, and mobile applications. He is also author or co-author of a number of commercial tools for developers, such as the VB Migration Partner (`http://www.vbmigration.com/`), the award-winning VBMaximizer add-in, CodeBox for .NET, and FormMaximizer for .NET.

Before the .NET era, Marco was a hardcore VB developer who specialized in Windows programming with advanced, low-level API techniques, as well as a COM and ASP developer.

Marco also frequently writes for programming magazines such as MSDN Magazine, MSDN Online, and Visual Studio Magazine, and other Italian magazines such as Computer Programming and Visual Basic & .NET Journal. Besides writing he has also done a lot of public speaking (both in English and Italian) at some of the most important Italian conferences organized by Microsoft Italy and other big companies.

About the Authors

In addition to his regular job, Marco runs a number of websites, projects, and services, such as www.pet-files.com and www.intellibits.com. In general, he has a lot of fun playing with the latest phones, gadgets, and technologies.

If you want to contact Marco to talk about anything related to the book, or maybe about other web/mobile projects, feel free to write to mbellinaso@gmail.com.

Credits

Development Editor
Adaobi Obi Tulton

Technical Editor
Doug Parsons

Production Editor
Rebecca Coleman

Copy Editor
Kim Cofer

Editorial Manager
Mary Beth Wakefield

Production Manager
Tim Tate

**Vice President and
Executive Group Publisher**
Richard Swadley

Vice President and Executive Publisher
Barry Pruett

Associate Publisher
Jim Minatel

Project Coordinator, Cover
Lynsey Stanford

Compositor
Jeff Lytle, Happenstance Type-O-Rama

Proofreader
Word One New York

Indexer
J&J Indexing

Acknowledgments

Wow, I am writing the acknowledgments for this book; that means that…this book is finally complete. I am not going to lie, writing a book is a very time-consuming process, and for the past year there hasn't been a day that has passed where this book hasn't been in the forethought of my mind. Mostly because this book has been a constantly evolving concept. When Jim Minatel first called me a year ago to write an update to the popular *ASP.NET 2.0 Website Programming* book, it started out as a simple update with only a small amount of code changes. But we quickly realized that to really show the power and grace of ASP. NET MVC we had to do a total rewrite of TheBeerHouse, which was a pretty major undertaking considering that we also had to rewrite a majority of the book. Combine all this with holding down a full-time job, running a growing business, and trying to steal some time to spend with my family, I could have really used an extra hour in each day.

This seems like a good transition for my first acknowledgment, which of course goes to my loving wife, Melinda. She has been my constant supporter with her love and patience she has shown me throughout this entire process of writing this book. She also played a large role as my in-house editor who made sure everything I wrote made sense technically and grammatically to the reader. Amazingly she has put up with this entire process for the last year, and that is why I love her.

Secondly I would like to thank my parents, Anthony and Linda Berardi, who taught me that good things come from hard work and perseverance. Without either of these teachings I would have never been able to finish writing this book. So thank you for your love, guidance, and support over the years; it has helped shape who I am today.

I would also like to acknowledge other family members, in addition to my parents, who have helped shape who I am today: My grandparents Dominick and Edith Berardi and Ken and Barb Hood, my brother Chris, and my sisters Catie, Terri, and Megan. All you guys have played a huge role in my life and mean the world to me, so thank you for that.

Additionally, I would like to thank my wife's parents, Don and Rena Gleiter, for being supportive and understanding about why we've had so little time to visit this past year. And for the amazing job they did raising their daughter and my wife, Melinda.

The next acknowledgment goes to Sam and Mary Bea Damico, who took a chance, in 2007, and hired me to start and build the technology division of Vovéo (www.voveo.com) and help make it a natural extension of their already successful marketing division. Without this necessary support and trust in my judgment, I wouldn't have had the chance to focus on ASP.NET MVC back in December 2007, and by proxy wouldn't be writing this book. So thank you Sam and Mary Bea and everybody at Vovéo, you guys played a pivotal role in this book.

My last acknowledgment goes to my best friend, my best man at my wedding, my sidekick since 1995, and now co-author Al Katawazi. If you weren't my co-author, this book would probably be about half the size it is now. You deserve a thank you, a good beer, and an even better cigar, for all the long nights you put in on this book. I wouldn't have been able to do it without you!

— *Nick Berardi*

Acknowledgments

This book was a monumental effort to complete, and I am very thankful for all the support everyone has given me in writing this book. Now that I think about it, writing this book while the MVC framework was still being developed was an insane task that led to many revisions. My co-author and I have worked very hard to ensure that this book is as up to date as reasonably possible. Now that I have patted my own back I think I will mention some of the real contributors, without whom this book would not have been possible. To my wife Heather, I thank you for allowing me the time to write this book, spending late nights reviewing what I had written, and being a great and supportive friend. I'd also like to thank Michael Staley; without his efforts you would have seen far more grammatical errors and typos in my writing. The man is a machine. To Nick Berardi, my best friend since 9th grade, who has been an absolutely critical resource on this project, who has kicked me when I was slacking, and who has been a lot of fun to work with.

On a more abstract level I would like to thank my parents Mohammad and Sarah Katawazi, who have always supported me (except that time I joined the army). I would also like to thank both my family and my wife's family for being so understanding these past 12 months while we were preoccupied with this book. And finally to my dog Scout, no matter how many walks or kayaking trips we miss you are always happy to see me. Thanks for being a great friend.

— Al Katawazi

Contents

Contents

Contents

Contents

Introduction

Dear reader, thanks for picking up this book, and welcome to the new edition of *ASP.NET MVC 1.0 Website Programming: Problem – Design – Solution*, fully updated to ASP.NET MVC 1.0! The idea for this book was born in 2001, with ASP.NET 1.0, from the desire to have a book that teaches how to create real-world websites. The first edition was published in 2002, and fortunately it was a success. Because of the success of the first edition, the concept was updated to use the new features in ASP.NET 2.0. The second edition was published in 2006, and again had a style that resonated with developers and was a success. We believe that this was due to the fact that most ASP.NET books on the market were (and still are) reference-type books, which describe every single control of the framework, and all their methods and properties, but the examples they provide are single-page demos showing how to use a singular feature. However, typically these references don't show how to integrate all ASP.NET features and controls into a single site with rich functionality, which is what readers have to do at work or at home. Designing and implementing a real-world site is very different from creating simple examples, and that's why we think a book like this is helpful for developers facing real problems in their everyday lives.

This new edition of the book was rewritten completely from scratch, to use all the features of ASP.NET MVC 1.0 as much as possible, and it is hoped that it is better in a number of ways: The project developed is much more complete (there's an updated e-commerce module, and a Web 2.0–style forum module, for example) and professional (the site was entirely updated to use CSS and modern design techniques, for example), and each chapter provides enough background information on ASP.NET MVC 1.0 to comfortably read the chapter even if you haven't already had experience with ASP.NET MVC 1.0 (this is something the first edition didn't provide).

First of all, this book is aimed at describing, designing, and implementing a site much like the ones you're probably working on or will be soon, while taking the opportunity to introduce and explain many of the new features that the new great ASP.NET MVC 1.0 framework offers. We don't hide difficult problems so that the solution can be simpler and shorter to develop; rather, we try to explain most of the problems you'll typically face when writing a modern website, and provide one or more solutions for them.

Second of all, we have broken up each chapter into different sections based on problem, design, and solution, and then to keep with the notion of separation of concerns we have broken up each section into subsections based on model, view, and controller (MVC). We did this with a specific goal in mind—to purposely break from the traditional way of explaining code in ASP.NET, using the database-to-user-interface-way, where you got everything in one shot and then moved on to the next page and started all over again. This traditional way of explaining ASP.NET was a massive injustice to the concept of MVC, and we felt it was important to truly understand ASP.NET MVC in an MVC way instead of an ASP.NET Web Forms way. Our hopes are that this way of explaining MVC in this book will solidify the concepts behind MVC in your mind, and the benefits that come from having your code separated into logical blocks of functionality (or separation of concerns) so that when you go off to develop your own MVC applications, you will have a firm understanding of the principals behind MVC, and not try to develop an MVC application in a Web Forms way.

The result of all of this is a website that features a CSS-based layout, a membership system, a Content Management System for publishing and syndicating articles, polls, mailing lists, Web 2.0–style forums, an e-commerce store with support for real-time credit card processing through PayPal, and localization (refer to Chapter 1 for a more detailed list of features to be implemented). We hope you enjoy reading this book, and that it offers guidance that speeds up the development of your next project and makes it more solid, extensible, and well organized.

What This Book Covers

This book is basically a large case study that starts from the foundation and works its way through to completion with a series of designs and solutions for each incremental step along the way. What sets the *Problem – Design – Solution* series apart from other Wrox series is the structure of the book and the start-to-finish approach to one completed project. Specifically, this book leads the reader through the development of a complete ASP.NET MVC 1.0 website that has most of the features users expect to find in a modern content-related and e-commerce site:

❑ Account registration

❑ News and events, organized into categories

❑ Opinion polls

❑ Newsletter

❑ Forums

❑ E-commerce store with shopping cart and order management

❑ Localization

From an administrative point of view, the following features and problems are also covered:

❑ Full online back-end administrative section, to manage practically all data from an intuitive user interface

❑ Site deployment

The implementation of each of these features provides the opportunity to teach various new features and concepts introduced by ASP.NET MVC 1.0, such as the following:

❑ The concepts of models

❑ Views

❑ What role View Engines play

❑ The use of View Master Pages, View Pages, and View User Controls

❑ The use of View Data and Temp Data to transfer data between controller actions and views

❑ The use of HTML and AJAX Extension Methods

❑ How jQuery is used in conjunction with MVC

❑ Controllers

❑ What role Controller Factories play

❑ The use of Routes to create REST-like URLs

❑ Controller Actions

❑ The use of Action filters, Action results, and Action selectors to enhance your application

We also use the following .NET 3.5 features that were added in C# 3.0:

- ❑ LINQ
- ❑ LINQ-to-SQL
- ❑ Extension methods
- ❑ Anonymous methods

In addition you learn how these new features and concepts will integrate with standard ASP.NET 2.0 features, such as:

- ❑ Master pages
- ❑ Membership and profile modules

Not only does this book cover the new features of ASP.NET MVC 1.0, it also demonstrates how to integrate all of them together, for the development of a single full-featured site. All the design options are explained and discussed (including the database design, the model, view, and controller design, and the overall site architecture); at the end of the book you will have learned many of the best practices for web development, based on a solid, scalable, and extensible architecture.

How This Book Is Structured

The book builds a complete project from start to finish. All the chapters (other than the first two) are self-contained modules within the larger project, and are structured in three sections:

- ❑ **Problem:** This defines the problem or problems to be addressed in the chapter: What do you want to do in this chapter? What features do you want to add to the site and why are they important? What restrictions or other factors need to be taken into account?
- ❑ **Design:** After the problem is defined adequately, this section describes what features are needed to solve the problem. This will give you a broad idea of how the solution will work or what will be entailed in solving the problem.
- ❑ **Solution:** After setting up what you are going to accomplish and why (and how that solves the problem defined earlier), we produce and discuss the code and any other material that will realize the design and solve the problem laid out at the beginning of the chapter. Just as the coverage of the book as a whole is weighted toward solution, so is each chapter. This is where you will get hands-on practice and create the code.

In Chapters 5 through 11 the *Design* and *Solution* sections are further broken down into sub-sections as we talked about earlier:

- ❑ Model
- ❑ Controller
- ❑ View

Each of these sub-sections will help solidify the concepts of MVC in a way that makes sense in the context of the *Design* or *Solution* sections of the chapter.

The book is intended to be read from cover to cover, so that you start with nothing and finish with a complete and deployed website ready to be launched. However, the book follows a modular structure, so every chapter is quite self-contained and implements a module that, if necessary, can be taken out of the proposed sample project and re-used in some other website.

Who This Book Is For

Let us state up front that this isn't a book for completely novice programmers, or for experienced developers that have never touched ASP.NET and the .NET Framework in general. This book teaches how to write a real-world website from scratch to deployment, and as such it can't explain every single detail of the technology, but must concentrate on designing and writing actual solutions. To comfortably read this book, you should already have had some experience with ASP.NET 2.0, even if not advanced solutions. You're not required to know ASP.NET MVC, because each chapter introduces the new concepts and features that you'll use in that chapter, providing enough background information to implement the solution. If you then want to go deeper and learn everything you can about a feature, you can refer to the MSDN official documentation or to another reference-type book such as Wrox's *Professional ASP.NET MVC 1.0*.

What You Need to Use This Book

To follow the book by building the project on your own computer, or to run the downloadable and ready-to-use project, you'll need the following:

❑   Windows XP, Windows Server 2003, Windows Vista, Windows 7, or Windows Server 2008.

❑   Any edition of Visual Studio 2008 for the C# language, including the freely available Visual Web Developer 2008 Express edition. The book depicts pictures from Visual Studio 2008 Professional edition.

    http://www.microsoft.com/express/vwd/

❑   Any edition of SQL Server 2008, including the freely available SQL Server 2008 Express edition. The book uses SQL Server 2008 Express edition for this project, but realistically any version of SQL Server 2008 will work just the same.

    http://www.microsoft.com/express/sql/download/

❑   Any edition of SQL Server Management Studio 2008, including the freely available Basic version that is distributed with *SQL Server 2008 Express with Tools* edition. The book depicts pictures from SQL Server Management Studio 2008.

    http://www.microsoft.com/express/sql/download/

The Companion Website

This book features a companion website that makes available to you the latest code, issue tracking, and discussions surrounding the TheBeerHouse application that you build in this book. To visit the companion website, please visit this address:

```
http://thebeerhouse.codeplex.com
```

You can visit as a guest and just browse our wiki, source code, and discussions, or you can get involved with the other active members of the TheBeerHouse community. New members are always welcome. And participation is always encouraged for members, who are using the TheBeerHouse application in their real-world scenarios, to share their knowledge with the rest of the community.

In addition to the companion website mentioned, there is a community supported demonstration site of TheBeerHouse. To visit the demonstration website, please visit this address:

```
http://www.TheBeerHouseExample.com
```

This demonstration website should act as an example of the final website that will be produced by this book, and can be used as a reference point as you are working through the code in the book.

Conventions

To help you get the most from the text and keep track of what's happening, we've used a number of conventions throughout the book.

> Boxes like this one hold important, not-to-be-forgotten information that is directly relevant to the surrounding text.

Tips, hints, tricks, and asides to the current discussion are offset and placed in italics like this.

As for styles in the text:

- ❑ We *highlight* new terms and important words when we introduce them.
- ❑ We show keyboard strokes like this: *Ctrl+A.*
- ❑ We show filenames, URLs, and code within the text like so: `persistence.properties`.
- ❑ We present code in two different ways:

```
We use a monospace font type with no highlighting for code examples.
```
```
We use gray highlighting to emphasize code that's particularly important in
the present context.
```

Source Code

As you work through the examples in this book, you may choose either to type in all the code manually or to use the source code files that accompany the book. All of the source code used in this book is available for download at www.wrox.com. Once at the site, simply locate the book's title (either by using the Search box or by using one of the title lists) and click the Download Code link on the book's details page to obtain all the source code for the book.

> Because many books have similar titles, you may find it easiest to search by ISBN; this book's ISBN is 978-0-470-41095-0.

Alternatively, you can download the source code from the CodePlex site mentioned earlier or go to the main Wrox code download page at www.wrox.com/dynamic/books/download.aspx to see the code available for this book and all other Wrox books.

Once you download the code, just decompress it with your favorite compression tool.

Errata

We make every effort to ensure that there are no errors in the text or in the code. However, no one is perfect, and mistakes do occur. If you find an error in one of our books, such as a spelling mistake or faulty piece of code, we would be very grateful for your feedback. By sending in errata you may save another reader hours of frustration, and at the same time you will be helping us provide even higher quality information.

To find the errata page for this book, go to www.wrox.com and locate the title using the Search box or one of the title lists. Then, on the book details page, click the Book Errata link. On this page you can view all errata that has been submitted for this book and posted by Wrox editors. A complete book list including links to each book's errata is also available at www.wrox.com/misc-pages/booklist.shtml.

If you don't spot "your" error on the Book Errata page, go to www.wrox.com/contact/techsupport .shtml and complete the form there to send us the error you have found. We'll check the information and, if appropriate, post a message to the book's errata page and fix the problem in subsequent editions of the book.

p2p.wrox.com

For author and peer discussion, join the P2P forums at p2p.wrox.com. The forums are a web-based system for you to post messages relating to Wrox books and related technologies and to interact with other readers and technology users. The forums offer a subscription feature to e-mail you topics of interest of your choosing when new posts are made to the forums. Wrox authors, editors, other industry experts, and your fellow readers are present on these forums.

At http://p2p.wrox.com you will find a number of different forums that will help you not only as you read this book, but also as you develop your own applications. To join the forums, just follow these steps:

1. Go to p2p.wrox.com and click the Register link.

2. Read the terms of use and click Agree.

3. Complete the required information to join as well as any optional information you wish to provide and click Submit.

4. You will receive an e-mail with information describing how to verify your account and complete the joining process.

You can read messages in the forums without joining P2P but in order to post your own messages, you must join.

Once you join, you can post new messages and respond to messages other users post. You can read messages at any time on the Web. If you would like to have new messages from a particular forum e-mailed to you, click the Subscribe to this Forum icon by the forum name in the forum listing.

For more information about how to use the Wrox P2P, be sure to read the P2P FAQs for answers to questions about how the forum software works as well as many common questions specific to P2P and Wrox books. To read the FAQs, click the FAQ link on any P2P page.

1

Introducing the Project: TheBeerHouse

This chapter introduces the project that you're going to develop in this book. I'll explain the concept behind the sample website that is the subject of this book, but as you read along you should keep in mind that this is a general-purpose, data-driven, content-based style of website that can easily be modified to meet the needs of a myriad of real-world website requirements. Although you'll use many of the older features of ASP.NET, the clear focus of this book is directed at showing you how to leverage the powerful new features of ASP.NET MVC in a real-world, non-trivial website.

This book follows a "Problem–Design–Solution" approach in each chapter: The Problem section explains the business requirements for the module designed in that chapter, the Design section is used to develop your roadmap for meeting those requirements, and the Solution section is where you write the code to implement your design. This is unlike traditional computer books because the focus is not on teaching basic concepts, but rather showing you how to apply your knowledge to solve real-world business requirements. If you are new to ASP.NET, perhaps this is not the best book to start with, but if you're generally familiar with the basic concepts of web development and ASP.NET (any version of ASP.NET), you're ready to put that knowledge to use, and perhaps you want to learn about the new features in ASP.NET MVC, so fasten your seat belt!

Problem

In State College, Pennsylvania, where I attended The Pennsylvania State University, more than half the population consists of students. With all these young people around, it goes without saying that there are a lot of pubs, bars, and places to spend the evenings and weekends with friends. Concerts, parties, shows, and other special events are commonplace. However, with all this competition, every pub must find something that the others don't have, something that's somehow appealing to its potential customers. Marketing plays a significant role, and your pub owner wants to be stronger in that area. He has always used traditional, printed marketing ads for his pub *TheBeerHouse* (a fictitious name), but he wants to expand into new media possibilities, starting with having his own exciting website. He thinks that this would be useful because, once customers become familiar with the site, they can go there to read about new specials and events, and possibly receive a newsletter right in their e-mail inbox. They can also browse photos of past events, rate them, and share messages with other website visitors, creating virtual relationships that they can later continue face-to-face right in the pub! The general idea is appealing, especially considering that the target audience is well accustomed to using computers and browsing the web to find out information about news and events. A pub is typically a fun place full of life, and it's perhaps more appropriate for this type of project, rather than, say, a classic restaurant. However, even classic restaurants may like to consider this type of website as well.

Design

The Design section of each chapter is devoted to discussing the problem and designing a solution. This usually means writing down a list of business requirements and desired features to implement, as well as the design of the necessary database objects for the data storage, and the structure of the classes to retrieve, manipulate, and present the data to the user. At the beginning of a project you start out by thinking about your client's needs, how you might meet those needs, and possibly even expand on them to give your client more functionality than the minimum needed, while still staying within your time limits and budgetary guidelines. As stated in the Problem section, your client in this scenario is a pub owner who wants to have a website to promote his pub, providing online information about upcoming events, reports about past events, and more. This initial idea can be expanded in many ways to create a site that has a lot more interesting things, which is good for its users who are also potential customers for the physical pub, and for the store owner. You can begin by writing down a list of features that a modern content-based site should have, and a few reasons why they are useful:

❑ **An appealing user interface.** Appearance is important, because it's the first thing users will notice — well before appreciating the site's functionality and services. But the graphics are not all that matters regarding the UI. The information on the site must be well organized and easily reachable. The site must be usable and provide a good (and possibly great) user experience, which means that users must find it easy to browse and interact with. Some attention should also be given to cross-browser compatibility; that is, ensuring that the site looks and behaves as desired from different platforms and browsers. This is especially true for sites like this one, where you can't know in advance which browser your customers will use, as you might know in the case of an intranet site for a corporation, for example.

❑ **A personalized user experience.** A successful content-based site owes its popularity to its users. Loyal users, who regularly visit the site, help write content, and participate in polls and special events, are those who guarantee that the site will keep growing. To build a vibrant community of active members, users must have some sort of *identity*, something that describes and distinguishes them among other members. Because of this, the site needs a registration feature as part of a larger authentication/authorization infrastructure. This will also be used to grant and restrict access to some areas of the site.

❑ **Dynamic content.** The site needs a constant supply of fresh content to stay alive and vibrant. If the content becomes stale, visitors will lose interest in the site and won't visit it anymore. A pub's site can't be very good unless it has regular updates about upcoming events, parties, and concerts. What's the point in visiting the site if it doesn't display photos that were shot at the last party? To facilitate a constant stream of new content, the site needs some mechanism that enables the editor to easily update it with dynamic content. Furthermore, the editor, who will be in charge of the content updates, will probably not be a technical person, so you must build some simple administration pages that make updates easy, even for nontechnical people.

❑ **Site-to-user communication.** Once the site has new content ready to be read, the site's manager must have some way to inform its users about this. Not all users visit the site every day, so the site manager must be proactive and notify the customers about recent updates. If customers have registered on the site and provided their e-mail address, they might also have requested to receive a newsletter notifying them about recent changes and additions to the site. Of course, there are also other ways to syndicate news, such as exposing syndication feeds to which users can register and then control from their favorite RSS reader, and get automatic notifications about news without having to visit the site daily to get the information.

❑ **User-to-site communication.** A site like this can also be a good opportunity to get feedback from customers about a variety of issues: What do they like most in a pub? What brand of beer do they prefer? Do they want to listen to live music while drinking with friends, or perhaps they don't like all that noise? Establishing some kind of user-to-site communication is important, and if you get a good number of responses it can even lead to strategic decisions and changes that may improve the business.

❑ **User-to-user communication.** If the presence of some sort of user-to-site communication is important, user-to-user communication may be even more so, because that's the central point of creating a community of loyal users who come to the site frequently to chat, discuss the news posted on the site, ask others about upcoming events, and more. This translates into more traffic on the site, and a feeling of membership that will pay off in both the short and long run.

❑ **An e-commerce store.** Once the pub's physical store has a strong customer base, the pub's owner may decide to expand it so that it supports an online store. In fact, the pub already offers a catalog of products for beer enthusiasts, such as glasses, T-shirts, key chains, and more. If the site has a lot of traffic, it may be a good way to promote these products so people can place orders without even visiting the pub in person. And once customers see a product and like it, they can rate that product to tell other people how much they like it. The online store must be easy to manage by nontechnical people, because it might possibly be the pub's owner who adds and edits products, and manages the orders, so there must be a module with a simple and intuitive UI that automates as many operations as possible, and guides the customers through the ordering process.

❑ **Localized content.** As mentioned previously, the pub is typically visited by a lot of customers coming from many different countries, and the pub's owner expects the same to happen for the website. Because of this, the site must be partially or fully translated into multiple languages, making it easy for most users to understand it. Not only text must be translated; information such as dates and numbers should also be displayed according to the user's preferred locale settings, so that nobody will misunderstand an announcement about an upcoming party or event.

To recap everything in a few words, the TheBeerHouse site will have everything a modern content-based site will have, including dynamic articles and news, polls for user-to-site communication, forums for user-to-user communication, newsletters and RSS feeds to notify members about new content on the site, an e-commerce store for selling products online, home page personalization, and content localization. Although the sample project is built around a fictitious pub, you'll recognize in this list of requirements the common features of the majority of content- and commerce-based sites you find online now, and sites that you're likely to develop in the near future, or maybe even sites you're developing right now.

Solution

The Solution section of each chapter contains the instructions and actual code for implementing all of the features and requirements outlined and designed in the previous sections. For this first chapter, however, I'll give you a more detailed description of exactly what the following chapters cover, so that you can get a good idea of what the final result will be like.

In Chapter 2 you learn about the general concept behind MVC and then learn about Microsoft's implementation of MVC called ASP.NET MVC. You learn how an ASP.NET MVC application is constructed and what the terms model, controller, action, filter, route, and view are used for and how they relate to give you a basic understanding of the framework before you dive into creating code in ASP.NET MVC.

In Chapter 3 you build the site's design, the graphics, and the layout that's shared among all pages of the site, through the use of master pages. This will create a flexible design that is easy to maintain and customize through the use of CSS.

In Chapter 4 you lay down the foundations for building a flexible, easily configurable, and instrumented site. First you design a model or data access layer (DAL) for use through the new language integrated query (LINQ) in .NET 3.5. Then you build a controller or business logic layer on the top of the model, with the required validation logic, transaction management, event logging, and caching as necessary. Finally, you look at the view or user interface (UI) as the presentation layer of the site, to create complex and feature-rich, data-driven pages.

In Chapter 5 you integrate ASP.NET's membership infrastructure into the site, to create user registration forms and supporting logic to authenticate/authorize users. You also use the `Profile` module, which allows you to declaratively define user-level properties that are automatically persisted to a durable medium, quite different from the well-known traditional `Session` state variables that only last as long as the user browses the site on one occasion. You build a complete management console to enable administrators to see the list of members, disable members that behave badly on the site, and view and edit each user's profile.

In Chapter 6 you build a sort of Content Management System, a module that enables administrators to completely manage the site's articles, news, and blog posts from an intuitive UI, accessible also by non-technical users. The module will integrate with the built-in membership system to secure the module and track the authors of the articles, and will have a syndication service that publishes a syndication feed of recent content for a specific category, or for every category, and will support ratings and comments, among many other features. The result will be quite powerful, enabling the editor to prepare richly formatted content in advance, and schedule it for automatic publication and retirement, so that the site's content updates are as simple as possible, and require the least effort and time. At the end of the chapter you will have an excellent understanding of how to create an MVC application and how all the working parts come together to give you a functional site.

In Chapter 7 you implement a solution for creating and managing multiple polls on the site. It will feature an administration console for managing the polls through a web browser, a way that enables you to change the polls that show on all the pages, as well as a history page for viewing archived polls.

In Chapter 8 you enrich the site with a complete module for sending out newsletters to members who registered for them in their profile page. The module will enable you to send out the e-mail newsletters from a background thread, instead of the main thread that processes the page request, so that the page won't risk timeouts, and more important, so that the editor will not be left with a blank page for minutes at a time. You use AJAX (Asynchronous JavaScript and XML Programming) to implement partial-page updates that provide real-time feedback about the newsletter being sent in the background. Finally, end users will be able to look at past newsletters listed on an archive page.

In Chapter 9 you create a forums system from scratch, which supports multiple subforums with optional moderation, lists threads and replies through custom pagination with different sorting options, crowd-sourcing mechanisms like those seen on Digg, Reddit, and Stackoverflow, and other features typical of the most recent forum-like software. You also provide complete administration features (deleting, editing, approving, and closing threads and posts).

In Chapter 10 you add a working e-commerce store with most of the essential features, including a complete catalog and order management system, a persistent shopping cart, integrated online payment via credit cards, product ratings, product stock availability, rich formatting of a product's descriptions, including text and images, configurable shipping methods and order statuses, and much more. You implement all this in relatively few pages, because it will leverage the good foundations built in previous chapters, and of course the ASP.NET built-in membership and profile systems, as well as other new features provided by ASP.NET MVC.

In Chapter 11 you make the site's home page fully localizable to an additional language and will support the user's preferred locale settings when displaying dates and numbers. All this can now be done easily with ASP.NET, thanks to its automatic resource generation, implicit and explicit localization expressions, and strongly typed and dynamically compiled global resources.

Finally, in Chapter 12 you look at the different ways to deploy an ASP.NET MVC site, either on a local IIS server, to a remote production site, or to an inexpensive shared hosting server. The new ASP.NET compilation model enables you to use a simple XCOPY deployment that includes everything. You also learn how to deploy the local SQL Server Express database to a remote full-featured SQL Server 2008 instance, and how you can create an installer package for distributing the application to automate as many installation tasks as possible.

Summary

In this first chapter you were given an overview of an aggressive plan to develop a highly functional content-based website that shows you how to use ASP.NET MVC to its full capability. I gave you a broad idea about what we're going to discuss, design, and implement throughout the rest of the book. In each chapter, you learn something new about ASP.NET MVC, and at the end of the book you will also have created a real-world site with most of the features required by modern content-centric sites and e-commerce stores. Furthermore, the site you develop in this book may provide a good deal more functionality than any site you've designed in the past, and the relatively small development effort will enable you to do more than you thought possible in a small amount of time. Microsoft has stated that one of its key goals in the ASP.NET MVC release is to make a developer's job easier and provide more flexibility and control over the HTML content sent to the browser from the server. You can do this by separating your concerns ahead of time into the model, view, and controller, reducing the amount of effort required to implement common functionality. This gives the developers more time to focus on business needs and enables them to offer more advanced functionality to empower users and site administrators, while keeping the site maintainable, testable, and scalable. This book will help you judge whether Microsoft has met this goal. Let the adventure begin!

2

Introducing the ASP.NET Model-View-Controller (MVC)

The first chapter introduced you to TheBeerHouse and the problem, design, and solution that we are going to focus on over the course of this book. But before you start creating the modules necessary to develop TheBeerHouse in ASP.NET MVC, this chapter teaches you a little about what MVC (or the Model-View-Controller) really is and how it is implemented on top of the ASP.NET framework.

The Model-View-Controller Pattern

The Model-View-Controller architectural pattern has been around since 1978 and was first described by Trygve Reenskaug while working on a programming language called Smalltalk at Xerox PARC. The implementation was first described in his now famous paper on the subject, titled "Applications Programming in Smalltalk-80: How to use Model-View-Controller," published in December 1979, and has been popping up in many different ways and forms since the original paper was published. Reenskaug maintains a page that explains MVC in his own words (http://heim.ifi.uio.no/~trygver/themes/mvc/mvc-index.html) and contains his publications on the subject; the 1979 publication is only two pages long and well worth the read.

The MVC pattern has been implemented in almost every programming language in use today, including ColdFusion, Java, JavaScript, Perl, PHP, Python, Ruby, Smalltalk, XML, and of course, .NET. In fact, in November 2002 the W3C (the main international standards body for the World Wide Web) voted to make the MVC pattern part of its XForms specification, which will be integrated directly into the XHTML 2.0 standard.

Reenskaug explains on his site that "the essential purpose of MVC is to bridge the gap between the human user's mental model and the digital model that exists in the computer," as illustrated in Figure 2-1.

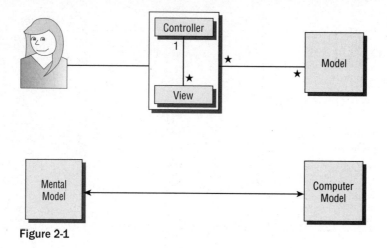

Figure 2-1

He goes on to explain that "the ideal MVC solution supports the user illusion of seeing and manipulating the domain information directly. The structure is useful if the user needs to see the same model element simultaneously in different contexts and/or from different viewpoints." This is important because it puts the emphasis not on the application, but on how the user perceives the data in your application. In other words, the controller and view are only a means to the end of allowing users to visualize the model in a way that they can understand.

Reenskaug defines the Model-View-Controller in the following way:

❑ **Model:** Represents knowledge. A model can be in the simplest case a single object in your application, or in a complex case a combination of objects. It should represent the world as seen by the developer for the application that is being developed; in other words, your database or domain.

❑ **View:** Visual representation of the *model*. It should highlight specific aspects of the model while minimizing the others where possible. According to Reenskaug, it should act as a presentation filter. What he describes as a presentation filter is the notion of a contract created between the *model* and the *view* that will provide the parts of the model requested for the presentation by the *view*.

❑ **Controller:** A controller provides a link between the user and the system. It provides the user with actions that can be taken against the *model*, which in other words creates a set of inputs that can be acted upon and represented to the user in one or more ways through a *view*.

Bringing MVC Down to Earth

The concepts and ideas behind MVC were honestly a little abstract for me when I was first getting started; it took me a while to understand how the model, view, and controller were supposed to work together to create an application. Unfortunately, at the time I didn't have any great examples that clearly defined the lines between the different parts of the model, view, and controller, so I had to learn the hard way.

Luckily, Jeff Atwood, of `codinghorror.com` fame, provided an example that really struck a chord with me that I want to share with you. Figure 2-2 is a visual representation of his example.

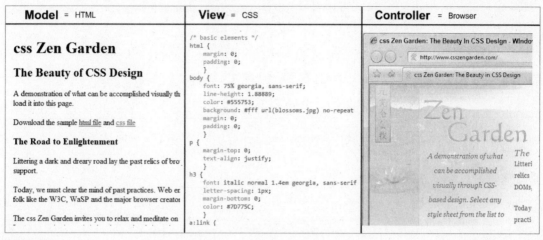

Figure 2-2

This example almost perfectly represents MVC in a way that any web developer with only basic knowledge of HTML and CSS can understand. From the example, MVC can be explained in this way:

❏ **Model:** The HTML is the "skeleton" or definition of the data to be displayed to the user.

❏ **View:** The CSS is the "skin" that gives the HTML a visual presentation. The CSS can be swapped out to view the original content in a different manner, without altering the underlying model. They are relatively, but not completely, independent of each other.

❏ **Controller:** The browser is responsible for combining the CSS and HTML into a final representation that is rendered out to the screen in the form of pixels. It gathers input from users, but it is restricted to the input defined by the HTML in the form of `input`, `select`, `textarea`, and `button` DOM objects.

We find this to be an awesome acknowledgment to the success of the Model-View-Controller, because the browser is a natural interface for a computer user who wants to visualize the World Wide Web. It successfully maps the Mental Model, from Figure 2-1, that a designer envisioned as an interface for the user to the Computer Model, which a developer coded for use on the World Wide Web. So we hope this helped you visualize MVC in a way that helps you break out and understand the concepts behind the model, view, and controller. If you would like to read Jeff's full article, it is available at `http://www .codinghorror.com/blog/archives/001112.html`.

For the purpose of this book we are going to define MVC as the following:

❏ **Model:** The classes that are used to store and manipulate the state of the database, through your domain objects, combined with some business logic.

❏ **View:** The user interface parts, coded in HTML, necessary for rendering the model to the user. It may also render the model as XML or JSON, if needed programmatically, by JavaScript.

❏ **Controller:** The application layer that will accept the input and save that information to the database through your model. It will also contain a small amount of business logic necessary for controlling and validating the inputs. The controller will also decide which view to render, the HTML, XML, or JSON, depending on the form that was requested by the browser.

This definition of MVC for your application, TheBeerHouse, is almost an exact representation of MVC as defined by the ASP.NET MVC team.

ASP.NET MVC vs. ASP.NET Web Forms

As you have seen in the previous section, and can probably imagine, MVC is an architectural pattern that is going to be around for the foreseeable future, especially on the Web. So it is very important to internalize and understand the major differences between ASP.NET MVC and the older ASP.NET Web Forms.

ASP.NET Web Forms

Starting with the .NET Framework version 1.0, in January 2002, Web Forms was Microsoft's first real attempt to provide a first-class web application layer that was both robust and flexible enough to meet the demands of the Web at that time. ASP.NET Web Forms has proven to be a mature technology that runs small- and large-scale websites alike. Web Forms was built around the Windows Forms construction, where you had a declarative syntax with an event-driven model. This allowed visual designers to take full advantage of the drag-and-drop, WYSIWYG interface that they had become accustomed to under Windows Forms development in Visual Studio 6.0. With that interface, they only needed to drop controls onto the ASP.NET page and then wire up the events, as was common in Visual Basic 6.0 development at the time. This made Web Forms a natural choice for Windows Forms developers, because the learning curve was low and the need to understand HTML and many of the web-centric technologies was almost zero.

Web Forms have many strengths and weaknesses:

Strengths

- ❑   Mature technology
- ❑   Provides very good RAD development capabilities
- ❑   Great WYSIWYG designer support in Visual Studio
- ❑   Easy state management
- ❑   Rich control libraries from Microsoft and third-party vendors
- ❑   Abstracts the need to understand HTTP, HTML, CSS, and in some cases JavaScript
- ❑   ViewState and PostBack model
- ❑   A familiar feel to Windows Forms development

Web Forms has grown so much since 2002 because it has the ability to do great things that are often much harder to accomplish in other frameworks.

Weaknesses

- ❑   Display logic coupled with code, through code-behind files
- ❑   Harder to unit test application logic, because of the coupled code-behind files
- ❑   ViewState and PostBack model
- ❑   State management of controls leads to very large and often unnecessary page sizes

Web Forms is not all roses and buttercups; some serious setbacks often show up when you try to optimize your code for scalability. The biggest problems are the ViewState and PostBack models. ViewState is a way to store the state of the controls, such as data, selections, and so on, which is needed to preserve the Windows Forms-like development habits of the developers. ViewState was necessary because the Web is a stateless environment, meaning that when a request comes in to the server it has no recollection of the previous request. So in order to give state to a stateless environment you need to communicate the previous state back to the server. In Web Forms this was accomplished using hidden <input /> fields that could become ridiculously large. This increased size becomes apparent when server controls such as GridView are added to the page. PostBack was another creation to facilitate the Windows Forms development feel; it renders JavaScript for every subscribed event, which leaves a web developer with less control over how the browser communicates with the server.

ASP.NET MVC

ASP.NET was often overlooked as a viable platform for modern, highly interactive websites that required a very granular control over the output of the HTML because of the lack of control over the rendered HTML. This granularity of control was sacrificed in Web Forms to make it more like Windows Forms development — in other words, easier for the drag-and-drop developers. The drag-and-drop nature of Web Forms had upsides for new developers, but had major downsides for advanced developers. The most notable downside is the lack of control over the HTML rendering. This forced these advanced developers to move to other platforms such as PHP and Ruby on Rails, which offered a higher level of control that they required and the MVC programming model that provided a necessary separation of concerns for their highly complex web applications.

This led Microsoft to announce in the fall of 2007 that it was going to create a platform based on the core of ASP.NET that would compete against these other popular MVC web-centric platforms. Microsoft implemented ASP.NET MVC to be a modern web development platform that gives a "closer to the metal" experience to the developers that program with it, by providing full control and testability over the output that is returned to the browser. This is the main and most important difference between Web Forms and MVC, in our opinion.

MVC has many strengths and weaknesses:

Strengths

❑   Provides fine control over rendered HTML

❑   Cleaner generation of HTML (well, as clean as you keep it)

❑   Clear separation of concerns

❑   Provides application-layer unit testing

❑   Can support multiple view engines, such as Brail, NHaml, NVelocity, XSLT, and so on

❑   Easy integration with JavaScript frameworks like jQuery or Yahoo UI frameworks

❑   Ability to map URLs logically and dynamically, depending on your use

❑   RESTful interfaces are used by default (this helps out with SEO)

❑   No ViewState and PostBack model

❑   Supports all the core ASP.NET features, such as authentication, caching, membership, and so on

❑   Size of the pages generated typically much smaller because of the lack of the ViewState

Weaknesses

❑ Not event driven by the framework, so it may be more difficult for ASP.NET Web Form developers to understand

❑ Requires the need to understand, at least at the basic level, HTTP, HTML, CSS, and JavaScript

❑ Third-party library support is not as strong

❑ No direct upgrade path from Web Forms

❑ No ViewState and PostBack model (makes it more difficult to preserve state)

As you can see, the pros and cons of MVC have to be weighed just as much as those of Web Forms, and MVC is not always the logical choice.

How Do I Choose?

It's up to you to decide and your choice needs to be weighted with a number of other factors, such as team and application requirements, when deciding which ASP.NET technology to implement. We have developed the following worksheet off of the strengths from the previous section, which will hopefully help you decide when you need to make this decision.

The worksheet is meant to be a guide for when you are trying to choose between Web Forms and MVC and will hopefully help you make your decision. We have provided seven "yes" or "no" statements that will help you flush out some basic MVC-centric application decisions. If you answer "yes" to any of them, you should consider MVC as a viable option for your application when weighing which way you should go.

You want...	This Book
... more control over the HTML rendering	yes
... more control over the URL	yes
... to do TDD (Test Driven Design)	no
... control over your content for SEO	yes
... to make a RESTful interface	no
... to support multiple view of the same application through mobile, web, and REST APIs	yes
... to support separation of concerns in your code	yes

Even if you don't answer "yes" to any of these statements, MVC still might be right for your application, so give it a chance and see if it works for you. You may just find out that MVC works more naturally with how you and your team develops software.

We want to mention one last thing before we move on: if you want to do new development in MVC, but you have to maintain some legacy Web Form pages, you can mix MVC and Web Forms in the same application. You just need to be aware of the differences between the two, and that you probably will not be able to share any of the Web Form front-end code with MVC, such as Themes, Master Pages, and User Controls.

Feel free to use the preceding decision table and modify it for your own team's decision process. The information provided should arm you with most of the important information that you need to know when deciding which way your project should go technology-wise.

Installing the Prerequisites

To start developing ASP.NET MVC, and to run the code in this book, you will need the following prerequisites installed on your system:

- Visual Web Developer 2008 Express
  http://www.microsoft.com/express/download/

- SQL Server 2008 Express
  http://www.microsoft.com/express/sql/download/

- Microsoft.NET Framework 3.5 SP1
  http://www.microsoft.com/net/

- SQL Server 2008 Management Studio Express (SSMSE)
  http://www.microsoft.com/express/sql/download/

- Microsoft ASP.NET MVC
  http://www.asp.net/mvc/

You can cover the first three prerequisites just by downloading the Visual Web Developer 2008 Express Edition installation file, which includes .NET 3.5 SP1 by default, and SQL Server 2008 Express Edition as an optional add-on during the install process.

If you have already installed all of the aforementioned software, or have a newer edition of the software installed, you can skip to the "Your First ASP.NET MVC Project" section.

Installing the Software

Now that all the prerequisites have been downloaded, you can install them to get your development machine ready for the ASP.NET MVC development you will be doing over the course of this book.

The first thing you want to do is double-click the Visual Web Developer 2008 Express Edition installation file. Figure 2-3 is the first window you will see during the installation process.

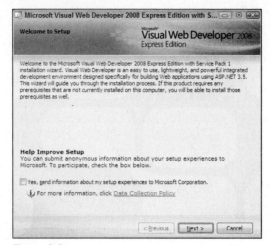

Figure 2-3

Click Next, and you will see the screen shown in Figure 2-4.

Figure 2-4

Now, read the license, accept the agreement, and click Next, and you will see the screen shown in Figure 2-5.

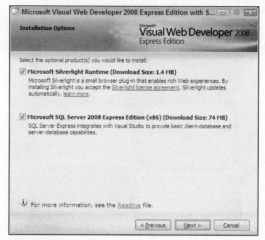

Figure 2-5

With this screen, if you don't already have SQL Server 2008 Express Edition installed, you will want to check the appropriate options. Then click Next, and you will see the screen shown in Figure 2-6.

Figure 2-6

Click Install, and you will see the screen shown in Figure 2-7.

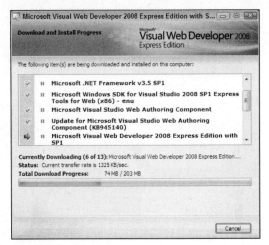

Figure 2-7

Next, the installer will download the required installation files to properly configure your machine. It may take anywhere from 10 minutes to an unspecified amount of time, depending on your Internet connection, to complete the download. After the download completes, you will see an installation screen that looks like Figure 2-8.

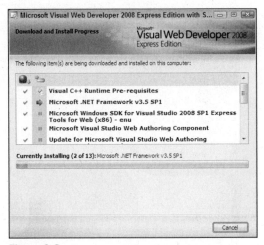

Figure 2-8

The last step is the installation of the software. Your machine may need to reboot, so make sure to reboot your machine right away, because Microsoft SQL Server 2008 Express Edition still needs to install. The installation will be automatically started after Windows restarts. Figure 2-9 shows what the installation screen looks like after the reboot.

If your machine automatically reboots during the installation process, it is because there was a required update that needed to occur before the installation of Visual Web Developer. If this happens you will need to start the installation process over, and follow the same steps from the beginning of this section. Don't worry, the download process will be much quicker because the downloads have already been cached in the Windows temporary directory.

Figure 2-9

When everything has completed successfully you will see the final screen, which looks like Figure 2-10.

Figure 2-10

The next thing you want to install is ASP.NET MVC. You can do this by double-clicking the installation file that you downloaded earlier. Figure 2-11 is what the screen will look like.

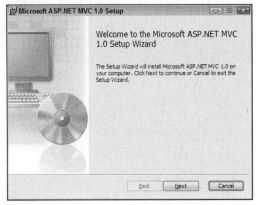

Figure 2-11

Now, click Next, and you will see the screen shown in Figure 2-12.

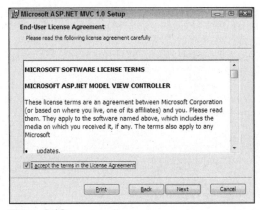

Figure 2-12

Read the license, accept the agreement, and click Next, and you will see the screen shown in Figure 2-13.

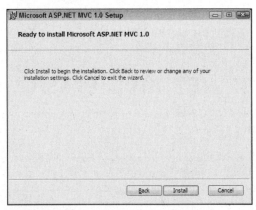

Figure 2-13

Click Install, and you will see the screen shown in Figure 2-14.

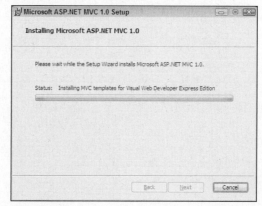

Figure 2-14

When everything has completed successfully, you will see the final screen, which looks like Figure 2-15.

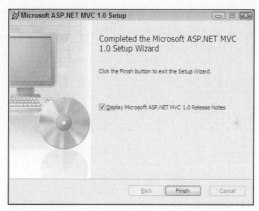

Figure 2-15

You are now ready to start developing your first ASP.NET MVC application project. So let's get started.

Your First ASP.NET MVC Project

To create your first ASP.NET MVC project, you only need the prerequisites listed in the previous section. To start, you first need to open Visual Web Developer 2008 or any version of Visual Studio 2008.

For the purpose of this section, we will be using Visual Studio 2008 Team Development Edition. We have, however, verified that this process works on Visual Web Developer 2008 SP1, Visual Studio 2008 Professional, and Visual Studio 2008 Team Development Edition.

After Visual Studio is open you need to create a new project (File ⇨ New ⇨ Project). See Figure 2-16 for an example.

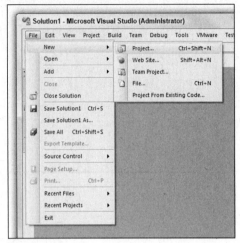

Figure 2-16

Doing this will put you in the New Project screen, where you will then select your preferred language (in our case Visual C#). From there you need to select Web ⇨ ASP.NET MVC Web Application, as depicted in Figure 2-17.

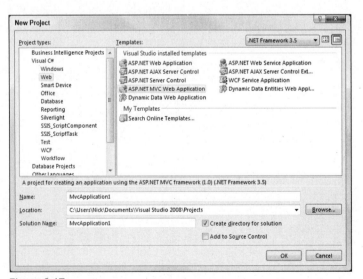

Figure 2-17

We are going to leave all of the project configuration fields set to their default values as shown in Figure 2-17, but you may configure them however you desire. When you are done, click OK, and you will see the screen shown in Figure 2-18.

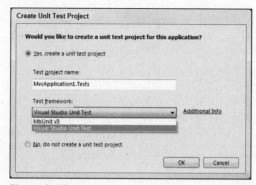

Figure 2-18

You have probably not seen a screen like this before, even if you have done ASP.NET Web Forms development. It is totally new to the ASP.NET MVC project creation process, and it automatically creates a unit testing project based on the default MVC project.

As an added feature, it also allows you to select the testing framework that you would like to use, even non-Microsoft ones, such as NUnit, MbUnit, XUnit, Visual Studio Unit Test, and any other unit test framework that decides to provide an interface to this Visual Studio dialog.

You can choose to create a unit project, or wait until later if desired. For the purpose of this demonstration, we are going to create a unit test project using MbUnit v3 from the drop-down menu. When you are done, click OK, and you will see a Solution Explorer that looks like Figure 2-19.

Figure 2-19

This is what the default folder and file structure looks like for the ASP.NET MVC project. It has a separate folder for Models, Views (as seen in Figure 2-21), and Controllers (as seen in Figure 2-20), as well as a set of default folders for storing JavaScript, CSS, or anything else you would want to deliver from your web application (as seen in Figure 2-22).

Figure 2-20

Two controllers are created by default. The `HomeController` is used to render the home page and the About page. The `AccountController` is used to authenticate a user with the standard ASP.NET membership provider. These two controllers provide you with everything you need to create a very basic web application.

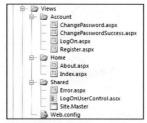

Figure 2-21

The views mirror the controllers that were created so there is one for `Account` and another for `Home`. In these folders there are `aspx` files that are called views. By default, each of these views mirrors an action method from the controller. As you will see later in this book there is a many-to-many relationship between the views and action methods. An action method can map to multiple views and a view can have multiple action methods that use it. We won't get too in-depth about the mapping of views and action methods at this point because we cover this in great detail later in this chapter and in future chapters when you implement your application.

There is also a shared folder called `Shared` which is, for lack of a better word, shared between all of the controllers and can be called by any of the controllers in the project.

The last thing we should discuss, before moving on to the rest of the files in the solution, is what appears to be a rogue `web.config` file located under the `Views` directory. This is a deliberate and strategic `web.config` file that is used, in addition to the one in the root, to block access to all the `aspx` files from getting accessed directly. This `web.config` file contains the following configuration information:

```
<?xml version="1.0"?>
<configuration>
    <system.web>
        <httpHandlers>
            <remove verb="*" path="*.aspx"/>
            <add path="*.aspx" verb="*" type="System.Web.HttpNotFoundHandler"/>
        </httpHandlers>
    </system.web>
```

```
<system.webServer>
    <validation validateIntegratedModeConfiguration="false"/>
    <handlers>
        <remove name="PageHandlerFactory-ISAPI-2.0"/>
        <remove name="PageHandlerFactory-ISAPI-1.1"/>
        <remove name="PageHandlerFactory-Integrated"/>
        <add name="BlockViewHandler" path="*.aspx" verb="*"
preCondition="integratedMode" type="System.Web.HttpNotFoundHandler"/>
    </handlers>
</system.webServer>
</configuration>
```

It contains configuration information for IIS 7, `<system.webServer />`, and IIS 6 and lower, `<system .web />`. So you will be covered on whichever server you decide to deploy your MVC application to.

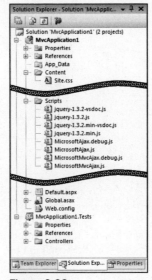

Figure 2-22

The rest of the solution files include JavaScript, style sheets, and other ASP.NET files that you should be familiar with. The JavaScript files that are included by default are Microsoft AJAX and jQuery, as well as debug versions of the files.

> *In the fall of 2008, Microsoft announced a partnership with jQuery (`jquery.com`) to provide support and deliver jQuery with Visual Studio 2010 and some key projects. One of the key projects that jQuery will be delivered with is ASP.NET MVC.*

If you are going to be using jQuery heavily in your application, as we are in this book, we highly recommend that you download the latest version of jQuery and the Visual Studio IntelliSense Documentation for jQuery. jQuery is constantly being developed and new features are getting added all the time, so it really pays to make sure you are running the latest version. You can get the latest production and development files from the jQuery website at `http://www.jquery.com`.

There are some standard ASP.NET files that you have seen before, but we would like to take this opportunity to give you a quick overview of the purpose of the `Global.asax` and `Default.aspx` files. These two files have a special purpose in an MVC application that you should be made aware of.

❑   **`Global.asax`:** This is a standard ASP.NET file. MVC takes advantage of this file to initialize all the URL routes, for mapping actions and controllers to URLs when the application is first started, using the `Application_Start` event handler as shown in the following code:

```
public static void RegisterRoutes(RouteCollection routes)
{
    routes.IgnoreRoute("{resource}.axd/{*pathInfo}");

    routes.MapRoute(
        "Default",
        "{controller}/{action}/{id}",
        new { controller = "Home", action = "Index", id = "" }
    );
}

protected void Application_Start()
{
    RegisterRoutes(RouteTable.Routes);
}
```

❑   **`Default.aspx`:** This is a standard ASP.NET file. It is not necessary on IIS 7, because of IIS 7's integrated pipeline. However, you should not worry about it being present on an IIS 7 MVC application because it will not interfere with the execution of the code. The sole purpose of this file is to handle root requests on IIS 6 and lower. It does this using the `Page_Load` event handler of the page and forcing the request through the `MvcHttpHandler` instead of rendering the page, which is empty. The `Page_Load` event handler is shown in the following code:

```
public void Page_Load(object sender, System.EventArgs e)
{
    HttpContext.Current.RewritePath(Request.ApplicationPath);
    IHttpHandler httpHandler = new MvcHttpHandler();
    httpHandler.ProcessRequest(HttpContext.Current);
}
```

The final thing we want to cover is what the default ASP.NET MVC application design looks like when running in a browser. You can see an example of this in Figure 2-23.

It is a pretty basic layout, but it is a good example of the Home and Account controllers and can be used to render to and interact with the browser.

The rest of this chapter covers the basics of the ASP.NET MVC framework, with a specific focus on the model, view, and controller.

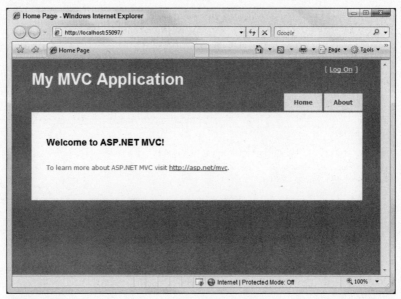

Figure 2-23

The Model

In ASP.NET MVC, the model refers to your application's business layer or domain objects. These objects are responsible for persisting the state of your application, which is often, but not necessarily, inside a database. There really isn't much to explain about the model as it relates to the ASP.NET MVC framework because it is based on your implementation and the design of your business layer. You can use any design pattern, methodology, and/or custom process to accomplish the creation of the model:

❑   DDD (Domain Driven Design)

❑   TDD (Test Driven Design)

❑   ALT.NET

❑   Repository Pattern

❑   Service Pattern

❑   Specification Pattern

❑   POCO (Plain Old CLR Object)

❑   LINQ-To-SQL

❑   ADO.NET Entity Framework

❑   NHiberante

❑ Data Tables

❑ Your own custom business layer

❑ Any combination of the above

The point behind all of this is to try to demonstrate that it is up to you to define the model. It is up to you to make the best decisions related to your requirements. You can make the model as simple or as complex as needed. Everything is up to you when talking about the M in MVC.

The View

In ASP.NET MVC, the view is the presentation of your application's business layer or model. Typically with ASP.NET MVC this is HTML, but your view can be rendered in any form that can be transmitted over the Internet, including JSON, XML, binary, RSS, ATOM, and your own customized protocol if you have one.

There is a dynamic range of views that allow it to be capable of such a wide range of delivery types in the ASP.NET MVC framework because of a provider engine appropriately called the view engine. The view engine is responsible for taking the controller and action names and then delivering the right view based on these names.

> *When we talk about the view engine from here forward, we will be specifically referring to the ASP.NET MVC implementation, called* WebFormViewEngine, *which is based on the* aspx, ascx, *and* master *files. Many other types of view engines exist, such as Brail, NHaml, NVelocity, and XSLT that are available from the MVC Contrib project located at* www.codeplex.com/mvccontrib, *if you are interested in learning more.*

ViewEngine

The default view engine in the ASP.NET MVC framework, the WebFormViewEngine, uses a hierarchy of folders and aspx and ascx files when rendering HTML pages to the browser. The WebFormViewEngine uses the standard ASP.NET Web Forms rendering engine that has been present in the framework since version 1.0, however the emphasis has been moved from control-based rendering to an inline code-based rendering that is reminiscent of its predecessor, plain old ASP. Let's take another look at the hierarchy that the default view engine uses, as seen in Figure 2-24.

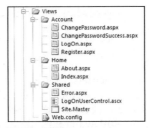

Figure 2-24

The view engine treats `aspx` and `ascx` files almost equally, so that it is possible to render your HTML from an `ascx` or user control file in the same way that an `aspx` or page file works. As you can probably imagine there needs to be a hierarchy or order to which an `aspx` or `ascx` file is picked from the controller or `Shared` directory in Figure 2-24. The default ASP.NET MVC view engine uses the following lookup order, from top to bottom, when trying to determine which view to render:

1. ~/Views/{controller}/{action}.aspx

2. ~/Views/{controller}/{action}.ascx

3. ~/Views/Shared/{action}.aspx

4. ~/Views/Shared/{action}.ascx

What this lookup order means is that:

❑ Controller directories are always checked before the `Shared` directory.

❑ `aspx` or page files are always checked before the `ascx` or user control files.

The lookup order even applies to `master` files, which allows you to select the master page template that you want to render with your view. The lookup order that the master pages follows is slightly different than the page and user controls:

1. ~/Views/{controller}/{master_name}.master

2. ~/Views/Shared/{master_name}.master

Now that you have learned how view pages, controls, and master pages are selected, let's take a little closer look at the files themselves.

ViewMasterPage, ViewPage, and ViewUserControl

In ASP.NET MVC, there are three new takes on old objects that you are probably familiar with from ASP.NET Web Forms. These types probably come as no surprise, given that we just covered them in the "ViewEngine" section and the title of this section, but they are as follows, listed with their Web Form equivalent.

MVC	Web Forms	Description
ViewMasterPage	MasterPage	Responsible for providing a template to the page object.
ViewPage	Page	Responsible for the main content of the web page being viewed.
ViewUserControl	UserControl	Used to sub-divide content and provide a modular design.

These object types in MVC are actually inherited from their Web Form counterparts, because they rely on their built-in execution, in the ASP.NET Core, as a way of delivering the content through the servers such as IIS. So all the interfaces you have become accustomed to (that is, `User`, `Context`, `Request`, `Response`, `IsPostBack`, and so on.) are still available in the MVC version of the page, user control, and master page.

However, when developing for MVC there is a primary difference in the way in which an MVC view is constructed in the code-behind compared to its Web Form counterpart. The best way to illustrate this difference is by showing you all that this required to have a fully functional view in MVC:

```
public partial class MyViewPage : ViewPage
{
}
```

Yup, that is all that is required. Pretty cool, huh? This is possible because all the application logic that used to be in button clicks and other event actions, via POST-backs, has been moved to the controller actions.

> **Since all application logic has been moved to the controller, it is now considered a bad practice in ASP.NET MVC to put any application logic code in the code-behind file.**

We have covered the basics of how views are rendered and found the differences between MVC views compared to their Web Form counterparts. We go into great detail about programming views in later chapters of this book, however we are not quite done; we want to cover a couple more basic things before moving on to "The Controller" section. These include special properties designed to allow easy communication between the model, controller, and view.

We have broken up the properties into logical sections, so that we can discuss the purpose and intended use of each of them as envisioned by the ASP.NET MVC team.

ViewData and Model

The ViewData property is used to store and transmit data from the model and controller to the view for rendering. It can either be used as a Dictionary object, such as:

```
<%= ViewData["text"] %>
```

or as a typed model object, such as:

```
<%= ViewData.Model.CustomerID %>
```

That is defined using generics in the inheriting object, such as a Customer type in the ViewPage:

```
public partial class EditCustomer : ViewPage<Customer>
```

or

```
<%@ Page Inherits="System.Web.Mvc.ViewUser<Customer>" %>
```

It is a very versatile collection that is available to both the views and the controllers, and is passed via the ViewContext, which inherits from the ControllerContext.

TempData

The TempData property is a session-backed temporary storage dictionary, much like ViewData, which is available for the current request, plus one. What this means is that any data you store in the TempData is kept in the session storage for one additional request, beyond the one you're currently processing.

You may be scratching your head like we were when we first learned about `TempData`, and wondering why this would be important enough to include in the framework. There is actually a very simple answer to this question: it allows you to pass data across requests, much like you have been accustomed to with the `ViewState` that is used in Web Forms. It is also great for passing data between redirects. Say you have the following scenario:

A user comes into your site unauthenticated and you have to redirect him to the login page. You want to display a message saying he needs to log in before viewing the content, but that message should display only when he doesn't visit the login page directly.

Previously, to accomplish this type of process you had to jump through hoops to determine if the user came from another page on your site, by checking the referrer or some other custom process that you had to come up with. Additionally, even after you got this done it was hard to customize that message to give the users some indication of where they came from or are going after they log in. `TempData` really comes to the rescue in this case, because the following is the only code that you need to display that message:

```
<% if (TempData["Message"] != null) { %>
    <div class="message"><%= TempData["Message"] %></div>
<% } %>
```

You can even put this code in your master page so that you can display a message to your user on any page in your site, and all that you need is these three lines of code in the view.

HTML and AJAX Extension Methods

The HTML and AJAX extension methods provide a way to generate snippets of code for such things as form inputs and links. For example, if you wanted to generate a text box with the name attribute set to `CustomerName`, you just need to put the following in your view:

```
<%= Html.TextBox("CustomerName") %>
```

which will generate the following HTML:

```
<input type="text" name="CustomerName" id="CustomerName" value="" />
```

As an added feature, if you actually wanted to render the page with `CustomerName` already filled in, you would just need to set `ViewData["CustomerName"]` in the controller equal to whatever you want to be rendered in the HTML.

An extension method for all of the form inputs available through HTML has been provided with the ASP.NET MVC framework, plus some other extensions such as AJAX implementations of the form inputs and anchor link generation for controller actions. The majority of all the HTML and AJAX extension methods that you will need to generate a web page have been provided in the framework, and if there is something that you must have, you can extend your own method from the HTML helper by doing the following:

```
public static string MyCustomControl (this HtmlHelper html, string name)
```

The `this` keyword is what is used to add these custom methods to the `HtmlHelper`, which is represented as `Html` in the view pages. We cover extension methods in greater detail in Chapter 6.

The Controller

In ASP.NET MVC, the controller contains the application logic for manipulating the model, handling user interactions, and choosing the view to display to the browser. It can be thought of as the glue that holds the model and views together.

The controller, in actuality, is just a class object that inherits from the `System.Web.Mvc.IController` interface. However, the typical implementation that you will encounter will be abstracted away from the `IController` interface, using an already-implemented `Controller` class. A properly implemented controller will contain one or more action methods, which we cover in a later section of this chapter.

URL Routes

Another important part of the controller is the routes that define the URL. The routes tell the controller factory which controller to instantiate and which action in the controller should be executed. Let's take the default route, which you learned about earlier in the chapter, as an example:

```
routes.MapRoute(
    "Default",
    "{controller}/{action}/{id}",
    new { controller = "Home", action = "Index", id = "" }
);
```

In this route definition, the URL can be constructed in the following manner:

```
{controller}/{action}/{id}
```

How the controller and routes work is one of those instances where it is easier to demonstrate the capabilities than to try to explain, so here is a table to demonstrate how the preceding route breaks up the following URLs:

URL	Controller	Action	ID
/	Home	Index	
/Home	Home	Index	
/Home/About	Home	About	
/Account	Account	Index	
/Account/User/1	Account	User	1

You may have noticed in the table that some of the parts of the URL are not defined, and in the first case none of the parts are defined. This is because a set of defaults are defined for each part of the URL, and if the part of the URL is missing, the default is used. The default is defined with the following line in the previous example code:

```
new { controller = "Home", action = "Index", id = "" }
```

In ASP.NET MVC, two parts need to be present in every route, and they are `controller` and `action`. This is because these two parts are required by the controller factory to find the correct controller object and then the correct action method in that controller. All the other parts can optionally map to the action methods' parameters.

> *When we talk about the controller factory from here forward, we will be specifically referring to the ASP.NET MVC implementation, called `DefaultControllerFactory`, which is based on the controller objects using the following format: {controller_name}Controller (that is, **Home**Controller, **Account**Controller). Many other types of controller factories exist, such as those based on the Inversion of Control principle, Castle Windsor, Sprint.NET, Structure Map, and Unity that are available from the MVC Contrib project located at `www.codeplex.com/mvccontrib`, if you are interested in learning more.*

Controller Factory

The default controller factory in the ASP.NET MVC framework, the `DefaultControllerFactory`, uses the following criteria, by default, when searching for available controllers for use:

❑ The namespace of the web assembly with `Controllers` added on the end (that is, `TheBeerHouse.Web.Controllers`).

❑ The objects in the namespace must be in the following format {controller_name}Controller (that is, **Home**Controller, **Account**Controller).

❑ The objects must also inherit from the `IController` interface.

These criteria can best be seen in the default solution that you saw earlier in this chapter. Take another look at the controllers, as shown in Figure 2-25.

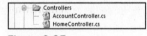

Figure 2-25

All of those criteria may have made the process of adding a new controller sound complex, but really all that you need to do to accomplish this is add a new code file to the `Controllers` directory and make sure the object in the code file inherits the `Controller` object from the `System.Web.Mvc` namespace.

Actions

The actions, like we talked about earlier in this chapter, are what binds the URL to the view being displayed. They are not that difficult to understand, but to help separate out the different parts that make up an action we have divided them into a couple of logical sections. We are going to use the following code example to help bring all of the different sections together:

```
[AcceptVerbs(HttpVerbs.Post)]
[OutputCache(Duration = 600)]
public ActionResult GetCustomer (string name, string email)
{
    // code for executing the GetCustomer action
    return View(customer);
}
```

Methods

When we refer to an action, we are actually talking about a standard .NET method with parameters, return values, and attributes just like any other in your code. The only thing that makes it an action is the fact that the method is inside of a controller class.

In the preceding example code, the whole thing can be considered your method, and is probably pretty similar to every other method that you have ever seen or developed.

Results

A result is just another name for the return value of the method. The only criterion for the return value is that it must be, or inherit from, the type `ActionResult`.

In the preceding example code, the result type is `ActionResult`, but it actually returns an object that inherits from `ActionResult` called `ViewResult`. The `ViewResult` is created from a protected method available on the controller called `View()`, which does all the necessary instantiating of the `ViewResult` to be returned.

Filters

The filters are implemented as attributes on the action methods. There are two types of filters: one for actions and another for results. The action filter refers to the action method and has two events. One is for custom processing before the action method has been executed and the other is for after the action method has been executed. The results filter refers to the HTTP response and has the same two events that the action has, one for before the response is sent and one for after the response is sent to the browser. We won't go into great detail about filters in this book; however, we will be using them for such things as authorization, caching, and RESTful service results.

In the sample code, the filter is the attribute called `OutputCache`.

Selectors

The selectors are implemented as attributes on the action methods. Because both filters and selectors are implemented using attributes, it is often difficult to determine the difference between them, but there is a huge difference. The selectors are used when the controller factory is trying to determine which action method is the correct one to process the request, so they really have nothing to do with the action method execution, just the selection of the action method by the controller factory.

In the sample code, the selector is the attribute called `AcceptVerbs`.

Summary

In this chapter, you've learned the basics of ASP.NET MVC that you need to know in order to understand the code you will be developing through the remaining chapters of this book. Everything that we covered in this chapter probably won't fully make sense until you start implementing your application, so you should use this chapter as a reference while reading the rest of the book. Don't hesitate to come back to this chapter and review anything that you need to understand better later on.

3

Developing the Site Design

The first step in developing a new site is to develop the visual site design consisting of the site's overall layout and use of graphics. This visual architecture defines the "look and feel" from the user's perspective. You start by establishing the user experience you want people to have, and then you design the plumbing behind the scenes that will provide that user experience. Some basic considerations that affect the user's experience are the menu and navigation, use of images, and the organization of elements on the page. The menu must be intuitive and should be augmented by navigation hints such as a site map or *breadcrumbs* that can remind users where they are, relative to the site as a whole.

You should consider the specific features included in the ASP.NET framework before writing any code, so you can take advantage of the work that's already been done by the developers at Microsoft. By laying a good foundation for the technical architecture, you can improve code reusability and enhance maintainability. This chapter looks at the overall visual layout of the site and explains how you can take advantage of a powerful feature called *master pages*. For many of you, master pages aren't anything new; they have been around since ASP.NET 2.0 and nothing about them has really drastically changed. They are still used to group functionality into templates that provide the common elements shared by many pages.

Problem

Many developers start out writing source code without paying attention to the primary goal of the site: to provide a simple but highly functional graphical application for users to interact with. Developing the user interface seems like a very basic task, but if not done properly, you may have to revisit it several times during development. Every time you go back and change fundamental features it will require a certain amount of rework, not to mention a whole new round of unit and integration testing. Even worse, if you take the user interface too lightly, you will likely end up regretting it because users may choose not to visit your site. You have various elements to consider when creating the site design. First, you must convince yourself of one simple fact: appearance *is* important! You should repeat this out loud a couple of times. If your site doesn't look good, people may regret being there. It's easy for a developer to get caught up with the difficult tasks of organizing source code into classes and coding the business logic — the cosmetics of the site just don't seem so important, right? Wrong! The user interface is the first thing presented to the end user: if it is ugly, unclear, and basically unusable, chances are good the user will be left with a bad impression of the site and the company behind it. Sadly, this will happen regardless of how fast and scalable the site is. Users are unable to see how neat and organized your source code is and how well-designed your business layer is, or how normalized your database is, so the only real impression that you can leave on your potential users is a nice clean interface that appeals to the masses. It is important to have an engaging design that keeps the users' confidence and trust high for your website, because it has been shown that poorly designed sites have less appeal and don't inspire confidence or trust in the website they are viewing.

After you choose the layout and colors to use, you need to ensure that the site will look the same on different browsers. A couple of years ago, Internet Explorer (IE) was the absolute dominant browser among Windows users, and if you were developing a site targeted to Windows users, you could assume that the majority of your user base would use IE to browse the site, and thus develop and test it only against IE. However, things have changed, Mozilla Firefox and the WebKit Project (examples of WebKit are Google Chrome or Apple Safari) are now gaining popularity among the Internetians and they are available to Windows users and non-Windows users, such as Linux and Mac OS alike. You are not targeting just a small niche of users (that is, not just Windows developers), but *all* people that go to your client's pub, and because other browsers besides IE are popular, it is absolutely necessary to ensure that your site works well for the most popular browsers. If you ignore this and just target IE, Firefox users may come to the site and find a layout much different from what they would expect, with wrong alignments, sizes, and colors, with panels and text over each other — in other words, a complete mess. As you can guess, a user who is presented such an ugly page would typically leave it, which means losing a potential client or customer for the online store. At the very least, this person's visit would have generated page views and thus banner impressions. Because you don't want to lose visitors, this book considers the latest versions of Internet Explorer, Chrome, and Firefox.

Designing the user interface layer doesn't mean just writing the HTML for a page; it also involves the navigation system and the ability of the webmaster or site administrator (if not the end user) to easily change the appearance of the site without requiring them to edit the actual content pages (which are numerous). It is helpful to develop a system that enables people to easily change the menus of the site, and modify the site appearance (the fonts, the colors, and the size of the various parts that compose the page) because this minimizes the work of administrators and makes users happy. Once you're done with the site's home page, developing all the other pages will take much less time because the home page establishes layout and navigation elements that will apply throughout the site. And if you need to modify something in the site's layout (for example, adding a new poll box to be displayed on the right-hand side of any page), you will be able to do this easily if you've developed a common user interface shared among many pages. This is why it's definitely worth spending some additional time thinking about a well-designed UI foundation layer instead of firing up Visual Studio and starting to code right away. This is really a strategic decision that can save you hours or even days of work later. Remember that fundamental changes applied later in the development phase will require more time and effort to implement.

Design

This section takes the problems described in the first section and discusses how to solve them by devising a technical system design. In practice, you will design and implement the following:

- ❑   A good-looking graphical template (layout) that appears the same with Internet Explorer, Chrome, and Firefox.

- ❑   A way to easily share the created template to all pages of the site, without physically copying and pasting the entire code to each page.

❑   A navigation system that enables you to easily edit the links shown in the site's menu, and clearly tells users where they currently are in the site map, enabling them to navigate backward.

❑   A way to apply not only a common design to all pages of the site, but also a common behavior, such as counting page views or applying the user's favorite style to the page.

We describe how you can utilize some of the new features in ASP.NET when implementing your reusability, menu, navigation, and customization requirements. Later, in the Solution section, you put these powerful new features into action!

Designing the Site Layout

When you develop a site design, you typically create a mock-up with a graphics application such as Adobe Photoshop or Paint.NET (if you want a free alternative) to show you what the final site may look like before you do any specific layout or coding in HTML. Once you have a mock-up, you can show this around to the various model users, testers, and managers, who can then make a decision to proceed with coding. You might create a simple picture, like the one shown in Figure 3-1, in which you show how the content will be laid out in the various areas of the page.

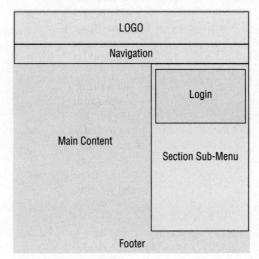

Figure 3-1

This is a typical two-column layout, with a header and footer. When the layout gets approved, you must re-create it with real graphics and HTML. Do this in the graphics program because, on average, it takes much less time for a graphic designer to produce these mock-ups as images, rather than real HTML pages. Once the client approves the final mock-up, the graphic designer can cut the mock-up image into small pieces that you can use in an HTML page.

Creating a mock-up is not always easy for those of us who aren't very artistic by nature. For a medium- or large-size company, this is not a problem because there is usually someone else, a professional graphic designer, to create the graphical design, and then the developers (people like us) will build the application around it. It is recommended that you find a person who specializes in interface design;

you can usually find a graphic designer at your local college or on one of the many websites that specialize in bringing together graphic designers with software developers. We find that having a graphic designer for creating a visually appealing website layout actually makes us more productive, because while they are developing a front-end layout we can feel free to start creating the database and hooking up the business layer. Usually, they are finished with the design and have had it approved by management by the time we are ready to start applying the layout of the website to the business logic, or in the case of MVC, hooking up the controller to the view.

However, sometimes it can be helpful and cheaper to enlist the assistance of a template store if you're faced with creating the graphical design by yourself and don't have the resources to hire a graphic designer. For the purpose of creating the website discussed in this book, we used Free CSS Templates (www.freecss templates.org) to create a good-looking site design that we could use as a starting point. It provided a CSS-based layout with all the necessary HTML and PNG files that we needed to get started. If you prefer a more sophisticated design you may want to try Template Monster (www.templatemonster.com). It includes the design as PSD files (to be opened with Photoshop), necessary image files, and some HTML pages with the images already cut in slices and positioned using CSS. We found that it was not possible to use its pre-built HTML pages verbatim because we wanted to create our own styles and customize our HTML markup, but it was very helpful to have a visual template to start with. This can give your site a professional feel early in the game, which can help you sell your design to the appropriate people.

Technologies Used to Implement the Design

ASP.NET is the overriding technology that makes the site work. This runs on the web server and takes advantage of the functionality provided by the .NET Framework. However, ASP.NET does not run on the user's computer; instead, it dynamically generates the elements a browser uses to render a page. These elements that are sent down to the browser consist of HTML, images, JavaScript, and Cascading Style Sheets (CSS), which provide colors, sizes, and alignments for various items in the HTML Document Object Model (DOM).

HTML is defined in several ways. You can use the visual form designer in Visual Studio to drop controls onto the form, and this automatically creates HTML code; however, this method is less useful in ASP.NET MVC because of the focus and emphasis on control over the HTML markup. Or, you can hand-edit or author your own HTML code to produce a tighter, more professional feel to your HTML code; this will give external users a bit of insight into your coding styles and habits if they care to look at the HTML.

ASP.NET 1.x used a "code behind" model: HTML (and some presentation-oriented C# code) was put in an .aspx file, and implementation C# code would go into a separate file that would be inherited by the .aspx file. We call the .aspx file "the page" because that's where the visual web page is defined. This provided some separation between presentation code and the related implementation code. One problem with this model is that the auto-generated code created by the form designer would be placed in the same files that the developer uses for his code.

This was slightly improved in the ASP.NET 2.0 code-behind model, which used a new feature of the .NET Framework called *partial classes*. The idea is simple: allow one class to span more than one file. Visual Studio will auto-generate at runtime the code for declaring the controls and registering events, and then it will combine that with the user-written code; the result is a single class that is inherited by the .aspx page. The @Page directive declared in the .aspx page uses the CodeFile attribute to reference the .cs code-behind file with the user-written code.

In ASP.NET MVC the concept of code separation was taken one step further by making it unnecessary to use code-behind files for your user interface or view. The code that the view interacted with was moved to the controllers; this provided a wonderful separation that now allows the views to be easily swapped out and replaced with a different kind of view without needing to copy or modify the underlying code that was used to drive the view.

Using CSS to Define Styles in Style Sheet Files

It is not possible to give an exhaustive explanation of Cascading Style Sheets (CSS) in this book, but we'll cover some of the general concepts. You should consult other sources for complete details about CSS. The purpose of CSS is to specify how visual HTML tags are to be rendered by specifying various stylistic elements such as font size, color, alignment, and so on. These styles can be included as attributes of HTML tags, or they can be stored separately and referred to by class or ID.

Sometimes, HTML files have the styles hard-coded into the HTML tags themselves, such as the following example:

```
<div style="align: justify; color: red; background-color: yellow; font-size:
12px;">some text</div>
```

This is bad because it is difficult to modify these stylistic elements without going into all the HTML files and hunting for the CSS attributes. Instead, you should always put the style definitions in a separate style sheet file with an extension of .css; or, if you insist on including styles inside an HTML file, you should at least define them in a <style> section at the top of the HTML file.

When you group CSS styles together, you can create small classes that syntactically resemble classes or functions in C#. You can assign them a class name, or ID, to allow them to be referenced in the class= attribute of HTML tags.

If you use style sheet classes and you want to change the font size of all HTML tags that use that class, you only need to find that class's declaration and change that single occurrence in order to change many visual HTML elements of that given type. In fact, this cascading of styles across the entire page is where the initial two letters of CSS come from. If the style sheet is defined in a separate file, you will benefit even more from this approach because you will change a single file and *n* pages will change their appearance accordingly.

The primary benefits of using CSS are to minimize the development effort required to maintain styles and to enforce a common look and feel among many pages. Beyond this, however, CSS also ensures safety for your HTML code and overall site. Let's assume that the client wants to change some styles of a site that are already in production. If you've hard-coded styles into the HTML elements of the page, you'd have to look in many files to locate the styles to change, and you might not find them all, or you might change something else by mistake — this could break something! However, if you've used style classes stored separately in CSS files, it's easier to locate the classes that need to be changed, and your HTML code will be untouched and safe.

Furthermore, separating the CSS files can make a site more efficient and help reduce bandwidth costs. The browser will download it once and then cache it (assuming that your server is set up correctly to tell the browser to cache the CSS file). The pages that include a reference to the cached .css file will not have to re-download the CSS file, so the request will be much smaller, and therefore faster to download. In some cases this can dramatically speed up the loading and rendering of web pages in a user's browser.

Here is an example of how you can redefine the style of the DIV object shown earlier by storing it in a separate file named styles.css:

```
.mystyle {
    align: justify;
    color: red;
    background-color: yellow;
    font-size: 12px;
}
```

Then, in the .aspx or .htm page, you link the CSS file to the HTML as follows:

```
<head>
    <link href="/Content/styles.css" text="text/css" rel="style sheet" />
    <!-- other metatags… -->
</head>
```

Finally, you write the HTML division tag and specify which CSS class you want it to use:

```
<div class="mystyle">some text</div>
```

Note that when the style was declared, we used the dot (.) prefix for the class name. This indicates to the browser that is rendering the styles that this style is a class and can be applied to any element that contains that class. You have to do this for all of your custom style classes.

If you want to define a style to be applied to all HTML objects of a certain kind (for example, to all <p> paragraphs, or even the page's <body> tag), you can write the following specification in the style sheet file:

```
body {
    margin: 0px;
    font-family: Verdana;
    font-size: 12px;
}

p {
    align: justify;
    text-size: 10px;
}
```

This sets the default style of all body tags and all <p> (paragraph) tags in one place. You could also specify a different style for some paragraphs by stating an explicit class name in those tags.

Yet another way to associate a style class to an HTML object is by ID. You define the class name with a # prefix, as follows:

```
#header {
    padding: 0px;
    margin: 0px;
    width: 100%;
    height: 184px;
    background-image: url(images/HeaderSlice.gif);
}
```

Then you could use the `id` attribute of the HTML tag to link the CSS to the HTML. For example, this is how you could define an HTML division tag and specify that you want it to use the #header style:

```
<div id="header">some text</div>
```

You typically use this approach for single objects, such as the header, the footer, the container for the left, right, and center column, and so on. This means that, unlike the class and element styles previously discussed where you could style multiple tags all on the same page, you are allowed to have only one ID tag of the same name on the page at once. So only one header, footer, and other named elements using ID are allowed under the HTML syntax and it is an error if you have more than one; that can cause problems with CSS and JavaScript that reference that ID.

You can also mix the various approaches. Suppose that you want to give a certain style to all links into a container with the `sectiontitle` class, and some other styles to links into a container with the `sectionbody` class. You could do it this way:

The .css file

```
.sectiontitle a {
    color: yellow;
}

.sectionbody a {
    color: red;
}
```

The .aspx/.html file

```
<div class="sectiontitle">
some text
<a href="http://www.wrox.com">Wrox</a>
some text
</div>

<div class="sectionbody">
some other text
<a href="http://www.wiley.com">Wiley</a>
some other text
</div>
```

Finally, you can mix the various approaches to target specific instances where you want to style certain elements with certain classes, or even the combination of two classes when together. The preceding code is like casting a large net to catch as many elements as you can; the following code is the reverse of that, in that it allows you to target certain corner cases. Suppose that you want to give a certain style to links that have only the class `sectiontitle`, and a different style to links that contain both `sectiontitle` and `first-instance` classes:

The .css file

```
a.sectiontitle {
    color: yellow;
}
```

```
a.sectiontitle.first-instance {
    color: red;
}
```

The .aspx/.html file

```
<a class=="sectiontitle first-instance" href="http://www.wrox.com">Wrox</a>
some other text
<a class=="sectiontitle" href="http://www.wiley.com">Wiley</a>
some other text
<a href="http://www.wiley.com">Wiley</a>
some other text
```

The first link will render as the color red, the second link will render as the color yellow, and the third link on the page will render normally.

Avoid Using HTML Tables to Control Layout

Sometimes developers will use HTML tables to control the positioning of other items on a web page. This was considered the standard practice before CSS was developed, but many developers still use this methodology today. Although this is a very common practice, the W3C officially discourages it (www.w3c.org/tr/wai-webcontent), saying:

> *"Tables should be used to mark up truly tabular information ("data tables"). Content developers should avoid using them to lay out pages ("layout tables"). Tables for any use also present special problems to users of screen readers."*

In other words, HTML tables should be used for displaying tabular data on the page, like a spreadsheet, not to build the entire layout of the page. For that, you should use container elements (such as DIVs) and their style attribute, possibly through the use of a separate <style> section or a separate CSS file. This is ideal for a number of reasons:

❑   If you use DIVs and a separate style sheet file to define appearance and position, you won't need to repeat this definition again and again, for each and every page of your site. This leads to a site that is both faster to develop and easier to maintain.

❑   The site will load much faster for end users! Remember that the style sheet file will be downloaded by the client only once, and then loaded from the cache for subsequent requests of pages until it changes on the server. If you define the layout inside the HTML file using tables, the client instead will download the table's layout for every page, and thus download more bytes, with the result that downloading the whole page will require a longer time and cost you more in bandwidth. Typically, a CSS-driven layout can trim the downloaded bytes by up to 50%, and the advantage of this approach becomes immediately evident. Furthermore, this savings has a greater impact on a heavily loaded web server — sending fewer bytes to each user can be multiplied by the number of simultaneous users to determine the total savings on the web server side of the communications.

❑   Screen readers, software that can read the text and other content of the page for blind and visually impaired users, have a much more difficult job when tables are used for layout on the page. Therefore, by using a table-free layout, you can increase the accessibility of the site. This is a very important requisite for certain categories of sites, such as those for public administration and government agencies. Few companies are willing to write off entire groups of users over simple matters like this. An easy way to see how a screen reader for the blind will read your site is to remove all the style sheets from your website. If it doesn't flow straight down and is broken up into content sections, they are going to have a tough time figuring out which content is important and how it should be read.

❑ CSS styles and DIVs provide greater flexibility than tables. You can, for example, have different style sheet files that define different appearances and positions for the various objects on the page. By switching the linked style sheet, you can completely change the appearance of the page, without changing anything in the content pages themselves. And it's not just a matter of colors and fonts — you can also specify positions for objects in CSS files, and thus have a file that places the menu box on the upper-left corner of the page, and another one that puts it on the bottom-right corner. Because you want to allow users to pick their favorite styles from a list of available themes, this is a particularly important point.

❑ CSS even enables you to create a specific layout for the printer. This is a very important point, because the user is usually interested in printing only the content of the page and not the sidebars and login information that is presented in the browser. These elements of the page can be easily set to not be displayed through CSS when they are being printed. Also, if you use a lot of dark background colors that would just use up ink, you can change the dark backgrounds to white to save the end user some money on the cost of ink and still have your website print in a way that you control.

❑ CSS enables you to target different classes of devices in some cases without requiring new HTML markup, such as mobile devices like PDAs or smartphones. Due to their constrained screen size, it is necessary to adapt the output for them, so that the content fits the small screen well and is easily readable. You can do this with a specific style sheet that changes the size and position of some containers (placing them one under the other, rather than in vertical columns), or hide them completely. For example, you might hide the container for the banners, polls, and the header with a big logo. Try to do this if you use tables — it will be much more difficult. You'll have to think about a custom skinning mechanism, and you'll need to write separate pages that define the different layouts available; this is much more work than just writing a new CSS file.

Sharing the Common Design Among Multiple Pages

Once you finish creating your beautiful site design, you need to find a way to quickly apply it to n pages, where n could be dozens or even hundreds of pages. The previous ASP.NET 1.x edition of this book followed the classic approach of isolating common parts of the design into user controls files, to be imported into all pages that needed them. Specifically, we had a user control for the header, and another for the footer. Although this was immensely better than actually replicating all code in all pages, and much better than including files of classic ASP (because of their object-oriented nature), it still wasn't ideal. The problem with this approach was that, for each and every page, you would still need to write some lines in .aspx files to import the controls, and other lines to place the controls where you wanted them to appear on the page. Thus, if you place them somewhere on the first page, and somewhere else on the second page, the two pages would appear differently at runtime. You don't want to pay attention to these details every time you create a new content page; instead, you want to focus on the content for that particular page, and have the common layout be applied to all pages consistently and automatically. What you really want is some sort of visual inheritance in practice, where you define a "base" page and have other pages inherit its layout. With ASP.NET 1.x, however, you could apply inheritance only at the code-behind level, and thus affect the behavior of the page (for example, what to do when the page loads, unloads, or renders), not its appearance. There were partial workarounds for this issue, but we personally didn't find any that really satisfied us with regard to functionality and design-time support. At last, the problem was solved in ASP.NET 2.0.

If you previously read the ASP.NET 2.0 edition of this book, nothing has really changed as far as master pages go with regard to ASP.NET MVC; you can probably skip the next section dealing with master pages and go to "Creating a Navigation System."

Enter the Master Page Model

ASP.NET 2.0 introduced a new "master page" feature that enables you to define common areas that every page will share, such as headers, footers, menus, and so on. A master page enables you to put the common layout code in a single file and have it visually inherited in all of the content pages. A master page contains the overall layout for your site. Content pages can inherit the appearance of a master page, and place their own content where the master page has defined a `ContentPlaceHolder` control. Although this has the effect of providing a form of visual inheritance, it's not really implemented with inheritance in an OOP sense — instead, the underlying implementation of master pages is based on a template model.

An example is worth a thousand words, so let's see how this concept turns into practice. A master page has a `.master` extension and is similar to a user control under the covers. The following is some code for a master page that contains some text, a header, a footer, and defines a `ContentPlaceHolder` control between the two:

```
<%@ Master Language="C#" AutoEventWireup="true" CodeFile="MasterPage.master.cs"
Inherits="MasterPage" %>

<html>
<head id="Head1" runat="server">
    <title>TheBeerHouse</title>
</head>

<body>
    <div id="header">The Beer House</div>
    <asp:ContentPlaceHolder ID="MainContent" runat="server" />
    <div id="footer">Copyright &copy; 2008 Nicholas Berardi</div>
</body>
</html>
```

As you see, it is extremely similar to a standard page, except that it has a `@Master` directive at the top of the page instead of a `@Page` directive, and it declares one or more `ContentPlaceHolder` controls where the `.aspx` pages will add their own content. The master page and the content page will merge together at runtime — therefore, because the master page defines the `<html>`, `<head>`, and `<body>` tags, you can easily guess that the content pages must not define them again. Content pages will only define the content for the master's `ContentPlaceHolder` controls, and nothing else. The following extract shows an example of a content page:

```
<%@ Page Language="C#" MasterPageFile="~/MasterPage.master" AutoEventWireup="true"
CodeFile="MyPage.aspx.cs" Inherits="MyPage" Title="The Beer House - My Page" %>

<asp:Content ID="MainContent" ContentPlaceHolderID="MainContent" Runat="Server">
    My page content goes here...
</asp:Content>
```

The first key point is that the `@Page` directive sets the `MasterPageFile` attribute to the virtual path of the master page. The content is placed into `Content` controls whose `ContentPlaceHolderID` must match the ID of one of the `ContentPlaceHolder` controls of the master page. In a content page, you can't place anything but `Content` controls, and other ASP controls that actually define the visual features must be grouped under the outermost `Content` controls. Another point to note is that the `@Page` directive has a new attribute, `Title`, which allows you to override the value specified in the master page's `<title>` metatag. If you fail to specify a `Title` attribute for a given content page, the title specified on the master page will be used instead.

Figure 3-2 provides a graphical representation of the master page feature.

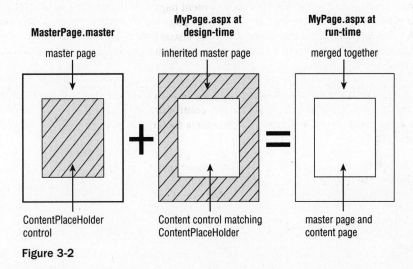

Figure 3-2

When you edit a content page in Visual Studio, it properly renders both the master page and the content page in the form designer, but the master page content appears to be "grayed out." This is done on purpose as a reminder to you that you can't modify the content provided by the master page when you're editing a content page.

> It is important to point out that your master page also has a code-behind file that could be used to write some C# properties and functions that could be accessed in the `.aspx` or code-behind files of content pages.

When you define the `ContentPlaceHolder` in a master page, you can also specify the default content for it, which will be used in the event that a particular content page doesn't have a `Content` control for that `ContentPlaceHolder`. Here is a snippet that shows how to provide some default content:

```
<asp:ContentPlaceHolder ID="MainContent" runat="server">
    The default content goes here…
</asp:ContentPlaceHolder>
```

Default content is helpful to handle situations in which you want to add a new section to a number of content pages, but you can't change them all at once. You can set up a new `ContentPlaceHolder` in the master page, give it some default content, and then take your time in adding the new information to the content pages — the content pages that haven't been modified yet will simply show the default content provided by the master.

The `MasterPageFile` attribute at the page level may be useful if you want to use different master pages for different sets of content pages. If, however, all pages of the site use the same master page, it's easier to set it once for all pages from the `web.config` file, by means of the `<pages>` element, as shown here:

```
<pages masterPageFile="~/Template.master" />
```

If you still specify the `MasterPageFile` attribute at the page level, that attribute will override the value in `web.config` for that single page.

Nested Master Pages

You can take this a step forward and have a master page be the content for another master page. In other words, you can have nested master pages, whereby a master page inherits the visual appearance of another master page, and the `.aspx` content pages inherit from this second master page. The second-level master page can look something like the following:

```
<%@ Master Language="C#" MasterPageFile="~/MasterPage.master"
AutoEventWireup="true" CodeFile="MasterPage2.master.cs" Inherits="MasterPage2" %>

<asp:Content ID="Content1" ContentPlaceHolderID="MainContent" Runat="Server">
   Some other content...
   <hr style="width: 100%;" />
   <asp:ContentPlaceHolder ID="MainContent" runat="server" />
</asp:Content>
```

Because you can use the same ID for a `ContentPlaceHolder` control in the base master page and for another `ContentPlaceHolder` in the inherited master page, you wouldn't need to change anything in the content page but its `MasterPageFile` attribute, so that it uses the second-level master page.

This possibility has great promise because you can have an outer master page that defines the very common layout (often the companywide layout), and then other master pages that specify the layout for specific areas of the site, such as the online store section, the administration section, and so on. The only problem with nested master pages was that they didn't have design-time support from within the Visual Studio IDE (as you do for the first-level master page). However, with the release of Visual Studio 2008 and the related Express products this is no longer a problem.

To be honest, we prefer editing content pages in the Source view in the editor, because it gives us more control over the HTML and we can structure it as we see fit, so not having design support never really bothered us as developers. Additionally, this is not much of a problem for most developers who prefer to write the code themselves. If you are not one of them we strongly encourage you to try it out; it will give you a deeper understanding of what the structure of your HTML looks like and ways you can cut down on the messy code that the visual editor generates.

Accessing the Master Page from the Content Page

You also have the capability to access the master page from a content page, through the page's `Master` property. The returned object is of type `MasterPage`, which inherits directly from `UserControl` (remember that we said master pages are similar to user controls) and adds a couple of properties. It exposes a Controls collection, which allows you to access the master page's controls from the content page. This may be necessary if, for example, in a specific page you want to programmatically hide some controls of the master page, such as the login or banner boxes. Accessing the Controls collection directly would work, but would require you to do a manual cast from the generic Control object returned to the correct control type, and you would be using the weakly typed approach. A much better and objected-oriented approach is to add custom properties to the master page's code-behind class — in our example, wrap the Visible property of some control. This is what you could write:

```
public bool LoginBoxIsVisible
{
    get { return LoginBox.Visible; }
    set { LoginBox.Visible = value; }
}
```

Now in the content page you can add the following line after the @Page directive:

```
<%@ MasterType VirtualPath="~/MasterPage.master" %>
```

With this line you specify the path of the master page used by the ASP.NET runtime to dynamically create a strongly typed MasterPage class that exposes the custom properties added to its code-behind class. We know that it seems like a duplicate for the MasterPageFile attribute of the @Page directive, but that's how you make the master page properties visible in the content page. You can specify the master type not just by virtual path (as in the preceding example), but also by name of the master page's class, by means of the TypeName attribute. Once you've added this directive, in the content page's code-behind file (or in a <script runat="server"> section of the .aspx file itself), you can easily access the master page's LoginBoxIsVisible property in a strongly typed fashion, as shown here:

```
protected void Test_OnClick(object sender, EventArgs e)
{
    this.Master.LoginBoxIsVisible = false;
}
```

When we say "strongly typed" we are implying that you'll have Visual Studio IntelliSense on this property, and that when you type the second period in "this.Master." you'll see your new property in the IntelliSense list!

This methodology of accessing master objects from content pages is also particularly useful when you want to put common methods in the master page, to be used by all the pages that use it. If you didn't have access to a strongly typed MasterPage object built at runtime by ASP.NET, you'd need to use reflection to access those methods, which is slower and certainly much less immediate to use (in this case, it would have been easier to put the shared methods in a separate class that every page can access).

For those of you who read the first edition of this book, we'd like to point out a difference between using an OOP base page and using a master page. In the first edition, we defined a base class called ThePhile that was inherited by all of the "content" pages. This was true OOP inheritance at work, but it was of limited usefulness because we couldn't inherit any kind of visual appearance from it; we still had to create user controls to achieve common visual elements. In the second edition, in ASP.NET 2.0, when you define a master page, you are able to get full visual inheritance (but not OOP code inheritance). The lack of code inheritance is not a serious limitation because you can access the code in the master page through a MasterType reference, as explained previously.

Switching Master Pages at Runtime

The last thing we want to describe in this introduction to master pages is the capability to dynamically change the master page used by a content page at runtime! That's right, you can have multiple master pages and pick which one to use after the site is already running. You do this by setting the page's `MasterPageFile` property from within the page's `PreInit` event handler, as follows:

```
protected void Page_PreInit(object sender, EventArgs e)
{
    this.MasterPageFile = "~/OtherMasterPage.master";
}
```

The `PreInit` event is new in ASP.NET, and you can only set the `MasterPageFile` property in this event handler because the merging of the two pages must happen very early in the page's life cycle (the `Load` or `Init` event would be too late).

When changing the master page dynamically, you must make sure that all master pages have the same ID for the `ContentPlaceHolder` controls, so that the content page's `Content` controls will always match them, regardless of which master page is being used. This exciting possibility enables you to build multiple master pages that specify completely different layouts, allowing users to pick their favorite one. The downside of this approach is that if you write custom code in the master page's code-behind file, you will need to replicate it in the code-behind class of any page; otherwise, the content page will not always find it. In addition, you won't be able to use the strongly typed `Master` property, because you can't dynamically change the master page's type at runtime; you can only set it with the `@MasterType` directive. For these reasons you will not use different master pages to provide different layouts to the user. You will instead have just one of them, to which you can apply different style sheet files. Because you're going to use a table-free layout, you can completely change the appearance of the page (fonts, colors, images, and positions) by applying different styles to it.

> The process described here for changing the master pages is the general way that this is done in ASP.NET. However, in ASP.NET MVC, Microsoft has vastly simplified this procedure by allowing the master page to be specified when returning `ActionResult` in the controller, as discussed in Chapter 2.
>
> So please treat this as just general information into the inner workings of ASP.NET and not the correct way to handle changing master pages in ASP.NET MVC.

Creating a Navigation System

As we said in the Problem section, you need to find some way to create a menu system that's easy to maintain and easy for users to understand. The previous book suggested that the use of the site map file was the best way to build a navigation structure. This doesn't really work well for dynamic content-driven sites such as the one you are building with ASP.NET MVC in this book because the site map file was really aimed at static sites where you know every page that is going to exist in the site at the time of development. You do not! So you are going to statically define the links to each module in the header of your master page and then let each module define its own link structure using the routes that were previously discussed in Chapter 2. This is the most efficient way to do this because it defines the top level of navigation that is needed across all pages in the master page file, which will in turn render the top level of navigation across all the pages that use that master page as their template. This eases the development process so, if you ever have to remove a module or add a new one to the top-level navigation, you only have to modify the master page file and it will propagate the changes across your entire site design.

Defining the Top-Level Navigation

The menu options are specified using the Html.ActionLink method that generates their names as based off of the routes in the global.asax file:

```
<div id="menu">
    <ul>
        <li><%= Html.ActionLink("Articles", "Index", "Article") %></li>
        <li><%= Html.ActionLink("Newletters", "Index", "Newsletter") %></li>
        <li><%= Html.ActionLink("Polls", "Index", "Poll") %></li>
        <li><%= Html.ActionLink("Forums", "Index", "Forum") %></li>
        <li><%= Html.ActionLink("Shop", "Index", "Commerce") %></li>
    </ul>
</div>
```

This is pretty basic and will render out to look like the following HTML when sent to the client browser from the server:

```
<div id="menu">
    <ul>
        <li><a href="/home">Articles</a></li>
        <li><a href="/newsletters">Newletters</a></li>
        <li><a href="/polls">Polls</a></li>
        <li><a href="/forums">Forums</a></li>
        <li><a href="/store">Shop</a></li>
    </ul>
</div>
```

The following routes were used to produce the preceding output:

```
// route for Articles or the Home Page
routes.MapRoute(
    "ArticleIndex",
    "home",
    new { controller = "Article", action = "Index" }
);

// route for Newsletters
routes.MapRoute(
    "NewslettersIndex",
    "newsletters",
    new { controller = "Newsletter", action = "Index" }
);

// route for the Polls
routes.MapRoute(
    "PollsIndex",
```

```
        "polls",
        new { controller = "Poll", action = "Index" }
    );

    // route for the Forums
    routes.MapRoute(
        "ForumsIndex",
        "forums",
        new { controller = "Forum", action = "Index" }
    );

    // route for the Store
    routes.MapRoute(
        "CommerceIndex",
        "store",
        new { controller = "Commerce", action = "Index" }
    );
```

As you can see, a human-readable route is defined for each module that you are going to create in this book. If you wanted to add an additional module, you would just create a new route in the `global.asax` file, and add that route to your navigation structure defined in your master page.

Creating Accessible Sites

All your code should render well-formatted XHTML 1.0 Strict code by default. XHTML code is basically HTML written as XML, and as such it must comply with much stricter syntax rules. For example, all attribute values must be enclosed within double quotes, all tags must have a closing tag or be explicitly self-closing (for example, no more <br> and <img src="...">, but <br /> and <img src="..." />), and nested tags must be closed in the right order (for example, no more <b><p>hello</b> Marco</p> but <p><b>Hello</b> Marco</p>). In addition, many HTML tags meant to format the text, such as <font>, <center>, <b>, and so on, are now deprecated and should be replaced by CSS styles (such as font-family: Verdana; font-weight: bold; text-align: center). The same is true for some attributes of other tags, such as width and align, among others. The reasoning behind this new standard is to attain a greater separation of presentation and content. This is what you are ultimately doing on the server side with ASP.NET MVC, but you should try to achieve the same principles of MVC on the client side by breaking up your content or model (HTML) from your presentation or view (CSS), and thus create cleaner code. You can find the official W3C documentation about XHTML 1.0 at http://www.w3.org/TR/xhtml1/.

As for accessibility, the W3C defines a set of rules meant to ease the use of the site by users with disabilities. The official page of the Web Content Accessibility Guidelines 1.0 (commonly referred as WCAG) is at www.w3.org/TR/WCAG10/. Section 508 guidelines were born from WCAG, and must be followed by U.S. federal agencies' sites. You can read more at www.section508.gov/. For example, you must use the alt attribute in <img> tags to provide an alternate text for visually impaired users, so that screen readers can describe the image, and you must use the <label> tag to associate a label to an input field. Other guidelines are more difficult to implement, so you can check out the official documentation for more information.

Sharing a Common Behavior Among All Pages

Master pages and themes do a great job of sharing the same design and look and feel among all pages of the site. However, you may also want the pages to share some common behavior, that is, code to run at a certain point of their life cycle. For example, if you want to log access to all pages so that you can build and show statistics for your site, you have to execute some code when the page loads. It's true that you can isolate the common code in an external function and just add a line of code to execute it from within each page, but this approach has two drawbacks:

❑   You must never forget to insert that line to call the external function when you design a new page. If multiple developers are creating .aspx pages — which is often the case — you will need to make sure that nobody forgets it.

❑   You may want to run some initialization from inside the PreInit event and some other code from the Load event. In this case, you have to write two separate xxxInitialize methods, and add more lines to each page to call the proper method from inside the proper event handler. Therefore, don't rely on the fact that adding a single line to each page is easy, because later you may need to add more and more. When you have hundreds of pages, I'm sure you'll agree that going back and modifying all the pages to add these lines is not a workable solution.

These two disadvantages are enough to make us discard that option. Another option is to write the common code in the master page's code-behind. This may be a very good choice in many situations. Not in your case, however, because you must handle the PreInit event, and the MasterPage class (and its base classes) does not have such an event. You can handle the Init or Load events, for example, but not PreInit, so you must think about something else.

In the previous edition of this book there was a BasePage class from which all the content pages would inherit, instead of inheriting directly from the standard System.Web.Page class. The base class approach was used to handle any page event from inside the page by overriding the bases' OnXXX methods, where XXX is the event name. This is no longer considered a best practice in ASP.NET MVC because the OnXXX methods were used to define application logic, in most cases, and that is supposed to be handled by the controller, not the view. You can usually accomplish these same behaviors in the controller with action filter attributes, the basics of which are covered when you dive into the implementation of your modules.

However, with all that being said, if you have a compelling reason to override the ViewPage class and use it as a base class for all your views, you should feel free to do this without prejudice. The snippet that follows is a basic skeleton for such a custom base class that inherits from ViewPage and overrides the OnPreInit and OnLoad methods:

```
public class BaseViewPage : System.Web.Mvc.ViewPage
{
    protected override void OnPreInit(EventArgs e)
    {
        // add custom code here...

        base.OnPreInit(e);
    }

    protected override void OnLoad(EventArgs e)
```

```
        {
            // add custom code here...

            base.OnLoad(e);
        }
    }
```

The classes in the pages' code-behind files will then inherit from your custom `BaseViewPage`, rather than the standard `ViewPage`, as shown here:

```
    public partial class Contact : BaseViewPage
    {
        // normal page code here...
    }
```

You still need to change some code in the code-behind class of every page, but once that's done you can later go back to `BaseViewPage`, add code to the existing methods or overload new methods, and you will not need to modify any additional lines in the code-behind classes. If you take this approach initially, you'll modify the code-behind classes one by one as you create them, so this will be easy and it gives you a future-proof design.

For ASP.NET MVC, this is usually not necessary because there are very few instances where you ever want to modify the code-behind file and even fewer when you want to do it in a global manner where all your pages inherit from the same base class. This is because, with MVC, the focus is on the view and just rendering the HTML code, not on the backend code that was so important in ASP.NET Web Forms. The following situations are most often the only times you would want to put custom code in the code-behind file:

❑   You need a helper method to facilitate the rendering of the HTML and it would be too messy to include in line with your HTML.

❑   You need to provide an application context that dictates how all pages render throughout your whole application. This application context might store important information such as permissions the current logged-in user has, some basic information about the user, and general information that you would like to persist across all your code for the current request.

Solution

At this point you should have a clear idea of what you have to build and how to do it, so let's start developing the solution! Earlier in this chapter we explained how you can create a mock-up of your site using a graphics application such as Photoshop or Paint.NET. Once you have been given the go ahead to start coding, you need to break out the individual images into `.gif`, `.jpg`, and `.png` files that can be referenced directly in a web page. Regardless of the method you used to create your images, you can now take those images and use them to create the website. The first step is to create a new website project, and then create a master page view to be used in conjunction with the rest of your MVC views.

First, create a new website project in Visual Studio 2008 (File ⇨ New ⇨ Project ⇨ Web ⇨ ASP .NET MVC Web Application). You will want to pick a location to store your new project (we used `C:\Projects\TheBeerHouse` as mine), and then click OK, as shown in Figure 3-3.

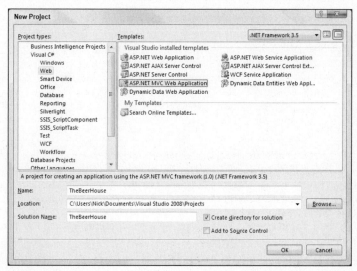

Figure 3-3

You may want to review Chapter 2 if you are not comfortable with the brief instructions that we just gave on creating a new ASP.NET MVC project in Visual Studio. You can find the instructions in the "Your First ASP.NET MVC Project" section of Chapter 2.

This enables you to create an ASP.NET MVC project. If you have never developed a web application in Visual Studio 2005 or 2008, it comes with an integrated web server, so you don't have to create a virtual directory in the IIS metabase (the metabase is where IIS stores its configuration data). The project is loaded from a real hard disk folder, and executed by an integrated lightweight web server (called ASP.NET Development Server) that handles requests on a TCP/IP port other than the one used by IIS. The actual port number used is determined randomly when you first create the web application. For example, it handles requests such as `http://localhost:1168/ProjectName/Home`. This makes it much easier to move and back up projects, because you can just copy the project's folder and you're done — there's no need to set up anything from the IIS Management console. In fact, Visual Studio 2008 does not even require IIS unless you choose to deploy to an IIS web server, or you specify a web URL instead of a local path when you create the website project.

If you've developed with any previous version of ASP.NET or Visual Studio, I'm sure you will welcome this new option. We say this is an option because you can still create the project by using a URL as the project path — creating and running the site under IIS — by selecting HTTP in the Location drop-down list. We suggest you create and develop the site by using the File System location, with the integrated web server, and then switch to the full-featured IIS web server for the test phase or as development dictates. Visual Studio 2008 includes a new deployment wizard that makes it easier to deploy a complete solution to a local or remote IIS web server. For now, however, just create a new ASP.NET website in any folder you want, and call it TheBeerHouse.

> The integrated web server was developed for making development and quick testing easier. However, you should never use it for final Quality Assurance or integration testing; you should use IIS for that. IIS has more features, such as caching, HTTP compression, and many security options that can make your site run much differently from what you see in the new integrated ASP.NET Development Server. It is also recommended that you use IIS 7.0 on Windows Server 2008 whenever possible with ASP.ET MVC, because it will provide the most support for the way MVC renders URLs using the routes.

After creating the new website, you have two different paths to take depending on your development environment:

1. If you are developing on and for IIS 7.0 (Windows Vista, Windows Server 2008, or better) and you are **NOT** using the integrated Web Server for development, you can right-click `Default.aspx` and delete it.

2. If you are developing on IIS 6.0 or less (Windows XP, Windows Server 2003, and so on) you need to **KEEP** the `Default.aspx` file. The reason you need this is because the `Default.aspx` file is used as a way to redirect the client browser to the `home` route, for servers like the integrated Web Server in Visual Studio and IIS 6.0 that still work on the dated assumption that the extension of the file name dictates the framework that will be executing the file. We encourage you to take a look at the code-behind of the `Default.aspx` to gather a better understanding of what it is doing.

For the purposes of TheBeerHouse, you are going to use option 2 to keep the development and setup simple and straightforward for the majority of development environments that exist at the writing of this book. If you choose to deploy TheBeerHouse on IIS 7.0, Chapter 12 covers the simple changes that need to take place in order to modify the application to run on IIS 7.0 and take advantage of not needing to have the `Default.aspx` file.

Creating the Site Design

Creating the master page with the shared site design is not that difficult once you have a mock-up image (or a set of images if you made them separately). Basically, you cut the logo and the other graphics and put them in the HTML page. The other parts of the layout, such as the menu bar, the columns, and the footer, can easily be reproduced with HTML elements such as DIVs. The template provided by Free CSS Templates (and just slightly modified and expanded by us) is shown in Figure 3-4.

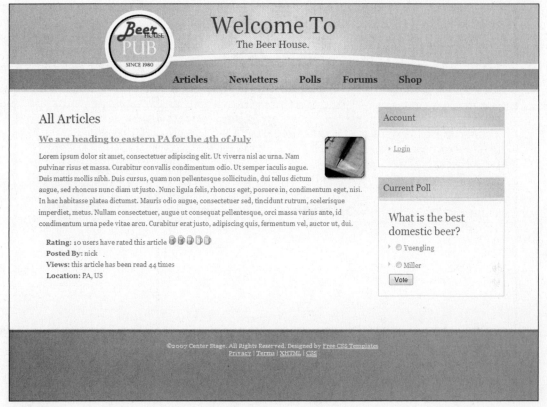

Figure 3-4

The trick to developing a good clean CSS site is to not fight the browser. Browsers love to lay things out from top to bottom, in the order that they appear in the HTML. So when you are designing your site, it is good to have an idea in your mind about the most natural way to lay out and design the DIVs so that they can flow as easily as possible. The preceding page can be broken down as follows and as seen in Figure 3-5:

1. Header
    1. Logo
    2. Menu
2. Page (as in the main body)
    1. Content (this is where your views from the controllers will render)
    2. Sidebar
3. Footer
    1. Legal
    2. Links

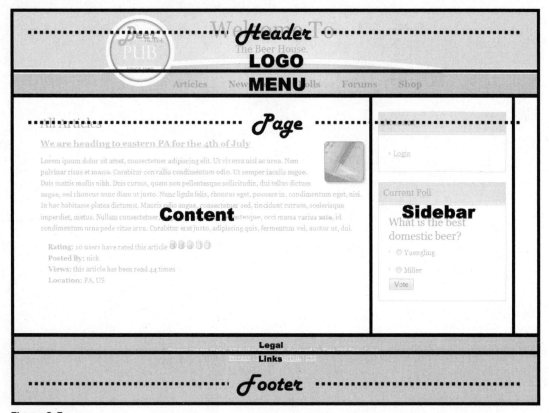

Figure 3-5

Figure 3-5 is a pretty typical site layout that you will find anywhere on the web. As you can see, it pretty much flows from top to bottom, which will make it very easy for the browser to render and save you from developing a lot of CSS. The only deviation from this is the sidebar, which needs to sit to the right of the content; you can support the sidebar by floating it to the right using a few lines of CSS.

Creating the Master Page

In this book we are assuming a certain amount of familiarity with ASP.NET and Visual Studio. More specifically, we assume you have a working knowledge of the basic operation of any previous version of Visual Studio. Therefore, the steps we explain here focus on the basics, but do not otherwise cover every small detail. If you are not comfortable following the steps presented here, you should consult a beginner's book on ASP.NET before following the steps in this book.

The default ASP.NET MVC application already comes with a default master page, located at ~/Views/Shared/Site.Master. However, if you would like to create a new master page file, right-click the folder in the Solution Explorer where you want to add the new master page, choose Add New Item ⇨ Master Page, and name it MyMasterFileName.master. We find it easier to work directly in the Source view, and write the code by hand. As we said earlier, creating the master page is not much different than creating a normal page; the most notable differences are just the @Master directive at the top of the file and the presence of `ContentPlaceHolder` controls where the `.aspx` pages will plug in their own content. What follows is the code that defines the standard HTML metatags, and the site's header for the file `Site.master`, which is where you will be developing your HTML:

```
<%@ Master Language="C#" AutoEventWireup="true" CodeBehind="Site.Master.cs"
Inherits="TheBeerHouse.Views.Shared.Site" %>

<!DOCTYPE html PUBLIC "-//W3C//DTD XHTML 1.0 Strict//EN" "http://www.w3.org/TR/
xhtml1/DTD/xhtml1-strict.dtd">

<html xmlns="http://www.w3.org/1999/xhtml">
<head>
    <title>The Beer House / <%= Html.Encode(ViewData["PageTitle"]) %></title>

    <meta http-equiv="content-type" content="text/html; charset=utf-8" />

    <link href="/content/styles/site.css" rel="style sheet" type="text/css" />
    <link href="/content/styles/modules.css" rel="style sheet" type="text/css" />

    <asp:ContentPlaceHolder ID="HeaderContent" runat="server" />
</head>
<body>
<div id="header">
    <div id="logo">
        <h1><a href="/">Welcome To</a></h1>
        <h2><a href="/">The Beer House.</a></h2>
    </div>
    <div id="menu">
        <ul>
            <li><%= Html.ActionLink("Articles", "Index", "Article")%></li>
            <li><%= Html.ActionLink("Newletters", "Index", "Newsletter")%></li>
            <li><%= Html.ActionLink("Polls", "Index", "Poll" %></li>
            <li><%= Html.ActionLink("Forums", "Index", "Forum")%></li>
            <li><%= Html.ActionLink("Shop", "Index", "Commerce")%></li>
        </ul>
    </div>
</div>
```

As you can see, there is nothing in this first snippet of code that relates to the actual appearance of the header. That's because the appearance of the containers, text, and other objects will be specified in the style sheet file.

Note that there is one `ContentPlaceHolder` control, `HeaderContent`, that allows you to insert custom code into the `<head/>` tag in the pages that will use this master page. You can use this for adding links for your feeds or other custom styles or content that you want to control on a page-by-page basis.

Proceed by writing the DIVs for the central part of the page, with the two columns:

```
<div id="page">
    <div id="content">
        <h1 class="title"><%= Html.Encode(ViewData["PageTitle"]) %></h1>
        <asp:ContentPlaceHolder ID="MainContent" runat="server" />
    </div>
```

```
    <!-- end content -->
    <div id="sidebar">
        <div id="account" class="boxed">
        <h2 class="title">Account</h2>
        <div class="content">
        <ul>
<% if (Context.User != null
        && Context.User.Identity != null
        && Context.User.Identity.IsAuthenticated)
        { %>
        <li class="first">Welcome <%= Context.User.Identity.Name %></li>
        <li>Html.ActionLink("Change Password", "ChangePassword", "User")%></li>
        <li><%= Html.ActionLink("Manage My Profile", "UserProfile", "User")%></li>
        <li><%= Html.ActionLink("Logout", "Logout", "User") %></li>
<% } else { %>
        <li class="first"><%= Html.ActionLink("Login", "Login", "User") %></li>
<% } %>
        </ul>
        </div>
        </div>
        <asp:ContentPlaceHolder ID="SidebarContent" runat="server" />
    </div>
    <!-- end sidebar -->
    <div style="clear: both;"> </div>
</div>
```

Note that two ContentPlaceHolder controls are defined in the preceding code, one for each column. This way, a content page will be able to add text in different positions. Also remember that filling a ContentPlaceHolder with some content is optional, and in some cases you'll have pages that just add content to the MainContent column, using the default content defined in the master page for the SidebarContent column.

The remaining part of the master page defines the container for the footer, with its subcontainers for the legal notice as well as some links that should be present at the bottom of every page:

```
<div id="footer">
    <p id="legal">
        &copy;2007 Center Stage. All Rights Reserved. Designed by
        <a href="http://www.freecsstemplates.org/">Free CSS Templates</a>
    </p>
    <p id="links">
        <a href="#">Privacy</a> |
        <a href="#">Terms</a> |
        <a href="http://validator.w3.org/check/referer" title="This page
validates as XHTML 1.0 Transitional"><abbr title="eXtensible HyperText Markup
Language">XHTML</abbr></a> |
        <a href="http://jigsaw.w3.org/css-validator/check/referer" title="This page
validates as CSS"><abbr title="Cascading Style Sheets">CSS</abbr></a>
    </p>
</div>

<script type="text/javascript" src="/content/scripts/jquery-1.2.6.min.js"></script>
<script type="text/javascript" src="/content/scripts/global.js"></script>
```

```
<script type="text/javascript" src="/content/scripts/poll.js"></script>
<asp:ContentPlaceHolder ID="ScriptContent" runat="server" />
</body>
</html>
```

Please pay special attention to the `ContentPlaceHolder` control, `ScriptContent`, that allows you to insert your JavaScript that is going to play a pivotal role in your user experience at the end of the pages that will use this master page.

Best Practices for Speeding Up Your Website

The `HeaderContent` and the `ScriptContent`, as well as the style sheet placement in the page `<head/>`, and the JavaScript placement after the footer, is based on some best practices for speeding the loading and rendering of your website. Yahoo did the research in an effort to optimize the rendering of its website in the browser. You can find the research at:

`http://developer.yahoo.com/performance/rules.html`

There is a lot of great information that every serious web developer should know and understand, regardless of whether some of it does not apply to you or your websites. In fact, the Yahoo research team found that only about 10% of the total perceived "slowness" of a website is actually the server rendering and returning the HTML that your code produces. This may come as a total shock to you because you spend countless hours optimizing your code to make it faster, but they found that you are probably spending an inordinate amount of time optimizing only 10% of the perceived "quickness" of your site.

The Yahoo research team also found that, by following the preceding performance guidelines, you can drastically speed up the "quickness" of your website by just making some pretty simple changes to the way your website is served up to the client-side browsers. If you would like to read more about this research, it is located at the following URL under the "Research" header on the page:

`http://developer.yahoo.com/performance/`

Creating the Style Sheet

It's time to create the first style sheet for the master page: `Site.Master`. The first thing you can do is move the `Site.css` file that the MVC project creates to `~/Content/styles/site.css`. This style sheet will hold the entire layout necessary for rendering the site. Next you are going to create a style sheet file in this same folder (right-click the folder and choose, Add ➪ New Item ➪ Style Sheet), named `modules.css`; this style sheet will contain all of your module's styles. We break up the style sheets for the same reason you have a master page file and a view page file: it allows you to have one file dedicated to the master page and the overall look of the site, and one file dedicated to the implementation and programming of the site in the modules. This way, if you ever want to swap out the style for a different one, you don't have to try and sort out the template styles from the implementation styles, which can be difficult if you don't take this precaution early. We usually give them names like the ones just created, but the names you give to the CSS files are not important, because all CSS files found in the folder will automatically be added by the master page at runtime.

For your reference, the code that follows includes part of the style classes defined in this file (refer to the downloadable code for the entire style sheet):

```
body {
    margin: 0;
    padding: 0;
    background: #FFFFFF url(/content/images/centerstage/img01.tif) repeat-x;
    font-family: Georgia, "Times New Roman", Times, serif;
    font-size: 13px;
    color: #666666;
}

h1, h2, h3 {
    margin: 0;
    font-weight: normal;
    color: #3F586B;
}

/* some styles omitted to move on to the more interesting styles */

/* Header */

#header {
    width: 700px;
    height: 175px;
    margin: 0 auto;
    background: #A4C0C8 url(/content/images/centerstage/img02.tif) no-repeat;
}

/* Logo */

#logo {
    height: 130px;
}

#logo h1, #logo h2 {
    text-align: center;
}

#logo h1 {
    padding-top: 16px;
    font-size: 350%;
}

#logo h2 {
    font-size: 150%;
}

#logo a {
    text-decoration: none;
    color: #3F586B;
}
```

```
/* Menu */

#menu {
    width: 600px;
    float: right;
    padding-top: 0;
}

#menu ul {
    margin: 0;
    padding: 10px 0 0 0;
    list-style: none;
    line-height: normal;
    text-align: center;
}

#menu li {
    display: inline;
    margin: 0;
    padding: 0;
}

#menu a {
    padding: 0 20px;
    text-decoration: none;
    font-size: 136%;
    font-weight: bold;
    color: #610720;
}

#menu a:hover {
    text-decoration: underline;
}

#menu .active a {
    color: #FFFFFF;
}

/* other styles omitted for the purpose of brevity */
```

Note the `#header` element uses `margin: 0 auto`; this is what you use to horizontally center an element on the page, and it means the top and bottom margin of the element should be `0pt` and the left and right should automatically adjust to be the same value (that is, center). Another thing to take note of is that in `#header` you are also setting the background image using CSS; this is the preferred way to add a non-content-related image to your site design. You should not under any circumstance use `<img />` to add design-related images to your design; it is bad practice and causes usability problems.

All images pointed to in this style sheet file are located in an Images folder under `/Content/images/ centerstage/`. *This way, you keep all related site design images together.*

Now that you have gone over the `site.css` file, we want to cover just a little more CSS that will start off your `modules.css` file. We always like to include a nice layout for messages to the user that gives them a nice and intuitive look and feel, which we believe goes really well with the lean site design. The original CSS was designed by Janko of `www.jankoatwarpspeed.com`, who we believe is one of the more talented designer/developers who has been able to straddle both sides of the fence that usually separates the designers from the developers.

```css
/* Message
************************************************************/

.info, .success, .warning, .error, .validation {
    border: 1px solid;
    margin: 10px 0px;
    padding: 15px 10px 15px 50px;
    background-repeat: no-repeat;
    background-position: 10px center;
}

.info {
    color: #00529B;
    background-color: #BDE5F8;
    background-image: url('/content/images/info.png');
}

.success {
    color: #4F8A10;
    background-color: #DFF2BF;
    background-image: url('/content/images/success.png');
}

.warning {
    color: #9F6000;
    background-color: #FEEFB3;
    background-image: url('/content/images/warning.png');
}

.error {
    color: #D8000C;
    background-color: #FFBABA;
    background-image: url('/content/images/error.png');
}

.validation {
    color: #D63301;
    background-color: #FFCCBA;
    background-image: url('/content/images/validation.png');
}
```

What we love about the preceding CSS is that it really shows the power of the C in the CSS, by creating a base style in the first block and then overloading just what needs to be changed in the cascading styles. Figure 3-6 is an example of what your message boxes will look like when rendered to the screen.

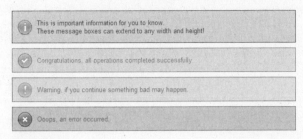

Figure 3-6

We think you can agree that these have a nice look and feel that your users can intuitively understand. On your screen the first block is blue, the second is green, the third is yellow, and the last is red. So the combination of the color, the text, and the icon gives instant feedback in three different ways as to what the message is suppose to convey to the user of the site.

In the chapters that follow, you add on to the `modules.css` style sheet as you develop your application for your client.

Summary

In this chapter, you've built the foundations for the site's user interface layer by finalizing your design, which will be the basis for the entire look and feel of the site you are going to develop throughout this book. You have laid the groundwork to start the development of your website with the ASP.NET MVC framework. Finally, you have designed and implemented a master page with common HTML and graphics, making it easy to change the layout and the graphics of the site by modifying a single file. The next chapter continues to talk about foundations, but for the business layer, or the M & C in MVC — in other words, the model and controller.

Planning an Architecture

This chapter lays the groundwork for the rest of the book by creating a number of basic services that will be shared among all future modules: configuration classes to process custom sections and elements in `web.config`, base business and data access classes, caching strategies, and more. It also introduces some of the new features afforded to us by using ASP.NET MVC, and some of the language extensions in the .NET 3.5 Framework.

Problem

Your website is made up of a number of separate modules for managing dynamic content such as articles, forums, and polls, and sending out newsletters. However, all your modules have a number of common "design problems" that you must solve:

❑ Separate the data access code from the business logic code and the presentation code (user interface) so that the site is much more maintainable and scalable. This is called a *multi-tier design*.

❑ Isolate the data access architecture so that it can allow the support of different underlying data stores — without requiring changes to the business object layer within the underlying data store. Similarly, changes to the business object or presentation layers should also be possible without changing another tier. This is called *decoupling* the tiers.

❑ Design the business object architecture to expose the data retrieved by the data access layer in an object-oriented format. This is the process of mapping relational data to OOP classes.

❑ Support caching of business objects to save the data you've already fetched from the data store so you don't have to make unnecessary fetches to retrieve the same data again. This results in less CPU usage, database resources, and network traffic, and thus results in better general performance.

❑ Leverage configuration files for your modules to make them easily customizable.

The task of this chapter is to discuss the best-practice approaches you can take to address the problems just outlined. Once you have finished this chapter you'll have a foundation upon which to build your website. In the previous version of the book, this chapter was much larger because we had to create a number of base classes to support our website. Using ASP.NET MVC and the .NET 3.5 Framework, these base classes became less necessary because of the design concepts implemented in the ASP.NET MVC framework and the new LINQ-to-SQL provided in the .NET 3.5 Framework. The implications of MVC and LINQ-to-SQL are that you need to focus less on building up a mini-framework to access the database and build your pages, so you can focus more on the problem that needs to be solved. By limiting the amount of code you have to write to get started on a project, you are able to have quicker turnaround times than in the past with ASP.NET 2.0. So let's get started designing the architecture for TheBeerHouse.

Design

As explained in the Problem section, many design decisions must be made before proceeding with the rest of the site, because they create the underpinnings used for all further development. It would be too late to design architecture to support multiple data stores once you've already developed half the site. Similarly, you couldn't decide on a strategy for handling configuration settings, such as database connection strings, after you wrote an entire module that uses the database. If you ignored these issues and started coding main modules first, you would end up with a poor design that will be difficult to correct later. As with this entire book, many of the new .NET 3.5 classes and features of the MVC framework are utilized, as they apply to each section of code you develop. Some of these new features even provide a complete and ready-to-go solution to a particular problem!

Architecture and the MVC Framework

With traditional ASP.NET Web Forms projects, you were never truly able to separate the user interface from your application logic. This is because .NET provided a lot of server-side controls that you could simply drag and drop onto your Web Forms. These controls, such as the GridView, would automatically do much of the legwork for you but often placed application logic code into the UI layer. An example you may be able to relate to is creating logic for sorting your GridViews or filtering data on the click events of buttons. Whatever the reasoning may have been, you often would find yourself with large code-behind files for your views. This was great for pushing out projects rapidly but tied your hands in terms of application efficiency and following of W3C standards. You always had the option to custom code your own modular solution but this always meant a huge investment in time to create your own framework. With the creation of the MVC framework this all changed. The code-behind files for your views were completely eliminated, creating a true separation of your UI from your application logic and your business/data layer. With the MVC framework you can easily and rapidly develop an architecture that separates the concerns of your application into an n-tier web application design.

Designing a Layered Infrastructure

If you've been doing any software development in recent years, you should be familiar with the multi-tier software design (also called *n-tier design*). To recap it in a few words, it divides the functionality, components, and code for a project into separate tiers, generally four or five of them:

❏ **Data Store:** Where the data resides. This can be a relational database, an XML file, a text file, or some other proprietary storage system that your application may use to persist data.

❏ **Data Access Layer (DAL):** The code that takes care of retrieving and manipulating the raw data persisted in the data store. It is also responsible for exposing the data store to the application in a more abstract and intuitive way, hiding low-level details such as the data store's schema, and adding all the validation logic to ensure that the data is persisted in a safe and consistent way.

❑ **Business Logic Layer (BLL):** The code that takes care of adding business rules and domain-specific objects that satisfy the requirements for the application.

❑ **Application Logic Layer (ALL):** The code that takes care of the interaction between the presentation layer and the business logic layer. An example of an application logic layer was the code-behind in ASP.NET Web Forms; this handled all the application logic related to button clicks, post backs, and any other events available to you through controls.

❑ **Presentation Layer (UI):** The code that defines what a user should see on the screen, including the user interface (UI) and user experience (UX), which may include formatted data and system navigation menus, for example. This layer will be designed to operate inside a web browser for the case of the World Wide Web and other more specific environments, such as WinForms, for desktop applications.

In the ASP.NET MVC framework, an n-tier application design would be broken down with the business logic layer and data access layer in the model, the application logic layer in the controller, and the presentation layer in the view. Figure 4-1 is a representation of this break down.

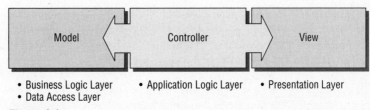

• Business Logic Layer   • Application Logic Layer   • Presentation Layer
• Data Access Layer

Figure 4-1

This figure is an optimal view of how you should break up your MVC application. It is the way that all the books, blogs, and evangelists will tell you how to build an MVC application. Remember that although this is an optimal way to design your MVC application, it may not fit your requirements in all circumstances. For instance, if you have a really simple application that you are developing, you may want to merge the BLL with the ALL to simplify your application architecture. This is a perfectly reasonable approach, but before you start coding you should gauge the depth and complexity of your application before you decide to merge the BLL and ALL together, because once this is done they are hard to separate. Because the TheBeerHouse application isn't that complex of an application, you are going to use the simpler of the two designs and for the most part merge your BLL and your ALL together into the controller. From here on out we will simply refer to the BLL + ALL as the BLL or controller.

In the second edition of the book we used ASP.NET 2.0 and traditional Web Forms to create our application. In this edition of the book we are going to take advantage of the MVC framework and the .NET 3.5 Framework. The major differences that you will see are a much clearer separation of your tiers, and the ability to modify the views without having to recompile the entire application. This is a really nice feature because it allows you to make minor design changes or modify your inline code without having to redeploy the entire application.

Choosing a Data Store

In this book you learn how to develop a flexible data access layer that enables you to support different data stores and quickly switch between them without any change on other layers. However, it will only be easy to switch between different data stores after you've developed the low-level data storage structures and a corresponding model for each data store you want to support. Therefore, it will still involve a considerable development effort if you want to support more than one data store, but the multi-tier design we're using should ease the pain if that is the route you take.

What kinds of data stores would be possible for this kind of application? You could use only XML files if you expect a fairly static site that doesn't change often, or you might use an Access database format. Access is better than XML files in many ways, but Access is mostly a desktop database and would not be appropriate for situations where you might have even a few concurrent users, or a large database. It doesn't scale at all, and because of this its use for websites is strongly discouraged. Moving up from there, you could consider any of the modern Relational Database Management Systems (RDBMSs), such as SQL Server, Oracle, DB2, MySQL, PostgreSQL, and so on; any of these would be great choices for your needs, but for the purposes of this book you'll choose only one data store as a target for your sample site.

In the real world, your customer may want you to use a specific RDBMS, or he may want you to change to a different RDBMS after the site has been deployed. Your customer may have reasons to use a specific RDBMS because he may already have corporate knowledge of a given platform/engine that would be necessary to maintain the site after you've sold it to him. Maybe he already has an installed/licensed copy of a particular RDBMS and wants to use it instead of purchasing a license for different software, or perhaps he just has a preference for a specific RDBMS. In this case you might try to explain your reasons for choosing something else, if you think that would be best (this is what a consultant is supposed to do, after all), but the customer may insist that his choice be honored.

Most .NET software developers choose Microsoft's SQL Server as their RDBMS for many reasons. These might include the excellent integration of SQL Server tools in Visual Studio, or the fact that it's easier to buy your IDE and RDBMS from the same company (you may have an MSDN software subscription that includes everything), but the reasons we personally favor are the relatively low cost and the high performance of SQL Server running on Windows, coupled together with easy administration. SQL Server also has the advantage of allowing you to use LINQ-to-SQL files, or the Entity Framework, which makes the creation of your models a snap. Having decided to use SQL Server as your data store, you now have to select one particular version. This edition of the book revolves around Visual Studio 2008, so it makes a lot of sense to couple this with the newest version of SQL Server, which is named SQL Server 2008. Microsoft has released a free variation of SQL Server 2008 that can be used on developers' computers and on production servers, called Microsoft SQL Server 2008 Express Edition. This is the 2008 replacement of its SQL Server 2005, which gives you some new data types, notably one that separates date from time, as well as a geospatial coordinate data type.

We will make the assumption that you will use either SQL Server 2008 Express Edition or one of the full editions of SQL Server 2008 (Workgroup, Standard, or Enterprise) for this sample website. For our purposes, these editions are functionally equivalent, with the main differences relating to the GUI administration tools, and not to the underlying RDBMS engine. All editions of SQL Server 2008 have great integration with Visual Studio 2008, whose Server Explorer tool enables developers to browse registered servers and databases; retrieve all details about a database's schema; add, delete, and modify tables, records, stored procedures, functions, triggers, views, types, and relationships. In fact, you can develop the entire database for this website from inside Visual Studio 2008, without using any of the

SQL Server administration tools! The Diagramming tool in Visual Studio 2008 even enables you to visually relate tables and set constraints and foreign key relationships without leaving the diagram.

At face value, SQL Server 2008 looks pretty much the same as SQL Server 2005, but under the covers it does a lot of really cool things. Some of the new features of the 2008 version include a new capability called database mirroring: this allows you to take an existing database and "mirror" it to another database on another server, in essence creating a failover or load-balancing cluster. All the work under the covers is handled for you without your interaction. Another great feature is the addition of new data types, which include a geospatial data type and a separate data type for both date and time. Microsoft also added the capability to compress backup files as well as allowing you to encrypt your data. Many other changes were implemented that can't be covered in the scope of this chapter but fill in a lot of the gaps that Oracle once had over Microsoft's SQL Server; for more information or white papers please visit the Microsoft SQL Server website.

Designing the Data Access Layer

The data access layer (DAL) is the code that executes queries to the database to retrieve data, and to update, insert, and delete data. It is the code that's closest to the database, and it must know all the database details, that is, the schema of the tables, the name of the fields, stored procedures, and views. You should keep database-specific code separated from your site's pages for a number of reasons:

❑ The developer who builds the user interfaces (that is, the pages and user controls) may not be the same developer who writes the data access code. In fact, for mid- to large-size sites, they are usually different people. The UI developer may ignore most things about the database, but still provide the user interface for it, because all the details are wrapped into separate objects that provide a high-level abstraction of the table, stored procedure, and field names, and the SQL to work with them.

❑ Some queries that retrieve data will typically be used from different pages. If you put them directly into the pages themselves, and later you have to change a query to add some fields or change the sorting, you'd have to review all your code and find every place where it's used. If, instead, the data access code is contained in some common DAL classes, you'd just need to modify those and the pages calling them will remain untouched.

❑ Hard-coded queries inside web pages would make it extremely difficult to migrate to a new RDBMS, or to support more than one RDBMS.

In relation to the MVC framework, it is almost a requirement to separate out the DAL because it is part of the MVC design pattern. For the purposes of our MVC projects, all DAL-related objects should ideally be placed into your models' folder, which is automatically generated for you. In this way you have a clear separation between your BLL, your DAL, and your UI.

Using the Provider Model Design Pattern to Support Multiple Data Stores

One thing that's important to consider for your site is that you may need to support different data stores. Our sample site is pretty generic, and as such could easily be adapted for different pubs, bars, and other places. However, as we said before, different clients may have different constraints about which data store to use, and may force you to install and configure the site to work with Oracle or MySQL instead of the SQL Server 2008 database you initially chose. If you don't plan for this possibility up front, you'll have a great deal of trouble trying to retrofit your code later. Different RDBMSs support different functionality and SQL dialects: stored procedures and the parameters for SQL statements are passed in with a different syntax, the data types are different, and so on. For a real-world site of medium complexity, it is impossible to have common data access code that works the same for all possible RDBMSs.

If you tried to write a common code base using the OleDb provider, you would soon start filling your code with an endless number of "if I'm using this database do this, else if I'm targeting this other database do something else"-style blocks. Even if you could put up with the mess in your code, that approach may not be workable in some cases. Say, for example, that you're developing a website that will be sold by other software companies, which would then integrate your code into a larger solution. You don't know what they'll be using as a data store, because you're developing a commercial product that could be sold to thousands of clients. As such, you can't implement support for all possible data stores. You can't even give them your source code so that they can customize it to add support for their own database because you want to protect your investment. This is exactly the situation with many of the ASP.NET 3.5 modules such as membership, profile, personalization, session storage, and more (you are introduced to some of these in the next chapter). Microsoft provided a built-in DAL for the SQL Server RDBMS and a few other data stores, but not all possible storage media; however, Microsoft wanted you to be able to add this support through the use of the provider model design.

Instead of writing the DAL class directly, you should first write a base abstract class that defines the public interface of the class (the signature of the data access CRUD methods), and the implementation of some helper methods if necessary. The real data access code is inside secondary classes that inherit from the base class, and provide the concrete implementation for its abstract methods. These classes are called *providers*, and are usually specific for one type of data store; when you implement one of them you don't have to worry about compatibility with any other data store.

Different providers are placed in different folders (for example, Model) and namespaces (for example, TheBeerHouse.Model) for organizational purposes. The base class has an Instance static property (or a GetInstance method, if you prefer) that creates and returns an instance of the provider class according to what's specified in the configuration file. This property/method is used by the business classes to get a reference for which concrete DAL object to use to retrieve/modify data. The business classes, in turn, are used by the user interface layer, which never accesses the lower-level DAL classes directly. This pattern enables the developer to write super fast code, because you can take advantage of all optimizations available for the specific data store. The code is also much cleaner, because you don't have to write confusing if...else blocks to manage all the differences of various RDBMSs. It also allows you to compile the whole site and give your customers the compiled assemblies. If they need to target a different data store from those you have implemented, they can create their own providers that inherit from your base abstract DAL classes, and they can point to them in the configuration file.

You may argue that if you implement this pattern you'll have to re-implement all of the DAL code for each data store. That's mostly true, of course. The question becomes whether you want to re-implement one DAL module or all the modules of your site. Also consider that you may only need this pattern for those methods that really must be implemented differently for different data stores. Simpler methods that would work fine on all data stores without any modification could use the OleDb provider with common code in the DAL base class so that all the providers inherit from it so they don't need to re-implement those simple methods. You can make them virtual to allow new providers to override this functionality if they need to. Figure 4-2 provides a graphical representation of the relationship between the user interface, BLL, and DAL and the data stores.

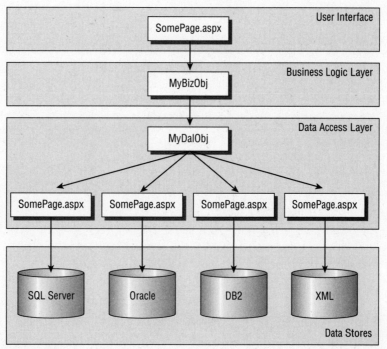

Figure 4-2

We talk about this pattern further in subsequent chapters. In Chapter 5 you see how the ASP.NET 3.5 team implemented this pattern for the authentication, membership, and profiling modules. In Chapter 6 you design and implement a DAL based on this pattern from scratch, to support the article management module.

The Impact of LINQ on the Data Access Layer

With the release of the .NET 3.5 Framework we saw the inclusion of a new feature called LINQ, or Language Integrated Query. Many developers will instantly mistake this new feature as a database-only feature, however they couldn't be more wrong. LINQ was designed as a way to perform queries on any type of collection in the framework, which includes arrays, dictionaries, lists, XML, and databases, to name a few. If you dig a little deeper into the technology you quickly discover that it has a lot to offer and directly impacts the creation of data access layers in .NET.

So you may ask what the big deal is and why not simply use typed data sets or custom entities. Although these routes are still available in .NET 3.5, LINQ is definitely worth consideration. In essence, LINQ gives you the capability to use SQL-like syntax in your .NET code to access data from your database. The following example shows how similar LINQ is to SQL:

SQL

```
select c.*
from Customer as c
```

LINQ

```
var customers = from c in dataContext.Customers
                select c;
```

In the example we are showing how to do a simple select in both SQL and LINQ. Both are doing exactly the same thing under the covers in terms of querying the data from the `Customers` table, but in the LINQ example the data is being dumped out into a custom collection, called `IQueryable<Customer>`, that you can loop through with a standard `foreach` loop. Something you may have noticed is a new keyword added to C# called `var`. You can think of `var` as an anonymously typed variable. What this means is that at compile time the compiler determines what the type of this variable should be and uses some "compiler magic" to replace the `var` keyword with the correct type. The nice part about using LINQ and the `var` keyword is that you do not need to go through the hassle of obtaining your data via the SQL provider and then stuffing it into an object; it is all done for you automagically.

Another significant advantage that LINQ affords us is type safety and rich querying options. Following is an example of a complex query, where we are trying to find out how much each customer paid for their orders in the year 2008:

SQL

```
select c.CustomerId, c.Name as CustomerName, sum(o.TotalPaid) as TotalPaid
from Customer as c
      inner join Orders as o
          on c.CustomerId = o.CustomerId
where o.OrderDate >= '1/1/2008'
      and o.OrderDate <= '12/31/2008'
group by c.CustomerId, c.Name
```

LINQ

```
var customers = from c in dataContext.Customers
                join o in dataContext.Orders on c.CustomerId equals o.CustomerId
                where c.OrderDate >= new Date(2008, 1, 1)
                    && c.OrderDate <= new Date(2008, 12, 31)
                group o by new { c.CustomerId, c.Name } into g
                select new {
                    CustomerId = c.CustomerId,
                    CustomerName = c.Name,
                    TotalPaid = g.Sum(o => o.TotalPaid)
                };
```

In the LINQ example the `OrderDate` field is actually of type `System.DateTime`. Therefore, if we attempt to compile our application and we try to compare it to a string or any object that isn't a `DateTime` type we will get a compiler error. This is extremely handy with agile development environments where database structures can change on a regular basis. Imagine changing a data type in your database from an integer to a double and recompiling your project; having the compiler tell you where all the failures are is a great advantage. In the past, developers would have to painfully search all of their stored procedures to ensure that they were all working properly, or worse yet, limit the type of changes allowed to the database schema. With LINQ you get back the flexibility to make changes as you see fit, and can rest assured that during compilation time your issues will be highlighted by the compiler.

LINQ also allows for more advanced querying such as taking base data and obtaining its corresponding dependency table information. The following is a quick example of how this can be accomplished with LINQ:

```
var order = (from o in dataContext.Orders
                where o.OrderId == 2
                select o).FirstOrDefault();

foreach(var orderInformation in order.OrderInformation)
    orderInformation.DateAdded = DateTime.Now;

dataContext.SubmitChanges();
```

As you can see from this example, we first selected a specific order from our orders table. The `FirstOrDefault()` part is important because it tells LINQ that we are only expecting a single entity or null returned. Once we have obtained the order information, we can get a collection of `OrderInformation` objects by requesting it through the order object. As soon as this request is made, LINQ goes to the database and grabs the information for consumption by our application. In the example, we are modifying the date added field in the order information table. Outside of the `foreach` loop we tell the `DataContext` to submit our changes. This is another great feature of LINQ because it allows you to cluster transactions before committing, similar to the `SqlTransaction` object you could use with the ADO.NET SQL Data Provider in .NET 2.0.

Can you imagine the amount of coding you can save by using LINQ?

LINQ-to-SQL

To get LINQ to work properly you need to initially design your model for use in your application. One of the ways this can be done is by using the LINQ-to-SQL designer provided with Visual Studio 2008. The designer for this tool allows you to connect to your SQL data store and literally drag and drop all the tables, views, and stored procedures you want to use. In the back end it is actually creating all the strongly typed entities based off your tables and views. The implications of this are that in minutes you can create an entire DAL for your application without having to write a single line of code! The downside, though, is that your LINQ-to-SQL designer will only work with SQL Server. If you want to use Oracle, DB2, MySQL, or any other database you will have to go elsewhere to get your fix. Some of the other issues we have found by using the LINQ-to-SQL files are that they do not automatically update when your database schema is updated. If you make a schema change to the database you will have to update your entities in LINQ-to-SQL by deleting them and re-adding them or modifying the XML file used to generate the entities. Both are easy to do, so pick the update that you want to perform and then save it and your updates will be applied to your entities. With these limitations aside though, if you want to rapidly develop an application the LINQ-to-SQL designer is definitely the way to go.

A LINQ-to-SQL Word of Caution

LINQ-to-SQL was originally developed by the team at Microsoft that worked on developing the entire framework for LINQ under the `System.Linq` namespace. There is also another competing project done by the Microsoft ADO.NET team called the Entity Framework.

Continued

> When the .NET 3.5 Framework was released, the Entity Framework was not ready to be released, so they released LINQ-to-SQL as the de facto way of working with databases using LINQ for the .NET 3.5 Framework. They did this because they wanted a way to show off the capabilities of LINQ when working with a database and to get developers started with and used to LINQ.
>
> LINQ-to-SQL came out the door first and has since gained a lot of popularity, followed by the Entity Framework that was released with .NET 3.5 SP1, but the ADO.NET team has been reticent to support and develop LINQ-to-SQL, because it would divide their time between the two competing frameworks. So don't be surprised if you see a retirement or at the very least a stagnant development of LINQ-to-SQL in the future. Don't let that stop you from using it, because Microsoft or a third party will probably provide a way to marry LINQ-to-SQL to the Entity Framework to make the conversion process easier for the developer.
>
> We chose LINQ-to-SQL because at the time of this writing, it is still the most widely used LINQ mechanism for connecting to and working with databases. In addition, we still see a bright future and a lot of developer support for the framework in the coming years.

Entity Framework

Another option available to you if you decide to use LINQ is the Entity Framework. This is a newer technology that the Microsoft ADO.NET team has released that allows you to have greater flexibility in building your DAL. It will allow you to build your own custom providers so you can theoretically use any database type you want. You can even connect to exotic data sources such as reporting services, business intelligence services, replication, and more.

The key difference with the Entity Framework is its flexibility in terms of data sources and mapping data structures to your custom entity classes. Where LINQ-to-SQL was a drag-and-drop solution, the Entity Framework allows you to deliberately map the relationship of entities you create to database objects. With it you can make a DAL that is abstracted away from the underlying database structure. All this flexibility comes at a cost though; the Entity Framework is more complex in the number of options it gives you for accessing and retrieving data compared with LINQ-to-SQL. But like any new framework, once you learn it and understand it, you will probably find that flexibility as a benefit instead of a hindrance.

Securing the Data Access Layer

In the past, when using concatenated inline SQL in your application you ran the risk of a SQL Injection attack. An example of this would be having a query string in a web request or text box in a post back request and having the contents of that field submitted to a database server unchecked and using inline concatenated SQL. A normal web request would look like this:

URL

```
http://www.somesite.com/Customers/Show.aspx?ID=22
```

You then take the ID from the query string and pass it into the database, like this:

C#

```
string sqlText = "select * from Customers";
            += "where ID = " + QueryString["ID"] + " ";
            += "and IsActive = 1";
// execute sqlText
```

When the code is executed, it would look like this to the database:

SQL

```
select * from Customers where ID = 22 and IsActive = 1
```

We have highlighted the text that was inserted into the SQL query string. In this case we just passed in a "22" and retrieved the customer with that ID. Nothing really wrong with that, right? You have probably seen this a hundred times if not more. However, this is a serious problem. Let's modify the URL slightly and follow the same code through the execution process.

URL

```
http://www.somesite.com/Customers/Show.aspx?ID=32;+drop+table+Customers;--
```

C#

```
string sqlText = "select * from Customers";
            += "where ID = " + QueryString["ID"] + " ";
            += "and IsActive = 1";
// execute sqlText
```

SQL

```
select * from Customers where ID = 32; drop table Customers;-- and IsActive = 1
```

Now that we have executed this and highlighted the text that was inserted into the SQL query string, do you see the problem? When the SQL executes, it will find the customer with the appropriate ID and then drop the Customers table from the database leaving you with no data for your customers and hoping that you have backed up your database. In addition, everything after the inserted ID in your C#, the and IsActive, will be commented out and not run.

In past editions of this book we have recommended using parameterized SQL queries, which eliminates the possibility of this occurring. The good news is that with LINQ this is done automatically for you so these types of attacks are not likely. The only major security concern should be where to keep your connection string, and what level of rights to grant the web application that will be accessing your database server. In most circumstances, granting the minimum possible rights while still making your application usable is ideal for securing your database. An example is granting the web application read and write access to only the database it needs and not any of the other databases on the server. This way, if the account is somehow compromised, other databases on your server will remain unaffected.

The second consideration is your connection string. A lot of times developers place the connection string right in the `web.config`; this strategy is alright but we would suggest that you use trusted connections. The advantage of trusted connections is that the password is not stored in clear text in the `web.config`; this is important because if for some reason your web server was compromised, the casual hacker would not be able to glance at your `web.config` file and gain access to your database.

Designing the Business Logic Layer

The DAL discussed in the previous section is made up of a number of classes that retrieve data from the database by using LINQ-to-SQL or the Entity Framework to return back collections of custom entity classes that wrap the fields of the retrieved data. The data returned by the DAL is still raw data, even though it's wrapped in classes, because these entity classes do not add anything; they are just a strongly typed container used to move data around. The BLL consumes this data and exposes it to the UI layer, but the BLL also adds validation logic and calculated properties, making some properties private or read-only (whereas they are all public and writable in the custom entity classes used between the DAL and the BLL), and adds instance and static methods to delete, edit, insert, and retrieve data. For a domain object named `Employee` that represents an employee, there may be a property named `Boss` that returns a reference to another object of type `Employee` that represents the first object's boss. In middle- to large-size projects, there are usually dozens, hundreds, or maybe even thousands of such objects with relationships between them. This object-oriented and strongly typed representation of any data provides an extremely strong abstraction from the database, which merely stores the data and provides a simple and powerful set of classes for the UI developer to work with, without needing to know any details about how and where the raw data will be stored, how many tables are in the database, or which relationships exist between them. This makes the UI developer's job easier and makes it possible for you to change low-level database structures without breaking any of the UI code, which is one of the primary reasons for using a multi-tier design. This will require more development time initially, and a good up-front architecture plan. If you follow the design pattern that we used to build the TheBeerHouse website you should be in great shape, and the initial time you spent doing it the right way will pay off in spades later on in terms of ease of maintenance and increased reliability.

Controllers

When initially creating a new MVC project you will notice a folder called "controllers" that you will use to develop your BLL. Within this folder you can create a new type of object called the *controller class*. This controller class, as mentioned in Chapter 2, coordinates the collection and processing of data through the model and renders the appropriate view. It completely eliminates the need for a code-behind class in your views. For the traditional ASP.NET developer this is going to be a massively huge paradigm switch, because all of your application and business logic is being processed in the controller. This is done to keep your interests separated so that the controller doesn't need to know anything about the view and vice versa.

Now that you have decided that you are going to implement your BLL in the controllers, you actually receive some great perks:

❏ Unit testing of your application is much more encompassing because all of your business logic is housed in either your controller or your model entities that you may have created; there are no server controls that you need to worry about failing.

❏ Security is much simpler to implement because all of your processing happens at the controller class. You no longer need to segregate higher-level authorization pages and commands into their own folders.

❑   You can render multiple views of your model off a single controller action method. A great example of this is using your actions to view standard web pages in HTML and also having it act as a RESTful interface to return XML or JSON, just by having the controller check the content type that is being requested from the browser. We talk about how this is useful later on in the book.

The transition is not all easy and does involve a moderate learning curve, one that we hope this book will help you overcome. In this section, we discuss in detail how to really take advantage of your new controller classes to make your application robust and elegant.

Security

In the past, we have always grappled with problems of ASP.NET and security. Traditionally, administrative sections would have to be placed into their own folders and given their own web.config files to limit the rights of users attempting to access these areas. We would also have to pepper in, in a seemingly chaotic manner, restrictions on specific controls or functionality. A great example is on a content page, having an edit button only visible to administrators. Our choices were to hack into the code-behind file to add explicit admin restriction, or create totally separate pages for our administrators to use, separate from the standard UI. With the MVC framework we can simply add tags to our actions that specify who can perform this action and under what conditions. Let's say that we only want administrators to edit the content page; the code would look something like this:

```
[Authorize(Roles = "Admin")]
public ActionResult EditContent(int id, ...)
{
    // logic that edits content

    return View();
}
```

In this very simple example we have locked down the action so that it allows only users with the role "Admin" to call and execute this action, which performs an edit of our content. So even if somehow users were able to get to the view that allows them to edit content, without having the right authorization they are rejected as unauthorized.

In some instances you may want to be able to render multiple views from one method. For example, you may have a "Content" method that presents the data and allows you to edit it based on the formation of the URL. Rather than including an attribute tag at the top of the method you can just as easily incorporate it right into your code with an if statement. Either way you choose, you are able to control access to your application and underlying data to a much higher degree with the MVC framework.

Direct navigation to .aspx pages is another thing that is no longer possible. Because the routing engine handles all requests, and subsequently sends its requests to your controller, a person cannot directly navigate to a view without going through a controller. This is a great feature because in the past you would always worry about sensitive content pages being accessed from outside users by some type of URL hack. An example of this would be a user who is at the ViewContent.aspx page and simply guesses that the EditContent.aspx page is the page that would allow him to edit content. Unless this page was under a secure folder, explicitly called out in the web.config, or specific to the authorization in the page load, any user could gain access to that page and its functionality. The MVC framework really helps developers to lock down their applications in a much more organized and logical manner.

Caching Data for Better Performance

In every site or web-based application there is some data that doesn't change very often that is requested very frequently by a lot of end users, such as the list of article categories, the e-store's product categories and product items, the list of countries and states, and so on. The most common solution to increase the performance of your site is to implement a caching system for that type of data, so that once the data is retrieved from the data store, it will be kept in memory for some interval, and subsequent requests for the same data will retrieve it from the memory cache, avoiding a round-trip to the database server and running another query. This will save processing time and network traffic to the database, and thus produce a faster output to the user.

The MVC framework again shines in this area by allowing you to manage caching at the controller level. The following code snippet shows you exactly how easy caching has become:

```
[OutputCache(Duration = 60)]
public ActionResult SomeControllerMethod()
{
    // some Logic
}
```

The example caches the output for this particular controller for a period of 60 seconds. Now, you may ask yourself what if you have variables associated with this method such as an id. The following code shows you how easy it is to use parameterized caching:

```
[OutputCache(Duration = 60, VaryByParam = "id")]
public ActionResult SomeControllerMethod(int id)
{
    // some Logic
}
```

Not only can you cache by duration, but also by the inputs that you receive into your controller classes. For very high-traffic sites this is essential! If you've ever done your own caching you can quickly realize this is a huge time saver, and it is based off of the same output caching available in ASP.NET Web Forms.

Content Delivery Networks

Are you planning for your site to be massively popular and gobble up an enormous amount of bandwidth that you servers will simply not be able to handle? Then you may want to look into a Content Delivery Network (CDN), which is a distributed network of servers that dish out your heavy content for you. This may include image files, JavaScript files, CSS files, documents, movies, audio — basically any static content that can be delivered to a browser. The CDN works by using a network of DNS servers that route your request to the geographically closest available server to distribute the requested content. An example of this is that you want to deliver static content that doesn't change a lot, like your styles, JavaScript, and images, from the closest server to the requesting browser so that you get the fastest transfer speeds and the lowest ping time.

The CDN fits in perfectly with an MVC application because all of your content is held in your "Content" folder. The way that most CDNs generally work is that you would need to install their software onto your server. You would then tell the software where your content folders are and it would propagate your content up to their CDN service. In your application's markup all of your linked references would point to another domain, possibly a subdomain, that was specifically created to deliver the content from the CDN service. Following is a quick example of a link to an image file:

```
<img src="http://static.TheBeerHouseExample.com/content/images/myhugeimage.png" />
```

Of course the gotcha is that you will need to make some modifications to your routing engine to facilitate the subdomain. If you are interested in using a CDN, pricing is usually pennies to the gigabyte used. Now, you may be thinking this is comparable to your current ISP, but you need to remember that dishing out content steals bandwidth away from running your website. A good way to think of this is that is that for each static file you have to deliver — images, JavaScript, CSS files, documents, and so on — you are reducing the number of requests that you server can handle by one, because it will be tied up transferring other files, which are sometimes large in the case of images.

To truly illustrate the power of a CDN, there was a popular dating website that delivered millions of hits a day running off only one or two servers. With the help of good architecture and a CDN, it was easily able to continue operating under these extreme loads with limited machines. If you plan on having a high-volume website or a website with very large static files that need to be distributed, this is the way to go.

Exception Handling

Sometimes things go wrong; you may believe that you are an unstoppable coding machine, but occasionally even the best of us make mistakes. Some bugs are so far in the system that only the most unlikely of circumstances will cause them to surface. With this in mind, you do not want your users seeing an ugly application error page.

By using custom error pages, your exceptions are handled in a very consistent way. Although this is not a generic buckshot approach as it was in .NET 2.0, in the MVC framework you actually need to specify an attribute tag at the controller or action level to handle errors. The advantage is that you can become a little more discriminate about what type of errors you want to catch and where they go. The following examples show you how to protect your action from returning an ugly, yellow-screen-of-death error page:

```
[HandleError]
public ActionResult SomeControllerMethod()
{
    // some Logic
}
```

This is the easiest way to handle an error. Essentially, all the exceptions generated out of the preceding method will go to a view in your shared folder called Error.ascx. A more granulated way of doing this is by adding a few more attributes to your tag:

```
[HandleError(ExceptionType = typeof(SecurityException), View = "UnauthorizedView"]
public ActionResult SomeControllerMethod()
{
    // some Logic
}
```

Here you can see we are creating a custom error handling tag only for situations where we get a security exception. We are also directing the user to a specific view, in this case the UnauthorizedView, which will most likely contain some text indicating the user does not have the necessary rights to proceed with the request.

So all this new error handling is wonderful but you may be asking yourself what good is error handling without logging? It's really of no use unless you have it integrated into your error handling strategy, and to do this you can take advantage of overrides. You need to create a new attribute based off of the `IExceptionFilter` interface stored in the `System.Web.Mvc` namespace. Your new attribute will emulate this except with the added benefit of recording your error into the database. Once this is in place you have a fully functional error handling system.

Expanded Output Choices

Controller classes are normally used for outputting HTML-based views but they can also output views in a variety of other formats. Imagine typing in a URL and getting a JSON or XML response, or even an HTML fragment. A controller action method can do all of these things, which in turn opens up a world of possibilities that were difficult to accomplish in ASP.NET Web Forms.

Integrated JSON support is one of our favorites because this format is being widely used by developers who create AJAX-based JavaScript for use in their websites. To use these new output types, all you have to do is simply point a JavaScript framework like jQuery at a URL and wait for the response to come back so that you can interact and use the data asynchronously without ever reloading the entire page.

We go more into how this is useful and different ways you can use this alternate output to create RESTful interfaces for your modules later in the book.

Transaction Management

A very important issue you must tackle when designing a business layer is how you plan to manage transactions. Many business methods call multiple DAL methods internally to update, insert, or delete multiple records, potentially in multiple tables. You must ensure that multiple calls run within a transaction, so that if one fails, all actions performed by previous methods are rolled back. If you don't do this, you'll end up having inconsistent and incorrect data. Managing transactions would be complicated if you had to do everything yourself, but fortunately LINQ saves the day again by providing you with the `DataContext` class. The `DataContext` class has a method within it called `SubmitChanges`; this is a critical item because no changes that you make to your custom LINQ entities will be propagated up to the database until you execute this method. In the past this process was a painful one involving the use of transaction objects, but with the help of LINQ-to-SQL, transaction management is a snap to accomplish.

Web.Config File Configuration

So far, while discussing the DAL and the BLL, we've mentioned that the site will have a number of configurable settings such as the membership, profile, e-mail server, the connection string to the database, and others. Managing these configuration settings is something that doesn't exactly fit into any of your layers, but rather an environmental setting that tells the layers what to expect and where to find certain resources.

For example, the DAL will need a connection string to find the database it is supposed to use. The BLL will need to be pointed to the SMTP server to send e-mails for the Newsletter module that you create in Chapter 8.

All these settings for your environment resources will be saved into the `web.config` file, so it's easy for an administrator to change them using only a text editor. Anytime the `web.config` file is changed, ASP.NET will automatically reload it, and its modified settings will be used for any new connections to the server.

In IIS 7 there is the capability to place IIS-specific configuration settings right into your web.config. In the past with IIS 6, if you wanted something trivial done, such as changing your default page, you would have to call the administrator to modify your website entry in the IIS 6 meta-base using the GUI provided on the server. The following example shows how to set a default page in your web.config for IIS 7:

```
<configuration>
    <system.WebServer>
        <defaultDocument>
            <files>
                <clear />
                <add value="default.aspx" />
            </files>
        </defaultDocument>
    </system.WebServer>
</configuration>
```

You are able to manage every aspect of the IIS 7 server from the web.config; this is a huge performance gain, because you no longer have to wonder if the administrator set up the website correctly through the GUI. You can simply store the settings for your IIS 7 in your source control repository and add or modify them through FTP whenever you want. Imagine being able to FTP your application for your website to its directory on the server and having 100% of your IIS settings already in place for you. The only thing that you need to make sure of is that the administrator of the server has created the website for you and set up the appropriate headers, IP addresses, and ports for the website. We go into great depth about setting up both IIS 6 and IIS 7 for MVC in Chapter 12.

User Interface

Now that we have discussed the DAL and the BLL, you come to the final layer of your web application: the presentation layer. This is the portion of your application the end user sees and directly interacts with. It is also one of the most important parts of your website, because it can literally make or break your reputation.

The reason why the UI is so important is because we use our sense of sight to instantly make assumptions about what we are seeing. In a split second we have sized up the whole site and decided if we deem it worth our time to continue to use the site. We look at many factors in that split second, such as whether the colors are pleasing, how intuitive the design is, and if there is enough organized content to make browsing around the site worth it.

Take, for example, when you meet somebody for the first time: in that split second before they say a single thing, you have already formed opinions about the person based on their clothing, hair, face, eyes, lips, and general posture.

The same logic can be applied to a website: the look and feel registers with the users' brains before they even start to read your content, so they have instantly formed opinions about your website. So that is why it is so important to make a design that appeals to your audience, or at the very least a design that doesn't make them want to run for the hills. But we already covered all this in Chapter 3, so here we focus on using what you learned about effective user interface design and learn to apply it to ASP.NET MVC views.

Best Practices in Engineering a Presentation Layer

The following is some advice we have gathered over the years that will make your user interfaces shine:

❑　Avoid pop-ups whenever possible; they obstruct the view of your website and aggravate your users. You also run the distinct possibility that your pop-up could be blocked by a pop-up blocker, thus causing further aggravation and loss of functionality.

❑　Test your user interface against as many different browsers as possible. The days of Internet Explorer being the only consideration are long gone; so many competitors are in this market with sizable market share that you need to consider at least testing the major browsers. Different interpretations of HTML markup may make things a little more difficult, but testing early and testing often is the key to staying on top of this.

❑　Avoid using tables to lay out your website; although this was common practice in the past, different browsers interpret tables in different ways. Your best bet is to use DIVs for website layout purposes and use tables only for situations where you have truly tabular data.

❑　Do use JavaScript to limit the number of full-page POST backs that actually occur. The only reason a full-page POST back should occur is if a person is going to a totally different page in your website. Things like drop-downs being selected or validation will aggravate your users to no end!

❑　Consider the colors you will use in your website. This is often overlooked but the brain naturally associates colors with ideas and concepts. For example, red text is more memorable to users because in our minds red is considered a danger or a warning color. On the other hand, a website with a blue scheme may invoke feelings of trust. There is a whole science behind the effect colors have on people's perceptions. Another consideration is that some people cannot differentiate certain colors such as red and green or are completely color blind. The best practice for these people is to have a website with high contrast. An example is a white background with black text. The difference between these two colors creates high contrast.

❑　Organize your data in a logical manner. Put your most important content in the center of your website and navigation and ancillary information on the peripheries. Ensure there are clear distinctions between the different sections such as using a beveled DIV boarder. Always place your most important information on your home page; users will frequently leave your website if they do not receive useful information within the first 30 seconds.

❑　Use section headings and large and bolded font to highlight them to the user. Within a few moments of arriving to a page a user should know exactly what it is all about. Section headings help the users organize the page's information, which in turn will encourage them to stay longer.

❑　Avoid long-running processes without giving the user some kind of feedback. If there is a process that is going to take several minutes, give the user a progress bar or process the request asynchronously. A slow and unresponsive interface is something that people will not want to use.

Views

We have already discussed models and controllers, so the last element of an MVC application is the view. The view is a representation of the model, but in this case it is HTML for rendering in a browser, and is equivalent to a standard ASP.NET Web Forms page except for the fact that it has no code-behind file. All of the code that ordinarily would have gone there is in your controller class. You may be wondering how all of your old ASP.NET server controls, that came with the .NET framework and that you acquired from third-party vendors, are going to work without a code-behind file. The bad news is that they won't; all your server controls that you loved such as your login control and your grid controls are totally non-functional with the MVC framework. The good news is that you won't really need them, and many alternatives are available that you will create and use later on in this book. One thing that you will notice, though, is that your rendered HTML markup will be cleaner and more efficient.

The MVC framework comes with a set of HTML helper extension methods that will automatically create and data-bind many of the controls that you were used to using in ASP.NET Web Forms.

```
<label for="title">Title</label><br />
<%= Html.TextBox("Title") %>
```

This is an example of an HTML text box being created. The name of that text box maps to our ViewData dictionary, which the controller uses to pass data to the view. We can also transfer an object directly into the view using a typed model. The following is an example of us using the model to populate what is in the text box:

```
<label for="title">Title</label><br />
<%= Html.TextBox("Title", ViewData.Model.Title) %>
```

We have the same end result, except in this example the data is coming from the typed model object that is bound to this view, and defined using generics. To give you an idea of how this is rendered, the following is the same exact text box after it has been rendered into HTML by the HTML extension method:

```
<label for="title">Title</label><br />
<input id="Title" name="Title" type="text" value="Chief Technology Officer" />
```

As you can see it is simply using an input tag to create this text box and there are absolutely no runat attributes involved. From the UI perspective this input will act as though it was all written purely in HTML.

You may be wondering why we are seemingly taking a step backwards in time. The answer is that many developers have wanted greater control over their HTML markup. When we used server controls we had to accept the bloated HTML and JavaScript that was rendered to the browser. We are also taking a negative hit by creating overly complicated and unnecessary JavaScript to force HTML to work like Windows Forms. We talked about this briefly in Chapter 2, but we encourage you to open up one of your old ASP.NET Web Form sites and view the source of the HTML when it is running. As you can probably see, the more complex the controls the uglier the markup becomes. This costs us in SEO, it costs us in bandwidth, and it costs us in performance. The MVC framework involves a greater level of initial planning but pays off in dividends later on.

Search Engine Optimization

Some websites are truly fantastic, but they get almost no traffic to them. This is because they are great for their human visitors but are lacking for their robot visitors. A great example of this is websites based entirely off of Flash animation. Although Flash is a great tool and it gives a "thick" client feel to a website, search engines simply cannot decipher their meaning. This is why it is important to use Flash in moderation. You must have valuable and unique content on your website in order to draw in visitors.

Some people are still stuck in the past with SEO; they still believe that the "description" and "keywords" meta tags are all that is needed to have a well-ranked site. Well we hate to burst your bubble, but these meta tags aren't really weighted any differently than anything else on your website:

```
<meta name="description" content="This website is all about SEO" />
<meta name="keywords" content="SEO, Search Engine Optimization" />
```

They used to matter back in the late 1990s, but in the 21st century they are no different than a paragraph of text in the body of your content.

A couple of things that you want to pay close attention to are the keywords that you enter in your title, h1, and h2 tags as well as your URL. You also want to make sure that each page only has one H1 and no more than three H2 tags; search engines now use these tags to determine the relevance of the content on the page in relation to the text people are using to link to this page.

Another strategy that is often used is to provide the search engine robot a sitemap so that it will have an easier time finding the relevant pages on your website. You can even assign relative importance and the frequency for which a particular page updates:

```
<url>
  <loc>http://www.TheBeerHouseExample.com/Article/SEO-Optimization</loc>
  <lastmod>2009-1-17</lastmod>
  <changefreq>daily</changefreq>
  <priority>12</priority>
</url>
```

This example is an XML sitemap definition that was standardized by a joint task force of all the major search engines, called sitemap.org, back in 2005. You probably wouldn't want to make this by hand every time your website changes so you would probably want a background process that periodically pings your database and writes out this XML sitemap to the root of your website. Normally it is called sitemap.xml.

Though you can do all the above perfectly, you can still fail if you don't have an easily searchable website. So we cannot stress enough the importance of having an easily searchable site that follows standard HTML and HTTP practices. A good rule of thumb is that if your HTML source looks clean when viewed through the browser you probably have an easily searchable site; if it looks like a garbled mess your site is probably not that easily searched.

Throughout this book and the code that we have written for it, we have paid special attention to creating concise and easily readable HTML for all of the public-facing pages that a search engine robot might visit. So rest assured that we have done our best to create a site that is easily indexed by a search engine robot, so now all that you need to get that number-one ranking in Google is some good engaging content that a user wants to link to.

JavaScript Integration

Most sites built today will have some level of JavaScript integration incorporated into them. You may not have realized this, but if you use ASP.NET Web Forms you are using JavaScript. That is because the ASP.NET server controls need JavaScript to be able to communicate back events that have occurred on the user's side. If you are unsure of what we mean, take the following example into consideration:

```
<input
    type="submit"
    name="ctl00$mainContent$SendEmailButton"
    value="Send"
    onclick="javascript:WebForm_DoPostBackWithOptions(new WebForm_PostBackOptions(
        &quot;ctl00$mainContent$SendEmailButton&quot;, &quot;&quot;, true,
```

```
              &quot;&quot;, &quot;&quot;, false, false
          ))"
      id="ctl00_mainContent_SendEmailButton"
  />
```

This was taken off of a website that used a standard ASP.NET 2.0 Web Form `Button` control to submit a simple form. As you can see, there is an enormous amount of markup to allow this to actually occur. Furthermore, we haven't even shown you the amount of code that was created to do the JavaScript POST back; it is measured in kilobytes, by the way.

Now take this same example, and do it using the MVC framework and you're using plain old standard HTML markup:

```
<input
    type="submit"
    name="send-email-button"
    value="Send"
/>
```

As you can see, you have much cleaner HTML that is being rendered. This eliminates the need for any kind of JavaScript to process the form action. However, if desired, you can still take advantage of JavaScript for doing asynchronous things like validating the inputs before they are submitted or partially rendering portions of your page to reduce load times.

If you are already familiar with the Microsoft AJAX framework we have some good and bad news for you. The bad news is that the ASP.NET AJAX server controls, namely the `UpdatePanel`, don't work in an MVC application. The good news is that the Microsoft AJAX framework, which drove all the controls, still does work in ASP.NET MVC. So you will probably soon see some community projects to get the type of functionality offered in the ASP.NET AJAX controls function in ASP.NET MVC.

You can, however, take this time to learn some well-documented and stable JavaScript frameworks that have been out for a couple years such as jQuery and Yahoo's YUI Framework. The jQuery Framework was an open-source JavaScript framework that the ASP.NET MVC development team liked so much they included the source files as part of the default project in Visual Studio. They even struck a deal with the jQuery team to provide IntelliSense support for their documented interface. Later in this book we go over how to use jQuery and integrate it into each of your modules in a natural and effective way, but it is important to note that JavaScript gives your users a richer experience by reducing POST backs that are oftentimes very annoying to users.

Solution

This section of this chapter is thinner than those found in most of the other chapters. In fact, in this chapter you've been presented with a general overview of good website design practices and some architectural considerations when working with the MVC framework. In the future chapters you actually take the principles that are laid out in this chapter and put them into real-world use. This includes actually building the various modules of the TheBeerHouse website by fully taking advantage of the new features in the MVC framework.

Summary

This chapter discussed the features that you will see in the future chapters. You are going to design articles, newsletters, a store, polls, and security for your web application. To do this you are going to use the full spectrum of new features that the MVC framework has provided. This includes building your DAL using the LINQ-to-SQL designer that we talked about earlier in this chapter, and the new LINQ syntax that was added as part of the .NET 3.5 Framework. As part of your BLL you will use the controllers and the routing engine. As we discussed in this chapter, the routing engine and the controller give you a much greater level of control over the flow of your application. Lastly, you are going to create some clean HTML markup and use the jQuery framework to provide some eye candy and perform AJAX calls against your controller actions. This will provide the user with a seamless and fluent user interface that will provided a greater level of control over the user experience.

We plan on following all the principles discussed in this chapter and adhering to them to create a great starting point for you to build your very own ASP.NET MVC-based web application called TheBeerHouse.

5

Membership and User Profiling

The sample website developed in this book contains dynamic content such as news, events, newsletters, polls, forum posts, and more. It can be considered a content-based site, where significant parts of the site can be easily changed or updated by privileged users. This functionality is sometimes called a *Content Management System* or *CMS* for short. Your site will be slightly different because you have also added an important e-commerce section that enables your client to sell merchandise at a profit. Here's a secret, although not a well-kept one: for any content-based site that wants to be successful, build a vigorous and thriving community of users! If you have a lot of loyal users, you can be sure that the site will increase its user base, and thus its size, its popularity, and your revenues. You want to encourage users to register for a free account on the site so you can enable them to customize their view, participate in message forums, and even order merchandise from e-commerce pages. Once they obtain a free account they will be members of the site. Membership is a form of empowerment — users will feel special because they are members, and you want to reward their loyalty by enabling them to customize certain visual aspects, and to remember their settings on their return visits. In order to track members, it is necessary to have some sort of *identity* to describe and distinguish them from other members and more importantly, against anonymous users who have not logged in. This chapter explains how to develop user registration functionality and user profiles. The user account will also be used to grant or deny access to special restricted pages of the site. The profile will be used by modules developed later in this book to customize content and give users a public "virtual face," visible to other members and users.

Problem

In reality, a membership system is a requirement for most websites — not only for community and content-based sites. Sites typically have a number of administration pages that visitors should not have access to. The administration section can be a complete application in itself, or just a couple of simple pages to allow people to change some settings. However, you always need to identify each user who tries to access those restricted pages, and check whether they are authorized to do so. The means of identifying a user is called *authentication*, and the means of determining what access a user has is called *authorization*. Unfortunately, it's easy to confuse these terms, so it helps to think of the root words: authenticate (who are you?) and authorize (what are you allowed to do?). The authentication and authorization processes are part of the site's membership system, which includes the creation of new user accounts, the management of the user's credentials, including protection mechanisms such as encryption and password recovery in case passwords are lost or forgotten, and roles associated with an account. For the sample site, the membership system must be as complete as possible, because it will be used by administrators and editors to access protected areas, and by users who want to have their own identity within the community, post messages to the forums, and be recognized by other members. It must also enable users to create their account interactively without administrator intervention and to update their profile information on demand.

Administrators must also be able to see a list of registered users, and control them. For example, if a user regularly posts spam or offending messages to the forum, a good administrator or forum moderator will want to temporarily or permanently disable this user's account. Conversely, if a user always behaves well and respects the site's policies, an administrator may decide to promote him to the status of moderator, or even editor. In other words, modifying users' account settings and their roles should be an easy thing to do, because the administrator may need to do it frequently. Thus, you require an easy-to-use administration section to manage user accounts.

To make it easier to manage security permissions, you'll create roles that are basically a group of users who have special permission in addition to the normal user permissions. For example, the Administrators role will be used to designate certain individuals who will have the capability to manage user accounts and site content.

Although a membership system is necessary for common security-related tasks, other things are needed to build an effective community of happy users. The users expect to have some benefits from their registration. For example, they could receive newsletters with useful information with links back to the website, and they could customize the home page so that it highlights the type of content they are most interested in. Furthermore, their preferred site template could be saved and restored between sessions. All this information makes up what's called a *user profile*. Implementing a system for profiling the user is a good thing not just for the end user, but also for the site administrators. Among the information stored in the profile is the user's age, gender, email address, and contact information. A savvy administrator could later make use of such data in a variety of ways:

❑ **Customize the user appearance for registered and profiled users:** For example, the news and events modules developed in the next chapter use the details stored in the user's profile to highlight the news and events that happen in the user's country, state, or city with different colors, to identify the items closer to home. This rather simple feature can improve the user experience, and gives users an incentive to provide such personal details in their profile.

❑ **Implement targeted marketing:** For example, you could send a newsletter about a concert or some other event to all users that reside in a particular country, state, or city. You can do the same with banners or text notices on the site. Multiple criteria could be used for targeting the sponsored news: other than the user's location, it could be according to age, gender, or a combination of multiple conditions. The more details you have about your users, the more chances you have to sell advertisement spaces on your site to external companies, or to effectively use the ad possibilities yourself.

The site administrators will need an intuitive console from which they can see and edit the profile of any user — to remove any offensive content from the user's profile.

Design

To recap, your client has commissioned a membership system that handles the following operations and features:

❑   Users must be able to create new accounts independently, by filling out an online registration form.

❑   Users must be able to later change their own credentials, or recover them if they forget them.

❑   The administrator must be able to grant or deny access to specific sections or individual pages by certain users.

❑   The administrator must be able to temporarily or permanently suspend a user account, for when a user does not respect the site's policy of conduct.

❑   The administrator may want to know when specific users registered, and the last time they logged in.

❑   The administrator must be able to view and edit the profile of each user. A profiling system enables each registered user to save data such as site preferences and personal details in a data store (such as a database), so that their information will be remembered on future visits.

ASP.NET 2.0 introduced some great features that help to develop a membership and profile subsystem for your website. You may have used the membership and profile provider in a past project using the built-in ASP.NET Web Form controls, but in this project you are going to use these providers without all the controls and call them directly to authenticate, authorize, and store profile information in the ASP. NET MVC way.

Password Storage Mechanisms

You have basically four methods for storing passwords, with each one offering different trade-offs between security and the ease of development, administration, and user experience:

1.   The most convenient method of password storage for developers and administrators is to store the password as plain text in a database field. This is also convenient for users because you can easily e-mail a user's password to him in case he forgets it. This is also the least secure option because all of the passwords are stored as plain text — if your database were compromised by a hacker, he'd have easy access to everyone's password. You need to be extremely careful about locking down your database and ensuring that you secure your database backup files.

2.   To enhance the security of password storage you can encrypt the passwords before storing them in a database. Many ways exist to encrypt passwords but the most common type is *symmetric encryption*, which uses a guarded system password to encrypt all user passwords. This is two-way encryption: you can encrypt a password and also decrypt it later. This offers medium convenience for developers, but still offers a lot of convenience for users because you can still e-mail them a forgotten password.

3.   Another frequently used method of storing passwords is called *hashing*. Hashing is not the most secure way to conceal your passwords, but it is the quickest. When hashing your passwords the hash function takes an arbitrary length data block and creates a fixed size jumble of data. The reason why a hash function is used is that it is fairly secure and extremely easy to deploy.

4. The last method is known as a distributed authentication system, which lets another website or service store and authenticate all the sensitive user information (passwords, verification questions, and so on) for your users. Distributed authentication systems have been around for a long time in the form of many different services, but have only recently caught on as a viable solution for small- and medium-sized websites. The most recent authentication system, called OpenID, has seen some massive gains in acceptance from many competing online authentication services, including Windows Live ID, Google, Yahoo, and AOL. The benefit to users is only having to keep track of one password that they can use on any website that supports the distributed authentication system. The benefit to the site owner is the low overhead for registration: the user simply has to log in to create an account with the website so this low overhead opens up the number of users that will want to register. Finally, the benefit to developers is that they can focus on building the application and not creating an authentication system that they have to spend countless hours making sure is protected from hackers trying to steal passwords.

The recommended encryption type to use would be the distributed authentication system (method 4), because of the excellent security. However, a distributed authentication system isn't an ideal solution for all business customers, so you are going to go with the next best thing — hashing (method 3), because it offers a good level of security without requiring a developer to provide an encryption key. Although hashing passwords will be used in this book for user security, we cover how making minor modifications in the web.config file will allow you to switch to a different method outlined in the preceding list. Keep in mind that if you opt to use symmetric encryption or asymmetric encryption you will need to provide a key for the encryption algorithm to use.

Authentication Modes: Windows or Forms Based?

The first thing you have to decide when you set up a security mechanism for a website is whether you want to use Windows or forms-based authentication. Windows authentication is the easiest to set up and use, whereas forms-based authentication requires you to create a custom database and a login form. Windows security is usually the best choice when you are developing an internal company website where all the users already have Windows logins managed by an Active Directory domain controller. With Windows security, users enjoy the capability to use restricted web pages without having to formally log in to the website. The page is executed under the context of the user requesting it, and security restrictions are automatically enforced on all resources that the code tries to access and use (typically files and database objects).

Another advantage is that Windows will securely store and encrypt user credentials so you don't have to. However, the requirement to have a local network account is a huge disadvantage that makes it a bad choice for the World Wide Web. If you use Windows security for users located outside of a company's network, the company would be required to create a network user account for each website user, which makes it slow for users to gain access and expensive for companies to administer. Though you could conceivably write some code to automate the creation of Windows network accounts, and could write a login page that uses Windows impersonation behind the scenes, it just doesn't make sense for this application. Employing Windows authentication with those nasty workarounds in your context, a public website with possibly thousands of users, would be a maintenance nightmare. It makes a lot more sense to use forms-based authentication, and store user account credentials and related profile data in a custom database.

The "Let's Do Everything on Our Own" Approach

Designing a module for handling user membership and profiling is not easy. It may not seem particularly difficult at first: you can easily devise some database tables for storing the required data (roles, account credentials and details, the associations between roles and accounts, and account profiles) and an API that allows the developer to request, create, and modify this data. However, things are rarely as easy as they appear at first! You must not downplay the significance of these modules because they are very crucial to the operation of the website. Properly designing these modules is important because all other site modules rely on them. If you design and implement the articles module poorly, you can go back and fix it without affecting all of the site's other modules (forum, e-commerce, newsletter, polls, and so on). If you decide to change the design of the membership module after you have developed other modules that use it, chances are good that you will need to modify something in those modules as well. The membership module must be both complete and simple to use. Developers should be able to use its classes and methods when they design administration pages. They should also be able to create and edit user accounts by writing just a few lines of code. Visual Studio 2008 and ASP.NET 3.5 offer a full set of controls that can be leveraged to create login and user administration pages. When using the MVC framework you want to steer away from these controls. Although extremely convenient, this book is about implementing a website that uses the Model-View-Controller design pattern. If you are worried about not using the ASP.NET security provider, don't be; you will still use much of the backend code that drives the security module, and some new code unique to the MVC framework.

This section introduces the built-in membership and profiling framework of ASP.NET 2.0 that you are probably familiar with if you have done any kind of ASP.NET development in the past. The membership and profiling framework hasn't been changed since ASP.NET 2.0, so your knowledge of those providers is still relevant in ASP.NET MVC. You also learn how to use these providers in your own project instead of inventing your own solution.

Using Membership for Authentication

The principal class of the ASP.NET 2.0's security framework is `System.Web.Security.Membership`, which exposes a number of static methods to create, delete, update, and retrieve registered users.

The following table describes the most important methods.

Method	Description
CreateUser	Creates a new user account.
DeleteUser	Deletes the specified user.
FindUsersByEmail	Returns an array of users with the specified e-mail address. If SQL Server is used to store accounts, the input e-mail can contain any wildcard characters supported by SQL Server in LIKE clauses, such as % for any string of zero or more characters, or _ for a single character.
FindUsersByName	Returns an array of users with the specified name. Wildcard characters are supported.

Method	Description
GeneratePassword	Generates a new password with the specified length, and the specified number of non-alphanumeric characters.
GetAllUsers	Returns an array with all the registered users.
GetNumberOfUsersOnline	Returns an integer value indicating how many registered users are currently online.
GetUser	Retrieves a specific user by name.
GetUserNameByEmail	Returns the username of a user with the given e-mail address.
UpdateUser	Updates a user.
ValidateUser	Returns a Boolean value indicating whether the input credentials correspond to a registered user.

Some of these methods (`CreateUser`, `GetAllUsers`, `GetUser`, `FindUsersByName`, `FindUsersByEmail`, and `UpdateUser`) accept or return instances of the `System.Web.Security.MembershipUser` class, which represents a single user, and provides quite a lot of details about that user. The following table describes the instance properties and methods exposed by this class.

Property	Description
Comment	A comment (typically entered by the administrator) associated with a given user.
CreationDate	The date when the user registered.
Email	The user's e-mail address.
IsApproved	Indicates whether the account is enabled, and whether the user can log in.
IsLockedOut	Indicates whether the user account was disabled after a number of invalid logins. This property is read-only, and the administrator can only indirectly set it back to false, by calling the `UnlockUser` method described later in the table.
IsOnline	Indicates whether the user is currently online.
LastActivityDate	The date when the user logged in or was last authenticated. If the last login was persistent, this will not necessarily be the date of the login, but it may be the date when the user accessed the site and was automatically authenticated through the cookie.
LastLockoutDate	The date when the user was automatically locked-out by the membership system, after a (configurable) number of invalid logins.
LastLoginDate	The date of the last login.

Property	Description
LastPasswordChangedDate	When the user last changed his or her password.
PasswordQuestion	The question asked of users who forget their password — used to prove it's really them.
ProviderName	Gets the name of the membership provider that stores and retrieves the user information for the membership user.
ProviderUserKey	Gets the unique user ID from the membership provider.
UserName	The user's username.

Method	Description
ChangePassword	Changes the user's password. The current password must be provided.
ChangePassword QuestionAndAnswer	Changes the question and answer asked of a user who forgets his or her password. Requires the current password as input (so someone can't change this for somebody else).
GetPassword	Returns the current password. Depending on how the membership system is set up, it may require the answer to the user's password question as input and will not work if only a password hash is stored in the database.
ResetPassword	Creates a new password for the user. This is the only function to change the password if the membership system was set up to hash the password.
UnlockUser	Unlocks the user if he was previously locked out by the system because of too many invalid attempts to log in.

When you change a user property, the new value is not immediately persisted to the data store; you have to call the UpdateUser method of the Membership class for that. This is done so that with a single call you can save multiple updated properties, and thus improve performance.

By using these two classes together, you can completely manage the accounts' data in a very intuitive and straightforward way. It's outside the scope of this book to provide a more exhaustive coverage of every method and overload, but we can show you a few examples about their usage in practice — please consult the MSDN Library for all the details on these classes.

❑ **Membership Class:**
   http://msdn.microsoft.com/en-us/library/system.web.security.membership.aspx

❑ **MembershipUser Class:**
   http://msdn.microsoft.com/en-us/library/system.web.security
   .membershipuser.aspx

The following is some highlighted code that outlines registering a new account in a typical MVC controller action and handling the exception that may be raised if an account with the specified username or e-mail address already exists:

```
try
{
    // creates account for user by passing in the username, password, and email
    MembershipUser newUser = Membership.CreateUser(
        "Al", "secret", "AKatawazi@wrox.com"
    );

    ViewData["Message"] = "Your account was created successfully.";
    return View();
}
catch (MembershipCreateUserException exception)
{
    string message = "Unable to create the user. ";
    switch (exception.StatusCode)
    {
        case MembershipCreateStatus.DuplicateEmail:
            message += " An account with the specified e-mail already exists.";
            break;
        case MembershipCreateStatus.DuplicateUserName:
            message += " An account with the specified username already exists.";
            break;
        case MembershipCreateStatus.InvalidEmail:
            message += " The specified e-mail is not valid.";
            break;
        case MembershipCreateStatus.InvalidPassword:
            message += " The specified password is not valid.";
            break;
        default:
            message += exception.Message;
            break;
    }

    ViewData["Message"] = message;
    return View();
}
```

If you want to change some of the user's information you first retrieve a `MembershipUser` instance that represents that user, change some properties as desired, and then update the user as shown in the following code:

```
MembershipUser user = Membership.GetUser("Al");

if (DateTime.Now.Subtract(user.LastActivityDate).TotalHours < 2)
    user.Comment = "Very knowledgeable user; strong forum participation!";

Membership.UpdateUser(user);
```

As discussed in Chapter 2, validating user credentials for an action on a controller requires only a single line of code, called an attribute, placed on the controller or action method that you want to secure:

```
[Authorize(Roles = "User")]
```

In the Solution section of this chapter, you use these classes to implement the following features in the site's Administration area:

❑   Find users by partial username or e-mail address.

❑   Display some information about the users returned by the search, listed in a grid, such as the date of the user's last activity and whether or not he or she is active. In another page you will display all the details of a specific user and will allow the administrator to change some details.

The Provider Model Design Pattern

We use the term "data store" to refer to any physical means of persisting (saving) data — this usually means saving data in a database or in Active Directory, but .NET abstracts the actual data storage mechanism from the classes that manipulate the data. The provider class is the one that stores the data on behalf of other classes that manipulate data. This *provider model design pattern* is pervasive in the .NET 2.0 Framework — you can frequently "plug in" a different back-end provider to change the mechanism used to save and retrieve data.

The Membership class uses a secondary class (called a *membership provider*) that actually knows the details of a particular data store and implements all the supporting logic to read and write data to/from it. You can think of the Membership class as a business layer class (in that it only manipulates data), and the provider class as the data access class that provides the details of persistence (even though a pure architect might argue the semantics). Two built-in providers are available for the membership system, and you can choose one by writing some settings in the web.config file. The built-in providers are the ones for Microsoft SQL Server (SqlMembershipProvider) and for Active Directory (ActiveDirectoryMembershipProvider), but you can also write your own or find one from a third party (for use with Oracle, MySQL, DB2, and so on, or perhaps XML files). Figure 5-1 provides a visual representation of the provider model design pattern.

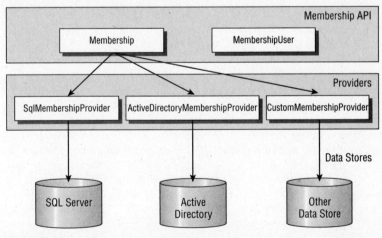

Figure 5-1

We find that the use of the provider model provides tremendous flexibility, because you can change the provider used by the Membership API under the hood without affecting the rest of the code. You just access the Membership "business" class from the pages of the other business classes, and not the providers directly. You may even ignore which provider is used, and where and how the data is stored (this is the idea behind abstraction of the data store). Abstraction is obviously provided to users in the sense that they don't need to know exactly how their data will be stored. We also have abstraction for developers because they, too, don't always need to know how the data is stored!

To create a new provider you can either start from scratch by building a completely new provider that inherits directly from System.Web.Security.MembershipProvider (which in turn inherits from System.Configuration.Provider.ProviderBase) or you can just customize the way some methods of an existing provider work. For example, let's assume you want to modify the SqlMembershipProvider so it validates a user's password to make sure that it's not equal to his username. You simply need to define your own class, which inherits from SqlMembershipProvider, and you can just override the CreateUser method like this:

```
class SqlMembershipProviderExample : SqlMembershipProvider
{
    public override MembershipUser CreateUser(
        string username, string password, string email,
        string passwordQuestion, string passwordAnswer, bool isApproved,
        object providerUserKey, out MembershipCreateStatus status)
    {
        if (username.ToLower() == password.ToLower())
        {
            status = MembershipCreateStatus.InvalidPassword;
            return null;
        }
        else
        {
            return base.CreateUser(username, password, email,
                passwordQuestion, passwordAnswer, isApproved,
                providerUserKey, out status);
        }
    }
}
```

The provider model design pattern is also very useful in the migration of legacy systems that already use their own custom tables and stored procedures. Your legacy database may already contain thousands of records of user information, and you want to avoid losing them, but now you want to modify your site to take advantage of the new Membership class. Instead of creating a custom application to migrate data to a new data store (or using SQL Server DTS to copy the data from your tables to the new tables used by the standard SqlMembershipProvider), you can just create your own custom provider that directly utilizes your existing tables and stored procedures. If you're already using a business class to access your account's data from the ASP. NET pages, creating a compliant provider class may be just a matter of changing the name and signature of some methods. Alternatively, you can follow this approach: keep your current business class intact, but make it private, and then move it inside a new provider class that delegates the implementation of all its methods and properties to that newly private legacy business class. The advantage of doing this instead of just using your current business class "as is" is that you can change to a different data store later by just plugging it into the membership infrastructure — you wouldn't have to change anything in the ASP.NET pages that call the built-in Membership class.

Once you have the provider you want (either one of the default providers, a custom one you developed on your own, or a third-party offering) you have to tell ASP.NET which one you want to use when you call the `Membership` class's methods.

The `web.config` file is used to specify and configure the provider for the membership system. Many of the default configuration settings are hard-coded in the ASP.NET runtime instead of being saved into the `Machine.Config` file. This is done to improve performance by reading and parsing a smaller XML file when the application starts, but you can still modify these settings for each application by assigning your own values in `web.config` to override the defaults. You can read the default settings by looking at the `Machine.config.default` file found in the following folder (the "*xxxxx*" part should be replaced with the build number of your current installation):

```
%windir%\Microsoft.NET\Framework\v2.0.xxxxx\CONFIG
```

The reason why we are pointing to the 2.0 framework folder instead of the 3.5 framework folder is because 3.5 was built on top of 2.0 and uses the same libraries and defaults still residing in the 2.0 folder.

What follows is the definition of the `<membership>` section of the file, where the `SqlMembershipProvider` is specified and configured:

```
<system.web>
    <membership>
        <providers>
            <add name="AspNetSqlMembershipProvider"
                type="System.Web.Security.SqlMembershipProvider, System.Web,
                    Version=2.0.0.0,
                    Culture=neutral,
                    PublicKeyToken=b03f5f7f11d50a3a"
                connectionStringName="LocalSqlServer"
                enablePasswordRetrieval="false"
                enablePasswordReset="true"
                requiresQuestionAndAnswer="true"
                applicationName="/"
                requiresUniqueEmail="false"
                passwordFormat="Hashed"
                maxInvalidPasswordAttempts="5"
                passwordAttemptWindow="10"
                passwordStrengthRegularExpression=""
            />
        </providers>
    </membership>

    <!-- other settings… -->
</system.web>
```

You can register more providers inside the `<providers>` section, and choose which one you want to use by specifying its name in the `defaultProvider` attribute of the `<membership>` element (not shown). Another attribute of `<membership>` is `userIsOnlineTimeWindow`, which specifies how many minutes after the last activity a user is still considered online. That way if a user logs in and brings up one page, but then closes the browser immediately, he will be counted as being online for this number of minutes. You need this kind of parameter because you have no definite way of knowing when a user has left the site or closed down his browser. This is because of the stateless nature of the Web. You can test this by checking the value returned by `Membership.GetNumberOfUsersOnline` as users come to your site and then leave.

For the sample site you will use SQL Server 2008 Express Edition, the free edition of SQL Server 2008, to store the accounts' credentials, and this database will also be used for all the dynamic content of the site. In the Solution section of this chapter, you'll see in practice how to add and configure the provider for this data store. Although this database edition is adequate for use on a developer's computer, it would be wise to use a more feature-laden edition of SQL Server 2008 for production deployment to get better development and analysis tools, and to get the best performance from high-end servers.

More Details About SqlMembershipProvider

In the previous code snippet, you saw the default settings used to register the `SqlMembershipProvider`. The following table lists the attributes you can specify when you register the provider, in the `<provider>` element.

Attribute	Description
applicationName	The name of the web application; used if you want to store data on user accounts for multiple websites in a single database.
connectionStringName	The name of the connection string, registered in the `<connectionStrings>` section of `web.config` that points to the SQL Server database used to store the data. *Important:* This is not the actual connection string! This is only a name that refers to `web.config`, where the actual connection string is stored.
description	A description for the provider.
enablePasswordReset	Indicates whether you want to enable the methods and controls for resetting a password to a new, auto-generated one.
enablePasswordRetrieval	Indicates whether you want to enable the methods and controls that allow a user to retrieve a forgotten password.
maxInvalidPasswordAttempts	The maximum number of invalid login attempts. If the user fails to log in after this number of tries, within the number of minutes specified by the `passwordAttemptWindow` attribute, the user account is "locked out" until the administrator explicitly calls the `UnlockUser` method of a `MembershipUser` instance representing the specific user.
minRequiredNonalphanumericCharacters	The minimum number of non-alphanumeric characters a password must have to be valid.
minRequiredPasswordLength	The minimum number of characters for a valid password.
name	The name used to register the provider. This is used to choose the provider by setting the `defaultProvider` attribute of the `<membership>` element.
passwordAttemptWindow	The number of minutes used to time invalid login attempts. See the description for `maxInvalidPasswordAttempts`.

Attribute	Description
passwordFormat	Specifies how the password is stored in the data store. Possible values are Clear, Encrypted, and Hashed.
passwordStrengthRegular Expression	The regular expression that a password must match to be considered valid.
requiresQuestionAndAnswer	Indicates whether the user must respond to a personal secret question before retrieving or resetting a password. Questions and answers are chosen by users at registration time.
requiresUniqueEmail	Indicates whether the same e-mail address can be used to create multiple user accounts.

By default, minRequiredPasswordLength *is set to 7 and* minRequiredNonalphanumericCharacters *is set to 1, meaning that you must register with a password that is at least seven characters long and contains at least one non-alphanumeric character. Whether you leave these at their default settings or change them to suit your needs, remember to list these values on your registration page to let users know your password requirements.*

These attributes let you fine-tune the membership system. For example, the ability to specify a regular expression that the password must match gives you great flexibility to meet stringent requirements. But one of the most important properties is certainly passwordFormat, used to specify whether you want passwords to be encrypted, or whether you just want a hash of them saved. Passwords are hashed or encrypted using the key information supplied in the <machineKey> element of the configuration file (you should remember to synchronize this machine key between servers if you will deploy to a server farm). The default algorithm used to calculate the password's hash is SHA1, but you can change it through the validation attribute of the <machineKey> element. Storing passwords in clear text offers the best performance when saving and retrieving the passwords, but it's the least secure solution. Encrypting a password adds some processing overhead, but it can greatly improve security. Hashing passwords provides the best security because the hashing algorithm is one way, which means the passwords cannot be retrieved in any way, even by an administrator. If a user forgets her password, it can only be reset to a new auto-generated one (typically sent by e-mail to the user). The best option always depends on the needs of each particular website: if you were saving passwords for an e-commerce site on which you might also save user credit card information, you would surely hash the password and use an SSL connection in order to have the strongest security. For a content-based website, however, we find that encrypting passwords is a good compromise. It's true that you're also building a small e-commerce store, but you're not going to store very critical information (credit card numbers or other sensitive data) on your site.

> Never store passwords in clear text. The small processing overhead necessary to encrypt and decrypt passwords is definitely worth the increased security, and thus the confidence that the users and investors have in the site.

Exploring the Default SQL Server Data Store

Even though the ASP.NET 2.0 membership system is pre-built and ready to go, this is not a good reason to ignore its design and data structures. You should be familiar with this system to help you diagnose any problems that might arise during development or deployment. Figure 5-2 shows the tables used by the `SqlMembershipProvider` class to store credentials and other user data. Of course, the data store's design of other providers may be completely different (especially if they are not based on relational databases).

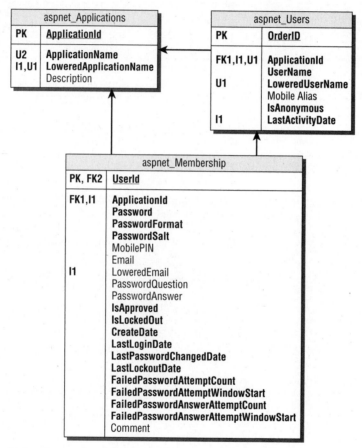

Figure 5-2

The interesting thing you can see from Figure 5-2 is the presence of the `aspnet_Applications` table, which contains a reference to multiple applications (that is, websites). Both the `aspnet_Users` table and the `aspnet_Membership` table contain a reference to a record in `aspnet_Applications` through the `ApplicationId` foreign key. This design enables you to use the same database to store user accounts for multiple sites, which can be very helpful if you have several sites using the same database server (commonly done with corporate websites or with commercial low-cost shared hosting).

In a situation where you have a critical application that requires the maximum security, you'll want to store the membership data in a dedicated database that only the site administrator can access. In your case, however, you're only using a SQL Server 2008 Express Edition database, and this requires you to use your own private database, deployed as a simple file under the App_Data special folder. In addition to these tables, there are also a couple of views related to membership (vw_aspnet_MembershipUsers and vw_aspnet_Users) and a number of stored procedures (aspnet_membership_xxx) for the CRUD (Create, Read, Update, and Delete) operations used for authorization. You can explore all these objects by using the Microsoft SQL Server Management Studio, which comes with the Express Edition, as shown in Figure 5-3.

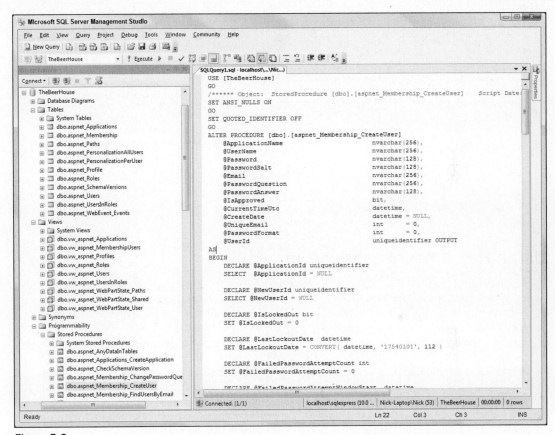

Figure 5-3

If you configure the provider so that it uses the default SQL Server Express database named ASPNETDB located under the App_Data folder, the ASP.NET runtime will automatically create all these database objects when the application is run for the first time! Because we are using this database for the sample site, we don't need to do anything else to set up the data store. However, if you're using the full edition of SQL Server 2008, you will need to set up the tables manually by running the aspnet_regsql.exe located at %windir%\Microsoft.NET\Framework\v2.0.xxxx. This little program lets you choose an existing database on a specified server, and it creates all the required objects to support membership, along with caching, profiles, personalization, and more. Figure 5-4 displays a couple of screens generated by this tool.

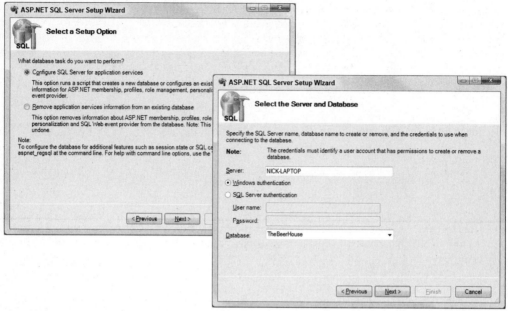

Figure 5-4

Using Roles for Authorization

An authentication/authorization system is not complete without support for roles. Roles are used to group users together for the purpose of assigning a set of permissions, or authorizations. You could decide to control authorizations separately for each user, but that would be an administrative nightmare! Instead, it's helpful to assign a user to a predetermined role and give him the permissions that accompany the role. For example, you can define an Administrators role to control access to the restricted pages used to add, edit, and delete the site's content, and only users who belong to the Administrators role will be able to post new articles and news. It is also possible to assign more than one role to a given user. ASP.NET has built-in support for roles, and it does it the right way with regard to performance, security, and flexibility. As is true in many other pieces of ASP.NET (membership, sessions, profiles, personalization), it is built on the provider model design pattern: a provider for SQL Server is provided, but if you don't like some aspect of how it works, or you want to use a different data store, you can write your own custom provider or acquire one from a third party.

The role management is disabled by default to improve performance for sites that don't need roles — role support requires the execution of database queries, and consequent network traffic between the database server and the web server. You can enable it by means of the <roleManager> element in the web.config file, as shown here:

```
<system.web>
    <roleManager
        enabled="true"
        defaultProvider="AspNetSqlRoleProvider"
    >
        <providers>
```

```
            <add name="AspNetSqlRoleProvider"
                type="System.Web.Security.SqlRoleProvider, System.Web,
                    Version=2.0.0.0,
                    Culture=neutral,
                    PublicKeyToken=b03f5f7f11d50a3a"
                connectionStringName="TheBeerHouseConnectionString"
                applicationName="TheBeerHouse"
            />
        </providers>
    </roleManager>

    <!-- other settings… -->
</system.web>
```

This snippet allows you to enable roles and configure some options.

System.Web.Security.Roles is the class that allows you to access and manage role information programmatically. It exposes several static methods, the most important of which are listed in the following table.

Method	Description
AddUserToRole, AddUserToRoles, AddUsersToRole, AddUsersToRoles	Add one or more users to one or more roles.
CreateRole	Creates a new role with the specified name.
DeleteCookie	Deletes the cookie locally storing the role information.
DeleteRole	Deletes an existing role.
FindUsersInRole	Finds all users who belong to the specified role, and who have a username that matches the input string. If the default provider for SQL Server is used, the username can contain any wildcard characters supported by SQL Server in LIKE clauses, such as % for any string of zero or more characters, or _ for a single character.
GetAllRoles	Returns an array with all the roles.
GetRolesForUser	Returns an array with all the roles to which the specified user belongs.
GetUsersInRole	Returns the array of usernames (not MembershipUser instances) of users who belong to the specified role.
IsUserInRole	Indicates whether the specified user is a member of the specified role.
RemoveUserFromRole, RemoveUserFromRoles, RemoveUsersFromRole, RemoveUsersFromRoles	Remove one or more users from one or more roles.
RoleExists	Indicates whether a role with the specified name already exists.

Using these methods is straightforward, and you will see some practical examples in the Solution section of this chapter, where you implement the administration console to add/remove users to and from roles. You can find more information on the MSDN Library related to the `Roles` class:

❑ **Roles Class:**

> http://msdn.microsoft.com/en-us/library/system.web.security.roles.aspx

> The roles system integrates perfectly with the standard `IPrincipal` security interface, which is implemented by the object returned by the page's `User` property. Therefore, you can use the `User` object's `IsInRole` method to check whether the current user belongs to the specified role.

The SQL Server provider retrieves and stores the data from/to `aspnet_Roles` and `aspnet_UsersInRoles` tables. The latter links a user of the `aspnet_Users` table (or another user table, if you're using a custom membership provider for a custom database) to a role of the `aspnet_Roles` table. Figure 5-5 shows the database diagram again, updated with the addition of these two tables.

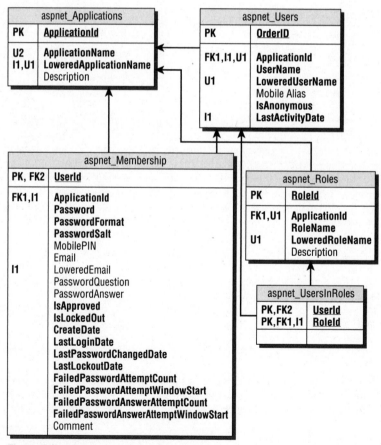

Figure 5-5

Securing the Controller Actions in ASP.NET MVC

As discussed earlier in this book, the `System.Web.Routing` class significantly changes the way you interact with views. In ASP.NET 2.0 you used to be able to directly restrict access to files and folders right in the `web.config` by using code similar to what is shown here:

```
<location path="Admin/EditUsers.aspx">
    <system.web>
        <authorization>
            <allow roles="Admin" />
            <deny users="*" />
        </authorization>
    </system.web>
</location>
```

In ASP.NET Web Forms you basically had two ways to control and protect access to sensitive pages: you could do it either imperatively (programmatically) or declaratively (using a `config` file).

This method of security essentially becomes obsolete in MVC because the MVC framework doesn't use file-based architecture for rendering pages anymore. Securing your website with MVC involves decorating your methods and controllers with the `Authorize` attribute. The following example shows how you would restrict access to only administrators with the same EditUser view in MVC:

```
[Authorize(Roles = "Admin")]
public ActionResult EditUsers()
{
    return View();
}
```

In the example we are locking down the `EditUsers` function to all people except for administrators. The only downside to this method is that if you need to make a change in security you will have to insert the code into the controller and then recompile your website. Most people want to avoid this scenario so, by using different roles to lock down the various controllers, you get the greatest level of flexibility. However, it does require a level of forethought into how you are going to design your authorization system and what type of users are going to be using it. Where flexibility is not a goal, you can always set one or two privileged roles to have most of the administrative rights.

Another security scenario is when you want a user to have access to a view but not necessarily all the functionality within it. This is common on views where editing and deleting are administrative privileges. ASP.NET MVC makes this really easy for you by allowing you to demand security rights both at the view level and at the controller level:

```
<% if (Roles.IsUserInRole("Admin")) { %>
    <button type="submit" id="delete-user-button">Delete</button>
<% } %>
```

This snippet shows an `if` statement being used in the markup to check to see if someone is an administrator before showing the control. In the corresponding controller method you would definitely want to check to see if the user is an administrator before allowing this button to do anything. This is important because it is possible for someone to emulate the click of this button without it actually being shown. It is interesting to note that when the view is rendered there will be no sign of this control in the page's source. You may remember that this was also typical with Classic ASP pages that used logic to determine what should not be displayed to a given user. This is also prevalent when you set the visibility of a server control to `false`.

Using Profiles for User Information

ASP.NET provides a built-in mechanism to manage user profiles in an easy, yet very complete and flexible, way. This feature can save you hours or even days of work! The Profile module takes care of everything — you just need to configure what the profile will contain, that is, define the property name, type, and default value. This configuration is done in the root `web.config` file, within the `<profile>` section. The following snippet shows how to declare two properties, `AboutMe` of type `String`, and `BirthDate` of type `DateTime`:

```
<system.web>
    <profile>
        <properties>
            <add name="AboutMe" type="String" />
            <add name="BirthDate" type="DateTime" />
        </properties>
    </profile>

    <!-- other settings… -->
</system.web>
```

Amazingly this is all you need to do to set up a profile structure! When the application is run, the ASP.NET runtime dynamically adds a `Profile` property to the `Page` class, which means you will not find such a property in the Object Browser at design time. The object returned is of type `ProfileCommon` (inherited from `System.Web.Profile.ProfileBase`); you will not find this class in the Object Browser either, or on the documentation, because this class is generated and compiled on-the-fly, according to the properties defined in the `web.config` file.

Having a class dynamically generated by Visual Studio 2008 with all the custom profile properties doesn't just speed up development, but also helps developers reduce inadvertent coding errors.

Using profiles in MVC can be a little trickier than they were in the traditional ASP.NET 2.0 applications. Because you want to use these objects in the controller, you have to access the profile information via the `HttpContext`. Once you have the profile you can then alter it as you see fit and pass the data on to the view that is about to be rendered. The following code demonstrates how to set up the controller method to accept the new profile information. If no new profile information is provided it simply uses what is on record for this user and sends it back.

```
public ActionResult ChangeProfileInformation (
    string themeName, DateTime? birthDate)
{
    ProfileBase profileBase = HttpContext.Profile as ProfileBase;

    if (!String.IsNullOrEmpty(themeName))
        profileBase.SetPropertyValue("FavoriteTheme", themeName);
```

```
    if (birthDate != null)
        profileBase.SetPropertyValue("BirthDate", birthDate);

    ViewData["FavoriteTheme "] = profileBase.GetPropertyValue("FavoriteTheme ");
    ViewData["BirthDate"] = profileBase.GetPropertyValue("BirthDate");

    Return View();
}
```

You may have noticed the question mark suffixed at the end of `DateTime` for the birth date variable. The question mark makes this variable a nullable generic type of `DateTime`. This is because you are going to hit this controller method every time you make a call to `ChangeProfileInformation`, so there is no distinction between an initial page load and a POST back. Logic has been added to this code to detect if the values are provided and to load them in. In this way both the submit button for this form and the initial page load call use the same controller method. It is definitely a paradigm switch from the more traditional ASP.NET Web Forms POST back model, but you'll find that this method actually reduces code and application complexity.

When you define a profile property, you can also assign a default value to it, by means of the `defaultValue` attribute:

```
<add
    name="AboutMe"
    type="String"
    defaultValue="I have not added my profile yet!"
/>
```

The default value for strings is an empty string, not null, as you may have thought. This makes it easier to read string properties, because you don't have to check whether they are null before using the value somewhere. The other data types have the same default values that a variable of the same type would have (for example, zero for integers).

When you declare profile properties, you can also group them into subsections, as shown here:

```
<system.web>
    <profile>
        <properties>
            <add name="AboutMe" type="String" />
            <add name="BirthDate" type="DateTime" />
            <group name="Address">
                <add name="Street" type="String" />
                <add name="City" type="String" />
            </group>
        </properties>
    </profile>

    <!-- other settings… -->
</system.web>
```

The `Street` property will be accessible as `profileBase.GetPropertyValue("Address.Street")`.

You should be aware that you can't define nested groups under each other, but can have only a single level of groups. If this limitation is not acceptable to you, you can define your own custom class with subcollections and properties, and reference it in the `type` attribute of a new property. In fact, you are not limited to base types for profile properties; you can also reference more complex classes (such as `ArrayList` or `Color`), and your own enumerations, structures, and classes, as long as they are serializable into a binary or XML format. The format will be dictated by the property's `serializeAs` attribute.

Accessing the Profile for Users Other Than the Current User

So far, all the examples have shown how to read and write the profile for the current user. However, you can also access other users' profiles — very useful if you want to implement an administration page to read and modify the profiles of your registered members. The `ProfileBase` class exposes a `Create` method that returns the profile for any specified user, and once you obtain this profile instance you can read and edit the profile properties just as you can do for the current user's profile.

The only difference is that after changing some values of the retrieved profile, you must explicitly call its `Save` method, which is not required when you modify the profile for the current user (in the case of the current user, `Save` is called automatically by the runtime when the page unloads). Here's an example of retrieving a profile for a specified user, and then modifying a property value in that profile:

```
ProfileBase profileBase = Profile.Create("Nick");
profileBase.SetPropertyValue("BirthDate", new DateTime(1980, 03, 14));
profileBase.Save();
```

Adding Support for Anonymous Users

The preceding code works only for registered users who are logged in. Sometimes, however, you want to be able to store profile values for users who are not logged in. You can explicitly enable the anonymous identification support by adding the following line to `web.config`:

```
<anonymousIdentification enabled="true"/>
```

After that, you must indicate what properties are available to anonymous users. By default, a property is only accessible for logged-in users, but you can change this by setting the property's `allowAnonymous` attribute to `true`, as follows:

```
<add
    name="SelectedTheme"
    type="String"
    defaultValue="CenterStage"
    allowAnonymous="true"
/>
```

This is useful to allow anonymous users to select a theme for their current session. This would not be saved after their session terminates because you don't have an actual user identity to allow you to persist the settings. Another important concern regarding profiles for anonymous users is the migration from anonymous to authenticated status. Consider the following situation: a registered user comes to the site and browses it without logging in. He or she then changes some profile properties available to anonymous users, such as the name of the favorite theme. At some point he or she wants to access a restricted page and needs to log in. Now, because the favorite theme was selected while the user was anonymous, it was stored into a profile linked to an anonymous user ID. After the user logs in, he or she then becomes an authenticated user with a different user ID. Therefore, that user's previous profile settings are loaded, and the user will get a site with the theme selected during a previous session, or the default one. What you wanted to do, however, was to migrate the anonymous user's profile to the authenticated user's profile at the time he logged in. You can do this by means of the `Profile_MigrateAnonymous` global event, which you can handle in the `Global.asax` file. Once this event is raised, the `HttpContext.Profile` property will already have returned the authenticated user's profile, so it's too late for you to save the anonymous profile values. You can, however, get a reference to the anonymous profile previously used by the user, and then copy values from it to the new profile. In the Solution section you see how to implement this event to avoid losing the user's preferences.

The Web Administration Tool

As you've seen so far, the preferred method of setting up all of the profiling and security configurations is directly in the `web.config` file. However, because you are using the MVC framework, you will want to put the group access rights directly into the controller classes and methods using the `Authorize` property shown earlier.

As of ASP.NET 2.0 we were given a great set of Web-based administration tools that you can launch by clicking the ASP.NET Configuration item from Visual Studio's Project menu item. This application provides help in the following areas:

❑   **Security:** It enables you to set up the authentication mode (you can choose between the Intranet/Windows and the Internet/forms-based model), create and manage users, create and manage roles, and create access rules for folders (you select a subfolder and declare which roles are granted or denied access to it). Figure 5-6 shows a couple of screenshots of these pages.

❑   **Application:** It enables you to create and manage application settings (those inside the `<appSettings>` section), and configure the SMTP e-mail settings, debugging and tracing sections, and the default error page.

❑   **Provider:** It enables you to select a provider for the Membership and the Roles systems. However, the providers must already be registered in the `web.config` file.

These pages use the new configuration API to read and write sections and elements to and from the `web.config` file. This tool, however, is intended to be used only on a local server, not a remote site. If you want to administer these kinds of settings for a remote site (as you want to do for your site), you will need to modify the web pages for this tool, or design your own pages. Fortunately, the complete source code for the ASP.NET Administration Tool is available under `%windir%\Microsoft.NET\Framework\v2.0.xxxxx\ASP.NETWebAdminFiles`. You can go look at these pages to see how Microsoft implemented the features, and then you can do something similar for your own custom administration console.

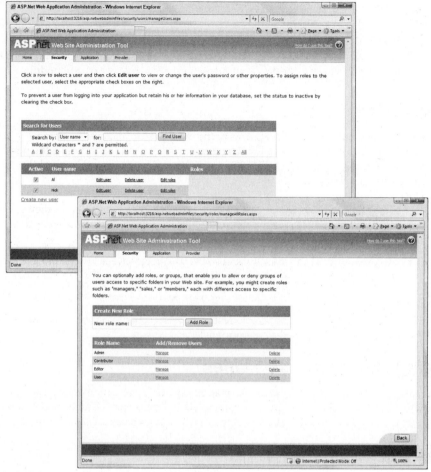

Figure 5-6

MVC Framework's Built in Security Module

Sometime during the development of the MVC Framework Microsoft released a built in security module that becomes available to you when you create a new MVC project with Visual Studio. You can find this module by looking for a controller in your project called `AccountController` and its views located in a folder called `Account`. Because of the complex nature of TheBeerHouse website this very basic implementation will not suit our needs. Specifically, it does not give you the capability to manage users, create roles, grant rights to users, and allow them to reset their passwords. If you are developing a website that only requires a basic authentication system then this might be a good option since it's already built. Like anything else, we would give it a try and see if it meets your needs before embarking on your own security module like we are about to.

Design

In this section we will go over the general design of our security module. We will discuss the design of the database tables, the model, the view, and the controller. At the end of this section you should have a good understanding of what our design goals are, and the exact layout of our module.

Features to Implement

So far we have described the general features of the membership and profile services initially introduced in ASP.NET 2.0. You can now build upon this knowledge and incorporate the powerful set of security classes and tools built into ASP.NET. Here's the summary of specific capabilities we want to integrate into our security module:

❑ Capability for visitors to create their own accounts and manage them as they see fit. This would include filling out an optional profile, changing their passwords, and being able to use their accounts to subscribe for services.

❑ The administrators of this site should be able to also manage accounts and grant or restrict access to users at will.

❑ The profile provider should be flexible enough to be used by other modules.

❑ Finally the system should be able to restrict access to sensitive areas of the website by forcing users to log in and posses the appropriate level of rights.

Desinging the Database Tables

This section will be relatively short since the majority of our tables are automatically designed and created for us by the membership and profile framework built into ASP.NET 2.0. In fact we only need to create a single table to drive our entire security module. That table is our Language table.

The Language Table

Our language table is extremely basic because all it is a simple reference that fills our language drop down box on our profile view.

Column Name	Type	Size	Allow Null	Description
LanguageID	int - PK	4	No	Unique ID for the category.
LanguageName	varchar	100	No	Category creation date/time.

Designing the Model

Similar to our database design, since many of our tables were designed and created for us, so too have our models. We will only be required to create two custom models that we will use in this module.

The UserInformation Class

Our system will have a number of views the user will use associated with login and management of their accounts. In order to pass back data without having to create a large number of variables for each of our action methods we are going create our own custom class.

The ProfileInformation Class

The ProfileInformation will be the more complicated of the two classes. This class will be used to manage profile information, as well as acting as a helper class to populate drop down information on our views. The property fields in this class will correspond in a one to one relationship with the profile fields we defined in our web.config file.

Designing the Views

This module is made up of many views. Some of the views will be used by your end users, and some of the views will be used to help you administer the security module. The following is a list of capabilities we would like our user interface to have.

❑ A login link will be visible in the top section of the right column of each page whenever the user is anonymous. After the user logs in, the login link will be hidden. Instead, you'll show actions that the users can do, such as logout, manage their profile, and change their password.

❑ A Registration view will allow new users to register (create their own account), and you'll populate some profile settings upon registration. The profile will have the following first-level properties: FirstName (String), LastName (String), Gender (String), BirthDate (DateTime), Occupation (String), and Website (String). A profile group named Address will have the following subproperties: Street, PostCode, City, State, and Country, all of type String. A final group named Preferences will have the Culture and Newsletter preferences.

❑ Your ForgotPassword view will allow users to reset their password; by answering a security question properly, it will allow the user access to the change password view and provide the option to change it to something different. You cannot reveal the existing password to the user because all passwords have been hashed and are therefore unrecoverable. This method offers the safest possible experience for your users. It is important to remember that just because you do not have sensitive content on your website does not mean that your users are not using the same password for a more critical account.

❑ Your UserProfile page will be accessible only to registered members, and it will allow them to change their account's password and the profile information they set up at registration time.

❑ You'll create some administration pages to allow the administrator to read and edit all the information about registered users (that is, members). A ManageUser view will help the administrator look up records for members either by their username or e-mail address. Among the data returned will be their username, e-mail address, when they registered or last accessed the site, and whether or not they are active. A second page, EditUser, will show additional details about a single user, and will allow the administrator to enable or disable the account, assign new roles to the user, or remove roles from the user. Finally, a ManageRole view will be used to create and delete roles from your security model.

With all of this in mind we will need the following views in order to provide us with the capabilities that we are looking for:

❑ **ChangePassword.aspx:** This page is used to change the user's password.

    ❑ `user/changepassword/`

❑ **EditUser.aspx:** This page allows the administrator to edit the rights of a user. It also gives them the ability to disable accounts and view when users have last logged in

    ❑ `user/edituser/{Id}`

❑ **ForgotPassword.aspx:** In the event the user forgets their password, this view will allow them to reset it without administrator intervention.

    ❑ `user/forgotpassword`

❑ **Login.aspx:** The login page for the website.

    ❑ `user/login`

❑ **ManageRole.aspx:** This is an administrative view that allows the admin to create and delete roles.

    ❑ `user/managerole`

❑ **ManageUser.aspx:** The manage user view shows all the users presently in the membership system. It also provides the capability to delete users.

    ❑ `user/manageuser`

❑ **Register.aspx:** This will allow any anonymous user to become a registered user by filling out the form on this view.

    ❑ `user/register`

❑ **UserProfile.aspx:** The profile view provides the user the ability to fill in demographical information about themselves that can later be used by our website in a variety of ways.

    ❑ `user/userprofile`

Designing the Controller

Throughout this book all of our controllers will only manage a single module. In this controller design section we will outline all the different methods available within our controller.

Action Method	Security	Parameters
Logout	--	--
Login	--	--
Login_OnPost	--	`string userName, string password, bool persistent, string returnUrl`
ForgotPassword	--	--
ForgotPassword_OnPost	--	`String username, string secretAnswer`

Action Method	Security	Parameters
Register	--	--
Register_OnPost	--	`UserInformation userInformation`
ChangePassword	--	`String resetPassword`
ChangePassword_ OnPost	--	`UserInformation userInformation`
UserProfile	--	--
UserProfile_OnPost	--	`ProfileInforamtion profileInformation`
GetErrorMessage	--	`MembershipCreateStatus membershipCreateStatus`
ManageUser	Admin	`String searchType, string searchInput`
DeleteUser	Admin	`String id`
ManageRole	Admin	--
CreateRole	Admin	`String newRole`
DeleteRole	Admin	`String id`
EditUser	Admin	`String id`
EditUser_OnPost	Admin	`String id, bool approved`

Solution

We'll get right into the implementation because the basic material and your objectives were already covered in the Design section of this chapter. Now you'll put all the pieces together to create the views and the supporting code to make them work. These are the steps used to tackle your solution:

1. Define the applicable settings required for membership, roles, and profiles in `web.config`.

2. Create a user administration box on the master page, and the user login view. To test the login process before creating the registration page, you can easily create a user account from the ASP.NET Web Administration Tool.

3. Create the registration and profiling views.

4. Create the password recovery view.

5. Create the view to change the current password and all the profile information.

6. Create the administrative view to manage the websites' roles.

7. Create the administration pages to display all users, as well as edit and delete them.

Initial Setup

To help keep things organized and manageable, all security-related items should be logically separated from the rest of your application. To accomplish this you should create a new MVC controller class under the ~/Controllers folder in your solution and a new subfolder in your ~/Views folder corresponding to the name of your controller class. In this example you are going to call the controller class UserController because it manages user information.

Before you even begin to dive in and start creating views to actually authenticate and manage users, you need to first add the appropriate web.config entries to configure security on your website. The following code snippet is an example of what you will need to put into your web.config under the system.web section:

```xml
<authentication mode="Forms">
    <forms defaultUrl="/" loginUrl="/user/login"/>
</authentication>
<membership>
    <providers>
        <clear/>
        <add name="AspNetSqlMembershipProvider"
            type="System.Web.Security.SqlMembershipProvider, System.Web,
                Version=2.0.0.0,
                Culture=neutral,
                PublicKeyToken="b03f5f7f11d50a3a"
            connectionStringName="TheBeerHouseConnectionString"
            enablePasswordRetrieval="false"
            enablePasswordReset="true"
            requiresQuestionAndAnswer="false"
            applicationName="TheBeerHouse"
            requiresUniqueEmail="false"
            passwordFormat="Hashed"
            maxInvalidPasswordAttempts="5"
            minRequiredPasswordLength="5"
            minRequiredNonalphanumericCharacters="0"
            passwordAttemptWindow="10"
            passwordStrengthRegularExpression=""
        />
    </providers>
</membership>
<roleManager enabled="true" defaultProvider="AspNetSqlRoleProvider">
    <providers>
        <clear/>
        <add connectionStringName="TheBeerHouseConnectionString"
            applicationName="TheBeerHouse"
            name="AspNetSqlRoleProvider"
            type="System.Web.Security.SqlRoleProvider, System.Web,
                Version=2.0.0.0,
                Culture=neutral,
                PublicKeyToken=b03f5f7f11d50a3a"
        />
    </providers>
</roleManager>
```

As you can see from this code sample, a number of different properties discussed earlier in this chapter can be set in the web.config to establish your security settings. It is also interesting to note that the role manager and the membership provider can be parsed out into two separate databases. This is why you see an individual entry in the web.config for both items as opposed to a singular, unified security entry.

To get profiles enabled and to set their properties and default values you will also need to insert the following piece of code into the web.config file:

```
<anonymousIdentification enabled="true" cookieless="AutoDetect"/>
<profile>
    <properties>
        <add name="Subscription" type="String"/>
        <add name="Language" type="String"/>

        <group name="PersonalInformation">
            <add name="FirstName" type="String" />
            <add name="LastName" type="String" />
            <add name="Gender" type="String" />
            <add name="BirthDate" type="DateTime" />
            <add name="Occupation" type="String" />
            <add name="Website" type="String" />
        </group>

        <group name="ContactInformation">
            <add name="Street" type="String" />
            <add name="City" type="String" />
            <add name="State" type="String" />
            <add name="ZipCode" type="String" />
            <add name="Country" type="String" />
        </group>
    </properties>
</profile>
```

As you can see in the code you have set various user profile attributes and set the location of your profile provider.

Finally, if you were interested in e-mailing reset passwords instead of allowing users to change their one password on the website, you would need to include this code in the web.config file:

```
<system.net>
    <mailSettings>
        <smtp deliveryMethod="Network" from="website@TheBeerHouse.com">
            <network defaultCredentials="true" host="localhost" port="25"/>
        </smtp>
    </mailSettings>
</system.net>
```

Of course the host setting should be replaced with whatever e-mail server you plan on using for your website. You may also be required to provide a username and password to access the mail server.

If you are looking to deploy your application to a web farm (more than one web server configured to distribute the load between the servers), you need to specify the same machine keys for each server. In addition to password encryption, these keys are also used for session state. By synchronizing these keys with all your servers, you ensure that the same encryption will be used on each server. This is essential if there's a chance that a different server might be used to process the next posting of a page. The following code snippet shows you the type of tag required for your `web.config` if you want to implement this feature:

```
<machineKey
    validationKey="287C5D125D6B7E7223E1F719E376CB741803........."
    decryptionKey="5C1D8BD9DF3E1B4E1D0D5EF772FE80AB........"
    validation="SHA1"
/>
```

When creating your own validationKey *and* decryptionKey *you need to use one that is unique to your server. We have truncated the preceding keys to fit the formatting of this book, and also so you will not compromise your own site by basing your security off of this published example key in the book.*

Database Configuration

With SQL Server 2008 Express Edition and Management Studio installed on your system, setting up a database is a snap. Launch Management Studio, right-click the Databases folder, and select New Database to create your database. A dialog that looks like Figure 5-7 will show up on your screen. Name your database and click the OK button to proceed. You will now see a brand new database under the database folder in Management Studio.

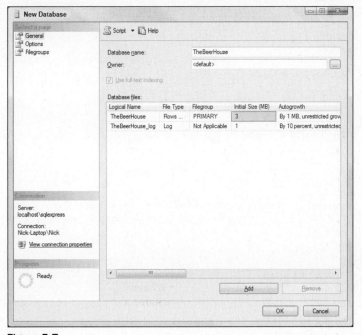

Figure 5-7

Once you have the database established you will also need to create a user for your application to use in order to access the newly created database. To do this, expand the Security folder, right-click the Logins folder, and select New Login. A dialog that looks like Figure 5-8 will appear. Here you should name the user and go to User Mapping; it is important to select the database you just created and give this new user read and write access to the database. You do this by selecting the db_datareader and db_ datawriter access; this gives the user the minimal rights to the database needed to enter and retrieve data from your tables, without providing access to modify the schema.

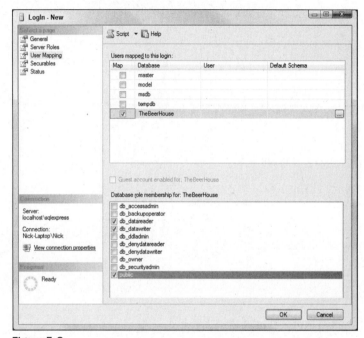

Figure 5-8

Now that you have a new user that has rights to your database, simply add the following code to your web.config file telling your application how to access this database:

```
<connectionStrings>
    <add name=" TheBeerHouseConnectionString"
        connectionString="Data Source=.\sqlexpress;
            Initial Catalog=TheBeerHouse;
            Persist Security Info=True;
            User ID=TheBeerHouseUser;
            Password=BeerIsGood;
            Application Name=TheBeerHouseWebsite"
        providerName="System.Data.SqlClient"
    />
</connectionStrings>
```

Finally, to set up your membership provider you need to run aspnet_regsql.exe, as discussed earlier in this chapter, against your new database. That will automatically install all the profile and security-related tables and stored procedures needed to run your website.

Implementing the Model

Even though we are using the built-in membership and profiling framework of ASP.NET 2.0 we are still going to need some of our own model objects. These objects will help to unclutter our security controller.

The UserInformation Class

This class is implemented in the ~/Models/UserInformation.cs file. This is a very simplistic class that will act a container of information for many controller methods and views in this module.

```
public class UserInformation
{
    public string UserName { get; set; }
    public string Password { get; set; }
    public string ConfirmPassword { get; set; }
    public string ChangePassword { get; set; }
    public string Email { get; set; }
    public string SecretQuestion { get; set; }
    public string SecretAnswer { get; set; }
    public string ReturnUrl { get; set; }
    public string Id { get; set; }
    public string[] Roles { get; set; }
}
```

Ordinarily these model objects would contain methods for obtaining information but we already have many of the methods built right into the membership framework. Therefore we will only be using this class to pass information back and forth in an efficient manner.

The ProfileInformation Class

This class is implemented in the ~/Models/ProfileInformation.cs file. The ProfileInformation class is used in our module to capture profile information. It also has methods within it that will be used to obtain drop down lists for our views. We will break this code into several small chunks to help you better understand what is going on.

```
public class ProfileInformation
{
    public string FirstName { get; set; }
    public string LastName { get; set; }
    public string GenderType { get; set; }
    public DateTime? BirthDate { get; set; }
    public string Occupation { get; set; }
    public string Language { get; set; }
    public string Country { get; set; }
    public string Website { get; set; }
    public string SubscriptionType { get; set; }
    public string Street { get; set; }
    public string City { get; set; }
    public string State { get; set; }
    public string Zipcode { get; set; }
}
```

This first part is like our last model class. We are defining the variables for our class that we will need for our profile controller methods and views. The next portion of code is exclusively for our views.

```
public static SelectList GetSubscriptionList(String subscription)
{
    List<SelectListItem> subscriptionList = new List<SelectListItem>()
    {
        new SelectListItem() { Value = "HTML", Text = "Subscribe to HTML Version"
},
        new SelectListItem() { Value = "Plain", Text = "Subscribe to Plain Text
Version" },
        new SelectListItem() { Value = "None", Text = "No Thanks" }
    };
    return new SelectList(subscriptionList, "Value", "Text", subscription ?? "HTML");
}

public static SelectList GetGenderList(String gender)
{
    List<SelectListItem> genderList = new List<SelectListItem>()
    {
        new SelectListItem() { Value = "M", Text = "Male" },
        new SelectListItem() { Value = "F", Text = "Female" }
    };
    return new SelectList(genderList, "Value", "Text", gender ?? "M");
}

public static SelectList GetCountryList(String country)
{
    return new SelectList(Iso3166CountryCodes.CountryDictonary, "Key", "Value",
country ?? "US");
}

public static SelectList GetOccupationList(String occupation)
{
    TheBeerHouseDataContext dataContext = new TheBeerHouseDataContext();
    var Occupations = from occupationList in dataContext.Occupations
                      orderby occupationList.OccupationName
                      select occupationList;
    return new SelectList(Occupations, "OccupationName", "OccupationName",
occupation ?? "Business Owner");
}

public static SelectList GetLanguageList(String language)
{
    TheBeerHouseDataContext dataContext = new TheBeerHouseDataContext();
    var Languages = from languageList in dataContext.Languages
                    orderby languageList.LanguageName
                    select languageList;
    return new SelectList(Languages, "LanguageName", "LanguageName", language ??
"English");
}
```

You may notice there are several new items you have not seen before specific to the .NET 3.5 Framework and the MVC framework. The biggest one being the SelectList which is an object that the views drop down lists will use to populate themselves with. The SelectList is one of those new objects that gives us the ability to truly separate out our user interface from our model and controller. You will also notice that in this action method we are using LINQ to obtain data from reference tables that were created for the occupation drop-down and the language drop-down. LINQ affords us a very easy way to implement query data against the database. In our code above we are using a combination of LINQ to obtain lists from our database, and we are creating some of our own lists programmatically. These methods will be used later on by our controller to render our profile view.

Implementing the Controller

When we first created our MVC solution in Chapter 2 you may have noticed that a controller folder was already created for you. If you right click on this folder and look under add you will see the very top item is called controller. You will want to select this and when the popup comes up, you will want to indicate the name of the controller as UserController and leave the checkbox in this dialog that automatically created CRUD methods for you unchecked. Once you have done this you will see a brand new class created in that folder called UserController.cs that will inherit from the Controller base class in System.Web.Mvc. Now that our controller is built, we can begin programming the various methods that this module will use in order to provide security for our application and manage our user's profiles.

Since this is the very first time you are encountering a controller section in this book we will briefly go over how this section is laid out. We will go over each and every action that is possible in our controller. This will involve a description of the action method, the variables it can accept, and the code that drives it. Once we have finished creating the controller we will then go over the creation of all the views in this module. In this way we separate our solution section like the MVC Framework separates out the Models, Views, and Controllers in our project. We hope that this will help you better acclimate yourself to thinking like an MVC programmer.

The Register Action

Our Registration action method will be the first method that we make because it is used to create user accounts. All of our other methods will in some way drive off of the user account that is created here. The action for registering the user looks like the following code snippet:

```
public ActionResult Register()
{
    ViewData["PageTitle"] = "Register New User";
    return View();
}
```

This method is very basic and simply returns back our Register view and sets the views page title information.

```
[AcceptVerbs("POST")]
public ActionResult Register(UserInformation userInformation)
{
    if (userInformation.Password != userInformation.ConfirmPassword)
    {
        TempData["ErrorMessage"] = "Registration failed! Your passwords must match,
please re-enter and try again";
    }
    else
    {
        MembershipCreateStatus membershipCreateStatus = new MembershipCreateStatus();
```

```
            try
            {
                Membership.CreateUser(userInformation.UserName, userInformation.
Password, userInformation.Email, userInformation.SecretQuestion, userInformation.
SecretAnswer, true, out membershipCreateStatus);
                if (membershipCreateStatus == MembershipCreateStatus.Success)
                {
                    if (Membership.ValidateUser(userInformation.UserName,
userInformation.Password))
                    {
                        FormsAuthentication.SetAuthCookie(userInformation.UserName,
false);
                        if (!String.IsNullOrEmpty(userInformation.ReturnUrl))
                            return this.Redirect(303, userInformation.ReturnUrl);
                        else
                            return this.Redirect(303, FormsAuthentication.DefaultUrl);
                    }
                    else
                    {
                        TempData["ErrorMessage"] = "Login failed! Please make sure you
are using the correct user name and password.";
                    }
                }
                else
                {
                    TempData["ErrorMessage"] = GetErrorMessage(membershipCreateStatus);
                }
            }
            catch (Exception exception)
            {
                TempData["ErrorMessage"] = exception.Message;
            }
        }

        ViewData["PageTitle"] = "Register New User";
        return View("Register", userInformation);
    }
```

Our next method which is an overloaded version of our first is designed to accept the form submission on that view. As you can see from the attribute decoration at the top of this method, it will only accept an HTML POSTs. The overloaded Register action method uses the built in membership framework classes to create our user account. In the event of an issue it returns the user back to the registration page with the error, otherwise they get sent back to the URL they came from.

The Get Error message Helper Method

You may have noted a supplemental method was used in our Registration action method called GetErrorMessage. This method interprets the MembershipCreateStatus object in the event of an error and provides useful feedback to the prospective registrant. This is how the method would look; you could customize these messages to meet your own needs, but these are the defaults used for the example application:

```
[NonAction]
private string GetErrorMessage(MembershipCreateStatus membershipCreateStatus)
```

```
    {
        switch (membershipCreateStatus)
        {
            case MembershipCreateStatus.DuplicateUserName:
                return "Username already exists. Please enter a different user name.";

            case MembershipCreateStatus.DuplicateEmail:
                return "A username for that e-mail address already exists. Please enter
a different e-mail address.";

            case MembershipCreateStatus.InvalidPassword:
                return "The password provided is invalid. Please enter a valid password
value.";

            case MembershipCreateStatus.InvalidEmail:
                return "The e-mail address provided is invalid. Please check the value
and try again.";

            case MembershipCreateStatus.InvalidAnswer:
                return "The password retrieval answer provided is invalid. Please check
the value and try again.";

            case MembershipCreateStatus.InvalidQuestion:
                return "The password retrieval question provided is invalid. Please
check the value and try again.";

            case MembershipCreateStatus.InvalidUserName:
                return "The user name provided is invalid. Please check the value and
try again.";

            case MembershipCreateStatus.ProviderError:
                return "The authentication provider returned an error. Please verify
your entry and try again. If the problem persists, please contact your system
administrator.";

            case MembershipCreateStatus.UserRejected:
                return "The user creation request has been canceled. Please verify
your entry and try again. If the problem persists, please contact your system
administrator.";

            default:
                return "An unknown error occurred. Please verify your entry and try
again. If the problem persists, please contact your system administrator.";
        }
    }
}
```

At the very top of this method you will notice an attribute flag called NonAction that will indicate this is not an action method. This will protect this method from being exposed by the controller as an action method and still allow it to be a publicly available method.

The ForgotPassword Action Method

We have all been in the situation where we have forgotten our passwords and needed a little extra help from our website to get us back on track. This action method will allow our users to do just that. As discussed earlier in this chapter, there is absolutely no way for you to recover a password that has been hashed. Since we cannot do that, the next best thing is to allow them to create a new password for themselves. Before we do that though we must ensure that the user is really who they say they are. You may recall that the `Register` action method asked a secret question and a secret answer. We are going to present the user with their secret question using this controller action method and see if they provide the right response:

```
public ActionResult ForgotPassword()
{
  ViewData["PageTitle"] = "Forgot Password";
    return View(new UserInformation());
}
```

Similar to our `Register` controller action method, we have a basic method to render our `ForgotPassword` view and set the title.

```
[AcceptVerbs("POST")]
public ActionResult ForgotPassword(string userName, string secretAnswer)
{
    if (!String.IsNullOrEmpty(secretAnswer))
    {
        string resetPassword = Membership.Provider.ResetPassword(userName,
secretAnswer);
        if (Membership.ValidateUser(userName, resetPassword))
            FormsAuthentication.SetAuthCookie(userName, false);
        return RedirectToAction("ChangePassword", new { resetPassword =
resetPassword });
    }

  MembershipUser membershipUser = Membership.GetUser(userName, false);
    UserInformation userinformation = new UserInformation();
  if (membershipUser != null)
  {
        userinformation.SecretQuestion = membershipUser.PasswordQuestion;
        userinformation.UserName = userName;
  }
  else
  {
        TempData["ErrorMessage"] = "The user you have specified is invalid, please
recheck your username and try again";
        userinformation.SecretQuestion = String.Empty;
  }

  ViewData["PageTitle"] = "Forgot Password";
    return View(userinformation);
}
```

The overloaded `ForgotPassword` action method above is being used to accept the form submissions from the `ForgotPassword` view. Since the view has two submissions, we process both actions in this one method. The first is obtaining the secret question for a particular username. In this scenario the secret answer variable would be empty so we would skip over that block of code. If the user is valid the view would be re-rendered with the secret question. On the second form submission we would ensure that the secret answer was correct and send the user to the `ChangePassword` action method with their hashed password.

The ChangePassword Action Method

The `ChangePassword` action method is the mechanism in our website that allows users to change their passwords. If the user has forgotten their password or simply would like to change it, they will need to use this action method:

```
public ActionResult ChangePassword(string resetPassword)
{
    UserInformation userInformation = new UserInformation();
    if (!string.IsNullOrEmpty(resetPassword))
    {
        userInformation.Password = resetPassword;
    }
    ViewData["PageTitle"] = "Change Password";
    return View(userInformation);
}
```

In the above code we are initially rendering our `ChangePassword` view. Since the user can invoke this action method from either the `ChangePassword` link on the website or the `ForgotPassword` action method, we will accept a reset password string. If this is populated then we pass in the base password into the view because the user will not know their password, and will therefore not be required to fill out that field in our form.

```
[AcceptVerbs("POST")]
public ActionResult ChangePassword(UserInformation userInformation)
{
    if (userInformation.ChangePassword != userInformation.ConfirmPassword)
    {
        TempData["ErrorMessage"] = "Your new passwords do not match, please retype
them and try again";
        return View(userInformation);
    }

    try
    {
        MembershipUser membershipUser = Membership.GetUser(HttpContext.User.
Identity.Name, false);
        membershipUser.ChangePassword(userInformation.Password, userInformation.
ChangePassword);
        TempData["SuccessMessage"] = "Your password has been sucessfully changed";
        ViewData["PageTitle"] = "Change Password";
        return View(userInformation);
    }
    catch (Exception exception)
    {
        TempData["ErrorMessage"] = "Password change has failed because: " +
exception.Message;
        return View(userInformation);
    }}
```

In the overloaded POST only version of our action method we accept an instance of our `UserInformation` object. You can see that in our method we are checking to see if the passwords match, and if they do we attempt to change them using the built in security provider classes. The try catch loop reports back any errors, otherwise the action is considered a success. Similar to the other controller methods, you are taking advantage of the ASP.NET security provider to do all the heavy processing work and are only doing basic validation on your end.

The UserProfile Action Method

In your initial setup you created the structure for your profiles in the web.config file. Now you can take advantage of the provider model initially introduced in ASP.NET 2.0 to handle your profile information. Using the provider model saves you the hassle of having to create tables that would have otherwise been dedicated to housing your visitor profile information. The controller method that manages the user profile information looks like this:

```
[Authorize]
public ActionResult UserProfile()
{
    string id = HttpContext.User.Identity.Name.ToString();

    ProfileBase profileBase;
    if (!String.IsNullOrEmpty(id))
    {
        profileBase = ProfileBase.Create(id);
    }
    else
    {
        profileBase = HttpContext.Profile as ProfileBase;
    }

    ViewData["subscriptionType"] = ProfileInformation.
GetSubscriptionList(profileBase.GetPropertyValue("Subscription").ToString());
    ViewData["genderType"] = ProfileInformation.GetGenderList(profileBase.GetProper
tyValue("PersonalInformation.Gender").ToString());
    ViewData["country"] = ProfileInformation.GetLanguageList(profileBase.GetPropert
yValue("ContactInformation.Country").ToString());
    ViewData["occupation"] = ProfileInformation.GetOccupationList(profileBase.GetPr
opertyValue("PersonalInformation.Occupation").ToString());
    ViewData["language"] = ProfileInformation.GetLanguageList(profileBase.
GetPropertyValue("Language").ToString());

    ProfileInformation profileInformation = new ProfileInformation()
    {
        FirstName = profileBase.GetPropertyValue("PersonalInformation.FirstName").
ToString(),
        LastName = profileBase.GetPropertyValue("PersonalInformation.LastName").
ToString(),
        BirthDate = (DateTime)profileBase.GetPropertyValue("PersonalInformation.
BirthDate"),
        Website = profileBase.GetPropertyValue("PersonalInformation.Website").
ToString(),
        Street = profileBase.GetPropertyValue("ContactInformation.Street").
ToString(),
        City = profileBase.GetPropertyValue("ContactInformation.City").ToString(),
        State = profileBase.GetPropertyValue("ContactInformation.State").
ToString(),
```

```
        Zipcode = profileBase.GetPropertyValue("ContactInformation.ZipCode").
ToString()
    };

    return View(profileInformation);
}
```

This first method is used to initially render our `UserProfile` view. I'm sure you can easily see that there is a lot more code in this action method than in our previous render action methods. This is because we have numerous dropdown lists that need to be populated. In order to do this we take advantage of our `ProfileInformation` object that we created in our model section. It provides us with all the `SelectLists` that this view will require. We are also checking to see if the user already has a profile and if not we create one. Lastly we pass in our `ProfileInformation` object to our view so it can repopulate the fields on the form if the user already had a profile in place.

```
[Authorize]
[AcceptVerbs("POST")]
public ActionResult UserProfile(ProfileInformation profileInformation)
{
    ProfileBase profileBase = HttpContext.Profile as ProfileBase;
    profileBase.SetPropertyValue("Subscription", profileInformation.
SubscriptionType);
    profileBase.SetPropertyValue("Language", profileInformation.Language);

    profileBase.SetPropertyValue("PersonalInformation.FirstName",
profileInformation.FirstName);
    profileBase.SetPropertyValue("PersonalInformation.LastName",
profileInformation.LastName);
    profileBase.SetPropertyValue("PersonalInformation.Gender", profileInformation.
GenderType);
    if (profileInformation.BirthDate != null)
  {
        profileBase.SetPropertyValue("PersonalInformation.BirthDate",
profileInformation.BirthDate);
  }
    profileBase.SetPropertyValue("PersonalInformation.Occupation",
profileInformation.Occupation);
    profileBase.SetPropertyValue("PersonalInformation.Website", profileInformation.
Website);

    profileBase.SetPropertyValue("ContactInformation.Street", profileInformation.
Street);
    profileBase.SetPropertyValue("ContactInformation.City", profileInformation.City);
    profileBase.SetPropertyValue("ContactInformation.State", profileInformation.
State);
    profileBase.SetPropertyValue("ContactInformation.ZipCode", profileInformation.
Zipcode);
    profileBase.SetPropertyValue("ContactInformation.Country", profileInformation.
Country);
 profileBase.Save();

    ViewData["subscriptionType"] = ProfileInformation.
GetSubscriptionList(profileBase.GetPropertyValue("Subscription").ToString());
    ViewData["genderType"] = ProfileInformation.GetGenderList(profileBase.GetProper
tyValue("PersonalInformation.Gender").ToString());
```

```
    ViewData["country"] = ProfileInformation.GetLanguageList(profileBase.GetPropert
yValue("ContactInformation.Country").ToString());
    ViewData["occupation"] = ProfileInformation.GetOccupationList(profileBase.GetPr
opertyValue("PersonalInformation.Occupation").ToString());
    ViewData["language"] = ProfileInformation.GetLanguageList(profileBase.
GetPropertyValue("Language").ToString());

    TempData["SuccessMessage"] = "Your profile information has been saved";
ViewData["PageTitle"] = "My Profile";
    return View(profileInformation);
}
```

Our second method is only used for our form POST action. Here we are looking up the user's profile with the information we just obtained from the form submission. Because all fields are optional, no real validation is done in this method. The only thing you want to be sure of is that the user is actually registered before allowing them to make modifications to their profile information. After saving the information we send the user a message that their profile has been updated, re-obtain all the SelectLists that the view will require, and pass back the ProfileInformation object that was originally passed into this action method .

The ManageUsers Action Method

Now that the end-user part of our controller is done, you can now begin work on the administrative action methods that will help you manage your website's membership and security. A nice administrative action method to start off with is the ManageUser action method. This method returns back to us a list of users that meet our search criteria. The code for the controller that drives this view is as follows:

```
[Authorize(Roles = "Admin")]
public ActionResult ManageUser(string searchType, string searchInput)
{
 List<SelectListItem> searchOptionList = new List<SelectListItem>()
    {
        new SelectListItem() { Value = "UserName", Text = "UserName" },
        new SelectListItem() { Value = "Email", Text = "Email" }
    };

 ViewData["searchOptionList"] = new SelectList(searchOptionList, "Value", "Text",
searchType ?? "UserName");
 ViewData["searchInput"] = searchInput ?? string.Empty;
 ViewData["UsersOnlineNow"] = Membership.GetNumberOfUsersOnline().ToString();
 ViewData["RegisteredUsers"] = Membership.GetAllUsers().Count.ToString();

 MembershipUserCollection viewData;

 if (String.IsNullOrEmpty(searchInput))
        viewData = Membership.GetAllUsers();
 else if (searchType == "Email")
        viewData = Membership.FindUsersByEmail(searchInput);
 else
        viewData = Membership.FindUsersByName(searchInput);

 ViewData["PageTitle"] = "Account Management";
 return View(viewData);
}
```

The `Authorize` tag at the top of the controller method ensures that a user must be an administrator to use this block of code. You can also see that a `viewData` object is being passed instead of the name of the view. This is because you want to pass a strongly typed collection right into the view without casting it in the markup. In this action you added the `MembershipUserCollection` as a strongly typed model to your view. Ordinarily this view would just inherit from `ViewPage` only, but by adding the collection object to the end of it, the model becomes available for use within the view's markup. To populate the model with actual data you pass the `viewData` object, which uses the model specified in the view. Because you are setting the model right in your markup, you have absolutely no need for a code-behind file for your views.

Within the controller you are making heavy use of the `Membership` and `MembershipUser` classes. Combined, these two classes offer a great deal of functionality with minimal effort. `Membership` gives you a complete list of all users; it also provides the capability to search against that list and return data populated into the `MembershipUser` class. The `MembershipUser` class contains a number of user properties that you are then using within your view to show pertinent information pertaining to that user.

The DeleteUser Action Method

Occasionally you may want to simply delete users out of your system. This could be because they haven't logged on in a very long time and are clogging up your database, or because you no longer wish to allow that user any rights to your website. To do this we are using the `DeleteUser` action method shown below.

```
[Authorize(Roles = "Admin")]
[Service, HttpPostOnly]
public ActionResult DeleteUser(string id)
{
    Membership.DeleteUser(id);
    return View(new { id = id });
}
```

Since this method will be invoked using javascript we only require an id field returned back to us so that our `javascript` knows which field to erase from our view. We will discuss how this is done further in our view section.

The EditUser Action Method

The next logical action method would be the `EditUser` action method. This controller method will allow us to view information pertaining to our selected user, modify rights, and accept an approval variable that can be passed in through our view's form. The code for your controller method for `EditUser` is as follows:

```
[Authorize(Roles = "Admin")]
public ActionResult EditUser(string id)
{
    ViewData["roles"] = (String[])Roles.GetAllRoles();
    MembershipUser membershipUser = Membership.GetUser(id);

    ViewData["PageTitle"] = "Edit " + id;
    return View(membershipUser);
}
```

This first method initially renders our `EditUser` view. On this view you will be able to add or remove user roles, so we are also passing in all the available roles in our system. Note too we are passing an instance of the `MembershipUser` object to the view. The overloaded method below is the one that will process the views form submission.

```
[Authorize(Roles = "Admin")]
[AcceptVerbs("POST")]
public ActionResult EditUser(string id, bool approved)
{
    //Is a list of all the user roles
    ArrayList removeRoleList = new ArrayList(Roles.GetAllRoles());

    //We are requesting the form variables directly from the form
    foreach (string key in Request.Form.Keys)
    {
        if (key.StartsWith("role."))
        {
            String userRole = key.Substring(5, key.Length - 5);
            removeRoleList.Remove(userRole);
            if (!Roles.IsUserInRole(id, userRole))
            {
                Roles.AddUserToRole(id, userRole);
            }
        }
    }

    foreach (string removeRole in removeRoleList)
        Roles.RemoveUserFromRole(id, removeRole);

    MembershipUser membershipUser = Membership.GetUser(id);
    membershipUser.IsApproved = approved;
    Membership.UpdateUser(membershipUser);

    TempData["SuccessMessage"] = "User Information has been updated";
    ViewData["roles"] = (String[])Roles.GetAllRoles();
    ViewData["PageTitle"] = "Edit " + id;
    return View(membershipUser);
}
```

Again you can see we are taking advantage of the `Authorize` attribute to lock the method down to only administrators. Unique from other pages you have looked at, you are actually calling your view's form keys directly:

```
foreach (string key in Request.Form.Keys)
```

What this does is give you a listing of all control values that were populated with values other than null. This is especially useful because on the view we will create in the next section, we are dynamically creating checkboxes based on our website's security roles. Each of our checkboxes' id properties of prefixed with `"role."` Because we are dynamically creating ids we are prevented from passing values back in the traditional MVC manner as variables in our method.

Since MVC Framework is only returning back true checkboxes and other controls with values other than null, we can iterate through the keys to find id properties that start with `"role."`. Then in our method you can see we are adding roles that we find, and removing roles that we do not. With these methods user administration is a snap. Adding and removing users from roles is made especially easy with the `Membership` and `Roles` classes.

The ManageRole Action Method

Our last set of controller action method for this module deals with the management of roles. The `ManageRole` controller method shown below renders our `ManageRole` view and lists all the available roles in our system.

```
[Authorize(Roles = "Admin")]
public ActionResult ManageRole()
{
 ViewData["TotalRoles"] = Roles.GetAllRoles().Count();
 ViewData["PageTitle"] = "Role Management";
 return View();
}
```

The CreateRole Action Method

This method is a little different than our other ones because we have named our form submission method for our `ManageRole` view differently than the action method that initially rendered it. This is a perfectly legitimate practice, and becomes very useful when you have multiple forms on a single view.

```
[Authorize(Roles = "Admin")]
[AcceptVerbs("POST")]
public ActionResult CreateRole(string newRole)
{
    Roles.CreateRole(newRole);
    return RedirectToAction("ManageRole");
}
```

In this controller method we are simply creating new roles using the `Roles` class to do all the heavy lifting for us. Something new that you may not have seen before is the `RedirectToAction` method. What this does for you as the name implies is allow you to use another action method to return back a result. In this case we want to re-render the `ManageRole` view so we will call on the `ManageRole` action method.

The DeleteRole Action Method

Now that we can view and create new roles, we will want to also be able to delete roles. This is easily done with our `DeleteRole` action method shown below:

```
[Authorize(Roles = "Admin")]
[Service, HttpPostOnly]
public ActionResult DeleteRole(string id)
{
    Roles.DeleteRole(id);
    return View(new { id = id });
}
```

Similar to the `DeleteUser` action method, it too will be invoked using javascript. Aside from that all of our heavy lifting is again done using the `Roles` class. This concludes the outline of your first controller; we hope that you were pleasantly surprised at how easy creating a controller can be.

Implementing the View

Once all of our action methods have been created in our controller we can now start to create our views. Similar to our controller section, we will briefly go over how this section is laid out. We will outline each view and user control for you, provide you an image of what that view or control will look like, and the HTML that will make it up. In this section our views will handle user logins, account creations, account management, and lastly user profiles.

The Register.aspx View

The view that makes the most sense to create first is our registration view. The `Register.aspx` view is located in `~/Views/User`. It is used to create new user accounts so that our visitors can view the member only portions of our website. We will also need this view built first to visit any of the proceeding views. An example of how this form will look is shown in Figure 5-9.

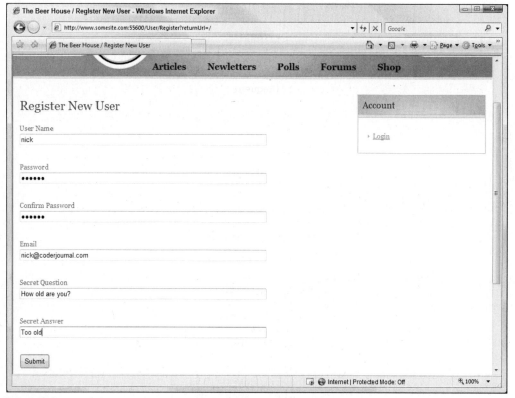

Figure 5-9

As you can see from Figure 5-9 this is a fairly standard user registration form. The only thing that is missing that you may want to add yourself is CAPTCHA (Completely Automated Public Turing Test to tell Computer and Human Apart) to this form to ensure your visitors are human and not automated web bots.

The header for this view will set the default `ViewPage` because you don't need to pass in a typed model for this view:

```
Inherits="System.Web.Mvc.ViewPage"
```

MainContent

The `MainContent` section in our form will contain all the fields you may expect when creating a new user account. This would include the username, password, email, secret question, and secret answer fields. Note that this view will `UserInformation` object as its model. You can set this when you initially create your view and the property box comes up. The markup below shows you how this would look in HTML:

```
<asp:Content ID="MainContent" ContentPlaceHolderID="MainContent" runat="server">

<% Html.RenderPartial("~/Views/Shared/Message.ascx"); %>

<form method="post" action="<%= Url.Action("Register", "User") %>" class="user-
login">

<input type="hidden" name="returnUrl" value="
<%= Html.If(!String.IsNullOrEmpty(Request.QueryString["returnUrl"]), () => Request.
QueryString["returnUrl"])
.ElseIf(Request.UrlReferrer != null, () => Request.UrlReferrer.ToString())
.Else(() => String.Empty) %>" />

    <p class="field input"><label for="UserName">User Name</label><br />
        <%= Html.TextBox("UserName")%>
      <span class="input-message"></span></p>

    <p class="field input"><label for="Password">Password</label><br />
      <%= Html.Password("Password")%>
      <span class="input-message"></span></p>

    <p class="field input"><label for="ConfirmPassword">Confirm Password</label><br />
      <%= Html.Password("ConfirmPassword")%>
      <span class="input-message"></span></p>

    <p class="field input"><label for="Email">Email</label><br />
        <%= Html.TextBox("Email")%>
      <span class="input-message"></span></p>

    <p class="field input"><label for="SecretQuestion">Secret Question</label><br />
        <%= Html.TextBox("SecretQuestion")%>
      <span class="input-message"></span></p>

    <p class="field input"><label for="SecretAnswer">Secret Answer</label><br />
        <%= Html.TextBox("SecretAnswer")%>
```

```
            <span class="input-message"></span></p>

        <hr />
        <p><button type="submit" id="user-registration-button">Submit</button></p>
    </form>

</asp:Content>
```

You may notice right off the bat that we are putting inline C# code directly into our markup. Since we are not using any code behind file for this view or any other view in this module, it becomes necessary. Fortunately the MVC Framework provides us with helper classes to create various form controls. If you look at our view markup you will notice we use the Html and Url extension classes to help form our form tag and create our textboxes. With our form method we specify that we want to post the contents of our form to Register action method in our UserController. When rendered in the browser this method call will be replaced by \User\Register. Similarly the textboxes we create will be replaced with standard HTML textboxes. The MVC Framework handles all the heavy lifting involved in matching up our controls to like named variables in our action method. So when this form posts the UserName textbox will match up to the corresponding UserName variable in the Register action method.

Swinging back to our view, you may notice that there is some embedded C# code to check to see if there is a return URL. This is handy because we want our users to be redirected back to the view that required authentication. In order to accomplish this we populate a hidden field called returnUrl with the URL of where the visitor just came from. In this way when the form is submitted the action method will know via the returnUrl variable in the action method where to redirect the user.

The last item that we would like to bring to your attention is the user control that we are rendering right before our form tag begins. We will use this user control throughout our application to display a message in case our controller returns one. As discussed at the end of Chapter 3 you need a common way like this user control to alert the user of messages on each page that requires one.

ScriptContent

This part of the view page contains the necessary references to your JavaScript that makes the user's browser validate your input fields and/or display informational messages about the textbox that the user is focused on.

```
<asp:Content ID="ScriptContent" ContentPlaceHolderID="ScriptContent"
runat="server">
<script type="text/javascript" src="/content/scripts/register.js"></script>
<% if (IsPostBack) { %>
<script type="text/javascript">
 ValidateRegistration();
</script>
<% } %>
</asp:Content>
```

The first thing you do is import the JavaScript file, located at /content/scripts/ register.js, which you will create a little later on. This file will specifically validate the inputs for this form so that you can ensure that your users will complete every field before our javascript file will allow the user to submit to the action method.

register.js

The `register.js` file is located under `~/Content/scripts/` and is used to perform custom client-side actions on the `Register.aspx` view. The javascript looks like this:

```
function ValidateUserName() {
    return VerifyRequiredField("#UserName", "required");
}

function ValidatePassword() {
    return VerifyRequiredField("#Password", "required");
}

function ValidateConfirmPassword() {
    return VerifyRequiredField("#ConfirmPassword", "required");
}

function ValidateEmail() {
    return VerifyRequiredField("#Email", "required");
}

function ValidateSecretQuestion() {
    return VerifyRequiredField("#SecretQuestion", "required");
}

function ValidateSecretAnswer() {
    return VerifyRequiredField("#SecretAnswer", "required");
}

function ValidateRegistration() {
    return ValidateUserName()
        && ValidatePassword()
        && ValidateConfirmPassword()
        && ValidateEmail()
        && ValidateSecretQuestion()
        && ValidateSecretAnswer();
}

$("form.user-registration").validate(ValidateRegistration);
```

The top six functions check each of the textboxes on the form to ensure that they all have values. The `ValidateRegistration` function runs the other six functions and if they all come back true then the original action proceeds. In our case it would be the form submission to the controller method. If one of the functions had failed then the submission would be short circuited and a message would appear near the empty field that was required.

Once your content and script sections are complete your view is now complete. Were you surprised at how easy that was? You probably didn't even have to jump back to the visual editor to see what the content would look like because the HTML is very clean and it is easy to picture what this is going to look like as you are writing it.

The Account Box

After the registration process, the user is directly logged in to the website with his new account and settings. When the user returns, he will need the capability to log back in to the website. You can do this via your login view and account box that you will set up.

You may have seen account boxes on other websites; they are a floating `div` that you place to give a visual indication as to the user's login status. If he has not logged in it will give him the option to do so, and if he has it will show information pertinent to his account. To accomplish this you need to add the following lines of code into your sidebar `div` in your master page:

```
<div id="account" class="boxed">
    <h2 class="title">Account</h2>
    <div class="content">
    <ul>
<% if (Context.User != null
    && Context.User.Identity != null
    && Context.User.Identity.IsAuthenticated) { %>
        <li class="first">Welcome <%= Context.User.Identity.Name %></li>
        <li><%= Html.ActionLink("Logout", "Logout", "User") %></li>
<% } else { %>
        <li class="first"><%= Html.ActionLink("Login", "Login", "User") %></li>
<% } %>
    </ul>
    </div>
</div>
```

Similar to the other examples, you use specific code in your markup to decide if the user is logged in and if so, to show the appropriate links and information.

The Login.aspx View

The `Login.aspx` view is located in `~/Views/User`. It is a standard login page that users will use in order to authenticate onto our website. An example of how this form will look is shown in Figure 5-10.

Figure 5-10

MainContent

The `MainContent` section for this section includes an input for a username, and password. It also gives the user the option to create a new user account or to reset their password in the event that they have forgotten it:

```
<% Html.RenderPartial("~/Views/Shared/Message.ascx"); %>

<form method="post" action="<%= Url.Action("Login", "User") %>" class="user-login">

    <input type="hidden" name="returnUrl" value="<%=
    Html.If(!String.IsNullOrEmpty(Request.QueryString["returnUrl"]), () =>
    Request.QueryString["returnUrl"])
        .ElseIf(Request.UrlReferrer != null, () => Request.UrlReferrer.ToString())
        .Else(() => String.Empty) %>" />

    <p class="field input"><label for="userName">User Name</label><br />
        <%= Html.TextBox("UserName")%>
    <span class="input-message"></span></p>

    <p class="field input"><label for="password">Password</label><br />
```

```
            <%= Html.Password("Password")%>
        <span class="input-message"></span></p>

    <p class="field">
        <%= Html.CheckBox("persistent")%> Remember Me?</p>

    <p>
        <%= Html.ActionLink("Forgot Password", "ForgotPassword") %>
        <%= Html.ActionLink("Join Now", "Register") %>
    </p>

    <hr />
    <p><button type="submit" id="user-login-button">Submit</button></p>

</form>
```

You will note that again we are using inline C# code to determine what the return URL will be for the visitor. You may recall from our `Login` action method that we will use this to redirect the user back to the view they originally came from.

Once you have built this view the log in functionality for this website should now be complete. You will notice that, once your user has logged in, the content of his account box changes. This is because we put some inline C# code into our account box markup. If you'd like to control other content on your master page such as navigation options this is also a very simple task with the MVC framework. In the TheBeerHouse website you have administrative menus that you want to keep hidden to all but administrators. To do this you use the following code:

```
<% if (Roles.IsUserInRole("Admin")) { %>
<div id="admin" class="boxed">
    <h2 class="title">Admin</h2>
    <div class="content">
    <ul class="list">
        <li><a href="<%= Url.Action("ManageUsers", "User") %>">Manage Users</a></li>
    </ul>
    </div>
</div>
<% } %>
```

From this example you can see that you are able to directly call into the markup demanding administrative rights to see the encapsulated list item. You may also have notice the `<% } %>` within the markup. This represents the closing brace in the `if` statement located at the top of this code block. In this way we are able to conditionally show markup, creating our dynamic content on the view. When rendered by the browser this will all appear as seamless HTML to the user.

The ForgotPassword.aspx View

The `ForgotPassword.aspx` view is located in `~/Views/User`. This view allows our users to reset their account password in the event that they forget. This view uses an instance of the `UserInformation` object as its model. An example of how this form will look is shown in Figure 5-11.

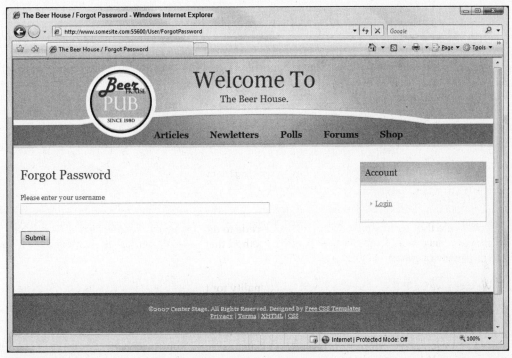

Figure 5-11

MainContent

The MainContent section for this section is a very simplistic form which simply asks the user for their username, secret answer, and what they would like their new password to be. To do this the following markup is required:

```
<% Html.RenderPartial("~/Views/Shared/Message.ascx"); %>

<form method="post" action="<%= Url.Action("ForgotPassword", "User") %>">

 <% if (!String.IsNullOrEmpty(Model.SecretQuestion)){ %>
        <%= Html.Hidden("UserName") %>

    <p class="field input"><label for="SecretQuestion">
        <%= Model.SecretQuestion %></label><br />
            <%= Html.TextBox("SecretAnswer")%>
        <span class="input-message"></span></p>
<% } else { %>
<p class="field input"><label for="userName">Please enter your username</label>
     <br />
            <%= Html.TextBox("UserName")%>
        <span class="input-message"></span></p>
<% } %>
```

```
<hr />
<p><button type="submit" id="user-login-button">Submit</button></p>
</form>
```

As you can see in our view some additional logic has been added to check to see if the username has been provided. Once the username is confirmed, the secret question is presented. If the user answers this properly they are given the chance to enter in a new password in our next view.

The ChangePassword.aspx View

The `ForgotPassword` view flows perfectly to the `ChangePassword` view. Not only do users need to occasionally change their password on their own, but you can also use this view to change it when users have forgotten their original password. The only difference between the two scenarios is that in the change password scenario you would ask them their old password, and in the forgot password scenario you'd automatically reset the password for them in the background. The `ChangePassword.aspx` view is located in `~/Views/User`. This view uses an instance of the `UserInformation` object as its model.

MainContent

Creating the view is fairly simple and the complete code for this is as follows:

```
<% Html.RenderPartial("~/Views/Shared/Message.ascx"); %>

<form method="post" action="<%= Url.Action("ChangePassword", "User") %>">

    <% if (Model.Password == null){ %>
     <p class="field input"><label for="Password">Old Password</label><br />
             <%= Html.Password("Password")%>
        <span class="input-message"></span></p>
  <% } else { %>
     <%= Html.Hidden("Password")%>
  <% } %>
        <p class="field input"><label for="ChangePassword">New Password</label><br
/>
             <%= Html.Password("ChangePassword")%>
        <span class="input-message"></span></p>

        <p class="field input"><label for="ConfirmPassword">Confirm New Password</
label><br />
             <%= Html.Password("ConfirmPassword")%>
        <span class="input-message"></span></p>

  <hr />
  <p><button type="submit" id="user-login-button">Submit</button></p>
</form>
```

This view consists mainly of textboxes. You may note that you are hiding the old password textbox if a reset password is present. The only scenarios where this would be present is if it was provided by the forgot password controller method. Figure 5-12 shows what the reset password view looks like in your sample application.

Figure 5-12

The UserProfile.aspx View

The `UserProfile.aspx` view is located in `~/Views/User`. This view is used to allow users to create a custom profile for themselves. Figure 5-13 shows what the profile view looks like in the sample application.

The profile information gathered on this page will be used in later modules to demonstrate how the website can be rendered in different languages based on the user's preferences, control newsletter subscriptions, drive marketing campaigns, and even pre-populate billing information automatically. This view uses an instance of our `ProfileInformation` object as its model.

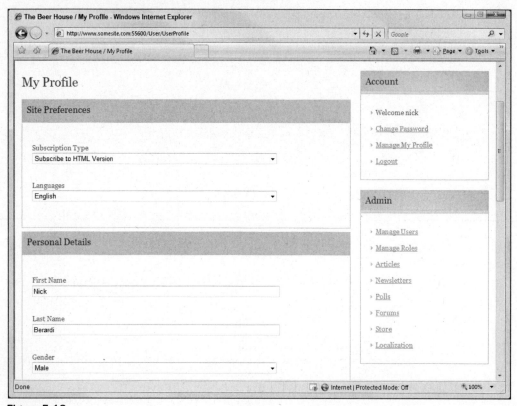

Figure 5-13

MainContent

The MainContent section of this view contains fields for subscription preference, language preference, first name, last name, gender, birth date, occupation, country, and user address information. The code for the view looks like this:

```
<% Html.RenderPartial("~/Views/Shared/Message.ascx"); %>

<form method="post" action="<%= Url.Action("UserProfile", "User") %>">

    <div id="SitePreferences" class="form">
          <h2 class="title">Site Preferences</h2>
            <div class="content">
          <p class="field input"><label
            for="subscriptionType">Subscription Type</label><br />
                <%= Html.DropDownList("subscriptionType")%>
          <span class="input-message"></span></p>

          <p class="field input">
           <label for="language">Languages</label><br />
                <%= Html.DropDownList("language")%>
```

```
            <span class="input-message"></span></p>
        </div>
</div>

<div id="PersonalDetails" class="form">
      <h2 class="title">Personal Details</h2>
      <div class="content">
        <p class="field input"><label for="firstName">First Name</label><br />
           <%= Html.TextBox("firstName")%>
        <span class="input-message"></span></p>

        <p class="field input"><label for="lastName">Last Name</label><br />
           <%= Html.TextBox("lastName")%>
        <span class="input-message"></span></p>

        <p class="field input"><label for="genderType">Gender</label>
        <br />
           <%= Html.DropDownList("genderType")%>
        <span class="input-message"></span></p>

        <p class="field input"><label for="birthDate">Birth Date</label><br />
             <%= String.Format(Html.TextBox("birthDate"))%>
        <span class="input-message"></span></p>

        <p class="field input"><label
          for="occupation">Occupation</label><br />
             <%= Html.DropDownList("occupation")%>
        <span class="input-message"></span></p>

        <p class="field input"><label for="website">Website</label>\
        <br />
             <%= Html.TextBox("website")%>
        <span class="input-message"></span></p>
      </div>
  </div>

<div id="Address" class="form">
    <h2 class="title">Address Information</h2>
      <div class="content">
        <p class="field input"><label for="street">Street</label>
        <br />
             <%= Html.TextBox("street")%>
        <span class="input-message"></span></p>

        <p class="field input"><label for="city">City</label><br />
             <%= Html.TextBox("city")%>
        <span class="input-message"></span></p>

        <p class="field input"><label for="state">State</label>
        <br />
             <%= Html.TextBox("state")%>
        <span class="input-message"></span></p>

        <p class="field input"><label
```

```
                for="zipcode">Zip / Postal Code:</label><br />
                    <%= Html.TextBox("zipcode")%>
                <span class="input-message"></span></p>

                <p class="field input"><label for="country">Country</label>
                <br />
                    <%= Html.DropDownList("country")%>
                <span class="input-message"></span></p>
            </div>
        </div>
        <hr />
        <p><button type="submit" id="user-login-button">Submit</button></p>

    </form>
```

The only thing of note with this view is the introduction of the `Html.DropDownList` object. This control is accessing the exact same `ViewData` object as the other controls except in this particular case it will be receiving a `SelectList` object that is MVC-specific. The `SelectList` object is very similar to a list object, except that it has an understanding of which item or items within it are selected. In this way the MVC framework is not reliant on the drop-down control for pertinent selection information.

> Note that the `ViewData` object is extremely flexible and can take almost any object that you place into it. It is your responsibility to ensure that you are accurately matching the type you pass into the `ViewData` object with the control it will go into. You will not receive any compile-time warnings of a mismatch. Your first indication of a problem will be at runtime when the object attempts to fill itself.

The ManageUser.aspx View

Now that we have completed the end user views we can now begin to build the administrative views. The `/User/ManageUser` and `/User/ManageRole` pages linked by the Admin navigation box represent the core of your security administration section. From these two views you will be able to make modifications to the security policies governing the entire website. We will start by outlining the `ManageUser.aspx` view is located in `~/Views/User`.

MainContent

This page's user interface can be divided into three parts:

1. The first part tells the administrator the number of registered users, and how many of them are currently online.

2. The second part provides controls for finding and listing the users. The search functionality in this part allows administrators to search for a user's username or e-mail address.

3. The third part of the page contains a grid that lists users and some of their properties.

The following code provides the user interface for the first two parts:

```
<% Html.RenderPartial("~/Views/Shared/Message.ascx"); %>

<form  method="post" action="ManageUser" class="manage-user">
```

```
<p><b>Total Registered Users: </b><%= ViewData["RegisteredUsers"]%></p>
<p><b>Users Online Now: </b><%= ViewData["UsersOnlineNow"] %></p>
<hr />

<!-- user search options -->
<p>Search Members: <%= Html.TextBox("searchInput", ViewData["searchInput"])%>
   <%= Html.DropDownList("searchType", (SelectList)ViewData["search
OptionList"])%>  <button type="submit" id="user-manageUser-button"
style="height:28px">Search</button></p>
<hr />

<!-- the user grid -->
<table cellpadding="2" cellspacing="0" align="left" summary="User Grid" border="1">
<tr style="font-weight:bold; background-color:#A8C3CB; ">
<td align="center">Username</td>
<td align="center">E-Mail</td>
<td align="center">Created</td>
<td align="center">Last Used</td>
<td align="center">Approved</td>
<td> </td>
<td> </td>
</tr>

<% foreach(MembershipUser membershipUser in ViewData.Model) { %>
<tr>
<td><%= membershipUser.UserName %></td>
<td><%= membershipUser.Email %></td>
<td align="center"><%= membershipUser.CreationDate.ToLocalTime() %></td>
<td align="center"><%= membershipUser.LastActivityDate.ToLocalTime() %></td>
<td align="center"><%= Html.CheckBox("","","",membershipUser.IsApproved, new
{disabled="true"}) %></td>
<td><a href="EditUser?id=<%= membershipUser.UserName %>"><img border="0" alt="Edit
User" src="/content/images/EditSymbol.png" title="Modify User" align="middle"/></
a></td>
<td><a href="ManageUser?id=<%= membershipUser.UserName %>"><img border="0"
alt="Delete User"  src="/content/images/DeleteSymbol.png" title="Delete User"
align="middle"/></a></td>
</tr>
<% } %>
</table>

</form>
```

You may notice in this code that we are using plain old tables to show our data. This is because the `GridView` control that we have used so frequently in ASP.NET 2.0 is now obsolete. Everything you could previously do with `GridView` can easily be done using simple HTML tables and a `foreach` loop. If you are still yearning for the slick sorting, filtering, and pagination capabilities of `GridView`, you can use a number of exceptional AJAX open source grids to accomplish this. These grids will be faster than the old `GridView` and use either XML or JSON. You can also avoid having all that ugly server control data in your `ViewState`!

Looking at Figure 5-14 you can see that styling is almost identical to a standard `GridView`. In fact, a `GridView` is an HTML table with a lot of code attached to it to make all the magic happen. With the delete and write functionality you are using standard HTML links and supplementing them with the ID of the target row as a URL variable. Although this doesn't use the `Html.ActionLink` to create a hyperlink, it does allow you to use a standard HTML `href` and `img` tag.

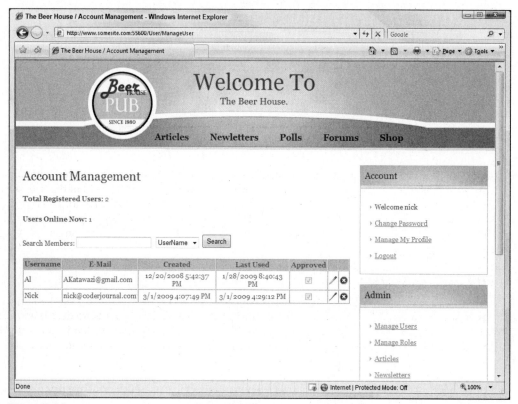

Figure 5-14

ScriptContent

The javascript portion of this view controls the deletion of users asynchronously. We do this by first registering our javascript file on our view using the following markup:

```
<asp:Content ID="ScriptContent" ContentPlaceHolderID="ScriptContent"
runat="server">
<script type="text/javascript" src="/content/scripts/manage-users.js"></script>
</asp:Content>
```

manage-user.js

The `register.js` file is located under `~/Content/scripts/` and it will be used to communicate with our `DeleteUser` action method that we discussed earlier. The javascript looks like this:

```
$(".delete-user-button").click(function() {
    var userId = $(this).attr("meta:id");
    $.post(
        "/User/DeleteUser",
        { id: userId },
        function(data) {
            $("#user-" + data.object.id).remove();
        },
        "json"
    );
    return false;
});
```

What is basically happening in this code is we are using javascript to first intercept the button click of the `delete-user-button`. Once we have intercepted that we obtain from it the id of the user that will be deleted. Using jQuery we execute a `HTTP POST` to our `DeleteUser` action method. You can also see that we are removing an element from our view. This element corresponds to the table row element with that same id. We therefore are able to delete the user in our database and also on our view, and all done asynchronously.

The EditUser.aspx View

The `EditUser` view is linked from a row of the `ManagedUsers` table. It takes a `username` parameter on the query string of the URL, and allows an administrator to see all the membership details about that user (that is, the properties of the `MembershipUser` object representing that user). It is therefore not surprising that this view takes `MembershipUser` object as its model. The user interface of the page is simple and is divided into two sections:

1. The first section shows the data read from `MembershipUser`. All controls are read-only, except for those that are bound to the `IsApproved` property.

2. The second section contains an array of `checkboxes` that displays all the roles defined for the application. This allows the administrator to add or remove users to and from roles.

MainContent

The following is the code for `EditUser.aspx`:

```
<% Html.RenderPartial("~/Views/Shared/Message.ascx"); %>

<form method="post" action="EditUser" class="manage-user">
<!-- The hidden control manages the username -->
<%= Html.Hidden("id") %>
```

```
<!-- Shows detailed information about member from MembershipUser object -->
<p><b>UserName:</b> <%= Model.UserName %> </p>
<p><b>E-Mail:</b> <%= Model.Email%></p>
<p><b>Registered:</b> <%= Model.CreationDate.ToLocalTime()%></p>
<p><b>Last Login:</b> <%= Model.LastLoginDate.ToLocalTime()%></p>
<p><b>Last Activity:</b> <%= Model.LastActivityDate.ToLocalTime()%></p>
<p><b>Online Now:</b> <%= Html.CheckBox("onlineNow", Model.IsOnline, new { disabled
= "true" })%></p>
<p><b>Approved:</b> <%= Html.CheckBox("approved", Model.IsApproved)%></p>
<p><b>Locked Out:</b> <%= Html.CheckBox("lockedOut", Model.IsLockedOut, new {
disabled = "true" })%></p>
<hr />

<!-- This portion allows you to actually edit the roles of the user -->
<h2>Edit User Roles</h2>
<ul>
<% foreach (string role in (string[])ViewData["roles"]){ %>
 <li><%= Html.CheckBox("role." + role,  Roles.IsUserInRole(Model.UserName, role))%>
 <label for="role.<%= role %>"><%= role %></label></li>
<% } %>
</ul>

<p>
 <button type="submit" id="user-editUser-button">Update User</button>
 <button type="button" onclick="location.href='/User/ManageUser'" style="margin-
left: 2em;">Return</button>
</p>

</form>
```

You may have noticed that in one of our `ViewData` object we are passing in an instance of the `MembershipUser` object. We are also casting it right in the view with line of code:

```
<% MembershipUser membershipUser = (MembershipUser)ViewData["membershipUser"]; %>
```

This makes the cast object available to you as a strongly typed object throughout the rest of the view. You may also notice that you are invoking the `ToLocalTime()` method for your timestamps; this is a very handy method that is attached to all `DateTime` objects allowing you to localize it to your region. For example, if you created an account at 6:00 AM UTC on Friday, the administrator on the east coast of the United States would have that number converted automatically to 1:00 AM to represent the equivalent United States Eastern Standard Time. For security purposes this is great because the time zone is rarely ever displayed. Figure 5-15 shows an administration page for the TheBeerHouse sample application.

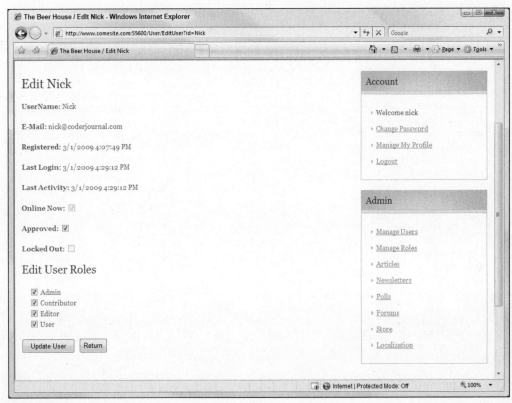

Figure 5-15

The ManageRole View

The very last thing that you need to wrap up for security is to be able to add and remove roles as you see fit. We have added a Manage Role link to the Admin navigation box to allow you to easily do this. This view is a simplified version of the manage user view.

MainContent

The `MainContent` section of this view contains a single textbox and button to allow you to add new roles. It also offers a delete button to help you remove existing roles. The views code is as follows:

```
<% Html.RenderPartial("~/Views/Shared/Message.ascx"); %>

<form  method="post" action="CreateRole" class="manage-role">
<p><b>Total Number of Roles: </b><%= ViewData["TotalRoles"].ToString()%></p>
<hr />

<!-- Functionality to add new roles -->
<p>Add New Role: <%= Html.TextBox("newRole")%>   <button type="submit"
id="user-manageRole-button" style="height:28px">Add Role</button></p>
<hr />
```

```
<!-- Table showing old rows -->
<table width="50%" cellpadding="2" cellspacing="0" align="left" summary="User Grid"
border="1">
<tr style="font-weight:bold; background-color:#A8C3CB; ">
<td align="center">Role Name</td>
<td> </td>
</tr>
<% foreach(String role in System.Web.Security.Roles.GetAllRoles()) { %>
<tr id="role-<%= role %>">
<td><%= role %></td>
<td align="center"><a class="delete-role-button" href="#" meta:id="<%= role
%>"><img border="0" alt="Delete Role"  src="/content/images/DeleteSymbol.png"
title="Delete Role" align="middle"/></a></td>


</tr>
<% } %>
</table>

</form>
```

Figure 5-16 shows a screenshot of this view in action.

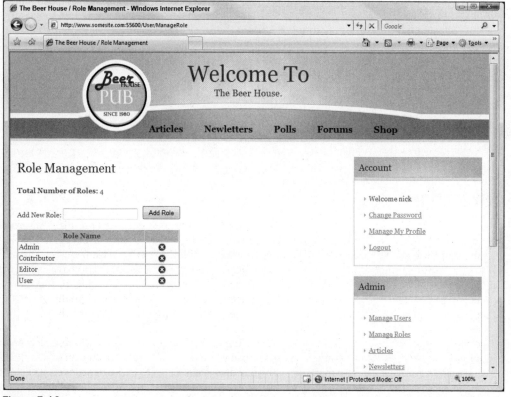

Figure 5-16

ScriptContent

Like the manage user javascript, this javascript section will also be responsible for asynchronously deleting items. We do this by first registering our javascript file on our view using the following markup:

```
<asp:Content ID="ScriptContent" ContentPlaceHolderID="ScriptContent"
runat="server">
<script type="text/javascript" src="/content/scripts/manage-users.js"></script>
</asp:Content>
```

manage-role.js

The `manage-role.js` file is located under `~/Content/scripts/` and it will be used to communicate with our `DeleteRole` action method that we discussed earlier. The javascript looks like this:

```
$(".delete-user-button").click(function() {
    var userId = $(this).attr("meta:id");
    $.post(
        "/User/DeleteUser",
        { id: userId },
        function(data) {
            $("#user-" + data.object.id).remove();
        },
        "json"
    );
    return false;
});
```

This javascript is exactly like the javascript that you saw with user deletion except it pertains to roles. Once you have this javascript and the content section complete you have finished the last of our security module. You should now have a fully functional MVC Framework compatible website security module and visitor profile system.

Summary

This chapter covered a great deal of information regarding the membership and profiling features introduced in ASP.NET 2.0. The Solution section contains surprisingly little code yet produces a complete membership system! We have even managed to re-implement and extend the Security area of the ASP.NET Web Administration Tool. In addition, the MVC framework has allowed you to have a true separation between the user interface and the business logic layer. You do accept, as a tradeoff, additional coding that is required to make security work. Instead of using the login controls seen originally in ASP.NET 2.0, you create simple HTML interfaces that access the membership and profile APIs directly.

Some significant improvements to security when using MVC include the capability to restrict access to individual methods within your web application. Because you use controllers to manage all of your business logic, all of the code that actually interacts with your data and your environment is conveniently located in one place. By using the `Authorize` attribute you are able to lock down specific controller actions rather than entire pages. Furthermore, the MVC framework by default will block direct access to almost every view in the web application except for the `default.aspx` page and the data held in the content folder.

The user profiling functionality remains largely unchanged from ASP.NET 2.0. You are still able to easily provide a list of your user attributes in the `web.config` file and have them saved directly to your provider with minimal coding. Using the MVC framework you do trade off the use of the `ProfileCommon` class used in the previous edition of this book. `ProfileCommon` is a dynamically generated class that is able to return a strongly typed object containing your profile attributes defined in the `web.config` file. Unfortunately this convenient class is only located in the code-behind file of views. Because you don't use code-behind files in your views, `ProfileCommon` is not an option. Fortunately you can still use the Profiling API using `ProfileBase`, the class that `ProfileCommon` directly inherits from. You get all the same functionality minus your strongly typed attributes. Even without type safety, the Profiling API makes retaining user data simple and easy to integrate.

Using the Membership and Profiling API is a no-brainer, especially with the MVC framework. Many of the features you would expect from a security system are already in place, and it is extremely easy to extend them to meet your specific needs.

6

News, Article, and Blog Management

The example site is basically a container for content targeted to beer, food, and pub enthusiasts. Content can be in the form of news, articles, reports of special events, reviews, photo galleries, blog entries, and so on. This chapter describes the typical content-related problems that should be considered for a site of this type. You'll then design and develop an online article manager that allows the complete management of your site's content, in terms of acquiring articles; adding, activating, and removing articles; sharing articles with other parties; and so on.

Problem

Different sites use different methods of gathering news and information. Some site administrators hunt for news events and write their own articles, whereas others get news and articles directly from their users (a great example of this is the Add Your News link at www.aspwire.com) or they rely upon a company whose business is to gather and organize news to be sold to third-party sites. In the old days, some sites did *screen-scraping*, retrieving data from an external site's page and showing it on their pages with a custom appearance (of course, you must have the authorization from the external company and you must know the format it uses to show the news from its pages). During the past few years you've seen an explosion in the use of Really Simple Syndication (RSS), a simple XML format for syndicating content, making it available to other clients. Atom is another XML-based syndication standard that was created to solve some problems of RSS — it has gained wide-scale acceptance because of an early adoption by Google and the standardization of the format by the World Wide Web Consortium (W3C) and Internet Engineering Task Force (IETF). The basic idea with RSS and Atom is for sites to provide an index of websites' content in the form of an XML document. A client program can fetch that XML document and provide users with a list of news items and hyperlinks that can direct them to the individual stories they are interested in. One site's XML index document is called a *newsfeed*. The client program is called a *news aggregator* (or *feed reader*) because it can extract newsfeeds from many sites and present them in one chronological list, possibly arranged by category. Users can subscribe to the XML feed and their aggregator program can periodically poll for new stories by fetching new XML documents automatically in the background. Because RSS and Atom are open standards, many web-based and fat-client desktop applications are available that can subscribe to any site that provides such feeds. Some popular feed readers are RSS Bandit (`www.rssbandit.org`), Microsoft Outlook 2007, Mozilla Firefox, and Google Reader (`reader.google.com`). RSS and Atom are very convenient for users who want to keep up on the latest news, articles, and published content. You can advertise your new content via RSS and Atom feeds by adding a feed link to your web page's header, which will automatically advertise your content to any feed reader. When users visit your site they will be presented with an icon, which is the universal sign that your website can be read via an RSS or Atom feed. You can even display a list of content from other sites by showing RSS links on one of your web pages. Your page can have an aggregator user control that makes it simple to display the content of specified RSS and Atom feeds. This adds to any unique content you provide, and users will find value in returning to your site frequently to see your own updated content as well as a list of interesting links to updated news items on other sites.

It doesn't matter which methods you decide to use, but you must have fresh and updated content as often as possible for your site to be successful and entice users to return. Users will not return regularly to a site if they rarely find new content. You should use a variety of methods to acquire new content. You can't rely entirely on external content (retrieved as an RSS feed, by screen-scraping, or by inserting some JavaScript) because these methods often imply that you publish just a small extract of the external content on your site and publish a link to the full article, thus driving traffic away from your site. It can be a solution for daily news about weather, stock exchanges, and the like, but not for providing real original content, which is why users surf the web. You must create and publish some content on your own, and possibly syndicate that content as RSS feeds, so that other sites can consume it, and bring new visitors to your site.

Once you have a source of articles, a second problem arises: how to add them to your site. You can immediately rule out manual updating of pages or adding new static HTML pages — if you have to add news several times a day, or even just every week, creating and uploading pages and editing all the links becomes an administrative nightmare. Additionally, the people who administer the site on a daily basis may not have the skills required to edit or create new HTML pages. You need a much more flexible system, one that allows the site administrators to easily publish fresh content without requiring special HTML code generator tools or knowledge of HTML. You want it to have many features, such as the capability to organize articles in categories and show abstracts, and even to allow some site users to post their own news items. You'll see the complete list of features you're going to implement in the Design section of this chapter. For now, suffice it to say that you must be able to manage the content of your site remotely over the web, without requiring any other tools. Think about what this implies: you can add or edit news as soon as it is available, in a few minutes, even if you're not in your office and even if you don't have access to your own computer; all you need is a connection to the Internet and a browser. And this can work the same way for your news contributors and partners. They won't have to e-mail the news to you and then wait for you to publish it. They can submit and publish content without your intervention (although in your case you will give administrators and editors the option to approve or edit the content before publication).

Once you have the article added to your site, a third problem arises: how to make the article's URL friendly to the search engines. The idea of making the URL friendly to the search engines is one of the many components that go into creating a good Search Engine Optimization (SEO)–friendly site. Search engines collect information on your website by sending out spider-bots to collect keywords from your web page's URL, title, and body, so that when a search engine's user searches for those specific keywords your web page comes up as one of the possible answers to the request. The rule of thumb for SEO is to treat the search engine bots just like you would treat any of your other users and to give it as much relevant information about your web page as possible. So you want to provide the bots a URL that is easy to read and gives a good amount of information about the content of the web page without having to visit it first. For example, `www.yoursite.com/articles/215/how-to-make-good-beer` is much easier to read than `www.yoursite.com/articles/?id=215`; the user, and the search engine bot, immediately understand that the web page that this URL points to is about "How to make good beer." So you definitely want to make your site easy to read no matter the audience.

The last problem is the implementation of security. You want to give full control to one or more administrators and editors, allow a specific group of users (contributors) to submit news, and allow normal users to just read the news. You could even prevent them from reading the content if they have not registered with the site.

To summarize the problem, you need the following:

❑ An online tool for managing news content that allows specific users to add, update, and delete articles without knowing HTML or other publishing software

❑ A method of allowing other sites to use your content so that they publish an excerpt and link to your site for the entire article, thus bringing your site more traffic

❑ A process for providing relevant and easily readable URLs for the articles you publish

❑ A system that allows various users different levels of access to the site's content

Design

This section introduces the design of the solution and an online tool for acquiring, managing, and sharing the content of your site. Specifically, you do the following:

❑ Provide a full list of the features you want to implement

❑ Design the database tables for this module

❑ Create a list and a description of the stored procedures needed to provide access to the database

❑ Design the object models of the data and business layers

❑ Describe the user interface services needed for content management, such as the site pages and reusable user controls

❑ Explain how you will ensure security for the administration section and for other access-restricted pages

Features to Implement

Let's start our discussion by writing down a partial list of the features that the article manager module should provide in order to be flexible and powerful, but still easy to use:

❑ An article can be added to the database at any time, with an option to delay publication until a specified release date. Additionally, the person submitting the article must be able to specify an expiration date, after which the article will be automatically retired. If these dates are not specified, the article should be immediately published and remain active indefinitely.

❑ Articles can have an approved status. If an administrator or editor submits the article, it should be approved immediately. If you allow other people, such as staff or users of the site (we will call them *contributors*), to post their own news and articles, this content should be added to the database in a "pending" state. The site administrators or editors will then be able to control this content, apply any required modifications, and finally approve the articles for publication once they are ready.

❑ The system must also track who originally submitted an article or news item. This is important because it provides information regarding whether a contributor is active, who is responsible for incorrect content, who to contact for further details if the article is particularly interesting, and so on.

❑ The administrator/editor must be able to decide whether an article can be read by all readers or only by registered users.

❑ There can be multiple categories, enabling articles to be organized in different virtual folders. Each category should have a description and an image that graphically represents it.

❑ The URL for the article should be automatically generated based on the title of the article.

❑ There should be a page with the available categories as a menu. Each category should be linked to a page that shows a short abstract for each published article. By clicking the article's title the user can read the whole text.

❑ Articles can be targeted to users from a specified location, for example, country, state/province, or city. Consider the case where you might have stories about concerts, parties, and special events that will happen in a particular location. In Chapter 5, you implemented a registration and profiling system that included the user's address. That will be used here to highlight events that are going to happen close to the user's location. This is a feature that can entice readers to provide that personal information, which you could use later for marketing purposes (ads can be geographically targeted also).

❑ Users can leave comments or ask questions about articles, and this feedback should be published at the end of the article itself, so that other readers can read it and create discussions around it (this greatly helps to increase traffic). You might recognize this approach as being common with *blogs*, which are web logs in which an individual publishes personal thoughts and opinions and other people add comments. As another form of feedback, users can rate articles to express how much they liked them.

❑ The module must count how many times an article is read. This information will also be shown to the reader, together with the abstract, the author name, the publication date, and other information. But it will be most important for the editors/administrators because it greatly helps them understand which topics the readers find most interesting, enabling administrators to direct energy, money, and time to adding new content on those topics.

❑ The new content must be available as an RSS feed to which a reader can subscribe, and read through his or her favorite RSS aggregator.

❑ Above all, the article manager and the viewer must be integrated with the existing site. In your case this means that the pages must tie in with the current layout, and that you must take advantage of the current authentication/authorization system to protect each section and to identify the author of the submitted content.

It's essential to have this list of features when designing the database tables, because you now know what information you need to store in, and what information you should retrieve from, existing tables and modules (such as the user account data).

Designing the Database Tables

As described in Chapter 3 (where you looked at building the foundations for your site), you're going to use `TheBeerHouse` as your database schema for all your tables, so that you avoid the risk of naming a table such that it clashes with another table used by another part of the site (this may well be the case when you have multiple applications on the site that store their data on the same shared database). You need three tables for this module: one for the categories, another one for the articles, and the last one for the user feedback. The diagram shown in Figure 6-1 illustrates how they are linked to each other.

How to Properly Name Database Tables

A common practice is to prefix table names with "tbl" or something related to your application, such as in the case of TheBeerHouse "tbh." This is called Hungarian Notation and you should not do this.

In the case of "tbl" this was done in the past to differentiate between tables, views, stored procedures, and other objects in the database; this is not necessary anymore in Microsoft SQL Server because of tools such as Microsoft Management Studio, which are smart enough to break up objects by their type.

In the case of prefixing the tables with the name of your application, for example, "tbh," this was done as a way to separate out different schemas (or applications) within the same database. This is also not necessary anymore because Microsoft SQL Server now supports schemas natively in the database, which helps separate entire applications of objects including tables, views, stored procedures, and so on, from other schemas in the same database.

I would encourage you to start using database schemas in your applications and make an active effort to forget the old ways of Hungarian Notation. As a developer it is important to stay up to date with the changes of the technologies you use so your understanding and application of the technology can grow with the technology.

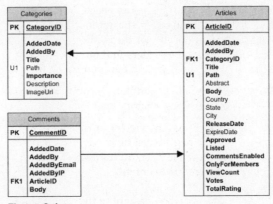

Figure 6-1

Let's start by looking at these tables and their relationship in more detail.

The Categories Table

Not surprisingly, the Categories table stores information about the article categories.

Column Name	Type	Size	Allow Null	Description
CategoryID	int - PK	4	No	Unique ID for the category.
AddedDate	datetime	8	No	Category creation date/time.
AddedBy	nvarchar	256	No	Name of the user who created the category.
Title	nvarchar	256	No	Category's title.
Path	nvarchar	256	No	Category-friendly URL part generated from the title.
Importance	int	4	No	Category's importance. Used to sort the categories with a custom order, other than by name or by date.
Description	nvarchar	4000	Yes	Category's description.
ImageUrl	nvarchar	256	Yes	URL of an image that represents the category graphically.

This system supports a single-level category, meaning that you cannot have subcategories. This is plenty for small to mid-sized sites that don't have huge numbers of new articles on a wide variety of topics. Having too many categories in sites of this size can even hinder the user's experience, because it makes it more difficult to locate desired content. Enhancing the system to support subcategories is left as an exercise if you really need it, but as a suggestion, the database would only require an additional ParentCategoryID column containing the ID of the parent category.

You may have noticed that the Path is generated from the Title and that they are the same length and type as each other, and ask: why not just generate the Path on the fly instead of storing it in the database? This is a very good question and it goes to the fact that, in a more advanced configuration, you may not always want to have your Path the same as your Title for SEO reasons. It is wise to keep your Path around four to six words, and to exclude common sentence structure words such as "a," "of," "and," and so on; search engines usually ignore these words anyway so there is no benefit to having them in your Path. For this project you are going to ignore this SEO recommendation, because it would involve creating an exclusionary dictionary for each language you wanted to support. However, we thought we would include the option in case you wanted to further develop the application outside of this book. There is also the added benefit of not having to do the transformation from Title to Path on the fly, which is good for performance.

AddedDate and AddedBy are two columns that you will find in all your tables — they record when a category/article/comment/product/message/newsletter was created, and by whom, to provide an audit trail. You may have thought that instead of having an nvarchar column for storing the username you could use an integer column that would contain a foreign key pointing to records of the `aspnet_Users` table introduced in Chapter 4. However, that would be a bad choice for a couple of reasons:

1. The membership data may be stored in a separate database, and possibly on a different server.

2. The membership module might use a provider other than the default one that targets SQL Server. In some cases the user account data will be stored in Active Directory or maybe in an Oracle database, and thus there would be no SQL Server table to link to.

The Articles Table

The `Articles` table contains the content and all further information for all the articles in all categories. It is structured as follows.

Column Name	Type	Size	Allow Null	Description
ArticleID	int – PK	4	No	Unique ID for the article.
AddedDate	datetime	8	No	Date/time the article was added.
AddedBy	nvarchar	256	No	Name of the user who created the article.
CategoryID	int – FK	4	No	ID of the category to which the news item belongs.
Title	nvarchar	256	No	Article's title.
Path	nvarchar	256	No	Article-friendly URL part generated from the title.
Abstract	nvarchar	4000	Yes	Article's abstract (short summary) to be shown in the page that lists the article, and in the RSS feed.
Body	ntext		No	Article's content (full version).
Country	nvarchar	256	Yes	Country to which the article (concert/event) refers.
State	nvarchar	256	Yes	State/province to which the article refers.
City	nvarchar	256	Yes	City to which the article refers.
ReleaseDate	datetime	8	No	Date/time the article will be publicly readable.
ExpireDate	datetime	8	Yes	Date/time the article will be retired and no longer readable by the public.
Approved	bit	1	No	Approved status of the article. If false, an administrator/editor has to approve the article before it is actually published and available to readers.

Column Name	Type	Size	Allow Null	Description
Listed	bit	1	No	Whether the article is listed in the articles page (indexed). If false, the article will not be listed, but will still be accessible if the user types the right URL, or if there is a direct link to it.
CommentsEnabled	bit	1	No	Whether the user can leave public comments on the article.
OnlyForMembers	bit	1	No	Whether the article is available to registered and authenticated users only, or to everyone.
ViewCount	int	4	No	Number of times the article has been viewed.
Votes	int	4	No	Number of votes the article has received.
TotalRating	int	4	No	Total rating score the article has received. This is the sum of all the ratings posted by users.

The ReleaseDate and ExpireDate columns are useful because the site's staff can prepare content in advance and postpone its publication, and then let the site update itself at the specified date/time. In addition to the obvious benefit of spreading out the workload, this is also great during vacation periods, when the staff would not be in the office to write new articles but you still want the site to publish fresh content regularly.

The Listed column is also very important, because it enables you to add articles that will be hidden from the main article list page, and from the RSS feeds. Why would you want to do this? Suppose that you have a category called Photo Galleries (you actually create this later in the chapter) in which you publish the photos of a past event or meeting. In such photo gallery articles you would insert thumbnails of the photos with links to their full-size versions. It would be nice if the reader could comment and rate each and every photo, not just the article listing them all, right? You can do that if, instead of linking the big photo directly, you link a secondary article that includes the photo. However, if you have many photos, and thus many short articles that contain each of them, you certainly don't want to fill the category's article listing with a myriad of links to individual photos. Instead, you will want to list only the parent gallery. To do this, you set the Listed property of all the photo articles to false, and leave it true only on the article with the thumbnails.

The Country, State, and City fields enable you to specify an accurate location for those articles that refer to an event (such as parties, concerts, beer contests, and so on). If the location for the article matches a specific user's location, even partially, you could highlight the article with a particular color when it's listed on the web page. You may be wondering why it was necessary to define the Country and State fields as nvarchar fields, instead of an int foreign key pointing to corresponding records of the Countries and States lookup tables. The answer is that we want to use the State field to support not only U.S. states, but states and provinces for any other country, so we defined this as a free text field. It's also good for performance if you de-normalize these fields. Using a lookup table is particularly useful when there is the possibility that some values may change; storing the information in one location minimizes the effort to update the data and makes it easier to ensure that you don't get out-of-sync. However, the list of countries will not realistically change, so this isn't much of a problem. In the remote case that this might happen, you will simply execute a manual update for all those records that have Country="US" instead of "United States", for example. This design decision can greatly improve the performance of the application.

You may be wondering why we decided to put the Votes and TotalRating columns into this table, instead of using a separate table to store all the single votes for all articles. That alternative has its advantages, surely: you could track the name and IP address of the user who submits the vote, and produce interesting statistics such as the number of votes for every level of rating (from one to five stars). However, retrieving the total number of votes, the total rating, and the number of votes for each rating level would require several SUM operations, in addition to the SELECT to the Articles table. We don't think the additional features are worth the additional processing time and traffic over the network, and thus we opted for this much lighter solution instead.

The Comments Table

The Comments table contains the feedback (comments, questions, answers, and so on) for the published articles. The structure is very simple.

Column Name	Type	Size	Allow Null	Description
CommentID	int - PK	4	No	Unique ID for the comment
AddedDate	datetime	8	No	Date/time the comment was added
AddedBy	nvarchar	256	No	Name of the user who wrote the comment
AddedByEmail	nvarchar	256	No	User's e-mail address
AddedByIP	nvarchar	15	No	User's IP address
ArticleID	int	4	No	Article to which this comment refers
Body	ntext		No	Text of the comment

You will track the name of the user posting the comment, but he could even be an anonymous user, so this value will not necessarily be one of the registered usernames. You also store the user's e-mail address, so that the readers can be contacted with private answers to their questions. Storing the IP address might be legally necessary in some cases, especially when you allow anonymous users to post content on a public site. In case of offensive or illegal content, it may be possible to geographically locate the user if you know the IP address and the time when the content was posted. In simpler cases, you may just block posts from that IP (not a useful option if it were dynamically assigned an IP, though).

Queries That Access the Database

To query the database, you will build a set of queries that you'll use later in the business layer of your application to query your categories, articles, and comments. I find it useful to define all your queries in the beginning of the design process so that it starts the brain-storming process of how your application will be used and what kind of pages will need to be developed in the later stages of the development process.

The queries you need, and their parameters, are listed in the following table (you'll be writing the queries later in the chapter in the Solution section):

Query	Description
GetArticle	Retrieves all details (the complete row) of the article identified by the specified ID.
GetArticleCount	Returns the total number of articles. This has one parameter: to specify the category to get the article count for; the category parameter is optional.
GetArticles	Retrieves a partial list of articles located. The list is partial because there are two parameters: one to specify the index of the page of articles to retrieve. This is used to implement a custom pagination system (because you can't fit all the articles on one page). The other is to specify the category to get the articles for; the category parameter is optional.
GetCategory	Retrieves all details of the category identified by the specified ID.
GetCategories	Returns all details about all categories.
GetComment	Retrieves all details of the comment identified by the specified ID.
(Category) Exists	Checks to see if the category supplied exists in the database already.
GetPublishedArticleCount	Returns the total number of published articles in any category. Similar to GetArticleCount, but gets only published articles, that is, articles that are approved, listed, and are not expired (whose ReleaseDate-ExpireDate interval includes the specified current date).
GetPublishedArticles	Retrieves a partial list of published articles located in any category. Similar to GetArticles, but gets only published articles, that is, articles that are approved, listed, and are not expired (whose ReleaseDate-ExpireDate interval includes the specified current date).

Many of these queries are pretty standard. However, it's worth noting some design decisions that could have an impact on the performance of the site:

❑　All queries that retrieve the list of articles accept two input parameters: one that indicates the index of the page of records to retrieve, and one that indicates which category, if any, to retrieve. This is done to support a custom pagination mechanism in the administration and user pages where you will show the list of items. Potentially, there can be thousands of articles, so implementing pagination is necessary both for performance and aesthetic reasons.

❑　The procedures that retrieve articles will be joined with the Categories table to retrieve the parent category's title, in addition to the ID stored in the Articles table. Similarly, the procedures that retrieve comments will be joined with the Comments table to retrieve the parent article's title. Returning this information together with the other data avoids running many separate queries when you have to list articles or comments on the page (an additional query would be needed for each article/comment otherwise).

❑ You may also notice that there are no queries listed to insert, update, and delete records from the database. This is because these queries are automatically handled by the data and business layer that is generated by LINQ (Language Integrated Query) to SQL, so it was only necessary to define the queries that were not automatically provided.

Designing the Configuration Module

Chapter 4 introduced a custom configuration section named <theBeerHouse> that you must define in the root folder's web.config file to specify some settings required in order for the site's modules to work. In that chapter you also developed a configuration class that would handle the <contact> sub-element of <theBeerHouse>, with settings for the Contact form in the Contact.aspx page. For the articles module of this chapter you'll need some new settings that will be grouped into a new configuration sub-element under <theBeerHouse>, called <articles>. This will be read by a class called ArticlesElement that will inherit from System.Configuration.ConfigurationElement, and that will have the public property shown in the following table.

Property	Description
PageSize	Default number of articles listed per page. The user will be able to change the page size from the user interface.

The settings in the web.config file will have the same name, but will follow the camelCase naming convention; therefore, you will use providerType, connectionStringName, pageSize, and so on, as shown in the following example:

```
<theBeerHouse>
        <contactForm mailTo="nick@coderjournal.com" />
        <articles pageSize="10" />
</theBeerHouse>
```

An instance of ArticlesElement is returned by the Articles property of the TheBeerHouseSection class, described in Chapter 4, which represents the <theBeerHouse> parent section.

Designing the Model

Now that you have a clear picture in mind of the database tables and how to retrieve data through the queries, you can design the model. As explained in Chapter 4, you will be using LINQ to SQL to generate your model. Generally, there is a one-to-one correspondence between the database tables and the entity classes. Figure 6-2 provides a graphical representation of these classes, with their inheritance relationships.

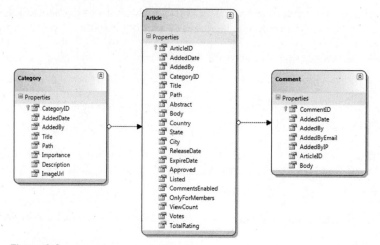

Figure 6-2

This diagram was created using LINQ to SQL in the `TheBeerHouse.Models` namespace. LINQ to SQL does a great job at creating a usable model from your SQL Server database that can quickly be applied to any application. You are able to query everything in these tables by simply calling them as outlined here:

```
TheBeerHouseDataContext dc = new TheBeerHouseDataContext();

foreach(var article in dc.Articles)
    // do something for articles

foreach(var category in dc.Categories)
    // do something for categories

foreach(var comment in dc.Comments)
    // do something for comments
```

This is much nicer than some of the ways you have had to access the database in the past. However, this doesn't accomplish everything you need to do and some of the queries that LINQ allows you to do can become pretty complex. So you will need to abstract these complex queries away from the code and make them natural extensions of the model.

Extending the Model

As discussed earlier there are some additional queries that you wanted available to you in the models of `Article`, `Category`, and `Comment`. .NET 3.5 introduced a language feature to call extension methods that you are going to use to extend your models in a natural way. An extension method provides a way for a programmer to attach a method to any object in the .NET Framework. So if you wanted to add a great new method to `System.String`, extension methods would allow you to do this, and have it show up on `System.String` as if it was always there. We have created a simple example that we hope will prove illustrative to you:

```
public static string PadBothEnds (this string s, char c, int count)
{
    string padding = new String(c, count);
    return padding + s + padding;
}
```

Notice the method signature starts with a `this` keyword; this is how the compiler knows that the method is an extension method for the `string` type. To use this method you simply make the following call:

```
string myString = "Extend Me";
string extendedString = myString.PadBothEnds('x', 5);
```

and the value of `extendedString` is

```
xxxxxExtend Mexxxxx
```

Obviously this example method probably isn't very useful in the real world, but hopefully it illustrates the basics of how extension methods work. We strongly recommend that you study extension methods by reading articles on the MSDN. Extension methods are going to be at the core of how you create queries for your entity objects, so it helps to have a good foundational knowledge in how they work. Figure 6-3 outlines a static class, called `ArticleQueries`, for all the extension methods that you are going to extend on to `Article`, `Category`, and `Comment` types.

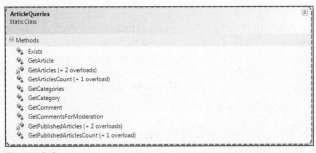

Figure 6-3

These extension methods will allow you to call the methods as if they were part of the original models that were created with LINQ to SQL. We have highlighted the methods that apply to each model object in Figures 6-3a through 6-3c and have given some examples of how each of these new extension methods will be used.

Article Extension Methods Queries

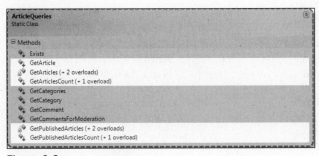

Figure 6-3a

```
TheBeerHouseDataContext dc = new TheBeerHouseDataContext();

// get single article
var article = dc.Articles.GetArticle(1);

// get articles for first page and then also for the general category
var firstPageArticles = dc.Articles.GetArticles(1);
var firstPageArticlesForGeneral = dc.Articles.GetArticles("general", 1);

// get articles count and then for the general category
var articlesCount = dc.Articles.GetArticlesCount();
var articlesCountForGeneral = dc.Articles.GetArticlesCount("general");

// get published articles for first page and then also for the general category
var firstPagePublishedArticles = dc.Articles.GetArticles(1);
var firstPagePublishedArticlesForGeneral = dc.Articles.GetArticles("general", 1);

// get published articles count and then for the general category
var articlesPublishedCount = dc.Articles.GetArticlesCount();
var articlesPublishedCountForGeneral = dc.Articles.GetArticlesCount("general");
```

Category Extension Methods Queries

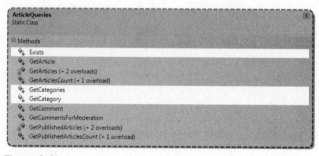

Figure 6-3b

```
TheBeerHouseDataContext dc = new TheBeerHouseDataContext();

// get single category
var article = dc.Articles.GetCategory(1);

// get all categories
var allCategories = dc.Categories.GetCategories();

// check to see if a category exists
bool categoryExists = dc.Categories.Exists(1);
```

Comment Extension Methods Queries

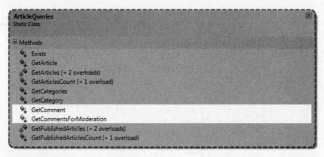

Figure 6-3c

```
TheBeerHouseDataContext dc = new TheBeerHouseDataContext();

// get first page of comments for moderation
var comments = dc.Comments.GetCommentsForModeration(1);

// get single comment
var comment = dc.Comments.GetComment(1);
```

Defining the Model

The Article, Category, and Comment classes have a series of instance public properties that fully describe a single element. Additionally, there are a number of methods to retrieve a list of instances as just described with the queries. One important aspect of the Getxxx methods is that they use IEnumerable<T> as the return type, where T is Article, Category, or Comment. This list type belongs to the System.Collections.Generic.IEnumerable class, which is a *generic* interface for a collection, provided in the .NET 2.0 Framework. This provides a strongly typed and specialized version of a collection class. Therefore, when you declare

```
IEnumerable<Article> articles = dc.Articles.GetArticles(1);
```

you're creating a collection that can only return and accept objects of the Article type — no casting, boxing, or unboxing are required because the internal type is being set as Article by this code, which instantiates the collection. The built-in collections in previous versions of .NET had to store everything as type System.Object, which required casting because they didn't hold objects of a known type.

> Generics are one of the best features in version 2.0 and we strongly recommend that you study this subject by reading articles on the MSDN website or Wrox's *Professional C# 2005* (ISBN 0-7645-7534-1).

The structure of the three main classes — Article, Category, and Comment — is very similar. Therefore, we'll only present the Article class in detail here, and just highlight the unique aspects of the others.

The Article Model Class

Some of the public properties of the `Article` class are just wrappers for the underlying database fields, but others return calculated values. These calculated properties can be derived from other columns in your `Article` entity object. Luckily the LINQ entities are created as a `partial class`, which means that you can add additional properties and methods in a different source file so you don't have to inherit and extend or modify the automatically generated code. We have created the classes shown in Figure 6-4 to help make our lives that much easier.

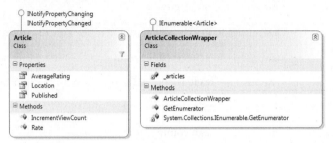

Figure 6-4

The `Article` class will get three additional properties, `AverageRating`, `Location`, and `Published`, which don't appear in the database, and two additional methods, `IncrementViewCount` and `Rate`. Also, we have created an object called `ArticleCollectionWrapper`, which exposes `IEnumerable<Article>`, which will handle the serving of each article to only the users who are allowed to see them.

The following table lists all the properties.

Properties	Description
ArticleID	Article's ID
AddedDate	Date/time the article was created
AddedBy	Name of the author
CategoryID	Parent category ID
CategoryTitle	Parent category title
Category	Reference to the article's parent Category object
Title	Title
Path	Path for the friendly URL
Abstract	Abstract (short description)
Body	Body

Properties	Description
Country	Country where the event described in the article will take place
State	State, region, or province where the event will take place
City	City where the event will take place
Location	Calculated read-only property that returns the full location of the event in the form: country, state, city
ReleaseDate	Date/time the article will be publicly readable by users
ExpireDate	Date/time the article will be retired and no longer readable by users
Approved	Whether the article is approved, or is waiting for approval
Listed	Whether the article is listed in the pages that list public articles
CommentsEnabled	Whether users can comment on this article
OnlyForMembers	Whether the article can only be read by registered and authenticated users, or by everyone
ViewCount	Number of times the article has been read
Votes	Number of votes received by the article
TotalRating	Total rating received by the article, that is, the sum of all votes
AverageRating	Average rating (as a double value), calculated as TotalRating/Votes
Published	Calculated value indicating whether the article is published (meaning the article is approved, and the current date is between the ReleaseDate and the ExpireDate)
Comments	List of comments submitted by users

The methods listed in the following table are instance methods.

Instance Method	Description
IncrementViewCount	Increment the ViewCount of the current article by one
Rate	Rate the current article; the rating value is passed as a parameter

Besides these instance members, several static methods allow the caller to retrieve a list of articles or a single article, or counts. Because they are static, they don't use any instance properties, and they get all the data they need as input parameters. These are all extension methods for Table<Article>, which is a queryable interface provided by LINQ.

Extension Methods	Description
GetArticles GetPublishedArticles	Returns a list of Article instances, and has two overloads to retrieve the list of articles (to retrieve all articles for a page, and optionally articles from a specific category) *Note:* articles retrieved from the `GetPublishedArticles` only allow articles that are approved and fall within the Release-Expires time frame.
GetArticleCount GetPublishedArticleCount	There are two overloads of this method that return the number of articles given no constraints (all articles), or optionally for a specific category *Note:* articles retrieved from the `GetPublishedArticleCount` only counts articles that are approved and fall within the Release-Expires time frame.
GetArticle	Returns an Article instance that fully describes the article identified by the input ID

LINQ uses the *lazy load* pattern, which means data is loaded only when requested and not when the object instance is queried. There are quite a few variations on this pattern, and you should refer to a patterns book for complete coverage of the subject. For the `Article` class, you don't need the list of comments or the article's body unless you're inside the specific article page that shows all details of the article. In the page that lists the available articles, you don't need those details, so you won't waste time retrieving them from the database. The `Article` class has a `Category` property that returns a full `Category` object with all the parent category's details. That object isn't retrieved when the `Article` object is created, but rather when that property is actually read. Also, once requested, you'll fetch the data and store it locally in case it is requested again from the same object instance. The implementation presented later in this chapter is very simple, but it can dramatically improve the performance of the application.

The `GetArticles` and `GetPublishedArticles` overloads take parameters to specify the index of the page to retrieve.

The Category Class

This class has instance properties that fully describe a category of articles. We won't describe all of them here because they are pretty similar to the corresponding methods of the `Article` class. They're actually a little simpler because you don't need multiple overloads to support pagination and other filters.

The Comment Class

The `Comment` class uses the lazy load pattern to load all details of a comment and any properties, such as the parent article, as needed. Another property it exposes is `EncodedBody`, which returns the same text returned by the `Body` property, but first performs HTML encoding on it. This protects you against so-called *script-injection* and *cross-site scripting* attacks. As a very simple example, consider a page on which you allow users to anonymously post a comment. If you don't validate the input, they may write something like the following:

```
<script>document.location = 'http://www.usersite.com';</script>
```

This text is sent to the server and you save it into the database. Later, when you have to show the comments, you would retrieve the original comment text and send to the browser as is. However, when you output the preceding text, it won't be considered as text by the browser, but rather as a JavaScript routine that redirects the user to another website, hijacking the user away from your website! And this was just a basic attack — more complex scripts could be used to steal users' cookies, which could include authentication tickets and personal data, with potentially grave consequences. For your protection, ASP.NET automatically validates the user input sent to the server during a post back, and checks whether it matches a pattern of suspicious text. However, in that case it raises an exception and shows an error page. You should consider the case where a legitimate user tries to insert some simple HTML just to format the text, or maybe hasn't really typed HTML but only a < character. In that case, you don't want to show an error page, you only need to ensure that the HTML code isn't displayed in a browser (because you don't want users to put links or images on your site, or text with a font so big that it creates a mess with your layout). To do so you can disable ASP.NET's input validation (only for those pages on which the user is actually expected to insert text, not for all pages!), and save the text into the database, but only show it on the page after HTML encoding, as follows:

```
&lt;script&gt; document.location = 'http://www.usersite.com'; &lt;/script&gt;
```

This way, text inserted by the user is actually shown on the page, instead of being considered HTML. The link will show as a link but it will not be a clickable link, and no JavaScript can be run this way. The `EncodedBody` property returns the HTML-encoded text, but it can't completely replace the `Body` property, because the original comment text is still required in certain situations — for example, in the administration pages where you show the text in a textbox, and allow the administrator to edit it.

> Scripting-based attacks must not be taken lightly, and you should ensure that your site is not vulnerable. One good reference on the web is `http://en.wikipedia.org/wiki/Cross-site_scripting`, but you can easily find many others. Try searching for XSS using your favorite search engine.

Sorting Comments

You will not implement sorting features for the categories and the articles. This is because categories will always be sorted by importance (the `Importance` field) and then by name, whereas articles will always be sorted by release date, from the newest to the oldest, which is the right kind of sorting for these features. However, comments should be sorted in two different ways according to the situation:

❑ From the oldest to the newest when they are listed on the user page, under the article itself, so that users will read them in chronological order so they can follow a discussion made up of questions and answers between the readers and the article's author, or between different readers.

❑ From the newest to the oldest in the administration page, so that the administration finds the new comments at the top of the list, and in the first page (remember that comments support pagination) so they can be immediately read, edited, and, if necessary, deleted if found offensive.

If you were to make a stored procedure that supports pagination of comments, it would become more complex than it needs to be. The alternative is to dynamically build the SQL SELECT statements, but then you lose the advantages of stored procedures. We came to the following compromise: you can use the stored procedure to retrieve all the article's comments (instead of a stored procedure that uses pagination), and it can be sorted from the newest to the oldest, and you can invert the order on the client by reordering the collection programmatically. We came to this conclusion by considering that the pagination would only be used on the administration pages, a single article will not have more than a few dozen short comments, and it's acceptable to retrieve all of them together when the article must be displayed. You could have sorted the comments from the oldest to the newest directly from a LINQ query, but we prefer to get it directly from the Article object in order to make it consistent with the other LINQ queries that use pagination.

The IQueryable<T> generic interface class has an OrderBy and OrderByDescending extension method that takes a functional expression as an input, and returns a typed collection of items with the specified sort order. In the Solution section you will see how simple it is to implement this technique to obtain a flexible and dynamic sorting mechanism. You should always take advantage of functionality built into the framework!

Designing the View

The design of the ASP.NET MVC view pages in this module is not particularly special, so there's not much to discuss. You have a set of pages, some for the administrators and some for the end users, which allow you to manage articles, and navigate through categories and read articles, respectively. The most important consideration for the view section, or UI, is the approach used to integrate the specific view pages into the rest of the site. You've already seen from previous chapters, and probably from reading done on your own, that this is very straightforward and naturally done in the ASP.NET framework, thanks to master pages. The MVC Framework handles master pages the same way as standard ASP.NET WebForms so all of your previous master pages that you have done for projects should work with very little tweaking. The following is a list of views and their related URL routes, which you will code later:

❑ **Index.aspx:** This lists the current articles with support for viewing by specific categories and the support for pagination.

> ❑ home
>
> ❑ articles/page{page}
>
> ❑ articles/categories/{category}
>
> ❑ articles/categories/{category}/page{page}

> *Adding* ?type=atom *to any of the preceding URL routes will not return HTML, but rather the XML, of the Atom Syndication feed for whatever articles would normally be rendered as HTML on the screen for that request. This is done by changing the* ViewEngine *from the standard* ViewPage *output to a custom syndication output. You will be doing this by implementing your own* ViewEngine *that monitors the URL for* ?type=atom *and renders the output accordingly from the* ViewData.

❑ **CategoryIndex.aspx:** This lists the available categories.

> ❑ articles/categories

❑ **ViewArticle.aspx:** This is used for viewing the article and adding comments to the article.

> ❑ articles/{id}/{*path}

❑ **ManageArticles.aspx:** This lists the current articles with support for pagination and links for editing or removing an article.

   ❑ `admin/articles`

   ❑ `admin/articles/page{page}`

❑ **ManageCategories.aspx:** This lists the available categories and links for editing or removing a category.

   ❑ `admin/articles/categories`

❑ **ManageComments.aspx:** This page displays the comments in descending order from most recent to least recent. It allows for the deleting of comments.

   ❑ `admin/articles/comments`

   ❑ `admin/articles/comments/page{page}`

❑ **CreateArticle.aspx:** This page allows you to create or edit an existing article.

   ❑ `admin/articles/create`

   ❑ `admin/articles/edit/{articleId}`

❑ **CreateCategory.aspx:** This page allows you to create or edit an existing category.

   ❑ `admin/articles/categories/create`

   ❑ `admin/articles/categories/edit/{categoryId}`

❑ **RemoveArticle.aspx:** This page asks you if you want to remove the article before it removes the article from the database.

   ❑ `admin/articles/remove/{articleId}`

❑ **RemoveCategory.aspx:** This page asks if you want to remove the category before it removes the category from the database.

   ❑ `admin/articles/categories/remove/{categoryId}`

Writing Articles with a WYSIWYG Text Editor

The first and most important challenge you face is that the site must be easily updatable by the client, without requiring help from any technical support people. Some regular employees working in the pub must be able to write and publish new articles, and make them look good by applying various formatting, colors, pictures, tables, and so on. All this must be possible without knowing any HTML, of course! This problem can be solved by using a WYSIWYG (the acronym for "what you see is what you get") text editor. These editors enable users to write and format text, and to insert graphical elements, much like a typical word processor (which most people are familiar with), and the content is saved in HTML format that can be later shown on the end-user page "as is." Various editors are available, some commercial and some free. Among the different options we picked the TinyMCE (`http://tinymce.moxiecode.com/`), which is developed and maintained by MoxieCode Systems, mainly because it is free to use, and it is compatible with all the major Internet browsers, including IE 6.0+, Firefox 2.0+, Safari 2.0+, and Opera 8.0+. You have to host these JavaScript files on your own server, but the files are small and take up a minimal amount of space. Figure 6-5 shows a screenshot of an online demo from the editor's website.

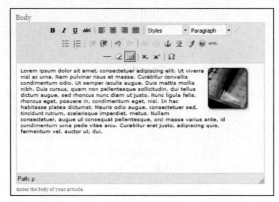

Figure 6-5

The editor is even localizable (language packs for many languages are already provided), and its user interface can be greatly customized, so you can easily decide what toolbars and what command buttons (and thus what formatting and functions) you want to make available to users.

Including Images in the Article

The editors must be able to include images in an article, or publish in a photo gallery, and include documents, screen savers, or other goodies that they want to distribute to their end users. An administrator of a site would be able to use an FTP program to upload files, but an editor typically does not have the expertise, or the credentials, needed to access the remote server and its file system. An online file manager might be very helpful in this situation. In the first edition of this book, an entire chapter was devoted to showing you how to build a full-featured online file manager that would enable users to browse and remove folders and files, upload new files, download, rename, copy, and delete existing files, and even edit the content of text files. However, this would be overkill in most situations, because the administrator is the only one who needs to have full control over the files and folders and structure of the site, and the administrator will presumably use an FTP client for this purpose.

The editors and contributors only need the capability to insert images that will be shown as part of the article. With all the great web services that have come out in the past couple of years, it has made it easier to cross-integrate websites and focus your application on accomplishing goals instead of reinventing the wheel. This is why you are going to forget about the hassles that come along with hosting images and making sure you have enough bandwidth to provide high-quality images to your users and take full advantage of Flickr (http://www.flickr.com/). Your goal is to create a high-quality application to manage a beer pub; Flickr's job is to create a high-quality application for hosting and delivery of images to include in articles.

Article Item View User Control

You will need a way to quickly add a defined reusable article format (with title, author, abstract, and a few more details) to any page for each article shown on that page. It's not enough to have entirely new articles; you also need to show them on existing pages so users will know about them! You'll need to show the list on the Index.aspx page for end users and on the ManageArticles.aspx page for administrators. If you have a good understanding of user controls, you may have already guessed that a user control is the best solution for this because it enables you to encapsulate this functionality into a single code unit (the .ascx file plus the .cs code-behind file), which enables you to write the code once and then reuse the user control on any page using one line of code. This user control will be named `ArticleItem.ascx`. This is also going to be done for the `Category` and `Comment`, which will be named `CategoryItem.ascx` and `CommentItem.ascx`, respectively.

Producing and Consuming Atom Feeds

You've already learned from the Introduction that you're going to implement a mechanism to provide the headlines of the site's new content as an Atom feed, so that external (online or desktop-based) aggregator programs can easily consume them, adding new content to their own site, but also driving new traffic to your site. This process of providing a list of articles via Atom is called *syndication*. The XML format used to contain Atom content is simple in nature, and here's an example of one Atom feed that contains an entry for two different articles:

```
<feed xmlns="http://www.w3.org/2005/Atom">
    <title type="text">Ideas</title>
    <subtitle type="text">Feed of ideas from IdeaPipe.</subtitle>
    <id>http://www.ideapipe.com/</id>
    <updated>2008-06-14T17:43:58-04:00</updated>
    <link rel="self" href="http://www.ideapipe.com/?type=atom" />
    <link rel="alternate" href="http://www.ideapipe.com/" />
    <link rel="first" href="http://www.ideapipe.com/?type=atom" />
    <link rel="next" href="http://www.ideapipe.com/page/2?type=atom" />
    <link rel="last" href="http://www.ideapipe.com/page/5?type=atom" />
    <entry>
        <id>http://www.ideapipe.com/ideas/40/...</id>
        <title type="text">I want to subscribe to IdeaPipe ...</title>
        <published>2008-05-28T20:41:19-04:00</published>
        <updated>2008-06-14T21:43:58Z</updated>
        <author>
            <name>nick</name>
            <uri>http://www.ideapipe.com/users/nick</uri>
        </author>
        <link rel="alternate" href="http://www.ideapipe.com/ideas/40/..." />
        <category term="Misc" />
        <content type="xhtml"><![CDATA[
            ...
        ]]></content>
    </entry>
    <entry>
        <id>http://www.ideapipe.com/ideas/32/...</id>
        <title type="text">IdeaPipe should support OpenID</title>
        <published>2008-05-15T22:13:42-04:00</published>
        <updated>2008-06-14T21:43:58Z</updated>
        <author>
            <name>nick</name>
            <uri>http://www.ideapipe.com/users/nick</uri>
        </author>
        <link rel="alternate" href="http://www.ideapipe.com/ideas/32/..." />
        <category term="Misc" />
        <content type="xhtml"><![CDATA[
            ...
        ]]></content>
    </entry>
</feed>
```

As you can see, the root node indicates that you are using Atom. It contains several required sub-elements, `<title>`, `<id>`, and `<updated>`, whose names are self-descriptive. There can also be a number of optional elements, including many forms of `<link>`, `<subtitle>`, and others defined by imported namespaces. After all of those feed-level elements is the list of actual posts/articles/stories, represented by `<entry>` subsections. An entry can have a number of optional elements, a few of which (`title`, `author`, `content`, `link`, `category`, and `publish`) are shown in the preceding example. For details on the full list of elements supported by RSS you can check this link, `http://tools.ietf.org/html/rfc4287`, or just search for "Atom Specification."

One important thing to remember is that this must be a valid XML format, and therefore you cannot insert HTML into the `<content>` element to provide a visual "look and feel" unless you ensure that it meets XML standards (XHTML is the name for tighter HTML that meets XML requirements). You must ensure that the HTML is well formed, so that all tags have their closing part (`<p>` has its `</p>`) or are self-closing (as in `<img.../>`), among other rules. If you don't want the hassle of making sure the HTML is XML-compliant, you can just wrap the text into a CDATA section, which can include any kind of data. Another small detail to observe is that the value for the `published` elements must be in the exact format "yyyy-MM-ddTHH:mm:ssZZZ," as in "1980-03-14T22:13:42-04:00." If you aren't careful to meet these Atom requirements, your users may get errors when they try to view your Atom feed. Some feed readers are more tolerant than others so it's not sufficient to make sure it works in your own feed reader — you need to meet the Atom specifications. This is why it is always a good idea to run your feed through validation that is provided by many websites; our favorite is `http://feedvalidator.org/`.

As mentioned before, the feed will be generated on any page that displays a list of articles by adding `?type=atom` to the query URL. This will be done by defining a custom `ViewEngine` that will handle the output anytime the query string `type` shows up in the URL. Coincidently you are also going to use this same custom `ViewEngine` to provide JSON and XML output serialization for your AJAX calls. So the custom `ViewEngine` will be very versatile in providing non-HTML output of your requests in the true spirit of a RESTful web experience.

You want to make your Atom feeds as discoverable as possible so you are going to add the following to the header of each page that displays a list of articles:

```
<link rel="alternate" type="application/atom+xml" title="IdeaPipe Feed"
href="http://www.ideapipe.com/?type=atom" />
```

This is a special META tag that is used to tell the web browser that your site has a feed and that it should alert the users to the fact that they can subscribe to the website.

Designing the Controller

The controller is probably one of the easiest things to design because all of the hard work was already done when you designed the model and the view. So you need to create an appropriate set of controller actions to map your model to your view. The following table lists these controller actions that are needed to support the functionality that we are designing. The first column of the table below lists the action method name, the second column lists the role that will have access to the action, and the last column lists the parameters for that action.

Action Method	Security	Parameters
Index	--	string category, int page
CategoryIndex	--	--
ViewArticle	--	int id, string path
RateArticle	--	int articleId, int rating
ManageArticles	Editor	int page
ManageCategories	Editor	--
ManageComments	Editor	--
CreateArticle	Contributor	int? categoryId, string title, string summary, string body, string country, string state, string city, DateTime? releaseDate, DateTime? expireDate, bool? approved, bool? listed, bool? commentsEnabled, bool? onlyForMembers
EditArticle	Editor	int articleId, int? categoryId, string title, string summary, string body, string country, string state, string city, DateTime? releaseDate, DateTime? expireDate, bool? approved, bool? listed, bool? commentsEnabled, bool? onlyForMembers
RemoveArticle	Editor	int articleId, string remove
CreateCategory	Editor	string title, int? importance, string imageUrl, string description
EditCategory	Editor	int categoryId, string title, int? importance, string imageUrl, string description
RemoveCategory	Editor	int categoryId, int? newCategoryId, string remove
CreateComment	--	int articleId, string name, string email, string body
EditComment	Editor	int commentId, string name, string body
RemoveComment	Editor	int commented

The Need for Security

The articles manager module is basically divided into two parts:

- ❏ The administration section allows the webmaster, or another designated individual, to add, edit, or delete the categories, publish articles, and moderate comments.

- ❏ The end-user section has pages to navigate through the categories, read the articles, rate an article or post feedback, and display the headlines on the homepage.

Obviously, different pages may have different security constraints: an administration page should not be accessible by end users, and an article with the `OnlyForMembers` flag set should not be accessible by the anonymous users (users who aren't logged in). In the previous chapter, you developed a very flexible module that allows you to administer the registered users, read or edit their profiles, and dynamically assign them to certain roles. For the articles manager module you will need the following roles:

- ❏ **Administrators and Editors:** These users have full control over the articles system. They can add, edit, or delete categories, approve and publish articles, and moderate comments. Only a very few people should belong to this role. (Note that administrators also have full rights over the user management system, and all the other modules of the site, so it might be wise if only a single individual has this role.)

- ❏ **Contributors:** These users can submit their own articles, but they won't be published until an administrator or editor approves them. You could give this permission to many users if you want to gather as much content as possible, or just to a selected group of people otherwise.

Enforcing these security rules is a simple task, as you learned in the previous chapter. In many cases it suffices to protect an entire page against unauthorized users by adding an `AuthenticationAttribute` to the action method on the controller. Settings done in a configuration file are called *declarative coding*, and settings made with C# source code are called *imperative coding*. I favor declarative coding whenever possible because it's easier to modify without recompiling source code, but in some more complex cases you have to perform some security checks directly from C# code. An example is the `ArticleCollectionWrapper`, which is used to control whether a certain article can be seen by the current user of the site.

Solution

In coding the solution, you'll follow the same path you used in the Design section: from database table creation, to the implementation of security, to the model, view, and controller.

Implementing the Configuration Module

The `ArticlesElement` class is implemented in the `~/Configuration/ArticlesElement.cs` file. It descends from `System.Configuration.ConfigurationElement` and implements the properties that map the attributes of the `<articles>` element under the `<theBeerHouse>` custom section in the web.

`config` file. The properties, listed and described in the Design section, are bound to the XML settings by means of the `ConfigurationProperty` attribute. Here's its code:

```
public class ArticlesElement : ConfigurationElement
{
    [ConfigurationProperty("pageSize", DefaultValue = "10")]
    public int PageSize
    {
        get { return (int)base["pageSize"]; }
        set { base["pageSize"] = value; }
    }
}
```

You added `Articles` as a new property to `TheBeerHouseSection` created in Chapter 4, now modified as shown here:

```
public class TheBeerHouseSection : ConfigurationSection
{
    [ConfigurationProperty("contactForm", IsRequired=true)]
    public ContactFormElement ContactForm
    {
        get { return (ContactFormElement) base["contactForm"]; }
    }

    [ConfigurationProperty("articles", IsRequired = true)]
    public ArticlesElement Articles
    {
        get { return (ArticlesElement)base["articles"]; }
    }
}
```

The updated `<theBeerHouse>` section in `web.config` looks like this:

```
<theBeerHouse>
        <contactForm mailTo="support@managedfusion.com" />
        <articles pageSize="10" />
</theBeerHouse>
```

To read the settings from code you can do it this way: `Configuration.TheBeerHouseSection.Current.Articles.PageSize`.

Implementing the Model

Creating the database tables is straightforward with Microsoft SQL Server Management Studio Express, so we won't cover it here. You can refer to the tables in the Design section to see all the settings for each field. In the downloadable code file for this book, you will find the complete database ready to go. Instead, here you'll create relationships between the tables.

Relationships Between the Tables

You create a new diagram from the Object Explorer: drill down from Server Connections to your database and then Database Diagrams. Right-click Database Diagrams and select Add New Diagram. By following the wizard, you can add the `Categories`, `Articles`, and `Comments` tables to your diagram. As soon as the three tables are added to the underlying window, Server Explorer should recognize a relationship between `Categories` and `Articles`, and between `Articles` and `Comments`, and automatically create a parent-child relationship between them over the correct fields. However, if it does not, click the `Articles`' `CategoryID` field and drag and drop the icons that appear over the `Categories` table. Once you release the button, a dialog with the relationship's properties appears, and you can ensure that the foreign key is the `Articles`' `CategoryID` field, and the primary key is `Categories`' `CategoryID`. Once the connection is set up, you also have to ensure that, when a category record is deleted or updated, the action is cascaded to the child table too. To do this, select the connection, go to the Properties window (or press F4), and set the Delete Rule and Update Rule settings to Cascade, as shown in Figure 6-6.

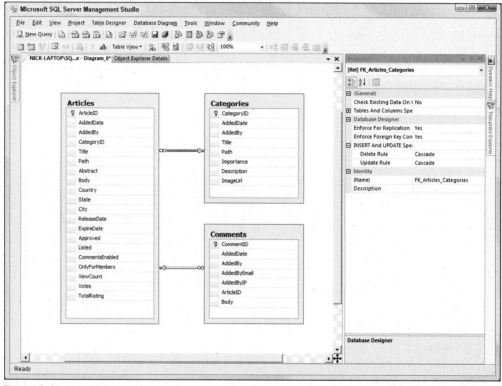

Figure 6-6

The `Update Rule = Cascade` option ensures that if you change the `CategoryID` primary key in the `Categories` table, this change is propagated to the foreign keys in the `Articles` table. The primary key should never be changed, because it is an identity and the administration pages won't allow you to change it. The `Delete Rule = Cascade` option ensures that if you delete a category, all the related articles are deleted as well. This means you won't have to delete the child articles from the stored procedure that deletes a category because they will be deleted automatically. This option is very important and must be checked, because if you forget it you'll end up with a database filled with unreachable articles because the parent category no longer exists!

Now you have to create a relationship between `Comments` and `Articles`, based on the `ArticleID` field of both tables. As before, click the `Comments`' `ArticleID` field, drag and drop the icon over the `Articles` table, and complete the Properties dialog. When you're done with the diagram, go up to the tab, right-click it, and save the diagram. Make sure you let it change your tables as specified in the diagram.

Create the LINQ Schema

You are first going to create the LINQ to SQL schema for your three tables: `Articles`, `Categories`, and `Comments`. You do this in the Server Explorer: drill down from Data Connections to your database (if you don't see your database you can add it as a new Data Connection), and then Tables. From here you select `Articles`, `Categories`, and `Comments` from the Server Explorer and drag them to your `TheBeerHouse.dbml` window (if you don't have a LINQ to SQL file yet, right-click in your ~/Models folder and add it). See Figure 6-7 for an example of how your LINQ to SQL file should look.

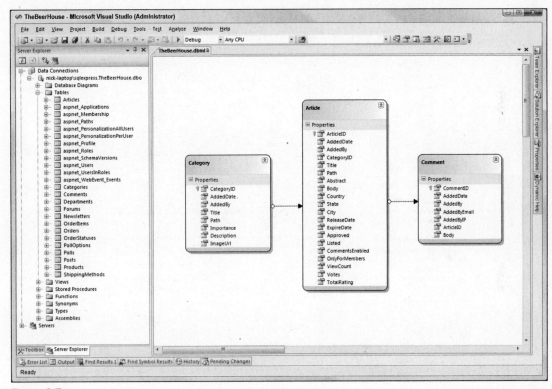

Figure 6-7

This file should represent the same schema and relationships seen in your database diagram.

The LINQ to SQL DBML

LINQ to SQL has a special Database Meta Language (DBML) for generating the objects needed in order to interact with the database. This special meta language is used to specify columns for records, and relationships between tables. This is all done in a defined XML structure based off of the `http://schemas.microsoft.com/linqtosql/dbml/2007` namespace. If we were to try and compare DBML to another similar meta language we would probably say that the XSLT DataSet, which you have probably created many times over for various applications you have worked on, is very similar in what the meta language is supposed to accomplish when creating a database interface for your compiled code.

We believe it is important to understand what is going on with all the aspects of your code even if it is generated automatically for you. So we have included copies of the DBML for `Articles`, `Categories`, and `Comments` so that you can review the structure of the meta language.

Please note that we have removed the `DbType` attribute from all of the columns to save room. The `DbType` attribute contains a string reference to the actual SQL datatype for that column in the table. This really has no use for queries except as a reference point to the actual database representation of that column.

The Articles Table

```
<Table Name="dbo.Articles" Member="Articles">
    <Type Name="Article">
        <Column Name="ArticleID" Type="System.Int32" IsPrimaryKey="true"
IsDbGenerated="true" CanBeNull="false" />
        <Column Name="AddedDate" Type="System.DateTime" CanBeNull="false" />
        <Column Name="AddedBy" Type="System.String" CanBeNull="false" />
        <Column Name="CategoryID" Type="System.Int32" CanBeNull="false" />
        <Column Name="Title" Type="System.String" " CanBeNull="false" />
        <Column Name="Path" Type="System.String" CanBeNull="false" />
        <Column Name="Abstract" Type="System.String" CanBeNull="true" />
        <Column Name="Body" Type="System.String" CanBeNull="false"
UpdateCheck="Never" IsDelayLoaded="true" />
        <Column Name="Country" Type="System.String" CanBeNull="true" />
        <Column Name="State" Type="System.String" CanBeNull="true" />
        <Column Name="City" Type="System.String" CanBeNull="true" />
        <Column Name="ReleaseDate" Type="System.DateTime" CanBeNull="false" />
        <Column Name="ExpireDate" Type="System.DateTime" CanBeNull="true" />
        <Column Name="Approved" Type="System.Boolean" CanBeNull="false" />
        <Column Name="Listed" Type="System.Boolean" CanBeNull="false" />
        <Column Name="CommentsEnabled" Type="System.Boolean" CanBeNull="false" />
        <Column Name="OnlyForMembers" Type="System.Boolean" CanBeNull="false" />
        <Column Name="ViewCount" Type="System.Int32" CanBeNull="false" />
        <Column Name="Votes" Type="System.Int32" CanBeNull="false" />
        <Column Name="TotalRating" Type="System.Int32" CanBeNull="false" />
        <Association Name="Article_Comment" Member="Comments" OtherKey="ArticleID"
Type="Comment" />
        <Association Name="Category_Article" Member="Category" ThisKey="CategoryID"
Type="Category" IsForeignKey="true" DeleteRule="CASCADE" DeleteOnNull="true" />
    </Type>
</Table>
```

One thing that you may want to check out are the `<association />` tags at the bottom of the `<table />`. These tags tell the generator of the table classes how your code could interrelate, and some precautions it needs to take in order to provide the code in the manner that it was meant to be retrieved from the database. For instance, in the `Category_Article` association, you can tell that this `Articles` table is a child of a `Category` class because the `IsForeignKey` is set to `true`. You also know that, if the `Category` is ever deleted, the delete action should cascade to all the children `Articles`.

The `IsDelayLoaded` on the `Body` column is interesting because this attribute is used to implement the lazy load pattern discussed earlier in this chapter. This will provide a mechanism to only pull the body text when it is necessary.

The Categories Table

```
<Table Name="dbo.Categories" Member="Categories">
    <Type Name="Category">
        <Column Name="CategoryID" Type="System.Int32" IsPrimaryKey="true"
IsDbGenerated="true" CanBeNull="false" />
        <Column Name="AddedDate" Type="System.DateTime" CanBeNull="false" />
        <Column Name="AddedBy" Type="System.String" CanBeNull="false" />
        <Column Name="Title" Type="System.String" CanBeNull="false" />
        <Column Name="Path" Type="System.String" CanBeNull="true" />
        <Column Name="Importance" Type="System.Int32" CanBeNull="false" />
        <Column Name="Description" Type="System.String" CanBeNull="true" />
        <Column Name="ImageUrl" Type="System.String" CanBeNull="true" />
        <Association Name="Category_Article" Member="Articles"
OtherKey="CategoryID" Type="Article" />
    </Type>
</Table>
```

The Comments Table

```
<Table Name="dbo.Comments" Member="Comments">
    <Type Name="Comment">
        <Column Name="CommentID" Type="System.Int32" IsPrimaryKey="true"
IsDbGenerated="true" CanBeNull="false" />
        <Column Name="AddedDate" Type="System.DateTime" CanBeNull="false" />
        <Column Name="AddedBy" Type="System.String" CanBeNull="false" />
        <Column Name="AddedByEmail" Type="System.String" CanBeNull="false" />
        <Column Name="AddedByIP" Type="System.String" CanBeNull="false" />
        <Column Name="ArticleID" Type="System.Int32" CanBeNull="false" />
        <Column Name="Body" Type="System.String" CanBeNull="false"
UpdateCheck="Never" />
        <Association Name="Article_Comment" Member="Article" ThisKey="ArticleID"
Type="Article" IsForeignKey="true" DeleteRule="CASCADE" DeleteOnNull="true" />
    </Type>
</Table>
```

The LINQ to SQL Classes

The classes generated from the preceding DBML are very lightweight and inherit directly from `System.Object`, which is one of the reasons to choose LINQ to SQL over some other database object mapping solutions. The `DataContext`, which maintains the connection to the database and the changed columns for the table records that need to be updated in the database, are monitored through a couple of events. These events are added to each record through a couple of interfaces designed to monitor for changes in a class; these interfaces are `INotifyPropertyChanging` and `INotifyPropertyChanged`. These interfaces add the following events to each table record:

```
public event PropertyChangingEventHandler PropertyChanging;
public event PropertyChangedEventHandler PropertyChanged;
```

The `DataContext` monitors these events automatically to watch for changes in the object. If it sees that a value has changed, it makes a record of that change, then when `SubmitChanges` is called from the `DataContext` all the changes that it has recorded for the object are compiled together and submitted back to the database. This process has the benefit of updating only the columns that have been changed, which has been a traditional problem with most object relational database models, in that it was either an all or nothing approach.

We are only going to provide the code for the `Article` object, and skip the `Category` and `Comment` objects, because they all look the same:

```
[Table(Name="dbo.Articles")]
public partial class Article : INotifyPropertyChanging, INotifyPropertyChanged
{

    private static PropertyChangingEventArgs emptyChangingEventArgs = new PropertyC
hangingEventArgs(String.Empty);

    private int _ArticleID;

    private System.DateTime _AddedDate;

    private string _AddedBy;

    private int _CategoryID;

    // same stuff repeated for all the other columns

    private EntitySet<Comment> _Comments;

    private EntityRef<Category> _Category;

#region Extensibility Method Definitions
partial void OnLoaded();
partial void OnValidate(System.Data.Linq.ChangeAction action);
partial void OnCreated();
partial void OnArticleIDChanging(int value);
partial void OnArticleIDChanged();
partial void OnAddedDateChanging(System.DateTime value);
partial void OnAddedDateChanged();
partial void OnAddedByChanging(string value);
partial void OnAddedByChanged();
partial void OnCategoryIDChanging(int value);
partial void OnCategoryIDChanged();

// same stuff repeated for all the other columns
#endregion

    public Article()
    {
        this._Comments = new EntitySet<Comment>(new Action<Comment>(this.attach_
Comments), new Action<Comment>(this.detach_Comments));
        this._Category = default(EntityRef<Category>);
        OnCreated();
    }

    [Column(Storage="_ArticleID", AutoSync=AutoSync.OnInsert, DbType="Int NOT NULL
IDENTITY", IsPrimaryKey=true, IsDbGenerated=true)]
    public int ArticleID
    {
        get
        {
            return this._ArticleID;
        }
```

```
        set
        {
            if ((this._ArticleID != value))
            {
                this.OnArticleIDChanging(value);
                this.SendPropertyChanging();
                this._ArticleID = value;
                this.SendPropertyChanged("ArticleID");
                this.OnArticleIDChanged();
            }
        }
    }

    [Column(Storage="_AddedDate", DbType="DateTime NOT NULL")]
    public System.DateTime AddedDate
    {
        get
        {
            return this._AddedDate;
        }
        set
        {
            if ((this._AddedDate != value))
            {
                this.OnAddedDateChanging(value);
                this.SendPropertyChanging();
                this._AddedDate = value;
                this.SendPropertyChanged("AddedDate");
                this.OnAddedDateChanged();
            }
        }
    }

    [Column(Storage="_AddedBy", DbType="NVarChar(256) NOT NULL", CanBeNull=false)]
    public string AddedBy
    {
        get
        {
            return this._AddedBy;
        }
        set
        {
            if ((this._AddedBy != value))
            {
                this.OnAddedByChanging(value);
                this.SendPropertyChanging();
                this._AddedBy = value;
                this.SendPropertyChanged("AddedBy");
                this.OnAddedByChanged();
            }
        }
    }

    [Column(Storage="_CategoryID", DbType="Int NOT NULL")]
    public int CategoryID
    {
```

```
        get
        {
            return this._CategoryID;
        }
        set
        {
            if ((this._CategoryID != value))
            {
                if (this._Category.HasLoadedOrAssignedValue)
                {
                    throw new
System.Data.Linq.ForeignKeyReferenceAlreadyHasValueException();
                }
                this.OnCategoryIDChanging(value);
                this.SendPropertyChanging();
                this._CategoryID = value;
                this.SendPropertyChanged("CategoryID");
                this.OnCategoryIDChanged();
            }
        }
    }

    // skip to the Body property because it implements lazy loading

    [Column(Storage="_Body", DbType="NText NOT NULL", CanBeNull=false,
UpdateCheck=UpdateCheck.Never)]
    public string Body
    {
        get
        {
            return this._Body.Value;
        }
        set
        {
            if ((this._Body.Value != value))
            {
                this.OnBodyChanging(value);
                this.SendPropertyChanging();
                this._Body.Value = value;
                this.SendPropertyChanged("Body");
                this.OnBodyChanged();
            }
        }
    }

    // same stuff repeated for all the other columns

    [Association(Name="Article_Comment", Storage="_Comments", OtherKey="ArticleID")]
    public EntitySet<Comment> Comments
    {
        get
        {
            return this._Comments;
        }
```

```
        set
        {
            this._Comments.Assign(value);
        }
    }

    [Association(Name="Category_Article", Storage="_Category",
ThisKey="CategoryID", IsForeignKey=true, DeleteOnNull=true, DeleteRule="CASCADE")]
    public Category Category
    {
        get
        {
            return this._Category.Entity;
        }
        set
        {
            Category previousValue = this._Category.Entity;
            if (((previousValue != value)
                || (this._Category.HasLoadedOrAssignedValue == false)))
            {
                this.SendPropertyChanging();
                if ((previousValue != null))
                {
                    this._Category.Entity = null;
                    previousValue.Articles.Remove(this);
                }
                this._Category.Entity = value;
                if ((value != null))
                {
                    value.Articles.Add(this);
                    this._CategoryID = value.CategoryID;
                }
                else
                {
                    this._CategoryID = default(int);
                }
                this.SendPropertyChanged("Category");
            }
        }
    }

    public event PropertyChangingEventHandler PropertyChanging;

    public event PropertyChangedEventHandler PropertyChanged;

    protected virtual void SendPropertyChanging()
    {
        if ((this.PropertyChanging != null))
        {
            this.PropertyChanging(this, emptyChangingEventArgs);
        }
    }

    protected virtual void SendPropertyChanged(String propertyName)
```

```
        {
            if ((this.PropertyChanged != null))
            {
                this.PropertyChanged(this, new PropertyChangedEventArgs(propertyName));
            }
        }

        private void attach_Comments(Comment entity)
        {
            this.SendPropertyChanging();
            entity.Article = this;
        }

        private void detach_Comments(Comment entity)
        {
            this.SendPropertyChanging();
            entity.Article = null;
        }
    }
```

We want to point out that the Body property is interesting because it implements the lazy load pattern discussed earlier in this chapter. The Body field is retrieved when the value of the Body property is requested by another class. Therefore, if the Body property is not accessed, this data will not be read from the database. Once it is requested and fetched, it will be held in memory in case it's requested again.

Some things to note are that the class is marked as a partial class; this means that you can add additional functionality to this object without modifying the generated code. You actually use this later on in the chapter to extend the Article and Comment objects to provide additional properties and methods that are specific to your business rules.

There is also the ability for you to define specific methods that allow you to control how the object is created, loaded, validated, and the value before and after changing a column. You can accomplish this by overloading the partial methods provided in the object.

Partial methods are a new feature in C# 3.0. These partial methods work very similar to how virtual methods work, except that if you do not define the partial method it just doesn't exist and any call made to it is simply ignored by the runtime; if you had a virtual method, you would have to define a base action for what it is supposed to do when it is called. A couple of examples of partial methods from the preceding code are:

```
partial void OnLoaded();
partial void OnValidate(System.Data.Linq.ChangeAction action);
partial void OnCreated();
partial void OnArticleIDChanging(int value);
partial void OnArticleIDChanged();
```

There is a partial method created for each column in the database on the Changing and Changed events. These events are called automatically from the property created for the column.

Extending the LINQ Objects

You need to extend the LINQ objects created from the DBML in order to add some necessary business functionality that your module will require. These extended properties and methods will save you from writing the code into your controller actions and views.

As you have done before, in the previous section for the `TheBeerHouse.dbml` file, you are going to add your partial classes that extend the functionality that you require in the `~/Models` folder.

The Article Class

This class is implemented in the `~/Models/Article.cs` file. The class starts with a `partial class` to declare that this class is part of another class and should be considered part of the same object when the compiler stitches everything together:

```
public partial class Article
{
    // code from the rest of the section goes here
}
```

The preceding object will include everything you previously reviewed in the "The LINQ to SQL Classes" section, as well as everything you are going to define in the rest of this section. At compile time they will be combined together to be one object called `Article` and referenced under the `TheBeerHouse.Models` namespace.

There are also a few calculated and read-only properties. The `Location` property returns a string with the full location of an event described in the article, consisting of the city, state/province, and country. Remember that the `state` and `city` fields could include more names separated by a semicolon (typically variations and abbreviations of the state name, such as "New York," "NY," "NewYork," and so on). For this reason the fields are split, and the first token is used. Here's the complete code:

```
public string Location
{
    get
    {
        string city = this.City ?? String.Empty;
        string state = this.State ?? String.Empty;
        string country = this.Country ?? String.Empty;

        string location = city.Split(';')[0];
        if (state.Length > 0)
        {
            if (location.Length > 0)
                location += ", ";
            location += state.Split(';')[0];
        }
        if (country.Length > 0)
        {
            if (location.Length > 0)
                location += ", ";
```

```
                    location += country.Split(';')[0];
            }
            return location;
        }
    }
```

The `AverageRating`-calculated read-only property checks whether the total number of votes is `0`; the division is not done in that case to avoid a `DivideByZeroException`, and `0` is returned instead:

```
public double AverageRating
{
    get
    {
        if (this.Votes >= 1)
            return ((double)this.TotalRating / (double)this.Votes);
        else
            return 0D;
    }
}
```

The other calculated read-only property is `Published`, which returns `true` if the article is approved and the current date is between the specified `ReleaseDate` and `ExpireDate`:

```
public bool Published
{
    get
    {
        return (this.Approved
            && this.ReleaseDate <= DateTime.Now
            && this.ExpireDate > DateTime.Now);
    }
}
```

In addition to properties, the `Article` class also has a number of instance methods such as `Rate` and `IncrementViewCount` that delegate the work away from the controller or the view so that the business rules are strongly defined and don't have to be tested in each case where they are used. Here are a few examples:

```
public bool IncrementViewCount()
{
    ViewCount++;
}

public bool Rate(int rating)
{
    Votes++;
    TotalRating += rating;
}
```

The Comment Class

This class, like the article class, is implemented in the ~/Models/Comment.cs file. The class starts with a partial class to declare that this class is part of another, in the same way that the article class does:

```
public partial class Article
{
    // code from the rest of the section goes here
}
```

The preceding object will include everything you previously reviewed in the "The LINQ to SQL Classes" section, as well as everything you are going to define in the rest of this section. At compile time they will be combined together to be one object called Comment and referenced under the TheBeerHouse.Models namespace.

The EncodedBody property is the only thing you need to add to the Comment class. As we talked about before with cross-site scripting attacks in the Design section, it is important to encode HTML that comes from sources that are not known to you. That is why we are going to offer this additional property that will encode the Body property of the comment:

```
public string EncodedBody
{
    get { return HttpContext.Current.Server.HtmlEncode(Body); }
}
```

It doesn't take much code to secure your site from cross-site scripting, just a little forethought on how you are going to access your data and the sources it comes from. Also, by adding this as a property, you don't have to worry about forgetting to encode the body in one of the multiple places you are going to use the Comment object in your site.

Creating a Page-able Collection

Many variables go into creating a web page that can be paged through by your users. There are also two main kinds of paging. The first kind is a linear type of paging that allows the user to only skip forward or back by one page; this type you will find in many common blogging platforms, because it is simple and easy to understand and also keeps the browsing of objects in the intended order that the programmer designed. The second kind is a non-linear type of paging that allows the user to jump around in no specific order (think of Google's paging mechanism), where you can jump from page one to page five and then back to three if you wanted to. This second kind is usually used to show the breadth of your content and to provide paging flexibility to your users. You are going to use the second non-linear type, so that you can show the breadth of your content, and so that you can program the more complex types together.

Much like everything else we find it easier to create a class to handle the variables that are going to be required for the operation. You are going to need a little information to accomplish your non-linear paging, which includes total page count and current page index. You calculate the total page count and current page index from a total count of records in the database for the query, the count requested, and the start index of the record. Your goals are to ultimately return this paging information along with the query to your view so that the correct paging can be rendered.

The class you are going to create is going to be called `Pagination<T>`; it will contain all the necessary variables we talked about for paging as properties of the class. These properties are `TotalCount`, `RequestedCount`, `StartIndex`, `PageIndex`, and `PageCount`. `PageIndex` and `PageCount` will be calculated properties based off of the first three properties. And because one of your requirements is to return the query, you may as well inherit your paging object from `IEnumerable<T>` so that it can be used as a natural collection by the controller or view. You will create this class alongside your other models, as `~/Models/Pagination.cs`, because it will be returned as part of the model queries you are going to define later on.

```csharp
public class Pagination<T> : IEnumerable<T>, IPagination
{
    private IEnumerable<T> _collection;

    public Pagination(
        IEnumerable<T> collection,
        int startIndex,
        int requestedCount,
        int totalCount
    ) {
        _collection = collection;
        StartIndex = startIndex;
        PageSize = requestedCount;
        TotalCount = totalCount;
    }

    public virtual int TotalCount { get; protected internal set; }

    public virtual int PageSize { get; protected internal set; }

    public virtual int StartIndex { get; protected internal set; }

    public virtual int PageNumber
    {
        get { return (StartIndex / PageSize) + 1; }
    }

    public virtual int PageCount
    {
        get {
            return (int)Math.Ceiling(
                    (double)TotalCount / (double)RequestedCount);
        }
    }

    #region IEnumerable<T> Members

    public IEnumerator<T> GetEnumerator()
    {
        return _collection.GetEnumerator();
    }

    #endregion
```

```
#region IEnumerable Members

System.Collections.IEnumerator System.Collections.IEnumerable.GetEnumerator()
{
    return this.GetEnumerator();
}

#endregion
}
```

> You may notice that we used a shortened declaration for properties that you might not
> be used to:
>
> ```
> { get; private set; }
> ```
>
> This syntax is a new feature in C# 3.0; when the compiler sees this kind of property defi-
> nition it automatically creates all the private members, setters, and getters that are nec-
> essary to set and retrieve this property. We find ourselves using this syntax more and
> more to replace all the old setup code that we used to have to do to create simple objects
> such as Pagination<T> above. It has saved us a ton of time when creating simple
> objects for passing data, and we just thought we would share this knowledge with you.

Securing the Viewing of the Articles

There is one last thing you want to do before you move on to writing the queries to grab the information
from the database. This one last thing is a collection wrapper for verifying that the current user is authorized to view the Article. This wrapper will act as a final transparent buffer before being sent to the view
for rendering to HTML. It is a very valuable pattern to use when you have to deal with a complex authorization model that cannot be easily queried from the database. This is not the case with your current authorization model where you just have to verify the user is authenticated in order to view the articles marked
OnlyForMembers. However, we want to make you aware of the power of a transparent collection enumerator, and it may become useful if you decide to expand upon The Beer House application.

> The main driver of the transparent collection enumerator is the yield keyword in C#.
> This keyword is only allowed to be used in an iterator block (a method that returns
> IEnumerable) to provide a value to the enumerator object or to signal the end of itera-
> tion. It takes one of the following forms according to MSDN:
>
> ```
> yield return <expression>;
> yield break;
> ```

The Transparent Collection Enumerator

The transparent collection enumerator is going to be called ArticleCollectionWrapper and
it will be alongside the other models at ~/Models/ArticleCollectionWrapper.cs. The
ArticleCollectionWrapper will implement the typed interface IEnumerable<Article>, which is
defined as a collection of Article objects.

```
internal class ArticleCollectionWrapper : IEnumerable<Article>
{
    private IEnumerable<Article> _articles;
```

```csharp
public ArticleCollectionWrapper(IEnumerable<Article> articles)
{
    _articles = articles;
}

#region IEnumerable<Article> Members

public IEnumerator<Article> GetEnumerator()
{
    bool isAuthenticated = false;
    HttpContext context = HttpContext.Current;

    if (context.User != null && context.User.Identity != null)
        isAuthenticated = context.User.Identity.IsAuthenticated;

    foreach (Article article in _articles)
    {
        // make sure that only members see articles marked as members only
        if (article.OnlyForMembers && !isAuthenticated)
            continue;

        yield return article;
    }
}

#endregion

#region IEnumerable Members

System.Collections.IEnumerator System.Collections.IEnumerable.GetEnumerator()
{
    return this.GetEnumerator();
}

#endregion
}
```

We have highlighted the important part of the code. You will notice that, if the current article is OnlyForMembers and the current user is not authenticated, the object doesn't get yield returned and is skipped for the next article.

We also created ArticleCollectionWrapper as an internal class because it is transparent outside of the assembly and really should be transparent outside of the TheBeerHouse.Model namespace. When this wrapper is returned from the queries it will be returned as IEnumerator<Article>, because IEnumerator<Article> is the interface this class is implemented from. The lack of referencing this wrapper directly is what makes it and its operation transparent to the consumer of this collection.

Create the LINQ Queries

The next step to setting up the model is to create the queries that will be called from the controller. As we talked about in the Design section, the queries are going to be extension methods for the LINQ tables. This is going to provide the ability to call these methods naturally from the code as if they were always designed into the class.

We always like to make our classes really descriptive so there is no question what they do, so you are going to name the class that is going to contain all the article queries `ArticleQueries.cs`. This class must be a static class, which means that only static methods and properties may be used in the class and the class cannot be instantiated.

The GetPublishedArticles Query

The following code returns a queryable instance that follows the rules already defined in the Design section for what a published article should be and the parameters it must follow:

```
private static IQueryable<Article> GetPublishedArticles(
TheBeerHouseDataContext dataContext,
string category
) {
    // make sure that category evaluates to null incase it is an empty string
    category = String.IsNullOrEmpty(category) ? null : category;

    bool isAuthenticated = false;
    HttpContext context = HttpContext.Current;

    if (context.User != null && context.User.Identity != null)
        isAuthenticated = context.User.Identity.IsAuthenticated;

    var query =
        from a in dataContext.Articles
        orderby a.ReleaseDate descending
        where
            a.Approved == true
            && a.Listed == true
            && (isAuthenticated == true || a.OnlyForMembers == false)
            && a.ReleaseDate <= DateTime.Now
            && (a.ExpireDate == null || a.ExpireDate > DateTime.Now)
            && (category == null || a.Category.Path == category)
        select a;

    return query;
}
```

The query is pretty simple, but a couple of details are worth taking note of when creating LINQ queries.

> LINQ uses a SQL-like syntax, but if you have ever worked with SQL you will notice right away that the select statement is last instead of first. There are reasons for this that we won't get into, but a quick search on the Internet for "LINQ Design" will yield the answers. In addition, instead of the typical SQL syntax like AND and OR, the equivalent C# syntax is used.

This next query has the same name and is an overload for the preceding query. The purpose of this query is to retrieve the articles for a certain category and page.

```
public static Pagination<Article> GetPublishedArticles(
this Table<Article> source,
string category,
int page
) {
    int count = Configuration.TheBeerHouseSection.Current.Articles.PageSize;
    int index = (page - 1) * count;

    return new Pagination<Article>(
        new ArticleCollectionWrapper(
        GetPublishedArticles(
                source.Context as TheBeerHouseDataContext,
                category
        ).Skip(index).Take(count)),
        index,
        count,
        GetPublishedArticlesCount(source, category)
    );
}
```

You may have noticed the `Skip` and `Take` methods that are used after calling the `GetPublishedArticles` method. This is how paging is done in LINQ; you skip to a certain spot in the query and then take as many items as you need returned. Pretty cool and simple, huh!

Also we just wanted to point out the use of the `this` keyword in the method parameters for defining an extension method again. This method will extend the `Table<Article>` class, so anytime this class is defined you will be able to use `GetPublishedArticles`.

The final query for getting published articles will be for retrieving all articles from all categories for a certain page. This method will most likely be used for the homepage where there is no category set to be retrieved.

```
public static Pagination<Article> GetPublishedArticles(
this Table<Article> source,
int page
) {
    int count = Configuration.TheBeerHouseSection.Current.Articles.PageSize;
    int index = (page - 1) * count;

    return new Pagination<Article>(
        new ArticleCollectionWrapper(
        GetPublishedArticles(
                source.Context as TheBeerHouseDataContext,
                null
        ).Skip(index).Take(count)),
        index,
        count,
        GetPublishedArticlesCount(source)
    );
}
```

The GetPublishedArticlesCount Query

This method returns the count of published articles, which is necessary for paging. This is necessary because, if you don't know how many articles there are in the database, you have no idea how many pages you need to display at the bottom of the page.

This first method returns the number of published articles for a certain category:

```
public static int GetPublishedArticlesCount(
this Table<Article> source,
string category
) {
    return GetPublishedArticles(
            source.Context as TheBeerHouseDataContext,
            category
        )
        .Count();
}
```

This next method returns the number of published articles in the entire database:

```
public static int GetPublishedArticlesCount(this Table<Article> source)
{
    return GetPublishedArticles(
            source.Context as TheBeerHouseDataContext,
            null
        )
        .Count();
}
```

The GetArticles Query

This code returns a queryable instance of the articles ordered by the release date in descending order and is meant to be used in the ManageArticles.aspx view:

```
private static IQueryable<Article> GetArticles(
TheBeerHouseDataContext dataContext,
string category
) {
    // make sure that category always evaluates to null incase it is an empty string
    category = String.IsNullOrEmpty(category) ? null : category;

    var query =
        from a in dataContext.Articles
        orderby a.ReleaseDate descending
        where category == null || a.Category.Path == category
        select a;

    return query;
}
```

This next query has the same name and is an overload for the preceding query. The purpose of this query is to retrieve the articles for a certain category and page.

```
public static Pagination<Article> GetArticles(
this Table<Article> source,
string category,
int page
) {
    int count = Configuration.TheBeerHouseSection.Current.Articles.PageSize;
    int index = (page - 1) * count;

    return new Pagination<Article>(
        new ArticleCollectionWrapper(
        GetArticles(
                source.Context as TheBeerHouseDataContext,
                category
        ).Skip(index).Take(count)),
        index,
        count,
        GetArticlesCount(source, category)
    );
}
```

The final query has the purpose of getting all articles for all categories, for a certain page. This query will be used for the ManageArticles.aspx view, where you have a long list of articles that you need to page through.

```
public static Pagination<Article> GetPublishedArticles(
this Table<Article> source,
int page
) {
    int count = Configuration.TheBeerHouseSection.Current.Articles.PageSize;
    int index = (page - 1) * count;

    return new Pagination<Article>(
        new ArticleCollectionWrapper(
        GetArticles(
                source.Context as TheBeerHouseDataContext,
                null
        ).Skip(index).Take(count)),
        index,
        count,
        GetArticlesCount(source)
    );
}
```

The GetArticlesCount Query

This method returns the count of articles, which is necessary for paging in the administration view.

This first method returns the number of articles for a certain category:

```
public static int GetArticlesCount(this Table<Article> source, string category)
{
    return GetArticles(
            source.Context as TheBeerHouseDataContext,
            category
        )
        .Count();
}
```

This next method returns the number of articles in the entire database:

```
public static int GetArticlesCount(this Table<Article> source)
{
    return GetArticles(
            source.Context as TheBeerHouseDataContext,
            null
        )
        .Count();
}
```

The GetArticle Query

This query gets a single article from the database for the requested identity. This will help you get specific articles for when you want to view the entire article with comments, or edit the article.

```
public static Article GetArticle(this Table<Article> source, int id)
{
    return source.SingleOrDefault(a => a.ArticleID == id);
}
```

This query uses the `SingleOrDefault` method, which you have not seen yet; this method returns either an instance of `Article` if it was found or a `null` value. There is also a method called simply `Single`; the reason you don't want to use this method to query the database is that if the query cannot find a record in the database it will throw an exception by design instead of returning a `null` value. In our opinion it is much more efficient to check to see if the return value is `null` than to catch an exception; that is why we always use `SingleOrDefault`.

The GetCategories Query

This query is going to give you all the categories in the database sorted first by `Importance` then by `Title`. The purpose of this procedure, even though it returns all the categories, is to abide by your business rules for sorting, so that the rule doesn't have to be done in the controller actions or the views.

```
public static IEnumerable<Category> GetCategories(this Table<Category> source)
{
    return from c in source
        orderby c.Importance, c.Title
        select c;
}
```

The Exists Query

This query tests an `id` to verify that it is a valid category. You are going to use this when you delete a category and need to update all of the articles that are mapped to the deleted category.

```
public static bool Exists(this Table<Category> source, int id)
{
    return source.Count(c => c.CategoryID == id) > 0;
}
```

The GetCategory Query

This query gets a single category from the database for the requested identity. This will help you get specific categories for when you want to edit the category.

```
public static Category GetCategory(this Table<Category> source, int id)
{
    return source.SingleOrDefault(c => c.CategoryID == id);
}
```

The GetCommentsForModeration Query

This query returns the comments for a specific page in descending order from when they were added to the article. This query will be used for administration only.

```
public static Pagination<Comment> GetCommentsForModeration(
this Table<Comment> source,
int page
) {
    int count = Configuration.TheBeerHouseSection.Current.Articles.PageSize;
    int index = (page - 1) * count;

    var query = from c in source
        orderby c.AddedDate descending
        select c;

    return new Pagination<Comment>(
        query.Skip(index).Take(count),
        index,
        count,
        source.Count()
    );
}
```

The GetComment Query

This query gets a single comment from the database for the requested identity. This will help you get specific comments for when you want to edit the comment.

```
public static Comment GetComment(this Table<Comment> source, int id)
{
    return source.SingleOrDefault(c => c.CommentID == id);
}
```

Implementing the Controller

As we talked about in Chapter 2, the controller has its own folder, just like the models and views. You will place your controller with the available actions in `~/Controllers` and call it `ArticleController.cs`. The actions in the controller use the model that you created in the previous section to provide access to the data and to enforce validation rules, check constraints, and provide an object-oriented representation of the data and methods for binding to the views. Thus, the controller serves as a mapping layer that creates a relationship between the models and views.

In this section you are going to create each action method that is needed for your controller. You are going to create two different kinds of action methods; one type is going to be used for creating the user interface and the other is going to be used to create your REST service that your AJAX requests will interface with.

The Index Action

The first action method you'll implement is used to display the published articles. This action takes two parameters, `category` and `page`:

```
public ActionResult Index(string category, int page)
{
    TheBeerHouseDataContext dc = new TheBeerHouseDataContext();
    var viewData = dc.Articles.GetPublishedArticles(category, page);
    var viewCategory = dc.Categories.GetCategory(category);

    ViewData["PageTitle"]
        = (viewCategory != null ? viewCategory.Title : "All") + " Articles";

    return View(viewData);
}
```

Earlier in the Design section of this chapter you defined all the routes that you needed to handle. You will be able to handle the viewing of any of the following routes with this action:

❑   home

❑   articles/page{page}

❑   articles/categories/{category}

❑   articles/categories/{category}/page{page}

The routes, for the actions and controllers, are defined in the `Global.asax` file. This section goes through each of the four routes that you need to create in order to get this action method working with the routes.

home

This route is used to define your homepage. The homepage is a pretty unique circumstance because when you are requesting the root of your domain there are no rules to pull out of the URL, so you need to define all these rules for yourself. This part is a little more challenging than the other routes, because you need to make a conscious decision about what data is going to display on your homepage. In this case it is relatively trivial because you already know you need to display a list of published articles that span across all categories and you probably want to start on page one.

```
routes.MapRoute(
    "ArticleIndex",
    "home",
    new {
        controller = "Article",
        action = "Index",
        category = (string)null,
        page = 1
    }
);
```

You will notice in this code sample that you have created an anonymous type for the defaults, and for each of the properties for this anonymous type, except `controller` and `action` because they are an exact match to the parameters in your `Index` action method.

> Anonymous types are new to C# 3.0 and are distinctive because they have no type; that is why they are called anonymous. They often look like this:
>
> ```
> new { ... }
> ```
>
> If you want to learn more about anonymous types and how they work, simply search for "anonymous types C#" in your favorite search engine.

The anonymous type defined in your route is parsed and turned into your `Defaults` collection for this route. The properties have an exact match to the parameters. This is not by accident; the MVC framework tries to match the action method's parameters from the URL. If it doesn't find the parameter name in the URL, it moves on and tries `Request.Params` (this includes the Query String and Form values); if that fails the framework finally looks for the parameter in the `Defaults` property of the route that you provided to it with the anonymous type.

articles/categories/{category}/page{page}

This route is used to get published articles for a specific `category` and `page`:

```
routes.MapRoute(
    "ArticleCategoryViewIndexPaged",
    "articles/categories/{category}/page{page}",
    new {
        controller = "Article",
        action = "Index",
        category = (string)null,
        page = (int?)null
    },
    new { category = "[a-zA-Z0-9\\-]+", page = "[0-9]+" }
);
```

In this route you set the defaults to `null`, so that if the URL route pattern you provided fails, it will be skipped and not considered as a valid source for your action method.

We want to point out something new that you haven't seen yet. In this route right below the `Defaults` definition there is another anonymous type that takes regular expressions; this is the `Constraints` collection and it is used to validate the rules in the URL route pattern. In this case you define that `category` can only contain characters A–Z (upper- or lowercase), numbers 0–9, and hyphens, and you also define that the `page` must be a number with at least one character. These constraints are very useful to prevent invalid data, such as letters in your page variables, from getting passed to your action method.

articles/categories/{category}

This route is used to get published articles for a specific `category` for the first page:

```
routes.MapRoute(
    "ArticleCategoryViewIndex",
    "articles/categories/{category}",
    new {
        controller = "Article",
        action = "Index",
        category = (string)null,
        page = 1
    },
    new { category = "[a-zA-Z0-9\\-]+", page = "[0-9]+" }
);
```

articles/page{page}

This route is used to get published articles for a specific `page` for all categories:

```
routes.MapRoute(
    "ArticleIndexPaged",
    "articles/page{page}",
    new {
        controller = "Article",
        action = "Index",
        category = (string)null,
        page = (int?)null
    },
    new { page = "[0-9]+" }
);
```

The CategoryIndex Action

The next action you need to create for your controller is one to display a list of your categories so that the users of the site can easily navigate between categories:

```
public ActionResult CategoryIndex()
{
    TheBeerHouseDataContext dc = new TheBeerHouseDataContext();
    var viewData = dc.Categories.GetCategories();

    ViewData["PageTitle"] = "All Categories";

    return View(viewData);
}
```

The route for this action is:

❑   `articles/categories`

articles/categories

This route is used to map your `CategoryIndex` action to this URL, so it is very basic and doesn't involve any variables:

```
routes.MapRoute(
    "ArticleCategoryIndex",
    "articles/categories",
    new { controller = "Article", action = "CategoryIndex" },
    new { category = "[a-zA-Z0-9\\-]+", page = "[0-9]+" }
);
```

The ViewArticle Action

This action is an important one; it is the one that is used to retrieve the necessary information for viewing the article, namely the `Article` object that you created in the model. This action is a little more complicated than the previous two that you have already done, so let's break this down into individual parts to make it a little simpler to understand.

```
public ActionResult ViewArticle(int id, string path)
{
    TheBeerHouseDataContext dc = new TheBeerHouseDataContext();
    Article viewData = dc.Articles.GetArticle(id);
```

In this part you are retrieving the `Article` for the `id` that is passed in as a parameter of the action.

```
    // throw a 404 Not Found if the requested article is not in the database
    if (viewData == null)
        throw new HttpException(404, "The article could not be found.");
```

In this part you are returning a `404 Not Found` to the client if the article was not found (that is, returned a `null` from the `GetArticle` method). The reason you want to do this is because the action should simulate a live file system on a web server where there is either a file that is returned to a browser or a response of `404 Not Found` if the file doesn't exist or, in this case, the requested article doesn't exist.

```
    // SEO: redirect to the correct location if the path is not
    if (!String.Equals(path, viewData.Path, StringComparison.OrdinalIgnoreCase))
        return this.RedirectToAction(301, "View",
            new { id = viewData.ArticleID, path = viewData.Path });
```

This part is insurance that your path is being displayed correctly in the URL. This is very important for SEO reasons, because the URL has a high ranking with all of the major search engines, so you want to make sure the keywords displayed in the URL are the correct ones. You should also be concerned about duplicate content — because you don't really use the path for anything, you could have multiple different paths all pointing the same `id`; we explain this later. Another more serious reason is the potential for allowing link bombs or Google bombs if you don't have this step.

A link bomb is an attempt to influence the ranking of a page for certain keywords within the search engine. This is not the same link bombing that was available back in 2003 (to read about this, search for "Google Bomb" on Wikipedia); this new link bombing relies on a lack of thoroughness caused by developers not checking their inputs. You could fall victim to this if you didn't check the path. So if you didn't check the `path` and just left it as is you would be allowing outsiders to define what keywords are placed in your URL for a given article. For example, the article URL `/articles/14/my-awesome-beer-recipe` would resolve to your article as you defined it, but so would `/articles/14/you-stole-this-recipe`, `/articles/14/go-to-our-competitor`, and `/articles/14/our-beer-is-watered-down`. The reason this would work with this action method is because all of your important information is derived from the `id`, 14 in this case, and nothing at all is derived from the `path`. So, if you never checked the `path`, all that your competitors would have to do is start linking to these bogus URLs, and because they resolved to your actual article a search engine would put them into its index and allow them to be searched. This is not something that you want your pub to be known for.

This is why it is important to be a defensive programmer and close the loop for potential future problems. In the preceding code you close this problem by checking that the `path` is equal to the path in your article and if it is not you do a `301 Permanent Redirect` to the actual URL. By doing this the search engines will interpret these bogus URLs as being wrong and they won't index the bogus URL.

```
// make sure the article is only viewed by members with permissions
if (viewData.OnlyForMembers
    && HttpContext.User != null
    && HttpContext.User.Identity != null
    && !HttpContext.User.Identity.IsAuthenticated)
    throw new HttpException(401,
        "The articles is only viewable for members.");
```

You must check that the articles that are only viewable for members are upheld. Even though you don't display the article link in the published articles page if the user is not logged in, you still need to make sure that an unauthorized user doesn't try to directly access the article. You do this by checking the `IsAuthenticated` property of the user's `Identity`, if the `OnlyForMembers` property is true. If the article is only for members and the user isn't authenticated, you need to send a `401 Unauthorized` response back to the client browser, which tells the browser that it is not authorized to view this URL and should redirect the user to the login page.

```
// update the view count
try
{
    viewData.ViewCount++;
    dc.SubmitChanges();
}
catch { /* ignore all conflicts because this action isn't critical */ }

ViewData["PageTitle"] = viewData.Title;

return View(viewData);
}
```

This last part updates the `ViewCount` of the article by one and updates the database. After this is completed it sends the articles to the View for rendering.

This action only has one route:

❑   articles/{id}/{*path}

articles/{id}/{*path}

This route is used to display your full article.

```
routes.MapRoute(
    "ArticleView",
    "articles/{id}/{*path}",
    new {
        controller = "Article",
        action = "ViewArticle",
        id = (string)null,
        path = (string)null
    },
    new { id = "[0-9]+", path = "[a-zA-Z0-9\\-]*" }
);
```

This route contains a new type of rule that you haven't seen before. This new rule is the wildcard route rule that is defined by putting a "*" before your rule. This allows anything to be put into this rule, including route delimiters (such as "/"), and is very useful for situations where you need delimiters to be passed in through the rule. In your case you don't care what is passed into the path because you are going to check the validity and reroute if wrong anyway, so you want to make sure anything beyond the id that is passed in is accepted and validated against the constraint even if it contains a delimiter.

You are also going to validate that the id is a number by setting a constraint for it. This is very important because the id shares the same spot with some of your other routes, such as /articles/**categories**… and /articles/**page**…. You validate the id so it creates a false-positive for "categories" or "page*n*" for your ViewArticle action.

The RateArticle Action

The next action method that you are going to create is a service that will not be directly accessed. Its job is to accept a POST via client-side AJAX and return an object serialized as JSON, so that the client-side AJAX can adjust the rating of the article accordingly.

```
[ServiceOnly, HttpPostOnly]
public ActionResult RateArticle(int articleId, int rating)
{
    TheBeerHouseDataContext dc = new TheBeerHouseDataContext();
    Article viewData = dc.Articles.GetArticle(articleId);

    try
    {
        viewData.Rate(rating);
        dc.SubmitChanges();
    }
    catch { /* ignore all conflicts because this action isn't critical */ }

    return View(new {
```

```
          articleId = articleId,
          averageRating = viewData.AverageRating
     });
  }
```

This action includes two attributes that you haven't seen before, `ServiceOnly` and `HttpPostOnly`; we have created these specifically for this book to allow you to limit the type of actions that can be performed on an action method. In this case only HTTP POSTs can be made to this action, so no HTTP GETs are allowed, and this action method can only render service data, such as JSON and XML, which means no HTML rendering is allowed. In a later chapter of the book, we go into detail on how to create your own action method attribute, so that you can create your own filters.

The route for this action uses the standard `{controller}/{action}` route, so requests to this action method can be accessed through:

❑   `article/ratearticle`

The ManageArticle Action

This action is used to display a list of articles, which can be managed, in descending order of when they are supposed to be released:

```
[Authorize(Role = "Editor")]
public ActionResult ManageArticles(int page)
{
    TheBeerHouseDataContext dc = new TheBeerHouseDataContext();
    var viewData = dc.Articles.GetArticles(null, page);

    ViewData["PageTitle"] = "Manage Articles";

    return View(viewData);
}
```

This action is relatively simple; however, you should take note of the `Authorize` attribute. This is a special attribute that we developed to authorize access to the action method based on the `IPrincipal` interface that is set through `Context.User`. In this case only users with the role of Editor are allowed to access this controller action; all others are redirected to the login page.

The `ManageCategories` and `ManageComments` action methods are just as simple to implement, so we are going to skip showing them because there is nothing new or remarkable about the way they are coded.

These actions have the following routes, respectively, for `ManageArticle`, `ManageCategories`, and `ManageComments`:

❑   `admin/articles`

❑   `admin/articles/page{page}`

❑   `admin/articles/categories`

❑   `admin/articles/comments`

❑   `admin/articles/comments/page{page}`

admin/articles

This route is used to show all the articles that can be edited on page one:

```
routes.MapRoute(
    "ArticleManage",
    "admin/articles",
    new { controller = "Article", action = "ManageArticles", page = 1 }
);
```

admin/articles/page{page}

This route is used to show all the articles that can be edited on a certain page:

```
routes.MapRoute(
    "ArticleManagePaged",
    "admin/articles/page{page}",
    new { controller = "Article", action = "ManageArticles", page = (int?)null },
    new { page = "[0-9]+" }
);
```

admin/articles/categories

This route is used to show all the categories that can be edited:

```
routes.MapRoute(
    "ArticleCategoryManage",
    "admin/articles/categories",
    new { controller = "Article", action = "ManageCategories" }
);
```

admin/articles/comments

This route is used to show all the comments that can be edited on page one:

```
routes.MapRoute(
    "ArticleCommentManage",
    "admin/articles/comments",
    new { controller = "Article", action = "ManageComments", page = 1 }
);
```

admin/articles/comments/page{page}

This route is used to show all the comments that can be edited on a certain page:

```
routes.MapRoute(
    "ArticleCommentManagePaged",
    "admin/articles/comments/page{page}",
    new { controller = "Article", action = "ManageComments", page = (int?)null },
    new { page = "[0-9]+" }
);
```

The CreateArticle and EditArticle Actions

The next actions you have to create are ones that will create and edit an article. We have combined these actions together in the same section because they contain mostly the same code concepts.

The CreateArticle Action

Just like we did for the `ViewArticle` action, we are going to break down the code so you can go through it piece by piece and make sense of what is going on.

```
[Authorize(Role = "Contributor")]
```

The first thing that you have for your `CreateArticle` is the `Authorize` attribute that tells the controller action that only users who are Contributors are allowed to proceed, which is one of the rules decided on in the Design section.

```
public ActionResult CreateArticle(
    int? categoryId, string title, string summary, string body, string country,
    string state, string city, DateTime? releaseDate, DateTime? expireDate,
    bool? approved, bool? listed, bool? commentsEnabled, bool? onlyForMembers)
{
    TheBeerHouseDataContext dc = new TheBeerHouseDataContext();
    var categories = dc.Categories.GetCategories();
```

The next thing you need to do is set up all the data that is going to be passed to your view. This includes any collections or data that you may need to pull from the database. You need to do this in the controller action because, unlike ASP.NET WebForms, where page rendering logic and data access were intertwined, the MVC views can only render the data that is provided from the actions. This is why you are pulling the categories that are available for the articles to be attached to at the top of the method.

```
if (categoryId.HasValue
    && !String.IsNullOrEmpty(title)
    && !String.IsNullOrEmpty(body))
```

This is where the logic can get complicated for the actions. This is what we like to call a validation block, which is basically just an `if` statement that prevents the action from trying to submit the article to the database if it doesn't pass some very basic validation. In this case your validation is that `categoryId`, `title`, and `body` are minimum requirements to try and submit the article to your database. Using this method, in combination with some client-side validation that we discuss when you create your view, will provide enough protection for most applications that need some kind of form in MVC.

```
    {
        try
        {
            Article article = new Article {
                CategoryID = categoryId.Value,
                Title = title,
                Path = title.ToUrlFormat(),
                Abstract = summary,
                Body = body,
                Country = country,
                State = state,
                City = city,
```

```
                ReleaseDate = releaseDate ?? DateTime.Today,
                ExpireDate = expireDate,
                Approved = approved ?? false,
                Listed = listed ?? false,
                CommentsEnabled = commentsEnabled ?? false,
                OnlyForMembers = onlyForMembers ?? false,
                AddedBy = User.Identity.Name,
                AddedDate = DateTime.Now
            };

        dc.Articles.InsertOnSubmit(article);
        dc.SubmitChanges();
```

If you make it into the preceding code it means that the parameters have passed the validation and the minimum requirements to submit the article to the database have been verified. Your next logical step is to create an instance of the article and set all the values from the actions parameters and the default values if necessary when a non-required parameter is `null`.

> The easiest way to set defaults is by using the `??` operator in C#, which returns the left-hand operand if it is not null, or else it returns the right operand. For example, another way of writing
>
> ```
> int? x = null;
> int y = x ?? -1;
> ```
>
> is probably a more common way that you have seen in C# or other languages:
>
> ```
> int? x = null;
> int y = (x != null ? x : -1);
> ```

After the `article` is created with all the properties set, you then need to save it to the database. You do this by using the `InsertOnSubmit` and `SubmitChanges` methods of your `DataContext`, which handles all of the SQL that is required to transform your `article` object to an entry in your `Article` table in the database.

```
            TempData["SuccessMessage"] = "Your article has been posted.";
            return RedirectToAction("ViewArticle", new {
                id = article.ArticleID,
                path = article.Path
            });
        }
        catch (Exception exc)
        {
            TempData["ErrorMessage"] = exc.Message;
        }
    }
```

The preceding code sets a message to be displayed to the user indicating that the article was saved successfully to the database, and then a redirect response is sent to the client browser, which will send the user to the article that was just created.

```
    ViewData["categoryId"] = new SelectList(
        categories, "CategoryID", "Title", categoryId);
```

```
ViewData["title"] = title;
ViewData["summary"] = summary;
ViewData["body"] = body;
ViewData["country"] = new SelectList(
    Iso3166CountryCodes.CountryDictionary, "Key", "Value", country ?? "US");
ViewData["state"] = state;
ViewData["city"] = city;
ViewData["releaseDate"] = releaseDate;
ViewData["expireDate"] = expireDate;
ViewData["approved"] = approved;
ViewData["listed"] = listed;
ViewData["commentsEnabled"] = commentsEnabled;
ViewData["onlyForMembers"] = onlyForMembers;
```

In the final part of code of this action, before you send the ViewData to the view, you need to set all the form fields that need a value in the view. This is an important step because, if the parameters are not valid or an error occurs on the submitting of the article to the database, you need to make sure that all the form fields retain their original value, as a convenience to the user of the form.

```
ViewData["PageTitle"] = "Create Article";

return View("CreateArticle");
}
```

The final step of your action method is always the same: send your ViewData to the view. This is slightly different than what you have seen before where you are passing the ViewData into the view that is returned. In this case, because you only have one view that handles both CreateArticle and EditArticle, you need to spell out which view you want the controller to use.

The EditArticle Action

In this section we are going to highlight the parts of the code that are different from what we just went over for CreateArticle:

```
[Authorize(Role = "Editor")]
public ActionResult EditArticle(
    int articleId,
    int? categoryId, string title, string summary, string body, string country,
    string state, string city, DateTime? releaseDate, DateTime? expireDate,
    bool? approved, bool? listed, bool? commentsEnabled, bool? onlyForMembers)
{
    TheBeerHouseDataContext dc = new TheBeerHouseDataContext();
    var categories = dc.Categories.GetCategories();

    if (IsPostBack)
    {
        approved = approved ?? false;
        listed = listed ?? false;
        commentsEnabled = commentsEnabled ?? false;
        onlyForMembers = onlyForMembers ?? false;
    }
```

```
    Article article = dc.Articles.GetArticle(articleId);

    // throw a 404 Not Found if the requested article is not in the database
    if (article == null)
        throw new HttpException(404, "The article could not be found.");

if (categoryId.HasValue
    && !String.IsNullOrEmpty(title)
    && !String.IsNullOrEmpty(body))
{
    try
    {
        article.CategoryID = categoryId.Value;
        article.Title = title;
        article.Abstract = summary;
        article.Body = body;
        article.Country = country;
        article.State = state;
        article.City = city;
        article.ReleaseDate = releaseDate ?? article.ReleaseDate;
        article.ExpireDate = expireDate;
        article.Approved = approved ?? false;
        article.Listed = listed ?? false;
        article.CommentsEnabled = commentsEnabled ?? false;
        article.OnlyForMembers = onlyForMembers ?? false;

        dc.SubmitChanges();

        TempData["SuccessMessage"] = "Your article has been updated.";
    }
    catch (Exception exc)
    {
        TempData["ErrorMessage"] = exc.Message;
    }
}
```

```
ViewData["categoryId"] = new SelectList(
    categories, "CategoryID", "Title", categoryId ?? article.CategoryID);
ViewData["title"] = title ?? article.Title;
ViewData["summary"] = summary ?? article.Abstract;
ViewData["body"] = body ?? article.Body;
ViewData["country"] = new SelectList(
    Iso3166CountryCodes.CountryDictionary, "Key", "Value",
    country ?? article.Country ?? "US");
ViewData["state"] = state ?? article.State;
ViewData["city"] = city ?? article.City;
ViewData["releaseDate"] = releaseDate ?? article.ReleaseDate;
ViewData["expireDate"] = expireDate ?? article.ExpireDate;
ViewData["approved"] = approved ?? article.Approved;
ViewData["listed"] = listed ?? article.Listed;
ViewData["commentsEnabled"] = commentsEnabled ?? article.CommentsEnabled;
ViewData["onlyForMembers"] = onlyForMembers ?? article.OnlyForMembers;
```

```
        ViewData["PageTitle"] = "Edit Article";

        return View("CreateArticle");
    }
```

The major things to take note of for `EditArticle` are the following:

❑   The `Authorize` attribute changed the authorized role from Contributor to Editor.

❑   An `articleId` is passed in from the route as a parameter, which is used to retrieve the original article for editing. Just as before in `ViewArticle` you need to check that a real article was returned, and if one wasn't you return a `404 Not Found` as the response.

❑   The block of code in the `if (IsPostBack)` may look weird to you if you have never had to deal with checkbox inputs in a raw POST back before. The reason this is necessary is because the value of the checkbox must be `true`, so that when the checkbox on the form is selected a true value is posted back to your controller action. However, and this is the key, when the checkbox is not checked, nothing is sent back to the controller action so it sets the boolean value to `null`. If you let this `null` value continue through the code all the way to the bottom where you are setting the form field values, your code would interpret this as a first occurrence and use the default from the article object, so the change wouldn't stick. This is why, when there is a POST back, you need to check all the booleans for a `null` value and set the value to `false` if one is found.

❑   You are also now populating the `ViewData`, to fill in the form fields, with either the new value that is passed in from the parameter or the original value from your `article` object.

These actions have the following routes, respectively, for `CreateArticle` and `EditArticle`:

❑   `admin/articles/create`
❑   `admin/articles/edit/{articleId}`

admin/articles/create

This route is used to create an article:

```
routes.MapRoute(
    "ArticleCreate",
    "admin/articles/create",
    new { controller = "Article", action = "CreateArticle" }
);
```

admin/articles/edit/{articleId}

This route is used to edit an article. It takes one rule, `articleId`, which provides the identity of the article that is being edited:

```
routes.MapRoute(
    "ArticleEdit",
    "admin/articles/edit/{articleId}",
    new { controller = "Article", action = "EditArticle", articleId = (int?)null },
    new { articleId = "[0-9]+" }
);
```

The RemoveArticle Action

The final action you are going to create for article administration is the remove action. This is the action you are going to call when you need to permanently get rid of an article from your database. This action method is mainly only a message pump that queues up the next message in a mini wizard that presents a "yes" or "no" question to the users about their intentions to delete the article in question.

Most of the code for the RemoveArticle action has been discussed previously, so we are only going to highlight the new code that you haven't seen before:

```
[Authorize(Role = "Editor")]
public ActionResult RemoveArticle(int articleId, string remove)
{
    TheBeerHouseDataContext dc = new TheBeerHouseDataContext();
    Article article = dc.Articles.GetArticle(articleId);

    // throw a 404 Not Found if the requested article is not in the database
    if (article == null)
        throw new HttpException(404, "The article could not be found.");

    if (String.Equals(remove, "yes", StringComparison.OrdinalIgnoreCase))
    {
        dc.Articles.DeleteOnSubmit(article);
        dc.SubmitChanges();

        TempData["SuccessMessage"] =
            "The article," + article.Title + ", has been deleted.";

        article = null;
    }
    else if (String.Equals(remove, "no", StringComparison.OrdinalIgnoreCase))
    {
        TempData["InformationMessage"] =
            "The article, " + article.Title + ", has NOT been deleted.";
    }
    else
    {
        TempData["WarningMessage"] =
            "Are you sure you want to delete " + article.Title
            + ". You will not be able to recover this article.";
    }

    ViewData["PageTitle"] = "Remove Article";

    return View(article);
}
```

In the view, to remove the article you are going to have two buttons, which provide a "yes" or "no" response to the RemoveArticle action; these buttons will correlate to whether or not you want to delete the article. If the editor selects "yes" you are going to delete the article from the database, and then respond by sending back a success message. If the editor selects "no" you are going to send back a message informing him that his article has not been deleted. There is also a third state to this that you need to take into account, and that is the state where the user is coming in to the remove article page fresh. This is the state of the action where you need to present your question asking them if they are sure they want to delete this article, and warning them that they will not be able to undo this deletion once it is completed.

This action has the following route:

❑   admin/articles/remove/{articleId}

admin/articles/remove/{articleId}

This route is used to remove an article:

```
routes.MapRoute(
    "ArticleRemove",
    "admin/articles/remove/{articleId}",
    new { controller = "Article",action = "RemoveArticle",articleId = (int?)null },
    new { articleId = "[0-9]+" }
);
```

The CreateCategory and EditCategory Actions

The category actions that you are going to develop for the ArticleController, to create and edit a category, must only be available to an editor, as laid out in the Design section. You are going to use many of the same techniques for CreateCategory and EditCategory that you used in CreateArticle and EditArticle.

The CreateCategory Action

The CreateCategory action is very similar to CreateArticle; you validate the required parameters, insert them in the database if they are valid, and set the view data for the return response:

```
[Authorize(Role = "Editor")]
public ActionResult CreateCategory(
    string title, int? importance, string imageUrl, string description)
{
    if (!String.IsNullOrEmpty(title)
        && !String.IsNullOrEmpty(imageUrl)
        && !String.IsNullOrEmpty(description))
    {
        try
        {
            TheBeerHouseDataContext dc = new TheBeerHouseDataContext();

            Category category = new Category {
                Title = title,
                Importance = importance ?? -1,
                ImageUrl = imageUrl,
                Description = description,
                AddedBy = User.Identity.Name,
                AddedDate = DateTime.Now,
                Path = title.ToUrlFormat()
            };
            dc.Categories.InsertOnSubmit(category);
```

```
            // save changes to database
            dc.SubmitChanges();

            TempData["SuccessMessage"] = "Your category has been created.";
            return RedirectToAction("ManageArticles");
        }
        catch (Exception exc)
        {
            TempData["ErrorMessage"] = exc.Message;
        }
    }

    ViewData["title"] = title;
    ViewData["importance"] = importance;
    ViewData["imageUrl"] = imageUrl;
    ViewData["description"] = description;

    ViewData["PageTitle"] = "Create Category";

    return View("CreateCategory");
}
```

Really the only thing different about this action compared to the `CreateArticle` action is the
fact that, instead of returning the users to the category they just created, you will send them to the
`ManageArticles` action so that they can create an article for the category.

The EditCategory Action

The `EditCategory` action allows the editors to update the selected category:

```
[Authorize(Role = "Editor")]
public ActionResult EditCategory(
    int categoryId, string title, int? importance, string imageUrl,
    string description)
{
    TheBeerHouseDataContext dc = new TheBeerHouseDataContext();
    Category category = dc.Categories.GetCategory(categoryId);

    // throw a 404 Not Found if the requested category is not in the database
    if (category == null)
        throw new HttpException(404, "The category could not be found.");

    if (!String.IsNullOrEmpty(title)
        && !String.IsNullOrEmpty(imageUrl)
        && !String.IsNullOrEmpty(description))
    {
        try
        {
            category.Title = title;
            category.Importance = importance ?? -1;
            category.ImageUrl = imageUrl;
            category.Description = description;
```

```
            // save changes to database
            dc.SubmitChanges();

            TempData["SuccessMessage"] = "Your category has been updated.";
        }
        catch (Exception exc)
        {
            TempData["ErrorMessage"] = exc.Message;
        }
    }

    ViewData["title"] = title ?? category.Title;
    ViewData["importance"] = importance ?? category.Importance;
    ViewData["imageUrl"] = imageUrl ?? category.ImageUrl;
    ViewData["description"] = description ?? category.Description;

    ViewData["PageTitle"] = "Edit Category";

    return View("CreateCategory");
}
```

These actions are associated with the following respective routes for CreateCategory and EditCategory:

❑ admin/articles/categories/create

❑ admin/articles/categories/edit/{categoryId}

admin/articles/categories/create

This route is used to create a category:

```
routes.MapRoute(
    "ArticleCategoryCreate",
    "admin/articles/categories/create",
    new { controller = "Article", action = "CreateCategory" }
);
```

admin/articles/categories/edit/{articleId}

This route is used to edit a category. It takes one rule, categoryId, which provides the identity of the category that is being edited:

```
routes.MapRoute(
    "ArticleCategoryEdit",
    "admin/articles/categories/edit/{categoryId}",
    new { controller = "Article",action = "EditCategory",categoryId = (int?)null },
    new { categoryId = "[0-9]+" }
);
```

The RemoveCategory Action

The RemoveCategory action is a little different from the RemoveArticle action because, when you remove a category, you need to move all the articles in the category to another category. If you didn't do this, all the articles under the category you are removing would also be removed. This could potentially cause many problems for The Beer House when and if it decided to reorganize its structure at a later point after the site has already been established.

```
[Authorize(Role = "Editor")]
public ActionResult RemoveCategory(
    int categoryId, int? newCategoryId, string remove)
{
    TheBeerHouseDataContext dc = new TheBeerHouseDataContext();
    var categories = dc.Categories.GetCategories();
    Category category = dc.Categories.GetCategory(categoryId);
    bool newCategoryExists =
        categoryId != newCategoryId && dc.Categories.Exists(newCategoryId ?? -1);

    // throw a 404 Not Found if the requested category is not in the database
    if (category == null)
        throw new HttpException(404, "The category could not be found.");

    if (String.Equals(remove, "yes", StringComparison.OrdinalIgnoreCase)
        && newCategoryExists)
    {
        foreach (Article article in category.Articles)
            article.CategoryID = newCategoryId.Value;

        dc.Categories.DeleteOnSubmit(category);
        dc.SubmitChanges();

        TempData["SuccessMessage"] =
            "The category, " + category.Title + ", has been deleted.";

        category = null;
    }
    else if (String.Equals(remove, "no", StringComparison.OrdinalIgnoreCase))
    {
        TempData["InformationMessage"] =
            "The category, " + category.Title + ", has NOT been deleted.";
    }
    else
    {
        ViewData["newCategoryId"] =
            new SelectList(categories, "CategoryID", "Title", newCategoryId);
        TempData["WarningMessage"] =
            "Are you sure you want to delete " + category.Title
            + ".  You will not be able to recover this category.";
    }

    ViewData["PageTitle"] = "Remove Category";

    return View(category);
}
```

You update the articles' categories after you have verified the required values, which are that a "yes" is sent back to the action and that the category the articles will be placed in has been verified. You then loop through all the Articles in the category you are going to remove and update them to the new category. After that a success message is returned to the user.

This action has the following route:

❑   admin/articles/categories/remove/{categoryId}

admin/articles/categories/remove/{categoryId}

This route is used to remove a category:

```
routes.MapRoute(
    "ArticleCategoryRemove",
    "admin/articles/categories/remove/{categoryId}",
    new { controller = "Article",action = "RemoveCategory",categoryId =(int?)null},
    new { categoryId = "[0-9]+" }
);
```

The CreateComment Action

The CreateComment action is different from the past create actions. This action is unique from the others you have created because the create form for the comments is in the ViewArticle view page. Because of this you have two options to add the comment to the article:

1.   You can do a POST to the CreateComment action on the server, which in return will redirect you back to the article. This is a valid solution that is used a lot on the Internet, but has the downside of causing the page to flicker from the browser refreshing the content.

2.   Or you can do an AJAX POST to the CreateComment action on the server, and then the server can send back all the necessary information to display the comment on the page. This option has the added advantage of not requiring the article page to refresh; however, it does require some client-side programming with JavaScript.

We prefer to take the extra step and develop the JavaScript so that the user of the website has a good experience and doesn't have to suffer through unnecessary POST backs. We discuss how to create the AJAX POST when you get to creating the views.

```
[ServiceOnly, HttpPostOnly]
public ActionResult CreateComment(
    int articleId, string name, string email, string body)
{
    TheBeerHouseDataContext dc = new TheBeerHouseDataContext();
    Article article = dc.Articles.GetArticle(articleId);

    // throw a 404 Not Found if the requested article is not in the database
    if (article == null)
        throw new HttpException(404, "The article could not be found.");
```

```
        Comment comment = new Comment {
            AddedBy = name,
            AddedByEmail = email,
            AddedByIP = Request.UserHostAddress,
            AddedDate = DateTime.Now,
            Body = body
        };
        article.Comments.Add(comment);

        // save changes to database
        dc.SubmitChanges();

        return View(new {
            commentId = comment.CommentID,
            name = comment.AddedBy,
            body = comment.Body
        });
    }
```

This action uses the `ServiceOnly` and `HttpPostOnly` attributes as talked about earlier in the article rating section. This request will return the `commentId`, `name`, and `body` back as a serialized JSON response, so that your client-side JavaScript can render the comment inline with the rest of the comments on the article.

The route for this action uses the standard `{controller}/{action}` route, so requests to this action method can be accessed through:

❑   article/createcomment

The EditComment Action

The `EditComment` action is very similar to the `CreateComment` action, except for the fact that only editors are allowed to edit a comment. This action is meant to be used in the `ManageComments` view page, and works also through JavaScript and AJAX. We chose to do this also through AJAX because there are only two fields that you need to support for modification and, because spamming is becoming more and more prevalent on comment forms, it is necessary to make the editing process easy on the moderator.

```
[Authorize(Role = "Editor")]
[ServiceOnly, HttpPostOnly]
public ActionResult EditComment(int commentId, string name, string body)
{
    TheBeerHouseDataContext dc = new TheBeerHouseDataContext();
    Comment comment = dc.Comments.GetComment(commentId);

    // throw a 404 Not Found if the requested article is not in the database
    if (comment == null)
        throw new HttpException(404, "The comment could not be found.");

    comment.AddedBy = name;
    comment.Body = body;
```

```
        // save changes to database
        dc.SubmitChanges();

        return View(new {
            commentId = comment.CommentID,
            name = comment.AddedBy,
            body = comment.Body
        });
    }
```

The route for this action uses the standard `{controller}/{action}` route, so requests to this action method can be accessed through:

❑   `article/editcomment`

The RemoveComment Action

The `RemoveComment` action, just like `EditComment`, is available only to users assigned to the Editors role and the action will be executed through AJAX to allow easy deletion. You are doing this so that comments can be easily removed from the articles, without the hassle of multiple steps. This simplistic approach to comment removal is one of the things I find is of great value to my blog, at www.coder-journal.com, because you get a ton of SPAM about everything under the sun, and it helps to be able to remove 100+ comments in only a couple minutes, since you don't have to go through an arduous process to remove an obviously inappropriate comment.

```
[Authorize(Role = "Editor")]
[ServiceOnly, HttpPostOnly]
public ActionResult RemoveComment(int commentId)
{
    TheBeerHouseDataContext dc = new TheBeerHouseDataContext();
    Comment comment = dc.Comments.GetComment(commentId);

    // throw a 404 Not Found if the requested article is not in the database
    if (comment == null)
        throw new HttpException(404, "The comment could not be found.");

    dc.Comments.DeleteOnSubmit(comment);
    dc.SubmitChanges();

    return View(new { commentId = commentId });
}
```

This works under the same process as the other actions for comments: the action is performed, and a value is returned to the client. In this case you are returning the `commentId` that you removed, so that on the successful response you can find the comment in the HTML and remove it with some client-side JavaScript. Use of the JavaScript will keep you from having to refresh the page, and speed up the process for removing a comment.

The route for this action uses the standard {controller}/{action} route, so requests to this action method can be accessed through:

❑   article/removecomment

Implementing the View

The model and controller for the articles module are now complete, so it's time to code the view. You will use the model to retrieve and manage Article data from the database. You'll start by developing the administration console, so that you can use it later to add and manage sample records when you code and test the views for end users.

The CategoryItem.ascx Control

This view control, located under the ~/Views/Shared/Article folder, allows for a consistent display of a Category object model in both ManageCategories.aspx and CategoryIndex.aspx. You will be able to use the same style sheet to keep everything consistent. The category will look like what is shown in Figure 6-8.

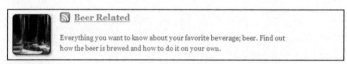

Figure 6-8

As you can see the layout is very simple. You provide a link with the category name that will take the users of the site to a listing of articles for that category, an image to identify the category, and a feed icon so that the users know that they can receive a feed of all the articles in that category.

In the header for the control you need to specify that the view model for this control is going to be of type Category. This is easily done by using the generic type specification for ViewUserControl:

```
<%@ Control Language="C#" Inherits="System.Web.Mvc.ViewUserControl<TheBeerHouse.
Models.Category>" %>
```

This is the full header required for your CategoryItem control. Not too complex, right! In the preceding code you are inheriting the generic ViewUserControl<T> type, where T is the type of your model, which happens to be Category in this case.

The HTML for the view control is equally simple. In the HTML that is rendered for each category, we usually like to give the primary wrapper two types of identification. The first type is a unique identifier, which in this case is the word category and the category identifier for the specific category you are rendering (that is, id="category-3"). The reason we do this is because it helps when you need to specifically reference the HTML DOM element in either JavaScript or CSS. The second type is a generic identifier, which will be applied to all HTML DOM elements of the same type; in this case the word is just plain category (that is, class="category"). The reason we also add a generic identifier is that it makes it easier to style all the HTML DOM elements the same way using CSS, and with most of the modern JavaScript frameworks they allow you to query your DOM for a collection of HTML elements using only this generic identifier called a `class`. You will see the real benefit of setting both of these types of identification when you get into client-side programming with JavaScript.

If you are just starting out with HTML, or are used to laying out HTML with tables, you may be shocked by the minimalistic approach that we took in creating the HTML for this category, shown in the following code, especially because the image is supposed to be positioned to the left of the category text according to Figure 6-8. The reason we took this approach is because it is now considered bad design practice to use tables to position elements on your screen, whereas only a few years ago it was an accepted practice. The new line of thought around HTML design says that tables should only be used to display tabular data, and you should use a combination of floats and widths to stylize and position your elements for display in the browser.

```
<div id="category-<%= ViewData.Model.CategoryID %>" class="category">
    <img src="<%= ViewData.Model.ImageUrl %>" title="<%= ViewData.Model.Title %>"
alt="<%= ViewData.Model.Title %>" class="main-image" />
    <h3>
        <a href="<%= Url.Action("Index", new { category = ViewData.Model.Path, page
= 1 }) %>?type=atom" rel="feed" type="application/atom+xml"><img src="/content/
images/feed.png" alt="RSS" /></a> 
        <a href="<%= Url.Action("Index", new { category = ViewData.Model.Path, page
= 1 }) %>"><%= ViewData.Model.Title%></a>
    </h3>
    <p><%= ViewData.Model.Description%></p>
</div>
```

The reference in the preceding code to `ViewData.Model` is where your `Category` object that is passed in to your view control is stored. It is typed specifically to `Category`, which is the generic type `T` that you set in the code-behind file in the previous code block.

You also reference `Url.Action` a couple of times; this utility method is used to generate your URL from the routes and actions you defined in your `ArticleController`. In the preceding cases you have

```
Url.Action("Index", new { category = ViewData.Model.Path, page = 1 }) %>
```

which references your `Index` action, that the parameters `category` and `page` should be the current path for the category that is your view model, and that the generated URL should start on the first page. The resulting URL, `/articles/category/the-model-path`, is created from the route and rules you defined for the `Index` action in the `Global.asax` file.

The next thing you want to define, as part of your design for the `CategoryItem` view control, is the CSS styles that are needed to style your HTML to look like Figure 6-8. These styles will be added into your main style sheet located in `~/Content/styles/site.css`.

```
/* Categories */

.category {
    min-height: 91px;
}
```

```
.category img {
    vertical-align: middle;
}

.category h3 {
    font-size: 1.3em;
}

.category .main-image {
    float: left;
    margin: 3px 15px 3px 3px;
}
```

If you are not familiar with CSS you may find it helpful to visit www.w3schools.com/css; it has great examples and an easy-to-learn tutorial that will get you up to speed on the basics of CSS. If you want to learn more and get past the basics provided by the W3 Schools, Wrox's *Professional CSS* (ISBN: 978-0-7645-8833-4) is very good.

The AdminSidebar.ascx Control

This view control, located under the ~/Views/Shared/Article folder, is used to create a set of links to edit and view categories, articles, and comments within the admin section for the article module. The real purpose of this view control, like most other view controls, is to make the reuse of common programming elements easier on us developers. This control will be used in the sidebar of seven different admin pages for the article module, so it will get a good amount of use before you are done.

```
<div id="articles-admin" class="boxed">
    <h2 class="title">Articles</h2>
    <div class="content">
    <ul>
        <li><%= Html.ActionLink("View Categories", "ManageCategories") %></li>
        <li><%= Html.ActionLink("Create Category", "CreateCategory") %></li>
        <li><%= Html.ActionLink("View Articles", "ManageArticles") %></li>
        <li><%= Html.ActionLink("Create Article", "CreateArticle") %></li>
        <li><%= Html.ActionLink("Comments", "ManageComments") %></li>
    </ul>
    </div>
</div>
```

The ManageCategories.aspx View

This view, located under the ~/Views/Article folder, allows the administrator and editors to add, delete, and edit article categories, as well as directly jump to the list of articles for a specific category. The screenshot of the page, shown in Figure 6-9, demonstrates what we're talking about, and then you'll learn how to build it.

Figure 6-9

There's a `foreach` loop that displays all the categories from the database (with the title, the description, and the graphical icon). Moreover, the links on the very far right of the category are, respectively, a hyperlink to edit the category and another one to remove it. When the edit link is clicked, the grid is not turned into edit mode as it was in the first edition of the book, and is not edited through the `DetailsView` box at the bottom of the page like in the second edition; you are taken to the `EditCategory` action so that it can be edited in its own page. This makes the page cleaner, and it doesn't mess with the layout, separates the view and edit logic, and also provides the ability to add more complex client-side validation to the page.

Now you'll examine the page's source code piece-by-piece. The first step is to set the `ViewData.Model` type through the generic `ViewPage`. The type of this page is going to be a collection of the `Category` object, from your model, so you will use `IEnumerable<Models.Category>` to define the type of object that this view will manage from the controller.

```
Inherits="System.Web.Mvc.ViewPage<IEnumerable<TheBeerHouse.Models.Category>>"
```

With ASP.NET MVC the header is usually only used to define the type of object that the view model will be. Unlike in ASP.NET WebForms, you don't need to have any code in the code-behind file, except if you want to define some utility methods to help the page render. This reduction in code is possible because most of the logic to handle the page setup is done by the controller and model, so the view is very slim; this is partly what makes ASP.NET MVC much faster at rendering the output compared to ASP.NET WebForms.

The HTML code for `ManageCategories.aspx` is broken down into two different `Content` sections. The master page template that you are using for this view has four sections defined: `HeaderContent`, `MainContent`, `SidebarContent`, and `ScriptContent`. For the purposes of this page you only are going to implement `MainContent` and `SidebarContent`.

MainContent

The `MainContent` placeholder uses a `foreach` loop and your `CategoryItem.ascx` control to create the HTML output for administering the categories. You also use `Html.ActionLink` to create your edit and remove links based off of your actions and the routes you defined earlier.

```
<asp:Content ID="MainContent" ContentPlaceHolderID="MainContent" runat="server">
<div id="categories">
<% foreach (Category category in ViewData.Model) { %>
    <div class="admin">
        <%= Html.ActionLink("Edit", "EditCategory", "Article", new { categoryId =
category.CategoryID })%> | 
        <%= Html.ActionLink("Remove", "RemoveCategory", "Article", new { categoryId
= category.CategoryID })%>
    </div>
    <%= Html.RenderUserControl("~/Views/Shared/Article/CategoryItem.ascx", category)%>
    <hr />
<% } %>
</div>
</asp:Content>
```

The `ViewData.Model` is typed to `IEnumerable<Models.Category>`, which you defined earlier in the code-behind, and will allow you to loop through all the categories returned from your `ManageCategories` action method in the `ArticleController`.

The `Html.RenderUserControl` method makes a call to render `CategoryItem.ascx` with the current `category` object from the loop. This method will generate the output from the control and insert it inline with the admin links and the horizontal ruler you are using to divide the categories.

SidebarContent

The `SidebarContent` has the sole purpose of rendering your `AdminSidebar.ascx` control, which contains the links for creating and viewing your categories, articles, and comments.

```
<asp:Content ID="SidebarContent" ContentPlaceHolderID="SidebarContent" runat="server">
<%= Html.RenderUserControl("~/Views/Shared/Article/AdminSidebar.ascx") %>
</asp:Content>
```

You also use `Html.RenderUserControl` to render the sidebar links. This is going to be the same on each of the administration pages so, in an effort not to repeat ourselves, any admin view that needs `SidebarContent` will use this exact same code.

The CreateCategory.aspx View

Like the `ManageCategories.aspx` view, this view is located under the `~/Views/Article` folder, and allows the administrator and editors to create or edit a category for an article. The screenshot of the page, shown in Figure 6-10, demonstrates the basic layout of what you are trying to accomplish.

Figure 6-10

The `CreateCategory.aspx` view will have two purposes: one is to create a category and the other is to edit the category. In the latter purpose the fields will be filled in with the values from the database so that they can be edited and submitted back for update.

In an effort to provide your users a great experience you want to specifically tell them what they need to enter into each field. The best way to do this is by providing a little message below the field explaining what kind of information should be entered into the selected field, as in Figure 6-11.

Figure 6-11

Or, if there is an error with the validation, explain what the error is and, if it is not obvious, what the user of the form should do to correct the error, as in Figure 6-12.

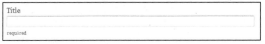

Figure 6-12

It probably doesn't come through very well in the black and white text of this book, but the message below the field in Figure 6-12 is actually red.

You can accomplish both of these usability requirements with a tiny bit of JavaScript. For the purposes of this book we use a JavaScript framework called jQuery, which is freely distributed at www.jquery. com. We are going to provide the basics for developing the usability features that your application requires with jQuery, but if you would like to learn about jQuery and the ease of development it offers you can find out more by searching for "jQuery help" in your favorite search engine.

As we did with the last section we will take a look at the source code piece-by-piece and the first place we will start is with the code-behind for `CreateCategory`:

```
Inherits="System.Web.Mvc.ViewPage"
```

The header for this view is as simple as it can get; you are using the built-in `ViewData` dictionary to hold the values so you can skip setting the model's type with the generic `ViewPage`.

The HTML code for `CreateCategory.aspx` has three different `Content` sections that you must implement to provide the desired look and feel; you are going to implement `MainContent`, `ScriptContent`, and `SidebarContent`.

MainContent

The `MainContent` for creating the category will hold your form with all the input fields, as well as the necessary HTML elements to hold the input field messages for information and validation errors

226

discussed for Figure 6-11 and Figure 6-12, respectively. The fields that you need to create textboxes for are `title`, `importance`, `imageUrl`, and `description`.

```
<asp:Content ID="MainContent" ContentPlaceHolderID="MainContent" runat="server">

<%= Html.RenderUserControl("~/Views/Shared/Message.ascx") %>

<form method="post" action="<%= Url.Action(this.ViewContext.RouteData.
Values["action"] as string, "Article") %>" class="category-create">

    <p class="field input"><label for="title">Title</label><br />
        <%= Html.TextBox("title", ViewData["title"], new { maxlength = 256 }) %>
        <span class="input-message"></span></p>

    <p class="field input"><label for="importance">Importance</label><br />
        <%= Html.TextBox("importance", ViewData["importance"],
                new { maxlength = 3 }) %>
        <span class="input-message"></span></p>

    <p class="field input"><label for="imageUrl">Image</label><br />
        <%= Html.TextBox("imageUrl", ViewData["imageUrl"],
                new { maxlength = 256 }) %>
        <span class="input-message"></span></p>

    <p class="field input"><label for="description">Description</label><br />
        <%= Html.TextArea("description", ViewData["description"]) %>
        <span class="input-message"></span></p>

<% if(this.ViewContext.RouteData.Values["action"] as string == "EditCategory") { %>
    <p><button type="submit" id="category-create-button">Update Category</button></p>
<% } else { %>
    <p><button type="submit" id="category-create-button">Create Category</button></p>
<% } %>

</form>
</asp:Content>
```

In the preceding code not everything is cut and dry because you are using this view page for dual purposes; however, it is much easier than trying to maintain two different view pages for creating and editing a category. In the form's `action` field you are creating the action URL from the routes using the current `action` contained in the `RouteData` for the page. What this means is that you are using the current controller action to pass into the utility method that creates your URL for the form to post back to. There is one other place you use the `action` value from the `RouteData`, but to be honest this is not required and it is only for vanity reasons that you change the button name from "Create Category" to "Update Category" depending if you are viewing this page from the `CreateCategory` action or the `EditCategory` action.

The code also uses a utility method, called `Html.TextBox`, that takes the `ViewData` value and, optionally, attributes that you want to add on to the textbox. For instance, in many of the cases, as in the preceding code, you are setting a name for a corresponding value in the `ViewData` to be pulled and entered in the textbox as a value, if one exists. Additionally you will see that you are defining a `maxlength` value in an anonymous type that will be added on to the textboxes' HTML as `maxlength="256"`.

ScriptContent

This part of the view page contains the necessary references to your JavaScript that makes the user's browser validate your input fields and/or display informational messages about the textbox that the user is focused on.

```
<asp:Content ID="ScriptContent" ContentPlaceHolderID="ScriptContent"
runat="server">
<script type="text/javascript" src="/content/scripts/manage-categories.js"></script>
<% if (IsPostBack) { %>
<script type="text/javascript">
    ValidateCategory();
</script>
<% } %>
</asp:Content>
```

The first thing you do is import the JavaScript file, located at `/content/scripts/manage-categories.js`, which you will create a little later on. Also if this page is a POST back, meaning that you have posted to the action and it was necessary to return to this view page, you will validate the textbox values to display any kind of validation issues as a hint to why the action might have returned you to this page. We always like to include this validation even though it is not always needed, because any validation messages that you can display to the user, in addition to the message that you will display at the top of the page, will help the user track down the problem if there is one.

manage-categories.js

The `manage-categories.js` file is located under `~/Content/scripts/` and is used to perform custom client-side actions on the `CreateCategory.aspx` view. We are going to break this JavaScript file up into three sections so that you can gain a better grasp of the different parts of this file needed to make everything work as you intended. The first part discussed is the information messages, then the validation and error messages, then, last but not least, the validation before the form is submitted.

```
$("#title").focus(function () {
    ShowMessage(this, "Enter the title for your category."); });

$("#importance").focus(function () {
    ShowMessage(this, "(optional) Enter the order of importance that you want the
categories shown in."); });

$("#imageUrl").focus(function () {
    ShowMessage(this, "The relative web path of an image you want to be shown with
articles in this category."); });

$("#description").focus(function () {
    ShowMessage(this, "Enter a short description of the category to display to
your users."); });
```

This code says that, when `title`, `importance`, `imageUrl`, or `description` textboxes receive focus from the browser, they should show the message that is being passed into the `ShowMessage` method.

```
function ValidateTitle () {
    return VerifyRequiredField("#title", "required");
}

function ValidateImageUrl () {
    return VerifyRequiredField("#imageUrl", "required");
}

function ValidateDescription () {
    return VerifyRequiredField("#description", "required");
}
```

These three functions perform a validation on the `title`, `imageUrl`, and `description` fields, making sure that they each contain a value because they are required in order to add a category record to the database.

```
function ValidateCategory () {
    var validTitle = ValidateTitle();
    var validImage = ValidateImageUrl();
    var validDescription = ValidateDescription();

    return validTitle && validImage && validDescription;
}

$("form.category-create").validate(ValidateCategory);
```

The `ValidateCategory` method is used to run all of your validations for this form and, if they all pass, you return a value of true, which will allow the form to continue the submit process; if any of the validation fails, the submit process is halted and error messages are displayed under the fields that have a validation error. The last line in the preceding code binds the `ValidateCategory` method to the `validate` event on your category form.

The RemoveCategory.aspx View

The `RemoveCategory.aspx` view is located under the `~/Views/Article` folder, and allows the administrator and editors to remove a category for an article. The view will look like Figure 6-13.

This view contains a "yes" and a "no" button and a category list to move all the articles to that are in the current category being removed. The header for `RemoveCategory` sets the model to the type of `Category`.

```
Inherits="System.Web.Mvc.ViewPage<TheBeerHouse.Models.Category>"
```

In this view you only need to implement two content sections of the master page: `MainContent` and `SidebarContent`.

Figure 6-13

MainContent

In this `MainContent` you are creating two submit buttons, one labeled "yes," which will confirm that the user wants to delete the category, and one labeled "no," which will cancel the removal of the category. The form should only be displayed when the view pages model has a non-`null` `Category` object in it.

```
<asp:Content ID="MainContent" ContentPlaceHolderID="MainContent" runat="server">

<%= Html.RenderUserControl("~/Views/Shared/Message.ascx") %>
```

```
<% if (ViewData.Model != null) { %>
<form method="post" action="<%= Url.Action("RemoveCategory", "Article", new {
categoryId = ViewData.Model.CategoryID }) %>" class="category-remove">

    <p class="field input"><label for="categoryId">Move Articles From <em><%=
ViewData.Model.Title %></em> To</label><br />
        <%= Html.DropDownList("newCategoryId")%>
        <span class="input-message"></span></p>

    <button type="submit" name="remove" value="yes" class="yes">yes</button>
    <button type="submit" name="remove" value="no" class="no">no</button>

</form>
<% } %>

</asp:Content>
```

Both submit buttons have the same name; this is because only one of them will be posting back a value for the `remove` name, which will be either "yes" or "no." If you remember from the `RemoveCategory` controller action, the `remove` parameter was an indicator for whether the category was deleted or the process was canceled. These buttons are where you get that value from.

CSS

The CSS styles needed to display the buttons red and green are:

```
button.yes {
    background-color: #DB0000;
    color: #ffffff;
    font-weight: bold;
    width: 75px;
    margin: 0 5px;
}

button.no {
    background-color: #00DB00;
    color: #ffffff;
    font-weight: bold;
    width: 75px;
    margin: 0 5px;
}
```

These styles will be reused for all of your other remove actions in this project.

The ArticleItem.ascx Control

As mentioned before, the code that lists articles in the administrative `ManageArticles.aspx` view page, and the end-user `Index.aspx` view page, is located not in the pages themselves but in a separate user control called `~/Views/Shared/Articles/ArticleItem.ascx`. This control displays a paginable list of articles for all categories or for a selected category. In Figure 6-14, you can see what the control will look like once it's plugged into the `ManageArticles.aspx` page.

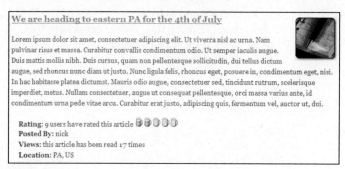

We are heading to eastern PA for the 4th of July

Lorem ipsum dolor sit amet, consectetuer adipiscing elit. Ut viverra nisl ac urna. Nam pulvinar risus et massa. Curabitur convallis condimentum odio. Ut semper iaculis augue. Duis mattis mollis nibh. Duis cursus, quam non pellentesque sollicitudin, dui tellus dictum augue, sed rhoncus nunc diam ut justo. Nunc ligula felis, rhoncus eget, posuere in, condimentum eget, nisi. In hac habitasse platea dictumst. Mauris odio augue, consectetuer sed, tincidunt rutrum, scelerisque imperdiet, metus. Nullam consectetuer, augue ut consequat pellentesque, orci massa varius ante, id condimentum urna pede vitae arcu. Curabitur erat justo, adipiscing quis, fermentum vel, auctor ut, dui.

Rating: 9 users have rated this article
Posted By: nick
Views: this article has been read 17 times
Location: PA, US

Figure 6-14

This control is a little different than the previous ones, because it contains a code-behind with a utility method that is used to generate the appropriate number of beer icons from the AverageRating.

```
namespace TheBeerHouse.Views.Shared.Article
{
    public partial class ArticleItem : System.Web.Mvc.ViewUserControl<Models.Article>
    {
        public string ImageRatingUrl
        {
            get
            {
                double value = ViewData.Model.AverageRating;
                string url = "/Content/images/stars{0}.gif";
                if (value <= 1.3)
                    url = String.Format(url, "10");
                else if (value <= 1.8)
                    url = String.Format(url, "15");
                else if (value <= 2.3)
                    url = String.Format(url, "20");
                else if (value <= 2.8)
                    url = String.Format(url, "25");
                else if (value <= 3.3)
                    url = String.Format(url, "30");
                else if (value <= 3.8)
                    url = String.Format(url, "35");
                else if (value <= 4.3)
                    url = String.Format(url, "40");
                else if (value <= 4.8)
                    url = String.Format(url, "45");
                else
                    url = String.Format(url, "50");

                return url;
            }
        }
    }
}
```

The `ImageRatingUrl` property helps the control create an image path from the average rating for displaying with the article. In addition to generating the graphical representation of the average rating, a more accurate numerical value is shown in the image's alternate text (aka tooltip).

The HTML to generate the control to look like Figure 6-14 contains the category image, title, abstract, rating, who posted it, number of views, and location of article. If the abstract is empty, you will display the body of the article.

```
<div id="article-<%= ViewData.Model.ArticleID %>" class="article">
    <img src="<%= ViewData.Model.Category.ImageUrl %>" class="category-image"
    title="<%= ViewData.Model.Category.Title %>" />
    <h3><%= Html.ActionLink(ViewData.Model.Title, "ViewArticle", "Article", new { id
= ViewData.Model.ArticleID, path = ViewData.Model.Path })%></h3>
    <p><%= !String.IsNullOrEmpty(ViewData.Model.Abstract) ? ViewData.Model.Abstract
: ViewData.Model.Body%></p>
    <ul>
        <li><strong>Rating: </strong><%= ViewData.Model.Votes%> <%= ViewData.Model.
        Votes == 1 ? "user has" : "users have"%> rated this article <% if
        (ViewData.Model.AverageRating > 0) { %><img src="<%= ImageRatingUrl %>"
        alt="<%= ViewData.Model.AverageRating %>" /><% } %></li>
        <li><strong>Posted By: </strong><%= ViewData.Model.AddedBy%></li>
        <li><strong>Views: </strong>this article has been read <%= ViewData.Model.
        ViewCount%> times</li>
        <li><strong>Location: </strong><%= ViewData.Model.Location%></li>
    </ul>
</div>
```

The next thing you need to create is the style sheet values to lay out each article. The CSS is not much different than the `CategoryItem` view control's styles, but we will go over them anyway.

```
.article {
    min-height: 91px;
}

.article h3 {
    font-size: 1.3em;
}

.article .category-image {
    float: right;
    margin: 5px;
}
```

The ManageArticles.aspx View

This view, located under the `~/Views/Article` folder, allows the administrator and editors to add, delete, and edit articles, as well as go to the articles being displayed. The screenshot of the page, shown in Figure 6-15, demonstrates what you need to build.

Just like you did in the `ManageCategories` view, you will be using a `foreach` loop to loop through the articles that are going to be displayed for the current page. The edit and remove links are positioned to the right of each of the articles they represent. The edit link will take you to the `EditArticle` action and the remove link will take you to the `RemoveArticle` action.

Figure 6-15

The header of this view takes a collection of `Article` objects for the model, which will be used to display.

```
Inherits="System.Web.Mvc.ViewPage<TheBeerHouse.Models.Pagination<TheBeerHouse.
Models.Article>>"
```

The `ManageArticles` view implements two content sections of the master page: `MainContent` and `SidebarContent`.

MainContent

The `MainContent` section of the master page will create the edit and remove links as seen in Figure 6-15 using the `Html.ActionLink` method.

```
<asp:Content ID="MainContent" ContentPlaceHolderID="MainContent" runat="server">
<div id="articles">
<% foreach(Article article in ViewData.Model) { %>
```

```
    <div class="admin"><%= Html.ActionLink("Edit", "EditArticle", "Article", new {
articleId = article.ArticleID })%> | <%= Html.ActionLink("Remove",
"RemoveArticle", "Article", new { articleId = article.ArticleID })%></div>
    <%= Html.RenderUserControl("~/Views/Shared/Article/ArticleItem.ascx", article) %>
    <hr />
<% } %>

<%= Html.RenderUserControl("~/Views/Shared/Pager.ascx", ViewData.Model) %>
</div>
</asp:Content>
```

The CreateArticle.aspx View

This page allows administrators, editors, and contributors to add new articles or edit existing ones. If it came from the `EditArticle` controller action, the page loads in edit mode for that article, but only if the user is an administrator or editor (the edit mode is available only to administrators and editors, whereas the insert mode is available to contributors as well). This security check must be done programmatically at the controller, instead of declaratively from the `web.config` file. Figure 6-16 is a screenshot of the page while in edit mode for an article.

Figure 6-16

235

As you might guess from studying this picture, it uses the same method to display the form fields as you used in the CreateCategory view. The Body field uses the open-source TinyMCE editor described earlier. It is declared on the page by importing the scripts and setting the configuration in your manage-article .js file. To set up TinyMCE you must download the packages from http://tinymce.moxiecode.com:

❑   TinyMCE includes the set of HTML pages and JavaScript files that implement the control. The control can be used not only with ASP.NET, but also with ASP, JSP, PHP, and normal HTML pages.

You unzip the package into the ~/Content/scripts/tinymce folder. The global TinyMCE JavaScript editor enables you to configure many properties that will be stored globally in your global.js file.

```
var __editorConfig = {
    mode: "textareas",
    theme: "advanced",
    plugins: "advhr,advimage,advlink,contextmenu,inlinepopups,media,paste,safari,
spellchecker,xhtmlxtras",

    theme_advanced_toolbar_location: "top",
    theme_advanced_toolbar_align: "center",
    theme_advanced_statusbar_location: "bottom",
    theme_advanced_resizing_use_cookie: false,
    theme_advanced_resize_horizontal: false,
    theme_advanced_resizing: true,
    theme_advanced_resizing_min_height: 200,

    convert_urls: false,

    gecko_spellcheck: true,
    dialog_type: "modal",

    paste_auto_cleanup_on_paste: true,
    paste_convert_headers_to_strong: true,
    paste_strip_class_attributes: "all"
};
```

You will use the __editorConfig later on in your manage-articles.js file.

The header for this view page is very plain, because you are using the internal dictionary of the ViewData to store your information about the form.

```
Inherits="System.Web.Mvc.ViewPage"
```

This page implements three sections from the master page: MainContent, SidebarContent, and ScriptsContent.

MainContent

In this content section you create the fields required to create or edit an article. The fields will be created in the same manner as the `CreateCategory` view; there are just more of them to put on the page because of the number of fields it takes to create an article.

```
<asp:Content ID="Content1" ContentPlaceHolderID="MainContent" runat="server">

<%= Html.RenderUserControl("~/Views/Shared/Message.ascx") %>

<form method="post" action="<%= Url.Action(this.ViewContext.RouteData.
Values["action"] as string, "Article") %>" class="article-create">

    <h3>Article</h3>

    <p class="field input"><label for="categoryId">Category</label><br />
        <%= Html.DropDownList("categoryId")%>
        <span class="input-message"></span></p>

    <p class="field input"><label for="title">Title</label><br />
        <%= Html.TextBox("title", ViewData["title"], new { @maxlength = 256 })%>
        <span class="input-message"></span></p>

    <p class="field input"><label for="summary">Summary</label><br />
        <%= Html.TextArea("summary")%>
        <span class="input-message"></span></p>

    <p class="field input"><label for="body">Body</label><br />
        <%= Html.TextArea("body", new { style = "height: 500px"})%>
        <span class="input-message"></span></p>

    <h3>Meta Data</h3>

    <p class="field input"><label for="country">Country</label><br />
        <%= Html.DropDownList("country") %>
        <span class="input-message"></span></p>

    <p class="field input"><label for="state">State</label><br />
        <%= Html.TextBox("state", ViewData["state"], new { @maxlength = 256 })%>
        <span class="input-message"></span></p>

    <p class="field input"><label for="city">City</label><br />
        <%= Html.TextBox("city", ViewData["city"], new { @maxlength = 256 })%>
        <span class="input-message"></span></p>

    <p class="field input"><label for="releaseDate">Release Date</label><br />
        <%= Html.TextBox("releaseDate")%>
        <span class="input-message"></span></p>

    <p class="field input"><label for="expireDate">Expire Date</label><br />
        <%= Html.TextBox("expireDate")%>
        <span class="input-message"></span></p>
```

Now that all the fields are created for the article you need to add the article options to the page, which control if the article is approved, listed, comments are enabled, and the member permissions to view. You only want to allow administrators and editors to modify these options so you are going to wrap them in an `if` statement that checks to see if the person visiting this page has an Editor role.

```
<% if (Roles.IsUserInRole("Editor")) { %>
    <h3>Options</h3>

    <p class="field"><ul class="options">
        <li><%= Html.CheckBox("approved") %>
            <label for="approved">Approved To Be Published</label></li>
        <li><%= Html.CheckBox("listed") %>
            <label for="listed">Listed</label></li>
        <li><%= Html.CheckBox("commentsEnabled") %>
            <label for="commentsEnabled">Enable Comments</label></li>
        <li><%= Html.CheckBox("onlyForMembers") %>
            <label for="onlyForMembers">Only Members Can View</label></li>
    </ul>
    <span class="input-message"></span></p>
<% } %>
```

The last part you need to add is the submit button. As you probably remember, with the `CreateCategory` view, we changed the name of the button for vanity reasons so that the user knew if they were updating or creating a category. You are going to do the same thing for the `CreateArticle` view except this time you are going to check for the `EditArticle` action instead of `EditCategory`.

```
    <hr />
<% if(this.ViewContext.RouteData.Values["action"] as string == "EditArticle") { %>
    <p><button type="submit" id="article-create-button">Update Article</button></p>
<% } else { %>
    <p><button type="submit" id="article-create-button">Create Article</button></p>
<% } %>
</form>

</asp:Content>
```

ScriptContent

In the `ScriptContent` section of the master page you need to include `tiny_mce_src.js` and `manage-articles.js` so that the appropriate source will be included for your TinyMCE Rich Text Editor.

```
<asp:Content ID="ScriptContent" ContentPlaceHolderID="ScriptContent" runat="server">
<script type="text/javascript" src="/content/scripts/tiny_mce/tiny_mce_src.js">
</script>
<script type="text/javascript" src="/content/scripts/manage-articles.js"></script>
<% if (IsPostBack) { %>
<script type="text/javascript">
    ValidateArticle();
</script>
<% } %>
</asp:Content>
```

Note that the order of these imports is very important. The `tiny_mce_src.js` *file must come before the* `manage-articles.js` *file because the latter file contains references to the former file. If they are out of order a JavaScript error will be displayed in the browser.*

manage-articles.js

The first part of the code used for information and validation we have already gone over, so we are just going to show the code because it is very similar for `manage-categories.js`.

```
$("#title").focus(function () {
    ShowMessage(this, "Enter the title for your article."); });

$("#summary").focus(function () {
    ShowMessage(this, "(optional) Enter a summary for your article to be displayed
instead of body."); });

$("#body").focus(function () {
    ShowMessage(this, "Enter the body of your article."); });

$("#country").focus(function () {
    ShowMessage(this, "(optional) Enter the country that is associated with this
article."); });

$("#state").focus(function () {
    ShowMessage(this, "(optional) Enter the state that is associated with this
article."); });

$("#city").focus(function () {
    ShowMessage(this, "(optional) Enter the city that is associated with this
article."); });

$("#releaseDate").focus(function () {
    ShowMessage(this, "(optional) This is the date that you want this article to be
first show on the site.  If left blank todays day is used."); });

$("#expireDate").focus(function () {
    ShowMessage(this, "(optional) This is the date that you want this article to
stop showing on the site."); });

function ValidateTitle () {
    return VerifyRequiredField("#title", "required");
}

function ValidateBody () {
    return VerifyRequiredField("#body", "required");
}

function ValidateArticle () {
    return ValidateTitle()
        && ValidateBody();
}

$("form.article-create").validate(ValidateArticle);
```

The next part of the JavaScript file is used to create and bind the TinyMCE instance to your `textarea` named `body`. This is an important step because, without this code, you would have just a plain `textarea` box that doesn't allow the rich formatting of TinyMCE.

In the first part of this code you are creating a variable called `bodyEditor` that will be used to initialize your rich text editor for `body`. As part of the process you bind an `onClick` and `onChange` event action to the editor so that, when data is changed, it is returned to the `textarea` for which it was created. This is a very important step because the rich text editor is actually an `iframe` that is written into your HTML to lay overtop of the textarea, but the rich text from the `iframe` doesn't get put into the `textarea` until the `save` method is called. Normally this `save` method would only be called when the submit button is clicked, but you need the information sooner so your inline validation will work.

```
var bodyEditor;

$(document).ready(function () {
    bodyEditor = new tinymce.Editor("body", __editorConfig);
    bodyEditor.onChange.add(function (ed) { bodyEditor.save(); });
    bodyEditor.onClick.add(function (ed) { ShowMessage("#body", "Enter the body of
your article."); });
    bodyEditor.render();
});
```

Because `bodyEditor` is actually a TinyMCE object, which represents an `iframe`, you need to duplicate your information and validation message queues to the user for this rich text box. The only way to do that, because the `focus` event is available like it is on the input fields, is to use the `onClick` event for the rich text box, so that you can simulate the same interaction.

Also, because there is no `blur` event or, in other words, leaving the focus of the rich text box, you need to rely on a trick that will simulate the same `blur` event that is available for the normal input fields. Normally the `blur` event, on a normal input field, clears the message below the input box, except in the case of a validation error. To accomplish this same effect for your rich text box you are using for `body`, you need to rely on the `focus` and `blur` events of all the other inputs on the page. So anytime another input receives focus or loses focus it will clear the message from the `body`.

```
// clears the message from the description when another input gets focus
$(":input")
    .focus(function () { HideMessage("#body"); })
    .blur(function () { HideMessage("#body"); });
```

This is an assumption that the users will click another field when leaving the rich text box, but it is an assumption that relies on standard use of WebForms to just page through from field to field until they reach the submit button at the bottom. So you have an almost perfect chance of the user finding focus on one of your other inputs, which include textboxes, drop-downs, textareas, checkboxes, and buttons. So that is why we are not worried about this assumption that we have made, especially for a non-critical mechanism like displaying an information message.

The RemoveArticle.aspx View

The `RemoveArticle.aspx` page view works in a similar fashion to that of the `RemoveCategory.aspx` page view in that the users are presented with a "yes" or "no" question of whether they want to permanently remove the article from the database. If they choose "yes," the article and all comments related to that article are permanently removed, and if they choose "no," no action is taken against the database. Figure 6-17 is a visual representation of what you are going to create for the `RemoveArticle.aspx` view page.

Figure 6-17

The header, like many of your other admin pages, is relatively simple, because you are only using it to set the view model to be an `Article` object.

```
Inherits="System.Web.Mvc.ViewPage<TheBeerHouse.Models.Article>"
```

The view is broken up into a `MainContent` section and a `SidebarContent` section.

MainContent

This is a very simple setup: you have a form with a "yes" or "no" button on it, and a message pane. The form with the buttons is only shown if the model is not `null`; you do this so that you can display a success message for whichever option the user chooses. Doing this gives the feel of a wizard, which most users are very comfortable with.

```
<asp:Content ID="MainContent" ContentPlaceHolderID="MainContent" runat="server">

<%= Html.RenderUserControl("~/Views/Shared/Message.ascx") %>

<% if (ViewData.Model != null) { %>
<form method="post" action="<%= Url.Action("RemoveArticle", "Article", new {
articleId = ViewData.Model.ArticleID }) %>" class="article-remove">

    <button type="submit" name="remove" value="yes" class="yes">yes</button>
    <button type="submit" name="remove" value="no" class="no">no</button>

</form>
<% } %>

</asp:Content>
```

The CommentItem.ascx Control

The `CommentItem.ascx` view control will be created with your other controls in the `~/Views/Shared/Article/` folder. This control will be used as a common way for displaying the `Comment` object in your views.

Figure 6-18

Figure 6-18 is how the comment will look in `ViewArticle.aspx` and `ManageComments.aspx`. The controls model is of the type of a `Comment` object, as seen in the code-behind:

```
Inherits="System.Web.Mvc.ViewUserControl<TheBeerHouse.Models.Comment>"
```

The HTML for the comment is broken into two elements: a header and a body. These two elements will help you format the comment to look like Figure 6-18:

```
<div id="comment-<%= ViewData.Model.CommentID %>" class="comment">
    <div class="comment-header">Comment posted by <span class="name"><%=
ViewData.Model.AddedBy%></span> <%= (DateTime.Now - ViewData.Model.AddedDate).
ToLongString()%> ago</div>
    <blockquote class="body"><%= ViewData.Model.Body%></blockquote>
</div>
```

The CSS needed to style the preceding HTML is pretty straightforward:

```
.comment {
    margin-top: 1.2em;
}

.comment .comment-header {
    margin: 0;
    padding: 5px 10px;
    background: #5F919E none repeat scroll 0% 0%;
    border-top: 5px solid #4C747E;
    font-size: 1.1em;
    color: #ffffff;
}

.comment blockquote {
    margin: .7em 2.5em;
}
```

The ManageComments.aspx View

This page is located under the ~/Views/Article/ folder and it displays all comments of all articles, from the newest to the oldest, and allows an administrator or an editor to moderate the feedback by editing or deleting comments that may not be considered suitable. The page allows the editing of comments inline through AJAX calls; this differs slightly from what you have done with the categories and articles but it provides a nice interface for your administrators to edit the comments. Figure 6-19 shows a screenshot of this page.

We won't cover the code for this page in detail because it's similar to other code that's already been discussed. You can refer to the downloadable code for the complete implementation.

To facilitate the inline editing of the comment you need to use some JavaScript and AJAX to replace the comment with a form that will allow the administrator to edit the name and body of the comment. The remove button is also done through an AJAX request. We will cover each separately so we can talk about the design decisions made.

Figure 6-19

Remove a Comment

The remove a comment script will actually bind itself to the click event of each of the Remove links. When the link is clicked, an asynchronous request is made to /article/removecomment with the id of the comment that is going to be removed. When a response is received from the server, the comment and the admin links are removed from the HTML DOM, and will not exist anymore in the database.

```
$(".remove-comment").click(function () {
    var id = $(this).attr("meta:id");

    $.post(
```

```
            "/article/removecomment",
            { commentId: id },
            function (data) {
                $("#comment-" + data.object.commentId)
                    .next(".admin")
                    .fadeOut("slow", function () { $(this).remove() });
                $("#comment-" + data.object.commentId)
                    .fadeOut("slow", function () { $(this).remove() });
            },
            "json"
        );

        return false;
    });
```

Edit a Comment

The edit a comment method is bound in the same way as the remove comment link. However, when the link is clicked, the header and body of the comment is hidden and replaced with a form that contains the name of the submitter and the body of the comment. The form will contain two buttons, update and cancel, which will be bound to their own set of actions. The cancel button on the form just reverses the changes made, and the comment is reverted back to look like Figure 6-18. When the update button is clicked, an AJAX request is sent to the /article/editcomment action in order to update the comment in the database. When the response for this update request is received, the values are updated on the page and the comment goes back to looking like Figure 6-18.

```
$(".edit-comment").click(function () {
    var id = $(this).attr("meta:id");
    var comment = $("#comment-" + id);
    var bodyText = comment.find(".body").text();
    var nameText = comment.find(".name").text();

    // hide all the childrend
    comment.children().hide();

    var commentText = "";
    commentText += "<form><div class=\"comment-header field\"><label for=\"name-" +
    id + "\">Commentor's Name</label><br/><input type=\"text\" id=\"name-" + id +
    "\" class=\"edit-name\" value=\"" + nameText + "\" /></div>";
    commentText += "<div class=\"field\"><label for=\"body-" + id + "\">Comment
Body</label><br/><textarea class=\"edit-body\" id=\"body-" + id + "\">" + bodyText
    + "</textarea><br/><button type=\"button\" class=\"update\" meta:id=\"" + id +
    "\">Update</button> <button type=\"button\" class=\"cancel\">Cancel</button>
</div></form>";

    var commentForm = $(commentText);

    // update the form
    commentForm.find(".update").click(function () {
        var id = $(this).attr("meta:id");
        var nameFormText = $(this).prevAll(".edit-name").val();
        var bodyFormText = $(this).prevAll(".edit-body").val();
```

```
            $.post(
                "/article/editcomment",
                { commentId: id, name: nameFormText, body: bodyFormText },
                function (data) {
                    var comment = $("#comment-" + data.object.commentId);
                    comment.children("form").remove();
                    comment.children(".body").text(data.object.body);
                    comment.children(".name").text(data.object.name);
                    comment.children().show();
                },
                "json"
            );
        });

        // cancel the update
        commentForm.find(".cancel").click(function () {
            $(this).parents(".comment").children(":hidden").show();
            $(this).parents("form").remove();
        });

        // add the form to the current comment
        comment.append(commentForm);

        return false;
    });
```

One interesting thing to note about this code is that we are defining the response functions inline, with the rest of the code. We did this because we don't need to reference the method anywhere else in the code, so it makes it easier to keep it all together in one place.

The CategoryIndex.aspx View

This is the first end-user page of this module, located in the site's root folder. Its only purpose is to display the article categories in a nice format, so that the reader can easily and clearly understand what the various categories are about and quickly jump to their content by clicking the category's title. Figure 6-9 is an exact representation of this page, minus the edit and remove buttons. Also the code is similar enough to the ManageCategories.aspx view page where we don't want to repeat ourselves by discussing it further. You can find the complete implementation in the downloadable code.

The Index.aspx View

This is the end-user version of the ManageArticles.aspx view page presented earlier. It shows only published content instead of all content, but otherwise it's the same because it just runs through a foreach loop from a collection of Article objects in the view model. Figure 6-15 represents an accurate screenshot of the page, minus the edit and remove buttons.

The ViewArticle.aspx View

This end-user page outputs the whole article's text, and all its other information (author, average rating, number of views, and so on). At the bottom of the page it has input controls to let the user rate the article (from zero to five glasses of beer) and to submit comments. All comments are listed in chronological order, on a single page, so that it's easy to follow the discussion. Figure 6-20 shows a screenshot of the page as seen by an end user.

Figure 6-20

The code that renders the title, rating, and other information in the upper box is very similar to the code used in the `ArticleItem.ascx` view control, so we won't list it here again. The article's content is displayed in a simple response block. Let's consider the elements that allow the user to rate the article and provide feedback. The possible rating values are listed in a drop-down list, and next to that is the button to submit the rating via an AJAX request back to the server. A message will be made visible only after the user rates the article, of course, and once that happens the drop-down list and button will be disabled.

```
<form method="post" action="#" class="rate-article">
    <p class="field input"><h3><label for="rating">What would you rate this
article?</label></h3><br />
        <select name="rating" id="rating">
```

```
                    <option value="0">0 Beers</option>
                    <option value="1">1 Beers</option>
                    <option value="2">2 Beers</option>
                    <option value="3">3 Beers</option>
                    <option value="4">4 Beers</option>
                    <option value="5">5 Beers</option>
                </select>
                <button type="submit" id="rate-button">Rate</button>
                </p>
        </form>
```

The rest of the page defines a list of comments and an accompanying form for submitting comments, but only if comments are enabled for the article.

```
<% if (ViewData.Model.CommentsEnabled) { %>
<div id="article-comments">
<h3>Comments</h3>
<% foreach(Comment comment in ViewData.Model.Comments) { %>
<%= Html.RenderUserControl("~/Views/Shared/Article/CommentItem.ascx", comment) %>
<% } %>
</div>

<form method="post" action="#" class="comment-create">
    <input type="hidden" id="articleId" name="articleId" value="<%=
ViewData.Model.ArticleID %>" />
    <input type="hidden" id="commentId" name="commentId" value="" />

    <p class="field input"><label for="name">Name</label><br />
        <%= Html.TextBox("comment-name", null, new { @maxlength = 256 })%>
        <span class="input-message"></span></p>

    <p class="field input"><label for="email">E-Mail</label><br />
        <%= Html.TextBox("comment-email", null, new { @maxlength = 256 })%>
        <span class="input-message"></span></p>

    <p class="field input"><label for="body">Body</label><br />
        <%= Html.TextArea("comment-body", String.Empty)%>
        <span class="input-message"></span></p>

    <hr />
    <p><button type="submit" id="comment-create-button">Add Comment</button></p>
</form>
<% } %>
```

One unique aspect of the preceding code is the fact that the action just contains a # sign as a place-holder. You did this because you are going to be submitting the comment though client-side script via an AJAX request. Use of this method, instead of including a URL in the action, has an upside and a downside that you have to weigh when you are making these kinds of decisions. The upside is that you pretty much reduce web-bot generated spam to nothing, which is a great thing because web-bots roam the web submitting WebForms with subversive marketing material. The downside is that anybody that doesn't have JavaScript enabled will not be able to use this comment form; however, we are at a point with the Internet and web browsers where you can say to people, if you don't have JavaScript enabled you have to use a limited set of functionality on your website.

There is a JavaScript component to rating the articles and adding a comment to an article. We are going to break down the JavaScript and go through it piece by piece so that you can understand what is going on. We will describe each of these code cross sections and what they do, but we are going to stay away from describing syntax because it is mostly specific to jQuery, but very easy to pick up and understand in very little time.

Rating an Article

The first thing you must do in order to rate an article is to bind your JavaScript routine to the submit event on the rating form. After the event is hooked up, anytime a user clicks the rate button an AJAX request will be sent to your /article/ratearticle action that you created earlier in the chapter.

```
$("form.rate-article").submit(function () {
    $.post(
        "/article/ratearticle",
        {   articleId: $("#articleId").val(),
            rating: $("#rating").val() },
        RateArticleSuccess,
        "json"
    );

    // don't allow submit because this is an ajax request
    return false;
});
```

Because the request is asynchronous, you provided a callback method called RateArticleSuccess that will be called when the response is successfully returned to the user's browser. The callback method is where most of the action usually occurs; by action we mean this is where you modify and update the HTML DOM depending on the response data returned.

```
function RateArticleSuccess (data) {
    var value = data.object.averageRating;
    var imagePosition = "50";

    if (value <= 1.3)
        imagePosition = "10";
    else if (value <= 1.8)
        imagePosition = "15";
    else if (value <= 2.3)
        imagePosition = "20";
    else if (value <= 2.8)
        imagePosition = "25";
    else if (value <= 3.3)
        imagePosition = "30";
    else if (value <= 3.8)
        imagePosition = "35";
    else if (value <= 4.3)
        imagePosition = "40";
    else if (value <= 4.8)
        imagePosition = "45";

    $("#article-rating-value")
```

```
            .replaceWith("<img src=\"/Content/images/stars" + imagePosition + ".gif\"
            alt=\"" + value + "\" />");

    $("form.rate-article :input").attr("disabled", "true");
    $("form.rate-article").append("Your rating has been applied!");
}
```

The response returned from the AJAX request is passed in through the `data` parameter in the `RateArticleSuccess` method. This `data` parameter is a JSON object which, just like objects in C#, can contain many levels, in this case everything returned from your service is serialized into `data.object`. So if you wanted to access the `averageRating` property set in the anonymous type in the `RateArticle` controller action, you would access it by referencing `data.object.averageRating`.

The preceding code is an exact representation of the `RatingImageUrl` utility that you used before in the `ArticleItem.ascx` view control. It calculates the correct image to use based on the average rating returned and then dynamically updates the image in the page for the new rating. Then, as we talked about before, it disables the drop-down list and submit button for the rating and displays the message "Your rating has been applied!"

Adding a Comment

Just like with rating an article you have two methods: one that makes the asynchronous request and one that handles the response. There is also some validation that is needed, but we will skip that because you have already seen how form fields are validated using JavaScript.

The AJAX request is made to `/article/createcomment` after the form fields have been validated:

```
$("form.comment-create").submit(function () {
    var valid = ValidateCommentName()
            && ValidateCommentEmail()
            && ValidateCommentBody();

    if (valid) {
        $.post(
            "/article/createcomment",
            {   articleId: $("#articleId").val(),
                name: $("#comment-name").val(),
                email: $("#comment-email").val(),
                body: $("#comment-body").val() },
            CreateCommentSuccess,
            "json"
        );
    }

    // don't allow submit because this is an ajax request
    return false;
});
```

The callback method for the add comment request is `CreateCommentSuccess`, which will construct the comment, in HTML, from the `data` object returned, and then append it to the bottom of the articles currently listed on the page.

```
function CreateCommentSuccess (data, textStatus) {
    $(".new-comment").removeClass("new-comment").show("normal");

    var commentText = "";
    commentText += "<div id=\"comment-"
                + data.object.commentId + "\" class=\"comment new-comment\">";
    commentText += "<div class=\"comment-header\">Comment posted by "
                + data.object.name + " 0 sec ago</div>";
    commentText += "<blockquote>" + data.object.body + "</blockquote>";
    commentText += "</div>";

    var comment = $(commentText);

    // clear the body box
    $("#comment-body").val("");

    // add the new comment to the other comments
    comment
        .hide()
        .appendTo("#article-comments")
        .slideDown("slow");
}
```

The very last method called in this code block actually provides a nice slide-down animation, so that the users visually see the comment rendering before their eyes. We like to provide this visual queue for a couple of reasons: one, because it looks nice, and two, it gives the users a visual queue so they know the comment has been added to the page. If you didn't have this animation, the comment would instantly appear on the page, and if the users weren't observant they might think the comment was never added.

The Atom Syndication View

Anytime `?type=atom` is added in the query string, to a page that contains a collection of articles, an Atom feed for that view model is returned. In the Design section of this chapter you saw the schema of a valid Atom document. Here you apply that structure to output a set of `Article` entries retrieved from the database using the same action filter that is used to serialize a response into JSON. After the feed is returned to the browser it may look something like Figure 6-21.

This is all easily done using a new Syndication model included in the .NET 3.5 Framework. To be specific you are going to use the `Atom10FeedFormatter`, located in `System.ServiceModel.Syndication`, to display your feed:

```
var articles = Data as Models.Pagination<Models.Article>;

SyndicationFeed feed = new SyndicationFeed {
    Title = new TextSyndicationContent("The Beer House Articles",
TextSyndicationContentKind.Plaintext),
    Description = new TextSyndicationContent("Feed of ideas from The Beer House.",
TextSyndicationContentKind.Plaintext),
    LastUpdatedTime = DateTime.Now
};
```

```
feed.Id = request.Url.GetLeftPart(UriPartial.Path);
feed.Links.Add(new SyndicationLink {
    Uri = request.Url,
    RelationshipType = "self"
});
/*  Purposely Removed */

List<SyndicationItem> items = new List<SyndicationItem>();

foreach (var article in articles)
{
    SyndicationItem item = new SyndicationItem {
        Title = new TextSyndicationContent(article.Title,
TextSyndicationContentKind.Plaintext),
        Content = new TextSyndicationContent(article.Body,
TextSyndicationContentKind.XHtml),
        PublishDate = article.ReleaseDate,
        Id = article.ArticleID.ToString()
    };

    item.Links.Add(new SyndicationLink {
        Uri = new Uri(HttpContext.Current.Request.Url, "/" + article.ArticleID +
"/" + article.Path),
        RelationshipType = "alternate"
    });

    item.Authors.Add(new SyndicationPerson {
        Name = article.AddedBy
    });

    item.Categories.Add(new SyndicationCategory {
        Name = article.Category.Title
    });

    items.Add(item);
}

feed.Items = items;

Atom10FeedFormatter atomFormatter = new Atom10FeedFormatter(feed);
atomFormatter.WriteTo(new XmlTextWriter(response.Output));
```

This code creates a variable called `feed` that will contain all the information needed to create the Atom syndication. To populate this variable with articles, the code loops through each `Article` object and builds a resulting `SyndicationItem` that is stored in a collection for the feed. After this is done, you pass this object through `Atom10FeedFormatter` to transform it into an Atom feed that you then write out to the response stream back to the feed client that requested the feed.

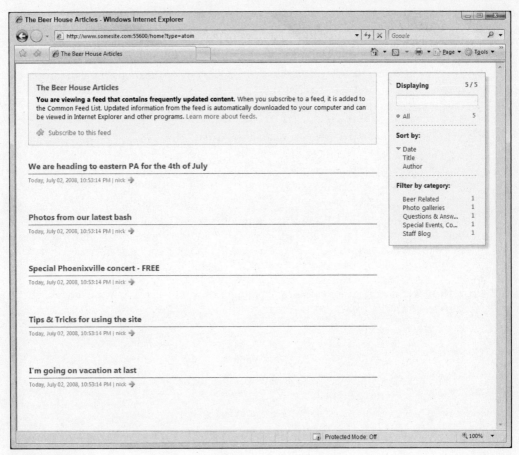

Figure 6-21

Summary

This chapter has shown you how to build a complex and articulate module to completely manage the site's articles, events, and possibly even photo galleries. It covered all of the following:

- ❑ An administrative section for managing the data in the database
- ❑ Pages for browsing the published content
- ❑ Integration with the built-in membership system to secure the module and track the authors of the articles
- ❑ A syndication service that publishes an Atom feed of recent content for a specific category, or for every category, by means of an `ActionResult`

By following along in this chapter you've seen some of the powerful things you can do with the models, views, controllers, and a properly designed infrastructure, and also created framework code for pagination that can be used in the upcoming chapters.

This system is flexible enough to be utilized in many real-world applications, but you can also consider making some of the following improvements:

❑ Support multilevel categories (subcategories management).

❑ A search engine could be added to the public section of the modules. Currently, when users want to find a particular article, they have to go through all the content (which could fill several pages in the article list). You could add a Search box that searches for the specified words in the selected category, or in all the categories, and with further options.

❑ Extend the `ViewArticle.aspx` page, or create a separate view, that outputs a printer-friendly version of the article, that is, the article without the site's layout (header, menus, footer, and right-hand column). This could be done easily by adding a new stylesheet to the page (when the page is loaded with a `printerFriendly=1` parameter on the querystring) that makes some DIVs hidden (use the `display:none` style).

In the next chapter you work on a module for creating, managing, displaying, and archiving opinion polls, to implement a form of user-to-site communication.

Opinion Polls

Opinion polls consist of questions with a set of options from which users can select their response. Once users vote in a poll it's customary to show them current statistics about how the poll is going at that particular time. This chapter explains why polls are useful and important for different websites, and shows you how to design and implement a simple and maintainable voting module for your TheBeerHouse site.

Problem

Polls are used on a website for basically two reasons: because the site managers may be interested in what their users like (perhaps so they can modify their advertising or product offerings, or maybe in a more general sense to understand their users better) and to help users feel like they have some input to a site and make them feel like they are part of a community of users. Good polls always contain targeted questions that can help the site's managers know who their users are and what they want to find on the site. This information can be used to identify which parts of the site to improve or modify. Armed with this information, e-commerce businesses can highlight those products, provide more detailed descriptions or case studies, or offer discounts to convince users to buy from their site. Another use for the information is to attract advertising revenue. If you look on a typical medium- to large-sized site, you will frequently see an "Advertise with Us" link or something similar. If you were to inquire about the possibility of advertising on a particular site, that site's advertising department would likely give you some demographics regarding the typical users of that site, such as age, the region or country they live in, common interests, and so on. This information is often gathered by direct or indirect polls. The more details you provide about your typical audience, the more chance you have of finding a sponsor to advertise on your site.

The other major benefit is user-to-user communication. Users generally like to know what their peers think about a product or a subject of interest to them. I must admit that I'm usually curious when I see a poll on a website. Even if I don't have a very clear opinion about the question being asked, I will often vote just so I can see the statistics of how the other users voted! This explains why polls are usually well-accepted, and why users generally vote quite willingly. Another reason why users may desire to cast a vote is because they think their opinion may influence other users or the site managers. In addition, their votes really are important, as you've seen, and the results can definitely drive the future content of the site and perhaps even business decisions. For these reasons, you or your client may realize that you want the benefits of a poll feature, and thus you will implement some form of polling on the website.

You should consider some design issues about web polls, namely the problems that you must address to successfully run a poll system. First of all, as with the news and other content, the same poll shouldn't remain active for too long. If you left the same poll on the page for, say, two months, you might gather some more votes, but you would lose the interest of users who voted early. If you keep a poll up for just a couple of days, you may not achieve significant results because some of your users may not have visited your site within that time frame. The right duration depends mostly on the average number of visitors you have and how often they return to your site. As a rule of thumb, if you know that several thousands of users regularly come to visit the site each week, that is a good duration for the active poll. Otherwise, if you have fewer visitors, you can leave the poll open for two or more weeks, but probably not longer than a month.

Finding Out How Many Visitors Your Site Has

Several services enable you to easily retrieve statistics for your site, such as the frequency and number of visitors, and much more. Some of these services are commercial, but you can also find some good free ones. If your website is hosted through a hosting company, you probably have access to some statistics through your hosting company's control panel or HTTP log parsing software (these gather information by analyzing the IIS log files).

If your hosting company doesn't provide a way to view your website's log or it is not detailed enough for what you need, you may want to consider some of the great alternatives like Google Analytics (`www.google.com/analytics`) or Stat Counter (`www.statcounter.com`). We personally use Google Analytics on all of our websites, because it provides in-depth statistics and visually appealing graphs about the visitor activity on the site.

So if you currently don't have a solution or are looking for a new one, give Google Analytics or Stat Counter a try; they are free.

When you change the active poll, a new question arises: what do you do with the old questions and their results? Should you throw them away? Certainly not! They might be very interesting for new users who didn't take part in the vote, and the information will probably remain valid for some time, so you should keep them available for viewing. Old polls can even be considered as part of the useful content of your site, and you should probably build an archive of past polls.

If you allow users to vote as many times as they want to, you'll end up with incorrect results; the overall results will be biased toward those users' personal opinions. Having false results is just as useless as having no results at all, because you can't base any serious decisions on them. Therefore, you want to prevent users from voting more than once for any given question. There are occasions when you might want to allow the user to vote several times, though. For example, during your own development and testing stage, you may need to post many votes to determine whether the voting module is working correctly. The administrator could just manually add some votes by entering them directly into the SQL table, or by directly calling the appropriate stored procedure, but that would not tell you if the polling front end is working right. If you enter votes using the polling user interface that you build in this chapter, it's more convenient and it thoroughly tests the module. Reasons exist for wanting to allow multiple votes after deployment, too. Imagine that you are running a competition to select the best resource on any selected topic. The resources might be updated frequently, and if the poll lasts a month, users may change their mind in the meantime, after voting. You may then decide to allow multiple votes, but no more than once per week (but you probably won't want to go to the trouble of letting users eliminate their earlier vote).

> *This discussion talks about polls that allow only a single option to be selected (a poll box with a series of radio buttons). Another type of poll box enables users to vote for multiple options in a single step (the options are listed with checkboxes, and users can select more than one). This might be useful if you wanted to ask a question like "What do you usually eat at pubs?" and you wanted to allow multiple answers through separate checkboxes. However, this type of poll is quite rare, and you could probably reword the question to ask what food they most like to eat at pubs if you want to allow only one answer. The design of a multiple-answer poll would needlessly complicate this module, so the example here won't use that kind of functionality.*

To summarize what we've discussed here: you want to implement a poll facility on the site to gauge the opinions of your users and to generate a sense of community. You don't want users to lose interest by seeing the same poll for a long time, but you do want a meaningful number of users to vote, so you'll add new questions and change the current poll often. You also want to allow users to see old polls because that helps to add useful content to your page, but they won't be allowed to vote in the old polls. Finally, you want to be able to easily add the poll to any page, and you want the results to be as unbiased and accurate as possible. The next section describes the design in more detail, and considers how to meet these challenges.

Design

This section looks at how you can provide poll functionality for the site. This polling stores the data (questions, answers, votes, and so on) in the database shared by all modules of this book. To easily access the database you'll need tables, a model, a view, and a controller to keep the presentation layer separate from the database and the details of its structure. Of course, some sort of user interface will allow administrators to see and manage the data using their favorite browser. You'll start with a list of features you want to implement, and then you'll design the database tables, model, view, controller, and security that you need for this module.

Features to Implement

Here's the list of features needed in the polls module:

❑   An access-protected administration console to easily change the current poll and add or remove questions. It should allow multiple polls and their response options to be added, edited, or deleted. The capability to have multiple polls is important because you might want to have different polls in different sections of your site. The administration pages should also show the current statistical results for each poll and the total number of votes for each poll, as a quick general summary.

❑   A user control that builds the poll box that can be inserted into any page. The poll box should display the question text and the available options (usually rendered as radio buttons to allow only one choice). Each poll will be identified by a unique ID, which should be specified as a custom property for the user control, so that the web master can easily change the currently displayed question by setting the value for that property.

❑ You should prevent users from voting multiple times for the same poll. Or, even better, you should be able to dynamically decide if you want to allow users to vote more than once, or specify the period for which they will be prevented from voting again.

❑ You can have only one poll question declared as the current default. When you set a poll question as being current, the previous current one should change its state. The current poll will be displayed in a poll box unless you specify a non-default poll ID. It's useful to set a default poll question because you'll be able to add a poll box without specifying the ID of the question to display, and you can change the poll question through the administration console, without manually changing the page and re-deploying it.

❑ A poll should be archived when you decide that you no longer want to use it as an active poll. Once archived, if a poll box is still explicitly bound to that particular poll, the poll will only be shown in Display state (read-only), and it will show the recorded results.

❑ A page that displays all the archived polls and their results. A page for the results of the current poll is not necessary, because they will be shown directly by the poll box — instead of the list of response options — when it detects that the user has already voted. This way, users are forced to express their opinion if they want to see the poll's results (before the poll expires), which will bring in more votes than you would get if you made the current results freely available to users that have not yet voted. There must also be an option that specifies whether the archive page is accessible by everyone, or just by registered users. You may prefer the second option to give the user one more reason to register for the site.

Handling Multiple Votes

As discussed in the Problem section, you want to be able to control whether users can cast multiple votes, and, if so, allow them to vote again after a specified period. Therefore, you would probably like to give the administrator the capability to prevent multiple votes, or to allow multiple votes but with a specified lock duration (one week in the previous example). You still have to find a way to ensure that the user does not vote more times than is allowed. The simplest, and most common and reliable, solution is writing a cookie to the client's browser that stores the ID of the poll for which the user has voted. Then, when the poll box loads, it first tries to find a cookie matching the poll. If a cookie is not found, the poll box displays the options and lets the user vote. Otherwise, the poll box shows the latest results and does not allow the user to vote again. To allow multiple votes, the cookie will have an expiration date. If you set it to the current date plus seven days, it means that the cookie expires in seven days, after which the user will be allowed to vote again on that same question.

Writing and checking cookies is straightforward, and in most cases it is sufficient. The drawback of this method is that the users can easily turn off cookies through a browser option, or delete the cookies from their machine, and then be allowed to vote as many times as they want to. Only a very small percentage of users keep cookies turned off — except for company users where security is a major concern — because they are used on many sites and are sometimes actually required. Because of this, it shouldn't be much of an issue because most people won't bother to go to that much trouble to re-vote, and this is not a high-security type of voting mechanism that would be suitable for something very important, such as a political election.

There's an additional method to prevent multiple votes: IP locking. When users vote, their computer's IP address can be retrieved and stored in the cache together with the other vote details. Later in the same user session, when the poll box loads or when the user tries to vote again, you can check whether the cache contains a vote for a specific poll by a specified IP. To implement this, the Poll ID and user's IP may be part of the item's key if you use the Cache class; otherwise, the Poll ID is enough if you choose to store it in Session state storage, because that's already specific to one user. If a vote is found, the user has already voted and you can prevent further voting. This method only prevents re-voting within the same session — the same user can vote again the next day. You don't want to store the user's IP address in the database because it might be different tomorrow (most users today have dynamically assigned IP addresses). Also, the user might share an IP with many other users if she is in a company using network address translation (NAT) addresses, and you don't want to prevent other users within the same company from voting. Therefore, the IP locking method is normally not my first choice.

There's yet another option to prevent undesired multiple votes: you could track the logged users through their username, instead of their computer's IP address. However, this will only work if the user is registered. In your case you don't want to limit the vote to registered users only, so we won't cover this method further.

In this module we provide the option to employ both methods (cookie and IP), only one of them, or neither. Employing neither of them means that you will allow multiple votes with no limitations, and this method should only be used during the testing stage. In a real scenario you might need to disable one of the methods — maybe your client doesn't want to use cookies for security reasons, or maybe your client is concerned about the dynamic IP issue and doesn't want to use that method. I personally prefer the cookie option in most cases.

In conclusion, the polls module will have the following options:

❑   Multiple votes per poll can be allowed or denied.

❑   Multiple votes per poll can be prevented with client cookies or IP locking.

❑   Limited multiple votes can be allowed, in which case the administrator can specify lock duration for either method (users can vote again in seven days, for example).

This way, the polls module will be simple and straightforward, but still flexible, and it can be used with the options that best suit the particular situation. Online administration of polls follows the general concept of allowing the site to be remotely controlled by managers and administrators using a web browser.

Designing the Database Tables

You will need two tables for this module: one to contain the poll questions and their attributes (such as whether a poll is current or archived) and another one to contain the poll response options and the number of votes each received. The diagram in Figure 7-1 shows how they are linked to each other.

Here you see the primary and foreign keys, the usual AddedDate and AddedBy fields that are used in most tables for audit and recovery purposes, and a few extra fields that store the poll data. The Polls table has a QuestionText field that stores the poll's question, an IsArchived bit field to indicate whether that poll is archived and no longer available for voting, and an ArchivedDate field for the date/time when the poll was archived (this last column is the only one that is nullable). There is also an IsCurrent bit field, which can be set to 1 only for a single poll, which is the overall default poll. The other table, PollOptions, contains all the configurable options for each poll, and makes the link to the parent poll by means of the PollID foreign key. There is also a Votes integer field that contains the number of user votes received by the option. In the first edition of the book we had a separate Votes table, in addition to these two, that would store every vote in a separate row with the date/time of the vote and the IP of the user who cast the vote.

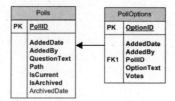

Figure 7-1

Queries That Access the Database

The stored procedures in the following table will be needed by the poll administration pages.

Property	Description
CurrentPoll	Gets the current poll for displaying on the front page.
GetPoll	Gets a single poll by the specified ID.
GetPollOptions	Gets a single poll option by the specified ID.
GetPolls	Retrieves all data for the rows of the Polls table, plus a calculated field that is the sum of all votes for the poll's child options. The procedure takes as input a couple of methods that enable you to specify whether you want to include the active (non-archived) polls in the results, and whether you want to include the archived polls in this poll box.

Designing the Configuration Module

I've already mentioned that the polls module will need a number of configuration settings that enable or disable multiple votes, make the archive public to everyone, and more. The following is the list of properties for a new class, named PollsElement, which inherits from the framework's ConfigurationElement class, and will read the settings of a <polls> element under the <the-BeerHouse> custom configuration section (this was introduced in Chapter 4, and then used again in Chapter 6).

Property	Description
VotingLockInterval	An integer indicating when the cookie with the user's vote will expire (number of days to prevent re-voting)
VotingLockByCookie	A Boolean value indicating whether a cookie will be used to remember the user's vote
VotingLockByIP	A Boolean value indicating whether the voter's IP address is kept in memory to prevent duplicate votes from that IP in the current session
ArchiveIsPublic	A Boolean value indicating whether the poll's archive is accessible by everyone, or if it's restricted to registered members

Designing the Model

The model of this module is based on the same pattern introduced in Chapter 4 and then implemented for the articles module in Chapter 6. The diagram shown in Figure 7-2 represents the two LINQ-to-SQL classes that you will be using as your model; the design should be self-explanatory.

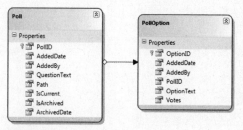

Figure 7-2

Just as before in Chapter 6 we created a static class that contained all the queries necessary to pull information from the database. In this case the static class is called `PollQueries`, and it provides extension methods for `Poll` and `PollOption`. The diagram in Figure 7-3 represents the queries available for the model.

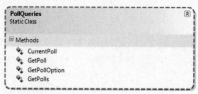

Figure 7-3

Designing the View

This section describes the views and routes necessary for this module. In particular the design of the view follows the same layout designed in Chapter 6.

- ❑ **Index.aspx:** This is the page through which you can view all the available polls and archived polls.

    - ❑ `/polls`

    - ❑ `/polls/page{page}`

    - ❑ `/polls?archived=true`

    - ❑ `/polls/page{page}?archived=true`

- ❑ **ManagePolls.aspx:** This is the page through which an administrator or editor can manage polls: add, edit, archive, and remove poll options, see current results, and set the current poll.

    - ❑ `/admin/polls`

    - ❑ `/admin/polls/page{page}`

❑ **CreatePoll.aspx:** This page will allow you to create or edit an existing poll.

    ❑ `/admin/polls/create`

    ❑ `/admin/polls/edit/{pollId}`

❑ **RemovePoll.aspx:** This page will ask you if you want to remove the current poll from the database.

    ❑ `/admin/polls/remove/{pollId}`

Designing the Controller

Just like in Chapter 6, the hard work was already done when you designed the model and the view. So you need to create an appropriate set of controller actions to map your model to your view.

Action Method	Security	Parameters
Index	—	bool? archived, int page
ViewPoll	—	int id, string path
Vote	—	int optionId
ManagePolls	Editor	int page
CreatePoll	Editor	string question, bool? current
EditPoll	Editor	int pollId, string question, bool? current, bool? archived
RemovePoll	Editor	int pollId
AddOption	Editor	int pollId, string text
RemoveOption	Editor	int optionId
SetCurrent	Editor	int pollId
SetArchived	Editor	int pollId, bool archive

Solution

Now that the design is complete, you should have a very clear idea about what is required, so you can consider how you're going to implement this functionality. You'll follow the same order as the Design section, starting with the creation of database tables and stored procedures, the configuration, DAL and BLL classes, and finally the ASPX pages and the `PollBox` user control.

Working on the Database

The tables and stored procedures required for this module are added to the same sitewide SQL Server 2005 database shared by all modules. It's easy to create the required objects with Visual Studio 2008 using the integrated Server Explorer, which has been enhanced in the 2008 version so that it's almost like using SQL Server 2005 Management Studio, but right from within the Visual Studio IDE. Figure 7-4 is a screenshot of the IDE when adding columns to the `Polls` tables and setting the properties for the `PollID` primary key column.

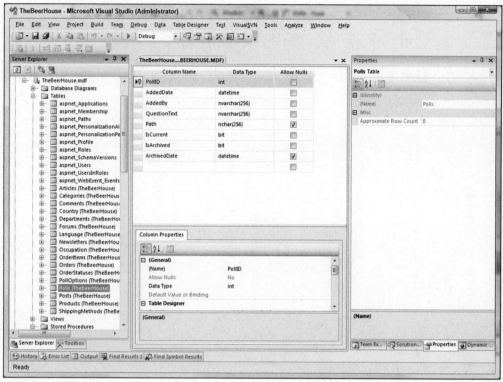

Figure 7-4

Implementing the Configuration Module

The custom configuration class must be developed before any other code because the custom settings are used in all other layers. This class is similar to the one seen in the previous chapter. It inherits from `ConfigurationElement` and has the properties previously defined:

```
public class PollsElement : ConfigurationElement
{
    [ConfigurationProperty("pageSize", DefaultValue = "10")]
    public int PageSize
    {
        get { return (int)base["pageSize"]; }
        set { base["pageSize"] = value; }
    }

    [ConfigurationProperty("archiveIsPublic", DefaultValue = "false")]
    public bool ArchiveIsPublic
    {
```

```
                get { return (bool)base["archiveIsPublic"]; }
                set { base["archiveIsPublic"] = value; }
        }
    }
```

To make this class map a <polls> element under the top-level <theBeerHouse> section, you add a
property of type PollsElement to the TheBeerHouseSection class developed in the previous chapter
and then use the ConfigurationProperty attribute to do the mapping:

```
public class TheBeerHouseSection : ConfigurationSection
{
    // other properties here…

    [ConfigurationProperty("polls", IsRequired = true)]
    public PollsElement Polls
    {
        get { return (PollsElement)base["polls"]; }
    }
}
```

If you want to make the archive available to everyone, you would use these settings in the web.config file:

```
<theBeerHouse>
        <contactForm mailTo="support@managedfusion.com" />
        <articles pageSize="10" />
        <polls archiveIsPublic="true" />
</theBeerHouse>
```

The default value will be used for all those settings not explicitly defined in the configuration file.

Implementing the Model

In this chapter we won't show the code for the entity classes, because there is no custom code in the
partial extension classes of the LINQ entities. The information in the diagram in Figure 7-2 is enough to
completely define the class.

Create the LINQ Queries

You still need to create some of the LINQ queries that we talked about in the Design section. Just like
in the last chapter you are going to use extension methods for the LINQ tables, which will provide you
with some useful queries when you are interacting with the model from your controller. This time you
only have a handful of queries to create and all but one of them is a single line query.

The CurrentPoll Query

The following query returns the current poll that will be displayed as part of the theme, and will be
present on each and every page:

```
public static Poll CurrentPoll(this Table<Poll> source)
{
    return source.FirstOrDefault(p => p.IsCurrent == true);
}
```

You may have noticed that we used a method called `FirstOrDefault` instead of the `SingleOrDefault` that you have seen before. There is a very logical reason for this, and it is because `SingleOrDefault` will throw an error if more than one result is returned from the database, and it is only really useful for queries where you know you will only get one result back, like when you query a unique field such as the `PollID`. `FirstOrDefault` will include a `TOP 1` statement in the SQL so that only the first result, if any, is returned; this is useful when you are querying a field that doesn't have a unique constraint on it, like the `IsCurrent` field. With the `IsCurrent` field you have a business rule that states that there should only be one row set to `true` at a time, however to achieve this uniqueness you would need to set up a custom trigger; that is probably overkill for this situation because you will only be selecting one from the database anyway.

The GetPoll Query

This query gets a single poll from the database for the requested identity. This will help you get specific polls for when you want to view just the poll with its results, or edit the poll:

```
public static Poll GetPoll(this Table<Poll> source, int id)
{
    return source.SingleOrDefault(p => p.PollID == id);
}
```

The GetPollOption Query

Like the `GetPoll` query, this query gets a single option from the database that is requested by its identity:

```
public static PollOption GetPollOption(this Table<PollOption> source, int id)
{
    return source.SingleOrDefault(o => o.OptionID == id);
}
```

The GetPolls Query

This query returns a paginable collection like you saw in Chapter 6. The query takes two parameters, one for the page you want to return and another one that tells the query if you want to return archived polls or not:

```
public static Pagination<Poll> GetPolls(
    this Table<Poll> source,
    bool? archived,
    int page
) {
    int count = Configuration.TheBeerHouseSection.Current.Polls.PageSize;
    int index = (page -1) * count;

    var query = from p in source
                orderby p.AddedDate descending
                where (archived == null ||
                    p.IsArchived == archived.GetValueOrDefault(false))
                select p;

    return new Pagination<Poll>(
        query.Skip(index).Take(count),
        index,
```

```
        count,
        query.Count()
    );
}
```

This is a slightly different query method structure than last time because your query and collection is constructed in the same method. The reason we didn't do this in Chapter 6 is because it was easier to have one query method handle the query creation for a handful of other methods; that way it was easy to update the one query in one place if you had to make changes.

Implementing the Controller

As we previously did in Chapter 6, we are going to walk through each action method that is needed for the polls controller, which is located in ~/Controllers and will be called PollController.cs. The actions of this controller will define business rules that enforce the data input and validation on your model and provide appropriate data for your view.

The Index Action

The first action you will implement displays all the polls that are requested for a certain page. It is also responsible for checking if the archived polls are public or private and rejecting the user if the requesting user doesn't have the permissions to view archived polls. The only exception to this is if the user is an editor of the website.

```
public ActionResult Index(bool? archived, int page)
{
    // if archived isn't set then we are only showing non-archived polls
    archived = archived ?? false;

    // make sure the current user is allowed to view archived polls
    if (archived.Value
        && !Configuration.TheBeerHouseSection.Current.Polls.ArchiveIsPublic
        && !Roles.IsUserInRole("Editor"))
        throw new HttpException(401,
            "The archived polls are only available to editors of the site.");

    TheBeerHouseDataContext dc = new TheBeerHouseDataContext();
    var viewData = dc.Polls.GetPolls(archived, page);

    ViewData["PageTitle"] = "Polls";
    return View(viewData);
}
```

The preceding code will throw a 401 Unauthorized HTTP exception if the poll archive is being requested and the website configuration has it set as only viewable by an editor and the user calling the action is not part of the Editor role.

This action has the following routes:

❑ polls

❑ polls/page{page}

/polls

This route is used to display a list of polls, for use on the first page:

```
routes.MapRoute(
    "PollsIndex",
    "polls",
    new { controller = "Poll", action = "Index", page = 1 }
);
```

/polls/page{page}

This route is used to display a list of polls for a certain page:

```
routes.MapRoute(
    "PollsIndexPaged",
    "polls/page{page}",
    new { controller = "Poll", action = "Index", page = (int?)null },
    new { page = "[0-9]+" }
);
```

The Vote Action

This action places one vote for the option identifier passed to the action. This action is a service, which you learned about in Chapter 6, which means that it cannot be viewed directly from the browser and can be accessed only by an AJAX call. This specific service only allows POST requests from the browser and will respond with a JSON response, which will contain the pollId, question, and a list of the options for this poll provided through the JSON property option, that the user just voted for.

```
[ServiceOnly, HttpPostOnly]
public ActionResult Vote(int optionId)
{
    TheBeerHouseDataContext dc = new TheBeerHouseDataContext();
    var option = dc.PollOptions.GetPollOption(optionId);

    if (option == null)
        throw new HttpException(404, "The poll option could not be found.");

    var poll = option.Poll;
    var options = new List<object>();
```

In the next block of code for the Vote action you are going to check that a cookie doesn't already exist for this poll. If a cookie exists it means that the user has already voted and shouldn't be allowed to vote for this poll again. Voting is also not allowed if the poll is archived.

```
if (poll.IsArchived || Request.Cookies["poll_" + poll.PollID] == null)
{
    option.Votes++;
    dc.SubmitChanges();
}
```

Next you are going to prepare a response for the poll to be rendered on the client side through AJAX:

```
foreach (var o in poll.PollOptions)
    options.Add(new {
```

```
                optionId = o.OptionID,
                text = o.OptionText,
                votes = o.Votes
            });

        return View(new {
            pollId = poll.PollID,
            total = poll.PollOptions.Sum(o => o.Votes),
            question = poll.QuestionText,
            options = options
        });
    }
```

The reason why we are providing a collection of all the options is because the poll results will actually be built by JavaScript on the client side to resemble an output that might have come from the server. We are doing this is because we are trying to provide a flicker-free and seamless experience wherever possible and that means we cannot do a POST-back when it is not necessary. In this case we don't need to go through a Herculean effort to provide that experience so it is well worth it for both the developers and the users of the site; the developers get a low overhead because they only have to transfer the necessary data for the poll results back to the client and the user ends up with a seamless experience.

The route for this action uses the standard `{controller}/{action}` route, so requests to this action method can be accessed through

❑   poll/vote

The ManagePolls Action

This action is a relatively simple action that is used to bind a set of polls to a view. The view will then be used as a launching point to edit, remove, set as current, and set as archived for the polls that you have created. This action is only allowed to be accessed by a user with the role of Editor.

```
[Authorize(Roles = "Editor")]
public ActionResult ManagePolls(int page)
{
    TheBeerHouseDataContext dc = new TheBeerHouseDataContext();
    var viewData = dc.Polls.GetPolls(null, page);

    ViewData["PageTitle"] = "Manage Polls";
    return View(viewData);
}
```

This works much like the `Index` action except that all polls are returned regardless of whether or not they are archived and even if the configuration doesn't allow them to be seen publicly. This is because this is an admin section that is only available for editors so you don't have to worry about anybody else entering the action.

This action has the following routes:

❑   admin/polls

❑   admin/polls/page{page}

/admin/polls

This route is used to display a list of polls for managing, for use on the first page:

```
routes.MapRoute(
    "PollManager",
    "admin/polls",
    new { controller = "Poll", action = "ManagePolls", page = 1  }
);
```

/admin/polls/page{page}

This route is used to display a list of polls to be managed for a certain page:

```
routes.MapRoute(
    "PollManagerPaged",
    "admin/polls/page{page}",
    new { controller = "Poll", action = " ManagePolls", page = (int?)null },
    new { page = "[0-9]+" }
);
```

The CreatePoll and EditPoll Action

The next actions you have to create are ones that will create and edit a poll. We have combined these actions together in the same section because they contain mostly the same code concepts.

The CreatePoll Action

This action is used to create your poll and it is only accessible to users with the role of Editor:

```
[Authorize(Roles = "Editor")]
public ActionResult CreatePoll(string question)
{
    TheBeerHouseDataContext dc = new TheBeerHouseDataContext();

    if (!String.IsNullOrEmpty(question))
    {
        try
        {
            Poll poll = new Poll {
                QuestionText = question,
                Path = question.ToUrlFormat(),
                AddedBy = User.Identity.Name,
                AddedDate = DateTime.Now
            };

            dc.Polls.InsertOnSubmit(poll);
            dc.SubmitChanges();

            TempData["SuccessMessage"] = "Your poll has been created.";
            return RedirectToAction("EditPoll", new { pollId = poll.PollID });
        }
        catch (Exception exc)
        {
            TempData["ErrorMessage"] = exc.Message;
```

```
                }
        }

        ViewData["question"] = question;

        ViewData["PageTitle"] = "Create Poll";

        return View("CreatePoll");
    }
```

As you can see from the preceding code, this is very similar to the create actions that you saw in Chapter 6. This pattern is very easy to implement and offers many advantages. The first is that you are not only verifying the input on the client side, but also on the server side; in addition, the verification process is used as a way to control whether or not the data should be inserted into the database. The second is that you only need one action to control the GET and POST of the page; this allows you to streamline while providing a reduction in code, which should result in fewer bugs and easier testing.

The EditPoll Action

This action is used to edit a poll that is defined by the parameter pollId; this action is only available to users who have the Editor role. In the EditPoll action we are going to highlight the parts of code you should pay specific attention to because they are the sections of code that differ from the CreatePoll action:

```
[Authorize(Roles = "Editor")]
public ActionResult EditPoll(int pollId, string question)
{
    TheBeerHouseDataContext dc = new TheBeerHouseDataContext();
    Poll poll = dc.Polls.GetPoll(pollId);

    // throw a 404 Not Found if the requested poll is not in the database
    if (poll == null)
        throw new HttpException(404, "The poll could not be found.");

    if (!String.IsNullOrEmpty(question))
    {
        try
        {
            poll.QuestionText = question;
            poll.Path = question.ToUrlFormat();

            dc.SubmitChanges();

            TempData["SuccessMessage"] = "Your poll has been updated.";
        }
        catch (Exception exc)
        {
            TempData["ErrorMessage"] = exc.Message;
        }
    }

    ViewData["pollId"] = pollId;
    ViewData["question"] = question ?? poll.QuestionText;
    ViewData["options"] = poll.PollOptions.ToList();
```

```
    ViewData["PageTitle"] = "Edit Poll";

    return View("CreatePoll");
}
```

In the first section of code you will notice that you are again checking if a poll is able to be returned from the database and, if one cannot be returned, a 404 Not Found HTTP exception is thrown. This will alert the browser that the requested URL is not valid on the server.

In the second section of code you are setting the ViewData for necessary information about the poll that is used to render the view in edit mode instead of create mode. This additionally includes the pollId and options of the poll object requested.

These actions have the following routes, respectively, for CreatePoll and EditPoll:

❑   admin/polls/create

❑   admin/polls/edit/{pollId}

/admin/polls/create

This route is used to create a poll:

```
routes.MapRoute(
    "PollCreate",
    "admin/polls/create",
    new { controller = "Poll", action = "CreatePoll" }
);
```

/admin/polls/edit/{pollId}

This route is used to edit a poll. It takes one rule, pollId, which provides the identity of the poll that is being edited:

```
routes.MapRoute(
    "PollEdit",
    "admin/polls/edit/{pollId}",
    new { controller = "Poll", action = "EditPoll", pollId = (int?)null },
    new { pollId = "[0-9]+" }
);
```

The RemovePoll Action

This action is what the users of the site will call when they need to remove a poll from the database. This action method is mainly only a message pump that queues up the next message in a mini wizard that presents a "yes" or "no" question to the users about their intentions to delete the poll in question. It is only available for users with the role of Editor:

```
[Authorize(Roles = "Editor")]
public ActionResult RemovePoll(int pollId, string remove)
{
    TheBeerHouseDataContext dc = new TheBeerHouseDataContext();
    Poll poll = dc.Polls.GetPoll(pollId);
```

```
// throw a 404 Not Found if the requested poll is not in the database
if (poll == null)
    throw new HttpException(404, "The poll could not be found.");

if (String.Equals(remove, "yes", StringComparison.OrdinalIgnoreCase))
{
    dc.Polls.DeleteOnSubmit(poll);
    dc.SubmitChanges();

    TempData["SuccessMessage"] = "The poll, "
    + poll.QuestionText + ", has been deleted.";

    poll = null;
}
else if (String.Equals(remove, "no", StringComparison.OrdinalIgnoreCase))
{
    TempData["InformationMessage"] = "The poll, "
    + poll.QuestionText + ", has NOT been deleted.";
}
else
{
    TempData["WarningMessage"] = "Are you sure you want to delete "
    + poll.QuestionText
    + ".  You will not be able to recover this poll if you select YES.";
}

ViewData["PageTitle"] = "Remove Poll";

return View(poll);
}
```

As in Chapter 6, the view for removing the poll has two buttons that provide a "yes" or "no" response to RemovePoll. If the editor selects "yes," the poll is removed from the database and a response is returned stating the poll has been successfully deleted. If the editor selects "no," an information message is displayed saying that the poll has not been deleted. The default state is a warning message telling the editor that, if he selects "yes," he will not be able to recover the poll.

This action has the following route:

❏   admin/polls/remove/{pollId}

/admin/polls/remove/{pollId}

This route is used to remove a poll. It takes one rule, pollId, which provides the identity of the poll that is being removed:

```
routes.MapRoute(
    "PollRemove",
    "admin/polls/remove/{pollId}",
    new { controller = "Poll", action = "RemovePoll", pollId = (int?)null },
    new { pollId = "[0-9]+" }
);
```

The AddOption Action

This action is used as a service to allow editors to add options to an already existing poll, which is defined by the identity of the poll, `pollId`:

```
[ServiceOnly, HttpPostOnly]
[Authorize(Roles = "Editor")]
public ActionResult AddOption(int pollId, string text)
{
    TheBeerHouseDataContext dc = new TheBeerHouseDataContext();
    var poll = dc.Polls.GetPoll(pollId);

    if (poll == null)
        throw new HttpException(404, "The poll could not be found.");

    var option = new PollOption {
        AddedBy = User.Identity.Name,
        AddedDate = DateTime.Now,
        OptionText = text,
        Votes = 0
    };
    poll.PollOptions.Add(option);
    dc.SubmitChanges();

    return View(new { optionId = option.OptionID, text = text });
}
```

The route for this action uses the standard `{controller}/{action}` route, so requests to this action method can be accessed through

❑   `poll/addoption`

The EditOption Action

This action allows an editor to edit a current option of a poll that is defined by the identity `optionId`:

```
[ServiceOnly, HttpPostOnly]
[Authorize(Roles = "Editor")]
public ActionResult EditOption(int optionId, string text)
{
    TheBeerHouseDataContext dc = new TheBeerHouseDataContext();
    var option = dc.PollOptions.GetPollOption(optionId);

    if (option == null)
        throw new HttpException(404, "The poll option could not be found.");

    option.OptionText = text;
    dc.SubmitChanges();

    return View(new { optionId = option.OptionID, text = text });
}
```

The route for this action uses the standard `{controller}/{action}` route, so requests to this action method can be accessed through

❑ poll/editoption

The RemoveOption Action

This action allows an editor to remove an option from a poll that is defined by the identity `optionId`:

```
[ServiceOnly, HttpPostOnly]
[Authorize(Roles = "Editor")]
public ActionResult RemoveOption(int optionId)
{
    TheBeerHouseDataContext dc = new TheBeerHouseDataContext();
    var option = dc.PollOptions.GetPollOption(optionId);

    if (option == null)
        throw new HttpException(404, "The poll option could not be found.");

    dc.PollOptions.DeleteOnSubmit(option);
    dc.SubmitChanges();

    return View(new { optionId = optionId });
}
```

The route for this action uses the standard `{controller}/{action}` route, so requests to this action method can be accessed through

❑ poll/removeoption

The SetCurrent Action

This action is a service for editors that sets one poll as the current poll that is displayed as part of the master theme:

```
[ServiceOnly, HttpPostOnly]
[Authorize(Roles = "Editor")]
public ActionResult SetCurrent(int pollId)
{
    TheBeerHouseDataContext dc = new TheBeerHouseDataContext();
    var poll = dc.Polls.GetPoll(pollId);

    if (poll == null)
        throw new HttpException(404, "The poll could not be found.");

    // reset all polls to not current
    dc.ExecuteCommand(
        "update TheBeerHouse.Polls set IsCurrent = 0;",
        new object[0]
    );

    poll.IsCurrent = true;
    dc.SubmitChanges();
```

```
        return View(new { pollId = pollId });
    }
```

You will notice that we are making a direct database call to SQL Server. We could have completed this same operation by pulling back all the poll objects and setting the IsCurrent property to false for each of them, except for the matching poll, which we would set to true. The reason we didn't go this route is because of the number of executions that SQL would have to deal with: O1(n), meaning that every poll you change is committed back to the database individually.

By going with the code that we laid out, doing a global update, it takes much less time for SQL Server to complete the execution for both a small and large number of polls. Then you just update the one poll, which you want to make current, and you have reduced the execution time down to O1 + O2.

> Whenever dealing with a mass update in LINQ, use the assumption that there are 1 million records in the database, and ask yourself the question "How will this perform with 1 million records?" and "Is there a better way to do this?" If you keep in mind both of those questions when developing your software you will usually wind up with a great solution.

The route for this action uses the standard {controller}/{action} route, so requests to this action method can be accessed through

❑   poll/setcurrent

The SetArchived Action

This action is a service for editors to archive a poll so that no more voting is allowed on the poll:

```
[ServiceOnly, HttpPostOnly]
[Authorize(Roles = "Editor")]
public ActionResult SetArchived(int pollId, bool archive)
{
    TheBeerHouseDataContext dc = new TheBeerHouseDataContext();
    var poll = dc.Polls.GetPoll(pollId);

    if (poll == null)
        throw new HttpException(404, "The poll could not be found.");

    poll.IsArchived = archive;
    poll.ArchivedDate = archive ? DateTime.Now : (DateTime?)null;
    dc.SubmitChanges();

    return View(new { pollId = pollId, isArchived = poll.IsArchived });
}
```

The route for this action uses the standard {controller}/{action} route, so requests to this action method can be accessed through

❑   poll/setarchived

Implementing the View

Now it's time to build the view: the controls, the administration, and finally the public viewable page.

The PollResultItem.ascx Control

This view control, located under the `~/Views/Shared/Poll` folder, allows for a consistent display of the `Poll` object in both the `ManagePolls.aspx` and `Index.aspx` views. The poll will look like Figure 7-5 when shown on the page.

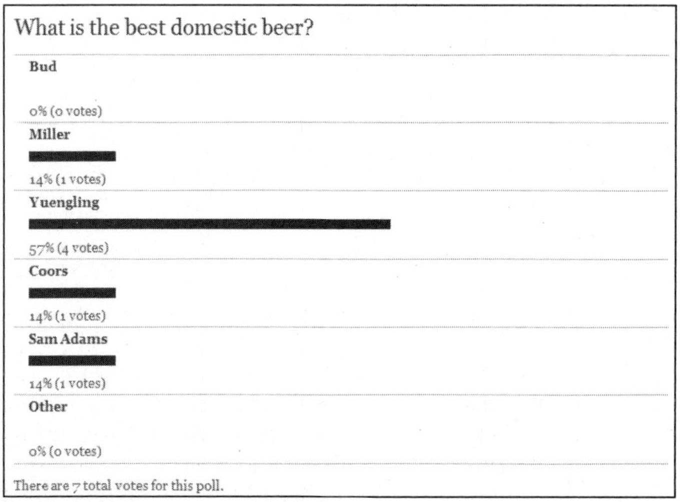

Figure 7-5

The layout of the results is pretty standard: you have a bar to show the results visually, you have the percentage of votes that the option received, and then you have the physical tally of the number of people who voted for each specific option.

> We apologize if your favorite domestic beer isn't mentioned or if the thought of this poll is making you thirsty for a tall frosty beer. It is making us thirsty just writing about it. The nice cold refreshing taste... But we digress.

In the header of the control you need to specify that the view model is going to be of the type Poll:

```
Inherits="System.Web.Mvc.ViewUserControl<TheBeerHouse.Models.Poll>"
```

This is pretty standard for the views that you have seen previously in Chapter 6, so the lack of code shouldn't catch you off guard. The next step is actually using the view model of the poll in the HTML of the control:

```
<div id="poll-<%= ViewData.Model.PollID %>" class="poll">
    <h2><%= ViewData.Model.QuestionText %></h2>

    <% var total = ViewData.Model.PollOptions.Sum(o => o.Votes); %>
    <ul class="poll-options">
```

```
<% foreach(var option in ViewData.Model.PollOptions) {
    var percentValue =
        Math.Round(((decimal)option.Votes / (decimal)total) * 100M); %>
    <li class="option" id="option-<%= option.OptionID %>">
        <h3><%= option.OptionText%></h3>
        <div class="graph">
            <img src="/Content/images/poll-graph.gif"
                height="10"
                width="<%= Math.Floor(percentValue) %>%" />
        </div>
        <div class="values">
            <%= Math.Floor(percentValue) %>%
                (<%= option.Votes %> votes)
        </div>
    </li>
<% } %>
</ul>
<div class="total">There are <%= total %> total votes for this poll.</div>
</div>
```

In this code, the first thing you do when rendering the poll results is to get a sum of all the votes in all the options for this poll. You then take this total and get the percentage value of each of the options by dividing the number of votes for each poll by the total number of votes. Then you use this percentage of votes to set the width of the image and to display the percentage of votes received. The image we are using is just a 1x1 blue pixel that is stretched by the browser to the appropriate height and width. The width of the image is correlated to the percentage of votes; by doing this the browser will automatically scale the image to the right width and visually give you what you want without too much acrobatics. Doing this was necessary because you are displaying the poll in both the body and sidebar, both of which vary in width, so, by letting the browser automatically calculate the width based on percentages, your poll easily scales visually for any size environment.

The next thing you want to define, as part of your design for the `PollResultItem` view control, and also the `PollItem` view control, is the CSS styles that are needed to style your HTML to look like Figure 7-5. These styles will be added into your main style sheet located in `~/Content/styles/site.css`.

```
/* Polls */

#polls {
    margin-top: 20px;
}

#polls .poll {
    margin-top: 10px;
}

#polls .poll-options .option:first-child {
    border-top: solid 1px #A8C3CB;
}

#polls .poll-options .option {
    border-bottom: solid 1px #A8C3CB;
}
```

The only thing you may not recognize from the preceding CSS is the `:first-child` special command; it is called a pseudo-class. This pseudo-class tells CSS that this styling only applies to the first child of the containing object, in this case the first `option` class in the `poll-options` class. We are using this to appropriately box the results of the options with the thin blue border. If you didn't have this pseudo-class in place each item would only have a bottom border, but visually it would look like each item had a top and bottom border except for the first option. You may ask, "Why don't you just define a top and bottom for each option?" Well, it is actually for a very simple reason visually: if you did that, where each option met another option it would visually look like a border twice as large as it should be, leaving the top of the first and the bottom of the last looking like half borders.

The PollItem.ascx Control

This view control, located under the `~/Views/Shared/Poll` folder, allows for a consistent display of the `Poll` object in both the `ManagePolls.aspx` and `Index.aspx` views. The poll will look like Figure 7-6 when shown on the page.

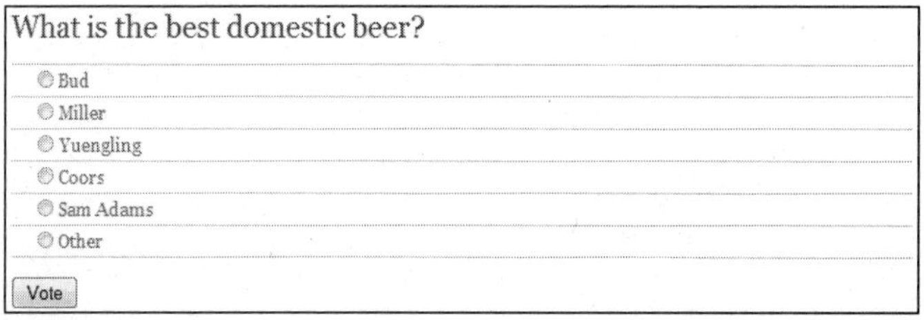

Figure 7-6

The layout is like the typical poll that you will see out on the Web, so there is nothing new about this control that you haven't seen a million times before.

In the header of the control you need to specify that the view model is going to be of the type Poll:

```
Inherits="System.Web.Mvc.ViewUserControl<TheBeerHouse.Models.Poll>"
```

The next step is actually using the view model of the poll in the HTML of the control, just as you did for the last control:

```
<div id="poll-<%= ViewData.Model.PollID %>" class="poll">
    <h2><%= ViewData.Model.QuestionText %></h2>

    <form action="#" method="post">
        <ul class="poll-options">
        <% foreach(var option in ViewData.Model.PollOptions) { %>
            <li class="option" id="option-<%= option.OptionID %>">
            <input type="radio"
                id="option-<%= option.OptionID %>"
                name="post-<%= ViewData.Model.PollID %>"
                value="<%= option.OptionID %>" />
            <label class="text"
                for="option-<%= option.OptionID %>">
                <%= option.OptionText %>
            </label>
            </li>
```

```
    <% } %>
    </ul>

    <button type="submit" name="poll-submit">Vote</button>
    </form>
</div>
```

As you can tell, this is pretty simplistic; you have the title of the poll with a form, and inside the form you have each poll option, which is rendered as a radio button that the user can select. The radio button contains the value of the `OptionID`, which corresponds to your input of the `Vote` action.

poll.js

The most difficult part of this control is the code in the `poll.js`, which is located under `~/Content/scripts`; the scripts in this file are necessary to make the AJAX request to the `Vote` action and render the results to resemble Figure 7-5.

The first thing you want to code in JavaScript is the binding event that will run every time a poll is submitted or, in other words, when the Vote button is clicked:

```
$(".poll form").submit(function() {
    var selection = $(this).find(":checked").val();

    if (selection != undefined) {
        $.post(
            "/poll/vote",
            { optionId: selection },
            function(data, textStatus) {
                SetCookie("poll_" + data.object.pollId, selection, 30);
                // render the poll for the given data
                RenderPoll($("#poll-" + data.object.pollId), data);
            },
            "json"
        );
    }

    return false;
});
```

This code is pretty straightforward. The script selects the object that is checked (that is, the radio button that is selected) in the form that is being submitted. If the script finds a selected radio button, an AJAX POST request is made to the URL `/poll/vote` with the `OptionID` that came from the selected radio button. When a response from the server is received, a cookie is set that indicates the poll has received a vote from this browser and should not be allowed to vote again. This also indicates that the poll results should be rendered instead of the voting form. After the cookie has been set, the `RenderPoll` function is called to format the results from the AJAX response.

```
function RenderPoll(obj, data) {
    var poll = $(obj),
        total = data.object.total,
        item, percentValue, rightValue, leftValue;

    // clears all child nodes
    poll.empty();
```

```
        poll.append("<h2>" + data.object.question + "</h2>");
        poll.append("<ul class=\"poll-options\">");

        // go through each option and render it
        for(var i = 0; i < data.object.options.length; i++) {
            item = data.object.options[i];
            percentValue = Math.round(item.votes / total * 100);

            poll.append("<li class=\"option\" id=\"option-" + item.optionId + "\">"
            + "<h3>" + item.text + "</h3>"
            + "<div class=\"graph\"><img src=\"/Content/images/poll-graph.gif\"
height=\"10\" width=\"" + percentValue + "%\" /></div>"
            + "<div class=\"values\">" + percentValue + "% (" + item.votes + " votes)</
div>"
            + "</li>");
        }

        poll.append("</ul>");
        poll.append("<div class=\"total\">There are " + total + " total votes for this
poll.</div>");
    }
```

This function is an exact copy of `PollResultItem.ascx`, except in JavaScript that runs in the browser instead of in C#/ASP.NET that runs on the server.

The AdminSidebar.ascx Control

This view control, located under the `~/Views/Shared/Poll` folder, is used to create a set of links that are common to the admin views:

```
<div id="polls-admin" class="boxed">
    <h2 class="title">Polls</h2>
    <div class="content">
    <ul>
        <li class="first"><%= Html.ActionLink("View Polls", "ManagePolls") %></li>
        <li><%= Html.ActionLink("Create Poll", "CreatePoll") %></li>
    </ul>
    </div>
</div>
```

The ManagePolls.aspx View

The `ManagePolls.aspx` view is located in `~/Views/Poll`. It is used to show editors current and archived polls so that they can monitor, add, edit, and remove both the polls and options on individual polls. An example of how this section will look is demonstrated in Figure 7-7.

As you can see from Figure 7-7, each poll is shown and you have the option to Archive, Edit, and Remove each poll, and for every poll that is not current (remember there can only be one current poll), a Make Current option. The Make Current and Archive links work through AJAX so the page will not have to be refreshed. The Edit and Remove links will take you to their respective views, `CreatePoll.aspx` and `RemovePoll.aspx`.

Figure 7-7

The header for this view will set the view model to `Pagination<Models.Poll>`:

```
Inherits="System.Web.Mvc.ViewPage<IEnumerator<Poll>>"
```

This view has been broken down into three `Content` sections that correlate to your master page for the site. We are going to go through each content part, `MainContent`, `SidebarContent`, and `ScriptContent`, separately so that each can be examined individually.

MainContent

The `MainContent` placeholder uses a `foreach` loop and your `PollItem.ascx` control to create the HTML output that is necessary to administer the polls for the site. The polls will be a combination of archived and currently available for voting, and each poll will contain the four admin links: Make Current, Archive, Edit, and Remove.

```
<asp:Content ID="MainContent" ContentPlaceHolderID="MainContent" runat="server">
<div id="polls">
<% foreach(Poll poll in ViewData.Model) { %>
    <div class="admin">
```

```
        <% if (!poll.IsCurrent) { %>
            <a id="set-current-<%= poll.PollID %>"
                class="set-current" meta:id="<%= poll.PollID %>"
                href="#current">Make Current</a> | 
        <% } %>
            <a id="set-archived-<%= poll.PollID %>"
                class="set-archived<%= poll.IsArchived ? " archived" : "" %>"
                meta:id="<%= poll.PollID %>" href="#archived">
                <%= poll.IsArchived ? "Allow Voting" : "Archive"%></a> | 
            <%= Html.ActionLink("Edit", "EditPoll", "Poll", new {
                pollId = poll.PollID })%> | 
            <%= Html.ActionLink("Remove", "RemovePoll", "Poll", new {
                pollId = poll.PollID })%>
    </div>
    <%= Html.RenderUserControl("~/Views/Shared/Poll/PollItem.ascx", poll) %>
    <hr />
<% } %>

    <%= Html.RenderUserControl("~/Views/Shared/Pager.ascx", ViewData.Model) %>
</div>
</asp:Content>
```

In this code, the View.Model is typed to Pagination<Models.Poll>, which you defined earlier in the code-behind. This allows you to loop through each of the polls and add the necessary links based on the current state of the poll object.

Similar to Chapter 6, you render the poll against the PollItem.ascx user control directly in your loop using the Html.RenderUserControl extension method. Then everything is topped off with a horizontal ruler to separate the polls visually when rendered in the browser.

SidebarContent

The SidebarContent placeholder's sole purpose is to render the AdminSidebar.ascx control, which contains links for creating and viewing your polls:

```
<asp:Content ID="SidebarContent" ContentPlaceHolderID="SidebarContent" runat="server">
<%= Html.RenderUserControl("~/Views/Shared/Poll/AdminSidebar.ascx")%>
</asp:Content>
```

This placeholder is the same for all of the admin pages so we are just going to show it this once and not show the code again.

ScriptContent

The ScriptContent placeholder contains a reference to the script you need for administrating the polls. The <script /> tag will reference /content/scripts/manage-polls.js, which we will go over after the code for the placeholder.

```
<asp:Content ID="ScriptContent" ContentPlaceHolderID="ScriptContent" runat="server">
<script type="text/javascript" src="/content/scripts/manage-polls.js"></script>
</asp:Content>
```

manage-polls.js

This JavaScript file contains code for both the `ManagePolls.aspx` view and the `CreatePoll.aspx` view. For the purposes of this part we are only going to go over the code necessary for the `ManagePolls.aspx` view and we will discuss the rest of the code in the `CreatePoll.aspx` view, so the JavaScript code will be in context with the view.

The first thing that you need to do is get rid of all the form-related elements on the page related to the polls. The reason you need to do this is because you are using the `PollItem.ascx` user control that contains radio buttons for the options and a vote button. We basically had two options when rendering the admin controls: either we could create a control specifically for rendering the poll, or we could reuse some code we have already written. In the effort for expediency, and because the admin page is used by a tiny set of users, we decided that it would be easier to just hide the inputs. This gives you one less control to change if you ever make changes to how the poll is laid out or rendered.

```
$(document).ready(function() {
    $("#polls :input").hide("fast");
});
```

This command is called when the `document` (your HTML page) is ready to start running the JavaScript. The `Hide` method is called on all `input`, `button`, and `textarea` tags within the `div` with an `id` of `polls`. When hiding these elements on the DOM, jQuery sets a special CSS style (`display:none` in the `style` attributes) on all the affected elements to hide them from being displayed in the browser.

Now you need to write the code to handle what happens when the Make Current link, which has a class of `set-current`, is clicked and the AJAX call needs to be made. The AJAX request will be made to `/poll/setcurrent` and the `pollId` of the poll you want to make current will be sent back to the server. After the response from the server is received, the link for Make Current is removed from the page because it cannot be used again to make the poll current.

```
$(".set-current").click(function() {
    var id = $(this).attr("meta:id");

    $.post(
        "/poll/setcurrent",
        { pollId: id },
        function(data) {
            var poll = $("#set-current-" + data.object.pollId);
            poll.remove();
        },
        "json"
    );

    return false;
});
```

Next you need to write code to handle setting the archive state of the poll. You are going to send the `pollId` and the `archive` state to the server address `/poll/setarchived` via an AJAX request. When the response comes back from the server you are going to flag the link as archived or not, depending on the state that you sent to the server, and you also need to change the wording of the text so that the administrator knows the state of the poll.

```
$(".set-archived").click(function() {
    var id = $(this).attr("meta:id"),
        archived = $(this).hasClass("archived");

    $.post(
        "/poll/setarchived",
        { pollId: id, archive: !archived },
        function(data) {
            var poll = $("#set-archived-" + data.object.pollId);
            poll.removeClass("archived");
            if (data.object.isArchived)
                poll.addClass("archived");
            poll.text(data.object.isArchived ? "Allow Voting" : "Archive");
        },
        "json"
    );

    return false;
});
```

So there really wasn't all that much you needed to do for managing the polls as far as JavaScript goes, just some basic handling of the dynamic links.

The CreatePoll.aspx View

The `CreatePoll.aspx` view is located in `~/Views/Polls` and is used for creating or editing a poll. This view is only available to users with the role of Editor. An example of how this view looks when a poll is being edited is demonstrated in Figure 7-8.

The `CreatePoll.aspx` view has two purposes: one is to create a poll and the other is to edit a poll. If the user is just creating the poll, the first form is shown, but if the user is editing the poll or adding options to the poll, the first and second forms are shown. After the user creates the poll she is transferred to the edit state of this view so that she can add options to the poll. The reason you have this process is twofold because adding options for the first time is the exact same process as editing the options, where the user might add, edit, or remove an option.

As with the last section, we will take a look at the source code piece-by-piece and the first place we will start is with the header for `CreatePoll`:

```
Inherits="System.Web.Mvc.ViewPage"
```

The code-behind for this view is as simple as it can get; you don't have any utility methods and you are using the built-in `ViewData` dictionary to hold the values so you can skip setting the model's type with the generic `ViewPage`.

The HTML code for `CreatePoll.aspx` has three different `Content` sections that you must implement to provide the desired look and feel. You are going to implement `MainContent`, `ScriptContent`, and `SidebarContent`.

Figure 7-8

MainContent

The MainContent for creating the poll is pretty straightforward because there are only two forms, which contain one textbox and one button each. We will break down the code into the poll form and the options form, respectively:

```
<asp:Content ID="Content1" ContentPlaceHolderID="MainContent" runat="server">
<%= Html.RenderUserControl("~/Views/Shared/Message.ascx") %>

<form method="post" action="<%= Url.Action(this.ViewContext.RouteData.
Values["action"] as string, "Poll") %>" class="poll-create">
    <p class="field input"><label for="question">Question</label><br />
        <%= Html.TextBox("question",ViewData["question"],new {@maxlength = 256})%>
        <span class="input-message"></span></p>

    <hr />
    <% if(this.ViewContext.RouteData.Values["action"] as string == "EditPoll") { %>
    <p><button type="submit" id="Button1">Update Poll</button></p>
    <% } else { %>
    <p><button type="submit" id="poll-create-button">Create Poll</button></p>
    <% } %>
</form>
```

There is nothing unique about this form, so we will not bore you with the details because you have seen all this before in Chapter 6.

The next form is the options form that should only be displayed if the calling action is EditPoll. You are going to display all the options with an edit and delete button next to each option. These buttons will provide you the necessary contact points for jQuery to bind to so that you can edit the options in line and submit the updates back to the server without a page refresh.

```
<% if(this.ViewContext.RouteData.Values["action"] as string == "EditPoll") { %>
    <h3>Poll Options</h3>

    <ul id="poll-options" class="manage-options">
    <% foreach(var option in ViewData["options"] as IEnumerable<PollOption>) { %>
        <li id="option-<%= option.OptionID %>" class="option">
            <span class="text"><%= option.OptionText %></span>
            <button type="button" class="edit-option-button" meta:id="<%= option.
OptionID %>">Edit</button> 
            <button type="button" class="delete-option-button" meta:id="<%=
option.OptionID %>">Delete</button>
        </li>
    <% } %>
    </ul>

<form method="post" action="#" class="poll-options-create">
    <input type="hidden" id="pollId" name="pollId" value="<%= ViewData["pollId"] %>"
/>

    <p class="field input"><label for="option">Option</label><br />
        <%= Html.TextBox("option", ViewData["option"], new { @maxlength = 256 })%>
        <span class="input-message"></span></p>

    <hr />
    <p><button type="submit" id="poll-option-create-button">Create Poll Option</
button></p>
</form>
<% } %>

</asp:Content>
```

You may have noticed that we didn't wrap the options list inside the form. We did this because each option is going to have its own separate form for submitting back edit or delete to the web server. This might be a hard thing to understand, especially if you have come from the ASP.NET Web Forms world where the whole page is wrapped in one form tag. The rule of thumb in MVC and HTML overall is to just put the necessary inputs inside the form, so that the browser has an easy time understanding what happens when a user submits a form, and also so that unnecessary data isn't posted back to the server.

ScriptContent

The ScriptContent placeholder will contain the other half of the manage-polls.js file that we promised you earlier in the chapter. Before we actually get to the JavaScript code, let's define what needs to be rendered to the HTML of the page first:

```
<asp:Content ID="ScriptContent" ContentPlaceHolderID="ScriptContent" runat="server">
<script type="text/javascript" src="/content/scripts/manage-polls.js"></script>
```

```
<% if (IsPostBack) { %>
<script type="text/javascript">
    ValidatePoll();
</script>
<% } %>
</asp:Content>
```

The first thing you do is import the JavaScript file, located at /content/scripts/manage-polls.js, which you will add a little later on. Also, if this page is a POST back, meaning that you have posted to the action and it was necessary to return to this view page, you will validate the textbox values to display any kind of validation issues as a hint to why the action might have returned you to this page.

manage-polls.js

The code for managing the edit and delete operations of the options is pretty complex, so we are going to break this JavaScript code down into four sections: form validations, edit options, delete options, and an add option, respectively.

```
$("#question").focus(function() {
    ShowMessage(this, "Enter the question you would like to ask in the poll."); });

function ValidateQuestion() {
    return VerifyRequiredField("#question", "required");
}

function ValidatePoll() {
    return ValidateQuestion();
}

$("form.poll-create").validate(ValidatePoll);
```

You have seen this code in Chapter 6 so we will skip it for now.

The edit option button works very similarly to how your edit comment code worked in Chapter 6. You replace the text of the option with an inline textbox and update and cancel buttons. The update button is bound to a function that posts the updated text to the URL /poll/editoption, and then swaps the form back to the updated text after the request has been completed. The cancel button just reverses the edit button actions without making any changes.

```
function EditOption() {
    var id = $(this).attr("meta:id"),
        option = $("#option-" + id),
        text = option.find(".text").text();

    // hide all the children
    option.children().hide();

    var optionForm = $("<form><span class=\"field\"><input type=\"text\" id=\"text-"
+ id + "\" class=\"edit-text\" value=\"" + text + "\" /> <button type=\"button\"
class=\"update\" meta:id=\"" + id + "\">Update</button> <button type=\"button\"
class=\"cancel\">Cancel</button></span></form>");
```

```
              // update the form
          optionForm.find(".update").click(function () {
              var id = $(this).attr("meta:id"),
                  formText = $(this).prevAll(".edit-text").val();

              $.post(
                  "/poll/editoption",
                  { optionId: id, text: formText },
                  function (data) {
                      var comment = $("#option-" + data.object.optionId);
                      comment.children("form").remove();
                      comment.children(".text").text(data.object.text);
                      comment.children().show();
                  },
                  "json"
              );
          });

          // cancel the update
          optionForm.find(".cancel").click(function () {
              $(this).parents(".option").children(":hidden").show();
              $(this).parents("form").remove();
          });

          // add the form to the current comment
          option.append(optionForm);

          return false;
      }

  $(".edit-option-button").click(EditOption);
```

The delete button is bound to the following JavaScript code, which posts the `optionId` of the option that you want to delete back to the URL `/poll/removeoption`. After the AJAX request completes, you just remove the option from the DOM.

```
  function DeleteOption () {
      var id = $(this).attr("meta:id");

      $.post(
          "/poll/removeoption",
          { optionId: id },
          function (data) {
              $("#option-" + data.object.optionId)
                  .fadeOut("slow", function () { $(this).remove() });
          },
          "json"
      );

      return false;
  }
  $(".delete-option-button").click(DeleteOption);
```

The next block of code deals with adding the options to the database and adding the option to the DOM for the options list in the HTML. The HTML generated for options lists is an exact replica of the code found in the `CreatePoll.aspx` view.

```
function AddOptionSuccess(data) {
    var optionItem = $("<li id=\"option-" + data.object.optionId + "\"
class=\"option\"><span class=\"text\">" + data.object.text + "</span> <button
type=\"button\" class=\"edit-option-button\" meta:id=\"" + data.object.optionId
+ "\">Edit</button> <button type=\"button\" class=\"delete-option-button\"
meta:id=\"" + data.object.optionId + "\">Delete</button></li>");

    optionItem.find(".edit-option-button").click(EditOption);
    optionItem.find(".delete-option-button").click(DeleteOption);

    // clear the option box
    $("#option").val("");

    // add the new option to the other options
    optionItem.appendTo("#poll-options");
}

$("form.poll-options-create").submit(function() {
    var option = $("#option").val(),
        pollId = $("#pollId").val();

    $.post(
        "/poll/addoption",
        { pollId: pollId, text: option },
        AddOptionSuccess,
        "json"
    );

    return false;
});
```

The RemovePoll.aspx View

The `RemovePoll.aspx` page view works in a similar fashion to what you did in Chapter 6 in that the users are presented with a "yes" or "no" question of whether they want to permanently remove the poll from the database. If they choose "yes," the poll and all comments related to that poll are permanently removed, but if they choose "no," no action is taken against the database. Figure 7-9 is a visual representation of what you are going to create for the `RemovePoll.aspx` view page.

The header, like many of your other admin pages, is relatively simple because you are only using it to set the view model to be a `Poll` object.

```
Inherits="System.Web.Mvc.ViewPage"
```

The view only contains a `MainContent` section because no JavaScript is required for this view to work.

Figure 7-9

MainContent

This is a very simple setup: you have a form with a "yes" or "no" button on it, and a message pane. The form with the buttons is only shown if the model is not `null`; you do this so that you can display a success message for whichever option the user chooses. Doing this gives the feel of a wizard, which most users are very comfortable with.

```
<asp:Content ID="MainContent" ContentPlaceHolderID="MainContent" runat="server">

<%= Html.RenderUserControl("~/Views/Shared/Message.ascx") %>

<% if (ViewData.Model != null) { %>
<form method="post" action="<%= Url.Action("RemovePoll", "Poll", new { pollId =
ViewData.Model.PollID }) %>" class="poll-remove">

    <button type="submit" name="remove" value="yes" class="yes">yes</button>
    <button type="submit" name="remove" value="no" class="no">no</button>

</form>
<% } %>

</asp:Content>
```

The Index.aspx View

This is the end-user version of the `ManagePolls.aspx` view page presented earlier. It shows archived or voteable content individually instead of all the content at once, but otherwise it's the same because it just runs through a `foreach` loop from a collection of `Poll` objects in the view model. Figure 7-10 represents an accurate screenshot of the page, minus the edit and remove buttons.

Figure 7-10

The header is an exact copy of the `ManagePolls.aspx` view because you are providing the same data, just without the administration features.

```
Inherits="System.Web.Mvc.ViewPage<TheBeerHouse.Models.Pagination<TheBeerHouse
.Models.Poll>>"
```

The view is broken up into a `MainContent` section.

MainContent

The `MainContent` placeholder runs through each loop in a similar way to what you have seen in the `ManagePolls.aspx` view, except for one critical piece of code that checks if the poll is archived or if the user has already voted and, if so, renders the `PollResultItem.ascx` control instead of the `PollItem.ascx` control.

We have highlighted the changed sections in the following code relating to the view, choosing if the results or the form should be displayed to the user:

```
<asp:Content ID="MainContent" ContentPlaceHolderID="MainContent" runat="server">

<% if (TheBeerHouseSection.Current.Polls.ArchiveIsPublic) { %>
    <%= Html.ActionLink("Public", "Index", "Poll") %> |
    <%= Html.ActionLink("Archived", "Index", "Poll", new { archived = true }) %>
<% } %>

<div id="polls">
<% foreach(Poll poll in ViewData.Model) { %>
    <% if (poll != null
        && !poll.IsArchived
        && Request.Cookies["poll_" + poll.PollID] == null) { %>
        <%= Html.RenderUserControl("~/Views/Shared/Poll/PollItem.ascx", poll) %>
    <% } else { %>
        <%=Html.RenderUserControl("~/Views/Shared/Poll/PollResultItem.ascx",poll)%>
    <% } %>
<hr />
<% } %>

<%= Html.RenderUserControl("~/Views/Shared/Pager.ascx", ViewData.Model) %>
</div>
</asp:Content>
```

The Current Poll

The current poll is displayed on the sidebar of the master page and is queried from the database for each result. It works in a similar fashion to the loop in the MainContent placeholder in the Index.aspx view. The current poll section of the master looks like Figure 7-11.

As you can see, this is where defining the widths of the images as percentages really helps out, because your graph is now scaled for the smaller-width sidebar instead of your larger-width main body like in Figure 7-10.

The following HTML is placed in the master page as part of the theme. The master page is actually responsible for pulling the CurrentPoll from your queries defined earlier in this chapter. Then, depending on whether or not the user has already voted, you show the poll's results or the form for voting.

```
<div id="current-poll" class="boxed">
    <h2 class="title">Current Poll</h2>
    <div class="content">
    <% var poll = (new TheBeerHouseDataContext()).Polls.CurrentPoll(); %>

    <% if (poll != null && Request.Cookies["poll_" + poll.PollID] == null) { %>
        <%= Html.RenderUserControl("~/Views/Shared/Poll/PollItem.ascx", poll) %>
    <% } else { %>
        <%=Html.RenderUserControl("~/Views/Shared/Poll/PollResultItem.ascx",poll)%>
    <% } %>
    </div>
</div>
```

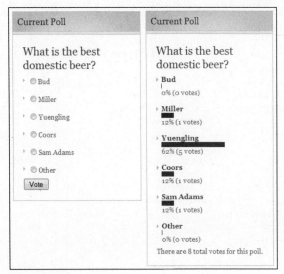

Figure 7-11

Summary

This chapter has presented a working solution for handling multiple dynamic polls on your website. The complete polls module is made up of an administration console for managing the polls through a web browser, integration with the membership system to secure the administration and archive pages, and a user control that enables you to show different polls on any page using only a couple of lines of code. This module can easily be employed in many real-world sites as it is now, but of course you can expand and enhance it as desired. Here are a few suggestions:

❏ Add the capability to remind users which option they voted for. Currently they can see the results, but the control does not indicate how they voted. The vote is stored in a cookie, which is easy to retrieve to provide this capability.

❏ Add a `ReleaseDate` and `ExpireDate` to the polls, so that you can schedule the current poll to change automatically. You do this type of thing with the articles module.

❏ Provide the option to allow only registered users to vote.

In the next chapter, you're going to continue the development of the TheBeerHouse site through the addition of another module that integrates with the rest of the site's architecture. This new module will be used for creating and sending out newsletters to users who subscribed to the newsletter at registration time.

8

Newsletters

In this chapter you design and implement a complete newsletter mailing list system. Your system will allow users to subscribe to online newsletters and allow administrators to manage the newsletter content. First, you look at what newsletters can offer to websites like the one developed in this book, and then you examine the various management aspects that must be addressed to make the mailing list administrator's life as easy as possible. By the end of the chapter, you'll have a powerful newsletter module fully developed and integrated into your site!

Problem

Throughout this book you have learned that the key to a successful site is having good content. This content must be logically organized to ease navigability, have an attractive design, and offer some interaction with the user. The content not only has to be interesting and accurate, but must also be fresh and regularly updated to ensure that users keep coming back to visit the site. To help you achieve this for the TheBeerHouse website, you developed an article management module in Chapter 6 to allow administrators and editors to easily manage and publish new content. Although you should try to publish new content on a regular basis, sometimes this simply is not possible. This is especially true when you cannot afford a dedicated team to publish content, or if your company has no news to pass on to its users. If your users see that content has not changed for a long time, chances are good that they won't come back very often, and they may end up forgetting about the site altogether. Even when you frequently add fresh content to the site, not every user will be aware of it. They might not visit the site daily or weekly to see the latest updates, particularly if the site is updated on a random basis with no public announcement.

A good way to inform users that some new content has been added to the site (for example, an article, a new product for sale, or a new layout design) is to send them an e-mail newsletter that lists all the new resources available on the site. Many sites offer the option of subscribing to a mailing list, which typically represents a group of users interested in a certain kind of news. A newsletter is created and sent to a mailing list to remind the community of users that the site is still worth visiting. However, many visitors do not like to submit their e-mail address just to be informed about changes to your website. To encourage people to maintain their subscriptions, and to drive more people to sign up, a webmaster should offer extra incentives available only to the mailing list's subscribers. These incentives, which are sometimes known as *kickers* in marketing lingo, could include free offers, special articles, or exclusive discounts.

The primary purpose of your mailing list system is to inform users that new material is available online so they will revisit your site. It is also possible to make money from your mailing list. If you have several thousand subscribers, you could sell some space in your newsletters for advertisement spots. These should not be anything too invasive, perhaps just a two- or three-line description of a partner site or company, or the manufacturer of a product you sell on your site. If you provide some valuable content in your newsletters, and the advertisement is short and preferably related to the theme of the site and the newsletter, the users will probably not complain about it. You can inform potential sponsors that this space in the newsletter is very valuable because it is sent only to users who have elected to receive it. This usually means that your subscribers will read the content more thoroughly, and therefore the advertisement in the newsletter will receive much more attention than it would have through a common banner ad on a site. Research shows that the average click-through from spots in newsletters is around 4%–5% compared to around 1% or less for common banner ads.

However you decide to promote your website to get more people to subscribe, you will face the problem of managing all the details of your clients. These include e-mail addresses, keeping track of the e-mail newsletter messages you send, and building a system to enable users to subscribe or unsubscribe easily (users must have the right to unsubscribe at any time). Some small sites manually collect the addresses with an HTML form, create a group of contacts in Outlook (or another messaging client), and use it to write a message to all their subscribers. This mostly applies to small, static sites, where ASP or other server-side code is not used. However, when the site grows and you get a significant number of subscribers, manually adding or removing users several times a week becomes a real chore, and if the number is on the order of thousands, it is almost impossible! Also, if you send out a newsletter to an Outlook group of contacts, you will not be able to personalize the newsletters in any way; they'll be exactly the same for every user. It would be much better to personalize every e-mail — for example, with the name of the subscriber if this information is available, because this will help to build a more personal relationship with subscribers. It is worth noting, however, that the most common way of subscribing to a list is for a user to enter an e-mail address in a form on the home page and click Submit. It is totally impersonal, and it will only enable you to personalize the newsletter with the user's e-mail address. To achieve a more extensive personalization, you have to ask the users to provide more details, such as their first and last name. You may remember that you placed your subscription option directly into the user's profile page in Chapter 5. You can access this information using the ASP.NET Profile Provider to obtain both personal information such as their name and location, and localization information such as their language of choice.

In summary, you may realize that you are losing traffic because you have no way of letting your users know that your content has been updated; the aim of this chapter is to build a newsletter mailing list system to inform subscribers of new site content. A secondary problem is that managing the system and personalizing newsletters is time-consuming, so you want to include a subscription and administration system that automates most of the tasks and enables the administrator to complete these tasks easily. Yet another problem is that you need to generate revenue, so you'll want to allow for the possibility of including advertising spots in the newsletters. Once you know what problems you want to solve, you can then move on to specifying the features you want it to have, that is, the design stage. The next section provides a more detailed list of features you need to implement to have a fully functional mailing list module.

Design

The first thing you need to think about is how you will store the subscription data, such as the user's e-mail address, first and last name, and other information that can be used to personalize the newsletters. In the previous edition of this book, you had to create your own tables to manage this information. Now you can simply take advantage of your membership and profile provider to maintain all this information for you.

As you may recall, the membership data includes the username and e-mail address, and the profile includes, among other things, the user's first and last name and the format of newsletter he would like to subscribe to (plain-text format, HTML format, or no newsletter at all). To make things simpler and prevent storing the same data in multiple places, you will use those same fields. You may think that this would require the user to register for the site just to receive the newsletter, and that this is not required by many other sites, so this may be a bad idea. Yes, you are requiring users to register for the site, but the only information strictly required by the registration system is just the username, e-mail address, and password; all the other profile information is optional. For this reason, we do not think that requiring users to choose a username and password, in addition to an e-mail address (needed anyway to send the newsletter), is much of a problem, or a valid reason to avoid using the membership system. The alternative would be to create a whole new user-membership system from scratch just for use by the newsletter module — no thanks! Our proposed solution is much better integrated with the site, and by registering the user will also gain access to protected articles, archived polls, the forums, and more. This approach also makes it easy for subscribers to change their registration type, or other information. For example, if subscribers want to switch from plain-text newsletters to HTML newsletters they can easily do this by going to the Profile Management section accessible from the Account menu.

In addition to the registration work, you have other parts of the module, and other features, to design. First, the administrator or editor needs a protected page from which he can send a newsletter to all subscribers, and to enter the body in both plain-text and HTML formats. You also need the option to send multi-part MIME messages (e-mails that contain both the plain-text and the HTML versions of the body), and leave it to the user's e-mail client program to decide which version to display. However, the reason why the user may wish to subscribe to the plain-text newsletter instead of the HTML version is not because the user's e-mail client software does not support HTML, but rather because the user does not want to download a large message, or for security reasons does not want (or cannot, as dictated by his company's policies) to download images and scripts with the e-mails. Because of this, we have decided it is better to send distinct versions of the newsletter according to each subscriber's preferences.

Because your membership registration system is already implemented, the next thing to design and integrate is the system that sends out the newsletters. Sending a single e-mail message is a relatively easy task. Sending out a newsletter to a mailing list of thousands of subscribers is a much more complex job that requires some analysis and a good design. The next section presents the classes of the .NET Framework that you can use to send e-mail messages, and then discusses the issues to consider and solve when delivering mass e-mails. After introducing this background information, we'll draw together all the considerations and techniques discussed, and design the module.

A Word About Spam

Before proceeding any further we want to clarify that this module is not intended to send unsolicited e-mail newsletters, or messages of any kind, to users who did not request them. Many countries have laws against this, but regardless of the legality, we strongly believe that it hurts a site's reputation considerably to participate in these kinds of actions. Spamming will inevitably end up damaging the favorable impression that you have worked so hard to create. This newsletter system is intended to send e-mail messages only to users who have specifically opted in. Furthermore, users must be allowed to easily change their mind and stop any further e-mails from the site.

Creating and Sending E-Mails

The System.Net.Mail namespace defined in the System.dll assembly contains all the classes used to send e-mails. The older System.Web.Mail namespace, and its related classes, that were used with ASP.NET 1.x are still there, but its use has been deprecated now in favor of these new classes in ASP.NET 2.0 that provide more features. The principal classes are MailMessage, which represents an e-mail message, and the SmtpClient class, which provides the methods used to send a MailMessage by connecting to a configured SMTP server. SMTP is the Simple Mail Transfer Protocol, which is the low-level protocol used by Microsoft Exchange and other mail servers.

MailMessage fully describes an e-mail message, with its subject, body (in plain-text, HTML, or in both formats), the To, CC, and BCC addresses, and any attachments that might be used. The simplest way to create an e-mail is using the MailMessage constructor, which takes the sender's address, the recipient's address, the mail's subject, and the body, as shown here:

```
MailMessage mail = new MailMessage(
    "from@somewhere.com", "to@somewhere.com", "subject", "body");
```

However, this approach will be too limited in most cases. You may want to specify the sender's display name in addition to his e-mail address. The display name is what is displayed by the mail client, if present, instead of the address, and makes the mail and its sender look more professional. You may also want to send to more than one recipient, use an HTML body (as an alternative, or in addition, to the plain-text version), include some attachments, use different encoding, modify the mail's priority, and so on. All these settings, and more, are specified by means of a number of instance properties of the MailMessage class. Their names should be self-explanatory, and some examples include the following: Subject, Body, IsBodyHtml, From, To, CC, Bcc, BodyEncoding, Attachments, AlternateViews, Headers, Priority, and ReplyTo. The class's constructor enables you to specify a From property of type MailAddress, which accepts as variables the e-mail address and a display name. The To, CC, and Bcc properties are of type MailAddressCollection, and thus can accept multiple MailAddress instances (you can add them by means of the collection's Add method). Similarly, the MailMessage's Attachments property is of type AttachmentCollection, a collection of Attachment instances that point to files located on the server. The following example shows how to build an HTML-formatted e-mail message that will be sent to multiple recipients, with high priority, and that includes a couple of attachments:

```
// create the message
MailMessage mail = new MailMessage();
// set the sender's address and display name
mail.From = new MailAddress("akatawazi@wrox.com", "Al Katawazi");
// add a first recipient by specifying only her address
mail.To.Add("john@wroxfans.com");
// add a second recipient by specifying her address and display name
mail.To.Add(new MailAddress("anne@wroxfans.com", "Anne Gentle"));
// add a third recipient, but to the CC field this time
mail.CC.Add("mike@wroxfans.com");
// set the mail's subject and HTML body
mail.Subject = "Sample Mail";
mail.Body = "Hello, <b>my friend</b>!<br />How are you?";
```

```
mail.IsBodyHtml = true;
// set the mail's priority to high
mail.Priority = MailPriority.High;
// add a couple of attachments
mail.Attachments.Add(
    new Attachment(@"c:\demo.zip", MediaTypeNames.Application.Octet));
mail.Attachments.Add(
    new Attachment(@"c:\report.xls", MediaTypeNames.Application.Octet));
```

If you also wanted to provide a plain-text version of the body in the same mail, so that the display format (plain text or HTML) would depend on the user's e-mail client settings, you would add the following lines:

```
string body = "Hello, my friend!\nHow are you?";
AlternateView plainView = new AlternateView(body, MediaTypeNames.Text.Plain);
mail.AlternateViews.Add(plainView);
```

Once a `MailMessage` object is ready, the e-mail message it describes can be sent out by means of the `Send` method of the `SmtpClient` class, as shown here:

```
SmtpClient smtpClient = new SmtpClient();
smtpClient.Send(mail);
```

Before calling the `Send` method, you may need to set some configuration settings, such as the SMTP server's address (the `SmtpClient`'s `Host` property), port (the `Port` property) and its credentials (the `Credentials` property), whether the connection in encrypted with SSL (the `EnableSsl` property), and the timeout in milliseconds for sending the mail (the `Timeout` property, which defaults to 100 seconds). An important property is `DeliveryMethod`, which defines how the mail message is delivered. It is an enumeration of type `SmtpDeliveryMethod`, which can be one of the following values:

❑   **Network:** The e-mail is sent through a direct connection to the specified SMTP server.

❑   **PickupDirectoryFromIis:** The e-mail message is prepared and the EML file is saved into the default directory from which IIS picks up queued e-mails to send. By default this is `<drive>:\Inetpub\mailroot\Queue`.

❑   **SpecifiedPickupDirectory:** The EML file with the mail being sent is saved into the location specified by the `PickupDirectoryLocation` property of the `smtpClient` object. This is useful when you have an external custom program that picks up e-mails from that folder and processes them.

The delivery method you choose can dramatically change the performance of your site when sending many e-mails and can produce different errors during the send operation. If you select the Network delivery method, the `SmtpClient` class takes care of sending the mail directly and raises an error if the destination e-mail address is not found or if other transmission problems exist. With the other two methods, instead of sending the message directly, an EML mail file is prepared and saved to the file system, where another application (IIS or something else) will pick them up later for the actual delivery. A queue accumulates the messages, which means the web application will not have to wait for each message to be sent over the Internet. However, when using the second and third delivery methods, your web application cannot be notified of any errors that may occur during transmission of the message, and it will be up to IIS (or another mail agent that might be used) to handle them. The `PickupDirectoryFromIis` method is the preferred one, unless your ASP.NET application is not given the right to write to IIS mail folders (check with your web hosting provider service if you don't use your own servers).

If you set all `SmtpClient` properties mentioned previously directly in your C# code, you will have to recompile the application or edit the source file every time you want to change any of these settings. This, of course, is not an option if you're selling a packaged application, or you want to let the administrator change these settings on his own without directly involving the developer. As an alternative to hard-coding the delivery method, you can set it declaratively in the `web.config` file, which supports a new configuration section named `<mailSettings>`, located under `<system.net>`, which allows you to specify delivery settings. The `SmtpClient` class automatically loads those settings from `web.config` to configure itself at runtime, so you should generally not have to set your own delivery and SMTP options directly in your C# code. The following code snippet is an extract of the configuration file that shows how to select `PickupDirectoryFromIis` as the delivery method, set up the sender's e-mail address and the SMTP server's name (or IP address) and port, and specify that you want to use the default credentials to connect to the server:

```
<configuration xmlns="http://schemas.microsoft.com/.NetConfiguration/v2.0">
    <system.net>
        <mailSettings>
            <smtp deliveryMethod="PickupDirectoryFromIis"
                from="akatawazi@wrox.com">
                <network defaultCredentials="true"
                    host="vmwin2003" port="25"></network>
            </smtp>
        </mailSettings>
    </system.net>
    <!-- other configuration sections… -->
</configuration>
```

The `SmtpClient`'s `Send` method used in the preceding code snippet sends the e-mail synchronously, which means that the task must complete before the execution of your application can resume. The term synchronous means "do what I asked and I'll stop and wait for you to finish." The term asynchronous means "do what I asked but let me continue doing other work, and you should notify me when you're done." The `SmtpClient` class also has a `SendAsync` method to send the mail asynchronously. It returns immediately, and the e-mail is prepared and sent out on a separate thread. When the send task is complete, the `SmtpClient`'s `SendCompleted` event is raised. This event is also raised in case of errors, and the `Error` and `Cancelled` properties of its second argument (of type `AsyncCompletedEventArgs`) tell you whether it was raised because the send was cancelled, because there was an error, or because the send completed successfully. Here's a sample snippet that shows how to send the mail asynchronously, and handle the resulting completion event:

```
SmtpClient smtpClient = new SmtpClient();
smtpClient.SendCompleted += new SendCompletedEventHandler(MailSendCompleted);
smtpClient.SendAsync(message, null);
…

public static void MailSendCompleted(object sender, AsyncCompletedEventArgs e)
{
    if (e.Cancelled)
        Trace.Write("Send canceled.");
    if (e.Error != null)
        Trace.Write(e.Error.ToString());
    else
        Trace.Write("Message sent.");
}
```

An asynchronous send operation can be cancelled before completion by calling the `SmtpClient`'s `SendAsyncCancel` method. Note that you cannot send a second e-mail while an `SmtpClient` has another send in progress; if you try to do so, you'll receive an `InvalidOperationException`.

Managing Long Operations on the Server

Due to the disconnected nature of the Web, when you submit a form, you typically have to wait some time to get a response. In the meantime you see nothing but a blank page. The browser cannot check how the server-side processing is going, and it cannot provide any feedback to the user. As long as the user only has to wait less than five seconds, that is normally fine. But if the application takes longer to produce a response, you have a problem because you cannot leave users stranded without visual feedback for more than a few seconds, or they will start to think that the application got stuck or had a serious problem, and they will close their browser and go away. If a user clicks the refresh button to resend the data and restart the processing, that is bad as well, because that action actually requests the same operation a second time, and the server will do the same work twice, causing duplication and possibly data integrity problems. In many situations the server-side processing might take a long time to complete: you may execute long-running SQL queries, call an external web service, or forward a call to an external application (a payment processing application, for example) and wait for a response, and so on. In your case, you will be sending potentially thousands of e-mails, and to do this you will need to retrieve the profiles for all registered members (that means multiple SQL queries), parse the newsletter's body and replace all the personalization placeholders, and insert the newsletter into the archive. This can possibly take many minutes, not just seconds! You cannot expect your newsletter editor to look at a blank page for such a long period of time.

To address this issue, you have to deal with two underlying problems. The first is that the process will take a while to complete, and the second is that the user needs to receive visual feedback on the status of the job. Much like installing an application on your computer, you need some type of progress bar or message from the system indicating the job is progressing without issue. To do this we propose several possible approaches with their pros and cons:

❑   When users click the Submit button, you can redirect them to a second page that shows a wait message. When this wait page arrives on the client browser it uses some simple JavaScript, or the refresh metatag, to immediately post back to the server — either to itself or to another page. For example, the following metatag declared at the top of the page makes the current page redirect to `processing.aspx` after two seconds:

```
<meta http-equiv="refresh" content="2;  URL=http://www.TheBeerHouse
.com/newsletter/processing">.
```

   After this second POST back, the long processing task will be executed. While the task is running on the server, the current wait page will remain visible on the client. You can provide an animated GIF representing an incrementing progress bar, in addition to the wait message, so that users get the idea that processing is taking place behind the scenes. This simple approach does not provide any real feedback about the task's actual progress, but it would suffice for many situations.

❑   When the user clicks the Submit button, on the server side you can start a secondary thread that will process the long task in the background. The page will then immediately redirect to a wait page that shows the user a message, while the real action continues on a separate worker thread. The code executing on the background thread will also update some server-side variables indicating the percentage of the task completed, and some other optional information. The wait page will automatically refresh every *n* seconds, and every time it loads it will read the variables written by the second thread and display the progress status accordingly. To refresh itself, it can use some JavaScript that submits the form, or it can use the refresh metatag, but without the URL of the page to load, as shown in the following:

```
<meta http-equiv="refresh" content="2">
```

This approach can be quite effective, because it gives the user some real feedback about the background processing. The problem arises with this method from the frequent flickering of the browser caused by the full-page POST back. A better solution would be to load the wait/progress page into a small IFRAME, which would show only the progress bar and nothing else. When the processing completes, the wait page will not show the progress bar again, but will instead redirect the user to the page showing the confirmation and the results. You should be aware that when the progress bar is updating, it will disappear for a short time while the page in the IFRAME refreshes, creating an ugly visual effect.

❑   Our final option is to spawn a worker thread to process the sending of the newsletter and immediately send the administrator to a newsletter management view. While the user is redirected the worker thread periodically reports its status by writing to the database row pertaining to this newsletter. In the newsletter management view, the user can see the status of all newsletters. To avoid having to place a refresh button on the page you can take advantage of jQuery to allow you to update the results seamlessly. jQuery gives you the ability to request data from your newsletter controller and then create a DOM object and directly inject it back into your view. The following example shows how you would go about doing this.

```
$.ajax({
    type: "GET",
    url: "/Newsletter/UpdateStatus",
    dataType: "html",
    sucess: function(result) {
        var domElement = $(result);
        $("#Newsletter_Status_Table").replaceWith(domElement);
    }
});
```

The advantage of using this approach is that you give the user the flexibility to watch the job complete on the newsletter management page or potentially do other things such as send another newsletter. You also eliminate the possibility that the user could potentially hit the refresh button on a wait screen and double-send the newsletter. Even if users do not have JavaScript enabled, they are more than welcome to hit the traditional refresh button to update the status information in the newsletter management view.

Instead of showing you how to implement all three possible solutions, we will go straight to the best one, which is of course the third one. In the next section we provide you with some background information about multi-threaded programming and script programming for partial page updating, which you will use in the Solution section to implement the newsletter delivery task.

Background Threads

Background or secondary threads can be used to execute long-running tasks without tying up the main UI tread. Creating new threads in .NET is simple to do, but you have to be careful about multiple threads trying to access the same memory spaces at the same time. .NET allows you to have a maximum of 250 threads total per CPU. New to .NET 3.5, the creation of threads requires your application to wait a certain amount of time (500ms for starters); this time becomes progressively longer as you approach the 250-thread limit. To begin creating new threads, all the classes you will need are under the `System.Threading` namespace, in the `mscorlib.dll` assembly.

Multi-Threaded Programming

Multi-threaded programming is a very complex subject, and you have further considerations regarding the proper way to design code so that it performs well and does not cause deadlocks that may freeze the entire application. You should avoid creating too many threads if it is not strictly required, because the operating system and the thread scheduler, the portion of the OS that distributes the CPU time among the existing threads, consume CPU time and memory for managing them. Other classes exist that we do not need to discuss here (such as `Monitor`, `Semaphore`, `Interlocked`, `ThreadPoll`, and so on) because they are outside the scope of what we are trying to accomplish in this chapter. If you are interested in digging deeper into the subject of multi-threading, we recommend you get a book that covers this subject in greater depth, such as *Professional C# 2008*, published by Wrox (ISBN 978-0-470-19137-8).

The basic steps required are as follows:

1. Create a `ThreadStart` delegate that points to the method that will run in the secondary thread. The method must return `void` and cannot accept any input parameters.

2. Create a `Thread` object that takes the `ThreadStart` delegate in its constructor. You can also set a number of properties for this thread, such as its name. The name property is particularly useful if you need to debug threads and identify them by name instead of by ID. You can also assign a thread priority, although this can be dangerous because it can seriously affect the performance of the whole application. It is of type `ThreadPriority`, an enumeration, and by default it is set to `ThreadPriority.Normal`, which means that the primary thread and the secondary thread have the same priority, and the CPU time given to the process is equally divided between them. Other values of the `ThreadPriority` enumeration are `AboveNormal`, `BelowNormal`, `Highest`, and `Lowest`. In general, you should never assign the `Priority` property an `AboveNormal` or `Highest` value for a background thread. Instead, it is usually a good idea to set the property to `BelowNormal`, so that the background thread does not slow down the primary thread to any noticeable degree, and it won't interfere with ASP.NET.

3. Call the `Start` method of the `Thread` object. The thread that started the worker thread has full control over it. For example, to affect the lifetime of the thread you can call the `Abort` method to start terminating the thread (in an asynchronous way), the `Join` method to make the primary thread wait until the secondary thread has completed, and the `IsAlive` property, which returns a Boolean value indicating whether or not the background thread is still running.

The following snippet shows how to start the `ExecuteTask` method, which can be used to perform a long task in a background thread:

```
// create and start a background thread
ThreadStart ts = new ThreadStart(Test);
Thread thread = new Thread(ts);
thread.Priority = ThreadPriority.BelowNormal;
thread.Name = "TestThread";
```

```
thread.Start();
// main thread goes ahead immediately
...

// the method run asynchronously by the background thread
void ExecuteTask()
{
    // execute time consuming processing here
    ...
}
```

As of .NET 2.0 you were given the ability to pass parameters into your thread by using the `ParameterizedThreadStart` delegate, which points to methods that take an object parameter. Because an object can be anything, you can pass a custom object with properties that you define as parameters, or simply pass an array of objects if you prefer. The following snippet shows how you can call the `ExecuteTask` method and pass an array of objects to it, where the first object is a string, the second is an integer (that is boxed into an object), and the last is a `DateTime`. The `ExecuteTask` method takes the object parameter and casts it to a reference of type `object` array, and then it extracts the single values and casts them to the expected types, and finally performs the actual processing:

```
// create and start a background thread with some input parameters
object[] parameters = new object[]{"val1", 10, DateTime.Now};
ParameterizedThreadStart pts = new ParameterizedThreadStart(ExecuteTask);
Thread thread = new Thread(pts);
thread.Priority = ThreadPriority.BelowNormal;
thread.Start(parameters);
// main thread goes ahead immediately
...

// the method run asynchronously by the background thread
void ExecuteTask(object data)
{
    // extract the parameters from the input data object
    object[] parameters = (object[])data;
    string val1 = (string)parameters[0];
    int val2 = (int)parameters[1];
    DateTime val3 = (DateTime)parameters[2];

    // execute time consuming processing here
    ...
}
```

The most serious issue with multi-threaded programming is synchronizing access to shared resources. That is, if you have two threads reading and writing to the same variable, you must find some way to synchronize these operations so that one thread cannot read or write a variable while another thread is also writing it. If you do not take this into account, your program may produce unpredictable results and have strange behaviors, it may lock up at unpredictable times, and possibly even cause data integrity problems. A shared resource can be any variable or field within the scope of the current method, including class-level public and private fields and static variables.

In C#, the simplest way to synchronize access to resources is through the `lock` statement. It takes a non-null object (that is, a reference type — value types are *not* accepted), which must be accessible by all threads, and is typically a class-level field. The type of this object is not important, so many developers just use an instance of the root System.Object type for this purpose. You can simply declare an object field at the class level, assign it a reference to a new object, and use it from the methods running in different threads. Once the code enters a lock block, the execution must exit the block before another thread can enter a lock block for the same locking variable. Here's an example:

```
private object lockObj = new object();
private int counter = 0;

void MethodFromFirstThread()
{
    lock(lockObj)
    {
        counter = counter + 1;
    }
    // some other work…
}

void MethodFromSecondThread()
{
    lock(lockObj)
    {
        if (counter >= 10)
            DoSomething();
    }
}
```

In many situations, however, you don't want to completely lock a shared resource against both read and write operations. Normally you would allow multiple threads to read the same resource at the same time, but no write operation can be done from any thread while another thread is reading or writing the resource (multiple reads, but exclusive writes). To implement this type of lock, you use the ReaderWriterLock object, whose AcquireWriterLock method protects code following that method call against other reads or writes from other threads, until a call to ReleaseWriterLock is made. If you call AcquireReaderLock (not to be confused with AcquireWriterLock), another thread will be able to enter its own AcquireReaderLock block and read the same resources, but an AcquireWriterLock call would wait for all the other threads to call ReleaseReaderLock. The following is an example that shows how you can synchronize access to a shared field when you have two different threads that read it, and another one that writes it:

```
public static ReaderWriterLock Lock = new ReaderWriterLock();
private int counter = 0;

void MethodFromFirstThread()
{
    Lock.AcquireWriterLock(Timeout.Infinite);
    counter = counter + 1;
    Lock.ReleaseWriterLock();

    // some other work…
}

void MethodFromSecondThread()
{
    Lock.AcquireReaderLock(Timeout.Infinite);
    if (counter >= 10)
```

```
        DoSomething();
    Lock.ReleaseReaderLock();
}

void MethodFromThirdThread()
{
    Lock.AcquireReaderLock(Timeout.Infinite);
    if (counter != 50)
        DoSomethingElse();
    Lock.ReleaseReaderLock();
}
```

In your specific case, you will have a controller class that runs a background thread to asynchronously send out the newsletters; periodically this process would update the database to indicate its current status. In the previous edition we would have updated server variables and potentially created locking issues, but in this edition, to keep the solution simple and streamlined, we have decided to write to the database directly. As you may already know, database locking is handled automatically for you by the SQL Server. While this is all happening your user will be on the main thread at the newsletter management view. This view, using a combination of JavaScript and jQuery, will update the user as to the status of the newsletter every few seconds. The user has the flexibility to stay on the view or go do other things and come back to review the newsletter's progress.

Partial View Updates with jQuery

To update the status of the newsletter on your newsletter management view, you must find some way to refresh parts of the view without posting the whole page to the server, because that would take time and temporarily show blank pages (which would appear as nasty flashes, even with fast computers and a broadband connection). The solution would be to use JavaScript to update only certain portions of your page, eliminating those unsightly page flashes. For this you are going to use jQuery, which gives you the ability to directly inject HTML data into a specific element on your view such as a div or a span. Consider the possibilities with MVC; you can request information from a refresh function on a controller class, which outputs data that is directly inserted into one of your page elements. The following code demonstrates an example of this:

```
function UpdateStatus()
{
    $.ajax({
        type: "GET",
        url: "/MyController/UpdateStatus",
        dataType: "html",
        sucess: function(data) {
            var domElement = $(data);
            $("#MyDiv").replaceWith(domElement);
        }
    });
}
```

In this example you are able to create a standard HTTP POST to the UpdateStatus method in your MyController controller. If data is returned via your results object, you create a domElement that contains the information in an HTML format, and inserts it into a div that was created on the page called MyDiv. What jQuery does for you in this example is handle the heavy lifting involved in manipulating the DOM directly to take your information. From the user's perspective, you see a seamless update of information in that div without having to do a full-page update.

You may have noticed several similarities in functionality with the preceding code and the ASP.NET AJAX UpdatePanel that was available for ASP.NET Web Forms. This is by design — even though the UpdatePanel cannot be used in MVC, it is a very useful concept and shouldn't be overlooked; that is why we re-created it in jQuery for use in MVC.

Designing the Database Tables

Now that you've covered all the background information, you can start the actual design for this module. As usual, you'll start by designing the database tables, then move on to designing the models and controllers, and finishing with the views. The database design, shown in Figure 8-1, is very simple: there's a single table to store newsletters that were sent out previously but were archived for future reference by online subscribers.

Figure 8-1

All fields are self-explanatory, so we won't spend time describing them, except to point out that `Subject` is of type `nvarchar(256)`, whereas `PlainTextBody` and `HtmlBody` are of type `ntext`. The other fields, `AddedDate` and `AddedBy`, are common to all of the other tables, and we've discussed them in previous chapters.

Designing the Configuration Module

This module will predominately use the `<mailsettings>` element under the `<system.net>` section of the `web.config`. Although most of your items will be set here, you do define a single custom key value pair in the `web.config` to indicate the e-mail address and name of the sender of the newsletter.

The first thing you need to look at is the `<system.net>/<mailSettings>/<smtp>` configuration, shown in the following table.

SMTP Properties	Description
DeliveryMethod	Setting this property to "network" indicates to the application that an external mail server will be used to send e-mails. This will require that the `<network>` element be used, which includes Host, Port, UserName, Password, and DefaultCredentials as shown in the following table.
From	Identifies the e-mail address that will be placed in the "From" section when the application sends an e-mail.
ConfigSource	Defines an external source for the mail configuration settings such as `mail.config`.

The next thing you want to look at is the `<system.net>`/`<mailSettings>`/`<smtp>`/`<network>` configuration:

Network Properties	Description
DefaultCredentials	A Boolean value indicating whether or not the credentials of the application are used. If this is true, UserName and Password are not required.
Host	The name of the mail server.
UserName	The username to be used to log in to the e-mail server and send the e-mails. This is not required if DefaultCredentials is set to true.
Password	The password to be used to log in to the e-mail server to send e-mails.
Port	The port that will be used to send out SMTP.

The next thing you want to define is the custom configuration for the module that sets the e-mail address that will be used to send out the e-mails:

Newsletter Property	Description
FromEmail	The actual e-mail address that will appear in your newsletter's "From" section of the e-mail header.
FromDisplayName	The display name used in conjunction with the FromEmail property.

The SMTP and Network properties are standard for configuring an e-mail server in the `web.config`. You may argue that the sender's e-mail address can be read from the built-in `<mailSettings>` section of the `web.config`, as shown earlier. However, that is usually set to the postmaster's or administrator's e-mail address, which is used to send service e-mails such as the confirmation for a new registration, the lost password e-mail, and the like. In other situations you may want to differentiate the sender's e-mail address, and use one for someone on your staff, so that if the user replies to an e-mail, his reply will actually be read. In the case of a newsletter, you may have a specific e-mail account, such as `newsletter@TheBeerHouse.com`, used by your newsletter editor.

Designing the Model

As usual, the model will be based off of the LINQ-to-SQL entity designer that will fulfill all of your CRUD needs. Unlike some of the other chapters, you will not require any kind of custom class in your model section to control any special data processing situations. The diagram in Figure 8-2 describes the model you will be using for this module. Your newsletter table will hold information pertaining to the content of the newsletter and the affiliated publishing information.

Figure 8-2

You may be wondering how the newsletter controller will know who to send the newsletters to without a table to manage that information. You may remember in Chapter 5 you allowed the user to opt-in to the site's subscription preferences in your custom user profiles page. Those preferences can be accessed by your newsletter controller to output a list of people interested in receiving your subscription. In this way you eliminate the need for unnecessary database tables and keep all the user preferences consolidated in your profile provider.

Designing the Views

Next you design the views that make up the module's presentation layer. Here is list of the user interface files that you develop later in the Solution section:

❑ **Index.aspx:** This view is used simply as a placeholder on the website.

   ❑   `newsletters`

❑ **CreateNewsletter.aspx:** This view allows the user to either create or edit a newsletter. A nice feature integrated into this view is a JavaScript WYSIWYG HTML editor. This is the same editor that was used in Chapter 6 for article creation.

   ❑   `admin/newsletters/create`

   ❑   `admin/newsletters/edit/{newsletterId}`

❑ **ManageNewsletters.aspx:** This view lists all past newsletters that were sent. It gives the user the ability to click any newsletter and review its contents, or delete newsletters that are no longer relevant. The page is updated every few seconds using jQuery to request information from the `UpdateStatus` action method that is only available to the administrators. The view then updates the newsletter status control.

   ❑   `admin/newsletters/remove/{newsletterId}`

   ❑   `admin/newsletters`

Designing the Controller

As in previous chapters, the hard work was already done when you designed the model and the view. So lastly, you need to create an appropriate set of controller actions to map your model to your view:

Action Method	Security	Parameters
Index	--	--
ManageNewsletters	Editor	--
UpdateStatus	Editor	--
CreateNewsletter	Editor	`string subject, string body`
EditNewsletter	Editor	`int? newsletterId, string subject, string body`
RemoveNewsletter	Editor	`int? newsletterId`

Solution

The solution implemented here is an elegant divergence from the solution shown in the previous version of this book. MVC's qualities really shine here at reducing the overall number of pages and lines of code necessary to create the newsletter module. With MVC, one view can be used to both create and edit the newsletters. Because there is no page load event to worry about, you can leverage a single method to perform both newsletter creations and newsletter modifications. Your management of newsletters is also streamlined using MVC by allowing you to display the relevant status information on a single page, and using jQuery to request information from a controller method to update your newsletter information periodically.

The design is complete, and you have all the information you need to start coding the solution. This module's database objects are simple (a single table, with no relationships and foreign keys) so we won't demonstrate how to create the tables. You can refer to previous chapters for general information about how you can work with these objects from Visual Studio 2008, and you can refer to the downloadable code to see the full implementation.

Configuring the Web.Config

For this module to work properly you must configure your `web.config` with all the appropriate information that your controller object needs in order to send newsletters. The following code outlines all the essential elements. Please refer to the "Designing the Configuration Module" section of this chapter if you would like to adjust some of these elements to suit your particular needs.

```
<theBeerHouse>
    <newsletter Email="Newsletter@TheBeerHouse.com"/>
</theBeerHouse>

<system.net>
    <mailSettings>
```

```
            <smtp deliveryMethod="Network"  from="website@TheBeerHouse.com">
               <network defaultCredentials="true" host="MailServer" port="25" />
            </smtp>
         </mailSettings>
      </system.net>
```

Note that this code snippet represents only a fraction of the web.config file. The items within the mailSettings tag can be changed to fit the unique requirements of your network.

Implementing the Model

This section is relatively simple because you have only a single database table to worry about. The rest of your subscription information will be handled by the infrastructure you put into place during the profiling chapter. The following script creates the newsletter table for you:

```
CREATE TABLE [TheBeerHouse].[Newsletters](
    [NewsletterID] [int] IDENTITY(1,1) NOT NULL,
    [AddedDate] [datetime] NOT NULL,
    [AddedBy] [nvarchar](256) NOT NULL,
    [Subject] [nvarchar](256) NOT NULL,
    [PlainTextBody] [ntext] NOT NULL,
    [HtmlBody] [ntext] NOT NULL,
    [Status] [nvarchar](50) NULL,
    [DateSent] [datetime] NULL,
    CONSTRAINT [PK_Newsletters] PRIMARY KEY CLUSTERED (
        [NewsletterID] ASC
    ) WITH (
        PAD_INDEX = OFF,
        STATISTICS_NORECOMPUTE = OFF,
        IGNORE_DUP_KEY = OFF,
        ALLOW_ROW_LOCKS = ON,
        ALLOW_PAGE_LOCKS = ON
    ) ON [PRIMARY]
) ON [PRIMARY] TEXTIMAGE_ON [PRIMARY]
```

You may notice that many of the fields use the nvarchar as opposed to simply varchar. The difference is that nvarchar gives you the ability to store Unicode data, which is used for multilingual support. Essentially, you are able to store the extended characters that would be found in other languages. If this is not a consideration for your particular application, feel free to simply use varchar and text instead of ntext.

Similar to the previous chapters, creating your model for the newsletter module is a snap with your LINQ-to-SQL file. Simply open up the database Tables folders, and drag and drop the newly created Newsletter table into the TheBeerHouse.dbml file. After saving the .dbml file, you are essentially finished creating your model.

Implementing the Controller

The Newsletter controller class is found under ~/Controllers/NewsletterController.cs. It is the code that allows the administrator to create, edit, and delete newsletters. It also provides functionality to retrieve lists of newsletters and provide status and publishing information pertaining to them. We have broken up the controller code example into four parts to cover the four available methods.

The Index Action

The first action you will implement will display a placeholder page for public viewing. This action will simply deliver the view and the page title.

```
public ActionResult Index()
{
    ViewData["PageTitle"] = "Newsletters";

    return View();
}
```

This action has the following route:

❑   newsletters

newsletters

This route is used to display a list of polls for use on the first page:

```
routes.MapRoute(
    "NewsletterIndex",
    "newsletters",
    new { controller = "Newsletter", action = "Index" }
);
```

The ManageNewsletters Action

This action is a relatively simple action that is used to bind all the newsletters in reverse order according to the AddedDate. The view will then be used as a launching point to create, edit, remove, and view the sending status of the newsletters. This action is allowed to be accessed only by a user with the role of Editor.

```
[Authorize(Roles = "Editor")]
public ActionResult ManageNewsletters()
{
    TheBeerHouseDataContext dc = new TheBeerHouseDataContext();
    var viewData = dc.Newsletters.OrderByDescending(n => n.AddedDate);

    ViewData["PageTitle"] = "Manage Newsletters";
    return View(viewData);
}
```

This action has the following route:

❑   admin/newsletters

admin/newsletters

This route is used to display a list of polls for use on the first page.

```
routes.MapRoute(
    "NewsletterManage",
```

```
    "admin/newsletters",
    new { controller = "Newsletter", action = "ManageNewsletters" }
);
```

The UpdateStatus Action

As we talked about earlier in this chapter, this is the main driver for the management screen so that the editors can keep track of when a newsletter has been successfully sent. This action is used only by AJAX requests, but unlike some of the other services that you have created in previous chapters this one will return an HTML representation of the action and is bound against a user control view called NewsletterStatus.

```
[Service]
[Authorize(Roles = "Editor")]
public ActionResult UpdateStatus()
{
    TheBeerHouseDataContext dc = new TheBeerHouseDataContext();
    var viewData = dc.Newsletters.OrderByDescending(n => n.AddedDate);

    return PartialView("Newsletter/NewsletterStatus", viewData);
}
```

This is useful because when jQuery calls this method, it can directly inject the new HTML returned from this action into the div housing this control on the ManageNewsletter view. In this way you avoid having to refresh the entire page and you get a seamless update of the newsletter grid.

The route for this action uses the standard {controller}/{action} route, so requests to this action method can be accessed through

❑   newsletter/updatestatus

The CreateNewsletter and EditNewsletter Actions

As in the previous chapters, the next actions you have to create are ones that will create and edit a newsletter. We have combined these actions together in the same section because they contain mostly the same code concepts and both map to the same view because they are so similar.

The CreateNewsletter Action

The CreateNewsletter action is a little more complex in that it handles the creating and sending of newsletters:

```
[ValidateInput(false)]
[Authorize(Roles = "Editor")]
public ActionResult CreateNewsletter(string subject, string body)
{
    TheBeerHouseDataContext dc = new TheBeerHouseDataContext();

    if (!String.IsNullOrEmpty(subject) && !String.IsNullOrEmpty(body))
    {
        Newsletter newsletter = new Newsletter() {
            AddedDate = DateTime.Now,
```

```
                AddedBy = User.Identity.Name,
                Status = "Queued",
                Subject = subject,
                HtmlBody = body,
                PlainTextBody = body
        };

        dc.Newsletters.InsertOnSubmit(newsletter);
        dc.SubmitChanges();

        Thread thread = new Thread(new ParameterizedThreadStart(SendNewsletter));
        thread.Priority = ThreadPriority.BelowNormal;
        thread.Start(new object[] { newsletter, dc });

        return RedirectToAction("ManageNewsletters");
    }

    ViewData["PageTitle"] = "Create Newsletter";
    return View();
}
```

You can see that you are creating a new parameterized thread to send e-mails out. You pass both the newsletter object and the data context into the newly created thread so that you can update the record once the mailing job is complete. We cover the `SendNewsletter` method that is used in the threading next.

The EditNewsletter Action

This action is used to edit a newsletter that is defined by the parameter `newsletterId`; this action is available only to users who have the Editor role. In the `EditNewsletter` action you can see the changed parts highlighted in the following code. You should pay specific attention to the highlighted parts because they are the sections of code that differ significantly from your `CreateNewsletter` action.

```
[ValidateInput(false)]
[Authorize(Roles = "Editor")]
public ActionResult EditNewsletter(int? newsletterId, string subject, string body)
{
    TheBeerHouseDataContext dc = new TheBeerHouseDataContext();
    var newsletter = dc.Newsletters.FirstOrDefault(
                        n => n.NewsletterID == newsletterId
                    );

    if (newsletter == null)
            throw new HttpException(404, "The newsletter could not be found.");

    if (!String.IsNullOrEmpty(subject) && !String.IsNullOrEmpty(body))
    {
        newsletter.Subject = subject;
        newsletter.HtmlBody = body;
        newsletter.PlainTextBody = body;

        dc.SubmitChanges();
```

```
        Thread thread = new Thread(new ParameterizedThreadStart(SendNewsletter));
        thread.Priority = ThreadPriority.BelowNormal;
        thread.Start(new object[] { newsletter, dc });

            return RedirectToAction("ManageNewsletters", "Newsletter");
    }

    ViewData["PageTitle"] = "Edit Newsletter";
    return View("CreateNewsletter" , newsletter);
}
```

In the highlighted section of code you will notice that you are again checking if a poll is able to be returned from the database and, if one cannot be returned, a 404 Not Found HTTP exception is thrown. This will alert the browser that the requested URL is not valid on the server.

These actions have the following routes, respectively, for CreateNewsletter and EditNewsletter:

❑   admin/newsletters/create

❑   admin/newsletters/edit/{newsletterId}

admin/newsletters/create

This route is used to create a poll:

```
routes.MapRoute(
    "NewsletterCreate",
    "admin/newsletters/create",
    new { controller = " Newsletter", action = "CreateNewsletter" }
);
```

admin/newsletters/edit/{newsletterId}

This route is used to edit a poll. It takes one rule, pollId, which provides the identity of the poll that is being edited:

```
routes.MapRoute(
    "NewsletterEdit",
    "admin/newsletters/edit/{newsletterId}",
    new { controller = "Newsletter",
        action = "EditNewsletter",
        newsletterId = (int?)null },
    new { newsletterId = "[0-9]+" }
);
```

The SendNewsletter Non-Action

This is a new type of method that you have not seen yet. This method, the SendNewsletter method, is a non-action method that is in the controller and is used to send your newsletters in a different thread:

```
[NonAction]
private void SendNewsletter(object data)
{
```

```
        object[] parameters = (object[])data;

        // get parameters from the data object passed in
        Newsletter newsletter = (Newsletter)parameters[0];
        TheBeerHouseDataContext dc = (TheBeerHouseDataContext)parameters[1];

        MembershipUserCollection membershipUserCollection = Membership.GetAllUsers();
        ProfileBase profileBase = new ProfileBase();
        NewslettersElement config =
            Configuration.TheBeerHouseSection.Current.Newsletters;

        // create the message
        MailMessage mailMessage = new MailMessage();
        mailMessage.Body = newsletter.HtmlBody;
        mailMessage.From = new MailAddress(config.FromEmail, config.FromDisplayName);
        mailMessage.Subject = newsletter.Subject;

        // add members to the BCC
        foreach (MembershipUser membershipUser in membershipUserCollection)
        {
            profileBase = ProfileBase.Create(membershipUser.UserName);
            if (profileBase.GetPropertyValue("Subscription").ToString() != "None")
                mailMessage.Bcc.Add(membershipUser.Email);
        }

        // send the e-mail
        SmtpClient smtpClient = new SmtpClient();
        try
        {
            smtpClient.Send(mailMessage);
            newsletter.Status = "Sent";
            newsletter.DateSent = DateTime.Now;
            dc.SubmitChanges();
        }
        catch (Exception ex)
        {
            newsletter.Status = "Failed: " + ex.Message;
            dc.SubmitChanges();
        }
    }
}
```

There is a special attribute that you have never seen before called NonActionAttribute. This attribute is used to tell the controller that this method is not an action and shouldn't be delivered and processed in the same way that an action is, and should basically be ignored by the controller.

You can also see from the preceding code that you are obtaining all your users and checking their profiles to see if they subscribe to your newsletter. If they do, they are added as a receiver of the MailMessage object you have created. Once you have all of your names, you send out the e-mail using the classes in System.Net.Mail, which obtain your mail server settings automatically from your web.config.

The RemoveNewsletter Action

This action is what the users of the site will call when they need to remove a newsletter form the database:

```
[Authorize(Roles = "Editor")]
public ActionResult RemoveNewsletter(int? newsletterId)
{
    TheBeerHouseDataContext dc = new TheBeerHouseDataContext();
    var newsletter = dc.Newsletters.FirstOrDefault(
                        n => n.NewsletterID == newsletterId
                    );

    if (newsletter == null)
        throw new HttpException(404, "The newsletter could not be found.");

    dc.Newsletters.DeleteOnSubmit(newsletter);
    dc.SubmitChanges();

    return RedirectToAction("ManageNewsletters");
}
```

This action has the following route:

❑   admin/newsletters/remove/{newsletterId}

admin/newsletters/remove/{newsletterId}

This route is used to display a list of polls for use on the first page:

```
routes.MapRoute(
    "NewsletterRemove",
    "admin/newsletters/remove/{newsletterId}",
    new { controller = "Newsletter",
          action = "RemoveNewsletter",
          newsletterId = (int?)null },
    new { newsletterId = "[0-9]+" }
);
```

Implementing the View

In this last part of the Solution section you implement the administration views for sending out a newsletter and checking its progress, as well as the end-user view that displays the list of newsletters. MVC affords you some great advantages in terms of being able to reuse your minimal set of views to provide all of the functionality that you are looking for in this newsletter module. The following section outlines how you will go about doing this.

The ManageNewsletter.aspx View

The ManageNewsletter.aspx view shown in Figure 8-3 allows you to see what newsletters have been sent out and what their status currently is. By clicking the subject of any of the newsletters listed in this view you can view the contents of the original newsletter. On the far right-hand of the grid you see little red x's; similar to Chapter 5, they allow you to delete the newsletter. Lastly, the Create Newsletter link allows you to send out a brand new newsletter.

Figure 8-3

When initially creating this view you will want to specify that you want to use a collection of the Newsletter object as your model. We have broken up this view into two Content sections that correlate to your master page for the site. We will go through each content part, MainContent and ScriptContent, separately so that each can be examined individually.

MainContent

The MainContent placeholder does only two things: it renders the NewsletterStatus.ascx control and adds a link to create a new newsletter, so there really isn't much to discuss with this view:

```
<asp:Content ID="MainContent" ContentPlaceHolderID="MainContent" runat="server">

<% Html.RenderPartial("~/Views/Shared/Newsletter/NewsletterStatus.ascx",
ViewData.Model); %>
<p><%= Html.ActionLink("Create Newsletter", "CreateNewsletter") %></p>

</asp:Content>
```

From this HTML you can see that you have very little in terms of actual controls on the page. You are leveraging a user control that contains the grid that you see in this particular view.

ScriptContent

The `ScriptContent` placeholder is a little more complex, but not by much. In this placeholder you have two scripts that need to be included in order for this view to function correctly:

```
<asp:Content ID="ScriptContent" ContentPlaceHolderID="ScriptContent" runat="server">
<script type="text/javascript" src="/content/scripts/tiny_mce/tiny_mce_src.js">
</script>
<script type="text/javascript" src="/content/scripts/manage-
newsletter.js"></script><script type="text/javascript">
    setInterval(UpdateStatus, 4000);
</script>
</asp:Content>
```

We have included some jQuery scripts that are being registered to ensure the grid is updated every four seconds.

manage-newsletter.js

This JavaScript file contains support for all of your admin pages, but the only function you are concerned about right now is the `UpdateStatus` function. This is the function that will fire at a given interval and retrieve the updated grid of statuses for the newsletters:

```
function UpdateStatus() {
    $.ajax({
        type: "GET",
        url: "/Newsletter/UpdateStatus",
        dataType: "html",
        sucess: function(result) {
            var domElement = $(result);
            $("#Newsletter_Status_Table").replaceWith(domElement);
        }
    });
}
```

What this function does is make a call to the `UpdateStatus` action on the controller, which returns back an HTML result for only your control. From there you use the magic of jQuery to insert the result object directly into the `Newsletter_Status_Table` div that you created in the `NewsletterStatus.ascx` control. Remember that this is all happening seamlessly to the user, so there are no page flashes!

The NewsletterStatus.ascx Control

The `NewsletterStatus.ascx` control is located in `~\Views\Shared\Newsletter\` because controls by their nature should be potentially reusable in other locations. In this particular case, though, the reason we made this grid its own control was because we wanted to be able to update only the grid using jQuery and the controller. Figure 8-4 shows only the area that represents the control. You will notice that built into this control, you have the capability of viewing newsletters and deleting them.

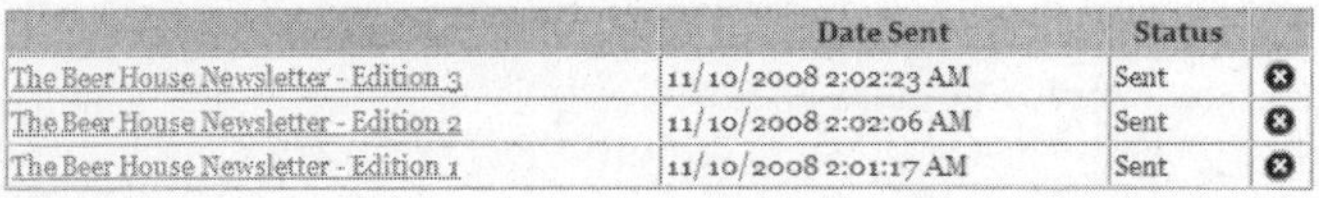

	Date Sent	Status	
The Beer House Newsletter - Edition 3	11/10/2008 2:02:23 AM	Sent	✖
The Beer House Newsletter - Edition 2	11/10/2008 2:02:06 AM	Sent	✖
The Beer House Newsletter - Edition 1	11/10/2008 2:01:17 AM	Sent	✖

Figure 8-4

To be able to present this information you must specify in the control which models you intend for it to receive. When creating this control you will want to indicate that you plan on using a collection of the `Newsletter` model object. This object is actually passed directly from the parent view. The HTML that drives this page is as follows:

```
<div id="Newsletter_Status_Table">

<table width="100%" cellpadding="2" cellspacing="0" summary="User Grid" border="1">
<tr style="font-weight:bold; background-color:#A8C3CB; ">
<td> </td>
<td align="center">Date Sent</td>
<td align="center">Status</td>
<td> </td>
</tr>

<% foreach (var newsletter in ViewData.Model) { %>
<tr>
<td><%= Html.ActionLink(newsletter.Subject, "EditNewsletter", new { newsletterId =
newsletter.NewsletterID }) %></td>
<td><%= newsletter.DateSent %></td>
<td><%= newsletter.Status %></td>
<td align="center"><a href="<%= Url.Action("RemoveNewsletter", new { newsletterId
= newsletter.NewsletterID }) %>"><img border="0" alt="Delete Newsletter" src="/
content/images/DeleteSymbol.png" title="Delete Newsletter" align="middle"/></a></
td>
</tr>
<% } %>
</table>

</div>
```

The CreateNewsletter.aspx View

The `CreateNewsletter.aspx` view, shown in Figure 8-5, is very similar to the create article view from Chapter 6 in that it has the same built-in WYSIWYG editor. This page essentially just provides you with a subject line and a body to enter in your information. The WYSIWYG editor will output both the standard text and the HTML format of this newsletter.

When you initially create this view you will want to specify that you plan on using the `Newsletter` object as your views model. For your convenience, we have broken this down into two `Content` sections that correlate to your master page for the site. We will go through each content part, `MainContent` and `ScriptContent`, separately so that each can be examined individually.

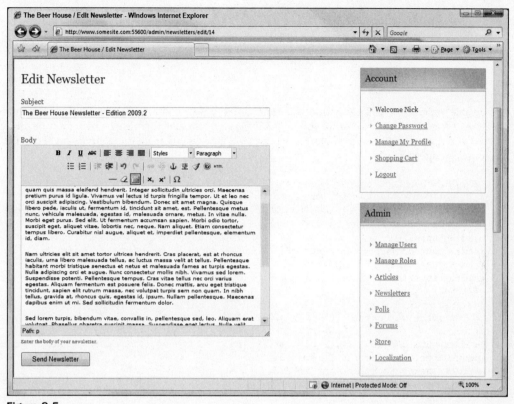

Figure 8-5

MainContent

The `MainContent` placeholder does only two things: it renders the `NewsletterStatus.ascx` control and adds a link to create a new newsletter, so there really isn't much to discuss with this view:

```
<asp:Content ID="MainContent" ContentPlaceHolderID="MainContent" runat="server">

<% Html.RenderPartial("~/Views/Shared/Message.ascx"); %>

<form method="post" action="<%= Url.Action(this.ViewContext.RouteData.
Values["action"] as string, "Newsletter") %>" class="newsletter-create">

    <p class="field input"><label for="title">Subject</label><br />
        <%= Html.TextBox("subject", ViewData["subject"], new { @maxlength = 256 })%>
        <span class="input-message"></span></p>

    <p class="field input"><label for="body">Body</label><br />
        <%= Html.TextArea("body", Model.HtmlBody, new { style = "height: 500px"})%>
        <span class="input-message"></span></p>
```

```
      <p><button type="submit" id="newsletter-create-button">Send Newsletter</
button></p>

   </form>

</asp:Content>
```

From this HTML you can see that you have very little in terms of actual controls on the page. You are leveraging a user control that contains the grid that you see in this particular view.

ScriptContent

The `ScriptContent` placeholder is pretty straightforward. You just include two scripts and a validate function, something that you have seen in previous chapters, so we won't elaborate on it any further than the following code:

```
<asp:Content ID="ScriptContent" ContentPlaceHolderID="ScriptContent" runat="server">
<script type="text/javascript" src="/content/scripts/tiny_mce/tiny_mce_src.js">
</script>
<script type="text/javascript" src="/content/scripts/manage-newsletter.js"></script>
<% if (IsPostBack) { %>
<script type="text/javascript">
    ValidateNewsletter();
</script>
<% } %>
</asp:Content>
```

manage-newsletter.js

The JavaScript that is needed for this view is no different than what you did back in Chapter 6 for the create article view and its WYSIWYG editor, so all of this may seem familiar to you:

```
var bodyEditor;

$(document).ready(function () {
    bodyEditor = new tinymce.Editor("body", __editorConfig);
    bodyEditor.onChange.add(function (ed) { bodyEditor.save(); });
    bodyEditor.onClick.add(function (ed) { ShowMessage("#body", "Enter the body of
your newsletter."); });
    bodyEditor.render();
});

// clears the message from the description when another input gets focus
$(":input")
    .focus(function () { HideMessage("#body"); })
    .blur(function () { HideMessage("#body"); });
```

As you can see from the code you are looking for a DIV called "body" on the form, and where it is located it replaces the TEXTAREA form input on the page with a WYSIWYG editor. The final thing that you want to provide your administrators with is some level of client-side validation and information about the form fields they are using. This is subsequently the last piece of JavaScript in your `manage-newsletter.js` file as well:

```javascript
$("#subject").focus(function () { ShowMessage(this, "Enter the subject for your
newsletter."); });

function ValidateTitle () {
    return VerifyRequiredField("#subject", "required");
}

function ValidateBody () {
    return VerifyRequiredField("#body", "required");
}

function ValidateNewsletter () {
    return ValidateTitle()
        && ValidateBody();
}
$("form.newsletter-create").validate(ValidateNewsletter);
```

Example Email

Finally, your end result, shown in Figure 8-6, is the e-mail that you had sent out using your new newsletter module.

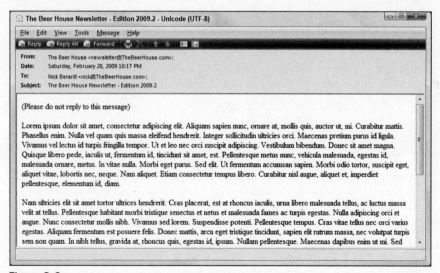

Figure 8-6

The Index.aspx View

The last view we are going to discuss is the public view for the newsletters module. Its only purpose is to serve as a reminder that the user can subscribe to newsletters that the site administrators may send out. The view will create a page that looks like Figure 8-7.

Figure 8-7

As you can see, this is just a reminder to the user of the site's functionality for sending newsletters. It actually only consists of a tiny bit of HTML in the `MainContent`.

MainContent

We have included the standard message display control that is used throughout the site and a paragraph tag that contains the text you want the users to see when they visit this view:

```
<asp:Content ID="MainContent" ContentPlaceHolderID="MainContent" runat="server">

<% Html.RenderPartial("~/Views/Shared/Message.ascx"); %>
<p>If you would like to subscribe to our newsletter, please go to <a href="/User/
UserProfile">your user profile</a>, and select your subscription type.</p>

</asp:Content>
```

You can customize this to whatever you would like; we kept it pretty generic for the example TheBeerHouse application. If you have something more poignant to say, feel free to modify this page for your own needs.

Summary

In this chapter you implemented a complete module for sending out newsletters to members who registered to receive them, either at initial registration time or later. The module sends out the e-mails from a background thread instead of the main thread used to process the page request, so that you don't risk page timeouts, and, above all, so that you don't leave the editor with a blank page that may last several minutes or more. To provide some feedback to the editor about the newsletter being sent, the administrator is sent to the newsletter management page. This page automatically updates on its own to allow the administrator to do other things and not risk interrupting the newsletter from being sent.

To implement all of this, you have used advanced features such as multi-threaded programming, script callbacks, and the `SmtpClient` and `MailMessage` classes to compose and send e-mail messages. You have also seen other new features provided with the MVC framework such as partial view renders.

Although this module works well for most basic newsletter needs, there's always room for enhancements. Here are some suggestions for improvements you may wish to make:

- ❑ Add the capability to send attachments with the newsletters. This can be very useful if you want to send HTML newsletters with images. Currently, you can only send e-mails with images by referencing the full URL of the images on your server.

- ❑ Add support for setting the priority of the newsletter e-mails.

- ❑ Add support for customized field insertion like the previous book had, so that you can insert the user's name, date, and other information into the newsletter dynamically before being sent.

- ❑ Add the capability to have different mailing lists, for different topics, such as Parties, New Articles, or New Products in your store. This would require having more profile properties, and an expanded `CreateNewsletter` page, so that you can choose the target mailing list.

- ❑ Add support for localization so that you can publish newsletters in multiple languages and have them delivered to the appropriate parties.

- ❑ Modify the `Index.aspx` view to show previously sent newsletters. This functionality should be pretty easy to implement, because you have essentially already done all the work for this functionality in Chapter 6.

- ❑ When the messages are sent out, you won't get an error or exception if the e-mail does not reach its destination because the e-mail address isn't valid. The SMTP server does its work without letting you know about the results. However, messages sent to non-existent addresses usually come back to the sender with an error message saying that the message couldn't be successfully delivered because the address does not exist. These error messages are sent to the server's postmaster and then forwarded to the site's administrator. At this point, when you get such a message, you can manually set that account's Newsletter profile property to none. However, a much better and automated approach would be to write a program (probably as a Windows service) that parses the incoming messages to find the error messages, automatically performing the unsubscribe operation.

In the last few chapters you've developed modules to strengthen the site-to-user communications, such as the polls module and this newsletter manager. In the next chapter you implement a module to manage forums, which is an important form of user-to-user communication.

9

Forums

Internet users like to feel they are part of a community of people with similar interests. A successful site should build a community of loyal visitors and be a place where they can discuss their favorite subjects, ask questions, and reply to others. Community members will return often to talk to other people with whom they've already shared messages, or to find comments and opinions about their interests. This chapter outlines some of the advantages of building such a virtual community, its goals, and the design and implementation of a new module for setting up and managing discussion boards.

Problem

User-to-user communication is important in many types of sites. For example, in a content site for pub enthusiasts, visitors to the site may want advice on the best way to brew their own beer, suggestions for good pubs in their area, to share comments on the last event they attended, and so on. Having contact with their peers is important so that they can ask questions and share their own knowledge. E-commerce sites have an added benefit of enabling users to review products online. Two ways to provide user-to-user communication are opinion polls and discussion boards. We've already looked at opinion polls in Chapter 7, and in this chapter we look at discussion boards, also known as forums. Visitors can browse the various messages in the forums, post their questions and topics, reply to other people's questions, and share ideas and tips. Forums act as a source of content, and provide an opportunity for users to participate and contribute. One reason why forums are especially attractive from a manager's perspective is because they require very little time and effort from employees because end users provide most of the content. However, a few minutes a day should be spent to ensure that nobody has posted any offensive messages, and that any problems that may be mentioned in a message receive some attention (maybe problems with the site, or questions about products, locations, and so on).

As for the TheBeerHouse site, you will offer discussion boards about brewing beers, pubs, concerts and parties, and more. These will be separate forums, used to group and categorize the threads by topic, so that it's easier for visitors to read what they are interested in. Early web-forum systems often threw up long lists of messages on a single page, which took ages to load. This can be avoided by displaying lists in pages, with each page containing a particular number of messages. The website already has a way to identify users, and the forums will need to integrate with that membership system. Besides being identified by username in the forums module, users may like something "catchy" in order to be recognized by the community: something such as an avatar image (a small picture that represents the users on their messages). This information will be added to every post, and will help readers quickly identify the post's author. Of course, like any other module you've developed so far, the site's administrators and editors must be able to add, remove, or edit forums, topics, and replies.

Design

Before looking at the design, let's consider a more accurate list of features to be implemented:

❑ Support for multiple categories, or subforums, that are more or less specific to a single topic/argument. Subforums are identified by name and description, and optionally by an image.

❑ Forums must support moderation. When a forum is moderated (this is a forum-level option), all messages posted by anyone except power users (administrators, editors, and moderators) are not immediately visible on the forum, but must be approved by a member of one of the power user roles first. This is a useful option to ensure that posts are pertinent, non-offensive, and comply with the forum's policy. However, this also places a bigger burden on the power users because posts have to be approved often (at least several times a day, even on weekends), or users will lose interest. Because of the timeliness needed for moderation, most forums are not moderated, but they are checked at least once a day to ensure that the policy has not been violated (with no particular need to check on weekends).

❑ The list of threads for a subforum, and the list of posts for a thread, must be paginable. In addition, the list of threads must be sortable by the last posting date, or the number of replies or views, in ascending or descending order. Sort options are very helpful if there are a lot of messages.

❑ Posting is only permitted by registered members, whereas browsing is allowed by everybody. An extension of the forum implemented in this chapter may include more options to specify that browsing also requires login, or that posting is allowed by anonymous users.

❑ Users will be able to format their messages with a limited, and safe, set of HTML tags. This will be done by means of the TinyMCE Editor already used in Chapter 6, with a reduced toolbar.

❑ If replies are allowed on a post, they can later be disabled (and thus the thread closed) only by administrators, editors, and moderators.

❑ The messages posted by users are counted. This count is a form of recognition, and it lets other users know that this person might be more knowledgeable, or at least that he's hung around in the forums a lot (it tends to lend more credibility).

❑ The user will have an avatar provided by the online service Gravatar, which stands for Globally Recognized Avatar, which works off of the users' e-mail address already provided to the site when they registered.

❑ Administrators, editors, and moderators can delete any post or reply.

Remember that you need some kind of policy statement somewhere in the forum pages that tells users what the rules are. This is usually needed for legal reasons in case a nasty, hateful, or untruthful message is posted and not caught quickly — just some kind of disclaimer to protect the site owners/administrators from lawsuits.

Designing the Database Tables

You need three tables for this chapter. In addition to the two tables provided in the previous book, you are going to add an additional table called Votes to give you the ability to vote the forum posts up and down, to hopefully create a set of high-quality posts voted on by the community. Figure 9-1 represents the UML diagram for this chapter.

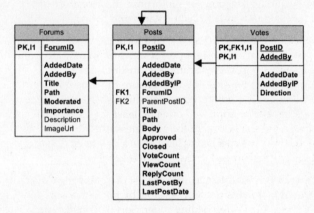

Figure 9-1

Here you see the primary and foreign keys, the usual AddedDate and AddedBy fields that are used in most tables for audit and recovery purposes, and a few extra fields that store the forum data. The Forums and Posts tables are similar to what you have seen previously in the book so we are not going to go over them in great detail. The Votes table is a pretty new concept in this book, so we should go through the primary key and why the decisions were made like they were. In the Votes table the primary key consists of the PostID and AddedBy field, which is also known as a composite key. Neither of these two fields is automatically generated like you have seen in other tables; they are based on the following rule: there can only be one vote per logged-in user for each post. So instead of creating an auto-generated identity for the row and then checking if the user has already added a vote before adding a new one, you are going to let the database manage this rule by setting a primary key to the two fields that make up your business rule. This way, even if there is a programming error, the data is still protected by not allowing more than one user to vote on a post.

Queries That Access the Database

The following table contains the list of stored procedures for the typical CRUD operations on the two database tables, plus some special updates to handle approving posts, moving threads, incrementing the view count, and so on.

Query	Description
GetVote	Get single vote based on the post and the user.
GetPost	Get single post based on the post identity.
GetForum	Get single forum based on the forum identity.
GetPosts	Get posts based on a forum and a page.
GetForums	Get all forums.
GetReplies	Get reply posts based on the parent post and a page.

Designing the Configuration Module

The configuration settings of the forums module are defined in a `<forums>` element within the `<theBeerHouse>` section of the `web.config` file. The class that maps the settings and exposes them is `ForumsElement`, which defines the following properties:

Property	Description
PostReplyPageSize	The number of post replies listed per page when viewing a post.
ForumPageSize	The number of posts listed per page when viewing a forum.

Designing the Model

As usual, the model consists of a number of entity classes that wrap data from the database tables (the `Forum`, `Post`, and `Vote` classes). The diagram shown in Figure 9-2 represents the two LINQ-to-SQL classes that you will be using as your model; the design should be self-explanatory.

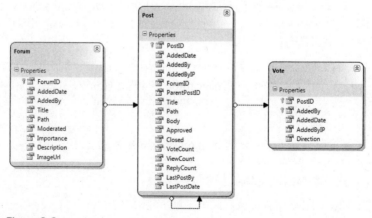

Figure 9-2

As in previous chapters you need to create a static class that contains all the queries necessary for the forum information for the database. The static class you are going to create, called ForumQueries, contains extension methods for Forum, Post, and Vote classes. The diagram in Figure 9-3 represents the queries available for the model.

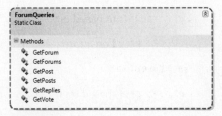

Figure 9-3

Designing the View

This section describes the views and routes necessary for this module. The design of the view follows the same layout you have previously used in the book:

❑ **Index.aspx:** This is the page through which you can view all the available forums.

    ❑ `forums`

❑ **ViewForum.aspx:** This is the page through which the posts in a specific forum are viewed.

    ❑ `forums/{forumId}/{*path}`

    ❑ `forums/{forumId}/{path}/page{page}`

❑ **ViewPost.aspx:** This is the page through which the post and the replies are reviewed.

    ❑ `forums/posts/{postId}/{*path}`

    ❑ `forums/posts/{postId}/{path}/page{page}`

❑ **CreatePost.aspx:** This is the page through which a user can post a new post to a forum or reply to a specific post.

    ❑ `forums/{forumId}/post`

    ❑ `forums/posts/{parentPostId}/reply`

❑ **ManageForums.aspx:** This is the page through which an administrator or editor can manage forums with functionality to add, edit, and remove content.

    ❑ `admin/forums`

❑ **ManagePosts.aspx:** This is the page through which an administrator or editor can approve or deny posts that are moderated.

    ❑ `admin/forums/posts`

❑ **CreateForum.aspx:** This page will allow you to create or edit an existing forum.

❑ `admin/forums/create`

❑ `admin/forums/edit/{forumId}`

❑ **RemoveForum.aspx:** This page will ask you if you want to remove the current forum from the database.

❑ `admin/forums/remove/{forumId}`

Designing the Controller

Just like in previous chapters, you already completed the hard work when you designed the model and the view, so now you just need to create the actions for your controller. The following table shows the actions that you will need in order for your forum to meet the requirements laid out in the Problem section.

Action Method	Security	Parameters
Index	--	—
ViewForum	--	`int forumId, string path, int page`
ViewPost	--	`int postId, string path`
Vote	--	`int postId, int direction`
ManageForum	Editor	—
CreateForum	Editor	`string title, string description, int? order, bool? Moderated`
EditForum	Editor	`int forumId, string title, string description, int? order, bool? Moderated`
RemoveForum	Editor	`int forumId, string remove`
CreatePost	--	`int? forumId, int? parentPostId, string title, string body`
ClosePost	Editor	`int postId, bool closed`
ApprovePost	Editor	`int postId, bool approved`
RemovePost	Editor	`int posted`

Solution

This section covers the implementation of key parts of this module, as described in the Design section. But you won't find complete source code printed here, because many similar classes were discussed in other chapters. See the code download to get the complete source code.

Implementing the Configuration Module

The custom configuration class must be developed before any other code because the custom settings are used in all other layers. This class is similar to the one seen in the previous chapter; it inherits from `ConfigurationElement` and has the properties previously defined:

```
public class ForumsElement : ConfigurationElement
{
    [ConfigurationProperty("postReplyPageSize", DefaultValue = "10")]
    public int ThreadsPageSize
    {
        get { return (int)base["postReplyPageSize"]; }
        set { base["postReplyPageSize"] = value; }
    }

    [ConfigurationProperty("forumPageSize", DefaultValue = "25")]
    public int PostsPageSize
    {
        get { return (int)base["forumPageSize"]; }
        set { base["forumPageSize"] = value; }
    }
}
```

To make this class map a `<forums>` element under the top-level `<theBeerHouse>` section, you add a property of type `ForumsElement` to the `TheBeerHouseSection` class developed in the previous chapter and then use the `ConfigurationProperty` attribute to do the mapping:

```
public class TheBeerHouseSection : ConfigurationSection
{
    // other properties here…

    [ConfigurationProperty("forums", IsRequired = true)]
    public ForumsElement Polls
    {
        get { return (ForumsElement)base["forums"]; }
    }
}
```

If you want to make the archive available to everyone, you would use these settings in the `web.config` file:

```
<theBeerHouse>
    <contactForm mailTo="support@managedfusion.com" />
    <forums postReplyPageSize="10" />
</theBeerHouse>
```

The default value will be used for all those settings not explicitly defined in the configuration file.

Implementing the Model

In this chapter, like the previous chapters, we are going to jump right into the LINQ queries needed and skip over the LINQ entities created for this chapter. The entities don't differ at all from what you saw in Chapter 6 and the diagram in Figure 9-2 is enough to completely define the queries you are going to create.

Extending the LINQ Objects

You need to extend the LINQ objects created from the DBML in order to add some necessary business functionality that your module will require; you previously did this in Chapter 6 and you need to add some extra functionality to the Post object to provide the Gravatar image URL.

The Post Class

For the post class you need to add two methods to your Post object to provide the Gravatar image URL for the AddedBy field and the LastPostBy field in the database:

```
public string GetAddedByAvatarUrl(int size)
{
    MembershipUser membershipUser = Membership.GetUser(AddedBy, false);
    string identity = AddedByIP;

    if (membershipUser != null && membershipUser.Email != null)
        identity = membershipUser.Email.ToLower();

    return String.Format("http://www.gravatar.com/avatar/{0}?s={1}&d=identicon",
        identity.ToHashString("MD5"),
        size);
}

public string GetLastPostByAvatarUrl(int size)
{
    MembershipUser membershipUser = Membership.GetUser(LastPostBy, false);
    string identity = AddedByIP;

    if (membershipUser != null && membershipUser.Email != null)
        identity = membershipUser.Email.ToLower();

    return String.Format("http://www.gravatar.com/avatar/{0}?s={1}&d=identicon",
        identity.ToHashString("MD5"),
        size);
}
```

This code uses the Membership provider that we first discussed in Chapter 5 to find the users by their UserName. You then use the membership name to get the e-mail address, and if there is no e-mail address you default to the IP address that was originally used in creating the post. Finally, you obtain the Gravatar image URL by taking the MD5 hash of the e-mail or IP address.

If you would like to learn more about how Gravatar works and the different options available in implementing it, you can visit http://en.gravatar.com/site/implement/url for more information.

Create the LINQ Queries

Next, you are going to create the LINQ queries that will drive your database access, through your model, and adhere to the requirements in the Design section of this chapter. The queries are pretty basic from our stand point, but over the course of the rest of the chapter you are going to see how some really advanced functionality can be driven by some very mundane queries. So let's get started!

The GetVote Query

This query gets a single vote from the database based on the user and post. This will help you get specific votes for when you want to show the specific vote for a specific poll:

```
public static Vote GetVote(this Table<Vote> source, int postId, string userName)
{
    var query = from v in source
                where v.PostID == postId && v.AddedBy == userName
                select v;

    return query.SingleOrDefault();
}
```

The GetPost Query

This query gets a single post from the database for the requested identity. This will help you get specific posts for when you want to view just the post with its results, or edit the post:

```
public static Post GetPost(this Table<Post> source, int postId)
{
    return source.SingleOrDefault(p => p.PostID == postId);
}
```

The GetForum Query

This query gets a single forum from the database for the requested identity. This will help you get specific forums for when you want to view just the forum with its results, or edit the forum:

```
public static Forum GetForum(this Table<Forum> source, int forumId)
{
    return source.SingleOrDefault(f => f.ForumID == forumId);
}
```

The GetPosts Query

This query returns a paginable collection of posts, like you first saw in Chapter 6. The query takes two parameters, one for the page you want to return and another for the forum that holds these posts:

```
public static Pagination<Post> GetPosts(this Table<Post> source, int forumId, int page)
{
    int count = Configuration.TheBeerHouseSection.Current.Forums.PostsPageSize;
    int index = (page - 1) * count;

    var query = from p in source
                where p.ParentPostID == null && p.ForumID == forumId && p.Approved
                orderby p.LastPostDate descending
                select p;

    return new Pagination<Post>(
        query.Skip(index).Take(count),
        index,
```

```
            count,
            query.Count()
        );
    }
```

The GetForums Query

This query returns all the forums in the database:

```
public static IEnumerable<Forum> GetForums(this Table<Forum> source)
{
    return source.OrderBy(f => f.Importance);
}
```

You may be asking what the point of this method is because you are doing little more than just returning the only parameter with a simple order by placed on it. We are doing this for consistency in the interface so that, just like GetPosts and GetReplies, you can call GetForums in a similar way to your other calls. Also, in the future you never know how the requirements might change for getting forums from the database, and if they change you won't have to worry about refactoring everywhere that you need to get forums in the application.

The GetReplies Query

This query returns a paginable collection of reply posts. The query takes two parameters, one for the page you want to return and another for the parent post that you want to get the replies for:

```
public static Pagination<Post> GetReplies(this Table<Post> source, int postId, int
page)
{
    int count = Configuration.TheBeerHouseSection.Current.Forums.ThreadsPageSize;
    int index = (page - 1) * count;

    var query = from p in source
                where p.ParentPostID == postId
                orderby p.AddedDate && p.Approved
                select p;

    return new Pagination<Post>(
        query.Skip(index).Take(count),
        index,
        count,
        query.Count()
    );
}
```

Implementing the Controller

As you have done in the previous chapters, you are going to implement the controller and each action it requires. In this chapter the controller will be appropriately named ForumController.cs and it will be located in the ~/Controllers folder. The actions of this controller will define business rules for your forums module and how it interacts with the database.

The Index Action

The first action you will implement displays all the forums that the website users can post to:

```
public ActionResult Index()
{
    TheBeerHouseDataContext dc = new TheBeerHouseDataContext();
    var viewData = dc.Forums.GetForums();

    ViewData["PageTitle"] = "Forums";
    return View(viewData);
}
```

This code retrieves all the forums from the database and sends them to the view to be displayed.

This action has the following route:

❑   forums

forums

This route is used to display a list of forums:

```
routes.MapRoute(
    "ForumsIndex",
    "forums",
    new { controller = "Forum", action = "Index" }
);
```

The ViewForum Action

This second action you are going to create allows the website users to view the posts for a specific forum. This action will display a list of posts for a specific forum and it will also be selected by the page that is passed in; if there is no page, it will default to the first page.

```
public ActionResult ViewForum(int forumId, string path, [Default(1)]int page)
{
    TheBeerHouseDataContext dc = new TheBeerHouseDataContext();
    var forum = dc.Forums.GetForum(forumId);

    // throw a 404 Not Found if the requested forum is not in the database
    if (forum == null)
        throw new HttpException(404, "The forum could not be found.");

    // SEO: redirect to the correct location if the path is not
    if (!String.Equals(path, forum.Path, StringComparison.OrdinalIgnoreCase))
        return this.RedirectToAction(301, "ViewForum",
            new { forumId = forum.ForumID, path = forum.Path });

    int count = Configuration.TheBeerHouseSection.Current.Forums.PostsPageSize;
    int index = (page - 1) * count;

    ViewData["PageTitle"] = forum.Title + " Forum";
```

```
        ViewData["count"] = count;
        ViewData["index"] = index;

        return View(forum);
    }
```

As you have done in previous chapters, you throw a 404 Not Found exception when the forumId passed in cannot be found in the database. In addition, you have a path being passed in; you need to verify it against the database and if it differs you redirect to the correct path. There are going to be similar actions for the rest of the actions in this controller, so we are not going to cover the 404 Not Found and 301 Permanent Redirect in the future actions because the pattern will likely not change.

This action has the following routes:

❑ forums/{forumId}/{*path}

❑ forums/{forumId}/{path}/page{page}

forums/{forumId}/{*path}

This route is used to display a list of posts, in a certain forum, for the first page:

```
routes.MapRoute(
    "Forum",
    "forums/{forumId}/{*path}",
    new { controller = "Forum", action = "ViewForum", forumId = (int?)null,
        path = (string)null, page = 1 },
    new { forumId = "[0-9]+" }
);
```

forums/{forumId}/{path}/page{page}

This route is used to display a list of posts, in a certain forum, for a certain page:

```
routes.MapRoute(
    "ForumPaged",
    "forums/{forumId}/{path}/page{page}",
    new { controller = "Forum", action = "ViewForum", forumId = (int?)null,
        path = (string)null, page = (int?)null },
    new { forumId = "[0-9]+" }
);
```

The ViewPost Action

This next action is for viewing the post. This is very similar in structure to the ViewForum action, and the only difference is that you need to increment the view count whenever the post is viewed.

```
public ActionResult ViewPost(int postId, string path, [Default(1)]int page)
{
    TheBeerHouseDataContext dc = new TheBeerHouseDataContext();
    var viewData = dc.Posts.GetPost(postId);

    // throw a 404 Not Found if the requested post is not in the database
```

```
        if (viewData == null)
            throw new HttpException(404, "The post could not be found.");

        // SEO: redirect to the correct location if the path is not
        if (!String.Equals(path, viewData.Path, StringComparison.OrdinalIgnoreCase))
            return this.RedirectToAction(301, "ViewPost",
                new { id = viewData.PostID, path = viewData.Path });

        viewData.ViewCount++;
        dc.SubmitChanges();

        int count = Configuration.TheBeerHouseSection.Current.Forums.ThreadsPageSize;
        int index = (page - 1) * count;

        ViewData["PageTitle"] = viewData.Title;
        ViewData["count"] = count;
        ViewData["index"] = index;

        var vote = dc.Votes.GetVote(postId, User.Identity.Name);
        ViewData["userVote"] = vote == null ? 0 : vote.Direction;

        return View(viewData);
    }
```

This action has the following routes:

❏   forums/posts/{postId}/{*path}

❏   forums/posts/{postId}/{path}/page{page}

forums/posts/{postId}/{*path}

This route is used to display a post and its replies for the first page:

```
routes.MapRoute(
    "ForumPost",
    "forums/posts/{postId}/{*path}",
    new { controller = "Forum", action = "ViewPost", postId = (int?)null,
        path = (string)null, page = 1 },
    new { postId = "[0-9]+" }
);
```

forums/posts/{postId}/{path}/page{page}

This route is used to display a post and its replies for a certain page:

```
routes.MapRoute(
    "ForumPostPaged",
    "forums/posts/{postId}/{path}/page{page}",
    new { controller = "Forum", action = "ViewPost", postId = (int?)null,
        path = (string)null, page = (int?)null },
    new { postId = "[0-9]+" }
);
```

The Vote Action

The next action that you are going to code gets at the real heart of the social media that this forum is going to provide to the patrons of the pub. It allows the users of the site to interact directly with the content and judge the validity of a post through a method called crowd sourcing. This feature is often referred to as the more generic term, social networking, but there isn't actually any networking going on like what happens on sites like Facebook or LinkedIn. This is why we use the term crowd sourcing, because we are out *sourcing* the judging of the posts to the *crowd*, or the registered users of the site in this case.

This action is used to vote up or down a post, and is only available to registered, logged-in users of the site through the provided service:

```
[Authorize, ServiceOnly, HttpPostOnly]
public ActionResult Vote(int postId, int direction)
{
    if (User == null || User.Identity == null || !User.Identity.IsAuthenticated)
        return View(new { error = "not-authenticated" });

    TheBeerHouseDataContext dc = new TheBeerHouseDataContext();
    var post = dc.Posts.GetPost(postId);
    var vote = dc.Votes.GetVote(postId, User.Identity.Name);

    if (vote == null)
    {
        vote = new Vote {
            AddedBy = User.Identity.Name,
            AddedDate = DateTime.Now,
            AddedByIP = Request.UserHostAddress,
            Direction = (direction > 0) ? (short)1 : (short)-1,
        };
        post.Votes.Add(vote);
        post.VoteCount += vote.Direction;

        dc.SubmitChanges();
    }

    return View(new { direction = vote.Direction, voteCount = post.VoteCount });
}
```

We have already covered what `Authorize`, `ServiceOnly`, and `HttpPostOnly` do in Chapter 6, so we will not cover them again for the sake of brevity. This action creates votes for a given post and increments the `VoteCount` on the post. This is all pretty simple to understand and nothing you haven't done before in previous chapters.

There are a couple of built-in protections that we haven't covered in any previous chapters. The first one we would like to discuss is the `direction` parameter for the action. It's typed as a signed 32-bit integer so it has the full spectrum of values that can be assigned to the `System.Int32` value-type structure, which is $-2,147,483,648$ to $2,147,483,647$. However, you want to limit this to either a vote up or a vote down, so you need to protect against a malicious user sending a value to your server that it wasn't designed for. You do this by using the following algorithm:

```
Direction = (direction > 0) ? (short)1 : (short)-1,
```

which says that if the `direction` parameter is greater than zero, then it should be considered a vote up, or +1, and everything else should be considered a vote down, or –1. This protects you against any faulty data being passed into the database and skewing your voting results with numbers that are too large or too small.

The second protection that you added in is gracefully failing if the user has already voted on this post. You do this by trying to retrieve a vote from the database for the currently logged-in user and the post; if it comes back as null, you know the user hasn't voted yet, but if a vote does exist you skip adding it and just return the vote result as if the user has voted. Many developers would throw an exception if the vote already existed, but by throwing an exception you essentially break the interface to the requesting browser. It is just as easy to return the object that you already pulled from the database and keep the interface constant and functioning the same. Doing things this way, the requesting browser never needs to know your internal logic, nor do they have to care, because the API for this service always returns the same data.

The route for this action uses the standard `{controller}/{action}` route, so requests to this action method can be accessed through:

❑   `forum/vote`

The ManageForums Action

This action is a relatively simple action that is used to bind a set of forums to a view. The view will then be used as a launching point to edit and remove forums that you have created. This action can only be accessed by a user with the role of Editor:

```
[Authorize(Roles = "Editor")]
public ActionResult ManageForums()
{
    TheBeerHouseDataContext dc = new TheBeerHouseDataContext();
    var viewData = dc.Forums.GetForums();

    ViewData["PageTitle"] = "Manage Forums";
    return View(viewData);
}
```

This action has the following route:

❑   `admin/forums`

admin/forums

This route is used to display a list of polls for managing and is for the first page:

```
routes.MapRoute(
    "ForumManager",
    "admin/forums",
    new { controller = "Forum", action = "ManageForums" }
);
```

The ManagePosts Action

This action is relatively simple, and very similar to the `ManageForums` action, and used to bind a set of posts that are awaiting approval to the view. The view will then be used as a launching point to approve and remove posts that need to be moderated. This action can only be accessed by a user with the role of Editor:

```
[Authorize(Roles = "Editor")]
public ActionResult ManagePosts()
{
    TheBeerHouseDataContext dc = new TheBeerHouseDataContext();
    var viewData = dc.Posts.Where(p => p.Approved == false);

    ViewData["PageTitle"] = "Manage Posts";
    return View(viewData);
}
```

This action has the following route:

❑   admin/forums/posts

admin/forums

This route is used to display a list of polls for managing and is for the first page:

```
routes.MapRoute(
    "ForumPostsManager",
    "admin/forums/posts",
    new { controller = "Forum", action = "ManagePosts" }
);
```

The CreateForum and EditForum Action

The next actions you have to create are ones that will create and edit a forum. We have combined these actions together in the same section, like we have done in previous chapters, because they contain mostly the same code in concept.

The CreateForum Action

This action is used to create your forum and it is only accessible to users with the role of Editor:

```
[Authorize(Roles = "Editor")]
public ActionResult CreateForum(
        string title, string description, int? order, bool? moderated)
{
    order = order ?? 0;
    moderated = moderated ?? false;

    TheBeerHouseDataContext dc = new TheBeerHouseDataContext();

    if (!String.IsNullOrEmpty(title) && !String.IsNullOrEmpty(description))
    {
        try
```

```
        {
            Forum forum = new Forum {
                AddedBy = User.Identity.Name,
                AddedDate = DateTime.Now,
                Title = title,
                Path = title.ToUrlFormat(),
                Description = description,
                Importance = order.Value,
                Moderated = moderated.Value
            };

            dc.Forums.InsertOnSubmit(forum);
            dc.SubmitChanges();

            TempData["SuccessMessage"] = "Your forum has been created.";
            return RedirectToAction("EditForum",
                new { forumId = forum.ForumID });
        }
        catch (Exception exc)
        {
            TempData["ErrorMessage"] = exc.Message;
        }
    }

    ViewData["title"] = title;
    ViewData["description"] = description;
    ViewData["order"] = order;
    ViewData["moderated"] = moderated;

    ViewData["PageTitle"] = "Create Forum";

    return View("CreateForum");
}
```

The EditForum Action

This action is used to edit a forum that is defined by the parameter `forumId`; this action is only available to users who have the Editor role. In the `EditForum` action we are going to highlight the parts of code you should pay specific attention to because they are the sections of code that differ from our `CreateForum` action:

```
[Authorize(Roles = "Editor")]
public ActionResult EditForum(int forumId,
        string title, string description, int? order, bool? moderated)
{
    order = order ?? 0;
    moderated = moderated ?? false;

    TheBeerHouseDataContext dc = new TheBeerHouseDataContext();
    Forum forum = dc.Forums.GetForum(forumId);

    // throw a 404 Not Found if the requested forum is not in the database
    if (forum == null)
        throw new HttpException(404, "The forum could not be found.");
```

```
              if (!String.IsNullOrEmpty(title) && !String.IsNullOrEmpty(description))
              {
                  try
                  {
                      forum.Title = title;
                      forum.Path = title.ToUrlFormat();
                      forum.Description = description;
                      forum.Importance = order.Value;
                      forum.Moderated = moderated.Value;

                      dc.SubmitChanges();

                      TempData["SuccessMessage"] = "Your forum has been updated.";
                  }
                  catch (Exception exc)
                  {
                      TempData["ErrorMessage"] = exc.Message;
                  }
              }

              ViewData["title"] = title ?? forum.Title;
              ViewData["description"] = description ?? forum.Description;
              ViewData["order"] = order ?? forum.Importance;
              ViewData["moderated"] = moderated ?? forum.Moderated;

              ViewData["PageTitle"] = "Edit Forum";

              return View("CreateForum");
          }
```

The only major difference that we wanted to point out between these two methods is the throwing of the 404 Not Found if the forumId that is passed in to the action as a parameter doesn't actually exist for anything in the database. You do this on the off chance that one of the managing editors has book-marked a URL for a forum that has been deleted. It is a basic protection that you should always take to report back the correct problem to the browser.

These actions have the following routes, respectively, for CreatePoll and EditPoll:

❑ admin/forums/create

❑ admin/forums/edit/{forumId}

admin/forums/create

This route is used to create a forum:

```
routes.MapRoute(
    "ForumCreate",
    "admin/forums/create",
    new { controller = "Forum", action = "CreateForum" }
);
```

admin/polls/edit/{forumId}

This route is used to edit a forum. It takes one rule, `forumId`, which provides the identity of the forum that is being edited:

```
routes.MapRoute(
    "ForumEdit",
    "admin/forums/edit/{forumId}",
    new { controller = "Forum", action = "EditForum", forumId = (int?)null },
    new { forumId = "[0-9]+" }
);
```

The RemoveForum Action

This action is what the users of the site will call when they need to remove a forum from the database. This action method is mainly only a message pump that queues up the next message in a mini wizard that presents a "yes" or "no" question to the users about their intentions to delete the forum in question. It is only available to users with the role of Editor:

```
[Authorize(Roles = "Editor")]
public ActionResult RemoveForum(int forumId, string remove)
{
    TheBeerHouseDataContext dc = new TheBeerHouseDataContext();
    Forum forum = dc.Forums.GetForum(forumId);

    // throw a 404 Not Found if the requested forum is not in the database
    if (forum == null)
        throw new HttpException(404, "The forum could not be found.");

    if (String.Equals(remove, "yes", StringComparison.OrdinalIgnoreCase))
    {
        dc.Forums.DeleteOnSubmit(forum);
        dc.SubmitChanges();

        TempData["SuccessMessage"] =
            "The poll, " + forum.Title + ", has been deleted.";

        forum = null;
    }
    else if (String.Equals(remove, "no", StringComparison.OrdinalIgnoreCase))
    {
        TempData["InformationMessage"] =
            "The poll, " + forum.Title + ", has NOT been deleted.";
    }
    else
    {
        TempData["WarningMessage"] =
            "Are you sure you want to delete " +
            forum.Title +
            ".  You will not be able to recover this forum if you select YES.";
    }

    ViewData["PageTitle"] = "Remove Forum";

    return View(forum);
}
```

We won't cover the exact process that is being used for removing a forum because it is the exact same process that you have used in the previous chapters.

This action has the following route:

❏   admin/forums/remove/{forumId}

admin/forums/remove/{forumId}

This route is used to remove a forum. It takes one rule, forumId, which provides the identity of the forum that is being removed:

```
routes.MapRoute(
    "ForumRemove",
    "admin/forums/remove/{forumId}",
    new { controller = "Forum", action = "RemoveForum", forumId = (int?)null },
    new { forumId = "[0-9]+" }
);
```

The CreatePost Action

This action is where most of the action for this module is going to occur; it is used to both create a new post for a forum and reply to an existing post. We decided to create one action to handle both situations because the same table is used for both actions and they really aren't that much different from each other. This action is rather long so we will break it apart so that we can go over each important part of the CreatePost action method.

Only authenticated users are allowed to create or reply to a post, so the first thing you need to do is add the AuthorizeAttribute to your action:

```
[Authorize]
public ActionResult CreatePost(int? forumId, int? parentPostId, string title,
string body)
{
```

The use of the AuthorizeAttribute is a little different than what you have seen before in the previous chapters. Previously, we have done Roles = "Editor" to define who can actually use the action in question, but this time we have just left it blank with no definition of who can use the action. This was done on purpose because this signifies that only authenticated people are allowed to call this action, so it doesn't matter if they are an administrator, editor, or just a user; if they are logged in to the site they are allowed to create or reply to a post.

Next, you need to set up your entity objects from the identities passed in through the parameters of the action; the two parameters that you are concerned with right now are forumId and parentPostId. For how you are using this action, you have two scenarios that you need to support:

1.   **Create New Post** — When a new post is created, only a forumId is passed in.

2.   **Reply to an Existing Post** — When a reply is made for a current post, only the parentPostId is passed in and you have to infer the forumId from the parent post.

```
TheBeerHouseDataContext dc = new TheBeerHouseDataContext();
Forum forum = null;
Post parentPost = null;
```

```
if (forumId.HasValue)
{
    forum = dc.Forums.GetForum(forumId.Value);
    TempData["InformationMessage"] =
        "You are creating a post in the \"" + forum.Title + "\" forum.";
}

if (parentPostId.HasValue)
{
    parentPost = dc.Posts.GetPost(parentPostId.Value);

    // throw a 404 Not Found if the requested parent post is not in the
    if (parentPost == null)
        throw new HttpException(404, "The post could not be found.");

    forum = parentPost.Forum;
    TempData["InformationMessage"] =
        "You are replying to \"" +
        parentPost.Title + "\" in the \"" +
        forum.Title + "\" forum.";
}

// throw a 404 Not Found if the requested forum is not in the database
if (forum == null)
    throw new HttpException(404, "The forum could not be found.");
```

The preceding code is structured so you do one operation if the forumId (New Post) is present and another operation if the parentPostId (Reply) is present. This complexity wouldn't be necessary if you had one action for new posts and one action for replies to posts. We are telling you this because we encourage you to do what you feel comfortable with. We did it this way to demonstrate a more complex action than what you have seen thus far.

We are not going to cover this next part in great detail because you have seen it many times over the course of this book.

```
if (!String.IsNullOrEmpty(title) && !String.IsNullOrEmpty(body))
{
    try
    {
        Post post = new Post {
            AddedBy = User.Identity.Name,
            AddedDate = DateTime.Now,
            AddedByIP = Request.UserHostAddress,
            ParentPostID = parentPostId,
            Title = title,
            Path = title.ToUrlFormat(),
            Body = body,
            ViewCount = 1,
            ReplyCount = 0,
            VoteCount = 0,
            Approved = !forum.Moderated,
            LastPostBy = User.Identity.Name,
            LastPostDate = DateTime.Now
        };
```

The only block of any significant meaning that you haven't seen in the past is this next code block:

```
if (parentPost != null)
{
    parentPost.LastPostBy = User.Identity.Name;
    parentPost.LastPostDate = DateTime.Now;
    parentPost.ReplyCount++;
    dc.Posts.InsertOnSubmit(post);
}
else
{
    forum.Posts.Add(post);
}
```

In the preceding code you are checking to see if there is a parentPost present. If there is, this action was a reply and you should update the parentPost accordingly. If there is not, this is a new post and should be added to the forum.

```
            if (forum.Moderated)
                TempData["SuccessMessage"] = "Your post has been created ";
                    + "and is awaiting approval from a moderator.";
            else
                TempData["SuccessMessage"] = "Your post has been created.";

            if (parentPost != null)
                return RedirectToAction("ViewPost", new {
                    postId = parentPost.PostID,
                    path = parentPost.Path });
            else if (forum.Moderated)
                return RedirectToAction("ViewForum", new {
                    forumId = forum.ForumID,
                    path = forum.Path });
            else
                return RedirectToAction("ViewPost", new {
                    postId = post.PostID,
                    path = post.Path });
        }
        catch (Exception exc)
        {
            TempData["ErrorMessage"] = exc.Message;
        }
    }

    ViewData["title"] = title;
    ViewData["body"] = body;

    ViewData["PageTitle"] = "Create Post";

    return View("CreatePost");
}
```

This action has the following routes:

- ❑ forums/{forumId}/post
- ❑ forums/posts/{parentPostId}/reply

forums/{forumId}/post

This route is used to add a new post to the specified forum:

```
routes.MapRoute(
    "ForumPostCreate",
    "forums/{forumId}/post",
    new { controller = "Forum", action = "CreatePost", forumId = (int?)null },
    new { forumId = "[0-9]+" }
);
```

forums/posts/{parentPostId}/reply

This route is used to add a reply to the specified post:

```
routes.MapRoute(
    "ForumPostReply",
    "forums/posts/{parentPostId}/reply",
    new { controller = "Forum", action = "CreatePost", parentPostId = (int?)null },
    new { parentPostId = "[0-9]+" }
);
```

The ClosePost Action

This next action is a service that forum moderators will use to close a post from future replies:

```
[ServiceOnly, HttpPostOnly]
[Authorize(Roles = "Editor")]
public ActionResult ClosePost(int postId, bool closed)
{
    TheBeerHouseDataContext dc = new TheBeerHouseDataContext();
    var post = dc.Posts.GetPost(postId);

    if (post == null)
        throw new HttpException(404, "The post could not be found.");

    // reset all posts to closed for a specific parent post
    dc.ExecuteCommand(
        "update TheBeerHouse.Posts set Closed = {0} where ParentPostID = {1}",
        new object[] { closed, postId }
    );

    post.Closed = closed;
    dc.SubmitChanges();

    return View(new { postId = postId });
}
```

The only thing in this code worth mentioning is that you are using the ExecuteCommand function of the data context to perform a quick bulk update. The last time you saw this being used was in Chapter 7 when you needed to update all the posts in the database to not be current before setting the poll you wanted to be current to true. You are doing something similar here, in that you are setting the closed status on all the reply posts in one bulk update, instead of individually.

Other than the bulk update in the preceding code, you just find the post and close it if it exists.

The route for this action uses the standard {controller}/{action} route, so requests to this action method can be accessed through:

❑   forum/closepost

The RemovePost Action

This last action is a service that forum moderators will use to remove a post from the system for whatever reasons they deem necessary. This is an important feature in case any of the users violate the site's policy for whatever reason and you need to remove the post:

```
[ServiceOnly, HttpPostOnly]
[Authorize(Roles = "Editor")]
public ActionResult RemovePost(int postId)
{
    TheBeerHouseDataContext dc = new TheBeerHouseDataContext();
    var post = dc.Posts.GetPost(postId);

    if (post == null)
        throw new HttpException(404, "The post could not be found.");

    dc.Posts.DeleteOnSubmit(post);
    dc.SubmitChanges();

    return View(new { postId = postId });
}
```

There is nothing really worth mentioning in the preceding code; you just find the post and delete it if it exists.

The route for this action uses the standard {controller}/{action} route, so requests to this action method can be accessed through:

❑   forum/removepost

Implementing the View

You are now at the last part of implementing this module. You need to create your views for the controller actions that you created in the last section. These views will manage, moderate, post, vote, and view the forum.

The AdminSidebar.ascx Control

This view control, located under the ~/Views/Shared/Forum folder, is used to create a set of links that are common to the admin views. This control is included on all of the admin sections for easy access to the links needed to manage the forum:

```
<div id="forums-admin" class="boxed">
    <h2 class="title">Forums</h2>
    <div class="content">
    <ul>
        <li class="first"><%=Html.ActionLink("View Forums", "ManageForums")%></li>
        <li><%= Html.ActionLink("Approve Posts", "ManagePosts") %></li>
```

```
    <li><%= Html.ActionLink("Create Forum", "CreateForum") %></li>
  </ul>
  </div>
</div>
```

The ManageForums.aspx View

The `ManageForums.aspx` view is located in `~/Views/Forum`. It is used to show administrators the current forums so that they can add, edit, and remove the forums. An example of how this section will look is shown in Figure 9-4.

Figure 9-4

As you can see from Figure 9-4, each forum is shown and you have the option to Edit and Remove each forum. The Edit and Remove links will take you to their respective views, `CreateForum.aspx` and `RemoveForum.aspx`.

The header for this view will set the view model to `IEnumerable<Forum>`:

```
Inherits="System.Web.Mvc.ViewPage<IEnumerable<TheBeerHouse.Models.Forum>>
```

This view has been broken down into three `Content` sections that correlate to your master page for the site. We are going to go through each content part, `MainContent` and `SidebarContent`, separately so that each can be examined individually.

MainContent

The `MainContent` placeholder uses a `foreach` loop to create the HTML output that is necessary to administer the forums on your site. Unlike in previous chapters where the management page was able to be paged, you are not that worried about the forums being paged because there are a finite number of them.

```
<asp:Content ID="MainContent" ContentPlaceHolderID="MainContent" runat="server">

<div id="forums">
<% foreach(var forum in ViewData.Model) { %>
    <div class="admin">
        <%= Html.ActionLink("Edit", "EditForum",
            new { forumId = forum.ForumID })%> | 
        <%= Html.ActionLink("Remove", "RemoveForum",
            new { forumId = forum.ForumID })%></div>
    <div id-"forum-<%= forum.ForumID %>" class="forum">
        <h2><%= Html.ActionLink(forum.Title, "ViewForum",
            new { forumId = forum.ForumID, path = forum.Path }) %></h2>
        <p><%= forum.Moderated ? "<strong>[moderated]</strong> " : "" %>
            <%= forum.Description %></p>
    </div>
    <hr />
<% } %>
</div>

</asp:Content>
```

In this code, the `View.Model` is typed to `Pagination<Models.Forum>`, which you defined earlier in the code-behind. This allows you to loop through each of the forums and add the necessary administration links.

Unlike previous chapters we have written, you render the `forum` right in the view instead of using a user control directly in your loop with the `Html.RenderUserControl` extension method. This was done because there is only a title and a description for each forum, so it is not really necessary to create a whole control for just two tags.

SidebarContent

The `SidebarContent` placeholder's sole purpose is to render the `AdminSidebar.ascx` control, which contains links for creating and viewing your forums:

```
<asp:Content ID="SidebarContent" ContentPlaceHolderID="SidebarContent"
runat="server">
<%= Html.RenderUserControl("~/Views/Shared/Forum/AdminSidebar.ascx")%>
</asp:Content>
```

This placeholder is the same for all the admin pages, so we are just going to show it this once and not show the code again.

The ManagePosts.aspx View

The `ManagePosts.aspx` view is located in `~/Views/Forum`. It is used for the moderation of posts that are awaiting approval by the moderator. The moderator will be allowed to approve or remove the posts from this page using the services you set up in the controller. An example of how this section will look is shown in Figure 9-5.

Figure 9-5

As you can see from Figure 9-5, each post is shown and you have the option to approve or remove each post; the Approve and Remove links will be executed using AJAX against your controller for this module.

The header for this view will set the view model to IEnumerable<Post>:

```
Inherits="System.Web.Mvc.ViewPage<IEnumerable<TheBeerHouse.Models.Post>>"
```

This view has been broken down into three Content sections that correlate to your master page for the site. We are going to go through each content part, MainContent and ScriptContent, separately so that each can be examined individually.

MainContent

The MainContent placeholder loops through each post that is passed in from the model and renders out the HTML for approving or removing the post:

```
<asp:Content ID="MainContent" ContentPlaceHolderID="MainContent" runat="server">

<% foreach(var post in ViewData.Model) { %>
```

```
      <div id="post-<%= post.PostID %>" class="post">
          <div class="admin">
              <a class="approve" meta:id="<%= post.PostID %>"
                  href="#approve">Approve</a> | 
              <a class="remove" meta:id="<%= post.PostID %>"
                  href="#remove">Remove</a>
          </div>
          <h3><%= post.Title %></h3>
          <div class="posted-last">
              <span class="posted-at">
                  <%= post.LastPostDate.ToUtcTimeSinceString() %> ago</span>
              <span class="posted-by">
                  by <img src="<%= post.GetLastPostByAvatarUrl(16) %>" />
                  <%= post.LastPostBy %></span>
          </div>
          <a class="toggle-body" href="#">Show Body</a>
          <div class="body" style="display:none"><%= post.Body %></div>
      </div>
      <hr />
  <% } %>

  </asp:Content>
```

In this code it looks just like any of your other administration screens except for one thing, you have the ability to expand and collapse the body of the post. This was done to save room on screen and to allow the administrator to easily browse through all the titles, and only look at the body of the content they are concerned with. You can create this feature using JavaScript, which we demonstrate next.

ScriptContent

The ScriptContent placeholder doesn't have much in it, only a reference to the JavaScript file that manages the AJAX calls for approving, removing, and closing posts:

```
<asp:Content ID="ScriptContent" ContentPlaceHolderID="ScriptContent"
runat="server">
<script type="text/javascript" src="/content/scripts/manage-forums.js"></script>
</asp:Content>
```

manage-forums.js

In this JavaScript file we are going to define the code that is used to toggle the display of the post body, approve a post, and remove a post. We will also define the JavaScript code that is used to close a post, which will be used later in this section.

We are going to break this code up into logical blocks; the first block of code you are going to look at deals with the toggling of the display of the post body, so that the administrator can view the body only if they need to:

```
$(".post .toggle-body").click(function() {
    $(this).next(".body").slideToggle("normal");

    return false;
});
```

As you can see, there is basically nothing to this because jQuery has done such a fantastic job at hiding away all the complex code that is required to make a function like sliding animation work.

The next block of code that you are going to look at deals with closing, approving, and removing posts in the database. Each of these actions will be done by creating a POST request to the appropriate controller action via an AJAX request:

```
$(".post .admin .close").click(function() {
    var postId = $(this).attr("meta:id");

    $.post(
        "/forum/closepost",
        { postId: postId, closed: true },
        function(data) {
            $("#post-" + data.object.postId)
                .fadeOut("normal", function() {
                    var title = $(this).find("h3");
                    title.text(title.text() + " [closed]");
                })
                .fadeIn("normal");
        },
        "json"
    );

    return false;
});

$(".post .admin .approve").click(function() {
    var postId = $(this).attr("meta:id");

    $.post(
        "/forum/approvepost",
        { postId: postId, approved: true },
        function(data) {
            $("#post-" + data.object.postId).fadeOut("normal", function() {
                $(this).remove();
            });
        },
        "json"
    );

    return false;
});

$(".post .admin .remove").click(function() {
    var postId = $(this).attr("meta:id");

    $.post(
        "/forum/removepost",
        { postId: postId },
        function(data) {
            $("#post-" + data.object.postId).fadeOut("normal", function() {
                $(this).remove();
            });
```

```
        },
        "json"
    );

    return false;
});
```

We have gone over most of this functionality and explained it in previous chapters, so we are just going to skip over the explanation because these actions are relatively simple compared to what you have seen in previous chapters.

The CreateForum.aspx View

The `CreateForum.aspx` view is located in `~/Views/Forum`. It is used to create new forums and edit existing forums for site users to post in. An example of how this form will look is shown in Figure 9-6.

The form in Figure 9-6 is pretty standard and nothing that you haven't seen before in this book. It follows the standard layout that provides a nice large form for input of information about the forum and provides room under each input for info or error messages.

Figure 9-6

The header for this view will set the default `ViewPage` because you don't need to pass in a typed model:

```
Inherits="System.Web.Mvc.ViewPage"
```

This view has been broken down into three `Content` sections that correlate to your master page for the site. We are going to go through each content part, `MainContent`, `ScriptContent`, and `SidebarContent`, which we have already discussed earlier in this section, but this time separately so that each can be examined individually.

MainContent

The `MainContent` for creating or editing a forum is much like you would expect — it has a title, description, order of appearance, and a flag indicating moderation all wrapped up in a form tag to submit back the results:

```
<asp:Content ID="MainContent" ContentPlaceHolderID="MainContent" runat="server">

<% Html.RenderPartial("~/Views/Shared/Message.ascx"); %>

<form method="post" action="<%= Url.Action(this.ViewContext.RouteData.
Values["action"] as string, "Forum") %>" class="forum-create">

    <p class="field input"><label for="title">Title</label><br />
        <%= Html.TextBox("title")%>
        <span class="input-message"></span></p>

    <p class="field input"><label for="description">Description</label><br />
        <%= Html.TextArea("description")%>
        <span class="input-message"></span></p>

    <p class="field input">
        <%= Html.CheckBox("moderated") %>
        <label for="moderated">Is Forum Moderated?</label>
        <span class="input-message"></span></p>

    <p class="field input"><label for="order">Order</label><br />
        <%= Html.TextBox("order") %>
        <span class="input-message"></span></p>

    <hr />
    <% if(this.ViewContext.RouteData.Values["action"] as string == "EditForum"){ %>
    <p><button type="submit" id="forum-create-button">Update Forum</button></p>
    <% } else { %>
    <p><button type="submit" id="forum-create-button">Create Forum</button></p>
    <% } %>
</form>

</asp:Content>
```

As we have done before, we are swapping the `action` on the `form` depending on whether this view is being displayed from the `CreateForum` or `EditForum` action, and changing the name of the button to keep the display simple and informative to the person using this view.

ScriptContent

The `ScriptContent` placeholder will contain a reference to the `manage-forums.js` file as well as the TinyMCE control that you first used in Chapter 6. Before we actually get to the JavaScript code, let's define what needs to be rendered to the HTML of the page first:

```
<asp:Content ID="ScriptContent" ContentPlaceHolderID="ScriptContent"
runat="server">
<script type="text/javascript" src="/content/scripts/tiny_mce/tiny_mce_src.js">
</script>
<script type="text/javascript" src="/content/scripts/manage-forums.js"></script>
<% if (IsPostBack) { %>
<script type="text/javascript">
    ValidateForum();
</script>
<% } %>
</asp:Content>
```

The first thing you do is import the JavaScript file, located at `/content/scripts/manage-forums.js`, which we will go over a little later on. Also, if this page is a POST back, meaning that you have posted to the action and it was necessary to return to this view page, you will validate the input values to display any kind of validation issues as a hint to why the action might have returned you to this page.

manage-forums.js

This code contains basic validation for the form and provides feedback to users to help them understand what you expect them to enter in each field and which fields are required to have a valid input in order to add the forum to the database:

```
$("#title").focus(function() {
    ShowMessage(this, "Enter the title for your forum."); });
$("#description").focus(function() {
    ShowMessage(this, "Enter the description of your forum."); });
$("#moderated").focus(function() {
    ShowMessage(this, "Do you want this forum to be moderated?"); });
$("#order").focus(function() {
    ShowMessage(this, "The order you want this forum to appear in, compared to the
other forums."); });

function ValidateTitle() {
    return VerifyRequiredField("#title", "required");
}

function ValidateDescription() {
    return VerifyRequiredField("#description", "required");
}

function ValidateForum() {
    return ValidateTitle()
        && ValidateDescription();
}

$("form.forum-create").validate(ValidateForum);
```

The RemoveForum.aspx View

The RemoveForum.aspx page view works in a similar fashion to what you have seen throughout this book, in that the users are presented with a "yes" or "no" question of whether they want to permanently remove the forum from the database. If they choose "yes," the forum and all posts related to that forum are permanently removed, but if they choose "no," no action is taken against the database. Figure 9-7 is a visual representation of what you are going to create for the RemoveForum.aspx view page.

Figure 9-7

The header is relatively simple, like many of your other admin pages, because you are only using it to set the view model to be a Forum object:

```
Inherits="System.Web.Mvc.ViewPage<TheBeerHouse.Models.Forum>"
```

The view only contains a MainContent section because no JavaScript is required for this view to work.

MainContent

This is a very simple setup: you have a form with "yes" or "no" buttons on it, and a message pane. The form with the buttons is only shown if the model is not null; you do this so that you can display a success message for whichever option the user chooses. Doing this gives the feel of a wizard, which most users are very comfortable with.

```
<asp:Content ID="MainContent" ContentPlaceHolderID="MainContent" runat="server">

<%= Html.RenderUserControl("~/Views/Shared/Message.ascx") %>

<% if (ViewData.Model != null) { %>
<form method="post" action="<%= Url.Action("RemoveForum", "Forum", new { forumId =
ViewData.Model.ForumID }) %>" class="forum-remove">

    <button type="submit" name="remove" value="yes" class="yes">yes</button>
    <button type="submit" name="remove" value="no" class="no">no</button>

</form>
<% } %>

</asp:Content>
```

The Index.aspx View

In the next view, `Index.aspx`, which is located in `~/Views/Forum`, you are going to create a user version of the `ManageForums.aspx` view page that was presented earlier in this section. It will show the exact same view of the forums that the administrators see under the forum admin section, minus the edit and remove buttons. Figure 9-8 shows a screenshot of this view.

Figure 9-8

The header is an exact copy of the `ManageForums.aspx` view because you are providing the same data, just without the administration features:

```
Inherits="System.Web.Mvc.ViewPage<IEnumerable<TheBeerHouse.Models.Forum>>"
```

It might strike you as odd that we are using the `Pagination<T>` object for the view model because the forums are not able to be paged. The reason we do this is more for simplicity's sake than anything else, because right now it is not hurting anything since it acts like a normal collection, but on the chance that you might want to page the forums in the future we included the typed reference to the collection.

The view only has a `MainContent` section.

MainContent

The `MainContent` placeholder runs through the loop in a similar way to what you have seen in the `ManageForums.aspx` view. The only difference is the lack of the admin buttons. We have taken the liberty to highlight where the admin buttons would be if this was in the `ManageForums.aspx` view as a way to demonstrate how similar these two code blocks are:

```
<asp:Content ID="MainContent" ContentPlaceHolderID="MainContent" runat="server">

<div id="forums">
<% foreach(var forum in ViewData.Model) { %>
    // the admin would be here <div class="admin">…div>
    <div id="forum-<%= forum.ForumID %>" class="forum">
        <h2><%= Html.ActionLink(forum.Title, "ViewForum",
            new { forumId = forum.ForumID, path = forum.Path }) %></h2>
        <p><%= forum.Moderated ? "<strong>[moderated]</strong> " : "" %>
            <%= forum.Description %></p>
    </div>
    <hr />
<% } %>
</div>

</asp:Content>
```

You can see this is an excellent reuse of code and keeps your DOM simple so that the styling doesn't have to vary much between the admin section and the public sections of the site.

The ViewForum.aspx View

The next view, `ViewForum.aspx`, which is located in `~/Views/Forum`, that you are going to create is a view for viewing the posts in the forum. Figure 9-9 shows a screenshot of this view.

Figure 9-9

The header is set to inherit from the `ViewPage` with a model for `Forum`, as shown here:

```
Inherits="System.Web.Mvc.ViewPage<TheBeerHouse.Models.Forum>"
```

The view has `MainContent` and `ScriptContent` sections.

MainContent

The `MainContent` has two different states, one if there are no posts for the forum and another if there are posts to show to the user. If there are no posts, you want to alert the user to this fact by showing a message stating that there are no posts currently. We did this right below the first `if` statement in the following code:

```
<asp:Content ID="MainContent" ContentPlaceHolderID="MainContent" runat="server">
<%= Html.ActionLink("Create A Post For This Forum", "CreatePost", new { forumId =
ViewData.Model.ForumID }, new { @class = "post-button" })%>

<% Html.RenderPartial("~/Views/Shared/Message.ascx"); %>

<% if (ViewData.Model.Posts.Count == 0) { %>
    <p>There are no posts in this forum yet, you can be the first.</p>
<% } else { %>
```

If there are posts to display, you want to show the users of the site as much information about the posts as possible while not overloading them. You can accomplish this by laying out each post in a visually appealing way and providing information that the users of the site would care about, such as votes, replies, views, the title of the post, and who was the last person to reply and when. The post will be laid out like Figure 9-10.

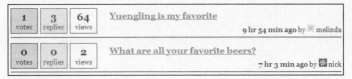

Figure 9-10

You can move these stats on each post anywhere within the post entity that you want, but we prefer them to be on the left side, like in Figure 9-10, because it provides a clean interface. In addition to providing a clean interface, the stats being on the left side provides a vertical line that the eye can line the post title up against. This is very important because it improves readability and keeps the eye from jumping around the screen trying to structure what it is seeing. If you were to structure the post to look like Figure 9-11, it would be harder for the eye to perceive an edge to the content, especially if the screen was filled with posts. Figure 9-10 shows how the page is currently structured with the post stats on the left, and Figure 9-11 shows how the posts would look if the stats were on the right. As a test, pay special attention to where your eye looks first and how much it has to jump around the image to acquire all the information about the post.

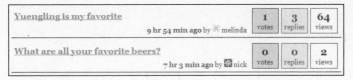

Figure 9-11

This is more of a design concept, but we wanted to take a moment to talk about some basic design concepts and how you can easily influence your users to stay on the site longer and explore more by just making things easier to read and making the site more visually appealing to them.

Get to Know a Graphic Designer

Design is very subjective to the person who is viewing it and the context with which that person is viewing it in. Not all developers have the knack for user interface design. If you are not a developer with a knack for the softer side of programming, we suggest you get to know somebody in the graphics arts field, a designer that you can trust and that can explain the psychology behind any design decisions. Having the psychology explained is both helpful to you as the developer and shows a deeper understanding from the designer, because it demonstrates that the designer is treating the web design as a user interface and not a painting. In addition, it gives you the added benefit of understanding the flow of the user interface so that your client-side code can interact appropriately.

The code to create Figure 9-9 is as follows:

```
<div id="posts">
<% var posts = ViewData.Model.Posts
             .Where(p => p.Approved)
             .OrderByDescending(p => p.LastPostDate)
             .AsPagination((int)ViewData["index"], (int)ViewData["count"]); %>
<% foreach(var post in posts) { %>
     <div id="post-<%= post.PostID %>" class="post">
<% if (User.IsInRole("Editor")) { %>
         <div class="admin">
             <a class="close" meta:id="<%= post.PostID %>"
                 href="#close">Close</a>  |  
             <a class="remove" meta:id="<%= post.PostID %>"
                 href="#remove">Remove</a>
         </div>
<% } %>
         <div class="stats">
             <div class="votes stat">
             <strong><%= post.VoteCount %></strong><small>votes</small>
             </div>
             <div class="replies stat">
             <strong><%= post.ReplyCount %></strong><small>replies</small>
             </div>
             <div class="views stat">
             <strong><%= post.ViewCount %></strong><small>views</small>
             </div>
         </div>
         <h3><%= Html.ActionLink(post.Title, "ViewPost",
         new { controller = "Forum", postId = post.PostID, path = post.Path }) %>
         </h3>
         <div class="posted-last">
             <span class="posted-at">
             <%= post.LastPostDate.ToUtcTimeSinceString() %> ago</span>
             <span class="posted-by">
             by <img src="<%= post.GetLastPostByAvatarUrl(16) %>" />
             <%= post.LastPostBy %>span>
         </div>
     </div>
     <hr />
<% } %>
</div>

<% Html.RenderPartial("~/Views/Shared/Pager.ascx", posts); %>
<% } %>

</asp:Content>
```

The only real thing to note in the preceding code is that the close and remove links are added to each post only if the current logged-in user has the Editor role assigned to him. If the current user is not an editor, the links will not be shown. The close and remove links use the same code in the `manage-forums.js` as the admin page, so you do not need to create any JavaScript code for them; you just import in the `manage-forums.js` file.

ScriptContent

The `ScriptContent` should only be included if the user is an administrator of the system, because the only JavaScript required for this view is related to the close and remove links so there is no use importing it for a user who does not require the code.

```
<asp:Content ID="ScriptContent" ContentPlaceHolderID="ScriptContent" runat="server">
<% if (User.IsInRole("Editor")) { %>
<script type="text/javascript" src="/content/scripts/manage-forums.js"></script>
<% } %>
</asp:Content>
```

The ViewPost.aspx View

The `ViewPost.aspx` view is located in `~/Views/Forum`. It is the view that shows your post and all the replies that it has received. It also acts as a way to post with the reply form at the bottom. This view follows the same principles as your articles in Chapter 6, as far as layout goes, because if you really think about it there isn't much difference between the functionality of a blog and a forum; the only real difference is the context and that you allow the site users to post instead of a specific set of editors. An example of how the post will look is shown in Figure 9-12.

Figure 9-12

The header for this view will have the `Post` type set as the model of your view:

```
Inherits="System.Web.Mvc.ViewPage<TheBeerHouse.Models.Post>"
```

This view has been broken down into two `Content` sections that correlate to your master page for the site. We are going to go through each content part, `MainContent` and `ScriptContent`, separately so that each can be examined individually.

MainContent

The `MainContent` for viewing a post is going to be easiest to explain if we break it up into three parts: the voting/main post, the replies, and the reply form. The first thing we are going to cover is the basic layout of the vote button and the necessary CSS to make it look nice:

```
<asp:Content ID="Content2" ContentPlaceHolderID="MainContent" runat="server">

<% var userVote = (int)ViewData["userVote"]; %>

<div id="posts">
    <div id="post-<%= ViewData.Model.PostID %>" class="post">
        <div class="vote-button">
            <a class="vote-up<%= userVote >= 1 ? " selected" : "" %>"
                href="#up">Like</a>
            <strong><%= ViewData.Model.VoteCount %></strong>
            <a class="vote-down<%= userVote <= -1 ? " selected" : "" %>"
                href="#down">Dislike</a>
        </div>
        <%= ViewData.Model.Body%>
        <div class="posted-last">
            <span class="posted-at">
                <%= ViewData.Model.AddedDate.ToUtcTimeSinceString()%>
                ago</span>
            <span class="posted-by"><%= ViewData.Model.AddedBy%></span>
        </div>
    </div>
</div>
<hr style="visibility:hidden;"/>
```

The vote button for your forum allows an up or down vote, or in this case a "like" or "dislike" vote. What is probably most notable at first glance is that the vote button isn't a button at all; it is a combination of anchor links and a `strong` tag. The following CSS is used to properly arrange the elements that we call the "vote button" into something the user can understand as a button without too much trouble:

```
#posts .post .vote-button {
    float: left;
    width: 60px;
    padding: 0 10px 10px 0;
    text-align: center;
}

#posts .post .vote-button .vote-up,
#posts .post .vote-button strong,
#posts .post .vote-button .vote-down  {
    display: block;
    font-weight: bold;
```

```
    padding: 3px;
}

#posts .post .vote-button strong {
    font-size: 2em;
}

#posts .post .vote-button .selected {
    border: solid 1px;
    color: #00529B;
    background-color: #BDE5F8;
}
```

This CSS defines the layout, colors, and styles of your "vote button." Some notable things to pay attention to are in the `#posts .post .vote-button` style; this is the styling that positions the button and makes it float within the text in the top left of the page. The one other thing we want to point out is the `display: block` style a couple of lines down from the end of the style we were just talking about. This styling tells the browser to interpret the tag like a `div` instead of a `span`; basically what this means is that instead of the tag just taking up as much space as needed like a `span` does, it should take up the whole line like a `div` does. This allows you to turn your anchor links into something that represents a button to the user, by making a big rectangular entity above and below the vote count.

The next part we want to look at is how the replies are generated:

```
    <h3>Replies</h3>
    <div id="forum-post-replies">
<% var replies = ViewData.Model.Posts
            .OrderBy(f => f.LastPostDate)
            .AsPagination((int)ViewData["index"], (int)ViewData["count"]); %>
<% foreach(var post in replies) { %>
    <div id="reply-<%= post.PostID %>" class="reply">
        <div class="reply-header">Reply posted by <span class="name">
            <img src="<%= post.GetAddedByAvatarUrl(16) %>" />
            <%= post.LastPostBy%></span>
            <%= post.LastPostDate.ToUtcTimeSinceString()%> ago</div>
        <% if (User.IsInRole("Editor")) { %>
        <div class="admin">
            <a class="remove" meta:id="<%= post.PostID %>"
                href="#remove">remove</a>
        </div>
        <% } %>
        <blockquote class="body"><%= post.Body %></blockquote>
    </div>
<% } %>
    </div>

<% Html.RenderPartial("~/Views/Shared/Pager.ascx", replies); %>
</div>
```

The replies are pretty simple to understand because you have a header and body that are similar to your comments in Chapter 6, with one exception in that you allow your users to post their own rich text using the WYSIWYG editor so the replies can have a much richer display. Another thing to note about the replies is that they have a remove link rendered if the current logged-in user is an editor, so that the editors can remove the reply if they desire.

The next thing you want to do is add a reply box to the bottom of your forum post. You want to make this reply mechanism simple, so you only give the user one input for the body of your reply. The title of the reply will be auto-generated to be "RE: {parent post title}" in the common e-mail format for replies:

```
<% if (!ViewData.Model.Closed) { %>
<form method="post" action="/forums/posts/<%= ViewData.Model.PostID %>/reply"
class="post-reply-create">
    <input type="hidden" id="postId" name="postId" value="<%= ViewData.Model.PostID
%>" />
    <input type="hidden" id="title" name="title" value="RE: <%= ViewData.Model.
Title %>" />
    <p class="field input">
        <label for="body">Enter Your Reply</label><br />
        <%= Html.TextArea("body", String.Empty, new { style = "height: 300px" })%>
        <span class="input-message"></span>
    </p>
    <hr />
    <p><button type="submit" id="post-reply-create-button">Add Reply</button></p>
</form>
<% } else { %>
<div class="info">This post has been closed, and no more replies can be made.</div>
<% } %>
</asp:Content>
```

The only thing that is really significant in this code is that the whole form is wrapped in an if statement that doesn't show the form if the post is closed. When the post is closed, an information message is shown saying that the post is closed, so the user doesn't look around for the form.

ScriptContent

The ScriptContent placeholder will contain a reference to the forums.js file as well as the TinyMCE control that you first used in Chapter 6 for formatting the reply. First, we will define what is needed to be rendered to the HTML of the page:

```
<asp:Content ID="ScriptContent" ContentPlaceHolderID="ScriptContent"
runat="server">
<% if (User.IsInRole("Editor")) { %>
<script type="text/javascript" src="/content/scripts/manage-forums.js"></script>
<% } %>
<script type="text/javascript" src="/content/scripts/tiny_mce/tiny_mce_src.js"></
script>
<script type="text/javascript" src="/content/scripts/forums.js"></script>
<% if (IsPostBack) { %>
<script type="text/javascript">
    ValidatePost();
</script>
<% } %>
</asp:Content>
```

The first thing you do is import the JavaScript file, located at /content/scripts/forums.js, which we will go over a little later on. Also, if this page is a POST back, meaning that you have posted to the action and it was necessary to return to this view page, you will validate the input values to display any kind of validation issues as a hint to why the action might have returned you to this page.

forums.js

This code contains the setup for the WYSIWYG editor and the JavaScript necessary to make your voting button work. We will break them up into two sections so that we can focus on the vote button code, because we have already covered the TinyMCE code previously in this book. First, the TinyMCE code:

```
var bodyEditor;

$(document).ready(function() {
    bodyEditor = new tinymce.Editor("body", __editorConfig);
    bodyEditor.onChange.add(function(ed) { bodyEditor.save(); });
    bodyEditor.onClick.add(function(ed) {
        ShowMessage("#body", "Enter the body of your article."); });
    bodyEditor.render();
});

// clears the message from the description when another input gets focus
$(":input")
    .focus(function() { HideMessage("#body"); })
.blur(function() { HideMessage("#body"); });
```

Next, we are going to cover the code that makes your voting system work. This code should post the up or down vote to the server using AJAX and receive an update of the vote count from the server to be displayed on the page in place of the old vote count. This feature is pretty cool for a couple of reasons: it is the basic concept behind the main feature of crowd-sourcing sites like Digg and Reddit, and it takes almost no JavaScript or server-side code to create.

```
function VoteSuccess(data) {
    var button = $(".post .vote-" + (data.object.direction > 0 ? "up" : "down"));
    var number = $(".post strong");

    // remove current selections and select correct button
    $(".post .vote-button a").removeClass("selected");
    button.addClass("selected");

    // set new count value
    number.text(data.object.voteCount);
}

$(".post .vote-button a").click(function() {
    var postId = $("#postId").val();
    var href = $(this).attr("href");
    var direction = (href == "#up") ? 1 : -1;

    $.post(
        "/forum/vote",
        { postId: postId, direction: direction },
        VoteSuccess,
        "json"
    );

    return false;
});
```

This code monitors your button for a click, either up or down, and then posts the vote to /forum/vote. When the request comes back to your VoteSuccess function, all the selected classes are removed from your anchor tags. The selected class is used to highlight the button in order to indicate the selection the user made. After the classes are removed from the anchors, the correct anchor is marked as selected and the vote count is updated. The reason you clear the selection is because the users have the option of changing their vote.

The CreatePost.aspx View

The CreatePost.aspx view is located in ~/Views/Forum. It is used to allow your users to create a new post in a forum where they want to ask a question or post about a subject that they think will be engaging to the other users of the site. An example of how this form will look is shown in Figure 9-13.

Figure 9-13

The form in Figure 9-13 is like what you have seen in this book so far: it follows the standard layout that provides a nice large form for the title and the content that the users want to post about. The only difference is that you provide an informational message at the top of the screen to explain to the users which forum they are currently posting in, in case they forgot.

The header for this view will set to the default ViewPage because you don't need to pass in a typed model:

```
Inherits="System.Web.Mvc.ViewPage"
```

This view has been broken down into two `Content` sections that correlate to your master page for the site. We are going to go through each content part, `MainContent` and `ScriptContent`, separately so that each can be examined individually.

MainContent

The `MainContent` for creating a post is just the standard form with two inputs — it is really basic with no frills attached. A title and a body are all wrapped up in a form tag to submit back the results:

```
<asp:Content ID="MainContent" ContentPlaceHolderID="MainContent" runat="server">

<% Html.RenderPartial("~/Views/Shared/Message.ascx"); %>

<form method="post" action="<%= Url.Action("CreatePost", "Forum") %>" class="post-create">

    <p class="field input"><label for="title">Title</label><br />
        <%= Html.TextBox("title")%>
        <span class="input-message"></span></p>

    <p class="field input"><label for="body">Body</label><br />
        <%= Html.TextArea("body", new { style = "height: 500px"})%>
        <span class="input-message"></span></p>

    <hr />
    <p><button type="submit" id="post-create-button">Post To Forum</button></p>

</form>

</asp:Content>
```

ScriptContent

The `ScriptContent` placeholder will contain a reference to the `forums.js` file as well as the TinyMCE control that you first used in Chapter 6. Before we actually get to the JavaScript code, let's define what needs to be rendered to the HTML of the page first:

```
<asp:Content ID="ScriptContent" ContentPlaceHolderID="ScriptContent"
runat="server">
<script type="text/javascript" src="/content/scripts/tiny_mce/tiny_mce_src.js"></script>
<script type="text/javascript" src="/content/scripts/forums.js"></script>
<% if (IsPostBack) { %>
<script type="text/javascript">
    ValidatePost();
</script>
<% } %>
</asp:Content>
```

The first thing you do is import the JavaScript file, located at `/content/scripts/forums.js`, which we will go over a little later on. Also, if this page is a POST back, meaning that you have posted to the action and it was necessary to return to this view page, you will validate the input values to display any kind of validation issues as a hint to why the action might have returned you to this page.

forums.js

This code contains basic validation for the form and provides feedback to users to help them understand what you expect them to enter in each field and which fields require valid input in order to add the forum to the database:

```
$("#title").focus(function() {
    ShowMessage(this, "Enter the title for your post."); });
$("#body").focus(function() {
    ShowMessage(this, "Enter the body of your post."); });

function ValidateTitle() {
    return VerifyRequiredField("#title", "required");
}

function ValidateBody() {
    return VerifyRequiredField("#body", "required");
}

function ValidatePost() {
    return ValidateTitle()
        && ValidateBody ();
}

$("form.post-create").validate(ValidatePost);
```

The code used to hook up the WYSIWYG editor comes from the previous view that also had the same WYSIWYG editor. Sharing the JavaScript works because both field names for the content portion of the post have an identity of body, which allows you to share the code and reduce duplicates in the file.

Summary

In this chapter you've built a forums system from scratch, and you did it by leveraging much of the work done in earlier chapters and many of the features in ASP.NET MVC. This was a further example showing how some simple client-side JavaScript code can be used, in conjunction with a small amount of server-side code, to produce some very engaging features for the site's users. Your forums module supports multiple forums, with optional moderation; it lists threads and replies through custom pagination (with different sorting options). You also created administration features for deleting, approving, and closing threads and posts. This is a fairly complete and modern forums module that should work well with many small- to mid-sized sites. However, the subject of user forums in general is a big area, and there are many possible options and features that you might want to consider adding to your forums module. Here are a few suggestions to get you started:

❑   Add support for some open forums, as a subforum-level option, which would be accessible by anonymous posters.

❑   Allow some subforums to have different moderators for more granular security control (especially useful for larger sites that may have multiple moderators who specialize in certain subforums).

❑ Add e-mail notification of new forum activity, or you can even send out e-mail message digests. E-mails could also be used by moderators to be notified about new messages waiting to be approved, and you might even allow the moderator to approve a message simply by clicking a link contained in the e-mail, after reviewing the post's body, also included in the e-mail.

❑ Support a list of banned words, and use regular expressions to replace them with acceptable alternatives, or maybe just a generic "###" pattern. Or you can just tag offending messages for moderation, even if the forum is not a moderated forum (this would require a little more work on the plumbing).

❑ Add private forums, whereby members can send each other messages, but each member can only read messages that were specifically addressed to them. This is a handy way to encourage people to communicate with each other, while allowing them to keep their own personal e-mail address hidden from other users (which is often desirable as a means of limiting spam). To make this easier to use, whenever you see the username of someone who posted a message in a forum, that username could have a link to another page that gives you the option to send that user a private message. To ensure that the user will notice the message, you could add an automatic check for private messages that would occur each time a registered user logs in.

❑ Implement a search feature to enable users to locate messages containing certain words or phrases.

❑ Allow members to vote on replies in the same way they vote on the post.

❑ Add full support for ATOM 1.0 feeds that allow users to track new messages in a syndication aggregator program, as you did in Chapter 6. There should be a flexible syndication system that provides distinct feeds to specific subforums, or all forums, that will sort posts in different ways. This enables users to get a feed with the ten newest threads posted into any forum, or with the ten most popular threads (if sorted by number of replies).

❑ Let members upload their own attachments, which would be accessed from a link in a forum message (be sure to make this an option, because some site owners may not like this idea for security and bandwidth reasons). You could allow configurable filename extensions (disallowing `.exe`, `.bat`, `.vbs`, and so on, but allowing `.doc`, `.txt`, and so on), and a configurable limit on allowable file size. You might also want to force any messages containing an attachment to be moderated so a power user can review the attachment before allowing it (this is especially important if you want to allow images to be uploaded).

There are numerous, very complex and complete forums systems for ASP.NET, and many of them are free. You might want to use one of them if the simple forums module presented here doesn't meet your needs, or you might just want to study the others to get ideas for features you might want to add to your own forums module. One of the best, and most feature-rich, forums modules for ASP.NET is the Community Server, available at www.communityserver.org. In the previous book we recommended Community Server because it was 100% free for non-profit sites, and fairly inexpensive for use on commercial sites. This is the same forums software used by the famous www.asp.net site, Microsoft's official ASP.NET developer site. If this doesn't work for you, or if you are looking for a forum that is open source, we would encourage you to take a look at YetAnotherForum, which you can find at www.yetanotherforum.net. It is 100% free and 100% open so you can download the code and modify it as you wish.

But don't be too quick to discard the forums module developed in this chapter, because even though it's missing some of the more advanced features, it still has several big benefits, including the fact that it's already integrated with the site's common layout and membership system (whereas others do not, unless you modify them, because they need to be installed on a separate virtual folder that makes it more difficult to share pieces of the parent site). It also uses many of the features in ASP.NET MVC and it is fairly easy to maintain and understand.

In the next chapter you will implement another common requirement in a modern, full-featured website: an e-commerce store with support for real-time electronic payments.

10

E-commerce Store

In this chapter, you implement a working e-commerce store for TheBeerHouse to enable users to shop for mugs, T-shirts, and other gadgets for beer fanatics. This again gives you the opportunity to implement a good model and controller that wraps and abstracts the database objects as well as a highly responsive user interface that is afforded to you by using the MVC framework. You also drill down into e-commerce-specific design and coding issues as you implement a persistent shopping cart, and you integrate a third-party payment processor service to support real-time credit card transactions. At the end of this chapter you will have a complete e-commerce module that you can easily adapt to suit your own needs.

Problem

Let's assume the site's owner wants you to implement some features to help him turn the site into a profit-making enterprise. You have a number of ways to do this: some sites gain revenue from renting advertising space (boxes and banners), some sell subscription-based access to their special content (articles, support forums, downloads, and so on), and some set up an e-commerce store for selling goods online. This chapter covers the design and implementation of an e-commerce store. This option was chosen for the demo website because it's a good example of non-trivial design and coding, and it gives you a chance to examine some additional ASP.NET 3.5 technology in a real-world scenario. In addition, it is much more common for small sites to sell products, rather than ads and articles, unless they are extremely popular and active (ad revenue is small until your hit and click-through counts get pretty high). Building an e-commerce store from scratch is one of the most difficult jobs for a web developer, and it requires a good design up front. It's not just a matter of building the site to handle the catalog, the orders, and the payments; a complete business analysis is required. You must identify your audience (that is, potential customers), your competitors, a marketing strategy to promote your site, marketing offers to convince people to shop on your site rather than somewhere else, and a plan for offers and other incentives to turn an occasional buyer into a repeat buyer. You also need to arrange for a supplier for products that you can sell, in the event that the site's owner is not the producer, which involves the order management and shipping functions and some consideration of local laws (licenses, tax collection, and so on). All of this could require a considerable amount of time, energy, and money unless the site owner is already running some kind of physical store that he merely wants to extend. In your case, we assume your sample site will be used by pubs that already have the business knowledge needed to answer the marketing-related questions, and we'll focus on the technical side of this project (a reasonable assumption because we are software developers and not marketing specialists).

For the sample project, let's say that the owner of TheBeerHouse wants to add an electronic store to the site — to sell beer glasses, T-shirts, key chains, and other gift items for beer enthusiasts. He needs the capability to create an online catalog that lists products divided into categories, one that provides a detailed and appealing description for each product, has pictures of products, and allows users to add them to an electronic shopping cart and pay for them online using a credit card. The owner needs the capability to run special promotions by setting up discounts for certain products, and to offer multiple shipping options at different prices. All this must be easily maintainable by the store keeper himself, without routine technical assistance, so you must also provide a very complete and intuitive administrative user interface. Finally, he also needs some kind of order reporting page that retrieves and lists the latest orders and the orders with a specific status (completed orders, orders that were confirmed but not yet processed, and so on). It should also enable him to change the order status, the shipment date, the shipment tracking information, and, of course, see all order details, such as the customer's full address and contact information. The next section contains a detailed list of requirements and features to be implemented.

Design

As you can gather from the Problem section, implementing a custom e-commerce module can easily be a big challenge, and entire books have been devoted to this subject. With this in mind, and because of space constraints, this is the only chapter to cover this subject so we've had to examine the feature set and select the basic and most common features that any such store must have. Although this module won't compete with sites like Amazon.com in terms of features, it will be complete enough to actually run a real, albeit small, e-store. As you've done in other chapters, you'll leverage much of the other functionality already developed, such as membership and profile management (Chapter 5), and your general model/controller design and transaction management (Chapter 4). Therefore, the following list specifies the new functionality you implement in this chapter:

❑   Support for multiple store departments used to categorize products so that they are easy to find if the catalog has a lot of items.

❑   Products need a description with support for rich formatting, and images to graphically represent them. Because customers can't hold the product in their own hands, any written details and visual aids will help them understand the product and may lead to a sale. A small thumbnail image will be shown in the products listing, and a bigger image can be shown when the user views the product detail page.

❑   Products will support a discount percentage that the store keeper will set when he wants to run a promotion for that item. The customers will still see the full price on the product page, along with the discount percentage (so that they can "appreciate" the sale, and feel compelled to order the product), and the final price to buy the product.

❑   Some simple stock availability management will be needed, such as the possibility to specify how many units of a particular item are in stock. This value will be decreased every time someone confirms an order for that product, and the store keeper will be able to see which products need to be re-ordered when inventory is running low.

❑ The store keeper will be able to easily add, remove, and edit shipping methods, such as Standard Ground, Next Business Day, and Overnight, each with a different price. Customers will be able to specify a preferred shipping option when completing the order.

❑ The module needs a persistent shopping cart for items that the customer wants to purchase. Making it persistent means that the user can place some items in the shopping cart, close the browser and end the session, then come back to the site later with the shopping cart unchanged. This makes it so the customers don't need to browse the entire catalog again to find the products they previously put in the cart. The customers may want time to consider the purchase before submitting it, they may want to compare the price with competitors first, or they may not have their credit card at that moment, so it's helpful for users to be able to put items in the cart and come back later to finalize the deal.

❑ You want to make the site as accessible as possible so you will not require the user to log in to your site in order to complete a transaction. Instead, users will be sent an e-mail confirming their order, and have the ability to use the link in the e-mail to review their purchase at a later date. This will prevent situations where people will cancel an order because of their registration aversion.

As anticipated, you may want, or need, to add many additional features. However, the features in the preceding list will give you a basic starting point with a working solution. In the following sections, you'll read more about some e-commerce-specific issues, such as choosing a service for real-time credit card processing, and then you'll create the typical design of the model, controller, and view parts of the module.

Choosing an Online Payment Solution

User have visited your site, browsed the catalog, read the descriptions of some products, and put them into the shopping cart. They finally decide that the prices and conditions are good and want to finalize the order; this means providing personal information (name, contact details, and shipping address) and, of course, paying. You should plan for, and offer, as many payment solutions as you can to satisfy all types of customers. Some prefer to send a check via snail mail, others prefer to provide the credit card information by fax or phone, and others are fine with paying via their credit card online. The best option for the store keeper is, of course, the online transaction, because it is the most secure (information is encrypted and no physical person sees it), it gives immediate feedback to the user, and it doesn't require the store keeper to do anything. Several third-party services, called *payment gateways*, provide this service. They receive some order details, perform a secure transaction for the customer, and keep a small fee for each order — typically a percentage of the transaction amount, but it may also be a fixed fee, or possibly a combination of the two. You can integrate your site with these services in one of two ways:

1. The customer clicks the button on your site to confirm the order and pays for it. At this point the user is redirected to the external site of the payment gateway. That site will ask the customer for his billing information (name, address, and credit card number) and will execute the transaction. The gateway's site resides on a secure server, that is, a server where the SSL protocol is used to encrypt the data sent between the customer's browser and the server. After the payment is processed, the customer is redirected back to your site. The process is depicted in Figure 10-1.

The Secure Sockets Layer (SSL) is a secure web protocol that encrypts all data between a web server and a user's computer to prevent anyone else from knowing what information was sent over that connection. SSL certificates are used on web servers and are issued by third-party certificate authorities (CAs), which guarantee to the customers that the site they're shopping on really has the identity it declares. A customer can identify the use of SSL by the presence of "https:" instead of "http:" in the URL, and by the padlock icon typically shown in the browser's status bar.

To learn more about SSL, you can search on Google or visit the websites of CAs such as VeriSign, Thawte, GeoTrust, or Comodo.

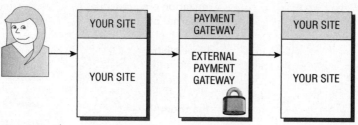

Figure 10-1

Your store's checkout page sends the payment gateway's page the amount to charge, the recipient account where it should place the money, the currency, and the URL where the customer will be redirected in case of a successful or cancelled order, using an HTML form that posts the data contained in a few hidden fields. The following form is an example:

```
<form method="post" action="https://payment_gateway_url_here">
    <input type="hidden" name="LoginName" value="THEBEERHOUSE">
    <input type="hidden" name="OrderAmount" value="46.50 ">
    <input type="hidden" name="OrderCurrency" value="USD">
    <input type="hidden" name="OrderID" value="#12345">
    <input type="hidden" name="OrderDescription" value="Beer Glass #2 (4
    pieces)"
    <input type="hidden" name="ConfirmUrl"
        value="http://www.yoursite.com/order_ok.aspx">
    <input type="hidden" name="CancelUrl"
        value="http://www.yoursite.com/order_ko.aspx">
    <input type="submit" value="CLICK HERE TO PAY NOW!">
</form>
```

Every payment gateway has its own parameters, with different names, and accepts data following their own conventions, but the overall principle is the same for all of them. Many gateways also accept the expected parameters through a GET request instead of a POST, which means that parameters are passed on the query string. In this case you can build the complete URL on your site, and then redirect the customer to it, but this method is less desirable because the query string is visible. Most of the information you pass to the gateway is also forwarded to the store site once the customer comes back to it, a feature you will use to commit the customer's order.

Some payment gateway services encrypt the data they send to you and give you a private key used to decrypt the data, so that you can ensure that the customer did not manually jump directly to your order finalization page. Others use different mechanisms, but you always have some way to be notified whether payment was made (despite this automatic notification, it would be wise to validate that the payment was actually processed to ensure that a hacker has not tried to give you a false indication that a payment was made). The advantage of using an external payment service is its ease of integration and management. You only forward the user to the external gateway (to a URL built according the gateway's specifications guide), and handle the customer's return after he has paid for the order, or cancelled it. You don't have to deal with the actual money transaction, nor do you have to worry about the security of the transaction, which would at least imply setting up SSL on your site, and you don't have to worry about keeping the customer's credit card information stored in a safe manner and complying with privacy laws (if you only keep the customer's name and address, laws that protect account numbers won't apply).

The disadvantage, however, is that the customer actually leaves your site for the payment process, which may be disorienting and inconvenient. Though it's true that most payment gateway services allow the site's owner/developer to change the payment page's colors and insert the store's logo inside it, the customization often does not go much further, so the difference between the store's pages and the external payment page will be evident. This would not be a problem if you've just created and launched an e-commerce site that nobody knows and trusts. A customer may be more inclined to leave her credit card information on the site of a well-known payment gateway, instead of on your lesser-known site. In that case, the visibility of the external payment service may actually help sales. For larger e-commerce sites that already have a strong reputation and are trusted by a large audience, this approach won't be as appealing, because it looks less professional than complete integration.

2. The second approach to handling online payments also relies on an external payment gateway, but instead of physically moving the user to the external site and then bringing him back to your site, he never leaves your site in the first place: he enters all his billing and credit card information on your page, which you then pass to the external service behind the scenes (and you don't store it within your own system). The gateway will finally return a response code that indicates the transaction's success or failure (plus some additional information such as the transaction ID), and you can display some feedback to the user on your page. This approach is depicted in Figure 10-2.

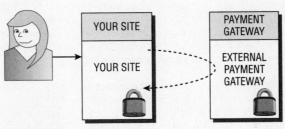

Figure 10-2

The manner in which your page communicates and exchanges data with the gateway service may be a web service or some other simpler server-to-server technology, such as programmatically submitting a POST request with the System.Net.HttpWebRequest class of the .NET Framework, and handling the textual response (usually a simple string with some code indicating success or failure). The obvious advantage of this approach is that the customer stays at your site for the entire process so that all the pages have the same look and feel, which you can customize as you prefer, and you won't need to worry about fake or customer-generated confirmation requests from the payment gateway because everything happens from server-to-server during a single HTTP post.

The disadvantages of this approach are that you're in charge of securing the transmission of sensitive information from the customer's browser to your site (even though you don't store the info, it will still be transferred to and from your web server), by installing an SSL certificate on your server, and using https to access your own checkout pages. If credit card information is hijacked somehow during the transmission, or if you don't comply with all the necessary security standards, you may get into big legal troubles and you may lose all your other customers if they hear about the problem. Another disadvantage is that if your site is small and unknown, some customers may be reluctant to give you their credit card number, something they would feel comfortable doing with a large and well-known credit card processing service.

It should be clear by now which of the two approaches you may prefer, and this will be influenced by the size of the store, its transaction volume, its popularity among the customers, and how much money the store owner wants to invest. Implementing the second approach requires buying and installing an SSL certificate (or arranging to share one via your hosting company), leaves more responsibilities to both you and the store's owner, and requires longer development and implementation. So you might choose the first approach, which is simpler, more cost effective, and still very good for small sites. Conversely, if you're implementing a new e-commerce storefront for a large site that is already selling online and is very popular, the complete integration of the payment process into the store is definitely the best and most professional option.

For the e-commerce store of TheBeerHouse, you'll follow the simpler approach and implement a payment solution that forwards the customer to the external payment service's page. As the store grows, you may want to upgrade the site to use a fully integrated payment mechanism in the future.

You have many payment services to choose from, but some of them can only be used in one country or may only accept a small variety of credit cards. Because we want to implement a solution that could work for as many readers as possible and still be relatively simple to integrate with, we selected PayPal. PayPal is widely known as the main service used by eBay, and it accepts many popular credit cards and works in many countries.

Using PayPal as the Payment Service

PayPal started as a service that enabled people to exchange money from one user's account to another, or to have payment sent to the user's home in the form of a check, but it has grown into a full-featured payment service that is used by a huge number of merchants worldwide as their favorite payment method, for a number of reasons:

❑ Competitive transaction fees, which are lower than most payment gateways.

❑ Great recognition among customers worldwide. At the time of writing, PayPal reports more than 105 million registered users. Much of its popularity stems from its relationship with eBay, but PayPal is definitely not restricted to use within eBay.

❑ Available to 56 countries, and it supports multiple languages and multiple currencies.

❑ Supports taking orders via phone, fax, or mail, and processes credit cards from a management console called Virtual Terminal (available to the U.S. only).

❑ Support for automated recurring payments, which is useful for sites that offer subscription-based access to their content and need to bill their members regularly — on a monthly basis, for example.

❑ Easy integration. Just create an HTML form with the proper parameters to redirect the customer to the payment page, and specify the return URL for confirmed and cancelled payments.

❑ For businesses located in the U.S. that demand more flexibility and greater integration, PayPal also exposes web services for implementing hidden server-to-server communication (for use with the second approach described earlier).

❑ Almost immediate setup. However, your store needs to use a validated PayPal account, which requires a simple process whereby PayPal sends a small deposit to your linked bank account, and you verify the amount and date of the transfer. This validation step is simple, but necessary to prove that the electronic transfer works with your bank account, in addition to proving your identity.

❑ Some good customization options, such as changing the payment page's colors and logo, so that it integrates, at least partially, with your site's style.

❑ Offers complete control over which customers can make a purchase (for example, only U.S. customers with a verified address) and enables merchants to set up different tax and shipping amounts for different countries and states.

❑ Best of all, there are no contract periods, and though you do need a merchant account, for basic accounts you are charged only when someone makes a transaction.

Choosing PayPal as the payment processor for TheBeerHouse allows you to start with its Website Payments Standard option (the HTML form that redirects the customer to the PayPal's pages) and later upgrade to Website Payments Pro if you want to completely integrate the payment process into your site, hiding PayPal from the customer's eyes. All in all, it offers a lot of options for flexibility, as well as support and detailed guides for merchants and developers who want to use it. We'll outline a few steps for setting up the PayPal integration here. See the official documentation at `www.paypal.com` and `http://developer.paypal.com` for further details and examples. Even without prior knowledge of PayPal, it's still easy to set up and works well.

Of special interest for developers is the Sandbox, a complete replication of PayPal, used for development and testing of systems that interact with PayPal (including all the administrative and management pages, where you configure all types of settings). This test environment doesn't make real transactions, but works with test credit card numbers and accounts. Developers can create an account for free (on `http://developer.paypal.com`), and then create PayPal test business accounts for use within the Sandbox. These test accounts can then be used as the recipients for sample transactions. You need to know only a few basic parameters, described in the following table.

Property	Description
cmd	Specifies in which mode you're using PayPal's pages. A value equal to _xclick specifies that you're using the Pay Now mode, whereby the customer lands on the PayPal's checkout page, types in his billing details, and completes the order. If the value is _cart, you'll be using PayPal's integrated shopping cart, which allows users to keep going back and forth from your store site to PayPal to add multiple items to a cart managed by PayPal, until the customer wants to check out. In your case, you'll be implementing your own shopping cart, and use PayPal only for the final processing, so the _xclick value will be used.
upload	A value of 1 indicates that you're using your own shopping cart.
business	The e-mail address that identifies the PayPal business account that will be the recipient for the transaction. For example, we've created the account thebeerhouse@ wrox.com through the Sandbox, to use for our tests. You should create a Sandbox account of your own for testing.
item_name	A descriptive string for the order the customer is going to pay for, for example, Order #25, or maybe "TheBeerHouse order 12345."
item_number	A number/string identifying the order.

Property	Description
amount	The amount the user will pay, in the currency specified by currency_code. You must use the point (.) as the separator for the decimal part of the number, regardless of the currency and language being used, for example, 33.80.
quantity	The total number of products that were ordered for this particular item.
shipping	The cost of the shipping, specified in the same currency as the amount, and in the same format. This will be added to the amount parameter to calculate the total price the customer must pay, for example, 6.00.

With the MVC framework and the assistance of your HTML helper class, this task is a snap. All you need to do is create a form on the page and some hidden inputs using some inline C# code and you are set! The HTTP post will redirect the customer to the Sandbox test environment. To handle real payments later, all you need to do is replace the `https://www.sandbox.paypal.com/us/cgi-bin/webscr` part with `https://www.paypal.com/us/cgi-bin/webscr`. Later in this chapter, we show you exactly how to build your very own form in your view that will post to PayPal. We also discuss how to redirect the users back to your site once they have completed processing their transaction with PayPal. For now, however, you should have enough background information to get started. So let's proceed with the design of the database, and then the model, views, and controller.

Designing the Database Tables

The e-commerce store module uses five tables for the catalog of products and for order management, as shown in Figure 10-3.

All catalog data is stored in Departments and Products, which contain the title, price, description, images, and other information about specific products. The relationship between the two tables makes DepartmentID a foreign key and establishes cascade updates and deletes, so that if a department is deleted, all of its products are automatically deleted as well.

A similar relationship exists between Orders and OrderItems. The former stores information about the order, such as its subtotal and shipping amount, the customer's complete contact information and shipping address, shipping method, current order status, and transaction and tracking ID. The latter stores the order information of each product, whereby a line describes each ordered product, with its title, ID, unit price, quantity, and stock-keeping unit (SKU) — a SKU is a marketing term designating a single product within the store.

There is also one additional support table: ShippingMethods. This table simply stores information, such as the title and price, on the different shipping methods the customer can choose.

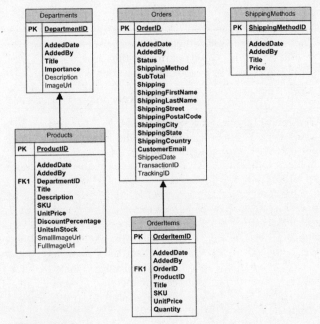

Figure 10-3

Preservation of Transactions

You may be wondering why the `Orders` and `OrderItems` tables maintain a copy of many values that could be retrieved by joining two tables. Take, for example, the `ShippingMethod` column and `Shipping*` columns in the `Orders` table, which you may assume could be replaced with a single `ShippingMethodID` foreign key that references a record in `ShippingMethod`. You may also wonder why the `OrderItems` table contains the title, price, and SKU of the ordered product, even if it already has a reference to the product in the `Products` table through the `ProductID` foreign key. However, think about the situation when a shipping method is deleted or edited, which changes its title and price. If you only linked an order record to a record of `ShippedMethods`, this would result in a different total amount and a different shipping method after the change. The same is true for products: you can delete or change the price of a product, but orders made before the change cannot be modified, and they must keep the price and all other information as it was at the time of the order. If a product is deleted, the store keeper must still be able to determine the product's name, SKU, and price, to identify and ship it correctly.

All this wouldn't be possible if you stored only the ID of the product, because that would become useless if the product were deleted. The product ID is still kept in the `OrderItems` table, but only as optional information that would enable you to create a hyperlink to the product page if the product were still available. The `Orders` and `OrderItems` tables are self-contained historical transaction tables. These tables should be considered as read-only for the most part, which is something you need to handle in the model, except for some information in the `Orders` table, such as the `Status`, `ShippedDate`, `TrackingID`, and `TransactionID` fields, which must be updatable to reflect the changes that happen to the order during its processing.

As in previous chapters, you are inserting these tables into your LINQ-to-SQL file to give you CRUD capabilities. You will not need to create any stored procedures or special views for this particular module.

Designing the Configuration Module

The configuration settings of the store module are defined in a `<store>` element within the `<the-BeerHouse>` section of the `web.config` file. The class that maps the settings is `StoreElement`, which defines the following properties:

Property	Description
PayPalServer	This is the PayPal server that you want to send the request to. This will be either the Sandbox server (`https://www.sandbox.paypal.com/cgi-bin/webscr`) or the live server (`https://www.paypal.com/cgi-bin/webscr`).
PayPalAccount	This is your PayPal ID or an e-mail address associated with your PayPal account. E-mail addresses must be confirmed with PayPal before they can be used for an account.
PayPalIdentityToken	This is the token used to identify you to PayPal. This is different than your PayPal account and can be acquired only through the PayPal website under your account options.
	For security, the identity token is not sent to you; however, once you have enabled PDT, it permanently appears below the Payment Data Transfer On/Off radio buttons on the Website Payment Preferences page.

Designing the Model

As usual, the model part of the module can be split into two virtual parts. The first part is the LINQ-to-SQL file that you have created with the five new tables that you are adding for this section. Figure 10-4 shows the LINQ entities classes.

The other part is the custom helper entities that you will create to help facilitate certain functions, such as the shopping cart. Your shopping cart class will actually be used by your profile provider to persist a user's shopping cart. In this way, any users can come onto the website and have their shopping cart persist, possibly days afterwards. Figure 10-5 shows a diagram of your custom entities.

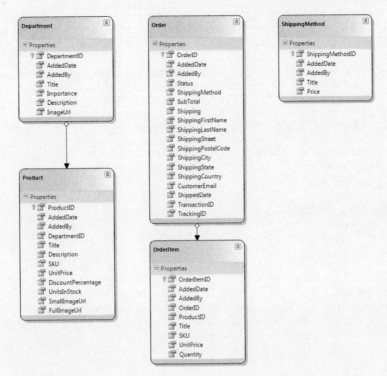

Figure 10-4

Figure 10-5

These two classes will be the only custom classes required to run your e-commerce module.

Just as before in Chapter 6, we created a static class that contains all the queries necessary to pull information from the database. In this case the static class is called `CommerceQueries`, and it provides extension methods for `Departments`, `Products`, and `ShippingMethods`. The diagram in Figure 10-6 represents the queries available for the model.

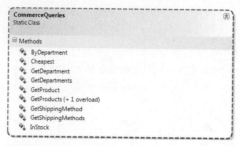

Figure 10-6

Designing the Views

This module is made up of many views. As usual, there is a complete administration console that allows you to edit practically all the data it uses other than the read-only fields such as those of the Orders and OrderItems tables, and a number of end-user pages that display departments, the product listings, and the specific products to the user; it also allows you to manage the shopping cart, the checkout process, and the order history page. In addition to the existing roles (Administrators, Editors, and Contributors) a new role named StoreKeeper should be created to designate which users will be allowed to administer the store. A new role, separate from the current Editors role, was necessary because people managing articles, polls, forums, and newsletters are not necessarily the same people who will manage products and orders (and vice versa). The following is a complete list of views and routes used by the module:

❑ **Index.aspx:** This is the page that shows the departments that will serve as a gateway for browsing products.

    ❑ `store`

❑ **ViewDepartment.aspx:** This page is used to show all the products in the selected department.

    ❑ `store/departments/{departmentId}`

❑ **ViewProduct.aspx:** This page shows a single product.

    ❑ `store/products/{productId}`

❑ **ViewShoppingCart.aspx:** The shopping cart page is among the most complex. It shows all the information pertaining to the shopping cart in addition to providing the user the ability to change shipping methods. Continuing with this form will actually send a request out to PayPal that will process the transaction.

    ❑ `store/cart`

❑ **CompleteOrder.aspx:** This page is used as a return point from PayPal after an order has been successfully processed.

    ❑ `store/order/completed`

❑ **TransactionError.aspx:** In the event that a transaction error occurs, the system does not process the order and indicates to the user that he should contact the store keeper to resolve the issue.

  ❑ *This does not contain a special path, the system-defined path will be used to display this error.*

❑ **ManageStore.aspx:** This view shows all the products in a specific department. It will allow the administrator to drill down further into the product detail view to make specific modifications or to delete a product.

  ❑ `admin/store`

❑ **ManageDepartments.aspx:** This view shows the user all the departments that are currently available.

  ❑ `admin/store/departments`

❑ **CreateDepartment.aspx:** This detailed view allows the administrator or store keeper to create a new department or edit information on an existing department.

  ❑ `admin/store/departments/create`

  ❑ `admin/store/departments/edit/{departmentId}`

❑ **ManageProducts.aspx:** Lists all the products of the store and allows the administrator or store keeper to view a product's details or delete it.

  ❑ `admin/store/products`

❑ **CreateProduct.aspx:** This detailed view allows the administrator or store keeper to create a new product or edit information on an existing product.

  ❑ `admin/store/products/create`

  ❑ `admin/store/products/edit/{productId}`

❑ **ManageOrders.aspx:** Lists all the orders that have been placed by this storefront, and it allows the administrator or store keeper to view the details associated with that order.

  ❑ `admin/store/orders`

❑ **OrderDetial.aspx:** Provides detailed information pertaining to an order. Will also allow administrators to include tracking information with an order.

  ❑ `admin/store/orders/{orderId}`

❑ **ManageShipping.aspx:** Shows all the available shipping options and allows the administrator to create or delete shipping methods.

  ❑ `admin/store/shipping`

Designing the Controller

Similar to other chapters, you will be designing a single controller that manages all of the e-commerce functions for you. This controller will be a little more complex than most because you are communicating with a payment gateway to process your transactions. The following table briefly describes what all of the actions in this controller class do.

Action Method	Security	Parameters
Index	--	--
ViewDepartment	--	`int departmentId`
ViewProduct	--	`int productId`
ViewShoppingCart	--	`int? shippingMethod`
AddShoppingCartItem	--	`int productId, int? quantity`
DeleteShoppingCartItem	--	`int productId`
CompleteOrder	--	`string tx, decimal amt`
ManageStore	StoreKeeper	--
ManageDepartments	StoreKeeper	--
CreateDepartment	StoreKeeper	--
CreateDepartment_OnPost	StoreKeeper	`string title, string imageUrl, string description, int? importance`
EditDepartment	StoreKeeper	`int departmentId`
EditDepartment_OnPost	StoreKeeper	`int id, string title, string imageUrl, string description, int? importance`
DeleteDepartment	StoreKeeper	`int id`
ManageProducts	StoreKeeper	--
CreateProduct	StoreKeeper	--
CreateProduct_OnPost	StoreKeeper	`int? departmentId, string title, string description, string sku, decimal? unitPrice, int? discountPercentage, int? unitsInStock, string smallImageURL, string fullImageURL`
EditProduct	StoreKeeper	`int productId`
EditProduct_OnPost	StoreKeeper	`int id, int? departmentId, string title, string description, string sku, decimal? unitPrice, int? discountPercentage, int? unitsInStock, string smallImageURL, string fullImageURL`
DeleteProduct	StoreKeeper	`int id`
ManageOrders	StoreKeeper	--

Action Method	Security	Parameters
OrderDetails	StoreKeeper	int id, string trackingId
ManageShipping	StoreKeeper	--
CreateShipping	StoreKeeper	string title, decimal price
DeleteShipping	StoreKeeper	int id

Solution

After creating some database tables to help drive this module, we will go over the creation of the e-commerce module by functionality because the solution can be broken down into several distinct subsystems. The first is store management with its associated options, the second is the payment processing portion, and the third is the user experience section. After implementing the code in this section, you should have a fully functional e-commerce module that you could attach to your very own storefront.

Building the Database

This module will probably be the most database-intensive module that you build in this book. This is because there are a lot of moving parts to e-commerce; you have order management, shipping options, products, inventory control, departments, and order tracking. To help facilitate all of these functions, you will be required to build five distinct database tables to drive them.

The ShippingMethod table will hold the shipping options available to the user. This table consists of an ID for the shipping method, a date added field, an added by field, a title or description, and a price. As usual, you can either use Visual Studio Server Explorer or SQL Server Management Studio (SSMS) to create your actual tables. Figure 10-7 shows you exactly how you will need to lay out your table.

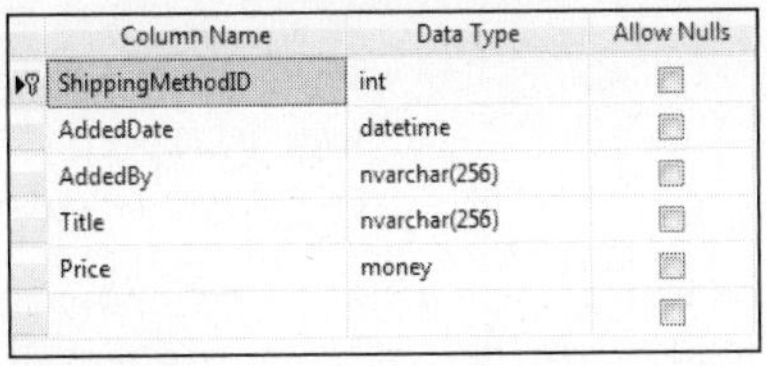

Figure 10-7

The second and third tables pertain to orders: you will need an Orders table to manage the overall order details of the purchase, and you will need an OrderItems table to manage the specific products associated with the order. The Orders table has a primary key field, along with meta data pertaining to who added the order and when, as well as an order status field, and contact/shipping information pertaining to the buyer. Most importantly, it has a transaction ID field which will be provided to you by PayPal once an order has been placed. This ID will be used to securely request data pertaining to the order from PayPal's systems. Figure 10-8 shows a quick diagram of the Orders table.

Column Name	Data Type	Allow Nulls
OrderID	int	☐
AddedDate	datetime	☐
AddedBy	nvarchar(256)	☐
Status	nvarchar(50)	☐
ShippingMethod	nvarchar(256)	☐
SubTotal	money	☐
Shipping	money	☐
ShippingFirstName	nvarchar(256)	☐
ShippingLastName	nvarchar(256)	☐
ShippingStreet	nvarchar(256)	☐
ShippingPostalCode	nvarchar(50)	☐
ShippingCity	nvarchar(256)	☐
ShippingState	nvarchar(256)	☐
ShippingCountry	nvarchar(256)	☐
CustomerEmail	nvarchar(256)	☐
ShippedDate	datetime	☑
TransactionID	nvarchar(256)	☑
TrackingID	nvarchar(256)	☑
		☐

Figure 10-8

You will notice that the last several fields are marked as nullable. This is because the information in these fields will not be made available until after the initial order has been placed. This is particularly true for the tracking information, which will have to be set manually by the users once they have the tracking information available.

The OrderItems table will hold the specific item information that will come from your shopping cart. This table has a primary key, meta data on who added the entry, and product-related information for that particular order. So for this table, if you had five different products that were purchased, you would expect five entries for that order, effectively creating a many-to-one relationship. The OrderItems table is shown in Figure 10-9.

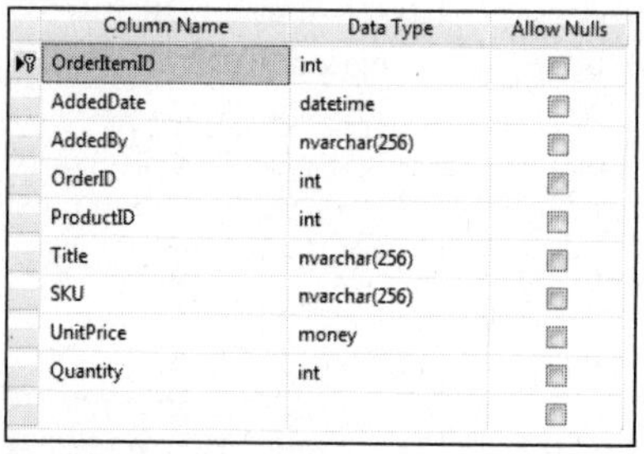

Column Name	Data Type	Allow Nulls
OrderItemID	int	☐
AddedDate	datetime	☐
AddedBy	nvarchar(256)	☐
OrderID	int	☐
ProductID	int	☐
Title	nvarchar(256)	☐
SKU	nvarchar(256)	☐
UnitPrice	money	☐
Quantity	int	☐
		☐

Figure 10-9

Finally, your last two tables deal with products and departments. The Products table holds the specific products that your storefront will offer, and the Departments table will be used to help better organize the products. Starting with the Departments table you have your primary key, the meta data pertaining to who added the entry, a title, an importance indicator, a description, and a URL field for the image representing that department, as shown in Figure 10-10.

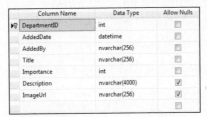

Figure 10-10

For your `Products` table you have your primary key, your meta data of who added the information, as well as a department ID tying it to the `Departments` table, a title, description, SKU, pricing information, discount information, inventory levels, and images, as shown in Figure 10-11.

Column Name	Data Type	Allow Nulls
ProductID	int	☐
AddedDate	datetime	☐
AddedBy	nvarchar(256)	☐
DepartmentID	int	☐
Title	nvarchar(256)	☐
Description	ntext	☐
SKU	nvarchar(50)	☐
UnitPrice	money	☐
DiscountPercentage	int	☐
UnitsInStock	int	☐
SmallImageUrl	nvarchar(256)	☑
FullImageUrl	nvarchar(256)	☑
		☐

Figure 10-11

The `Products` table has a lot of information packed into it, and believe it or not, this table is actually pretty light. You can include many other pieces of information in this table that may be valuable. An example of this would be associating other related products to the product your customer is attempting to buy. This is referred to as up-selling. Up-selling is when you have a customer who is committed to buying a specific product, and then you show her another product that would complement her original product well. An example is buying a digital camera and then offering to sell a tripod or a larger memory card for that camera. Other product-related fields could include keywords for search engines, bulk discounts, special taxation rules, and color options among numerous other possibilities. With that said, this base table should provide an excellent starting point for a basic product offering.

In terms of relationships of your tables, you are only creating a relationship between the `Orders` and the `OrderItems` tables, and the `Departments` and the `Products` tables. You are purposefully not tying in the `Products` or `ShippingMethod` tables to the `Orders` or `OrderItems` tables because you want to be able to remove products or shipping methods from your storefront without affecting order history. This is also the reason why the `OrderItems` table has redundant information in it.

Implementing the Configuration Module

The custom configuration class must be developed before any other code because the custom settings are used in all other layers. This class is similar to the one seen in Chapter 6. It inherits from `ConfigurationElement` and has the properties previously defined:

```
public class CommerceElement : ConfigurationElement
{
    [ConfigurationProperty("payPalServer", DefaultValue = "https://www.paypal.com/
cgi-bin/webscr")]
    public string PayPalServer
    {
        get { return (string)base["payPalServer"]; }
        set { base["payPalServer"] = value; }
    }

    [ConfigurationProperty("payPalAccount", IsRequired = true)]
    public string PayPalAccount
    {
        get { return (string)base["payPalAccount"]; }
        set { base["payPalAccount"] = value; }
    }

    [ConfigurationProperty("payPalIdentityToken", IsRequired = true)]
    public string PayPalIdentityToken
    {
        get { return (string)base["payPalIdentityToken"]; }
        set { base["payPalIdentityToken"] = value; }
    }
}
```

To make this class map a `<commerce>` element under the top-level `<theBeerHouse>` section, you add a property of type `CommerceElement` to the `TheBeerHouseSection` class developed in Chapter 6 and then use the `ConfigurationProperty` attribute to do the mapping:

```
public class TheBeerHouseSection : ConfigurationSection
{
    // other properties here...

    [ConfigurationProperty("commerce", IsRequired = true)]
    public CommerceElement Commerce
    {
        get { return (CommerceElement)base["commerce "]; }
    }
}
```

If you want to make the archive available to everyone, you would use these settings in the `web.config` file:

```
<theBeerHouse>
    <!-- other modules -->
    <commerce
        payPalServer="https://www.sandbox.paypal.com/cgi-bin/webscr"
        payPalAccount="store@TheBeerHouseExample.com"
```

```
            payPalIdentityToken="your-token-here" />
</theBeerHouse>
```

The default value will be used for all those settings not explicitly defined in the configuration file.

Implementing the Model

Once you have created your five core e-commerce tables you can create the model that will drive your module. As usual, all you have to do is drag and drop your five tables onto your LINQ-to-SQL file to create the entities that are important to your model.

Extending the LINQ Objects

After creating your LINQ-to-SQL entities, you need to create two more classes to handle the storage of the shopping cart information. These special classes are your ShoppingCartItem class and your ShoppingCart class.

The ShoppingCartItem Class

The first class you want to create is your ShoppingCartItem class, which is used to store the products and quantities that the shoppers on the site want to buy:

```
[Serializable]
public class ShoppingCartItem
{
    public ShoppingCartItem(Product product)
    {
        Product = product;
    }

    public Product Product { get; set; }

    public string Title { get { return Product.Title; } }

    public int Quantity { get; set; }

    public decimal Price { get { return Product.UnitPrice; } }

    public string SKU { get { return Product.SKU; } }

    public decimal TotalPrice
    {
        get { return Price * Quantity; }
    }
}
```

This class is very basic, and for the most part it acts as a wrapper around the Product LINQ entity. It also adds a property to store the quantity of the products that the shopper wants to purchase. It also has a calculation property that calculates out the total price based on Price and Quantity purchased.

The ShoppingCartItem class is the serialized class that you will use in conjunction with the profile provider to retain your shopping cart information.

The ShoppingCart Class

The last class you want to create is your `ShoppingCart` class, which is used to store each `ShoppingCartItem` that the users want to purchase as part of their order:

```
[Serializable]
public class ShoppingCart : List<ShoppingCartItem>
{
    public ShippingMethod ShippingMethod { get; set; }

    public decimal ShippingPrice { get { return ShippingMethod.Price; } }

    public decimal SubTotal
    {
        get
        {
            decimal totalPrice = 0M;
            foreach (var item in this)
                totalPrice += item.TotalPrice;

            return totalPrice;
        }
    }

    public decimal Total
    {
        get { return SubTotal + ShippingPrice; }
    }
}
```

This entity extends the generic `List<T>` class to create a collection of `ShoppingCartItem`; by creating a collection of the items you can use the `ShoppingCart` just like any other collection to `Add`, `Remove`, `Set`, and `Get` the items from the cart. You are also able to add a couple more properties to further define the shopping cart, such as the `ShippingMethod` that will be used for shipping this order, and the `SubTotal` and `Total` amount owed for this order. The `SubTotal` is the `TotalPrice` from each item in the shopping cart and the `Total` is the `SubTotal` and the `ShippingPrice`.

In order to persist your shopping cart, you will be registering the `ShoppingCart` class with your profile provider. To do this, simply go into your `web.config` and make the following entry:

```
<anonymousIdentification enabled="true"/>

<profile>
  <properties>
    <!-- Add the line below to enable our shopping cart -->
    <add name="ShoppingCart"
        type="TheBeerHouse.Models.ShoppingCart"
        serializeAs="Binary"
        allowAnonymous="true"/>
  </properties>
</profile>
```

By adding the `"ShoppingCart"` item in your properties section of the profile and ensuring that your class has a serialized attribute, it can be included as part of a user's profile. In addition, by adding the `allowAnonymous` tag with a value of `true`, any user that comes onto the site, whether or not they are logged in, will be able to have a shopping cart.

Create the LINQ Queries

You still need to create some of the LINQ queries that we talked about in the Design section. Just like in Chapter 6, you are going to use extension methods for the LINQ table classes, which will provide you with some useful queries when you are interacting with the model from your controller.

The GetShippingMethod Query

This query gets a single shipping method from the database for the requested identity:

```
public static ShippingMethod GetShippingMethod(this Table<ShippingMethod> source,
int id)
{
    return source.FirstOrDefault(sm => sm.ShippingMethodID == id);
}
```

The GetShippingMethods Query

The following query gets all the shipping methods ordered by the `Price`. This query should return `IQueryable<ShippingMethod>` so that it can be used in combination with other queries.

```
public static IQueryable<ShippingMethod> GetShippingMethods(this
Table<ShippingMethod> source)
{
    return from sm in source
           orderby sm.Price ascending
           select sm;
}
```

This method is used for simplicity in keeping the ordering the same across all uses of the shipping methods. The `IQueryable<ShippingMethod>` that you are returning is important because it allows it to be combined with other queries.

The Cheapest Query

This query is one of the queries that can be combined with `GetShippingMethods`. Its purpose is to return the cheapest shipping method for when you are initially creating the `ShoppingCart` and need to set a `ShippingMethod` on creation.

```
public static ShippingMethod Cheapest(this IQueryable<ShippingMethod> source)
{
    return source.OrderBy(sm => sm.Price).FirstOrDefault();
}
```

The GetDepartment Query

This query gets a single department from the database for the requested identity:

```
public static Department GetDepartment(this Table<Department> source, int id)
{
    return source.SingleOrDefault(d => d.DepartmentID == id);
}
```

The GetDepartments Query

This query returns all the departments in the database ordered by the title:

```
public static IEnumerable<Department> GetDepartments(this Table<Department> source)
{
    return from d in source
           orderby d.Title
           select d;
}
```

The GetProduct Query

This query gets a single product from the database for the requested identity:

```
public static Product GetProduct(this Table<Product> source, int id)
{
    return source.SingleOrDefault(p => p.ProductID == id);
}
```

The GetProducts Query

This query gets all the products ordered by the `Title`. This query should return `IQueryable<Product>` so that it can be used in combination with other queries.

```
public static IQueryable<Product> GetProducts(this Table<Product> source)
{
    return from p in source
           orderby p.Title
           select p;
}
```

This next `GetProducts` query gets all the products ordered by the `Title` that are in the provided `ShoppingCart` instance. This query should return `IQueryable<Product>` so that it can be used in combination with other queries.

```
public static IQueryable<Product> GetProducts(this Table<Product> source,
ShoppingCart cart)
{
    var productIds = cart.Select(item => item.Product.ProductID);
    return from p in source
           where productIds.Contains(p.ProductID)
           orderby p.Title
           select p;
}
```

The previous code will get all the products from the database that are contained in the `productIds` collection. This may look like an odd LINQ-to-SQL statement, but it is the same as the following highlighted SQL below.

SQL

```
select *
from Products
where ProductID in (/* the product IDs from the shopping cart */)
order by Title
```

The above highlighted SQL code uses the `IN` statement, which determines whether a specified field (`ProductID`) matches any of the values in the list between the two parentheses. So in other words the above SQL which is the same as our LINQ-to-SQL statement above brings back only the list of products that match the `ProductID` supplied from our shopping cart.

The ByDepartment Query

This query is one of the queries that can be combined with `GetProducts`. Its purpose is to return all the products for a given department identifier. This query should return `IQueryable<Product>` so that it can be used in combination with other queries.

```
public static IQueryable<Product> ByDepartment(this IQueryable<Product> source, int departmentId)
{
    return from p in GetProducts(source)
           where p.DepartmentID == departmentId
           select p;
}
```

This query returns all products that match the specified department as an `IQueryable<Product>` object so that it can be chained with other queries.

The InStock Query

Your last query and one that can be chained with `GetProducts` or `ByDepartment` is this query, which only returns products that are in stock. This query should return `IQueryable<Product>` so that it can be used in combination with other queries.

```
public static IQueryable<Product> InStock(this IQueryable<Product> source)
{
    return from p in source
           where p.UnitsInStock > 0
           select p;
}
```

Implementing the Controller

As we have previously done in other module chapters, we are going to walk through each action method that is needed for the commerce controller, which is located in `~/Controllers` and will be called `CommerceController.cs`. The actions of this controller will define business rules that enforce the data input and validation on your model and provide appropriate data for your view.

The Index Action

The first action you will implement will display all the departments for the e-commerce shop for your shoppers:

```
public ActionResult Index()
{
    TheBeerHouseDataContext dc = new TheBeerHouseDataContext();
    var viewData = dc.Departments.GetDepartments();

    ViewData["PageTitle"] = "Welcome to The Beer House Shop";
    return View("ViewDepartment", viewData);
}
```

This action has the following route:

❑ store

store

This route is used to display the preceding action.

```
routes.MapRoute(
    "CommerceIndex",
    "store",
    new { controller = "Commerce", action = "Index" }
);
```

The ViewDepartment Action

In this action you are going to get all the products for a specific department, based on the department identifier passed in to this action:

```
public ActionResult ViewDepartment(int departmentId)
{
    TheBeerHouseDataContext dc = new TheBeerHouseDataContext();
    var department = dc.Departments.GetDepartment(departmentId);
    var viewData = dc.Products.GetProducts().ByDepartment(departmentId).InStock();

    ViewData["PageTitle"] = "Available Products for " + department.Title;
    return View(viewData);
}
```

This action has the following route:

❑ store/departments/{departmentId}

store/departments/{departmentId}

This route is used to display the preceding action.

```
routes.MapRoute(
    "CommerceDepartment",
    "store/departments/{departmentId}",
```

```
        new { controller = "Commerce",
            action = "ViewDepartment",
            departmentId = (int?)null
        }
    );
```

The ViewProduct Action

In this action you are going to get a specific product, based on the product identifier passed in to this action:

```
public ActionResult ViewProduct(int productId)
{
    TheBeerHouseDataContext dc = new TheBeerHouseDataContext();
    Product viewData = dc.Products.GetProduct(productId);

    ViewData["PageTitle"] = viewData.Title;
    return View(viewData);
}
```

This action has the following route:

❏   store/products/{productId}

store/products/{productId}

This route is used to display the preceding action.

```
routes.MapRoute(
    "CommerceProduct",
    "store/products/{productId}",
    new { controller = "Commerce", action = "ViewProduct", productId = (int?)null }
);
```

The ViewShoppingCart Action

This next action is arguably one of the most important actions outside of actually completing the order. This is the cart where the user will manage her order before continuing on to purchase the items listed in the shopping cart.

```
public ActionResult ViewShoppingCart(int? shippingMethod)
{
    TheBeerHouseDataContext dc = new TheBeerHouseDataContext();
    ProfileBase profileBase = HttpContext.Profile as ProfileBase;
    ShoppingCart shoppingCart =
        (ShoppingCart)profileBase.GetPropertyValue("ShoppingCart");

    if (shoppingCart == null)
    {
        shoppingCart = new ShoppingCart();

        // get the cheapest shipping method for our user
        var cheapestShippingMethod =
```

```
            dc.ShippingMethods.GetShippingMethods().Cheapest();
        shoppingCart.ShippingMethod = cheapestShippingMethod;

        profileBase.SetPropertyValue("ShoppingCart", shoppingCart);
    }

    // set the shipping method if one exists
    if (shippingMethod.HasValue)
        shoppingCart.ShippingMethod =
            dc.ShippingMethods.GetShippingMethod(shippingMethod.Value);

    // make sure the shipping method is set
    if (shoppingCart.ShippingMethod == null)
        shoppingCart.ShippingMethod =
            dc.ShippingMethods.GetShippingMethods().Cheapest();

    ViewData["shippingMethod"] = new SelectList(
        dc.ShippingMethods.GetShippingMethods(),
        "ShippingMethodID",
        "Title",
        shoppingCart.ShippingMethod.ShippingMethodID
    );

    ViewData["PageTitle"] = "Your Shopping Cart";
    return View(shoppingCart);
}
```

As you can see from this code, the viewing of the shopping cart is not that complex. You first try and get the user's ShoppingCart from her profile. If it doesn't exist, you create a new ShoppingCart for her with the cheapest shipping method already set, and then put it in the profile for storage and retrieval at a later time.

After you are done retrieving the shopping cart, you need to set the shipping method on the ShoppingCart object if one was passed in to the action. From there you populate the shippingMethod drop-down so that the view can render the available shipping methods that the shoppers can select to have their products shipped through.

This action has the following route:

❑   store/cart

store/cart

This route is used to display the preceding action.

```
routes.MapRoute(
    "CommerceCart",
    "store/cart",
    new { controller = "Commerce", action = "ViewShoppingCart" }
);
```

The AddShoppingCartItem Action

This action is a non-view action that acts as an intermediary between the product page and the cart page that adds the product and quantity to the cart:

```
[AcceptVerbs("POST")]
public ActionResult AddShoppingCartItem(int productId, int? quantity)
{
    TheBeerHouseDataContext dc = new TheBeerHouseDataContext();
    ProfileBase profileBase = HttpContext.Profile as ProfileBase;
    ShoppingCart shoppingCart =
        (ShoppingCart)profileBase.GetPropertyValue("ShoppingCart");

    if (shoppingCart == null)
    {
        shoppingCart = new ShoppingCart();

        // get the cheapest shipping method for our user
        var cheapestShippingMethod =
        dc.ShippingMethods.GetShippingMethods().Cheapest();
        shoppingCart.ShippingMethod = cheapestShippingMethod;

        profileBase.SetPropertyValue("ShoppingCart", shoppingCart);
    }

    Product product = dc.Products.GetProduct(productId);

    // throw a 404 Not Found if the requested forum is not in the database
    if (product == null)
        throw new HttpException(404, "The product could not be found.");

    ShoppingCartItem item = new ShoppingCartItem(product) {
        Quantity = quantity ?? 1
    };

    shoppingCart.Add(item);

    return RedirectToAction("ViewShoppingCart");
}
```

The part that isn't highlighted is the exact same code you used in `ViewShoppingCart` for setting up a shopping cart if one doesn't exist after you get it from the user's profile, so that needs no further discussion.

After you have your shopping cart available, you need to add the selected product to it. You do this by getting the product from the database based on the product identifier passed in to the action. However, if the product doesn't exist in the database, you need to throw a `404 Not Found`, as you have done in previous chapters when a certain entity is not found in the database. You do this to signify to the caller that the requested product is not real.

Now that you have retrieved a product from the database and verified that it is a real item in the database, you then need to create a new `ShoppingCartItem` with the quantity based on this product, and then add it to your shopping cart with any other items that might also be in the shopping cart.

After everything is completed you redirect the user to the `ViewShoppingCart` action that we talked about previously. This is why we call this type of action a non-view action, because it doesn't actually have a view that it binds against; it works much like your service actions, except instead of returning a JSON response, it gets redirected to another action that will handle the viewing of the data.

The route for this action uses the standard `{controller}/{action}` route, so requests to this action method can be accessed through

❑   commerce/addshoppingcartitem

The DeleteShoppingCartItem Action

The next logical action that you need to create is one for deleting shopping cart items from your shopping cart. This will be done by deleting a single product from the shopping cart, by passing in the product identifier for the product that needs to be removed. This action will be completed as a service called by an AJAX script, so you need to add your normal service-related attributes to the action.

```
[Service, HttpPostOnly]
public ActionResult DeleteShoppingCartItem(int productId)
{
    ProfileBase profileBase = HttpContext.Profile as ProfileBase;
    ShoppingCart shoppingCart =
        (ShoppingCart)profileBase.GetPropertyValue("ShoppingCart");

    if (shoppingCart == null)
        throw new HttpException(404, "The shopping cart could not be found.");

    foreach (var item in shoppingCart)
    {
        if (item.Product.ProductID == productId)
        {
            shoppingCart.Remove(item);
            break;
        }
    }

    return View(new { id = productId });
}
```

As you have done in the past, you look for a shopping cart in the user's profile; however, in this case if the shopping cart isn't found, you don't create a new one, you just throw a `404 Not Found` to alert the user that the shopping cart was not found and the action was invalid.

After you have successfully retrieved the shopping cart from the user's profile, you need to search through each item trying to find the first match with the product identifier that was passed in. If you find that match, you simply want to remove the item from the cart and break out of the loop.

Note that you have not called the database at all in this action, because everything you are currently working with is stored in memory, in the user's profile. By not calling the database you have created a really fast action that doesn't have all the unmanaged overhead of having to call a database and wait for a response. Whenever it is possible to achieve an action without going to an unmanaged data store, it is preferred, because it will keep your application efficient and fast.

When everything is completed and the item is removed from the shopping cart, you just want to return back the identifier that was originally passed in to the action method. This is done as an indication that the operation completed smoothly and also serves as a dual purpose to indicate which remove item action was completed. Because AJAX is asynchronous it is possible to have as many delete operations running at the same time as you need. Nine times out of ten you are going to want to do some kind of post-completion operation in your JavaScript code, so you need to pass back some kind of referential-context so that the JavaScript code understands which asynchronous operation it is working with. That is why you are passing back the same identifier that the AJAX code originally passed to the action, because the identifier obviously meant something to the JavaScript code, so passing it back as an indication that the operation completed is both a very lightweight response and one that preserves the context of the request.

The route for this action uses the standard `{controller}/{action}` route, so requests to this action method can be accessed through

❑   `commerce/deleteshoppingcartitem`

The CompleteOrder Action

This next action is the most important action in the entire system; if it doesn't work correctly, you are going to have a lot of mad customers and TheBeerHouse won't make any money. This action is responsible for processing the transaction that is sent back from PayPal, so that you know the user has paid for the products in his cart and that you need to ship the products he ordered to his shipping address. This action is probably one of the more complex that you are going to run across in this book, so we are going to break it apart and talk about each part of the code, so that you can understand how it is working in conjunction with the PayPal servers.

But before you jump into creating the code for the action, let's discuss for a moment how the PayPal servers work and communicate with your code. Figure 10-12 is a flow diagram of all the requests and responses going back and forth between your shopper's computer, your website server, and the PayPal server.

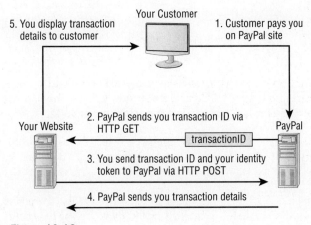

Figure 10-12

This looks pretty complex, but if you break down the five different steps occurring in the figure, you will soon see that they are not that complicated to process. We will walk through each step and to make it easier we will put each step in context of the application that you are building.

1. In the first step your customer is on your `ViewShoppingCart.aspx` view and has clicked the checkout button. (We discuss this view later on in the chapter, but don't worry, the majority of the processing that is in the figure happens on the backend. So you aren't missing much contextually by learning about the full process here.) When the checkout button is clicked it sends the request to the PayPal server, where your shopper enters her payment information, shipping address, and other relevant information to the transaction and completes her order. (This process is covered in the views later on.)

2. The shopper has completed the order on PayPal and the transaction record is being sent back to your servers via an HTTP GET request to your `CompleteOrder` action. Two query string variables are included in the request, `tx` and `amt`, as outlined in the following code:

```
[AcceptVerbs("GET")]
public ActionResult CompleteOrder(string tx, decimal amt)
{
```

You are accepting these two parameters from PayPal as your action's input parameters. They will be used later on in the process.

3. In this step you are sending a POST request back to PayPal to retrieve all the information about the transaction. This extra step is necessary, because with the transaction ID you send a unique identity token back and this acts as a security authorization to say you are allowed to view the transaction information. This is accomplished within the code by calling a non-action method in the controller called `TransactionDataRequest`:

```
// get transaction response from PayPal
string response = TransactionDataRequest(tx);
```

Beginning The TransactionDataRequest Method

We are including the code for the `TransactionDataRequest` *method here, because it contains a number of the steps in Figure 10-12. But you should take note that the code does not occur in this order when implemented in the controller. It is just being shown in this manner to continue the conversation.*

In the first part of this method you are going to create a POST request to send to PayPal as part of step 3.

```
[NonAction]
private string TransactionDataRequest(string tx)
{
    // read the original IPN post
    string payPalServer =
        Configuration.TheBeerHouseSection.Current.Commerce.PayPalServer;
    string formValues =
        Encoding.ASCII.GetString(
            HttpContext.Request.BinaryRead(HttpContext.Request.ContentLength)
        );
    string requestFormValues =
        formValues +
        String.Format("&cmd={0}&at={1}&tx={2}",
            "_notify-synch",
```

```
                    Configuration.TheBeerHouseSection.Current.Commerce.
                    PayPalIdentityToken,
                    tx
            );
```

In the preceding code you create the response you would like to send to PayPal. It includes your PayPal Identity Token and your transaction ID that was passed in as a parameter called tx. In addition to that you also include all the data originally passed to you from PayPal. In the next part of the method you are actually going to make the POST request to the PayPal server.

```
        // create the pay pal request
        HttpWebRequest payPalRequest = (HttpWebRequest)WebRequest.
        Create(payPalServer);
        payPalRequest.Method = "POST";
        payPalRequest.ContentType = "application/x-www-form-urlencoded";
        payPalRequest.ContentLength = requestFormValues.Length;

        // write the request back IPN strings
        using (StreamWriter writer =
            new StreamWriter(payPalRequest.GetRequestStream(), Encoding.ASCII))
        {

            writer.Write(requestFormValues);
            writer.Close();
        }
```

In this code you create an HttpWebRequest object and set the necessary properties to create a POST request to the PayPal server. It should be noted that it is also necessary to write the request data to the request stream as shown at the end of the preceding code block. So now that the request has been sent to PayPal it is time to move on to step 4, where you will get the actual response back.

4. In this step, PayPal is sending back the transaction details that were requested by the transaction ID and your authorization token sent to the PayPal severs in step 3.

```
        // send the request to pay pal
        using (HttpWebResponse payPayResponse =
            (HttpWebResponse)payPalRequest.GetResponse())
        {
            // get the response from pay pal
            using (Stream payPalResponseStream = payPayResponse.
            GetResponseStream())
            {
                // read the response from pay pal
                using (StreamReader reader =
                    new StreamReader(payPalResponseStream, Encoding.UTF8))
                {
                    string ipnStatus = reader.ReadToEnd();
                    return ipnStatus;
                }
            }
        }
    }
```

This code is a little convoluted because you need to open three different kinds of streams to read the request sent back from PayPal. But if we were to boil all this code down to what is actually happening, it is as easy as saying you are reading the response from PayPal back as text. This text from PayPal is then returned from the method to be used in the rest of the order completion process.

Continuing The CompleteOrder Action

5. This last step is totally up to you, the developer. Once you have received the transaction details from PayPal, you need to create an order in your database and store all the information that is contained in the cart in the database so that it can be shipped to your buyer. The first thing you want to do is retrieve your shopping cart from the profile like you have done in previous actions.

```
ProfileBase profileBase = HttpContext.Profile as ProfileBase;
ShoppingCart shoppingCart =
    (ShoppingCart)profileBase.GetPropertyValue("ShoppingCart");

// save transaction to database
if (shoppingCart.Total == amt)
{
```

Notice that you have a check to see if the amount paid corresponds to the total amount in your shopping cart. If there is a discrepancy, the user is sent to an error page and directed to call support. Otherwise, you use the returned PayPal data to create an order for the customer. The reason why you aren't using the information stored from the profile provider is because the billing information from PayPal is confirmed, whereas your information is not. You do not want to be caught in a situation where someone stole a credit card and shipped the order to his own house, while the unknowing card holder later gets an unknown bill and files a chargeback against your storefront. For those of you not familiar with the way credit cards work, chargebacks are when the bank reverses a transaction for one of its credit card holders unless the merchant can prove they sent out the order and followed due diligence procedures. Using the address provided by PayPal will certainly reduce the odds of you or your customers being robbed.

```
TheBeerHouseDataContext dc = new TheBeerHouseDataContext();
Order order = new Order() {
    AddedBy = User.Identity.Name,
    AddedDate = DateTime.Now,
    CustomerEmail = ExtractValue(response, "payer_email"),
    Shipping = shoppingCart.ShippingPrice,
    ShippingCity = ExtractValue(response, "address_city"),
    ShippingCountry = ExtractValue(response, "address_country"),
    ShippingFirstName = ExtractValue(response, "first_name"),
    ShippingLastName = ExtractValue(response, "last_name"),
    ShippingMethod = shoppingCart.ShippingMethod.Title,
    ShippingStreet = ExtractValue(response, "address_street"),
    ShippingPostalCode = ExtractValue(response, "address_zip"),
    ShippingState = ExtractValue(response, "address_state"),
    Status = "Order Recieved",
    TransactionID = tx,
    SubTotal = shoppingCart.Total
};
```

In this code you are saving all the values from the PayPal transaction details to your `Order` entity object to be saved to the database. To get this information from the transaction details you use the `ExtractValue` method, which is another non-action method in your controller. The purpose of this method is to search through the text response you received from PayPal and pick out the information being requested.

Beginning The ExtractValue Method

```
[NonAction]
private string ExtractValue(string pdt, string key)
{
    string[] keys = pdt.Split('\n');
    string output = String.Empty;
    string thisKey = String.Empty;

    foreach (string item in keys)
    {
        string[] bits = item.Split('=');
        if (bits.Length > 1)
        {
            output = bits[1];
            thisKey = bits[0];
            if (thisKey.Equals(key, StringComparison.InvariantCultureIgnoreCase))
                break;
        }
    }

    return HttpContext.Server.UrlDecode(output);
}
```

We are going to avoid talking about this method too much, because it is very specific to how PayPal works and really just acts like a lookup table for extracting the information from the transaction details that you really care about.

Continuing The CompleteOrder Action

```
        foreach (ShoppingCartItem item in shoppingCart)
        {
            order.OrderItems.Add(new OrderItem() {
                AddedBy = User.Identity.Name,
                AddedDate = DateTime.Now,
                ProductID = item.Product.ProductID,
                Quantity = item.Quantity,
                Title = item.Title,
                UnitPrice = item.Price,
                SKU = item.SKU
            });

            var productToUpdate = products
                .FirstOrDefault(p => p.ProductID == item.Product.ProductID);
            productToUpdate.UnitsInStock -= item.Quantity;
        }
```

After the order is completely filled out with the transaction details from PayPal, you need to save the shopping cart items to the OrderItems table in the database. You do this by adding a new OrderItem object to the OrderItems collection property off of the Order entity that you created previously. When you connect the objects like this, LINQ-to-SQL is smart enough to save the Order to the database first and then retrieve the OrderID to be used with the

`OrderItems` collection. This saves you from having to worry about the minutia of finding out what the `OrderID` is and set it for each of the `OrderItem` objects.

```
dc.Orders.InsertOnSubmit(order);
dc.SubmitChanges();

profileBase.SetPropertyValue("ShoppingCart", new ShoppingCart());
ViewData["OrderNumber"] = order.OrderID;

ViewData["PageTitle"] = "Order Received";
return View();
```

In the preceding code you save the order to the database, and then clear the shopping cart by creating a new one. You also set the `OrderNumber` in the `ViewData` and return the view as having completed successfully.

```
    }
    else
    {
        return View("TransactionError");
    }
}
```

However, if the transaction wasn't successful because the amounts didn't match what was in the cart, you want to alert the users so that they can take the appropriate actions with the TheBeerHouse support staff. You alert the users of this by returning the `TransactionError` view.

This action has the following route:

❑   store/order/completed

store/order/completed

This route is used to display the preceding action.

```
routes.MapRoute(
    "CommerceCompleted",
    "store/order/completed",
    new { controller = "Commerce", action = "CompleteOrder" }
);
```

The ManageStore Action

This next action is for the StoreKeeper role only. The StoreKeeper is a new role that you haven't seen before. The user with this role acts as the store administrator in charge of everything to do with the TheBeerHouse store. This action is the main entry point for administering the store.

```
[Authorize(Roles = "StoreKeeper")]
public ActionResult ManageStore()
{
    ViewData["PageTitle"] = "Manage Store";
    return View();
}
```

This action has the following route:

❑   `store/admin`

store/admin

This route is used to display the preceding action.

```
routes.MapRoute(
    "CommerceManageStore",
    "store/admin",
    new { controller = "Commerce", action = "ManageStore" }
);
```

The ManageDepartments Action

This action is used to manage the store's departments. It will be available only to the StoreKeeper role.

```
[Authorize(Roles = "StoreKeeper")]
public ActionResult ManageDepartments()
{
    TheBeerHouseDataContext dc = new TheBeerHouseDataContext();
    var viewData = dc.Departments.GetDepartments();

    ViewData["PageTitle"] = "Manage Departments";
    return View(viewData);
}
```

This action has the following route:

❑   `store/admin/departments`

store/admin/departments

This route is used to display the preceding action.

```
routes.MapRoute(
    "CommerceManageDepartments",
    "store/admin/departments",
    new { controller = "Commerce", action = "ManageDepartments" }
);
```

The CreateDepartment Action

This action is used to create departments. It will be available only to the StoreKeeper role.

The code for this action is a little different than what you have seen before, because it is broken up into two different actions based on the GET and POST HTTP methods. This breakup is very useful if you want to keep your retrieval and update actions separate, but interacting with the same view.

The following code is used for HTTP GET requests:

```
[Authorize(Roles = "StoreKeeper")]
public ActionResult CreateDepartment()
```

```
    {
        ViewData["PageTitle"] = "Create Department";
        return View();
    }
```

The next piece of code is for the HTTP POST requests. It can be identified as such by the `AcceptVerbs` attribute and the `ActionName` attribute as seen here:

```
[Authorize(Roles = "StoreKeeper")]
[AcceptVerbs("POST"), ActionName("CreateDepartment")]
public ActionResult CreateDepartment_OnPost(string title, string imageUrl, string
description, int? importance)
{
    // Create new Department
    if (!String.IsNullOrEmpty(title)
        && !String.IsNullOrEmpty(imageUrl)
        && !String.IsNullOrEmpty(description))
    {
        try
        {
            TheBeerHouseDataContext dc = new TheBeerHouseDataContext();
            Department department = new Department {
                Title = title,
                Importance = importance ?? -1,
                ImageUrl = imageUrl,
                Description = description,
                AddedBy = User.Identity.Name,
                AddedDate = DateTime.Now
            };
            dc.Departments.InsertOnSubmit(department);

            // save changes to database
            dc.SubmitChanges();

            TempData["SuccessMessage"] = "Your department has been created.";
            return RedirectToAction("ManageDepartments");
        }
        catch (Exception exc)
        {
            TempData["ErrorMessage"] = exc.Message;
        }
    }

    // Bring up blank form
    ViewData["PageTitle"] = "Create Department";
    return View();
}
```

This code handles the adding of a department to the database.

Let's briefly talk about what these two new attributes do and how you can get them to work for you to create some pretty advanced controller actions. The `AcceptVerb` attribute tells the controller which HTTP method verb should be used when the controller is looking for the action it should execute based on the route information. The `ActionName` attribute allows you to make this action appear as a different name to the controller. When you combine these two attributes, you have a powerful new tool for breaking up your actions based on the HTTP method verb.

This action has the following route:

❑   `store/admin/departments/create`

store/admin/departments/create

This route is used to display the preceding actions. Both of them will use the same URL, because they are treated as the same action by the controller, but like other actions they are retrieved based on their HTTP method and name.

```
routes.MapRoute(
    "CommerceCreateDepartment",
    "store/admin/departments/create",
    new { controller = "Commerce", action = "CreateDepartment" }
);
```

The EditDepartment Action

This action is used to edit an existing department in the database. It will accept the department identifier to indicate which department will be edited. It will be available only to the StoreKeeper role.

Just like in the `CreateDepartment` action, the code for this action is a little different because the action is based on the GET and POST HTTP methods.

The following code is used for HTTP GET requests:

```
[Authorize(Roles = "StoreKeeper")]
public ActionResult EditDepartment(int departmentId)
{
    TheBeerHouseDataContext dc = new TheBeerHouseDataContext();
    Department viewData = dc.Departments.GetDepartment(departmentId);

    ViewData["id"] = viewData.DepartmentID;
    ViewData["PageTitle"] = "Update Department";
    return View(viewData);
}
```

The next piece of code is for the HTTP POST requests:

```
[Authorize(Roles = "StoreKeeper")]
[AcceptVerbs("POST"), ActionName("EditDepartment")]
public ActionResult EditDepartment_OnPost(int id, string title, string imageUrl,
string description, int? importance)
{
    // Update Exsisting Department Data
    if (!String.IsNullOrEmpty(title)
        && !String.IsNullOrEmpty(imageUrl)
        && !String.IsNullOrEmpty(description))
    {
        try
        {
```

```
            TheBeerHouseDataContext dc = new TheBeerHouseDataContext();
            Department department = dc.Departments.GetDepartment(id);

            department.Importance = importance ?? -1;
            department.Title = title;
            department.ImageUrl = imageUrl;
            department.Description = description;
            department.AddedBy = User.Identity.Name;
            department.AddedDate = DateTime.Now;
            dc.SubmitChanges();

            TempData["SuccessMessage"] = "Your department has been modified.";
            return RedirectToAction("ManageDepartments");
        }
        catch (Exception exc)
        {
            TempData["ErrorMessage"] = exc.Message;
        }
    }

    ViewData["PageTitle"] = "Update Department";
    return View();
}
```

This code handles the updating of a department in the database, after all the validation criteria have been met. To validate this action you need to check that `title`, `imageUrl`, and `description` strings are not empty.

This action has the following route:

❑   store/admin/departments/edit/{departmentId}

store/admin/departments/edit/{departmentId}

This route is used to display the preceding action.

```
routes.MapRoute(
    "CommerceEditDepartment",
    "store/admin/departments/edit/{departmentId}",
    new { controller = "Commerce",
          action = "EditDepartment",
          departmentId = (int?)null
    }
);
```

The DeleteDepartment Action

This action is used to delete an existing department from the database. Like your other actions that deal with one object, you will accept the department identifier to indicate which department will be deleted. It will be available only to the StoreKeeper role.

```
[Authorize(Roles = "StoreKeeper")]
[Service, HttpPostOnly]
```

```
public ActionResult DeleteDepartment(int id)
{
    TheBeerHouseDataContext dc = new TheBeerHouseDataContext();

    Department department = dc.Departments.GetDepartment(id);
    dc.Departments.DeleteOnSubmit(department);
    dc.SubmitChanges();

    return View(new { id = id });
}
```

The preceding action is a service that will be used through an AJAX call on the `ManageDepartments` view. After this action is completed it should return the `id` as an indication that everything succeeded; this is the same process that we talked about earlier in the `DeleteShoppingCartItem` action.

The route for this action uses the standard `{controller}/{action}` route, so requests to this action method can be accessed through

❑   `commerce/deletedepartment`

The product-related actions are almost identical to the department actions you just created, so for the next set of actions relating to products, we highlight only the code you should pay special attention to.

The ManageProducts Action

This action is used to manage the store's products. It will be available only to the StoreKeeper role.

```
[Authorize(Roles = "StoreKeeper")]
public ActionResult ManageProducts()
{
    TheBeerHouseDataContext dc = new TheBeerHouseDataContext();

    var viewData = dc.Products.GetProducts();

    ViewData["PageTitle"] = "Manage Products";
    return View(viewData);
}
```

This action has the following route:

❑   `store/admin/products`

store/admin/products

This route is used to display the preceding action.

```
routes.MapRoute(
    "CommerceManageProducts",
    "store/admin/products",
    new { controller = "Commerce", action = "ManageProducts" }
);
```

The CreateProduct Action

This action is used to create products. It will be available only to the StoreKeeper role.

The following code is used for HTTP GET requests:

```
[Authorize(Roles = "StoreKeeper")]
public ActionResult CreateProduct()
{
    ViewData["PageTitle"] = "Create Product";
    return View();
}
```

The next piece of code is for the HTTP POST requests:

```
[Authorize(Roles = "StoreKeeper")]
[AcceptVerbs("POST"), ActionName("CreateProduct")]
public ActionResult CreateProduct_OnPost(int? departmentId, string title, string
description, string sku, decimal? unitPrice, int? discountPercentage, int?
unitsInStock, string smallImageURL, string fullImageURL)
{
    // Populate Drop Downs
    TheBeerHouseDataContext dc = new TheBeerHouseDataContext();
    var departments = dc.Departments.GetDepartments();

    // Create new Product
    if (!String.IsNullOrEmpty(title))
    {
        try
        {
            Product product = new Product {
                Title = title,
                Description = description,
                DepartmentID = departmentId ?? -1,
                DiscountPercentage = discountPercentage ?? 0,
                FullImageUrl = fullImageURL,
                SmallImageUrl = smallImageURL,
                SKU = sku,
                UnitPrice = unitPrice ?? 0,
                UnitsInStock = unitsInStock ?? 0,
                AddedBy = User.Identity.Name,
                AddedDate = DateTime.Now
            };
            dc.Products.InsertOnSubmit(product);

            // save changes to database
            dc.SubmitChanges();

            TempData["SuccessMessage"] = "Your product has been created.";
            return RedirectToAction("ManageProducts");
        }
        catch (Exception exc)
        {
```

```
                TempData["ErrorMessage"] = exc.Message;
            }
        }

    ViewData["departmentID"] = new SelectList(departments, "DepartmentID", "Title",
departmentId);

        // Bring up blank form
        ViewData["PageTitle"] = "Create Product";
        return View();
    }
```

This code handles the adding of a product to the database.

This action has the following route:

❏   store/admin/products/create

store/admin/products/create

This route is used to display the preceding action.

```
routes.MapRoute(
    "CommerceCreateProduct",
    "store/admin/products/create",
    new { controller = "Commerce", action = "CreateProduct" }
);
```

The EditProduct Action

This action is used to edit an existing product in the database. It will accept the product identifier to indicate which product will be edited. It will be available only to the StoreKeeper role.

The following code is used for HTTP GET requests:

```
[Authorize(Roles = "StoreKeeper")]
public ActionResult EditProduct(int productId)
{
    // Populate Drop Downs
    TheBeerHouseDataContext dc = new TheBeerHouseDataContext();
    var departments = dc.Departments.GetDepartments();
    Product viewData = dc.Products.GetProduct(productId);

    ViewData["id"] = viewData.ProductID;
    ViewData["title"] = viewData.Title;
    ViewData["sku"] = viewData.SKU;
    ViewData["description"] = viewData.Description;
    ViewData["smallImageURL"] = viewData.SmallImageUrl;
    ViewData["FullImageURL"] = viewData.FullImageUrl;
    ViewData["discountPercentage"] = viewData.DiscountPercentage;
    ViewData["unitPrice"] = viewData.UnitPrice;
    ViewData["unitsInStock"] = viewData.UnitsInStock;
```

```
        ViewData["departmentID"] =
            new SelectList(departments, "DepartmentID", "Title", viewData.DepartmentID);

    ViewData["PageTitle"] = "Update Product";
    return View(viewData);
}
```

In this code, you are setting all the necessary view data to populate the form that will be edited.

The next piece of code is for the HTTP POST requests:

```
[Authorize(Roles = "StoreKeeper")]
[AcceptVerbs("POST"), ActionName("EditProduct")]
public ActionResult EditProduct_OnPost(int id, int? departmentId, string title,
string description, string sku, decimal? unitPrice, int? discountPercentage, int?
unitsInStock, string smallImageURL, string fullImageURL)
{
    // Populate Drop Downs
    TheBeerHouseDataContext dc = new TheBeerHouseDataContext();
    var departments = dc.Departments.GetDepartments();

    // Update Exsisting Department Data
    if (!String.IsNullOrEmpty(title))
    {
        try
        {
            Product product = dc.Products.GetProduct(id);

            product.Title = title;
            product.Description = description;
            product.AddedBy = User.Identity.Name;
            product.AddedDate = DateTime.Now;
            product.DepartmentID = departmentId ?? -1;
            product.DiscountPercentage = discountPercentage ?? 0;
            product.FullImageUrl = fullImageURL;
            product.SmallImageUrl = smallImageURL;
            product.SKU = sku;
            product.UnitPrice = unitPrice ?? 0;
            product.UnitsInStock = unitsInStock ?? 0;

            dc.SubmitChanges();

            TempData["SuccessMessage"] = "Your product has been modified.";
            return RedirectToAction("ManageProducts");
        }
        catch (Exception exc)
        {
            TempData["ErrorMessage"] = exc.Message;
        }
    }
```

```
        ViewData["departmentID"] = new SelectList(departments, "DepartmentID", "Title",
    departmentId);

        // Bring up blank form
        ViewData["PageTitle"] = "Create Product";
        return View();
    }
```

This code handles the updating of a product in the database, after all the validation criteria have been met. To validate this action you need to check that `title` is not an empty string.

This action has the following route:

❑   `store/admin/products/edit/{productId}`

store/admin/products/edit/{productId}

This route is used to display the preceding action.

```
routes.MapRoute(
    "CommerceEditProduct",
    "store/admin/products/edit/{productId}",
    new { controller = "Commerce",
          action = "EditProduct",
          productId = (int?)null
    }
);
```

The DeleteProduct Action

This action is used to delete an existing product from the database. It will accept the product identifier to indicate which product will be deleted. It will be available only to the StoreKeeper role.

```
[Authorize(Roles = "StoreKeeper")]
[Service, HttpPostOnly]
public ActionResult DeleteProduct(int id)
{
    TheBeerHouseDataContext dc = new TheBeerHouseDataContext();

    Product product = dc.Products.GetProduct(id);
    dc.Products.DeleteOnSubmit(product);
    dc.SubmitChanges();

    return View(new { id = id });
}
```

The route for this action uses the standard `{controller}/{action}` route, so requests to this action method can be accessed through

❑   `commerce/deleteproduct`

The ManageOrders Action

This next action is necessary when you want to manage the orders that your shoppers have created. This action will be available only to the StoreKeeper role and will display all the orders in the system sorted by when they were ordered, in descending order.

```
[Authorize(Roles = "StoreKeeper")]
public ActionResult ManageOrders()
{
    TheBeerHouseDataContext dc = new TheBeerHouseDataContext();
    var orders = dc.Orders.OrderBy(o => o.AddedDate);

    ViewData["PageTitle"] = "Manage Orders";
    return View(orders);
}
```

This action has the following route:

❑   store/admin/orders

store/admin/orders

This route is used to display the preceding action.

```
routes.MapRoute(
    "CommerceManageOrders",
    "store/admin/orders",
    new { controller = "Commerce", action = "ManageOrders" }
);
```

The OrderDetail Action

Now that you have an action to manage your orders, you need one to view the order details of one specific order. This action should take an order identifier that will be used to look up the order the store administrator wants to view. It is available only to users with the StoreKeeper role.

This code will be broken up into a GET and POST action for handling the different HTTP methods from the view.

This is the code that shows the order details for the GET request:

```
[Authorize(Roles = "StoreKeeper")]
public ActionResult OrderDetail(int orderId)
{
    TheBeerHouseDataContext dc = new TheBeerHouseDataContext();
    Order viewData = dc.Orders.FirstOrDefault(o => o.OrderID == orderId);

    ViewData["PageTitle"] = "Order Details";
    return View(viewData);
}
```

This next block of code updates the tracking ID for the shipment for the POST request:

```
[Authorize(Roles = "StoreKeeper")]
[AcceptVerbs("POST"), ActionName("OrderDetail")]
public ActionResult OrderDetail_OnPost(int orderId, string trackingId)
{
    TheBeerHouseDataContext dc = new TheBeerHouseDataContext();
    Order viewData = dc.Orders.FirstOrDefault(o => o.OrderID == orderId);

    if (!String.IsNullOrEmpty(trackingId))
    {
        viewData.TrackingID = trackingId;
        viewData.Status = "Shipped";
        dc.SubmitChanges();

        // send tracking information to shopper
        SendTrackingEmail(viewData.TrackingID, viewData.CustomerEmail);

        TempData["SuccessMessage"] =
        "Order Status has been changed to SHIPPED, " +
        "and the customer has been notified.";
    }

    ViewData["PageTitle"] = "Order Details";
    return View(viewData);
}
```

This code works much like the GET request except for one fact; it takes a parameter called `trackingId`, which is the tracking code for the shipment. You need to update the order object and save this tracking e-mail back to the database. But before you return the result, you need to send an e-mail announcing to the shopper that her order is being shipped. You do this through a method called `SendTrackingEmail` that just sends a simple e-mail to the user saying:

```
to: {shopper e-mail}
from: {pay pal account}
subject: Order has been shipped

Your package has been shipped, your tracking # is {tracking id}
```

After the e-mail is sent you set a success message for the administrator and return the result to the view.

This action has the following route:

❑   store/admin/orders/{orderId}

store/admin/orders/{orderId}

This route is used to display the preceding action.

```
routes.MapRoute(
    "CommerceOrderDetail",
    "store/admin/orders/{orderId}",
    new { controller = "Commerce", action = "OrderDetail", orderId = (int?)null }
);
```

The ManageShipping Action

The last part of your administration of the store is to create and manage shipping methods for your shoppers. This action will be available only to the StoreKeeper role and will display all shipping methods ordered by title.

```
[Authorize(Roles = "StoreKeeper")]
public ActionResult ManageShipping()
{
    TheBeerHouseDataContext dc = new TheBeerHouseDataContext();
    var viewData = dc.ShippingMethods.OrderBy(sm => sm.Title);

    ViewData["PageTitle"] = "Manage Shipping";
    return View(viewData);
}
```

This action has the following route:

❑   store/admin/shipping

store/admin/shipping

This route is used to display the preceding action.

```
routes.MapRoute(
    "CommerceManageShipping",
    "store/admin/shipping",
    new { controller = "Commerce", action = "ManageShipping" }
);
```

The CreateShipping Action

This next action is a service for creating a shipping method through an AJAX call. It is available only to the StoreKeeper role and its only return value is the identity of the shipping method that was just created by the administrator.

```
[Authorize(Roles = "StoreKeeper")]
[Service, HttpPostOnly]
public ActionResult CreateShipping(string title, decimal price)
{
    TheBeerHouseDataContext dc = new TheBeerHouseDataContext();
    ShippingMethod shippingMethod = new ShippingMethod() {
        Title = title,
        Price = price,
        AddedDate = DateTime.Now,
        AddedBy = User.Identity.Name
    };
    dc.ShippingMethods.InsertOnSubmit(shippingMethod);
    dc.SubmitChanges();
    var viewData = dc.ShippingMethods.OrderBy(sm => sm.Title);
    return View("ManageShipping", viewData);
}
```

The route for this action uses the standard `{controller}/{action}` route, so requests to this action method can be accessed through

❑   `commerce/CreateShipping`

The DeleteShipping Action

The last action we are going to discuss in this chapter is a service for deleting a shipping method through an AJAX call. Like your other administration methods it will be available only to users with the StoreKeeper role.

```
[Authorize(Roles = "StoreKeeper")]
[Service, HttpPostOnly]
public ActionResult DeleteShipping(int id)
{
    TheBeerHouseDataContext dc = new TheBeerHouseDataContext();
    ShippingMethod shippingMethod = dc.ShippingMethods.GetShippingMethod(id);

    dc.ShippingMethods.DeleteOnSubmit(shippingMethod);
    dc.SubmitChanges();

    var viewData = dc.ShippingMethods.OrderBy(sm => sm.Title);
    return View("ManageShipping", viewData);
}
```

As you can see, this action follows your standard AJAX request model of just returning the ID to indicate success for the action.

The route for this action uses the standard `{controller}/{action}` route, so requests to this action method can be accessed through

❑   `commerce/deleteshipping`

Implementing the View

Now that your model and controller actions are complete you can focus on your views. As you may have expected, your commerce module is full of different kinds of views. To help keep things organized in your mind, we will break down the views into several different sections. The first section discusses the administrative views that will allow you to manage departments, products, shipping methods, and orders. The second section goes over what the customer will see, such as the department views, product views, and the shopping cart. The last section discusses order processing with PayPal and shows you how to set up the order confirmation view.

Storefront Administration Views

Every store has to have a store administration section so that you can initially set up your product offering and organize it in a way that your customers can easily navigate. Because you can't even test your store without your store administration section being completed, we will go over how to create these views first. These views include all the views pertaining to department management, product management, shipping management, and order management.

The ManageStore.aspx View

Your first view will be a simple store administration landing view. This view contains links that will allow you to jump right into product management, department management, shipping management, and order management. Figure 10-13 shows you what this looks like in the sample application.

Figure 10-13

Fortunately for you, there is no dynamic content on this view so setup is extremely simple. You will want to create a new folder called `Commerce` in your `Views` folder. Like the other sections, this folder will house the majority of your commerce views. Once that is done, place the following markup in your view:

```
<asp:Content ID="Content2" ContentPlaceHolderID="MainContent" runat="server">
    <div class="commerce">
        <h2><%= Html.ActionLink("Manage Departments", "ManageDepartments") %></h2>
        <p>This section will allow you to add "Departments" to your store. A
department is like a category such as Mugs, Brews, and Accessories</p>
    </div>
```

```
                <hr />

                <div class="commerce">
                    <h2><%= Html.ActionLink("Manage Products", "ManageProducts") %></h2>
                    <p>This section will allow you to add Products to your store.</p>
                </div>
                <hr />

                <div class="commerce">
                    <h2><%= Html.ActionLink("Manage Shipping Options", "ManageShipping") %></
h2>
                    <p>You can configure different shipping options and pricing here.</p>
                </div>
                <hr />

                <div class="commerce">
                    <h2><%= Html.ActionLink("Manage Orders", "ManageOrders") %></h2>
                    <p>View currently active orders placed in the store and update their
statuses here.</p>
                </div>
                <hr />
        </asp:Content>

        <asp:Content ID="Content3" ContentPlaceHolderID="SidebarContent" runat="server">
        <% Html.RenderPartial("~/Views/Shared/Commerce/CommerceSidebar.ascx"); %>
        </asp:Content>
```

Again, you are just creating simple HTML markup with the exclusion of the links you are using. The description text of the different areas can be changed to whatever you like. This view will also be invoked by the `ManageStore` method that you created earlier in your controller.

Store Sidebar

You may have noticed that at the bottom of your landing page you created a commerce sidebar. This sidebar is similar to other administrative sidebars you have previously built. Because it is being used by this particular view, we will go over its creation next. As with other sidebars, you will need to place it in the `Shared` folder under `Views` and create a separate commerce folder for it. Once that is done, all you need to do is create a control called `CommerceSidebar` and include the following HTML:

```
        <div id="commerce-admin" class="boxed">
        <h2 class="title">Store</h2>
        <div class="content">
        <ul>
            <li class="first">
                <%=Html.ActionLink("Manage Departments","ManageDepartments") %></li>
            <li><%= Html.ActionLink("Create Department", "CreateDepartment") %></li>
            <li><%= Html.ActionLink("Manage Products", "ManageProducts") %></li>
            <li><%= Html.ActionLink("Create Product", "CreateProduct") %></li>
            <li><%= Html.ActionLink("Shipping Options", "ManageShipping") %></li>
            <li><%= Html.ActionLink("Manage Orders", "ManageOrders") %></li>
        </ul>
        </div>
        </div>
```

This sidebar is not very complex and includes pretty much the same links listed for your storefront administration landing page.

The CreateDepartment.aspx View

Once your landing view is in place, you can get started creating the contents of your storefront. The first step is to create product categories that you will call departments. To do this you need to create a new view called `CreateDepartment` that will look like Figure 10-14 once it is completed.

Figure 10-14

The CreateDepartment view is a simple form that allows you to enter in the name of the department, its order in the sort, an image you may affiliate with it, and a description. The view is rendered by the CreateDepartment and the CreateDepartment-OnPost methods you created earlier in your controller. Because this view is so similar to editing a department, it will also be used by EditDepartment and the EditDepartment-OnPost methods. The markup for this view is shown here:

```
<asp:Content ID="Content2" ContentPlaceHolderID="MainContent" runat="server">
<% Html.RenderPartial("~/Views/Shared/Message.ascx"); %>

<form method="post" action="<%= Url.Action(this.ViewContext.RouteData.
Values["action"] as string, "Commerce") %>" class="department-create">

    <p class="field input"><label for="title">Title</label><br />
        <%= Html.TextBox("title", null, new { maxlength = 256 })%>
        <span class="input-message"></span></p>

    <p class="field input"><label for="importance">Importance</label><br />
        <%= Html.TextBox("importance", null, new { maxlength = 3 })%>
        <span class="input-message"></span></p>

    <p class="field input"><label for="imageUrl">Image</label><br />
        <%= Html.TextBox("imageUrl",null, new { maxlength = 256 })%>
        <span class="input-message"></span></p>

    <p class="field input"><label for="description">Description</label><br />
        <%= Html.TextArea("description") %>
        <span class="input-message"></span></p>

    <%= Html.Hidden("id", ViewData["id"])%>
    <p><button type="submit" id="deparment-create-button"><%= ViewData["PageTitle"]
%></button></p>

</form>
</asp:Content>

<asp:Content ID="SidebarContent" ContentPlaceHolderID="SidebarContent"
runat="server">
<% Html.RenderPartial("~/Views/Shared/Commerce/CommerceSidebar.ascx"); %>
</asp:Content>

<asp:Content ID="ScriptContent" ContentPlaceHolderID="ScriptContent"
runat="server">

<script type="text/javascript" src="/content/scripts/manage-department.js"></
script>

<% if (IsPostBack) { %>
<script type="text/javascript">
    ValidateDepartment();
</script>
<% } %>
</asp:Content>
```

You are able to use this view for both editing and creating departments because the MVC framework is smart enough to automatically populate data in the model that corresponds to the name of the element on your form if it is available. Thus for creation, because no data is available, all the fields are empty, but when the view is used for editing, data is available and those fields will be populated. Your second area of interest is the JavaScript that you will be using to validate your form.

manage-department.js

This JavaScript is similar to your previous modules in that it uses jQuery to verify that certain fields in your form are populated. The following code outlines how this is accomplished:

```
$("#title").focus(function() { ShowMessage(this,
    "Enter the title for your department."); });

$("#importance").focus(function() { ShowMessage(this,
    "(optional) Enter the order of importance that you want the departments shown
in."); });

$("#imageUrl").focus(function() { ShowMessage(this,
    "The relative web path of an image you want to be shown with products in this
department."); });

$("#description").focus(function() { ShowMessage(this,
    "Enter a short description of the department to display to your users."); });

function ValidateTitle() {
    return VerifyRequiredField("#title", "required");
}

function ValidateImageUrl() {
    return VerifyRequiredField("#imageUrl", "required");
}

function ValidateDescription() {
    return VerifyRequiredField("#description", "required");
}

function ValidateDepartment() {
    var validTitle = ValidateTitle();
    var validImage = ValidateImageUrl();
    var validDescription = ValidateDescription();

    return validTitle && validImage && validDescription;
}

$("form.department-create").validate(ValidateDepartment);
```

You are also using jQuery to show hover-over instructions to the users while they are completing the form. In your validation, if any of the items do not validate properly you return a `false`, which short-circuits the POST request and shows the appropriate error messages.

The ManageDepartment.aspx View

Now that you have actually created departments you can start to manage them. Your management view will give you the ability to edit existing departments and delete them when they become obsolete. Your `ManageDepartments` view will be invoked by the `ManageDepartments` controller method that you created earlier. You will also accept a collection of the `Departments` as your model. The markup for this view looks like this:

```
<asp:Content ID="MainContent" ContentPlaceHolderID="MainContent" runat="server">

<% Html.RenderPartial("~/Views/Shared/Message.ascx"); %>

<div id="departments">
<% foreach (Department department in ViewData.Model) { %>
    <div class="admin" id="admin-<%= department.DepartmentID %>">
        <%= Html.ActionLink("Edit", "EditDepartment", new { = department.
DepartmentID })%> | 
        <a href="#" class="delete-department-button" meta:id="<%= department.
DepartmentID %>">Remove</a>
    </div>
    <% Html.RenderPartial("~/Views/Shared/Commerce/DepartmentItem.ascx",
department); %>
    <div id="spacer-<%= department.DepartmentID %>"><hr /></div>
<% } %>
</div>
</asp:Content>

<asp:Content ID="SidebarContent" ContentPlaceHolderID="SidebarContent"
runat="server">
<% Html.RenderPartial("~/Views/Shared/Commerce/CommerceSidebar.ascx"); %>
</asp:Content>

<asp:Content ID="ScriptContent" ContentPlaceHolderID="ScriptContent"
runat="server">
<script type="text/javascript" src="/content/scripts/commerece.js"></script>
</asp:Content>
```

This view uses a collection of the `Department` entities as its model. As you have done in the past, you need to set the `Inherits` property in the `@Page` header as follows:

```
Inherits="System.Web.Mvc.ViewPage<IEnumerable<TheBeerHouse.Models.Department>>"
```

As mentioned earlier, this view shows you your departments and gives you links to edit and delete departments. You can see that you have created a custom user control called `DepartmentItem` that you are using to render your department information. This control will also be used later on to display your department information to your customers. It is for this reason that the editing and deletion links have been purposefully left out of this user control. Figure 10-15 gives you an idea of what this view will look like.

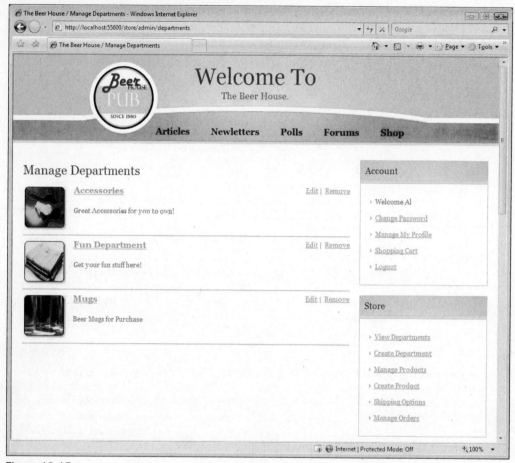

Figure 10-15

The edit link in your view fires off the `EditDepartment` controller method, which will use the `CreateDepartment` view. You will notice that your view is passing this `actionlink` to your `departmentID`, which it will use to render the right department information. Your remove link, on the other hand, doesn't appear to do anything at face value. This is because you are using JavaScript to invoke the `DeleteDepartment` method in your controller and remove the department from your view without causing a full POST back. This is a really nice feature because it reduces the amount of information being transmitted both ways, and it gives the view a thick-client feel.

commerce.js for Departments

Your `commerce.js` file will be used as a generic script throughout your commerce module. For management of departments you will want to put into this file the ability to intercept the delete-department-button click and also to remove divs pertaining to the deletion. The following code snippet shows you how this is accomplished:

```
$(".delete-department-button").click(function() {
    var departmentId = $(this).attr("meta:id");
    $.post(
        "/Commerce/DeleteDepartment",
        { id: departmentId },
        function(data) {
            $("#department-" + data.object.id).remove();
            $("#admin-" + data.object.id).remove();
            $("#spacer-" + data.object.id).remove();
        },
        "json"
    );
    return false;
});
```

Your first method, which does the click interception, sends out the departmentID to your DeleteDepartment controller method. If the call is successful, it calls a second method, which removes the department div, the admin div, and the spacer div. This second method is what makes the department information magically "disappear" from your view without the use of a POST back. Of course your return false ensures that the link's post request is short-circuited.

Department Item

The final element to making your ManageDepartments view work properly is to create the DepartmentItem.ascx control. As mentioned earlier, this control will show generic information pertaining to a particular department. This control will be used both in your store administration section and your actual store itself. The control expects an instance of the Department model object. From the ManageDepartments markup you can see you are using a foreach loop to pass it individual departments. The markup for this control looks like this:

```
<div id="department-<%= ViewData.Model.DepartmentID %>" class="department">
    <img src="<%= ViewData.Model.ImageUrl %>" title="<%= ViewData.Model.Title %>"
alt="<%= ViewData.Model.Title %>" class="main-image" />
    <h3><a href="<%= Url.Action("ViewDepartment", new { DepartmentID = ViewData.
Model.DepartmentID}) %>"><%= ViewData.Model.Title%></a></h3>
    <p><%= ViewData.Model.Description%></p>
</div>
```

As you can see from this code snippet, you are using the department object to show the title, the department's image, and its description. Once this control is built, you now will have all the elements necessary to manage your departments.

The CreateProduct.aspx View

Now that you have created your departments, you will want to fill these departments with all the products you plan on offering. Building a product selection for a storefront will probably involve a lot of legwork depending on how large the storefront is. Many online storefronts offer dozens if not hundreds of different products. The task gets especially complicated when you are dealing with variations of products, such as special pricing for extra large and small items. If possible, we would suggest you use the supplier's in-house inventory system to help populate most of this data for you automatically. SSMS offers several very easy-to-use conversion wizards that can make this process a snap. In the interests of keeping this chapter to the point though, we will go right into building a user interface for the store keeper to directly enter the products right into the website. To do this, you will first need a create/modify product view. The markup for this view looks like this:

```
<asp:Content ID="Content2" ContentPlaceHolderID="MainContent" runat="server">

<% Html.RenderPartial("~/Views/Shared/Message.ascx"); %>

<form method="post" action="<%= Url.Action(this.ViewContext.RouteData.
Values["action"] as string, "Commerce") %>" class="product-create">

    <p class="field input"><label for="departmentID">Department</label><br />
        <%= Html.DropDownList("departmentID")%>
        <span class="input-message"></span></p>

    <p class="field input"><label for="title">Title</label><br />
        <%= Html.TextBox("title")%>
        <span class="input-message"></span></p>

    <p class="field input"><label for="description">Description</label><br />
        <%= Html.TextArea("description")%>
        <span class="input-message"></span></p>

    <p class="field input"><label for="sku">SKU</label><br />
        <%= Html.TextBox("sku")%>
        <span class="input-message"></span></p>

    <p class="field input"><label for="unitPrice">Unit Price</label><br />
        <%= Html.TextBox("unitPrice")%>
        <span class="input-message"></span></p>

    <p class="field input"><label for="discountPercentage">Discount Percentage</
label><br />
        <%= Html.TextBox("discountPercentage")%>
        <span class="input-message"></span></p>

    <p class="field input"><label for="unitsInStock">Units In Stock</label><br />
        <%= Html.TextBox("unitsInStock")%>
        <span class="input-message"></span></p>

    <h3>Image Data</h3>

    <p class="field input"><label for="smallImageURL">Thumnail URL</label><br />
        <%= Html.TextBox("smallImageURL")%>
        <span class="input-message"></span></p>
```

```
<p class="field input"><label for="fullImageURL">Full Image URL</label><br />
    <%= Html.TextBox("fullImageURL")%>
    <span class="input-message"></span></p>

<%= Html.Hidden("id", ViewData["id"])%>
<hr />
<p><button type="submit" id="product-create-button">Save Product</button></p>

</form>

</asp:Content>

<asp:Content ID="Content3" ContentPlaceHolderID="SidebarContent" runat="server">
<% Html.RenderPartial("~/Views/Shared/Commerce/CommerceSidebar.ascx"); %>
</asp:Content>

<asp:Content ID="ScriptContent" ContentPlaceHolderID="ScriptContent"
runat="server">
<script type="text/javascript" src="/content/scripts/tiny_mce/tiny_mce_src.js"></
script>
<script type="text/javascript" src="/content/scripts/manage-product.js"></script>
<% if (IsPostBack) { %>
<script type="text/javascript">
    ValidateArticle();
</script>
<% } %>
</asp:Content>
```

This form is very similar to your create/edit department form except for the fact that it has more fields. Those fields include the product title, its description, SKU, unit price, discount percentage, units in stock, assigned department, thumbnail image location, full-sized image location, and a hidden input to track the product ID. Note that in the markup you are registering the tinyMCE JavaScript; that is because you want to use a rich text editor for your description. This control will be absolutely critical for putting rich HTML into your product description to include possible product charts, images, extensive descriptions, and reviews. Remember that users absolutely love valuable information and if you've ever been to Amazon.com, you can easily see that it includes everything it possibly can about its products. Amazon.com also has an extensive review section that you may want to integrate into your storefront if you have a lot of user activity in your store.

manage-product.js

Now that your view is complete, you will need a custom JavaScript file to do the validation and hover-over text like the rest of your forms. The code for this file looks like this:

```
$("#title").focus(function() { ShowMessage(this,
    "Enter your product name here."); });
$("#sku").focus(function() { ShowMessage(this,
    "Enter your SKU number here."); });
$("#unitPrice").focus(function() { ShowMessage(this,
    "Enter the unit price of this product."); });
$("#discountPercentage").focus(function() { ShowMessage(this,
    "Enter the percent off you want to give for this product."); });
```

```
$("#unitsInStock").focus(function() { ShowMessage(this,
    "Total number of units of this product you have in stock."); });
$("#smallImageURL").focus(function() { ShowMessage(this,
    "The url to the thumbnail for this product."); });
$("#fullImageURL").focus(function() { ShowMessage(this,
    "The url to full sized image of this product."); });

function ValidateTitle() {
    return VerifyRequiredField("#title", "required");
}

function ValidateDescription() {
    return VerifyRequiredField("#description", "required");
}

function ValidateProduct() {
    return ValidateTitle()
        && ValidateDescription();
}

$("form.product-create").validate(ValidateProduct);

/********************************************************************************
* Rich Text Editor
********************************************************************************/

var bodyEditor;

$(document).ready(function() {
    bodyEditor = new tinymce.Editor("description", __editorConfig);
    bodyEditor.onChange.add(function(ed) { bodyEditor.save(); });
    bodyEditor.onClick.add(function(ed) { ShowMessage("#description",
        "Enter the description of your product here."); });
    bodyEditor.render();
});

// clears the message from the description when another input gets focus
$(":input")
    .focus(function() { HideMessage("#description"); })
    .blur(function() { HideMessage("#description"); });
```

Don't let the size of this file scare you; you have a lot more inputs that need to be validated and described. You are also using a WYSIWYG editor and have to build in some logic to bind it to the description text area. All of this code is very similar to the code you have already created in your articles module. Once these two files are in place and bound to the `CreateProduct` and `EditProduct` controller method, your result should look like Figure 10-16.

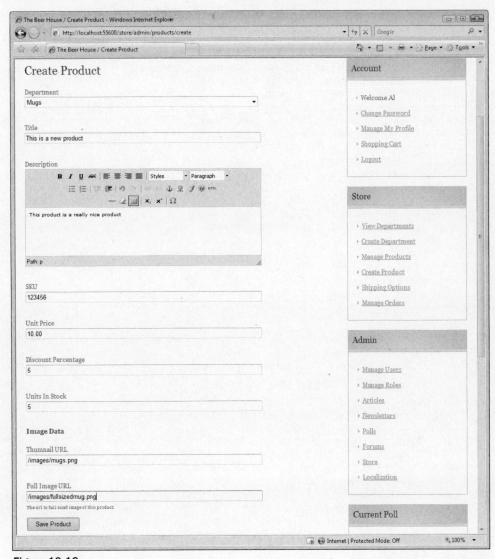

Figure 10-16

The ManageProducts.aspx View

Once you are able to create and edit products, you will want a management page similar to your department management page, except for products. The designs of the two views are almost identical. Your ManageProducts view will be tied into your ManageProducts controller method and will accept a collection of your Product model object. The following example shows the markup in this view:

```
<asp:Content ID="Content2" ContentPlaceHolderID="MainContent" runat="server">
<% Html.RenderPartial("~/Views/Shared/Message.ascx"); %>
<br />
<div id="products">
```

```
<% foreach (Product product in ViewData.Model) { %>
    <div class="admin">
        <%= Html.ActionLink("Edit", "EditProduct", new { controller = "Commerce",
productID = product.ProductID })%> | 
        <a href="#" class="delete-product-button" meta:id="<%= product.ProductID
%>">Remove</a>
    </div>
    <% Html.RenderPartial("~/Views/Shared/Commerce/AdminProductItem.ascx",
product); %>
        <div id="spacer-<%= product.ProductID %>"><hr /></div>
<% } %>
</div>

</asp:Content>

<asp:Content ID="Content3" ContentPlaceHolderID="SidebarContent" runat="server">
<% Html.RenderPartial("~/Views/Shared/Commerce/CommerceSidebar.ascx"); %>
</asp:Content>

<asp:Content ID="ScriptContent" ContentPlaceHolderID="ScriptContent"
runat="server">
<script type="text/javascript" src="/content/scripts/commerece.js"></script>
</asp:Content>
```

Similar to the departments management view, you have a custom control for product item details that you will use in your main storefront. You also have a separate administrative `div` that allows your user to edit and delete products. Finally, you are registering your `commerce.js` file that will have JavaScript within it to allow you to delete a product without doing a full POST back.

Admin Product Item

Your `AdminProductItem.ascx` control takes in an instance of your `Product` model, which you are populating using a `foreach` loop in your `ManageProduct` view. This view is a little different from your department item control because you are providing some additional information. Not only does this control contain a thumbnail image, a product name, and a description, but it also shows regular pricing information, sale pricing information, and units available. When done correctly, your control should look like what you see in Figure 10-17.

The markup to accomplish this is fairly simple:

```
<div id="product-<%= ViewData.Model.ProductID %>" class="product">
    <img src="<%= ViewData.Model.SmallImageUrl %>" title="<%= ViewData.Model.Title
%>" alt="<%= ViewData.Model.Title %>" class="main-image" />
    <h3><a href="<%= Url.Action("CreateProduct", new { ProductID = ViewData.Model.
ProductID}) %>"><%= ViewData.Model.Title%></a></h3>
    <p><%= ViewData.Model.Description%></p>
    <p>Regular Price: <b><%= ViewData.Model.UnitPrice.ToString() %></b> |
    Sale Price: <b><font color="red"><%= ((ViewData.Model.UnitPrice * (100 -
ViewData.Model.DiscountPercentage)) / 100 ).ToString("C") %></font></b> |
    Units Available: <b><%= ViewData.Model.UnitsInStock %></b></p>
</div>
```

The only element that really requires explanation is the globalization settings. Because you are calling the data directly from your model, you are invoking currency formatting right in the view. This will format your amounts with the symbol associated with currency in your particular area. This could include the pound symbol, or the euro symbol, or the dollar symbol, to name a few. We go into globalization in further detail in the next chapter.

Figure 10-17

commerce.js for Products

You already created a JavaScript file called `commerce.js` when you built your departments section; you will want to add to this file the following code:

```
$(".delete-product-button").click(function() {
    var productId = $(this).attr("meta:id");
    $.post(
        "/Commerce/DeleteProduct",
        { id: productId },
        function(data) {
            $("#product-" + data.object.id).remove();
            $("#admin-" + data.object.id).remove();
```

```
            $("#spacer-" + data.object.id).remove();
        },
        "json"
    );
    return false;
});
```

As before, you are intercepting the delete button click event; this will fire off your `DeleteProduct` controller method and then erase the product from the view. Again, you are also short-circuiting the click event of the hyperlink. Once these views and support files are created you should be able to create, remove, edit, and view products in your storefront.

The ManageShipping.aspx View

Now that you have created the views to build your departments and products, you will also need a view to add shipping options. We decided to consolidate the creation of shipping options, management, and removal all into a single view. This view will accept a collection of the `ShippingMethod` model object and it will be rendered by your `ManageShipping` controller method. The code for this view looks like this:

```
<asp:Content ID="Content2" ContentPlaceHolderID="MainContent" runat="server">

<table width="95%" cellpadding="2" cellspacing="0" align="center" summary="User
Grid" border="1" id="shipping-table">
<thead>
<tr style="background-color:#A8C3CB;">
    <th>Shipping Option</th>
    <th>Price</th>
    <th style="width:100px"> </th>
</tr>
</thead>
<tbody>
<% foreach(ShippingMethod shippingMethod in ViewData.Model) { %>
<tr id="shipping-method-<%= shippingMethod.ShippingMethodID %>">
<td align="center"><%= shippingMethod.Title %></td>
<td align="center"><%= shippingMethod.Price.ToString("C") %></td>
<td align="center"><a href="#" class="delete-shipping-method-button" meta:id="<%=
shippingMethod.ShippingMethodID %>"><img border="0" alt="Delete Role" src="/
content/images/DeleteSymbol.png" title="Delete Role" align="middle"/></a></td>
</tr>
<% } %>
</tbody>
<tfoot>
<tr style="background-color:#A8C3CB;">
    <td align="center"><%= Html.TextBox("title")%></td>
    <td align="center"><%= Html.TextBox("price")%></td>
    <td align="center"><button id="add-shipping-method-button" type="submit">Add</
button></td>
</tr>
</tfoot>
</table>

</asp:Content>

<asp:Content ID="Content3" ContentPlaceHolderID="SidebarContent" runat="server">
<% Html.RenderPartial("~/Views/Shared/Commerce/CommerceSidebar.ascx"); %>
```

```
</asp:Content>

<asp:Content ID="ScriptContent" ContentPlaceHolderID="ScriptContent" runat="server">
<script type="text/javascript" src="/content/scripts/commerece.js"></script>
</asp:Content>
```

We would like to point out several elements of note with this view. First off, you have a form at the top to allow you to create new shipping methods, and at the bottom of the view you have a table you are creating to show you the current shipping options. This table also gives the user the ability to remove any shipping options at will. Finally, you are registering the commerce.js because you have code in there that allows you to delete shipping options without having to do a full POST back. If everything was implemented properly, your view should look like Figure 10-18.

Figure 10-18

commerce.js for Shipping Methods

In the next section of your commerce.js file, you are adding in the code that allows you to delete shipping methods without causing a full POST back. This code will also remove the table row that pertains to that shipping method because you have given each table row its own ID in your ManageShipping view.

```
$(".delete-shipping-method-button").live("click", function() {
    var shippingMethodId = $(this).attr("meta:id");
    $.post(
        "/Commerce/DeleteShipping",
        { id: shippingMethodId },
        function(data) {
            $("#shipping-method-" + data.object.id).remove();
        },
        "json"
```

```
        );
        return false;
    });

    $("#add-shipping-method-button").click(function() {
        var title = $("#title").val();
        var price = $("#price").val();

        $.post(
            "/Commerce/CreateShipping",
            { title: title, price: price },
            function(data) {
                var html = '<tr id="shipping-method-' + data.object.id + '">';
                html += '<td align="center">' + title + '</td>';
                html += '<td align="center">' + price + '</td>';
                html += '<td align="center"><a href="#" class="delete-shipping-method-
button" meta:id="' + data.object.id + '"><img border="0" alt="Delete Role" src="/
content/images/DeleteSymbol.png" title="Delete Role" align="middle"/></a></td>';
                html += '</tr>';

                $("#shipping-table tbody").append(html);
                $("#title").val("");
                $("#price").val("");
            },
            "json"
        );

        return false;
    });
```

That basically wraps up managing shipping methods. There are really only two fields involved, the name and the cost, and that's about it. Of course, you may want to factor weight into your shipping options, or charge more for certain geographical areas. For the purposes of this demonstration we decided to keep it simple and to the point.

Storefront

After building your product, department, and shipping management sections you can move on to the most important part: your storefront. The storefront is the portion of your online shop that the general public will use to browse your selection of products or services. This subsystem, like the store management subsystem, will require a landing page for people to go to initially.

The Index.aspx View

To keep things simple, we decided that for the TheBeerHouse storefront we would send people directly to the Index view. This view is going to be very similar to your ManageDepartments view except for the fact that you are not giving the user any capability to edit or delete departments. Like ManageDepartments, we are using a collection of the Department model object and the view is actually being rendered by the ViewDepartments controller method. The markup that will drive this view is listed here:

```
<asp:Content ID="MainContent" ContentPlaceHolderID="MainContent" runat="server">

<% Html.RenderPartial("~/Views/Shared/Message.ascx"); %>
```

```
<div id="departments">
<% foreach (Department department in ViewData.Model) { %>
    <% Html.RenderPartial("~/Views/Shared/Commerce/DepartmentItem.ascx",
department); %>
    <hr />
<% } %>
</div>
</asp:Content>
```

The user control that you are using to display the description and image of your department is the exact same one used for the ManageDepartment view. Don't you just love being able to reuse code! The Index view, the first page of your e-commerce store that customers will see, is shown in Figure 10-19.

Figure 10-19

The ViewDepartment.aspx View

Now that a landing page is in place, your prospective customer will hopefully be interested in one of your departments and click on it. You will then want to list all of the available products under that department. For the TheBeerHouse website we created a new commerce view called `ViewDeparment` that accepts a collection of the `Product` model object and is rendered by the `ViewDepartment` controller method. The following markup was used to create this view:

```
<asp:Content ID="Content2" ContentPlaceHolderID="MainContent" runat="server">
<% Html.RenderPartial("~/Views/Shared/Message.ascx"); %>
<br />
<div id="products">
<% foreach (Product product in ViewData.Model) { %>
    <% Html.RenderPartial("~/Views/Shared/Commerce/ProductItem.ascx", product); %>
    <hr />
<% } %>
</div>

</asp:Content>
```

The only thing special about this view is the `ViewProductItem` control that we are populating with a `foreach` loop that passes in a product. You will need to create this control, set the product entity as its model, and place it into the shared `Commerce` folder.

Product Item

Because you have slightly different requirements than the `AdminProductItem` control you built earlier, namely the ability to add products to a customer's cart, you are forced to create a new control. The code for this control is as follows:

```
<div id="department-<%= ViewData.Model.ProductID %>" class="department">
    <img src="<%= ViewData.Model.SmallImageUrl %>" title="<%= ViewData.Model.Title
%>" alt="<%= ViewData.Model.Title %>" class="main-image" />
    <h3><a href="<%= Url.Action("ViewProduct", new { ProductID = ViewData.Model.
ProductID}) %>"><%= ViewData.Model.Title%></a></h3>
    <p><%= ViewData.Model.Description%></p>
    <p>Regular Price: <b><%= ViewData.Model.UnitPrice.ToString("C") %></b> |
    Sale Price: <b><font color="red"><%= ((ViewData.Model.UnitPrice * (100 -
ViewData.Model.DiscountPercentage)) / 100 ).ToString("C") %></font></b> |
    Units Available: <b><%= ViewData.Model.UnitsInStock %></b></p>
    <form method="post" action="<%= Url.Action("AddShoppingCartItem",new {
ProductID = ViewData.Model.ProductID, Price = (ViewData.Model.UnitPrice * (100
- ViewData.Model.DiscountPercentage)) / 100, Title = ViewData.Model.Title, SKU =
ViewData.Model.SKU}) %>" class="add-cart">
        <p><button type="submit" id="add-item-button">Add to Cart</button></p>
    </form>
</div>
```

To understand what is going on with this view and control, please refer to Figure 10-20. This view shows the sale price of your product, the actual price, units available, its description, image, and the option to add it to the cart. Let us take a moment to say that this product page is extremely basic. It is enough to get the job done, but you might want to think about putting in a review rating, or possibly some additional info. If you want to get really fancy about it, you could even build a system that presents products based on a particular user's purchasing history. You may notice that the Amazon.com home page implements this feature.

For the sake of simplicity, we present a basic e-commerce product summary page and leave it to you to determine what additions would be relevant and useful to include for your particular store.

Figure 10-20

The ViewProduct.aspx View

The final part of your storefront, before you begin the checkout process, is being able to see detailed information about your products. It's nice to have a list of products available organized by department, but sometimes you just need more information. To accomplish this, we created a view called

`ViewProduct` that does just that for you. It is an entire page dedicated to a single product, and with your WYSIWYG editor on your edit products view, you can show pictures, specifications, reviews, and much more in this view. The `ViewProduct` view is very straightforward; of course you are going to accept an instance of your product entity as your model, and you will use the following markup:

```
<asp:Content ID="Content2" ContentPlaceHolderID="MainContent" runat="server">

<% Html.RenderPartial("~/Views/Shared/Message.ascx"); %>
<div class="left">
<img src="<%= ViewData.Model.FullImageUrl %>" title="<%= ViewData.Model.Title %>"
alt="<%= ViewData.Model.Title %>" class="main-image" />
</div>

<div class="right">
<h3><%= ViewData.Model.Title%></h3>
<p>SKU: <%= ViewData.Model.SKU%></p>
<p><%= ViewData.Model.Description%></p>

<p>Regular Price: <b><%= ViewData.Model.UnitPrice.ToString("C") %></b> |
Sale Price: <b><font color="red"><%= ((ViewData.Model.UnitPrice * (100 - ViewData.
Model.DiscountPercentage)) / 100 ).ToString("C") %></font></b> |
Units Available: <b><%= ViewData.Model.UnitsInStock %></b></p>

</div>
<br />
<hr />
<form method="post" action="<%= Url.Action("AddShoppingCartItem","Commerce", new
{ ProductID = ViewData.Model.ProductID,  Price = (ViewData.Model.UnitPrice * (100
- ViewData.Model.DiscountPercentage)) / 100, Title = ViewData.Model.Title, SKU =
ViewData.Model.SKU}) %>" class="add-cart">
    <p class="field input"><label for="quantity">Quantity: </label><%= Html.
TextBox("quantity", 2, new { style = "width: 50px" })%>
    <p><button type="submit" id="add-item-button">Add to Cart</button></p>
</form>

</asp:Content>
```

Figure 10-21 shows you exactly how this page should look if everything is implemented properly.

You have your larger image to the left and a very detailed description to the right of the page that includes a bullet list. You also could put in some of your own custom HTML to include images and a specifications chart for this mug. Finally, toward the end of your view, you offer information pertaining to pricing, units available, how many items the customer is interested in having, and the ability to add the item to the shopping cart, which we talk about next.

Figure 10-21

The ViewShoppingCart.aspx View

Now that you have a customer who is interested in a particular product and actually clicked your Add to Cart button, you will want him to go to a shopping cart page that will summarize his order. At the end of your AddShoppingCartItem controller method call you are rendering the ViewShoppingCart view; the code for this is listed here:

```
<table width="100%" cellpadding="2" cellspacing="0" align="left" summary="User
Grid" border="1">
<tr style="font-weight:bold; background-color:#A8C3CB; ">
<td align="center">Item</td>
<td style="width:100px" align="center">Quantity</td>
<td style="width:100px" align="center">Price</td>
<td style="width:20px"> </td>
</tr>
```

Because this view is absolutely massive, we are going to break it down into its component parts. In the first section, you are simply providing a drop-down for the user to select a shipping method and the header portion of your table that will display your shopping cart information. In your header, you provide a field for the item's title, the quantity, and the unit price.

```
<% foreach(ShoppingCartItem shoppingCartItem in ViewData.Model) { %>
<tr id="item-<%= shoppingCartItem.Product.ProductID %>">
<td align="center"><%= shoppingCartItem.Title %></td>
<td align="center"><%= shoppingCartItem.Quantity %></td>
<td align="center"><%= shoppingCartItem.Price.ToString("c") %></td>
<td align="center"><a class="delete-item-button" meta:id="<%= shoppingCartItem.
Product.ProductID %>" href="#"><img border="0" alt="Delete Role"  src="/content/
images/DeleteSymbol.png" align="middle"/</a></td>
</tr>
<% } %>
```

In this second section you are doing a simple `foreach` loop against your model, which is your shopping cart, and pulling the individual shopping cart items out of it. Notice also that you are providing a link for the users to allow them to delete a shopping cart item. This will post back to the `DeleteShoppingCartItem` controller method that we discussed earlier in this chapter.

```
<tr style="font-weight:bold; background-color:#A8C3CB;">
<td> </td>
<td align="right">Subtotal:</td>
<td align="center"><%= ViewData.Model.SubTotal.ToString("c")%></td>
<td> </td>
</tr>

<tr style="font-weight:bold; background-color:#A8C3CB;">
<td align="right"><form method="post" action="<%= Url.Action("ViewShoppingCart","Co
mmerce") %>" class="add-cart"><%= Html.DropDownList("shippingMethod")%></form></td>
<td align="right">Shipping:</td>
<td align="center"><%= ViewData.Model.ShippingPrice.ToString("c") %></td>
<td> </td>
</tr>

<tr style="font-weight:bold; background-color:#A8C3CB;">
<td> </td>
<td align="right">Total:</td>
<td align="center"><%= ViewData.Model.Total.ToString("c") %></td>
<td> </td>
</tr>
```

Of course, no shopping cart would be complete without a totals section. The preceding code will calculate out the shipping price and the total price for you. Note that we are not including any tax calculations or tax fields. Generally with online shopping, with the exception of a few states, there are no taxes for online purchases if you live outside the state of the storefront. For simplicity purposes, we did not build a taxation class for the e-commerce module, but they are relatively simple to create, especially if your state uses a flat sales tax.

```
<tr>
<td> </td>
<td> </td>
<td align="center">
```

We are going to break here, because there is an order processing form that goes between the preceding code block and the following code block, but we need to take a special look at it so we will specifically look at the PayPal integration piece of this page in the next section called "Order Processing."

```
</td>
<td> </td>
</tr>
</table>

</asp:Content>

<asp:Content ID="ScriptContent" ContentPlaceHolderID="ScriptContent" runat="server">
<script type="text/javascript" src="/content/scripts/commerece.js"></script>
</asp:Content>
```

The last part of your view will either update your shopping cart information or check you out via the PayPal system. We discuss in much greater detail in the next section how the online payment piece of this works. For now, take note that you are filling in input information that you will then post over to PayPal's servers for processing. We'd also like you to be aware of two attributes that you will be calling from the `web.config`; they are the `PaypalAccount` attribute and the `PaypalServer` attribute. The `PaypalAccount` attribute is the e-mail that corresponds to your account, and the `PaypalServer` attribute defines where the HTML data post goes to. Again, this is discussed in much greater detail in the order processing section. Figure 10-22 shows how your shopping cart will look.

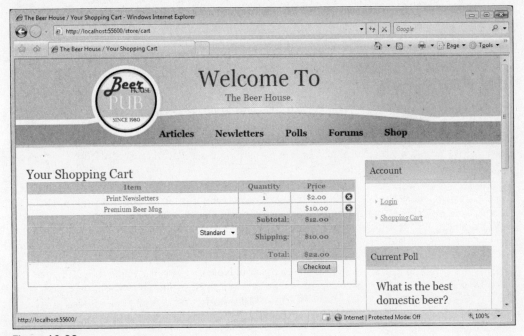

Figure 10-22

Remember that because you used your profile provider, and because this saves your information into a database, a user's shopping cart will persist every time he comes back to the website. Its contents will only be cleared if the user executes the order or manually deletes the contents of the cart. This is a great strategy because oftentimes a user may find that he wants to purchase a particular item, but doesn't have a credit card on him at the time, or in my case has to ask his wife for permission. Regardless of the reason, it is a really good practice to retain this information as a reminder to the user.

Note that you may have your membership table fill up with shopping carts of anonymous users. We have not discussed it in this chapter but you should come up with your own mechanism for clearing this table of data on a semi-regular basis.

commerce.js for Shopping Cart

The last piece of the shopping cart is the `commerce.js` section that will handle the deletion of shopping cart items. Similar to the other JavaScript in this file, you are doing a post to your `DeleteShoppingCartItem` controller method, which will handle the actual deletion of the item. The `RemoveItem` method will delete the product from your shopping cart without a POST back.

```
$(".delete-item-button").click(function() {
    var productId = $(this).attr("meta:id");
    $.post(
        "/Commerce/DeleteShoppingCartItem",
        { id: productId },
        function(data) {
            $("#item-" + data.object.id).remove();
        },
        "json"
    );
    return false;
});
```

Order Processing

The order processing system will probably be the most difficult system to implement in this book. The main reason is because you are doing integration, and as any seasoned developer will tell you, all of your pain and suffering usually involves integrating one system to another (preferably not a legacy system). Because you are relying on PayPal to do your payment processing, you must configure your e-commerce module to submit requests in a format PayPal likes, and decipher the data that it returns back to you.

Let's start with a brief overview of how the PayPal service will be expecting information from you. In your shopping cart view, you saw that you were making a post to the PayPal payment processing server at the end of it. The post included the passing over of multiple pieces of information that you populated using hidden input fields on your page. You added multiple items to the post by using a `foreach` loop and incrementing the hidden input `id` field names. See the following code:

```
<form id="Paypal" name="Paypal" action="<%= TheBeerHouse.Configuration.
TheBeerHouseSection.Current.Commerce.PayPalServer %>" method="post">
<input type="hidden" name="cmd" value="_cart" />
<input type="hidden" name="upload" value="1" />
<input type="hidden" name="business" value="<%= TheBeerHouse.Configuration.
TheBeerHouseSection.Current.Commerce.PayPalAccount %>" />

<input type="hidden" name="shipping" value="<%= ViewData.Model.ShippingPrice.
ToString("N2") %>" />
```

```
<input type="hidden" name="amount" value="<%= ViewData.Model.Total.ToString("N2")
%>" />

<% int count = 1; %>
<% foreach(ShoppingCartItem shoppingCartItem in ViewData.Model) { %>
    <%=Html.Hidden("amount_" + count, shoppingCartItem.Price.ToString("N2"))%>
    <%=Html.Hidden("item_name_" + count, shoppingCartItem.Title) %>
    <%=Html.Hidden("item_number_" + count, shoppingCartItem.Product.ProductID) %>
    <%=Html.Hidden("quantity_" + count, shoppingCartItem.Quantity) %>
    <%count++;%>
<% } %>

<button type="submit" id="paypal-checkout-button" value="PayPal">Checkout</button>
</form>
```

Note that in this example you are not using every possible field available, such as a taxation field or a currency field. If you want an in-depth understanding about how the PayPal API works, we suggest that you visit its website at `developer.paypal.com`; it has tons of resources to assist you with your integration. After taking a look at how the PayPal API, works you will need to create PayPal test accounts. To do this visit `developer.paypal.com` and click the Sign Up Now button. You will be required to fill out a form and agree to their policies, but once you have completed that you should be taken to a screen that looks like Figure 10-23.

Figure 10-23

this section

Once you are there, click "Create a preconfigured buyer or seller account" under the Test Accounts menu. Create both a buyer account and a seller account; you will need both because you want to test out the user experience and ensure your seller account receives funding from the buyer. Figure 10-24 should be what you receive from the Sandbox when you successfully created the accounts. Take note of both accounts and their passwords because you will need them later.

Figure 10-24

Now that you have a PayPal account set up properly, copy and paste the login e-mail of your store test account into your web.config. Insert the following line into the TheBeerHouse node of your web.config:

```
<commerece PaypalServer="https://www.sandbox.paypal.com/cgi-bin/webscr"
PaypalAccount="Store@TheBeerHouseExample.com" />
```

This defines both your store test account and the PayPal server URL you want your transactions to post to. After this is complete you will want to log in to your store account via the PayPal Sandbox so you can set some additional information. In Figure 10-24, you see an orange button that says Enter Sandbox Test Site. Make sure that the store account is selected and then click that button. It will send you into a dummy account that looks just like a real one, except for the fact the subdomain is the Sandbox.

You can set a multitude of different options here, from what you plan on taxing people, to your business name, to its address, home page, what you want the invoices to look like, and much more. For the purposes of getting this e-commerce module processing transactions, you will want to log in and click the Profile node under My Account. If you are in the right place, your screen should look like Figure 10-25.

Once here you will want to click Website Payment Preferences under the Selling Preferences section of this page. In this page, shown in Figure 10-26, you are going to explicitly tell PayPal where to send the users once they have completed their transactions. This is a very important step because on their return you get an order number for each transaction and you can use those order numbers to complete their orders.

Unfortunately, this is where your setup begins to get convoluted. Because PayPal uses its own servers, you can't simply put `localhost` into the return URL because PayPal has no idea where you are. Therefore, you have to provide an IP address and then a valid URL that will receive the order information. This may sound straightforward, but believe us it's not! The first step only applies if you have a router in your house that has DHCP activated. In most homes this is the case, so you will have to log in to your router and set a redirection rule to send all incoming port 80 traffic to your local IP address. This setup varies from router to router, so we recommend consulting your router manual for specific instructions on port forwarding.

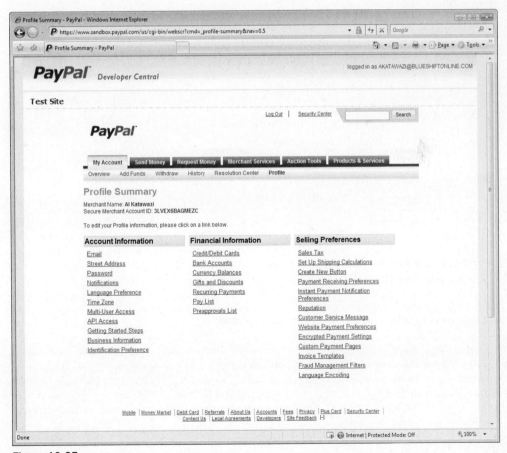

Figure 10-25

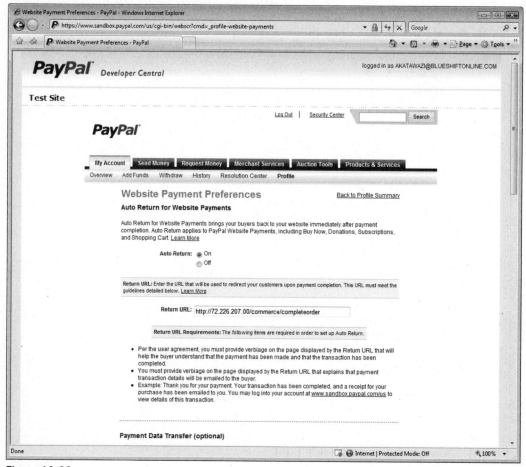

Figure 10-26

The second step is to set up your website to use IIS instead of Cassini. This is seemingly a straightforward operation by just right-clicking your website project file and going to properties. Once there, you would click the Web tab and select "Use Local IIS Web server" under Servers. Figure 10-27 shows the screen where you would make this adjustment.

We personally had a lot of trouble getting this to work properly because we were using IIS 7 and we had to add a number of things that were not running by default. Hopefully, this process will go a lot smoother for you.

If you really want to avoid having to set up a website on IIS or simply do not have access to your router, there is another less elegant method. When PayPal sends you back to your IP and it fails to load because it's not set up properly, simply change your IP address in the address bar manually to localhost and add the port that Visual Studio is using, and that should work.

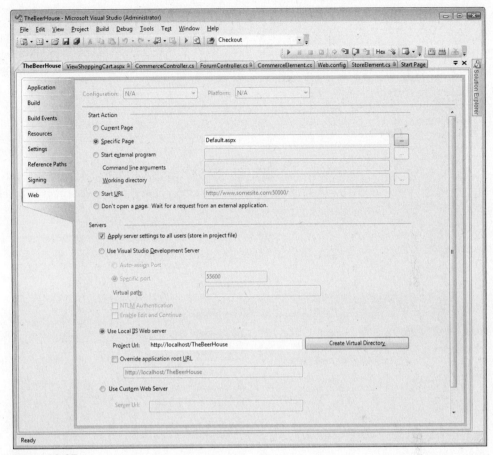

Figure 10-27

Now that PayPal has been completely set up you can tie your online checkout process with PayPal's checkout process. Because PayPal will be sending you back to your original site once the user has made payment, you will want to create two new views the user can come to.

The CompleteOrder.aspx View

Your first view is the CompleteOrder.aspx view, the page the user will come to if the transaction has successfully completed. The CompleteOrder controller method will be responsible for rendering this view. This very simple view tells the users that their order has been processed and gives them their confirmation number. The markup for this view is as follows:

```
<asp:Content ID="Content2" ContentPlaceHolderID="MainContent" runat="server">
<h3>Order Sucess</h3>
<p>Your order has been sucessfully recieved. Your order number is <%=
ViewData["OrderNumber"].ToString() %>. You will recieve an email when your order
has shipped out, thank you for your business.</p>
</asp:Content>
```

The TransactionError.aspx View

This view is rendered by the `CompleteOrder` controller method when something has gone wrong with the transaction. It, too, is a simple form that provides instructions to the user to contact technical support. Of course, you are free to change this to meet your own purposes. The markup for this view looks like this:

```
<asp:Content ID="Content2" ContentPlaceHolderID="MainContent" runat="server">
<h3>Problem with your order</h3>
<p>We aplogize but there seems to be an issue processing your order. Please call
The Beer House at 1-888-555-5555 or email us at support@TheBeerHouseExample.com</p>
</asp:Content>
```

To review what the entire checkout process should look like, your users will pick a basket of goods that they would like to purchase (resulting in a screen that looks like Figure 10-22) and then click the Checkout button.

Once they have done this, they will be sent out of your website and to PayPal's payment processing service, as shown in Figure 10-28. Note that if you are using the Sandbox, you must be logged in for this to work properly.

Figure 10-28

Now if you expand the shopping cart as shown in Figure 10-28, you should see all the items you picked plus the shipping price for the shipping type the user would have selected in the shopping cart. If you put in taxation rules into PayPal, those should appear as well. Now log in with the test customer account and click the Pay Now button on the next page to complete the order. You should be sent to a page that looks like Figure 10-29, which indicates you are going to be redirected.

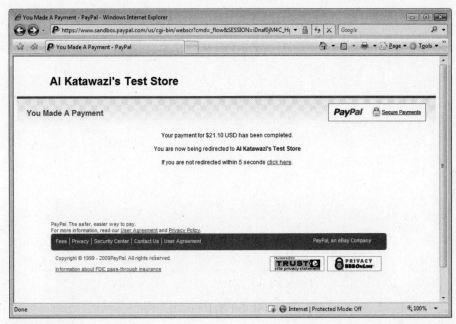

Figure 10-29

If the redirection went well, and the request for information from the PDT system was successful, and if the transaction amount expected matches the transaction amount made, an order will be put through and you should go to the `CompleteOrder` view, shown in Figure 10-30.

If, on the other hand, your order failed to process for whatever reason, you will go to the `TransactionError` view, shown in Figure 10-31.

That's basically it for payment processing. Once you have completed your transaction, the owner of the storefront will have to potentially ship out items, and update order information as discussed in the next section.

Figure 10-30

Figure 10-31

Order Management

The last part of your e-commerce module is going to be the order management system. This consists of two parts. The first part is through PayPal; you should be able to log in to PayPal and view transactions that have been processed within its system. The second part is managing the transactions through your own system, because you keep your own records in your database.

After a customer has placed an order, he will usually expect an e-mail immediately afterwards indicating that his order has been received and is being processed. Fortunately, you can simply rely on PayPal's system to send out that initial notification for you. The second notification, however, needs to come from your website; this notification will pertain to the item being shipped. If you run a store that sells online widgets, you don't need to worry about this, but if you actually ship physical goods you'll want to continue reading on.

The ManageOrder.aspx View

You may recall that at the beginning of the Solution section you created an administrative landing page for your storefront. One of the links on that page was Managing Orders. You are now going to create the view that this link points to. The controller method that will fire off this view will be called ManageOrders and it will take a collection of your Order model object. Take a look at the markup in this view:

```
<asp:Content ID="Content2" ContentPlaceHolderID="MainContent" runat="server">

<table width="95%" cellpadding="2" cellspacing="0" align="center" summary="User
Grid" border="1">
<thead>
<tr style="background-color:#A8C3CB; ">
    <th>ID#</th>
    <th>Status</th>
    <th>Paypal Transaction #</th>
    <th>Order Placed Date</th>
    <th>Amount</th>
    <th> </th>
</tr>
</thead>
<tbody>
<% foreach(Order order in ViewData.Model) { %>
<tr>
<td align="center"><%= order.OrderID%></td>
<td align="center"><%= order.Status%></td>
<td align="center"><%= order.TransactionID%></td>
<td align="center"><%= order.AddedDate%></td>
<td align="center"><%= order.SubTotal.ToString("C")%></td>
<td align="center"><%= Html.ActionLink("view", "OrderDetail", new { orderId =
order.OrderID }) %></td>
</tr>
<% } %>
</tbody>
</table>

</asp:Content>

<asp:Content ID="Content3" ContentPlaceHolderID="SidebarContent" runat="server">
<% Html.RenderPartial("~/Views/Shared/Commerce/CommerceSidebar.ascx"); %>
</asp:Content>
```

This view essentially contains a very simple table that you are using to indicate the general information pertaining to this order. It provides the status of the order, its ID number, its PayPal ID number, the date the order was purchased, and its price; pretty standard information for an `OrderManagement` view. This view also provides the store keeper or admin the ability to drill down into the details of an individual order by clicking the View Details link shown in Figure 10-32.

Figure 10-32

The OrderDetail.aspx View

View Details actually invokes the `OrderDetail` controller method, which will render the `OrderDetail` view. The code for this view is broken down into several sections to help better explain what is going on:

```
<asp:Content ID="Content2" ContentPlaceHolderID="MainContent" runat="server">

<% Html.RenderPartial("~/Views/Shared/Message.ascx"); %>
```

```
<p><%= Html.ActionLink("Return to Order Management", "ManageOrders") %></p>

<div id="OrderInformation" class="form">
<h2 class="title">Order Information</h2>
<div class="content">
    <strong>Order ID: </strong><%= ViewData.Model.OrderID %><br />
    <strong>Paypal Transaction ID: </strong> <%= ViewData.Model.TransactionID %><br
/>
    <strong>Order Placed By: </strong> <%= ViewData.Model.AddedBy %><br />
    <strong>Order Date Placed: </strong> <%= ViewData.Model.AddedDate %><br />
    <strong>Order Status: </strong> <%= ViewData.Model.Status %>
</div>
</div>
```

The first section of this view gives you all the basic information such as transaction ID, PayPal transaction ID, who placed the order, the date of the order, and its current status.

```
<div id="ShippingInformation" class="form">
<h2 class="title">Shipping Information</h2>
<div class="content">
    <address><%= ViewData.Model.ShippingFirstName %> <%= ViewData.Model.
ShippingLastName %><br />
    <%= ViewData.Model.ShippingStreet %><br />
    <%= ViewData.Model.ShippingCity %>, <%= ViewData.Model.ShippingState %> <%=
ViewData.Model.ShippingPostalCode %></address><br />

    <strong>Email:</strong> <a href="mailto:<%= Model.CustomerEmail %>"><%= Model.
CustomerEmail %></a><br /><br />
    <strong>Shipping Details: </strong><%= ViewData.Model.ShippingMethod %><br />

    <% if(String.IsNullOrEmpty(ViewData.Model.TrackingID)) { %>
    <form method="post" action="<%= Url.Action(this.ViewContext.RouteData.
Values["action"] as string, "Commerce") %>" class="product-create">
    <%= Html.Hidden("id", ViewData["id"])%>
        <label for="trackingID"><strong>Tracking Number:</strong></label>
        <%= Html.TextBox("trackingId")%>
        <button type="submit" id="product-create-button">Save</button>
    </form>
    <% } else { %>
    <strong>Tracking Number: </strong><%= ViewData.Model.TrackingID %>
    <% } %>
</div>
</div>
```

This second part shows shipping details, and provides the option for the store keeper or admin to enter in a tracking number if one isn't already present. If they click the Submit button here, it will return the transaction ID to your controller method and send out your e-mail message to your customer.

```
<table width="100%" cellpadding="2" cellspacing="0" align="left" summary="User
Grid" border="1">
<thead>
```

```
<tr style="background-color:#A8C3CB;">
    <th>Item</th>
    <th style="width:100px">Quantity</th>
    <th style="width:100px">Price</th>
</tr>
</thead>
<tbody>
<% foreach(OrderItem orderItem in ViewData.Model.OrderItems) { %>
<tr>
    <td align="center"><%= orderItem.Title%></td>
    <td align="center"><%= orderItem.Quantity%></td>
    <td align="right"><%= (orderItem.UnitPrice * orderItem.Quantity).
ToString("C")%></td>
</tr>
<% } %>
</tbody>
<tfoot>
<tr style="background-color:#A8C3CB;">
    <th align="right" colspan="2">Sub Total:</th>
    <td align="right"><%= Model.SubTotal.ToString("C")%></td>
</tr>
<tr style="background-color:#A8C3CB;">
    <th align="right" colspan="2">Shipping:</th>
    <td align="right"><%= Model.Shipping.ToString("C")%></td>
</tr>
<tr style="background-color:#A8C3CB;">
    <th align="right" colspan="2">Total:</th>
    <td align="right"><%= (Model.SubTotal + Model.Shipping).ToString("C")%></td>
</tr>
</tfoot>
</table>
</asp:Content>

<asp:Content ID="Content3" ContentPlaceHolderID="SidebarContent" runat="server">
<% Html.RenderPartial("~/Views/Shared/Commerce/CommerceSidebar.ascx"); %>
</asp:Content>
```

The last section provides very detailed information as to what exactly was ordered. If you decide not to build your own automatic order fulfillment system, this section will be useful in seeing what you need to ship out to your customer. If you were able to integrate all this properly in the view, you should see something like Figure 10-33.

That concludes the Solution section. As you have now realized, quite a bit of work is involved in building an e-commerce system. The solution you built here is very basic and there is a lot of room for improvement. We are sure you already have some of your own ideas!

Figure 10-33

Summary

In this chapter you implemented a fully working e-commerce store with most of the basic features including complete catalog and order management, a persistent shopping cart, integrated online payment via credit card, and more. All this required a fairly short amount of time to design and implement, and this was due in no small part to the powerful new features in ASP.NET 3.5 such as profiles (which enable you to implement persistent shopping carts in minutes instead of several hours or days) and the way the MVC framework is well-suited for the dynamic creation of views. Some improvements that we would suggest are:

❑ Improving the correspondences between the system and the customer by customizing the order e-mails and expanding on the order completion view.

❑ For a professional-looking site you could use a seamless payment gateway to allow you to keep your customers on your site while they are submitting their payment information.

❑ Numerous improvements could be made in terms of the product description, up-selling, and integration to other storefronts such as Amazon or Google using file or RSS feeds.

❑ Expanding the order management section by allowing administrators or store keepers to change any element of the order or create their own custom order statuses.

❑ Building a review system so that your users can indicate whether or not they liked the product.

For some additional great ideas on building a successful e-commerce site, visit some of your favorite storefronts and see what they are doing. Some of ours are Amazon.com and NewEgg.com because they seem to know what we want even before we do! If you were not put off by all the work that was involved in building an e-commerce module, expanding its capabilities should not be an issue. On the other hand, if you just want a quick-and-dirty solution, many fantastic third-party order management systems and e-commerce modules are available that you could buy outright. As you may know, classic ASP.NET forms will work with your MVC without any major issues, especially if you have a server with IIS 7.

11

Localizing the Site

We live in a global community consisting of people from many countries. The term *localizing* refers to the capability to present a site in the language of the local user and to use the correct symbols for currency, decimals, dates, and so on. ASP.NET 2.0 added some new features to its arsenal for localizing a site that made localization a snap. The developer was free from writing clumsy code for managing multiple languages, locale settings, translated strings, and other resources that can be compiled into independent files that could easily be plugged into the site. The localization features in ASP.NET 2.0 also gave the developer the ability to add additional localization support even after the site had been deployed. With the release of the MVC framework, these same localization features are still available but should be customized to work under the Model-View-Controller design pattern. In this chapter you learn how to use these features in MVC to create a truly globalized site with little effort on your part.

Problem

These days, it seems that the word *globalization* is used everywhere. The beauty of the Internet and the World Wide Web is that you can reach anyone who has a computer and a phone line or some other sort of Internet connection, be it for fun, passion, business, or so on. Nevertheless, if you want to be able to communicate with people, you must speak (or write) a language the people can understand. Due to the great proliferation of English as a primary or secondary language, many sites use English as their base language, even if they are not run by people for which English is their native language. However, offering a site in the user's first language is often a great advantage over competitors that don't, because all users find it easier and more comfortable reading their primary language even when they can understand others. This is true not only for text but also for the format used to display and parse numbers, dates, and currency names. In fact, an Italian reader would interpret 07/02/2006 as February 7, whereas an American would interpret it to be July 2. And though this may cause misunderstandings when reading the date, it may also cause errors when users insert data in one format when the system expects a different one. For this reason, any modern site that wants to target a worldwide audience must be multi-language, displaying numbers and dates according to the user's local settings, and translating the full site's text (or at least the most important parts) into the user's primary language.

Fully localizing a site based on dynamic content (articles, products, forums, polls, and so on) is an extremely difficult task, and you can approach it in a number of ways. The difficulty varies considerably depending on whether you intend to localize everything or just static content (text on the page layouts, menus, links, and page, section and field titles and descriptions, and so forth). ASP.NET contains features that significantly simplify localizing static parts of a site, and this is what we cover in this chapter. Conversely, localizing the dynamic content would be much harder and would require quite a lot of rework on the database, the UI structure, and the object model. If that's what you really need to achieve, it's usually better to create separate language-specific sites with their own content.

Design

The first thing you need to decide when localizing a site is whether you want to localize only static content (menus, links, copyright notices, the usage agreement, titles and descriptions for pages, tables, fields, buttons, and other controls) or whether you want to provide a translation for everything including articles, poll questions, product listings, and so on. Let us state up front that adding support for complete localization would be very difficult at this stage of development, because it would require a complete rework of the database design, the DAL, the BLL, and the UI; it's something that should be planned very early during the initial site design and the foundation development. Complete localization in a single website is not a common requirement. You normally wouldn't translate every article on the site, forums, polls, and newsletters, but rather only those that have a special appeal to one country or language-specific audience. You may also want to present information differently for different languages — changing something in the site's layout, for example. Because of this, most sites that want to be fully localized "simply" provide multiple copies of their pages under different subdomains or folders, one copy for each language. For example, there could be www.contoso.com/en and www.contoso.com/it or http://en.contoso.com/ and http://it.contoso.com/. Each copy of the site would target an independent database that only contains data for that specific language. If you take this approach, you'll only need to make static content localizable, and then install the site multiple times for multiple languages. Another advantage of this strategy is that with completely separate websites, you can have different people managing them independently who would be able to create content that best suits the audience for that particular language. In this chapter you localize the site's static content, and support the different locale settings for dates and numbers in different languages.

Your sample site will be installed only once, and the language for which the site is localized will be specified by each user at registration time or later from the Edit Profile page. This setting is mapped to the `Preferences.Culture` profile property, which was described and implemented in Chapter 5. An alternative would be to detect the user's favorite language from the browser's settings, which are sent to the web server with the request's header. However, many nontechnical users don't understand how to set this, and it would be difficult to explain it on your site and answer support questions from people who don't understand it. Therefore, it's better to directly ask users which language they'd like to use, so they understand what it's for and how to change it. The next section provides an overview of the new features introduced by ASP.NET 2.0 regarding localization of static content.

A Recap of Localization in ASP.NET 1.x

ASP.NET (and the .NET Framework in general) has always supported localization to some extent. Displaying and parsing dates and numbers according to a specific culture, for example, only requires you to create a `System.Globalization.CultureInfo` instance for that culture (for example, "en-US" for American English or "it-IT" for Italian of Italy), and use it as the value for the `CurrentCulture` property of the current executing thread (`System.Threading.Thread.CurrentThread`). For example, after executing the following statement, all dates and numbers displayed to the user would follow the Italian format by default:

```
System.Threading.Thread.CurrentThread.CurrentCulture =
    System.Globalization.CultureInfo.CreateSpecificCulture("it-IT");
```

The preceding code would have been typically placed into the page's `Init` or `Load` event handlers, or even better in the `Application_BeginRequest` event handler accessible from the `Global.asax` file, so that it would execute for all pages of the site without replicating the code in each of them. Putting it into a custom base class from which all pages' code-behind class would inherit is another great solution.

Localizing static content by dynamically setting the properties of the various controls on a page (such as `Text`, `ToolTip`, and so on) with values translated to a specific language was much less easy in ASP.NET 1.x, though. You needed to create one or more resource files for each language you wanted to support (such as `Messages.resx` for the generic default culture, `Messages.it-IT.resx` for Italian, `Messages.fr-FR.resx` for French, and so on) and write key-value pairs into these files (they are XML files, but Visual Studio has an editor that allows editing them in a grid), where the *value* was some string translated into the language of the resource file. Then, from the code-behind class of every page that you wanted to localize, you had to manually write something like this:

```
using System.Resources;
using System.Reflection;

ResourceManager rm = new ResourceManager(
    "WebProjectName.Messages", Assembly.GetExecutingAssembly());
Title.Text = rm.GetString("Title");
```

This would instantiate a `ResourceManager` object for the resources stored in a class called `WebProjectName.Messages` (created from the `.resx` file). Then, it would load the string resource with a key equal to `"Title"`, and use it for the `Text` property of a label control. `ResourceManager` automatically loads the resource class from the current assembly, or from one of the satellite resource-only assemblies, according to the culture specified by the `CurrentUICulture` property of the current thread. If the resource for the current UI culture is not found, the `ResourceManager` will fall back to the resources for the default neutral culture.

Note that the property used by `ResourceManager` to load the correct satellite assemblies is `CurrentUICulture` and not `CurrentCulture`, which is instead used to display and parse numbers and dates. The two properties are often set to the same culture, but not necessarily.

Localization Features in ASP.NET 2.0

Although ASP.NET 1.x had technology for localizing sites, the solution outlined in the preceding section had a number of problems that made the process unwieldy and prone to error. The most significant issues were as follows:

❑ You had to create the resource files manually, in a folder of your choice. However, the final name of the resource class would change because of the inclusion of the folder name, and many developers didn't realize this. This often resulted in errors whereby resources could not be found.

❑ You had to specify the resource key as a string, and if you misspelled this string it resulted in errors whereby resources could not be found. If this were an enumeration it could avoid the possibility of misspelling it.

❑ You had to invent your own naming convention to choose key names that would identify the same resource but for different pages, such as `Page1_Title` and `Page2_Title`. This is because there were only site-wide global resources, and not page-specific resources. You could also create different `.resx` files, one for each page, and thus simulate page-specific resources. This was merely a way to physically separate resources as they were still accessible by any other page.

❑ Above all, you had to manually write the code to set the `Text` property (or any other localizable property) to the proper string loaded by means of a `ResourceManager`, because there wasn't a declarative way to do it from the `.aspx` markup file.

With ASP.NET 2.0 all this changes considerably, and even though under the covers things work pretty much the same, from the developer's vantage point things are much easier and more intuitive now. Here is a list of improvements, which are described in detail in the following subsections:

❑ **Strongly typed global resources:** Once you create a global resource file (like the ones you may have used under ASP.NET 1.x), it is dynamically compiled into a class, and you can immediately see and access the class listed under the `Resources` namespace. Each resource of the file is accessible as a property, and IntelliSense is provided by Visual Studio to make it easier to select the right one. No more mistyped resource names!

❑ **Page-level resources:** In addition to global resource files, you also have page-specific resource files, so that you can place the resource strings only in the page that uses them. This enables you to have a resource called `Title` for every view, with different values, because they are stored in separate files. You no longer have to come up with a naming convention such as using the page name as the prefix for the resource keys.

❑ **New localization expressions:** Similar to data binding expressions, these enable a developer to associate an expression to the properties to localize directly in the `.aspx` markup file, so you don't need any C# code. A special declarative syntax is also available to bind all localizable properties to resources in a single step. Programmatic localization is still possible, of course, and has been improved as mentioned before for the global resources.

❑ **Improved Visual Studio designer support:** This enables you to graphically associate a localization expression to a resource string from a dialog box, without requiring the developer to write any code. There's also a command to automatically generate the neutral language view-level resource file for the current view, which you can copy, rename, or translate to another language.

❑ **Auto detection of the Accept-Language HTTP header:** This is used to automatically set the page's UICulture and Culture properties, which correspond to the current thread's CurrentUICulture and CurrentCulture properties.

❑ **Custom providers:** Should you want to store localized resources in a data store other than .resx files, such as a database, you can do that by writing your own custom provider. This enables you to build some sort of online UI for managing existing resources, and create new ones for additional languages, without the need to create and upload new resource files to the server.

Localization Features in ASP.NET 3.5 and MVC

The latest version of ASP.NET 3.5 has had no changes or additional features added for localization since the .NET 2.0 Framework. The only thing that has changed is that with the ASP.NET MVC framework the implementation of localization has become slightly more complex due to the separation of the model, view, and controller. This section talks about how to use the same powerful localization features in ASP.NET with the MVC framework.

Using Global Resources

Global resources are shared among all models, views, and controllers, and are best suited to store localized data used in different places. When we say "data," we don't just mean strings, but also images, icons, sounds, and any other binary content. Now you access a resource file item (from the Add Item dialog box) under a folder named App_GlobalResources, which is a special folder handled by the ASP.NET runtime and Visual Studio 2008; you can insert data into the grid-style editor represented in Figure 11-1.

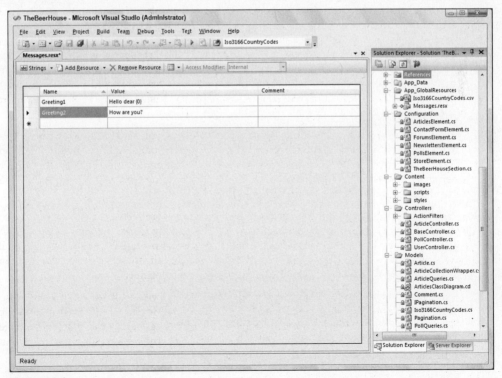

Figure 11-1

If you click the arrow on the right side of the editor's Add Resource toolbar button, you will be able to create an image or icon, or insert any other file. Figure 11-2 shows the window after choosing Images from the drop-down menu of the first toolbar icon (where Strings was selected in Figure 11-1) and after adding a few image files.

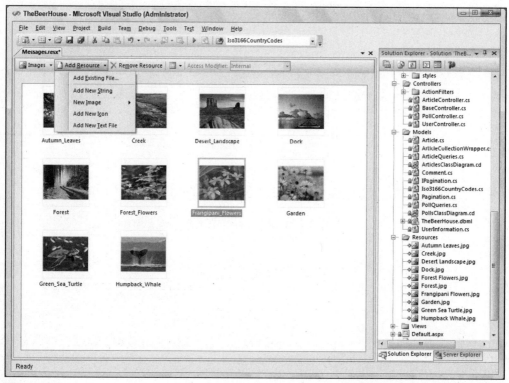

Figure 11-2

Once you have added a few strings and a few images, you can go to a controller class in the editor and type "Resources": IntelliSense will pop up a drop-down list with the names of the resource files added to the project; that is, Messages in the example shown in Figure 11-1. Then, when you type "Resources. Messages," it will list the string and image resources added earlier, and if you look closely at Figure 11-3, you'll also note that image resources are returned with the proper type of System.Drawing.Bitmap.

This results in less manual typing, less probability of mistyping a resource or key name, and thankfully less casting.

Programmatic access of resources is necessary in some cases, particularly when you need to retrieve data from controllers, and in this case you'll be happy to know that IntelliSense for dynamically compiled resources is also an option! Resource files can be accessed directly from the view as well, an especially useful technique when populating label information. The following code snippet shows an example of us accessing the first greeting:

```
<p class="field input">
    <label for="greeting">
```

```
        <%= HttpContext.GetGlobalResourceObject("Messages", "Greeting1")%>
    </label>
    <%= Html.TextBox("greeting") %>
</p>
```

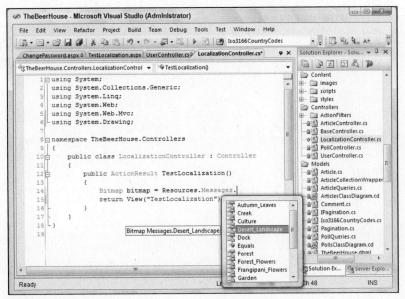

Figure 11-3

Our `HttpContext` contains the specific global and local resources within it necessary for us to extract our information. The `GetGlobalResourceObject` and `GetLocalResourceObject` allows you to enter in the class name and key of the object you would like from the resource file and returns it back to you. The preceding example shows how we got the first greeting message from our messages resource file.

Using Page-Level Resources

You can create page-level resources by creating resource files just as you do for global resources, but placing them under a folder named `App_LocalResources` (as opposed to `App_GlobalResources` used for global resources) located at the same level of the page to localize. For example, if the view is in the view folder, you'll create the `App_LocalResources` under the view folder, but if the view is under a subdirectory of the view folder, you'll create a `/[SubdirectoryName]/App_LocalResources` folder. This means you can have multiple `App_LocalResources` folders, whereas you can only have one `App_GlobalResources` folder for the whole site. The name of the resource file is also fundamental, because it must be named after the page or control file for which it contains the localized resources, plus the part with the culture name. For example, a culture-neutral resource file for `TestLocalization.aspx` would be named `TestLocalization.resx`, whereas it would be named `Localization.it-IT.resx` for the Italian resources. In Figure 11-4, you can see the organization of files in the Solution Explorer, and the resource file being edited in the grid editor.

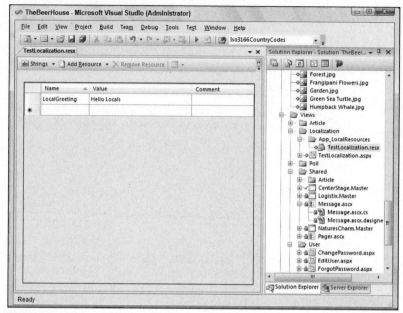

Figure 11-4

Once your local resource file is established, accessing it is easy. Simply use the following code snippet in your markup:

```
<%=HttpContext.GetLocalResourceObject("~/Views/Localization/TestLocalization",
"LocalGreeting", System.Globalization.CultureInfo.CurrentUICulture) %>
```

The `GetLocalResourceObject` method is slightly different from the `GetGlobalResourceObject` method because it relies on you to provide the actual path of the resource file. Remember that because you are using the MVC framework, you need to drop the extensions from your file name. In the preceding example we are accessing the `TestLocalization.resx` resource that is located in the localization folder under views. The second parameter in our method defines the element we are looking for within that resource file. In this case our local greeting should return back "Hello Locals." Lastly, we are passing in the current culture that is being used in this particular session so we can identify which message version should be displayed.

Using the Cultural Information Class

This handy but often overlooked class looks directly into the current thread and provides a wide array of cultural information about the user. This information can be manipulated by your controller classes to change the cultural information of the thread to align with the information stored in the user's profile. In this way you can allow the end users to determine in what way the website's information will be displayed to them.

The following table describes the most important properties.

Method	Description
CurrentCulture	Returns a `CultureInfo` object that provides information on the culture being used in the current thread.
CurrentUICulture	Returns a `CultureInfo` object that provides information on the culture being used by the resource manager of the operating system.
DateTimeFormat	Supplies you with the `DateTimeFormatInfo` object that is culturally specific.
InstalledUICulture	Returns a `CultureInfo` object that provides cultural information on the installed operating system. For example, if you were using the Italian version of Vista OS, this property would return Italian regardless of how you have configured your system.
NumberFormat	Provides you with the `NumberFormatInfo` object that provides culturally specific data for numbers, currencies, and percentages.

Setting the Current Culture

Once you've modified your page with localization expressions for the various controls displaying static content, and you've created local or global resource files for the different languages you want to support, it's time to implement a way to enable users to change the page's language. One method is to read the Accept-Language HTTP header sent by the client to the server, which contains the array of cultures set in the browser's preferences, as shown in the dialog box in Figure 11-5.

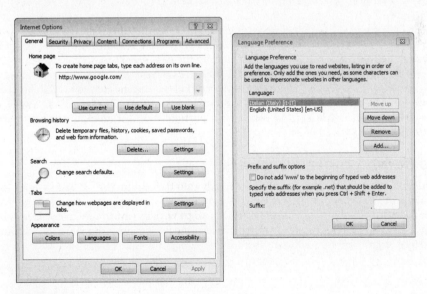

Figure 11-5

In ASP.NET 1.x, you would set the current thread's `CurrentCulture` and `CurrentUICulture` properties to the first item of the `UserLanguage` array of the `Request` object, which would contain the first language in the list. You would execute this code in the `Init` or `Load` event of a page (typically a `BasePage` class, so that all others would inherit the same behavior), or from the application's `BeginRequest` event, as shown here:

```
void Application_BeginRequest (Object sender, EventArgs e)
{
    if (Request.UserLanguages.Length > 0)
    {
        CultureInfo culture = CultureInfo.CreateSpecificCulture(
            Request.UserLanguages[0]);
        Thread.CurrentThread.CurrentCulture = culture;
        Thread.CurrentThread.CurrentUICulture = culture;
    }
}
```

In ASP.NET 2.0 you had to set the `culture` and `uiCulture` attributes of the `web.config` file's `<globalization>` element to `"auto"`, so that the user's favorite language would be retrieved and used automatically:

```
<configuration>
    <system.web>
        <globalization culture="auto" uiCulture="auto" />
        ...
    </system.web>
</configuration>
```

With the MVC framework and ASP.NET 3.5 you don't need to make any changes to your application to make it globalization-ready; it's already done for you automatically.

Figure 11-6 shows what the same page looks like when loaded for the American English or Italian language selected in the browser.

Automatically obtaining the culture using the `CultureInfo` object is nice but in some situations you'll prefer to set the culture yourself. This is because you'll need to extract the current culture from the user's profile, a session variable, or according to some other logic (we discussed earlier how it's a good idea to let users specify their language of choice). Setting a new culture within your controller based on the user's profile is simple to do; here is our example:

```
Thread.CurrentThread.CurrentCulture = new CultureInfo(HttpContext.Profile.
GetPropertyValue("Language") + "-" + HttpContext.Profile.GetPropertyValue("ContactI
nformation.Country"), false);
```

In this code we are directly modifying the culture of the current thread to whatever the users put down as their country of origin and their language of choice during registration. Because both are drop-downs with defaults we can rest assured that this code will function without issue.

> Note that thread information can only be changed when the code is fully trusted by the server. In many cases you will not want your application to have the capability to modify threads because it presents a material security risk to your web server.

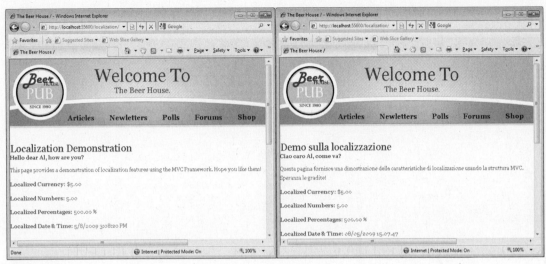

Figure 11-6

Solution

As a sample implementation for this chapter, we decided to create a small section in our application dedicated to demonstrating localization using the MVC framework. We opted not to use localization throughout the application because it would make the rest of the code unnecessarily complex and probably add another 20 pages of code! The examples provided here can be easily applied to the rest of the application if you wish; just remember that localization as a process needs to start very early in the software development cycle. Without further ado, these are the steps to make this solution a reality:

1. Develop both local and global resource files that will be used to provide culturally contextual localization data.

2. Create a localization controller that will assign the local culture based on the user's profile, and pass the sample data in a culturally contextual manner.

3. Create a localization test view that will present the data to us.

Creating the Resource Files

As previously discussed, your resource files will contain the information required to present culturally relevant information to your users. In our example we will create two global resource files, and two local resource files. Each will have one resource file with information in English, and the other with information in Italian. If you wanted to provide support for additional languages you would simply have to create additional resource files to provide the culturally relevant information.

To create a global resource file, you first need to create a global resource folder (remember only one of these can be created per web application). To create one of these, right-click your project, select Add, then Add ASP.NET Folder, and then App_GlobalResources, as shown in Figure 11-7.

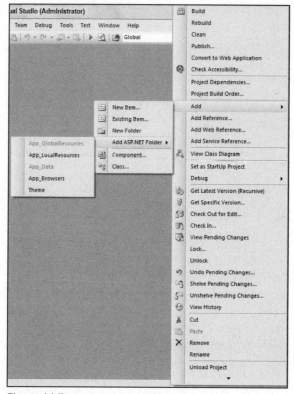

Figure 11-7

Once you have created the new App_GlobalResources folder you can now right-click it and add a new item to it. In the list you should see a resource file; label the resource file "Message." You should also create a second resource file called "Messages.it-IT." Open each and create a new string entry in both called "LocalGreeting." Add a local greeting in English for the default resource file and one in Italian for the Italian-specific resource file. An example of this screen is shown in Figure 11-8.

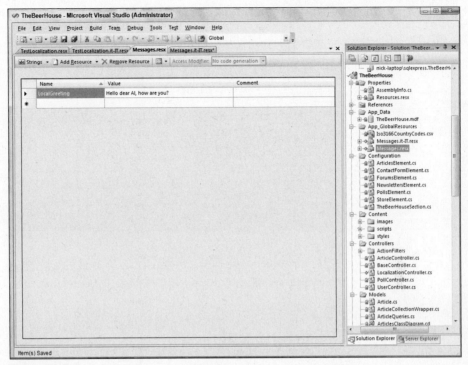

Figure 11-8

Creating the local resource file occurs in much the same way except you want your local resource file to fall in the same folder as your localization view page. In this case you will want to create a new folder called "localization" under the "views" folder. Right-click it, select Add New Item, then add ASP.NET Folder, and select App_LocalResources. Once the `App_LocalResources` folder is created, add a new resource file to it and make sure the name of the resource file corresponds with the name of the test view, in this case it will be "TestLocalization." Create a second resource file but instead of calling it just "TestLocalization," append the ".it-IT" to the end of the name to denote it is specifically for Italian users.

To demonstrate the local resource files, you will be adding the following strings to the resource files. The default English resource file looks like Figure 11-9.

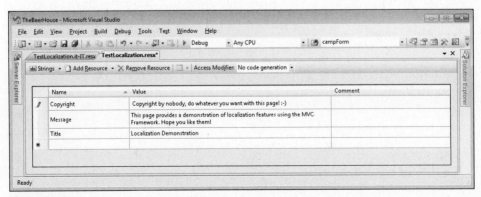

Figure 11-9

The local Italian resource file looks like Figure 11-10.

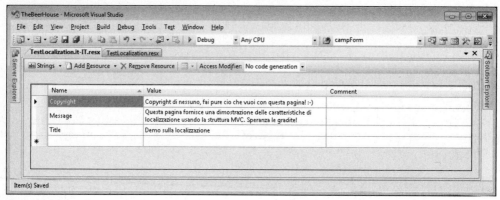

Figure 11-10

Once you have created these four files, at this point you should have all the contextual data necessary to demonstrate localization.

Creating a Localized View

Although you do not have access to many of the nice wizards and auto generation tools present in a traditional ASP.NET application, you are still able to use localization in your views. To demonstrate this you will start by creating a new view under your newly created localization folder called "TestLocalization." Within it you will place the following code:

```
<%@ Page Title="" Language="C#" MasterPageFile="~/Views/Shared/CenterStage.Master"
AutoEventWireup="true" Inherits="System.Web.Mvc.ViewPage" culture="auto" meta:resou
rcekey="PageResource1" uiculture="auto" %>

<asp:Content ID="Content2" ContentPlaceHolderID="MainContent" runat="server">

<h1><%= HttpContext.GetLocalResourceObject("~/Views/Localization/TestLocalization",
"Title", System.Globalization.CultureInfo.CurrentUICulture)%></h1>

<h3><%= HttpContext.GetGlobalResourceObject("Messages", "LocalGreeting", System.
Globalization.CultureInfo.CurrentUICulture)%></h3>

<p><%= HttpContext.GetLocalResourceObject("~/Views/Localization/TestLocalization",
"Message", System.Globalization.CultureInfo.CurrentUICulture)%></p>
<p><b>Localized Currency:</b> <%= ViewData["CurrencyExample"] %></p>
<p><b>Localized Numbers:</b> <%= ViewData["NumberExample"] %></p>
<p><b>Localized Percentages:</b> <%= ViewData["PercentageExample"] %></p>
<p><b>Localized Date & Time:</b> <%= ViewData["DateExample"] %></p>
<p><b><%= HttpContext.GetLocalResourceObject("~/Views/Localization/
TestLocalization", "Copyright", System.Globalization.CultureInfo.
CurrentUICulture)%></b></p>

</asp:Content>
```

You may notice that the uiculture is mentioned at the top of this view. This is something that the MVC framework automatically does for you, saving you from worrying about your site being globalization-ready. Some of the static information that you see on this view is being accessed directly from the appropriate resource file. This saves you the effort of having to go through the controller to obtain static, culturally appropriate content through the ViewData object. The example formatting items, on the other hand, require some level of logic to prep them before presenting them on the view.

Creating a Localized Controller

To bring this entire solution together you will need a new controller in your controllers folder called "LocalizationController." This controller will allow you to set the current culture of the thread based on the user's profile and to format various types of information into culturally appropriate formats. The code for the controller is as follows:

```
namespace TheBeerHouse.Controllers
{
    public class LocalizationController : Controller
    {
        public ActionResult TestLocalization()
        {
            Thread.CurrentThread.CurrentCulture = new
              CultureInfo(HttpContext.Profile.GetPropertyValue("Language") + "-" +
              HttpContext.Profile.GetPropertyValue("ContactInformation.Country"),
              false);
            Decimal amount = new Decimal(5);

            ViewData["CurrencyExample"] =
              String.Format(CultureInfo.CurrentCulture.NumberFormat,"{0:c}", amount);
            ViewData["PercentageExample"] =
              String.Format(CultureInfo.CurrentCulture.NumberFormat,"{0:p}", amount);
            ViewData["NumberExample"] =
              String.Format(CultureInfo.CurrentCulture.NumberFormat,"{0:N}", amount);
            ViewData["DateExample"] =
              Convert.ToDateTime(DateTime.Now,
              CultureInfo.CurrentCulture.DateTimeFormat);

            return View("TestLocalization");
        }
    }
}
```

In this controller you are setting the CultureInfo at the top of your controller to that specified by the user during registration. Because you asked for a country of origin separate from the language, you are creating a composite of profile properties to create an acceptable cultural region. You then use the CultureInfo class to provide you with culturally relevant formatting information for your various examples. The final result is shown in Figure 11-11, where it all comes together.

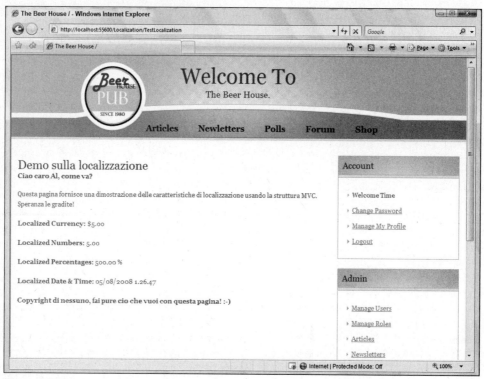

Figure 11-11

Summary

This chapter has covered how to use the localization features built into ASP.NET within the MVC framework. Using the MVC framework you are not able to take advantage of the resource auto generation tools originally available in ASP.NET 2.0, but our lives are made much easier by being able to retrieve cultural information directly from our markup. More complex logic is easily accomplished by taking advantage of the CultureInfo class found in System.Globalization. The resource files that you created were all strongly typed and allowed you to insert a variety of different types of objects into them.

The Solution section of this chapter was fairly short because you only need to follow a few simple steps, repeating them for all the pages you want to localize. It only took us a couple of hours to create the localization example that was outlined in the Solution section. We know from personal experience that without ASP.NET localization features, this task would have taken significantly longer. If this power and flexibility still isn't enough for your needs, we invite you to go deeper and study the provided model for localization, which enables you to store and retrieve resources to and from any data store you prefer.

Now that the site is 100% feature complete, you can start thinking about its packing, distribution, and publication to the Internet for global usage. The next chapter shows you how to deploy the site to your very own dedicated server under your control.

12

Deploying the Site

You've finally come to the end of the development: your site is ready, you have tested it locally and it all works fine, and now you have to publish it online. If you have ever had any experience with older legacy ASP/COM applications, and later with ASP.NET Web Form applications, you already know that .NET made deployment much easier. You no longer had any COM components to register, or shared components that might overwrite an existing version and thus break other applications. For pure ASP.NET applications it may suffice to do an XCOPY of all your deployment-related files (such as .aspx, .ascx, .dll, .config, and static files) to the remote server, and possibly deploy the database. With the release of the MVC framework and ASP.NET 3.5, the ease of deployment has not changed. However, in the real world, things usually tend to get a little more complex than that because you have constraints and company policies to respect regarding the deployment of your application. Database deployment and configuration can also be nontrivial, and you should consider this carefully before you start rolling out the site. This final chapter guides you through all of the different options to successfully deploy your website's files and the database, explaining why and when some techniques are more suitable than others.

Problem

The problem described and solved here was a real problem that we faced while completing the sample site. We wanted to put the site online somewhere so that potential readers could browse it and consider whether it was worth the purchase, and so that we could show it to clients and colleagues during presentations about the ASP.NET MVC framework.

Not having a private dedicated server connected to the Internet available for this project, we had to make a choice between a shared hosting environment and a dedicated server. Fortunately, it is now extremely affordable to buy your own dedicated or virtual dedicated servers for a small monthly fee. A quick check on the Internet showed prices that are very reasonable, especially if you are on a budget. Of course, your specific hosting requirements may vary according to the type of project you're working on. For high-usage sites or sites that require high availability, you'll want dedicated servers configured as a web farm, whereby a number of servers are running the same applications and load-balancing is used to determine which server will process a specific web request. Because our sample project uses the MVC framework, and it requires the .NET 3.5 Framework to operate and potentially use some special configurations in IIS 6.0, some low-cost shared hosting plans may not work.

The good news is that Windows Server 2008 shared hosting environments will not require any special configurations to host your MVC applications. The following is an outline of some things you should consider when choosing a hosting option:

❑ What files do I need to deploy?

❑ How do I deploy those files?

❑ How can I protect my source code against prying eyes, once the website has been published on a shared remote server?

❑ What installs and updates will I need to complete to make my server ready for my MVC framework application?

❑ How will different versions of IIS affect my deployment?

This chapter shows how different hosting options answer these questions.

Design

The complete deployment is basically split into two parts: deploying the database and deploying the site. If your web server supports SQL Server Express (only recommended for small sites), the database will automatically be attached when you publish your application. If you have the desire to place this application on a non-Express version of SQL Server, you will need to attach the database files manually or create them using a script. The advantage to using a non-Express version of SQL Server is that it provides you the ability to easily create a cluster using the premium options in SQL Server 2008. Some of these new features include Database Mirroring, which makes the process of clustering painless: you simply specify the database you want mirrored and it will keep another server on standby if anything happens to the first one, without losing any transactions. The following table provides a cursory comparison between the SQL Server 2008 versions. For a complete list please visit Microsoft's website.

Feature	Express	Web	Enterprise
Number of CPUs	1	4	OS Max
RAM	1 GB	OS Max	OS Max
Database Size	4 GB	Unlimited	Unlimited

Special Considerations for MVC Framework Applications

The MVC framework is great to develop with but presents its own set of challenges when deploying. You must ensure several things are installed prior to publishing your application. You must ensure you have at least ASP.NET 3.5 SP1 installed and that you have installed the latest version of the MVC framework or included the MVC assembly, `System.Web.Mvc.dll`, in your bin folder of your application. At some point, Microsoft will decide to bundle the MVC framework with the ASP.NET framework like it did with the AJAX framework, but as of this writing that hasn't been done. The other piece is that you will be required to make special modifications to IIS 6.0 to be able to handle the dynamic nature of the URL routes used in the MVC framework. The following sections discuss how to properly deploy your MVC application.

Deploying the Database to SQL Server 2008

You have several options to choose from when deploying your database out to the SQL Server. The option that you choose will be entirely dependent on the amount of control you have over the database and the server it lives on. Following is a list of your options from easiest to most difficult along with their pros and cons:

❑ **Attach the Database Automatically:** Making some slight modifications to your web.config file and having a SQL Express database means that deploying your server is a snap. In fact, there is literally no database configuration that needs to be done other than to make sure that the user and password in your web.config corresponds to what is on the production SQL Express database. If it does not you'll know pretty quickly when your application gives you an error indicating the database could not be attached due to rights. This works only for SQL Server Express editions!

❑ **Attach the Database using SSMS (SQL Server Management Studio):** So you've decided SQL Express will not meet your needs and you want to use a more powerful version. In a virtual server or dedicated server environment this should be no problem. You will need to modify your web.config and place your database file and log files in a logical place. We discuss how this is accomplished later in this section.

❑ **Script out Database:** This is by far the most difficult to initially set up. You literally have to make a script file for every single object in the database and then script files for critical data that you want replicated as well. Although this can be very tedious, it makes creating installers for your application very simple. This is also a great solution if you do not have administrator-level privileges on the SQL Server. You will almost certainly have to go this route if you are using a shared hosting environment.

Deploying the MVC Web Application

Like all other web applications, you have a set of files and folders you need to transfer over to your web server. These files will include your views, the contents of your /bin directory, and any other static dependencies such as images, styles, and JavaScript files. Once that is complete, you start getting into the sticky business of configuring IIS to work properly with your MVC application. IIS 7 and IIS 6 both have different requirements; whereas IIS 7 can be a drag-and-drop solution, configuration settings on the web application need to be modified in IIS 6 to work properly. The key things to remember when deploying an MVC application and getting it to work properly are:

❑ **Ensure dependencies are met:** That will include a SQL Server instance, the latest version of the .NET Framework, and the MVC assemblies. If any of these are missing, your application will simply not work.

❑ **Configuring IIS 6 to work with an MVC application:** Aside from the usual configurations that you need to make in IIS for a new web application, you must also disable a critical check that ensures the files actually exist before rendering them and creating a wildcard mapping to the .NET 2.0 Internet Server Application Protocol Interface (ISAPI) library. This is because the URLs that you use in MVC do not actually correspond to real files. If you have ever delved into IIS, you know that extensions are associated with programs in IIS and with MVC you have to create a wildcard rule to properly route extensionless URLs.

❑ **Configuring IIS 7 to work with an MVC application:** IIS 7 gives you the ability to set configuration preferences for IIS directly in the web.config, making deployment of your MVC application much simpler and easier to manage. All the necessary configurations for IIS 7, of which there are very few, are provided by default in the Visual Studio MVC solution file.

❑ **Modify** web.config **file:** Based on the way you plan on deploying this application and your own personal requirements, the web.config file will need to have certain elements changed within it. Most notably, the connection string setting will probably need to be modified in order to work properly.

Solution

This section discusses how to deploy your MVC application to a web server. Several methods of deploying the database are discussed to provide you the greatest amount of flexibility when choosing hosting environments and SQL Server editions. This section also walks you through how to publish your web application and configure both IIS 6 and IIS 7 to work properly with it.

Attaching a Database

As discussed in the Design section, attaching a database can be done automatically by configuring the web.config properly or by using SSMS to do it manually. Following is a sample of what the connection string should look like in order to get your database to attach automatically to your SQL Server Express instance.

Integrated Security

```
<connectionStrings>
    <add name="TheBeerHouseConnectionString"
    connectionString="Data Source=.\SQLEXPRESS;
    AttachDbFilename=|DataDirectory|\TheBeerHouse.mdf;
    Integrated Security=True;
    User Instance=True"
    providerName="System.Data.SqlClient" />
</connectionStrings>
```

From this example you can see that we are indicating to the application that this particular database will be attached by the application to the local SQL Server Express instance that we have specified. This example uses trusted connections, but if you wanted to actually enter in a special username or password the connection string would look like this:

Username & Password

```
<connectionStrings>
    <add name="TheBeerHouseConnectionString"
    connectionString="Data Source=.\SQLEXPRESS;
    AttachDbFilename=|DataDirectory|\TheBeerHouse.mdf;
    User ID=MyUserName;
```

```
        Passowrd=MyPassword;
        User Instance=True"
        providerName="System.Data.SqlClient" />
   </connectionStrings>
```

The only difference here is, instead of specifying integrated security, we spell out the username and password. Note that we are using a relative path for the location of the database; this is because we are not always certain what the directory structure above the path is going to look like. In this example we simply have to make sure that our database file and our log file are located in the |DataDirectory| folder within our application. In the case of our web application the data directory is the App_Data folder in the root of our web application.

Of course, for all this to work properly you must ensure that an instance of SQL Server Express is installed and the data source attribute is properly pointed to where your database lives. In our example, we specify a period in front of the SQL Express instance, which tells our application that it lives on the same box the application resides on (that is, localhost).

Alternatively, if you decide to use a non-Express edition of SQL Server the connection string in the preceding code will fail. Microsoft will require you to actually attach the database manually or use a script. Here is how to manually attach the database yourself using SSMS. First, open up SSMS and expand your server node, right-click the folder named Database, and select Attach Databases. A dialog like the one in Figure 12-1 will come up for you.

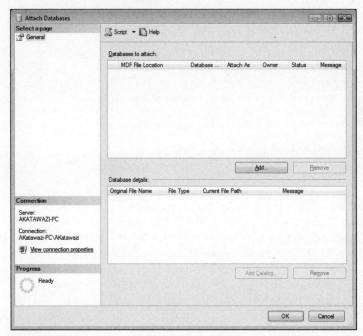

Figure 12-1

At this point you would click the Add button and find your `.mdf` file in the directory structure and attach it. That's pretty much it for deploying your database manually. As a security precaution you may want to create a user that only has rights to that specific database and does not have admin rights over the entire SQL Server. That way, in your `web.config` file you can specify that user in your connection string instead of your administrator account. To do this, you simply expand your Security tab and right-click the Logins folder to add a new login. You should get a dialog that looks like Figure 12-2.

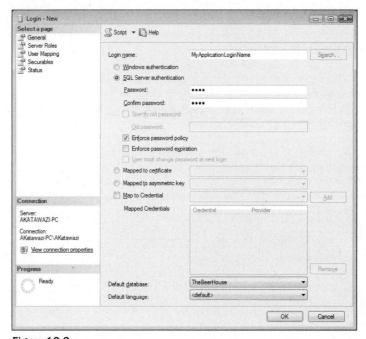

Figure 12-2

If you create a new user, make sure to uncheck Enforce Password Expiration so your application doesn't go down after the expiration period. Now, we are not condoning never changing your password, you just want to avoid accidently forgetting it and having your application lose connectivity to the database. When you are creating your user you will also need to go to the User Mapping page and set up the rights of the user. The page should look like Figure 12-3.

As you can see from Figure 12-3, we have set the rights to only the TheBeerHouse database and have given this user account rights to read and write data. This is a good practice because if somehow security is compromised via a SQL Injection attack or other method, the amount of damage that can be caused is limited. In the preceding example, the user cannot drop any tables or access in any way from any of the other databases on this server.

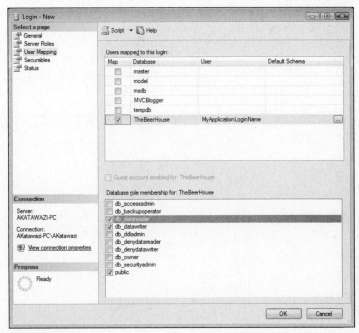

Figure 12-3

Setting Up a Backup and Maintenance Plan

Creating a backup and maintenance plan is perhaps one of the most important things you can do with your database, but it is often glossed over. Something very important to remember is that all hardware will fail given a long enough time frame. Using database mirroring helps to mitigate this problem by replicating the data between two databases, but sometimes you simply need to roll data back. There is nothing worse than losing or corrupting your data and this can be very costly. Because of this, we have decided to spend some time talking about how to set up a basic backup plan in SSMS that offers some level of protection. If you expand out the Management node, right-click Maintenance Plans, and select New Maintenance Plan, you get the maintenance plan designer window shown in Figure 12-4.

> You will only be able to create a backup and maintenance plan with versions that are greater than SQL Server Express. If you are using the Express version of SQL Server, you may want to either create your own program that will back up your data or purchase an off-the-shelf solution.

In the preceding example, we have already added some items to the designer, but they are simple to create. In the Toolbox, simply drag over a database backup task highlighted in Figure 12-4 and a shrink database task. The shrink task is important because the log files tend to get huge over time. You will need to double-click the Shrink Database Task box to bring up its dialog, shown in Figure 12-5, and set up the database and settings properly.

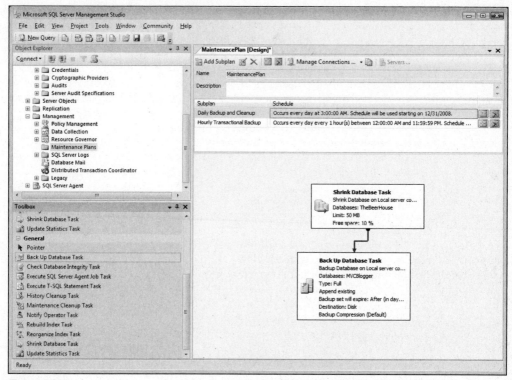

Figure 12-4

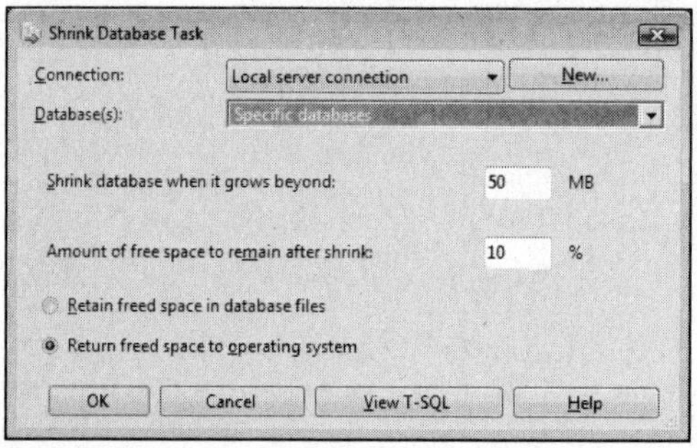

Figure 12-5

Figure 12-5 shows how we have set up the shrink task for this particular plan. In the form we have specified that shrinks only happen if the log file gets bigger than 50 megabytes. We are also allowing the operating system to take back that reclaimed space to allocate to other things.

Now that the shrink task is in place, we can set up our backup strategy. For this project we have set up two different backup options. The first is a full backup of the entire database that will happen once a week. The second is going to be an hourly transaction log backup. The advantage of the latter is that the transaction log backups will allow us to roll back our information to any point in time starting from the latest transaction backup. So let's say we are getting junk data inserted into the database starting yesterday. With this backup plan we can roll back to the exact moment the junk data started. This is a really great way to recover databases that have become corrupted.

In contrast, our full backup is a simple backup of all the contents of the database at the moment the backup happens. The reason why we want one of these is because a full backup restores very rapidly. The way a transaction log backup restores is by executing all the transactions that have occurred from the restore point you have specified up to the point of the last full backup. This can be lengthy and you should feel free to experiment with this to find the combination that works best for you. As always, you have many other backup options you can pursue. Entire books have been written on this and we encourage you to research more.

Getting back to our backup task, when you double-click Back Up Database Task, the dialog screen in Figure 12-6 will come up.

Figure 12-6 shows the full backup that we are doing. To change this to do a transaction log backup you simply need to change the backup type. You will notice that we have specified an ftp address for the folder that the backup is going to. It is very important for you to store your backups on a separate disk and preferably on a separate server. Many low-cost secure ftp services are available that you can sign up for that will give you this capability.

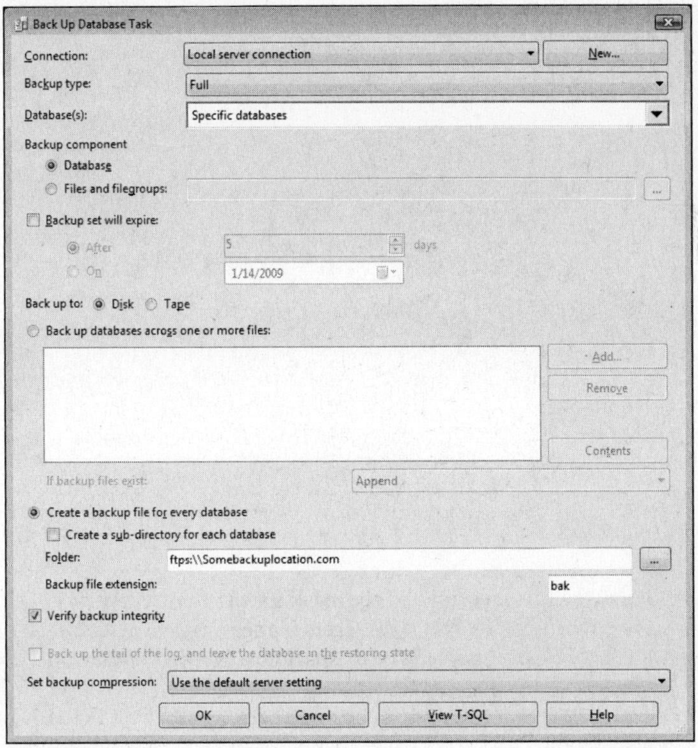

Figure 12-6

If you look back to Figure 12-4, you will see under the Subplan section that we have created two sub-plans. Next to those plans is also a calendar. Your full backup and your shrink plan should go under one subplan and your transactional backup should go under the other. You would click the calendar icon to set up the appropriate intervals. These basic steps establish a backup plan that should protect you against most things that could go wrong with your database. As always, you should periodically check your backups by doing a restore on a test database to be safe.

Scripting Your Database

If you have decided that you would rather go with a scripted solution for your database deployments, you can easily do this using a combination of Visual Studio and SSMS. On the Visual Studio side, simply open up your Server Explorer and navigate to your database. Right-click it and select Publish to Provider. This will bring up the Database Publishing Wizard and you will come to a dialog that looks like Figure 12-7.

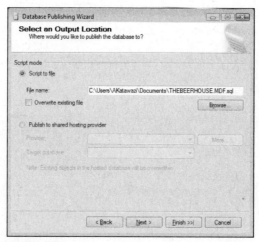

Figure 12-7

In the previous edition of this book, there were many pages dedicated to scripting out your database. With Visual Studio 2008 and this new wizard, scripting is a snap. In the preceding dialog you simply specify where you want your `.sql` file to end up and your databases schema is created. You will have a few other options but if you accept all the other options with their default presets, you should have a completely scripted database.

Importing Existing Data

If you used the attach method of moving your database, you can completely skip this section because the data automatically migrates with you using this method. If you have decided to script out your database, things get a little sticky. This is because neither Visual Studio's Server Explorer nor your local installation of SSMS has the ability to create `SQL INSERT` scripts for your data. Several options are available to you, as discussed in this section.

The first and probably the most popular option for moving your database is using the Import/Export Wizard in SSMS. As you can see from Figure 12-8, you would right-click your database, select Tasks, and then either select Import Data if you were in your target database, or Export Data if you were in your source database.

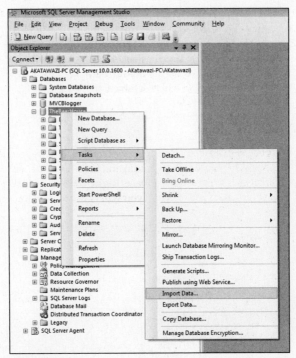

Figure 12-8

When you use the tool's Import/Export Data feature, it allows you to choose all tables, but you can't select the order in which they will be imported, and you'll get many import errors if the tool tries to insert data into a detail table that has a foreign key to a master table for which the data hasn't been imported yet. To solve the problem, you need to temporarily disable the referential integrity checks during the import, so that the tool can insert data into a table even if the records reference other records that are not present in the master table yet. To do this you use the ALTER TABLE <tablename> NOCHECK CONSTRAINT ALL statement for every table, as follows:

```
ALTER TABLE Articles NOCHECK CONSTRAINT ALL
ALTER TABLE Categories NOCHECK CONSTRAINT ALL
ALTER TABLE Languages NOCHECK CONSTRAINT ALL
…do the same for all other tables required by ASP.NET and your application
```

You can run this script from SSMS by clicking the New Query button at the top and selecting the appropriate database. After disabling constraints, select the target database in which you want to import the data (this may be a local database or a database on the remote server) in the Object Explorer, and select Tasks ➪ Import Data from its context menu to open the SQL Server Import and Export Wizard shown in Figure 12-9.

In the first step you select the source database, which will be the TheBeerHouse database attached to the .mdf SQL Server Express file. In the second step you choose the destination database, which will already be selected. If you're targeting a remote database (one not on your own computer), you probably also need to modify the options to choose SQL Server Authentication, and enter your credentials to connect to the database. In the next step, shown in Figure 12-10, you are asked to select the tables for which you want data replicated.

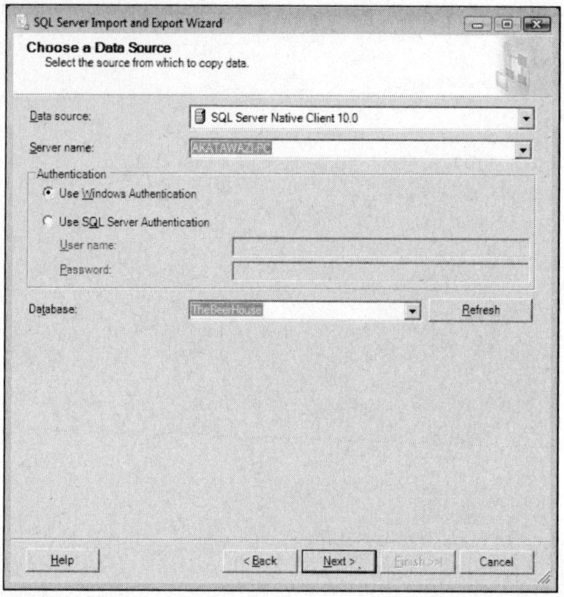

Figure 12-9

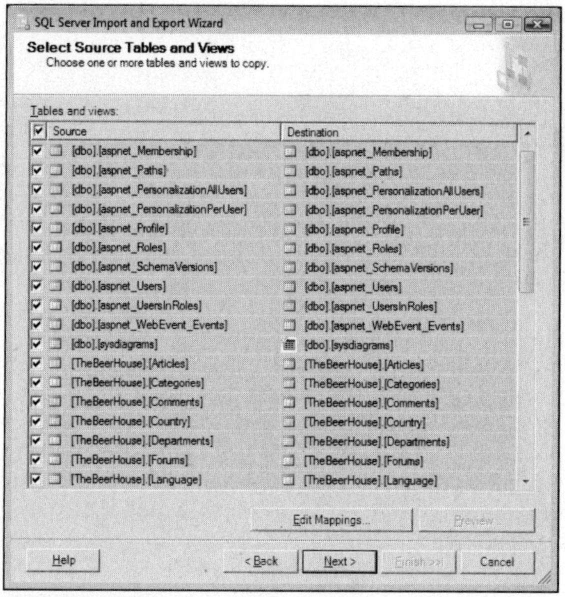

Figure 12-10

Figure 12-10 shows you should select all of the tables. You could omit the following tables if you prefer: sysdiagrams and aspnet_WebEventEvents. Also, make sure you do not select the objects beginning with vw_aspnet, because these are views that don't contain their own data in reality. Before proceeding to the next step, you must go into the import options of each selected table by clicking the Edit Mappings button on the bottom of the grid listing the objects. This will open up the Column Mappings dialog shown in Figure 12-11.

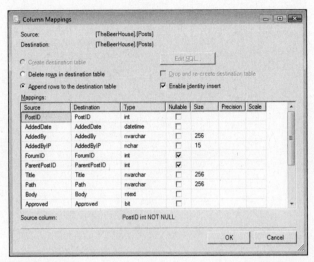

Figure 12-11

Select the Enable Identity Insert checkbox to ensure that records are imported with their original identity values (for columns such as `ApplicationID`, `CategoryID`, `ArticleID`, `PollID`, and so on). This is necessary so inserted rows will respect the referential integrity (other tables have foreign keys that reference the specific values in these identity columns, so you have to insert the original values instead of letting it assign new values). You might think it's a good idea to select Delete Rows in Destination Table so that you won't get duplicate key errors if you're re-importing the data. This won't work, however, because it will try to use truncate statements that don't work on any table that has foreign keys (even if the constraints are off). So you need to use a script to delete all rows first if you want to re-import data, rather than use this checkbox.

Complete the wizard, check the box that lets you save the SSIS package, and check File System. When you see the Package Protection dialog, select Encrypt All Data with Password and specify a password. Select a file name for this package and run the actual process; it will import all rows as specified. Save the SSIS package in a file so you can easily rerun this import in the future without having to do all the setup steps again (just double-click that file). However, be careful because you have to empty your tables before doing this and you don't want to do this once you have real users in a production environment! Figure 12-12 shows the screen providing feedback about the process, with the number of rows successfully imported for each table.

The last thing to do is re-enable the constraints you previously disabled by running the following statements on the remote database from a Query window:

```
ALTER TABLE Articles CHECK CONSTRAINT ALL
ALTER TABLE Categories CHECK CONSTRAINT ALL
ALTER TABLE Languages CHECK CONSTRAINT ALL
...do the same for all other tables required by ASP.NET and custom features
```

489

Figure 12-12

The entire import takes a couple of minutes to complete and you end up with a perfect replication of the local SQL Server database.

The other option available to you is to either manually write the insert statements for each row of data or obtain one of the many third-party tools that does this for you. Doing a simple search of the Internet, we found several that were completely free of charge.

If you do create insert scripts, make sure that the scripts are ordered so they don't create any foreign key conflicts. For example, in our database the data in the Polls table would need to be inserted before the data in the PollOptions table.

Deploying Your MVC Web Application

Now that your database has been properly set up, you need to move your web application over to the web server. This can be easily accomplished in a number of ways.

Preparing for Deployment

Before you get ready to move your MVC application to the server, you need to make sure the server will be able to handle your MVC application. It is very important that you install .NET 3.5 SP1 or later; without this your MVC framework application will not work. You will also need to either install the MVC framework on your web server or make sure the MVC assembly appears in your /bin directory for deployment. If you'd like to /bin deploy the assemblies, you will need to include the System. Web.Mvc from your References folder in your TheBeerHouse project. Select the assembly, as shown in Figure 12-13, and right-click to get its properties. You must set the Copy Local attribute to True so that when you publish, this assembly is transferred over.

Note that doing a /bin deployment will only allow that particular application to use the MVC framework's assembly. This is because the assemblies are not registered in the global assembly cache.

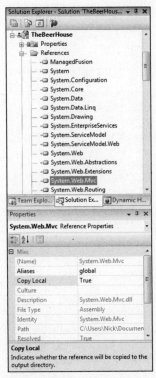

Figure 12-13

Deploying TheBeerHouse

The easiest way we have found to deploy a website has been by using the Visual Studio website publishing capability; to do this, simply right-click your project in the Solution Explorer and click the Publish button. You will also need a location to publish to. This is a good time to actually create your web application folder on your web server. By default, IIS will use `C:\Inetpub\www\` for web applications; all you need to do is create a folder called TheBeerHouse. If you are in a shared environment, your hosting company generally provides you with an ftp that you can upload files to. Figure 12-14 shows the Publish Web dialog.

From the example you can see that we are publishing to an ftp site that we set up for the TheBeerHouse website. Once you click the Publish button, all the files you need will be moved over.

Some people have complained that Publish works extremely slowly over the Internet and we have found this to be true in some isolated cases. If you are experiencing this problem, we suggest creating a folder on your local drive and publishing to it instead. Once you have done that you can manually transfer the files yourself using your preferred method; that's all there is to moving the files themselves. The next section discusses configuring IIS.

Note that before publishing, if you want you can specify that your application be built in debug mode or in release mode. This option will be available in a pull-down docked at the top of the Visual Studio window. The advantage of publishing in release mode is that the debug information is excluded from your assemblies, which makes them smaller and allows them to run faster.

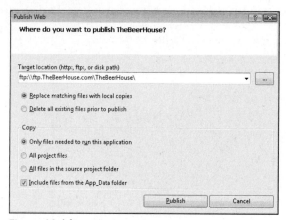

Figure 12-14

Configuring IIS 6 for MVC Framework

In IIS 6, you will first need to create your application pool. To do this, open up IIS by going to Start ➪ Control Panel ➪ Administrative Tools ➪ Internet Information Services. Once in there you can expand the server node, and then expand the Application Pools node. Right-click it and select New and then Application Pool, as shown in Figure 12-15.

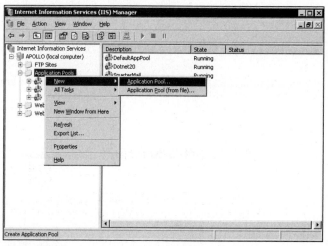

Figure 12-15

From here you will name the new pool and use the default settings as shown in Figure 12-16.

Right-clicking the pool and going into Properties will reveal a lot of different options that you can apply such as limiting bandwidth usage or monitoring health. We could go over this in more detail but that is beyond the scope of this book.

Now that an application pool has been created, it is time to create your actual website. Right-click the website folder under the server node in IIS and select New Web Site; from there IIS 6 will take you to the Web Site Creation Wizard, shown in Figure 12-17.

Continue past the wizard splash screen and give a description of the website. The next screen you will come to is shown in Figure 12-18.

Figure 12-16

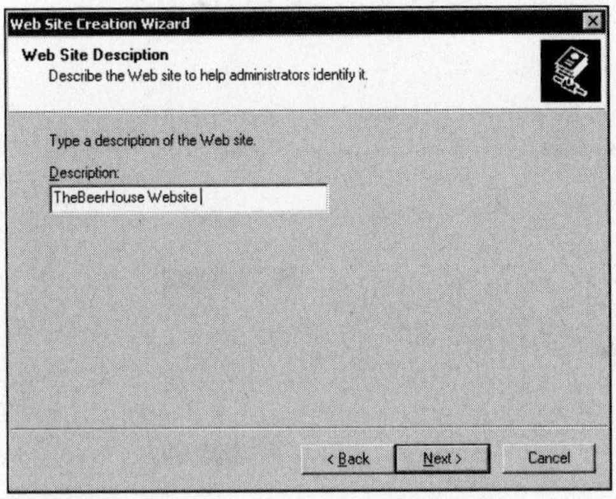

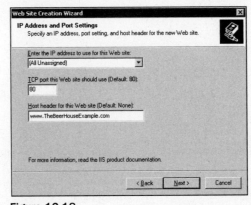

Figure 12-17

Figure 12-18

This screen will ask you what IP you would like to use and what the header of the website is. As shown in the figure, the Host header will be the root URL address that IIS will key in on to know that this application is responsible for the TheBeerHouse website. Because an IIS server can have many websites, the header is critical to directing traffic appropriately. Your next step will be to specify the path that the application actually resides in, as shown in Figure 12-19.

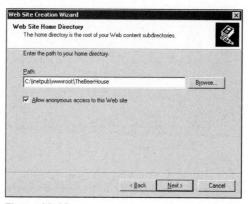

Figure 12-19

Navigate through the file system until you find the folder you created and click Next. Once you have completed this step, you will be asked what type of rights you would like to give the application, as shown in Figure 12-20.

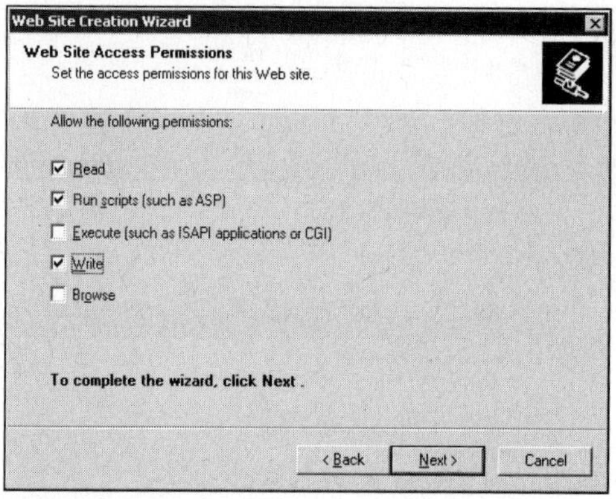

Figure 12-20

We normally select the permissions for Read, Write, and Run scripts so that most scenarios are covered. You may need to give Execute rights if you plan on allowing your web application to fire off executable files.

After you have specified the application's rights, the wizard should complete. You are not done setting up the application though; you will need to right-click your website and select Properties under the website folder. You will be presented with a dialog that looks like Figure 12-21.

Figure 12-21

Once there, select the Home Directory tab and change the Application Pool to the TheBeerHousePool that you created previously. After you are done setting the application pool, you need to configure the website for wildcards.

To do this you need to click the Configuration button and then select the Insert button to add a wildcard mapping. You will then need to specify the location of the asp_isapi.dll (this should be `c:\ windows\microsoft.net\framework\v2.0.50727\aspnet_isapi.dll` for IIS 6 systems), and uncheck the option that verifies if the files actually exist, as shown in Figure 12-22. Suppressing this check is critical because our URLs will not correspond to real files thanks to the magic provided by the `System.Web.Routing` framework that MVC uses to make the actions' URL Routes.

Figure 12-22

Configuring IIS 7 for MVC Framework

IIS 7 is significantly easier than configuring IIS 6. You will not need to set up wildcard rules but you will have to ensure that all the features you need are installed. By default, Windows Server 2008 has certain server roles not installed.

Standard Setup of IIS 7

To resolve this, you simply need to go into the Server Manager and select Roles from the tree on the left-hand side of the screen as shown in Figure 12-23.

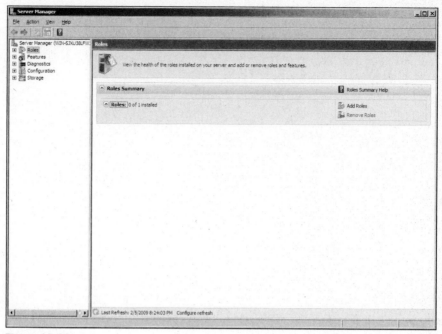

Figure 12-23

From this screen, select Add Roles on the right side. Once you have selected this, you will get a new dialog, which will look like Figure 12-24.

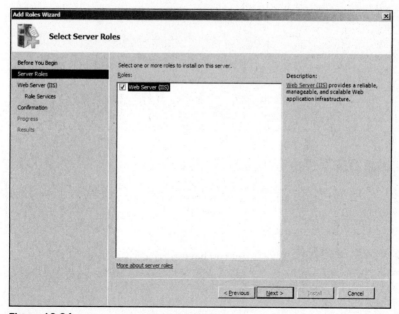

Figure 12-24

In this dialog, select Server Roles and select Web Server (IIS); click Next and you will see a screen that looks like Figure 12-25.

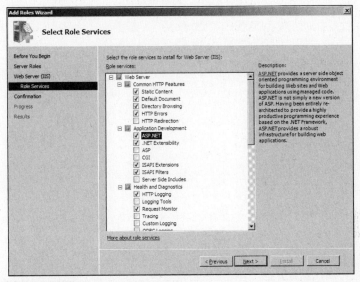

Figure 12-25

When you see this screen, click ASP.NET and a dialog may pop up that looks like Figure 12-26.

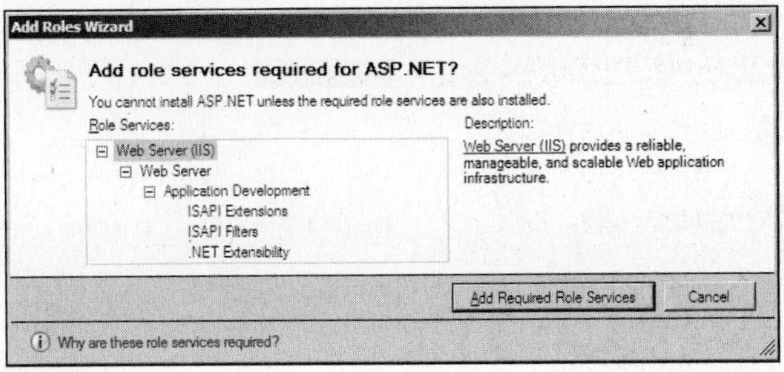

Figure 12-26

This dialog asks you to confirm additional services required to run ASP.NET. Click Add Required Role Services and you will be taken back to the screen shown in Figure 12-25. Just continue through the screens normally until you are finished. If everything completes successfully you will be presented with a screen that looks like Figure 12-27.

When you are presented with this screen, you have successfully installed IIS 7 and you are ready to exit the Add Roles Wizard. When you click Close, you will be taken back to the Server Manager screen, except all the new services you have installed will show on the screen, as shown in Figure 12-28.

Once all the services you need are installed, you are done.

This may not be the optimal solution for you, because it is very involved and requires a lot of knowledge about the Server Manager. Luckily for us, Microsoft has created a new tool that makes installing everything we need to get our MVC application up and running as easy as selecting a couple of checkboxes.

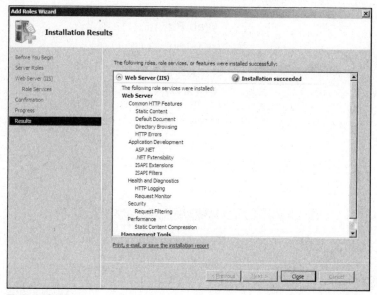

Figure 12-27

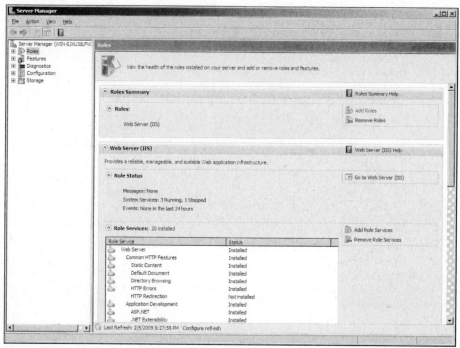

Figure 12-28

Alternative Setup of IIS 7 Using Microsoft Web Platform Installer

This new tool is called Microsoft Web Platform Installer (Web PI), and you can download it from `http://www.microsoft.com/web/downloads/platform.aspx`.

> ### Microsoft Web Platform Installer
>
> The Web Platform Installer (Web PI) is a simple tool that installs Microsoft's entire Web Platform, including IIS, Visual Web Developer 2008 Express Edition, SQL Server 2008 Express Edition, and the .NET Framework. Using the Web Platform Installer's user interface, you can choose to install either specific products or the entire Microsoft Web Platform onto your computer. The Web PI also helps keep your products up to date by always offering the latest additions to the Web Platform.

After you have download Web PI, double-click the install file and you will be presented with a screen that looks like Figure 12-29.

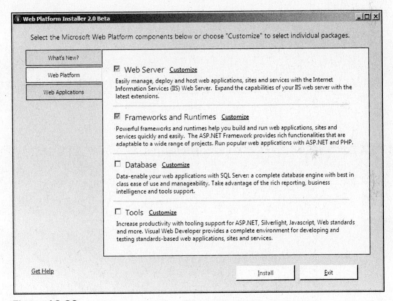

Figure 12-29

You will want to select the Web Platform tab to get started. On this tab, the first thing we want to do is ensure that ASP.NET MVC will get installed. To do this click the Frameworks and Runtimes customize link, as seen in Figure 12-30.

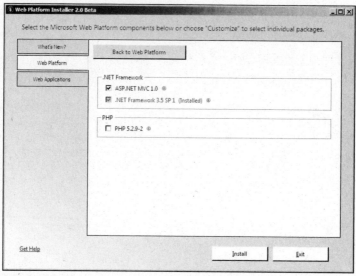

Figure 12-30

On this screen, make sure to select the latest .NET Framework and ASP.NET MVC. After you are done selecting the features you want to install, click the Back to Web Platform button. This will take you back to the previous screen, from here you will want to select the Database customize link and you will be presented with a screen that looks like Figure 12-31.

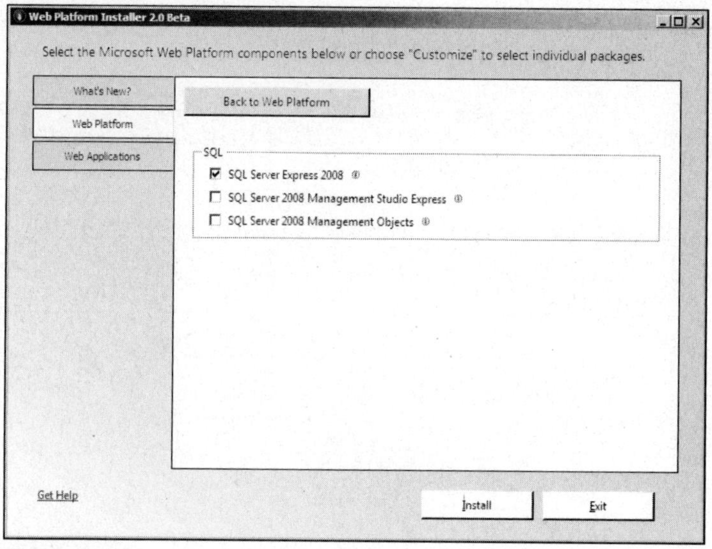

Figure 12-31

If you are going to be installing SQL Express to run your MVC application, make sure to also choose it from the list to streamline your installation so all the components are installed at once. Now that we have selected all the requirements to run our MVC application, we can click the Install button. After doing this you will be presented with a screen that looks like Figure 12-32.

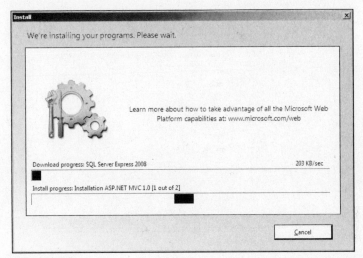

Figure 12-32

In this screen, the tool is downloading the necessary requirements from the Internet that we selected. After the installation process is completed, a screen will be shown detailing all the services and applications that have been installed. After this is complete, you will need to configure IIS 7 for the TheBeerHouse application.

Adding the TheBeerHouse Site

Next, you need to create the site for TheBeerHouse. To do this, open up IIS by going to Start ➪ Control Panel ➪ Administrative Tools ➪ Internet Information Services. This will open the Internet Information Services (IIS) Manager, shown in Figure 12-33.

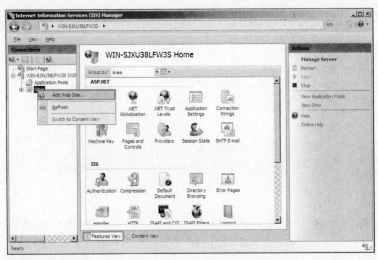

Figure 12-33

Once in the IIS Manager, expand the server node, right-click Sites, and select Add Web Site. You will be presented with a dialog that looks like Figure 12-34.

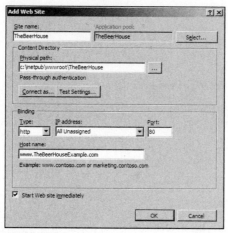

Figure 12-34

Here you are setting things up pretty much the same way you did in IIS 6. You simply need to name the new website, specify its physical path, and assign the host header to direct traffic. Believe it or not, that is all you need to do. Assuming that your prerequisites were already installed, this would literally be a two-step deployment. That should be it; if you check your URL your website should be up and fully functional.

Summary

In this chapter, you've looked at all the options for deploying a site that uses the MVC framework and ASP.NET 3.5. If you ever had experience with traditional ASP.NET applications, you can see that deploying an MVC framework site can be tricky, especially with IIS 6; more prerequisites are required and this could potentially limit you from using certain shared hosting environments. As the MVC framework enters the mainstream, we should begin to see the prerequisite issues go away because many servers will already have the needed assemblies by default. Don't feel put off though; the MVC framework is worth the extra effort to create more elegantly designed websites. With that, we come to the end of our journey together. We hope that you have thoroughly enjoyed this book and we wish you the best of luck. Happy coding!

Index

D

P

Q

forum controllers, 340–341
opinion poll controllers, 267–268
votes, handling multiple votes in opinion polling, 258–259

W

W3C
RSS and, 151
XHTML and, 48
WCAG (Web Content Accessibility Guidelines), 48
Web browsers
best practices for presentation layer, 80
search engine optimization and, 81
site design and browser compatibility, 34
Web Content Accessibility Guidelines (WCAG), 48
Web Forms. *See ASP.NET Web Forms*
Web sites
best practices for speeding up, 57
companion site for this book, xxv
deploying. *See site deployment*
designing. *See site design*

list of features in content-based sites, 2–3
revenue options, 375
statistics services, 256
uses of opinion polls on, 255
`web.config` **file**
configuring, 310–311
configuring membership providers, 95
environment resources saved in, 78–79
modifying when deploying MVC web applications, 480
`WebFormViewEngine`, **26–27**
WebKit Project, 34
Website Payments Standard option, PayPal, 381
Windows authentication, 88
Windows Server 2008, as hosting server, 478
WYSIWYG editors, 171–172

X

XHTML, 48
XML
data store options, 66
newsfeeds, 151

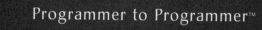